TIME SERIES IN PSYCHOLOGY

TIME SERIES IN PSYCHOLOGY

Robert A. M. Gregson

University of New England
Armidale, New South Wales
Australia

LEA LAWRENCE ERLBAUM ASSOCIATES, PUBLISHERS

1983   Hillsdale, New Jersey   London

Copyright © 1983 by Lawrence Erlbaum Associates, Inc.
   All rights reserved. No part of this book may be reproduced in
   any form, by photostat, microform, retrieval system, or any other
   means, without the prior written permission of the publisher.

Lawrence Erlbaum Associates, Inc., Publishers
365 Broadway
Hillsdale, New Jersey 07642

Library of Congress Cataloging in Publication Data
Gregson, R. A. M. (Robert Anthony Mills), 1928–
   Time series in psychology.

   Bibliography: p.
   Includes index.
   1. Time-series analysis.   2. Psychometrics.
I. Title.   [DNLM: 1. Psychology, Experimental—Methods.
2. Time factors.   3. Time.   BF 181 G819t]
BF39.G74   1983   150'.724   83-1462
ISBN 0-89859-250-X

Printed in the United States of America
10 9 8 7 6 5 4 3 2 1

Contents

Preface

Psychological data are segments of life histories; as such they are ordered sequences of observations and by definition time series. Yet they are often anything but well behaved; what regularities and invariances they have are buried from all but the most persistent investigator. The most common methods of representing quantitative results in psychology are frozen outside time; thus they deliberately average out much of the sequential structure that holds any sparse clues to the nature of processes within the organism.

It might be thought, looking at the problem from an uncommitted stance, that the developments of time series analysis and systems identification, both of which have expanded dramatically in the last decade, would have made an immediate and profound impact on our notions of how to conduct, analyze, and report on sequences of human action and experience. The increase in the depth and diversity of quantitative analysis and the ready facility with which new methods are packaged into and disseminated by computers make many problems tractable that but a short time ago were incomprehensible or insoluble. The foundations of time series analysis do, it is true, date back to the 1880s, contemporary with the early growth of experimental psychology. The two areas ought to have cross-fertilized before, as workers on both sides of the fence have repeatedly lamented, but real and imaginary difficulties got in the way. There is no denying that the real difficulties are demanding ones.

This review, whose simple aim is to bring together in an illuminating juxtaposition basic results in both time series analysis and in experimental psychology, thus cuts across traditions within psychology. It raises many unsolved questions in time series analysis and attempts to build bridges where some would think foundations hardly exist. The exposure of common themes and problems in diverse substantive areas can be surprising and painful because of the erroneous preconceptions and wasted reduplicative effort brought to light; it can also be the start of a small paradigm revolution. Much has been written of the paradigm shift from behaviorism to cognitive psychology, helping us to see in retrospect that some periods of intense activity were interludes rather than progress; if we seriously seek to build psychological explanations in the manner of other systems sciences, then we are forced to question the point and relevance of traditions reaching back to Wundt.

The conceptual and mathematical bases of time series models vary in their intricacy and depth; quite deliberately the examples presented in this book do progress in difficulty, being generally more complex in the later chapters. The treatment of the mathematics is not intended to be, nor is, at one level; prerequisites for ready comprehension vary considerably. An engineering or user-oriented approach has been taken by choice, rigorous existence theorems and formal axiomatic proofs are to be found in the cited literature. Even so, many parts of time series theory do require a competence that is different in content and direction from that usually associated with training in psychometrics. The reader who wants to do creative work, as opposed just to getting a feel of what it is all about, would need both reading and practical experience in the ways reviewed. In the long run there is no substitute for doing exploratory time series analysis on data, collected by the investigator, whose structure is partly understood to begin with. Cookbook analysis of entirely new situations can be disastrous or deceptive in its apparent but misleading simplicity. Repeated emphasis has been placed upon the interplay between psychological and mathematical ideas that has to occur for some meaningful results to emerge. It is this interplay that cannot be learned passively; it is not a catalog of methods but a style of reasoning. In this author's view, it is what scientific psychology is all about.

To use time series analysis and systems modeling seriously in psychology, as we show can be done and has been done in a diversity of fields, is not just to graft new algebra onto old results; instead it is to rethink the very nature of description, prediction, and explanation, in themselves. What were three separate conceptual tasks now flow together; to model the structure of a dynamic process is to do all three at once. So the changes do not just reflect the power of new analytical procedures, they demand a different perspective on scientific objectives. This in turn raises questions about how experimental psychology, which is more recognized for its methodology than for the cohesion of its empirical findings, ought to be taught. I am bold enough to suggest that it would be better to aim at system identification and to forget hypothesis testing, hence the occasionally iconoclastic tone of the book.

Thanks are due to many people, in various countries, who have expressed friendly interest and so given me strong encouragement to complete this work. Some small sections have been given in advance at seminars at the Universities of Melbourne in 1979 and Newcastle in 1980. Part was started in New Zealand

and the whole finished in Australia, though it would be rash speculation to look for the zeitgeist of the antipodes. I am above all indebted to my family for putting up with another book-in-progress around the home and to the skill and accuracy of secretaries who have typed somebody else's private language.

Robert A. M. Gregson
University of New England

1 General Considerations in the Representation of Real Psychological Processes

1.1 ANALYSES OUTSIDE AND INSIDE TIME

Analyses of data that are treated as time series are found in many different scientific disciplines, and a few examples have accumulated in psychology. There are interesting and important reasons why psychological data should be particularly suitable for such analyses, and there are also historical reasons why time series analysis has neither been developed nor used in psychology to the same extent as in other disciplines that do not, on the face of it, seem any more or any less suitable areas of application. This monograph surveys the elementary theory of time series in a selective manner and indicates by example and by contrast where its use increases our insight into the nature of psychological processes that extend through time. Because time series analysis is an abstract mathematical activity that cuts across problems of great diversity, it is not always immediately apparent when it matches, or is relevant to the problems of, theoretical and experimental psychology. For this reason it is helpful to examine some models of processes in time that have evolved in psychology, alongside the recent explosion in the volume and sophistication of time series theory. Time series are not studied here as an end in themselves; consequently we are selective in considering their mathematics and focus on aspects that may appear to lead more naturally into developments that link to systems theory on the one hand and psychology on the other. It is quite valid to regard time series analysis as a body of techniques and also a bridge between system theory and psychology in particular. Indeed, in the long run this may be the best justification for attempting to make more explicit use of time series analysis within the methodological repertoire of the psychologist.

A time series is a sequence of events ordered in time, which we may have good reason to believe is generated by some lawful underlying process that itself persists throughout the whole duration of the observations made. This is a very abstract idea, but it recurs in many different areas of scientific inquiry and in very tangible and obvious forms.

When, for example, records are collected at regular, or nearly regular, intervals in time, on the milk yield of cows or the number of spots seen on the surface of the sun or the birth rate of first-generation immigrant families, then patterns or regularities may be immediately apparent, or they may be suspected to generate trends and variations that emerge if the records are collected from a long enough sequence. Some sciences are observational rather than experimental in emphasis, so that series running through time are their typical data. The economics of animal, crop, or industrial production is such a science, and a classical example of an economic time series is the record of annual wheat production in Europe over the last 200 years.

Brief reflection will show that many psychological experiments are deliberately set up in such a way that their data records are time series; stimuli are selected from a pool, a rule is decided on for drawing from that pool and presenting one at a time, a response is recorded to each stimulus, and the data record is then two time series, one of stimuli and one of responses. Thus the bare bones of experimental records have a sequential structure because the human or animal subject is required to perform a series of tasks. We are sequential organisms; our lives do not exist only at one point in time and our capacities to do different things simultaneously, as in parallel rather than in series, are limited.

There should, therefore, be methods of investigating how a time series is generated, and how it sustains itself, that have a bearing on the particular time series that are of interest to psychologists. If we are abstract enough then any psychological experiment, or quasi-experiment (to use an accepted term for observational studies whose progression is not wholly under the control of the investigator) will be a potential case for time series analysis. But to be useful a more restricted definition of what we can do is needed.

To plan a psychological experiment with predominantly time series analysis in mind is quite feasible but has not often been done. The examples are so few that at the time of writing a good proportion of extant cases have been collected in this monograph. Traditions in experimental and social psychology usually go at the problem of analyzing data from a different stance. Let us take a very simple experiment, which has been done many times in the last century, and expand its description to illustrate the contrasts in approach.

It is required to investigate the relation between sucrose (cane sugar) concentration in water and the perceived sweetness of the liquid. The more concentrated the solution, the sweeter it tastes, and it is known that if there is not enough sucrose present, then the liquid will not taste sweet at all. Commonly, solution concentrations below 0.5% weight per volume are said to be below threshold. Our motives for doing such experiments are threefold:

1. To find out if there is a regular, quantifiable, relationship between concentration and sweetness, because this is a fundamental problem in the psychophysics of taste.

2. To find out, already knowing something about objective 1, if this sucrose tastes the same as some other chemical substances of related or unrelated molecular structure.

3. To see if the observer is anomalous in his/her perception of the taste of sucrose.

The experiments actually done can be much the same, in practical details, whichever of the three objectives is chosen. Indeed, item 1 must be done at some stage as a calibration before going on to study objectives 2 or 3.

Typically, the investigator is counselled to create, from a range of sucrose concentrations, equally spaced in log units such as 0.25, 0.5, 1.0, 2.0, 4.0, 8.0, 16.0% weight per volume, a random sequence of presentations. The idea is that any one of these seven concentrations should be equally likely to appear on a given trial or, to put this condition slightly differently, that the occurrence of a particular value, say 2.0%, at one point in time should provide no real information to the subject about what will occur next. In doing this, a random sequential structure has been imposed on the stimulus sequence; there is nothing intrinsically normative about such a series and it is not commonly met in nature. There are obvious practical limitations; concentrations that are very low (like water) or very high (like syrup) are not going to be used. But they are not part of the sequential structure of the experiment; their exclusion is a prior consideration before the series is generated. All that can be said about the stimulus series is that it is randomly chosen or, in better modern statistical terminology, it is exchangeable with any other comparably drawn sequences and that the intertrial intervals between stimuli are known and controlled within limits. Ideally the variation in the interstimulus intervals, in seconds, is very small compared with the mean interval. The minimum interval is determined from practical considerations; stimuli are not presented too close together in time lest the subject become confused or lose sensations. It so happens that these constraints on spacing are also necessary to support the legitimate use of some forms of time series analysis, which is a convenient matching of conditions for experiment and for theory.

The responses may be freely selected by the subject from a range of numbers or be predetermined by the experimenter; there may, for example, be seven alternative permitted responses, each a labeled key from a set of which the subject presses one for each stimulus tasted. It is true that changing the number of permitted responses relative to the number of alternative stimuli can alter the stimulus–response relationships that the subject will exemplify in the experiment. For our immediate purposes this is peripheral; all that we need is an agreed method of coding the responses into numbers that in some way comprises a scale of the perceived intensity of sweetness.

The objectives 1, 2, and 3 are usually met by plotting the set of employed stimulus values, $\{S_a, S_b, S_c, \ldots, S_h, \ldots, S_n\}$ against the response values nominated or observed (perhaps lumped into a number of categories) that can correspondingly be symbolized as $\{R_{a'}, R_{b'}, R_{c'}, R_{d'}, \ldots, R_{h'}, \ldots, R_{n'}\}$. The different suffices a, a', b, b', . . . are used to show that the set of S can be ordered, as can the set of R but that there is no necessary correspondence one-to-one or one-to-many, between h and h' suffices. It is precisely this relationship that the experimenter seeks to determine and express as a response

$$R^* = f(S) = \alpha + \beta S^* + e \qquad (1.1.1)$$

where R^* is some scaling of $R_{h'}$ values, S^* is some scaling of the concentrations, α and β are constants, and e is independent mismatch that $f(S)$ cannot express. The whole experiment may be replicated over conditions and analyzed by ANOVA, but the logic is the same; a relationship is sought like (1.1.1) for which we may predict the following:

1. Further behavior by the same subject to the same stimuli.
2. Further behavior by the same subject to stimuli not used but not very different from the values used originally (interpolation or slight extrapolation).
3. What other subjects may do.
4. Detectable differences in responses to other substances like sucrose.

There are many refinements available to estimate α and β and the response confidence limits, given the form of $f(S)$.

Now consider what this approach does *not* tell us, and what the conceptual approach of time series analysis would aim to clarify.

The form of (1.1.1) tells us the end result, standing in a relationship outside time, for the S and R values used and hopefully for some others. It is not, as given, a model of the fine process by which the R are generated from the S values unless very strong assumptions are made that each S_h generates a family of R_h, which has a central, modal, value $\hat{R}_h$, and that

$$\hat{R}_h^* = \alpha + \beta S_h^* \qquad (1.1.2)$$

with the variance properties of the family centered on R_h, captured by the assumptions made about e; typically e is assumed for reasons of mathematical tractability to be distributed normally with zero expectation and to be uncorrelated with $\{S_h\}$. This powerful assumption makes a rich diversity of statistical methods available to the experimenter.

If instead it is desired to model the process by which successive R_h, are generated from the stimulus sequence, because interest is not in the average outcome but in the process itself, then the sequential character of the experiment returns to the center of the stage. Equations (1.1.1) and (1.1.2) say nothing at all about when or in what order the stimuli were presented or the responses made. All instances of an S_h are treated as equivalent; all instances of responses to S_h are treated as members of one centrally tending distribution. Thurstone's discriminal dispersion is one name for this classic idea. The cause of the variability is not examined further in the sense of being decomposed; it is one residual error. It is the only error given that (1.1.1) is a priori defined as the model sought. The error can, of course, be decomposed, for example, into sources associated with a particular stimulus and with a particular observer. This is done in some psychometric theories, such as that of Rasch.

Both empirically, in terms of experimental design, and conceptually, in terms of the assumption that the model appropriately fitted is of the form (1.1.2), the investigator strives for independence between successive responses. Diagrammatically if the locality of the experimental sequence where we are at present is shown by Fig. 1.1.1, where j is a subscript marking off steps in time, not designating particular stimulus values, the pattern of causal dependencies leads from prior events onto R_j.

If a form like (1.1.1) is accepted, then in effect a strong simplifying assumption is being made, namely that only the link from S_j to R_j matters in Fig. 1.1.1, and the rest are negligible or sources of error. The reader may like to call these causal links "influence lines"; this representation will be used repeatedly throughout this monograph, either diagrammatically or in its mathematical equivalents as soon as quantification is the objective. Note that quite deliberately the notation in Fig. 1.1.1 says nothing about *what* the stimuli and responses are; it says that their temporal connections are *relative to the present* point of observation, j. Thus $j + 1$, $j + 2$ are in the future, and $j - 1$, $j - 2$ are in the past.

The two series, $\{S_j\}$ and $\{R_j\}$, are treated as occurring at equal intervals (j as a counter taking integer values only) but the actual values that S_j takes from the possible alternatives $\{S_h\}$ are now shown. If there is to be a theory with special influence lines associated with particular stimulus values, which is quite possible both logically and psychologically, then it obviously needs a more complicated

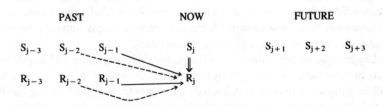

FIG. 1.1.1   The experiment as two time series with some postulated causal links.

representation. Such theories, though tempting, can become intractable in analysis and should be set up with caution.

In time series analysis, which can be in discrete time as quantized or in continuous time, questions are asked and answered about the processes that the influence lines suggest are operating. Instead of setting up the simple model $R_j = f(S_j)$, the general model

$$R_j = f(\{S_j, S_{j-1}, \ldots, S_{j-k}\}, \{R_{j-1}, \ldots, R_{j-m}\}) + e' \quad (1.1.3)$$

is taken as starting point. It says that the present response is a function of the present stimulus and all the previous stimuli back to $j - k$, or in other words R lags up to k steps on S. Also, the response is a function of previous responses back m steps. Actually, though this form looks complex, it is a simplification for a more general form that will be shown to be necessary in some cases whose consideration we may defer. Most of time series analysis is based on simple restricted cases of (1.1.3), which means both k and m are small. As in all theory construction one seeks a minimum complexity model or equation, given the objectives of process representation.

Consider two questions: What will (1.1.3) suggest as questions to be asked of the data, and why ask such questions instead of being content with representations like (1.1.1)? Recall that the paradigm experiment is about sucrose and sweetness.

If (1.1.3) is set up as an hypothesis, then it has to be matched to data structures, and the nature of the function f and the magnitude of k and m (maximum lag effects) determined. In pictorial terms this is the same as asking for a map, with numerical annotations, of the influence lines. The lines have to have their relative strengths indicated in some way. In statistical terms such influence is expressible as covariance, whereas in a deterministic model scalar weights can convey the notion, their values perhaps being normed to some fixed sum.

The solution to (1.1.3) in the sucrose experiment will depend, it is known, on the actual times in seconds between tastings and the volume of liquid ingested; for illustrative purposes we can take these things as fixed by the experimenter, but if interest is in the details of methodology, then the variations in k, m, and f as a function of procedural parameters can themselves be information about underlying psychophysiological processes that take some time to complete. For example, reactions on the surface of the tongue involve molecular movements from a water-soluble to a fat-soluble medium, and these reactions impose a biological time scale on some aspects of the psychophysics.

So, because of physiological and psychological adaptation and lingering effects in the mouth, two things can be expected to happen; in the short run there will be carry-over from a stimulus for one or two trials at least after it has been tasted. In the long run the sensitivity of a subject, either to detect sensation at all at a given stimulus concentration or to detect differences in sensations, may attenuate. It is also possible to obtain recovery of sensitivity and to obtain abrupt shifts in the subject's use of response scale values. All these things can in principle occur simultaneously; the object of the study is to disentangle (1) stable patterns in the influence lines, (2) long-term trends, (3) transient effects that can be modeled because they are recurrent in form though perhaps occurring randomly distributed in time, and (4) transient effects that cannot be modeled.

These four sources of response variability, given the $\{S_j\}$ series as input, might be thought of as four independent outputs. In time series analysis conceptually they may be separate because they can be looked at and described in data records and in trial solutions of the equations like (1.1.3), but in practice one may seek a single model that will encompass in its structure the means of generating all of items 1, 2, and 3 at once. This implies that the residual error, e', of (1.1.3) will be item 4 and some other noise but it will not be the same as e in (1.1.1). One would expect that the percentage residual variance associated with e' after fitting (1.1.3) would always be less than that associated with e in (1.1.1), not just because (1.1.3) has or can have many more parameters but because it has a different structure. If it is the case that (1.1.1) is sufficient, then it will come out as such in a search to identify the minimum complexity form of (1.1.3). However, what constitutes complexity, beyond conventions about the order of the model (the value of max (k, m) is the order here) is not simply defined. Prior considerations of the relative plausibility of different model structures with comparable numbers of free parameters come into the picture. The psychology of the situation precedes the model identification as well as follows it.

The motivation for attacking the modeling problem this way and giving little attention to the approximation of (1.1.3) by (1.1.1) (the approximation (1.1.1) is itself called a first-order gain function and computationally is obtained from any time series analysis as an intermediate step; standard library computer programs will do this automatically) rests not on knowing (1.1.3) in parametrised form but on the fact that (1.1.3) is a form of equation that is necessary and in some cases sufficient to identify the dynamic properties of the system. Mathematically it is an analog, in discrete time, of a differential equation in which the rates of change in a process are expressed as a consequence of environmental changes.

The form (1.1.1) is essentially static, not just by being outside time but by telling us nothing about how the system will behave if the inputs change atypically, such as very rapidly or very slowly. Biological and psychological systems have to respond to change and to restore their internal equilibrium in the face of change. There are naturally limits on how quickly they can do this; there are also limits on what changes they can detect and adjust to; rates of change of environmental parameters can be too low to be detected and consequently are not corrected for but induce slow drift in mean response levels. By excluding processes that extend over real time (continuous or discrete), we exclude any information on the capacity of a system to regulate itself in the face of change, other than to predict to what asymptotic values it will settle down, after a given change in input (i.e., *after* it has responded in a temporally extended manner). As no psychologist, hopefully, would wish to assert that (1.1.1) represents instantaneous response behavior to stimuli presented at unextended points in time, for to do so is to deny the existence of thresholds for stimulus durations and of response latencies, it is interpretable as a sort of steady-state description. The steadiness is attained after the system is perturbed by short-term transient input changes. Yet it is not the steady state that tells us anything about how the system regulates itself. To discover that, it is necessary to have data about the paths that the system takes, in time, to get to or back to a steady state. There are a great many systems, including that which actually mediates the taste of sucrose, that might, over a restricted range of S_h values, give the same set of $\hat{R}_h{}^*$ values in (1.1.2) if handled slowly and carefully. But their equivalence under steady-state conditions is precisely what stops the investigator from predicting how they respond to different rates of changes, given only data sufficient to establish the form of (1.1.1).

Pursuing this argument further, both empirically and mathematically, leads us from the solution of equations like (1.1.3), which is generally part of *system identification,* into the theory of dynamic systems. This theory is neutral with respect to the subject matter; it is not psychology until it is interpreted in specific instances as modeling a defined and circumscribed psychological process. In technical parlance, we only seek to model closed systems in time series analysis; the history of relevant inputs to the system has to be known in full. System theory is a broad and mathematically advanced area that extends to considerations well beyond identifying the structure or processes underlying relations like (1.1.2) or (1.1.3); it includes the design of systems to achieve specific objectives of controllability, which is a formal problem in engineering but not yet in psychology. Hence at many places the use of systems theory in psychology stops well short of the ramifications to which engineering applications naturally lead.

Thus, in the example chosen, the form (1.1.1) as a representation of the concentration–intensity relationship between sucrose and sweetness is intrinsically incomplete, and before it is of any theoretical importance or practical use, it needs augmentation. One step that has to be taken is to stipulate boundary conditions; namely

$$R = f(S), \qquad c_1 \leqslant S \leqslant c_2 \tag{1.1.4}$$

which restricts $f(S)$ to hold only between c_1 and c_2, and in this particular case we would further need to define

$$f(c_1) = 0 \tag{1.1.5}$$

$$f(c_2) = \max R \tag{1.1.6}$$

which means that stimuli of concentration lower than c_1 evoke no response, and stimuli more concentrated than c_2 are all perceived as equally sweet. The interesting complications that could arise because increasing concentration to syrups, molasses, and solids can in fact decrease the sweetness per unit of substance are just a peculiarity of the example that in other respects is chosen because it is typical of a very wide range of input–output relationships in psychology.

Traditionally (1.1.5) defines, perhaps probabilistically, a detection threshold, and (1.1.6) defines an upper threshold. Graphically the situation is shown in Fig. 1.1.2, again without any temporal considerations:

The form (1.1.4) is thus expanded to

$$R^* = a + bS^*, \qquad c_1^* \leqslant S^* \leqslant c_2^* \tag{1.1.7}$$

where the c^* are new limits defined because of the shift in the scales of S and R made so that the linear form of (1.1.7) will suffice between c_1^* and c_2^*.

The slope of (1.1.7), b, is an overall measure of sensitivity on the range $c_1^*-c_2^*$ but it turns out that it is not a measure of the discriminability of different S^* within that range, because there is no simple association or necessary relation between the two things; discriminability of adjacent S^* points varies along the line of slope b with the value of S^* and may be much poorer near to c_1^* or c_2^*.

The model (1.1.7) therefore requires amplification to answer basic questions about concentration–sweetness relationships for any one of the three objectives that motivate the study. That this is so implies, in turn, that the ordinary notion that "sweetness" (of sucrose, or whatever) can be characterized by a single number is empirically and conceptually wrong; the measure of sweetness demands information on thresholds *and* sensitivity *and* discriminability.

Yet we still have no insight, from this model (1.1.7), into how the organism comes to evaluate a given S_h^* by a given R_h^*, because the process takes place in time and is only representable by a model whose form is extended through time. The form of this process model should be invariant, but there is not necessarily some R that is a unique fixed response to an S, as (1.1.7) might erroneously be read to imply.

Birch, Latymer, and Hollaway (1980) have reexamined the question of sugar–sweetness relations with more precise methodology. They find a characteristic relationship, in time, for fixed concentration S_h for a given sugar. This is shown as a general case in Fig. 1.1.3. That is, a pattern of variation of sweetness

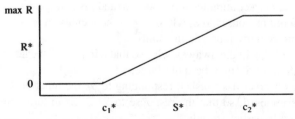

FIG. 1.1.2   The input–output relationship with boundary or threshold conditions imposed.

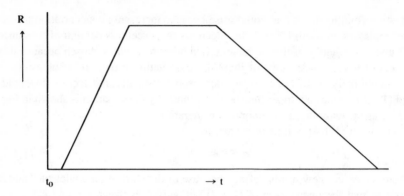

FIG. 1.1.3 Relation between time and perceived sweet taste intensity for a fixed sugar concentration.

in time, after ingestion at some point t_0, is a necessary characterization of sweetness as perceived, and the shape of the rise and the fall is specific to a particular stimulus substance. The height to which it rises reflects the concentration. Some substances have a long initial delay before a response is elicited. Clearly equations like (1.1.7) say nothing about Fig. 1.1.3; the $R_h{}^*$ in (1.1.7) is some sort of average or integral or peak value of the shape of Fig. 1.1.3, though precisely how the response "R_h," that we get a subject to make, in terms of a rating on a scale, has some sort of fairly stable relation to the parameters of the shape in Fig. 1.1.3, is unknown. This relationship could be teased out by time series analysis of a diversity of data.

The fact that responses are extended and variable in time to a given stimulus means that the observed responses in a series

$$R_{j-2} \quad R_{j-1} \quad R_j \quad \cdots$$

are not simply explained as corresponding to

$$S_{j-2} \quad S_{j-1} \quad S_j \quad \cdots$$

because Fig. 1.1.3 tells us, qualitatively:

1. R_j will not be an immediate response to S_j because of the initial delay after t_0; here, obviously, t is a continuous time measure and j is in large discrete steps.
2. The maximum responses to S_j will occur in the vicinity of $R_{j+1}, R_{j+2}, R_{j+3}$ (depending on how long j is in t units).
3. The effects of S_j will die away slowly, so that k in R_{j+k}, the last response that owes something to S_j, may be quite large.
4. Before the observer has finished responding to S_j, the input of S_{j+1} will begin to be superimposed, so that the response to S_{j+1} is in turn confounded with that to S_j and to earlier stimuli.

5. The observed response series $\{R_j\}$ is not a series of independent responses to $\{S_j\}$ but rather consists of what are called *convolutions* of responses to $\{S_j\}$.

A *convolution* is a mixing of shapes like Fig. 1.1.3, staggered in their starting times, as in Fig. 1.1.4. The response at any t, or at the sampled points $j, j + 1, j + 2, \ldots$ is a weighted sum of the curves at that point. In order to get back to discovering what the underlying Fig. 1.1.3 is for a prototypical stimulus and to discover how R_h^* in (1.1.7) relates to the parameters of the shape in Fig. 1.1.3, it is necessary to find ways of effecting a *deconvolution* of the observed response series; we can only observe the sum of the shapes in Fig. 1.1.4, and a great diversity of component shapes could generate the same sum or envelope curve, or series of points if we observe in discrete time steps. The way that the shapes convolute is under partial experimenter control in psychology, which sets that discipline apart from the purely observational sciences.

Biological subsystems like this sweetness perception process, which fluctuate in time, can be conceptualized and studied through a diversity of mathematical methods. Which method is chosen depends strongly on what the investigator is interested in and what is known at the outset. As soon as we move away from a simple unique model like (1.1.2) to the great flexibility of (1.1.3), the analysis demands much greater a priori consideration of what is a plausible psychological structure; the mathematics of *deconvolution* from observed outputs to underlying processes extended in time can be, and often is, almost fully automated by computer library programs. But the investigator's decision process concerning what sort of representation is sought is much more fluid; it is precisely that area where substantive psychological theory and the mathematics of data analysis have critically to interact.

Time series analysis cannot effectively be used without knowing, at least tentatively, some of the range of models consequent upon different assumptions. The sort of explanation or model that is sought is consequently chosen from a

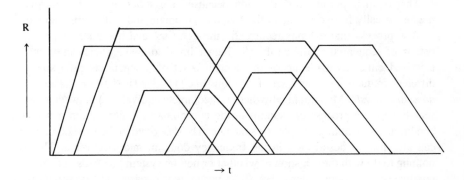

FIG. 1.1.4 Successive responses to a series shown as superimposed, though they actually sum at any point in time.

repertoire different from that of models outside time, though such models can occur as special restricted cases if they fit the data. That is, approaching theoretical psychology via time series analysis does not exclude time-independent models; it subsumes them as special limiting approximations. Computationally they are usually much simpler and can therefore be produced as an interim stage or a by-product of a full time series analysis. But psychologically what they mean, from the context of time series analysis, is no longer the same; they are no longer models of stimulus-response relationships but are artifacts of averaged or cumulative behavior under steady-state conditions. This last point can be emphasized in a slightly different way. In traditional psychophysics, whose methods can be used to find estimates of the parameters in (1.1.2) or (1.1.7), data are not collected until the organism has stabilized; the early trials of an experiment are characterized as contaminated practice trials, or warm-up, and discarded because including their results in the data for estimating (1.1.4) decreases validity. There is thus an admission that the process is not homogeneous through time as (1.1.7) suggests. But, if it is represented as a time series, it can be homogeneous in the sense of having fixed parameters and a structure like (1.1.3); yet at the same time it can behave on early trials in quite a different way from later on. If the process in Fig. 1.1.4 starts at t_0, then until about four complete patterns like Fig. 1.1.3 have been generated, the system is not the convolution of four or more patterns.

The fact that the microstructure of a response (the pattern in Fig. 1.1.3) is not a value at a point in time but rises and falls over a time span comparable in order of magnitude with the length of a trial, suggests two possibilities:

1. That the system may have a natural periodicity, which means it has within it regular fluctuations of fixed amplitude and frequency.
2. That the very act of doing an experiment and eliciting responses at fixed intervals induces some periodicity.

This is an important consideration because time series analysis is pursued mathematically in two ways, in the frequency domain and in the time domain.

Any process that extends recurrently through time and has a stable internal pattern of sequential relations, the "influence lines" drawn earlier, can be characterized either as made up of the sum of a set of independent processes of different frequencies or as a set of relations like (1.1.3). The latter is called *time domain analysis*. Mathematically there is a complete equivalence between representations (of a process or system) in the two domains under certain technical conditions, so that in principle if a system can be described in the time domain, it can also have a description in the frequency domain, and vice versa. This is nothing to do with the question of whether or not the system proceeds in continuous time or in discrete steps. For some purposes it is easier and clearer to see what is happening by working in the frequency domain of analysis, but generally it is here suggested that an intuitive feel for psychological time series is easier and more obviously gained in a discrete time representation. In computational terms there is little to choose, as standard library programs such as IMSL will give both time and frequency domain analyses on the same data input as a routine. If the meaning of the phenomena is sought in a physiological substrate, it may be easier to use the frequency domain representation. Again, it must be reiterated that it is not necessary to do this and in no sense more "accurate." Accuracy and interpretability are not the same thing in time series analysis, nor are they really so in any other modeling.

The distinction between the natural periodicity (or quasi-periodicity if the system does not exactly repeat itself in time) and a periodicity induced by the experimental procedure can be illustrated in a psychophysical problem that arises in olfaction (Berglund, 1974; Gregson, 1982). When a subject is asked to estimate the intensity of an odor in an airstream, the subject sniffs repeatedly, mainly as part of breathing but also as a consequence of being told to try and detect a smell.

If the airstream is continuous but varying in concentration, it will be sampled as the subject sniffs. As a consequence of sniffing there is intensity adaptation and the subject alters temporarily in sensitivity. What goes into the olfactory receptors, and hence generates signals to the brain, and what is reported to the experimenter, are not of course the same thing. The sniffing produces an *inner sampled data system,* of irregular spacing in time, and from this quasi-periodic series is further sampled a series of equally spaced responses, by the experimenter's spaced trials, which may be designated an *outer sampled data system.*

In a sense, therefore, the stimulus available, a continuous variable in time, is sampled twice, by sniffing and by choosing, less often, to respond. The original sampled data series is censored by the response process, and some of the information about fluctuations, periodic or aperiodic, in the behavior of odor intensity and its more rapid changes, is lost. It will be inevitably lost if the frequency of sniffing is too low. Losing information about periodic variations in a time series just by sampling too infrequently is called *aliasing.* The mathematical analysis of aliasing and its avoidance is thus a recurrent topic in time series analysis.

Summarizing the conclusions that follow from this introductory example, seven points are noted:

1. Input–output functional analyses outside time are restricted representations that are produced within a time series analysis and are called *first-order gain functions.* Plots of stimulus–response relations are examples of such functions.

2. Time series analysis takes into account the nature of processes that extend through time; they are thus concerned with rates of change. They are constructed to model the way that systems behave in the face of changes in inputs.

3. Time series analysis is an area of statistical mathematics that is rich and diverse in the models it potentially offers the psychologist. Consequently the

choice between models has to be made on psychological as much as on mathematical grounds.

4. Any experiment or quasi-experiment that makes systematic repeated observations in time may potentially be analyzed as a time series or as a set of time series.

5. Time series may be deconvoluted in the time or in the frequency domains. These two forms of representation are mathematical counterparts of one another, but their ease of interpretability, relative to one another, varies with the psychological or psychophysiological content of the problem.

6. Because time series analysis is concerned with the representation of fairly stable processes that exist through time, it leads naturally into systems theory and to the identification of processes or psychological subsystems that have the capacity for self-regulation.

7. The results and methods of linear modeling and associated experimental design techniques commonly found in psychology are not readily extended to time series analysis; conceptually it is expedient to start afresh.

1.2 WAYS OF ENCODING DYNAMIC BEHAVIOR

The problem of how appropriately to describe dynamic behavior that persists through time has been with us since the start of human discourse; until recently negligible progress was made. Perhaps it is true to say that persisting dynamic behavior presents us with cognitive and conceptual problems that are beyond the talents of most to understand and to solve; if such problems are simplified to make them comprehensible, in the sense that the reader or listener enjoys a warm feeling of understanding, then in most cases the problems are trivialized out of shape and reduced to insolvability. To put the problem a little more optimistically, the amount of learning, of conceptual frameworks and algorithms, necessarily is so extensive that relatively few will be attracted to the effort even if the component steps in such learning are surmountable. This matters to the theoretical psychologist because there is a good case to be made for arguing that psychology is or should be the science of dynamic systems, but the literature of dynamic systems analysis is mostly about problems that arise outside psychology, though not necessarily in any better-defined contents. It could be that there is a natural sequence of progression in constructing theories about dynamic systems and that a science may get stuck at the wrong level for the appropriate solution of its own data-generated problems. Let us see how this might have come about, because our objective is to get out of and past the verbal phase of system description in which much of psychology is presently locked.

Consider the example of a child riding a bicycle along the road. The dynamics of riding a bicycle were early considered by engineers, because there are design problems centering on the castor action of the front wheel; if the axle of the front wheel is vertically under a steering column that is itself vertical, then the machine is much harder to ride. Most of us learn to ride a bicycle and learn that leaning and turning the front wheel a little, as we go, first to one side and then to the other, seems to keep us upright. To explain precisely how this happens is another story, which is peripheral to the current theme.

Now our hypothetical child rides along the road, and his front wheel hits a stone, say about 10 cm in diameter, and he temporarily loses control and wobbles erratically from side to side uttering cries of distress. He may fall off or he may gradually or even abruptly regain control of his movement and stop the wobble, so that he goes on as if nothing had happened.

This story is a slice out of the history of a dynamically steady-state system, comprising rider and machine and road surface. If we do not consider the energy loss involved in riding the bicycle, then it may be called a closed system, nothing else comes into the story. The actual situation is, of course, a sequence of events in the space and time of the physical world and in the experience of the rider. If a film is made of the episode, then we have a record in discrete time, one frame of film per arbitrary unit of time. In fact we shall have then some of the raw data that lead, with selective numerical encoding, to a multivariate discrete time series. Such a time series is itself the starting point for the construction of models of behavior; it is not the behavior itself. In making this distinction the precedent of Coombs (1964) demarcating between events and what we choose to record of events, when we make decisions about the form that data to be recorded will take, is closely and deliberately followed.

All the ways that we have of describing a series of events are intrinsically incomplete, in the sense that a map of terrain is always incomplete; if it were complete, it would become an exact copy of the terrain, which is not a map. The purpose of making descriptions of time series of events is to hold onto regularities and pattern or structure and to lose, hopefully, trivia. Any description is thus a *partial encoding*. There are five major ways of partially encoding the situation of the boy nearly falling off his bicycle; they are interesting not only for their limitations but because they illustrate the progression of human thought and the inadequacies of much of psychological writing on dynamic topics. An interesting problem posed for the developmental psychologist is whether historical progression is a model for the education of the single individual or whether some stages can profitably be skipped.

Partial Encoding 1

Pictorial representation: the discrete time form dates from about 7000 B.C. and the continuous form from the cinematograph. This method is useless for making quantitative predictions about the stability of a system; it communicates with impact even to the illiterate and is sufficient basis for the creation of typologies of event sequences but little else. This sort of encoding has become increasingly popular in elementary university textbooks and in filmstrips.

Partial Encoding 2

Verbal or written language representation: this dates from about 500 B.C. This needs more skill to interpret and can be less redundant in encoding than level 1. The ideas of stability and limits on stability, which are abstract notions of powerful generality, have to be introduced by examples and are not quantifiable. Thus level 2 represents the limit of what can be conceptualized in nonmathematical models, though recently the concepts of fuzzy set theory provide some limited bridge between this encoding 2 and quantification. It is intrinsically dangerous, precisely because we can repeatedly reencode within this level and never get any more precise or predictive. Translation can be made into other languages, or into another verbal theory, and still be as far from quantification. So-called dynamic theories of behavior in clinical psychology characteristically show these features. Discussions of metatheory are usually at this level, even at the price of vacuity.

Partial Encoding 3

Flow diagram representation: this dates from the early twentieth century. This level is interesting because it is the first at which the encoding presents, deliberately, a picture of functional relationships in which the physical details are lost. The actual shapes or sizes of the boy, the bicycle, and the stone are minimally represented, but the sequence of events in time may be taken out of time and into simultaneous pictorial representation. This form of partial encoding superficially resembles a cross between levels 1 and 2 but is neither. Its proper use is as an aid to functional modeling involving quantification, but it is unfortunately used commonly as a starting point for retrogression to level 2, in which case it says nothing that cannot be said, with characteristic imprecision, at 2.

The feedback loop is most readily presented this way; see Fig. 1.2.1. In fact

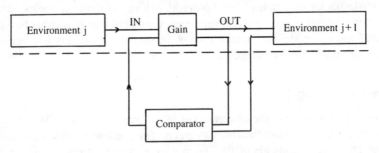

FIG. 1.2.1   Feedback partially encoded at level 3.

feedback is so commonly shown in this way that the picture may become synonymous with the theory or with the phenomenon, which is to commit the error of equating an encoding with the process it represents. Figure 1.2.1 is drawn slightly differently from the manner commonly used in many texts in order simply to be able to chop off the bottom part of the diagram as required. In this system signals go IN from the environment, and later responses go OUT to the environment; some time necessarily elapses, which can be one unit of time in duration, while the process in the middle boxes is taking place. The box labeled Gain simply increases or decreases the extent to which the input is modified to obtain the output. In the Gain box we could write a familiar psychological equation:

$$[R_j] \qquad\qquad [S_j]$$
$$\log (\text{environment}, j + 1) = a + b{\cdot}\log (\textit{environment}, j) \qquad (1.2.1)$$

and if we do this, then the equation is called, in this context, the *first-order gain equation*. As written, it says nothing about the part of the diagram below the dashed line that divides the figure horizontally. It says nothing about control or stability or self-regulation or the correctness or incorrectness of responses.

The Comparator box takes its own two inputs, compares them, and sends out a signal whose only purpose is to adjust the gain, so that the two inputs to the comparator are brought into a close match or correspondence with each other.

If the total loop (Gain + Comparator) is present, then we have closed-loop or *feedback* behavior. If only the part of the system above the dotted line is present, then we have open-loop behavior, and no self-regulation. When the system is dynamically stationary, then we may have no evidence of the existence of the part below the dotted line if we can only look at the system from the outside, that is, if we have only the record of the input and the output as is usual in psychophysical experiments. This is a serious conceptual problem.

The feedback loop exists in many forms: as the TOTE pattern in psychology (Miller, Galanter, & Pribram, 1965) or as part of a computer flow diagram (early 1950s) or in industrial studies of process control (early 1920s).

This sort of encoding has the limitations of the first two encodings, but if we can write equations into the boxes, then the whole situation becomes predictive and capable of precise description. As an unquantified model it is rather trivial, but put the exact values of the parameters in the equations for the gain and the comparator and it is powerful. Historically it appeared in psychology nearly 200 years after James Watt invented the governor in 1788.

Partial Encoding 4

Classical control theory (in the form given here, originates with Liapunov in 1892). To make any more progress we have to leave picture thinking and use process thinking: We have to consider abstract systems that extend in time. We consider an abstract system with output z and input x, so that $z = g(x)$ is the gain function when the system is in its simplest form. *But,* we are concerned with questions of stability and the capacity of the system to regulate itself. Time must now come explicitly into the encoding: In fact, this is what happens when we turn the previous form into an encoding that is any use. That is, the differential equations that we now must use are the consequence of filling in the boxes in the previous picture.

The rate of change of x with time is $dx/dt = y$. The rate of change of change of x (that is, the acceleration of x) is

$$\frac{d^2x}{dt^2} = \frac{dy}{dt} = f(x, y) \tag{1.2.2}$$

This means that the rate at which input accelerates in this system is a function both of the input itself and the rate of change of the input. This is the way in which we express the problem if we want to represent motor skills used in such tasks as riding a bicycle.

Note that we do not just move into mathematics and out of picture thinking, we move out of the real world of concrete images into a style of thinking that is removed from the real world. So the encoding is now formal, powerful: It is known to work sometimes; it is known not always to work; the conditions under which it does not work are partly known.

From the initial assumptions we set up Fig. 1.2.2.

This is the abstract model: δ is the *zone of influence of equilibrium of the phase plane.* A system that is self-regulating is stable inside this region. This means that if the input, or the rate of change of the input, are changed within the limits of the shaded region in Fig. 1.2.2, then the system can adjust itself and keep its input–output relations stable in a dynamic sense. It doesn't mean that the output remains static. If we move into G (a zone that can vanish, mathematically), then we are in the *zone of influence of the stable state.* Normally we can, within some small time, come back into the zone δ. The path in time, through the variable values of x and y that the system takes in returning to equilibrium, is mathematically tractable in the stable equilibrium region. Liapunov (1892) showed that the path can be approximated by linear equations of the form

$$\frac{dy}{dt} = ax + by, \qquad \frac{dx}{dt} = y \tag{1.2.3}$$

and we can calculate the actual path back into stability on the plane and how long it will take to get back into stability. This is what McFarland has done (1971, 1974) with some work in the psychophysiology of thirst regulation in animal behavior.

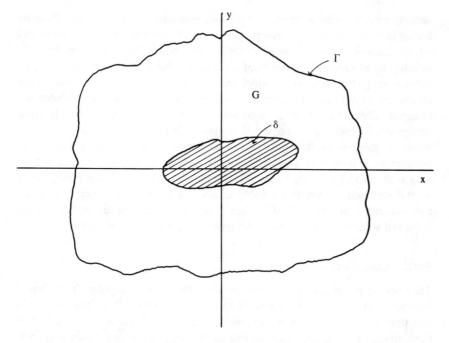

FIG. 1.2.2   Liapunov Phase Plane.

But when we get near to Γ, the boundary of G, the system becomes unstable; it may not be able to get back into δ, and certainly if it can get back, then the path that it takes is not predictable from simple equations. This path that I refer to is of course a path in time and in parameter values, not a path in space. The rate of return to stability decreases as we approach Γ. All this theory matters a great deal to people who design such things as nuclear power stations. If a potentially lethal system gets near to its Γ, then you have to evacuate one or two cities nearby. A system has to be monitored continuously to know where it is in the phase plane.

This sort of theory became more usable when means of calculating the behavior of complex systems became generally available, when computers allowed the investigator to set up the model as in Fig. 1.2.2 and see how it behaved. But the classical theory is written in continuous variables, and computers and psychological experiments that are composed of sequences of trials in time are both discontinuous. So a shift in theory construction has taken place again.

Once a breakthrough into abstract modeling has occurred, the way is opened to refinement and to variations in the basic structure of ideas. Of particular importance to the life scientist is the possibility of considering various different sorts of stability or of considering the performance of systems that function intermittently or with limited efficiency. The idea of stability intorduced by Liapunov (1892) turns out to be not always the most pertinent, and alternative definitions offered by Andronov (1956) are potentially of greater use: Remembering that *stability* is an overall property of a system whereby it can return to a steady dynamic input–output relationship after being displaced from that relationship by extraneous sequences of stimuli, a stable system in the coarse sense defined by Andronov is one in which the values of some internal parameters can be altered, though an appreciable range and yet leave the overall stability unchanged. The same system may be said to be robust (or insensitive) to some changes in its own internal detailed structure. In other words, the system as a whole is stable when it is not critically sensitive to the values of some of its parameters. It is obviously advantageous for a biological system to have robustness with respect to some of its parameters; for example, if our ability to do mental arithmetic was not reasonably unaffected by the environmental temperature within a range of 16°–30°C, then it is possible that the evolution of technological societies would have been appreciably slower or negligible.

Partial Encoding 5

The latest step it is plausible to distinguish is the digital computer simulation of systems, with origins in the early 1950s. The abstract structure of a process in real time is represented by a computer program that itself is extended in real time, though not the same time as that of the original process, necessarily, and time can be represented within the program. All that could be done in partial encoding 4 can be done, and the internal time scale of the program can be changed as we wish, and the process stopped or started or opened up for inspection as desired.

It was originally thought that systems that operated in continuous time should be properly modeled in continuous time, but for all practical purposes this is not true, and without loss of generality any psychological model, whether concerned with processes that are plausibly continuous such as the biochemistry of neural transmission or plausibly discontinuous such as repeated plays of a prisoners' dilemma game, can be adequately simulated in discrete time. The fact that most of the data of psychology are time series constitutes no obstacle to encoding in this sense. There are other advantages that make timely the use of encoding at this level; some of the theory in artificial intelligence, mathematical learning theory, and time series analysis in statistical dynamics has come into a mutual correspondence. There are parallels in the way theory is written so that results that were developed for one application can readily be used for another seemingly diverse purpose. This form of abstraction is lacking, except in the sense of literary metaphors, at the lowest level of encoding.

The layman, and indeed the psychologist with little sympathy for quantification and modeling, will often complain that ideas are not expressed in ordinary language. It might be well, therefore, to note that ordinary language is the partial encoding at what has been called level 2, and only when this level was abandoned did progress in our self-imposed task begin, historically, to be made. It is possible to write about different levels of partial encoding in fairly ordinary language, as is being done now, but this does not solve any of the problems that the later partial encodings solve; it only points out that things can be done. In distinguishing among these levels, three objects are achieved; to remind the reader that no description of behavior is complete, to give at least a hint of why time series are the recurrent theme of this study, and to show why much of what is said is not in everyday prose though it is very much about the recurrent structure of human experience. The boy on the bicycle can have his behavior in both observed and hypothetical situations represented precisely and powerfully at the level of partial encodings 4 and 5, but in doing so the bicycle and the boy have, like the smile on the face of Alice's Cheshire cat, disappeared; all that is left is abstract structure. At the end of the exercise we can predict the appropriateness of descriptions at levels 1 and 2 though the reverse direction of inference is impractical. It is for this reason that the order of development, historically, of the various forms of describing dynamic sequences can be regarded as moving toward more powerful conceptualization.

1.3   SOME COMMENTS ON THE STATE OF THE ART

Time series analysis has gone through sweeping changes and expansion in the last decade; new developments with obvious potential for psychological modeling and data analysis appear frequently. Generalizations should therefore be made with great caution concerning either the strength or the limitations of pertinent forms of time series analysis. The comments of this section are offered as an introduction to some questions of identifiability; this topic is approached as it is in the early 1980s and is also in a state of flux. Any experimental psychologist entering this area will be concerned with questions of identifiability, and hence this section is a preamble to the more detailed treatment given later.

The initial motivation for moving into time series analysis is to be able to represent the behavior of a system that is itself able to respond to rates of change, as opposed to responding only to amounts of change, even when the system can only be observed at discrete points in time. It is thus a way of investigating the problems raised in Section 1.2. As noted, different dynamic systems can, if perturbed, eventually come to a static response level or can correct for input displacements or perturbations by compensating so that their observed output stays, quantitatively, about the same. A system that is capable of controlling its own stability may, at the black box level of description, show virtually no abrupt changes for *large but not too rapid* input changes. This leads to the indistinguishability, at the black box level, of systems that apparently blithely ignore their environments. There are basically two ways of failing to respond to change, either the system is dead or it is alive and a perfect compensator. Some animals will feign near-death, from insects up the phyletic ladder to humans in psychotic states, so the distinction has interest for the neuropsychologist.

Figure 1.3.1 depicts the two cases: (1) is independence of the environment and (2) is perfect compensation.

As shown, the two systems considered in terms of input–output relations, at the level of resolution in time that the observer uses (observations are made, say, every n msec) are indistinguishable up to the point in time where recording stopped. There are two ways in which the two systems might be distinguished without opening the black boxes, apart from waiting forever, given that the human observer does not know that Fig. 1.3.1(a) has no inside connections and that Fig. 1.3.1(b) has a well-designed feedback loop inside with rapid and good response characteristics. Note that poker players value (b) positively because it resembles (a); (b) is dynamic and (a) is static.

The first way to distinguish the two systems is to increase the resolution of observation (i.e., make observations more frequently). This will show up second-order perturbations in the output of Fig. 1.3.1(b) that cannot be found in the output of (a). These will be of higher frequency and will be correlated with some

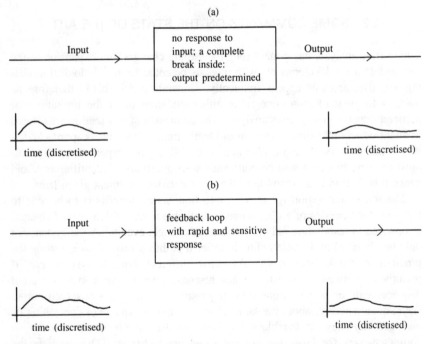

FIG. 1.3.1   Comparison of two indistinguishable systems, one static and one dynamic. (a) A system independent of input, generating its own output, that can be described by a stationary model. (b) A system with perfect compensation to input changes, and a predetermined rule for converting inputs to outputs, that can match the output of (a).

events in the input, say, with high acceleration. This strategy may not be possible in practice; there is a limit to resolution because observations cost money.

The second way is to give each system a large violent brief input; an impulse that is a sharp peak or single value with negligible duration or a step that shifts the mean level of input up or down a large amount relative to its local variability. This case is reviewed to emphasize that time series analysis and experimental manipulation together are needed to answer questions concerning what sort of system is functioning, when the internal structure is not directly observable. Systems that have equivalent responses (which can include no response at all) are not distinguishable simply by passive observation, and time series analysis can be merely a sophisticated form of passive observation.

Proceeding now to a more detailed consideration of identification, in the sense of deciding what sort of dynamic structure will most simply describe behavior, it is presupposed that the system is like Fig. 1.3.1(b).

Figure 1.3.2 presents a framework for this evaluation; it can be seen that both the environment and the organism include aspects of the time series as subsystems. The part inside a double frame is treated as a closed subsystem (CSS) and is the total scope of the time series analysis; it includes all the quantitative data that is available to the investigator who wants to investigate environment–organism relationships, within some defined problem area such as vision or memory.

The alternative ways in which the current stimulus can be written as a function of past stimuli only, or as a function of past responses, are formalized as models within the closed subsystem, though obviously how this comes about is determined by processes in the environment or in the organism, respectively. It is the *stability* in time that is a capacity for being representable by a comprehensible model of low complexity and few changes in its internal structure in time that enables us to treat the stimulus and response sequences as a closed system.

More complex models will allow intermittent interaction by environment or organism with the CSS; such interaction can be spaced evenly or at random or be contingent on specific events outside or in the CSS. This is not shown in Fig. 1.3.2, but the wider situation can be thought of as a sequence of models like Fig. 1.3.2 placed end to end in time, so that the pattern is repeated but with different parameters in each segment. This sequence leads inevitably to theories of hierarchical control systems, because rules are needed to go from one pattern, which is a state, to another.

In Fig. 1.3.2 it is convenient to consider alternative structures within the CSS by labeling the functional linkages, each of which may be the subject of one or more algebraic time series models. Call the complete set of linkages $\{l\}$ and the component linkages that are possible:

ls = link within the stimulus series
lc = current stimulus–response link

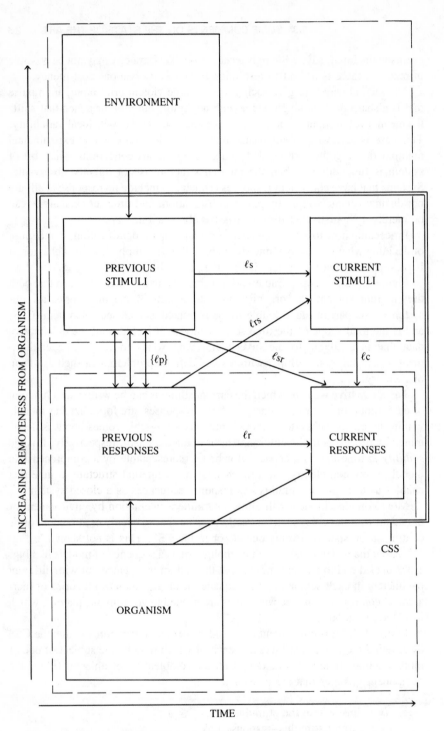

FIG. 1.3.2   A closed subsystem.

lrs = link from previous responses
to the current stimulus

(This will be absent unless the stimuli are contingent upon previous responses; such a link can exist if feedback has been introduced by the environment, which includes the actions of the experimenter.)

lsr = link from previous stimuli to
the current response bypassing the
current stimulus
lr = link within the response series
$\{lp\}$ = past set of linkages, stimuli to
responses and responses to stimuli

Each of the defined linkages can be extant, or absent, in a time series model of current response generation; obviously therefore one way to proceed would be to classify time series in terms of their extant linkages as given in Fig. 1.3.2, and indeed to some degree this is what is actually done. However, seeking too tight a correspondence would include some models of little apparent use in psychology and would exclude some recent developments that are potentially exciting and point the way that progress can be made.

A partial correspondence with models that have been systematized by Box and Jenkins (1970), and workers deriving therefrom since 1970, is useful because it makes clear some issues of identifiability apart from the one already raised at the beginning of this section.

Given the set of linkages $\{l\}$, the *general* problem of identification is to decide, from input–output records and contextual configurations of causes and influences, which links are extant and which are absent.

In contradistinction, the *specific* problem of identification is one of deciding on the details of the algebraic structure and parameter values that most accurately represent what the links do, given that it is known which are extant. These specific objectives need not be met in the same way for description and for forecasting; in fact a best-fit model for the description of a data sample may be inferior for purposes of prediction into the future. Hence the investigator's objectives are part of the definition of specific identification but need not be, nor hopefully would be, part of general identification.

Correspondence between the structure of time series models and substantive psychological theories can be sought after general identification has been achieved or assumed. This assertion is contrary to the sense of some time series identification procedures, even semiautomated ones, where attempts are made directly to choose between alternate parametrized models within $\{l\}$, but it is compatible with attempts to decide between more specific models involving ls and lc. The sense of recent analyses (Anderson, 1980) is to show that there are cases where on real data samples, or samples of comparable length but simulated, it is not possible to distinguish with confidence in the general identification sense, but it is possible to distinguish alternative parametrizations within a set of models that assume the same linkages. To put this another way, given only input–output relations, there may be different models with incompatible $\{l\}$ structures, having comparable complexity, that are equivalent in their efficiency as describers or predictors.

Heuristically different models can be arranged in a two-dimensional plot, the axes of which are complexity and goodness of fit, and the areas in this plot that models characterized by different $\{l\}$ structures occupy will overlap and not be separable.

For illustration, eight different cases are listed in Table 1.3.1. These are not exhaustive but would cover a great diversity of psychological theories. In every case, the stimuli and responses can be understood as either single variables or as multivariate; for example, the responses can be vectors incorporating a magnitude estimation, a latency, and a degree of confidence or subjective probability. In this table MA = moving average, AR = autoregressive, SETAR = self-exciting threshold autoregressive (Tong & Lim, 1980).

Case 1 in Table 1.3.1 is the simplest modeling of psychophysics outside time and involves no time series analysis.

Cases 2 and 3 treat the responses as a weighted function of the recent stimulus history of the CSS; this idea has been used extensively in an ad hoc fashion, for example, by Helson (1964a) in adaptation level theory, or by N. Anderson (1974) in functional measurement theory to represent sequential effects in judgment.

Case 4 represents situations where the responses are an autonomous process.

TABLE 1.3.1

Some correspondences between linkages and time series models in common use

Case	Formal Description	Linkages	Time Series Model Names Gain Function
1	$R = f(\text{current } S)$	ℓc	
2	$R = f(\text{previous } S)$	ℓsr	MA
3	$R = f(\text{current}+\text{previous } S)$	$\ell sr + \ell c$	MA
4	$R = f(\text{previous } R)$	ℓr	AR
5	$R = f(\text{current } S + \text{previous } R)$	$\ell r + \ell c$	ARMA
6	$R = f(\text{current } + \text{previous } S \text{ and } R)$	$\ell sr + \ell r + \ell c$	ARMA
7	$R = f(\text{previous } S + \text{previous } R + \text{products of previous } S, R)$	$\{\ell\}$	Bilinear
8	$R = f[\text{cutoff level, } c^*;$ if current $S > c^*$, then f_1 if current $S < c^*$, then f_2 f_1 (previous + current S) f_2 (previous + current S)]		SETAR

Cases 5 and 6 are examples of the most general prior hypothesis for which Equation (1.1.3) has been used. In time series analysis the identification problem is approached either by assuming ARMA structure and then estimating the parameters within it or by seeking directly for an MA or AR solution; as the latter two are restricted forms of ARMA, this can eventually give the same result.

Case 7 is of interest because it can temporarily explode; the output flares up like an episode of high energy release and then subsides. When this occurs is not predictable, but its form can be simulated from random inputs. In particular, such episodes are not the result of responses just to specific stimuli as would be the situation in Cases 1, 2, or 3.

Case 8 is of very recent construction but is potentially revealing as it can show rapid jumps in output for continuous changes in input; it thus resembles and is related to catastrophe models that are discussed in Chapter 3. It is worth re-emphasising that the properties of time series models are not clear to intuition; it is rarely possible without considerable experience to predict from the algebraic shape of a model how it will behave, though many standard cases have now been described in the literature. Quite complex phenomena can be generated by models in Table 1.3.1 with only a few lags or cross-product terms.

The choice between models, either between cases like 1–8, which corresponds to the general identification problem, or within a case like ARMA, which is specific identification, is not made solely on data. Contextual information about how sequences are generated in the organism or in the environment and how they persist in real time create the boundary conditions within which an explanation has to be sought.

Thus, *input–output data cannot be, in general, sufficient for psychological subsystem identification through time series analysis.* This principle implies that a continual interplay between psychological theory and statistical analysis is necessary to produce economical and sensible models. There will exist very simple cases, which are often studied for preference, where time series analysis should be sufficient because the range of alternatives is small and certainly within the set of cases given in Table 1.3.1. It may be noted that procedures like analysis of variance are a sort of $\{lc\}$ modeling in their familiar forms.

1.4   OVERVIEW AND PLAN FOR LATER CHAPTERS

There is not just one way of representing time series of quantified observations, but at least three main methods of importance. Representations in terms of serial dependencies in discrete time, which correspond generally to the approach used in the example discussed in Section 1.1, lead to autoregressive models and what are called *transfer functions*. These have been extensively studied in some particular forms in econometrics. Their general theory is a branch of mathematical statistics and particular computational methods for solving practical problems have developed strongly in control engineering. Representations in time are appropriate when the way a process is conceptualized is in a set of steps equally spaced in time, and there is relatively little interest in, or little information to be gained from, considerations of the variations in intervals between discrete events. Hence representations in time are useful when the situation is one that the experimenter can pace or that goes on continuously but can be sampled at evenly spaced points in time. This covers a very wide range of psychological investigations and has some intuitive appeal as some of the statistics are clearly related to simpler and more familiar methods, as in regression and the general linear model.

If interest is in the variations between successive events in terms of when they occur, as a function of when the last previous events occurred, then a different approach is needed. In this monograph a brief coverage of this specialized approach is made to show its relation to time series analysis, but it is not the main thrust of the monograph.

When it is known or suspected that it would make good psychological sense to regard a process as made up of the sum of independent processes each of which is periodic; that is, it fluctuates regularly and repeatedly in time, then a representation in the frequency domain is used. This means that a conversion is made from a set of points in time to a set of frequencies, each with associated measures that describe the relative contribution of a particular frequency to the overall process. The frequencies become the basic building blocks of the model instead of the sequential dependencies in time.

The third main method is state space representation that has evolved in systems theory. This approach is mathematically a development of equations that deal with rates of change in a framework of discrete time. Because the theorist introduces additional transformations, called *states,* between the inputs and the outputs of the system and can have a diversity of such states each with its own characteristics and can further introduce rules by which the system switches between states, the approach is far more powerful than the first two but necessarily leads to more abstract and complex mathematical treatment. Some elementary notions are introduced for their potential application in psychology toward the end of the monograph. The problem that psychologists have to face is that their data will often only yield evidence of some underlying structure to the more powerful methods, precisely because biological and psychological systems are untidy and change their structure in time as they evolve, through learning or through maturation or through fatigue and decay.

To be historically superficial, then, transfer functions emerged in economics, frequency decompositions in physics, and state space equations in engineering, and frequency decomposition came first. In some cases these methods have a long history, but the topic has exploded in scope and depth since around the mid-1960s. It is now possible to find problems that are subtle and of great intrinsic complexity, such as the question of how subjects keep a system under dynamic control when faced by an interfering adversary who disrupts the control (Speyer, Samn, & Albanese, 1980), being treated quantitatively, but necessarily by using state space methods beyond the scope of this introductory monograph.

The earlier methods go back to the beginning of the nineteenth century, but applications in psychology really only date from the 1930s and were hardly successful. So far as psychology is concerned, the available mathematics has run well ahead of demonstrable applications (Anderson, 1980), or alternatively often the postulated psychological structures that are intrinsically dynamic and should be amenable to time series analysis are so put together that they do not lend themselves so readily to analysis as would some engineering theories. In areas of experimental psychology such as the study of motor skills, where engineering approaches have been used, then also time series analysis has found obvious employment. Though there are obvious difficulties in bringing time series analysis in an elementary form and models in traditional experimental psychology into close correspondence, the few examples where this has been done are of great interest. They raise new and potentially very creative issues in theoretical psychology and special problems for the applied mathematician who wishes to contribute both to theory and to methodology.

Although three main methods of time series analysis have been mentioned and were developed rather separately, it must not be thought that they are distinct. Indeed, much of the mathematical endeavor in this area has gone into demonstrating equivalences among the three approaches and into finding ways of transforming a representation of a system from one form into another.

Contemporary research has produced algorithms, now usually computerized (because it is virtually impossible to do the task any other way) to transform from time series to frequency domain representation or vice versa and from time series to state space equations and vice versa. These transformations are usually much easier to do in one direction than in the other, and in some practical cases of importance the transformation may be possible in one direction and impossible in the other. Precisely what the conditions are, under which these transformations from one mode of representation to another are legitimate and possible, is impossible to state in elementary terms or may not be known. The difficulties of proving general theorems at such a level of abstraction are considerable but need not detain the investigator from exploratory analysis. With library programs now available, it takes no more work and time to do a multivariate time series analysis than it takes to do a factor analysis or multivariate analysis of variance; the problems are ones of making sense of the answers.

In order for the results of a time series analysis to be interpretable, the investigator has to bring strong prior knowledge and hypotheses about the psychology of the situation to the exercise of interpretation, because one of the costs of powerful analytic methods is a rich diversity of alternative solutions that can have very different properties when extrapolated from the situation where the data were originally collected. Interestingly, in time series modeling of more complex forms, the solutions that fit data samples most closely may not be the best basis for predicting future behavior of the same series. The choice of mode of representation is thus partly determined by the ease with which it may be possible to marry psychological ideas to statistical structures.

But examination of the starting points of theory construction in transfer functions, frequency decompositions, or state space models, and the way they may have to be changed to accommodate the known sequential properties of the sorts of data the psychologist collects, is valuable. It is valuable both to see how time series analysis gives new insights and to sharpen up ideas of what constitutes a meaningful representation of a dynamic psychological or psychophysiological process. None of the methods of time series analysis are to be found in the run-of-the-mill introductory texts of statistics applicable to psychology. Thus the terms and the sorts of structures sought are unfamiliar and yet surprisingly are devised specifically to answer abstract questions in systems theory that look as though they have been borrowed from theoretical psychology. It is precisely because systems theory has pervaded the style of writing in sciences concerned with self-regulating and dynamic processes, including living organisms, that the common vocabulary seems familiar, even though the methodology that makes system theory rigorous and not just heuristic has had little use outside control engineering and cybernetics. Major themes that are introduced in the following chapters are outlined as follows.

Chapter 2 brings together concepts and definitions that underlie the common and usually computerized methods of time series analysis. The reader who is already familiar with parts of this work, whose original sources are very scattered, will choose to omit parts. The descriptive methods introduced are loosely interconnected because it is possible to progress in this way: Starting with a series of events, each of which is treated as either present or not present, yes or no, hit or miss, or degenerated into a binary measure because of doubts about its intrinsic measurability, such as pass–fail in an interview situation, it is possible to construct models that identify lawfulness in the temporal distribution of intervals, measured in time units, between successive events. This situation is considered first because it makes the fewest assumptions about the measurement of psychological units, such as perceived or reported sensation intensities used as responses or system outputs. As such it leads to statistical descriptions of single series under the control of stochastic generating mechanisms.

Sections 2.2 to 2.7.   The main concern of this monograph is with series spaced evenly in time. This common situation arises either because observations are made deliberately at even intervals or because the process only generates outputs at such intervals in time. In the first case, where the underlying process is continuous or almost continuous, the procedure of taking records at discrete points in time, and only at those points, yields what is called a *sampled data system.* Such systems have evolved to the point where their theory has its own specialized literature (Krut'ko, 1969).

When a series is considered at evenly spaced points in time, and interest focuses on the magnitude of the discrete input and output events, the natural role of autocorrelation within a time series arises. This basic idea, of measuring the serial dependence with a series by autocorrelating it over different lags or separations in time, leads naturally into a large family of models, studied in detail by Box and Jenkins (1970), which have already found some use in psychophysics and in experiments, such as can arise in operant psychology, which are basically interrupted time series. An episode is superimposed on, or inserted in, a time series, and its precise location and/or what happens in it is to be identified.

Sections 2.4 to 2.6.   Any series that can be represented by an autocorrelation structure, or a linear transfer function that can be derived from its autocorrelation, can also be represented in the frequency domain, within wide limitations. Psychophysiological time series, of which EEG (electroencephalogram) records are one of the best sorts of example, are usually analyzed in terms of their activity levels within a priori defined frequency ranges. It is known that this approach can lead to meaningful clinical diagnoses.

Sections 2.7 to 2.8.   There are extensive practical difficulties in constructing accurate frequency domain models for short error-loaded data samples, or as these are often called, *realizations* of time series. At the same time, as well as being methods of data analysis, representations in the frequency domain also serve as models of component subsystems or processes that transform series of inputs by creating changes in periodicity or in phase. Such processes are called *filters.* The idea of a filter is again extremely general, any human sensory, perceptual, or cognitive process could be called a sort of filter, but filters that are mathematically precise and well-defined, in terms of what they do to quantified inputs, are a rather more useful and restricted idea.

Section 2.9.   In both the time and frequency domains there are many available statistical measures that can be used to express the form and magnitude of functional dependencies between input and output time series properties. Unlike simpler measures such as a product–moment correlation they measure covariation between patterns each of which extends through time as well as involving the variances of the variates involved. Adequately to characterize a situation may require a complete set of such measures. Diagrammatically we can suggest what is implied, as a minimum complexity analysis, by Fig. 1.4.1.

In the left-hand column is a representation of what is done if the analysis is outside time. Two series of observations in numerical form (u represents input values and y output values; the notation shows that concern is with more general

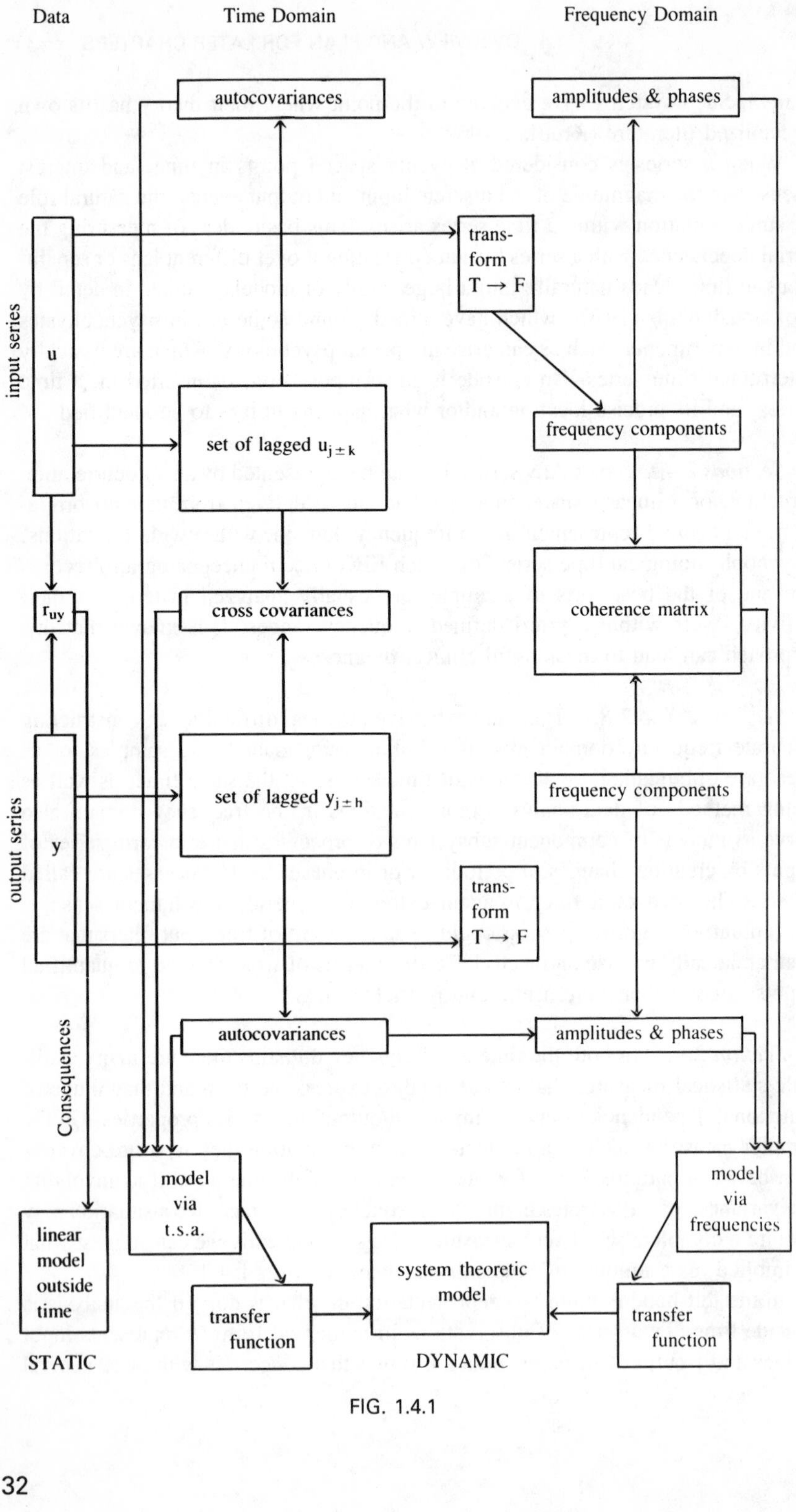
Data
Time Domain
Frequency Domain
autocovariances
amplitudes & phases
trans-
form
T → F
input series
u
set of lagged $u_{j \pm k}$
frequency components
r_{uy}
cross covariances
coherence matrix
output series
y
set of lagged $y_{j \pm h}$
frequency components
trans-
form
T → F
Consequences
autocovariances
amplitudes & phases
model
via
t.s.a.
model
via
frequencies
linear
model
outside
time
system theoretic
model
transfer
function
transfer
function
STATIC
DYNAMIC

FIG. 1.4.1

issues than a strict S, R representation) are related through a single number, typically a correlation r_{uy}, or a linear model outside time, a regression equation such as (1.1.2).

By strong contradistinction, analysis in either the time or the frequency domains is much more complex, though the actual computational effort is immaterial as the whole operation is commonly computerized. Parenthetically, the distinction between the three different solutions in Fig. 1.4.1 could represent computation time of less than a second for Data, about 5 sec for Time Domain, and about 15 sec for Frequency Domain with a large computer and a small experiment. The lines and boxes in Fig. 1.4.1 are actual program steps, in gross but not detailed terms, and show data movements and computations within the analysis. Only in the lower part of the figure, labeled Consequences are the boxes merely schematic, each containing some sort of equation or set of equations, which when interpreted constitutes a model of behavior. The crucial distinction is between static mode and dynamic mode representations, as labeled; the time versus frequency domains distinction is of less metatheoretical importance but obviously of great practical concern.

The long narrow boxes are vectors; the three large rectangles are matrices. Note that the representation of a process in time series analysis, so far as the descriptive statistics are concerned, requires many more terms than the single r_{uy} or the few parameters of the static model. This is the logical and necessary price of being able to demonstrate or, better, to identify a dynamic process with such intrinsic features as feedback or self-regulation.

Sections 3.1 to 3.7. The pathways of Fig. 1.4.1 are by now standard and have become library package programs for the routine analysis of well-behaved time series with stationarity and linearity in their appropriate representation.

As more complex models of systems, showing discontinuities or mathematically perverse characteristics, can be produced by breaking the difficult systems into tractable component parts, the methods of Fig. 1.4.1 continue to be useful for part-system analysis. In practice, exploratory analysis comparing different models, which the investigator can specify a priori, would be done within the framework of Fig. 1.4.1, unless strong information about the particular nonlinearities in the system was available (as in Section 2.5).

Psychological data are typically ill-behaved, however, though perhaps not more than those of other disciplines that have made better use of time series analysis. The nature of "ill-behaved" is not simply defined, because there are at least three problems that face the investigator:

1. The closeness of observation points in time, or in other words the *resolution* of the sampled data system, may not be sufficient to capture all the variations of importance. This is the problem of *aliasing* mentioned earlier.

2. The process being studied is not stationary, which means that the input–output relations may change gradually with time. Thus either there is needed a model of a time series in which the parameters themselves are functions of time (they are usually written as constants) or it is necessary to partial out trends in time. Such trends are either slow drifts in the levels of responding or are very low-frequency components. It is necessary to examine the remainder of the process decontaminated of such nonstationarities. Removing low-frequency components is probably more common in econometrics, and setting up models with time-varying parameters is more common in engineering. The experimental psychologist must decide on the basis of how much is known in advance which approach to adopt; detrending is somewhat atheoretical and exploratory.

3. The process is not linear, which means that none of the models implicit in Fig. 1.4.1 are appropriate. The simplest way to approach this question is to test if there is serial dependence of the form of deconvoluted responses to two or three repeated identical inputs. In analyses outside time, it is expected that repeating the same stimulus will, within error limits, yield the same response. This assumption is the cornerstone of much of classical psychophysics. In stationary linear time series it is not expected that the same response will always occur to the same stimulus, because of prior effects unique at a given point in a time series; but if the process is stationary and linear, then a repeated long series of the same input will give, after a lag, stable and consistent outputs. Under some circumstances, however, a nonlinear system will give a very different response to the second presentation of the same stimulus in immediate repetition, in the deconvoluted analysis. To recall the example of sucrose–sweetness in Section 1.1, marked short-term adaptation, which is a loss of sensitivity or of first-order gain, means that the peak value and the form of the characteristic response to a sweet substance would be shifted on successive presentations, as a direct consequence of the spacing of the testing points in time. This example serves to make another point, namely, that what is linear and what is nonlinear may depend also on the experimenter's choice of the spacing of trials in real time of the serial process studied. One may thus "tune" an experiment to approximate linearity and then analyze it as such, but with implicit loss of generality in the findings. Indeed this is a classical psychophysical approach; in so tuning the experiment, the evidence of nonlinearity that is necessary for a valid insight into process stability and self-regulation can be destroyed.

A summary of various types of time series analysis that make different demands on the data, so far as stationarity and linearity are concerned, is given in Table 1.4.1. Not all of these methods have found application so far in psychology, and the more complex methods (those lower down in the table) may demand so much prior quantitative information for their proper use that they could only be used in areas that have already been studied in depth with more traditional approaches.

TABLE 1.4.1

Commonest Forms of Time Series Analysis Potentially Applicable in Psychology

Type of Analysis	Input Continuous or Discrete	Magnitudes of Input/Output Specifiable	Intervals Constant or Variable	Process Stationary/ Nonstationary	Compatibility with Linear or Nonlinear Representations	Psychologically Relevant Paradigm
Renewal processes	Both	Not spec.	Variable dependent	Stationary	Linear	Successive reaction times
Autocorrelated or Moving average or Mixed (ARIMA)	Discrete or continuous via a sampled data system	Specified	Constant	Stationary	Linear	Steady state psychophysical series of judgments
Bivariate	Discrete	Specified	Constant	Stationary	Nonlinear	Behavior with random episodes
Fourier decomposition	Continuous	Specified	Constant and second-order or continuous	Stationary	Linear	Psychophysiological extended response processes
Hybrid ARIMA with periodicities	Mixed	Specified	Constant	Stationary	Linear	Longterm social group behaviour
Walsh decomposition	Discrete or continuous via a sampled data system	Constant value or zero	Constant and second-order	Stationary	Linear	Pattern recognition
Volterra functions	Usually discrete	Specified	Constant	Stationary	Nonlinear	Complex psycho-physiological processes
Wiener functions	Usually continuous	Specified	Constant and second-order	Stationary		
Kalman filtering	Discrete	Specified can be degenerate	Constant	Both	Both	Adaptive and predictive behaviour
Bayes filtering	Both	Specified	Both	Both, but particularly nonstationary	Both	Optimisation of sequential decision making
(Multivariate versions of the above correspond to the univariate cases)						

Sections 4.1 to 4.7.   Applications, varying in their complexity and in their tractability from the standpoint of stationary linear modeling, are reviewed in Chapter 4. Attention has to be drawn to the limitations and potential applicability of the time series approach. The problems of system representation peculiar to different areas of psychology, and the consequent diversity of time series analyses needed, is emphasised.

Section 5.1.   In state space representation, intermediate variables, usually denoted as some set $\{x\}$, are used as well as the inputs u and the outputs y. As soon as states are introduced, the observed outputs become, algebraically, a sort of weighted compromise between input information and information already stored in the system. The values of the states can be used as a form of memory of the past inputs and outputs of the system. The rules for combining the two sorts of information, from inputs and from states, are fixed, but the actual parameter values of the internal states can also be subject to systematic and modelable changes in time. The skeleton of these very general ideas is suggested in Fig. 1.4.2, though obviously the way in which it is done in any given case is the subject of a precise algebraic structure.

Any of the lines φ_i, φ_o, and φ_s in Fig. 1.4.2 may be broken in a particular case; if all three are broken at once, then the process is stationary and even may be appropriately modeled outside time.

The state generation can use current u values through φ_i and/or current y values through φ_o or integrate the history of the recent inputs and outputs and then use that integration. The whole system then begins to look "intelligent" and have a qualitatively different feel. These are the sorts of model that are needed, particularly if the subject being represented has different strategies and can jump between them as a consequence of some particular input or output sequences occurring.

In engineering the impetus for theorizing in this way was provided by the need to gain an understanding of control and stable self-regulation, which should cue the reader to see that when these concepts emerge in psychological theory, as they do for example in motor skills, consummatory drives, attitude shifts, and interpersonal dynamics, then the minimum complexity model that is logically adequate to describe what is going on is going to resemble Fig. 1.4.2. Handling such systems quantitatively is more complex than just using the forms of time series analysis set out in Fig. 1.4.1, and identifying structures like Fig. 1.4.2 merely from input–output records is not always possible. The task is more difficult and more ambiguous than a standard sort of deconvolution. Methods that have been developed, although often computerized, are not universally valid and the mathematical and substantive conditions for their legitimate application are not yet fully understood. It is precisely here that we reach beyond the current limits of conceptual and empirical understanding and see where quantitative psychology can develop.

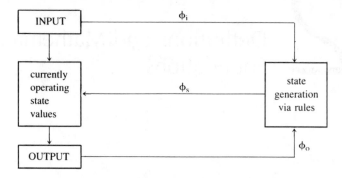

FIG. 1.4.2   Conceptual outline of state space approaches to time series.

Sections 6.1 to 6.4.   Time series analysis is often employed in the context of forecasting, though the two are not synonymous. The accuracy of prediction into the future may obviously be increased if a dynamic process is correctly modeled from a sample or realization of relatively short length, but the distinction between description and forecasting has psychological importance in situations where a series of observations are made during treatment, and the future progression is thereafter intended to have practical therapeutic usefulness. It is required to forecast if behavior induced during therapy will persist, to the advantage or to the disadvantage of the patient, after the therapist withdraws from the scene.

Analogs of time series but extended in space, in one or more dimensions, can be created or used as stimulus classificatory devices. Any periodic series can have a pictorial representation in a space of sufficient dimensionality, and two dimensions is quite adequate for many psychological applications, though three have found use in linguistics.

The extension of time series analysis to more complex situations, as an additional analytic tool in the repertoire of the scientist, is illustrated by a few real examples in cognitive psychology. The necessary departure from traditional forms of experimental design in order to gain insights into dynamic and multivariate psychological processes is shown.

2

Definitions and Mathematical Foundations

2.0 STATISTICAL THEORY OF SERIES IN DISCRETE TIME

The data collected in the psychological laboratory are, to the statistician, often samples from processes that are amenable to representation by univariate stochastic difference equations. This is a rich area of theory, and consequently there are often available alternative models, generated in very disparate ways, that would fit the results of a given experiment about equally well. Furthermore, it can be possible, by choosing terms or transformations, to make an equation stationary, or covariance stationary (see Section 1.4) or not stationary at all! The notion that psychological processes are inherently nonstationary may be good empirical science, but the inference that such processes are inherently irreducible to forms that permit tractable modeling is as a generalization quite wrong.

Two commonly met classes of time series models used in the representation of dynamic processes are called, after Box and Jenkins terminology (1970),

ARMA = autoregressive moving average
ARIMA = autoregressive integrated moving average

The latter class may be considerably more difficult to deal with because it does not usually exhibit covariance stationarity. This ARIMA class is implicated when the equation describing a time series is written in a form using the nth differences of the output,

$$\Delta_n y = y_{j+n} - y_j \qquad (2.0.1)$$

and we may remark that fortunately what little evidence exists in psychology suggests that it is unnecessary or unrewarding to go beyond $n = 4$ in (2.0.1) to obtain meaningful predictions. Because ARIMA models are difficult, it is a sensible strategy to start with ARMA alternatives in analyzing any real data and move on to more complex models if the simpler ones prove inadequate (Aigner, 1971).

It should also be observed that the units of discrete time are at choice; the trial of an experiment is conceptually taken as the unit in this monograph, but this presupposes that all the trials are of the same length in real, clock, time or alternatively that the differences in real-time length of the trials, as time segments, are second-order or irrelevant. These assumptions are actually found in other sciences that have cause to use discrete time series, but they do not excuse the investigator from checking, on every analysis, the reasonableness of taking the variations in real time at which events occur within a trial to be noise and orthogonal with respect to the parameters of the process being modeled. If these variations play a critical role, then a new unit of discrete time, small enough to capture these variations, has to be used and a new model created.

The implications of being able to model the same process in discrete time scales of different resolution are twofold: The solution given by any model has to be taken as applicable only for the unit of discrete time used until it can be shown to be more generally valid, and the best-fitted model for making predictions or representations between sessions, say days apart, can be quite different from that which is a best fit for making trial-to-trial predictions; one may be simpler and more tractable than the other. Hence the problem of what is a best fit and the problem of what is an appropriate time unit in real time for a discrete time representation are two interlocked problems; the choice of model, in both senses, requires consideration of psychological plausibility and mathematical tractability.

The learning curves of the psychology of the 1930s and 1940s, particularly those advanced by Hull, are examples of deterministic models with an arbitrary time scale; variations on the theme of an exponential growth curve

$$Y_T = A(1 - \exp(-kT)) \tag{2.0.2}$$

are common and were not implausible first approximations, though they gave no insight into the processes they represented. Growth curves that show an inflection are commonly represented by a function (the Volterra equation)

$$\frac{dy}{dt} = Cy\left(1 - \frac{y}{K}\right) \tag{2.0.3}$$

integrating to

$$Y_T = \frac{K}{(1 + B \cdot \exp(-CT))} \tag{2.0.4}$$

and examples may be found reviewed in Stevens (1951). It is not usual for these deterministic models to fit data very well, even if they are made complicated, so they have been superseded by the stochastic models that can do a better job with fewer inbuilt assumptions. A bibliography of earlier stochastic models is given by Wold (1965).

2.1 RENEWAL PROCESSES

If a series of events in time is characterized not by the events themselves, each of which may be thought of as occurring instantaneously, at fixed or specified intervals but instead characterized by the intervals themselves, then a different sort of time series is involved from that sort where the interest lies in the identity and sequences of the events. In this situation the events may have no identities; that is, they may be reducible to a single event repeated many times. Or, equivalently, the differences in the events, although readily discernible, may be uninteresting, and so all the events are treated as equivalent; "all cats are grey in the dark."

In a sequence of this sort the variable of interest is the time elapsing between two successive observations of the event. This set of elapsed times we call X (following notational precedents by Bartlett, 1966; Cox & Lewis, 1966; and other statisticians, but note that Parzen, 1962, is slightly different), and the distributional properties of X under processes of random or stochastic generation or perturbation are themselves of interest. Examples in psychophysiology arise when the details of sequences of spike potentials moving along a neuron are studied by on-line recording, or recordings are made of pulses in blood flow along a capillary in the peripheral circulatory system by attaching a monitoring device to the thumb of a subject.

In psychophysics, models have been advanced (Green & Luce, 1974, Luce & Green, 1972, McGill, 1962, McGill & Gibbon, 1965) that require a notional observing process to monitor sequences of signals passing, and make "no response versus response" decisions based on statistical properties of samples of the events passing; the two simplest and most obvious things such a monitor might do are (1) count events until some fixed total is exceeded and then note how much time has elapsed; or (2) count events until a fixed time has elapsed and then note how many events happened. The resultant statistics have distributional properties that may be examined analytically and so may serve in models of the process monitored. These models, which are time series versions of the classical threshold or signal detection processes, owe something to precedents at a much grosser scale of human behavior, namely, road traffic flow, and to the modeling of events in molecular physics. A diversity of systems from the microscopic to the macroscopic is amenable to representation in time series form.

The analysis of the behavior of vehicles (understood in the sense of man–machine subsystems) at traffic signs and road intersections has long been an activity in operations research or traffic engineering; it could equally well be thought of as a special problem in social psychology. If a less mechanical example makes the traditionally minded psychologist more happy, he might study the intervals, in time, between successive letters of protest arriving at a television station after it has shown a film that some viewers thought indecent. That would not in fact be very interesting, because the process would tail off rapidly and because the letters would come in bunches through the selective filtering of a mail delivery service, so that the time units would be discretized into multiples of the shortest mail interdelivery time. However, those who wish to conduct such experiments should not be deterred by lack of ingenuity; in fact, the methods of Chapter 3 where responses to pulse inputs are studied could be more pertinent for this contrived example, particularly if the experiment is repeatable with a series of potentially distasteful programs.

Perhaps the most important class of time series characterized by variable intervals between point events has been generated by operant psychologists; for a time the cumulative record, popularized by B. F. Skinner as a picture of response-emitting behaviour extending through time, was a major descriptive tool for the experimental analysis of behavior, even though the results were not often subjected to detailed statistical treatment but instead presented in their own right as characteristic patterns in response to specifiable stimulus and reinforcement schedules. It is well known that elaborate typologies of schedules of reinforcement have been developed by operant psychologists, and though these are, in a sense, deterministic or stochastic time series, they are outside the scope of this monograph because the experimenter is not typically faced with the problem of identifying his own schedules, after doing an experiment, because the schedules are the input over which he has control from and which he may select.[1] To an outside observer, an operant experiment sometimes appears to be a film or magnetic tape loop emitting an input sequence to a box, in which an unseen organism has its lonely existence, and from which is output a cumulative record. The experimenter takes long time samples because the processes he studies may take considerable time to converge to what is regarded as a stable input–output configuration. Generally the definitions of input, output, and stability were developed by operant psychologists from their own first principles and descriptive data analysis and owe little to the mathematics of control theory. This is not invariably true, however, and some links between operant studies and, for example, semi-Markov chains have been published, notably by Gibbon (1972).

Thus there are three questions arising in the operant experiment that might be treated by time series analysis: the sequential structure of a stimulus series, as

---

[1]If, however, an investigator were to be given a record of an experiment and wished to discover, post hoc, what the rules governing the generation of the stimulus series had been, because for some reason they were missing from the records, then the series of stimuli used could be submitted to a time series analysis, and that problem of identification would be central to this review. It still is not quite typical, however, because in an operant experiment one would expect to have very strong prior information concerning the alternative schedules the experimenter could be using.

events and as intervals; the sequential structure of the response intervals; and the relations between the two series. It is the first that is not expected to be a subject for identification, precisely because it is already identified by its stated generation rules; the second (of response intervals) is describable, hopefully, as resembling one of the models in this section. The fact that it is generated in an operant experiment does not necessarily make it mathematically any different from sequences in other areas of psychology, psychophysics, or psychophysiology.

Here the general statistics of sequences characterized solely by their interevent time distribution will be reviewed; the substantive applications may be in any of the areas mentioned previously. Operant data output sequences (cumulative records) are not a unique form of series; in fact, such sequences were found in engineering control processes some years before they became popular with animal psychologists. But the wider problem of analyzing input–output relations (necessarily involving the relations between two series in time) is a different problem from those covered in this chapter (see instead Chapters 3 and 5); at this stage we are solely concerned with asking questions about a single output sequence or record and its internal structure. Particularly, the nature of randomness in univariate time series demands examination.

Let us suppose there is some mechanism to count time, in integer units (each equivalent to n sec) and that this mechanism records the arrival of each event in a sequence to the nearest integer of the measurement unit used.

If the interarrival times, the intervals between two successive events, are independent (i.e., knowledge of the last interval, X_{j-1}, is of no value in predicting the next interval, X_j) and each X_j is generated by some underlying probabilistic process that remains the same in terms of the frequency distribution of different X that it emits, then the sequence of $\{X_j\}$ is called a *renewal process*. It has been given this name by statisticians because it is the sort of series that aptly describes situations where a component is run until it becomes defective and then is replaced by a new component, and that in turn runs until it becomes defective and is replaced, and so on. Replacing the electric light bulbs in my desk reading

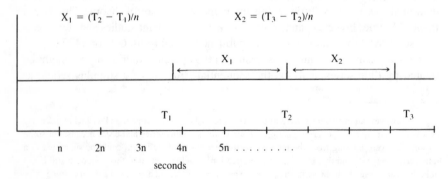

FIG. 2.1.1   Times between the occurrence, or arrival, of successive events.

lamp is such a process; the X_j are the times in hours of illumination that successive bulbs provide. One might like to postulate that the reigns of successive monarchs in a dynasty constitutes a renewal process, but political activities make these nonindependent in some countries. Obviously presidents who are elected for a fixed term do not fit into this model. But if one studies small psychotherapy groups where the leadership role moves about, then the X_j are minutes between a shift of leadership within the group, and these X_j may conform to a renewal process. It is known that a renewal model of conversational changes in dialogues is plausible, so this wider conjecture is sensible even if it should prove to be false.

The first way in which a time series of the renewal process type might be analyzed is by turning it into a variable output fixed discrete interval series. This is done most readily by chopping it up into successive intervals of length nT;

$$\text{lumping interval} = nT \tag{2.1.1}$$

and counting in each interval, as response variable, the number of events observed. This series is a sequence of estimates of the rate of responding; if the series is generated by a stable probabilistic process, then the variance and limits of such estimates can be derived, and such stationarity becomes an alternative hypothesis to a trend in time. It may make more intuitive sense to a psychologist if the series is expressed in this way. The fact that a renewal process can be treated as a discrete time series indicates that there is a mapping from one representation to the other, but this mapping cannot be as readily reversed; the distributional properties of the renewal process cannot be reconstructed from the discrete time series of response rates in lumped intervals. If the distribution properties of the renewal process are critically important for an interpretation of how the process is generated, then the analysis must proceed at an appropriate level. In particular, if the observed process is converted into a discrete time series of response rates, all evidence of interresponse independence (or functional dependence at the fine-grain level) is lost, unless the interval T is so small as to be much less than the average interarrival time, which is completely pointless in this case. It is not, of course, pointless in sampled data systems where aliasing is to be avoided (see Chapters 1 and 3). Discretization of a renewal process, if done at all, would be done on a coarse metric, which expresses another way of regarding the role of nT.

Renewal processes are important because they are a form of null hypothesis against which observed sequences can be compared for internal evidence of some sort of nonrandomness. However, the problems of making comparisons are statistically difficult, even if the precaution is taken of initially removing any long-term trend from data samples before commencing analysis. It is necessary to set up a probabilistic process representation of the way interevent times are generated, and some alternative possibilities that have received use or mention in psychological applications are briefly reviewed. Before doing this, however, one further comment is pertinent. The type of analysis upon which we embark depends on the perspective or scale of the representation that theory demands. For example, consider the sequence of pulses in a neurone, as a model of information transmission in the nervous system. At the most detailed, the form of an individual spike may be modeled in detail, as a sum of components each of approximately sinusoidal form; the data for such an analysis are records in continuous time of many spikes, statistically averaged to produce a single wave-form or an envelope of waveforms. Such an analysis is of main interest to the physiologist or the physiological psychologist. When we step back from such close detail, then the sequence of spikes becomes a sequence of pulses; the fine detail of each pulse is jettisoned and attention focused on the interpulse intervals by treating each pulse as located at a point in time, or if discretization is employed, then the duration of a pulse is taken as less than that of lumping interval. The information at this level is contained necessarily and sufficiently in the interevent intervals. It is this level that is of interest to psychologists working in the tradition of what Fechner (1860) called "inner psychophysics," or using models of the brain that derive from network and transmission theories. Stepping back yet again, a representation of a whole sensory channel becomes a picture of a bundle of individual channels, each characterized by some measure of information transfer capacity and working in parallel with some interdependence. At this level a multivariate model of information channels is needed and the individual time series properties of the channels are lost, or they become part of a statistical distribution of transmission parameters across a bundle of channels; the identity of single channels no longer matters, though the relative incidence of channels with different transmission properties could be very important. There is no sense in which one of these perspectives is more true than another; they each have their appropriateness for some level of description, and as the perspective recedes, so the possibility or even the necessity of taking a large systems view increases. But when the large systems view is taken, then the dynamics of the most complex channel have to be reduced to some set of control or feedback or transmission characteristics in order to be tersely and explicitly comprehensible. At this level the time series representation of the whole system comes into its own, but it is not the same analysis as that which was used in the intermediate perspective needed to represent a single idealized neuron. At the intermediate level, each series may be a renewal process, but hundreds or thousands of such processes acting in parallel, and in networks in the central nervous system, create new dynamic relationships that are not themselves necessarily thought of as renewal processes. There are some writers who are still troubled about the separate existence of psychology and physiology; their troubles appear to stem from an inability to appreciate that a complex system may only be dynamically describable at a level that is unique to itself; in no sense do we attempt to reduce a psychological model to an aggregate of renewal processes in all its components, except in a statistical sense in which detailed information is lost.

A sequence in discrete time in which successive observations take independent values is, of course, a *random walk*. The values of the successive steps in a random walk can be anything we wish, positive or negative, real or imaginary numbers. But with additional constraints it is possible to regard a renewal process as a special sort of random walk. If the discrete time steps are notional and associated with counting the steps of the renewal process, so that we regard the jth interval X_j as being indexed to discrete time step j and not to the elapsed time in seconds that X_j actually represents, then all the X_j are real and greater than zero, and hence their expectation $\Sigma (X) > 0$. The distribution of the sum of n such intervals X_j, $S_n (X_j)$, will by the central limit theorem, tend to normality as n increases, irrespective of the distribution of the X_j themselves. This property is useful if we wish to model systems where sums of X_j are monitored and decisions taken when the sum $S_n (X_j)$ exceeds some critical value.

The Poisson Process

In the case of a Poisson process, the rate of occurrence of events in time is λ. This is a mean rate over long periods, once the process has settled down, if λ is interpreted as a sampling theory statistic.

The process has to be without trend, so it cannot be a model of learning, though it might be used as a model of residual fluctuations once a linear trend, which is well identified, has been removed. The investigator beginning a study will not be in such a position. It is also necessary that no two events (in the operant case, responses) can occur simultaneously and that the chance of an event occurring is independent of what happens previously. There can thus be no "dead time" after an event, but if the dead time's upper limit is known, then one might take as discrete time unit the duration, δT, needed to make a response, plus dT, the dead time, and make $\delta T + dT$ the metric of time measurement. The Poisson process is a mathematical abstraction but requires some sensible interpretation of its basic assumptions.

Properties that follow by definition are as given:

1. The unit of time is T (take $nT = T$, for $n = 1$ without loss of generality) and the number of responses in $T = N_T$.

$$E(N_T) = \lambda T \tag{2.1.2}$$

and

$$p(N_T = x) = \frac{(\lambda T)^x e^{-\lambda T}}{x!} \qquad x = 0, 1, 2, \ldots \tag{2.1.3}$$

2. The additive property of Poisson distributions holds, so if the metric T is coarsened to T', then the resultant rate $\lambda T'$ will also have a Poisson distribution but with a tendency to normality.

The distribution of times between successive events can be obtained by considering the first event in the observed sequence as happening at t_0; then the probability distribution of the time X elapsing before the next event (where x is a value taken by X) will be

$$P(X, x) = \lambda e^{-\lambda x} \qquad (2.1.4)$$

which has

$$E(X) = \lambda^{-1}, \qquad \text{var }(X) = \lambda^{-2} \qquad (2.1.5)$$

This distribution is actually more general than its derivation suggests; it does not just hold between two responses in a sequence, it holds between any two arbitrary time points in the record of a sequence. To test for a Poisson process, the actual distribution of X and its first two moments have to be calculated, and compared with predictions; tests also must be made on the independence of successive interevent times.

The generalization of (2.1.4) is a representation of the probability density function (p.d.f.) of the nth event after t_0, instead of the first event after t_0 as in (2.1.4) (which contrariwise may obviously be considered as a special case when $n = 1$) and is

$$F(X_n, x) = \frac{\lambda(\lambda T)^{n-1} e^{-T}}{(n-1)!} \qquad T \geqslant 0 \qquad (2.1.6)$$

The distribution of $2\lambda X_n \sim \chi^2$, d.f. $= 2n$, and

$$E(X_n) = n\lambda^{-1}, \qquad \text{var}(X_n) = n\lambda^{-2} \qquad (2.1.7)$$

As n increases,

$$(\lambda X_n)^{0.5} \sim N((n - .25)^{0.5}, .25) \qquad (2.1.8)$$

An alternative approach is to use $\log X_n$, whose distribution properties are given by Bartlett and Kendall (1946) as the log chi-squared distribution.

As the important parameter is λ, tests of the appropriateness of a Poisson model are sometimes expressed in terms of sufficient statistics for λ.

For a sample of fixed duration, θ, the number of events in that period, θ_n, is a sufficient statistic for λ. Note that, if θ is not fixed in advance but is determined in any way that is independent of the events themselves (and hence independent of λ), then it is legitimate to proceed as if θ were fixed a priori. For determining λ, it is not necessary to know the distribution of events in subperiods θ', $\theta' <<$ θ, only the total θ_n ($= \Sigma \ \theta_n'$) is necessary; but if it is not clear that the process is indeed Poisson, then the variability across subsamples is relevant information. An exact probability expression relating θ_n to a hypothesized rate λ_0 is given by

$$P\left(\frac{\theta_n > v}{\lambda T = \lambda_0}\right) = \sum_{r=v} \frac{\lambda_0^r e^{-\lambda_0}}{r!} \tag{2.1.9}$$

though in practice simpler tests can be constructed by using (2.1.6) or the normal approximation (2.1.8) and appropriate credibility intervals.

The two-dimensional extension of a given Poisson process may also be of some potential psychological interest, as a representation of relations between events distributed over a surface. We might, for example, wish to study the way members of a crowd, who are not forced spatially together as they might be by seating arrangements in a theater, distribute themselves in a city square when listening to music from a grid network of loudspeakers that gives approximately even sound density over the square.

Parzen (1962) shows that if events (subjects, stimuli) are distributed on a plane at a mean rate of λ per unit area, and X is the distance between an independent event and its nearest neighbor,[2] then

$$F(\pi \lambda X^2 > x) = \exp(-x) \tag{2.1.10}$$

which has a mean of 1.

The Hazard Function

It is sometimes important to be able to predict the conditional probability that an event will occur between two points in time, t_j and t_{j+1}, given that it has not occurred up to that point and having a record of the process since t_0. One can think readily of many psychological problems that fit this paradigm; for example, will a parachutist have an attack of paralytic anxiety between his jth and $(j + 1)$th jumps, given that he has not shown one so far, and given that a personality test predicting the probability of such attacks was administered before the parachutist started his series of jumps? A delightful example is given by Parzen (1962) about that tiresome habit of compulsive outbursts of coughing that some patrons show at the beginning of concerts. It is conjectured that a conductor hears an average rate of coughing and then can employ rules to decide when to begin the overture, such as waiting until there has been at least 20 sec silence. There always seems to be one very persistent cougher in any concert audience who waits to begin coughing in the pianissimo passages, so the rules suggested are probably doomed to failure.

---

[2]Note that *nearest neighbor* in two-dimensional space replaces *adjacent event* on a one-dimensional line; the definitions parallel the previous notation, and if the model is extended to higher dimensionality, which in psychology would be unlikely unless, say, the distribution of fish swimming in shoals or swarms of bees were being studied, the distance to a nearest neighbor remains the interpretation of X.

The function that expresses the probability of a first event between t_j and t_{j+1} (or the first absence of an event; there is freedom of definition here) is a hazard function. In general, by definition,

$$\mu(X, x) = \frac{F(X, x)}{1 - F^*(X, x)} \qquad (2.1.11)$$

where $\mu(X, x)$ is the hazard function of X, $P(X, x)$ is the p.d.f. of X, and $P^*(X, x)$ is the distribution function, $P(X < x)$. In the case of the Poisson distribution $\mu(X, x) = \lambda$, $x > 0$. Hazard functions for a number of distributions are given in standard references.

The Erlang or Waiting-Time Distribution

The Danish statistician Erlang was interested in the problem of estimating the probability and characteristics of queues that form in telephone networks on busy lines. In the context of the problem, which is now perhaps less severe than it was in his time except in periods of festivity or crisis, he defined a process (sometimes also called a discrete gamma distributed interarrival time process) where

$$F(X, x) = \frac{\lambda}{\Gamma(k)} \cdot (\lambda T)^{k-1} e^{-\lambda T} \qquad \text{for } T > 0 \qquad (2.1.12)$$

$$= 0 \qquad \text{for } T < 0$$

Here k takes only integer values; the distribution (2.1.12) also arises as the sum of k independently exponentially distributed random variables.

Luce and Green (1972) have used this as an interevent distribution on a notional neural pathway in the context of a time series psychophysical model. The Erlang distribution should always be considered as an alternative competing model to the Poisson for psychological processes of uncertain stochastic structure. When k can take all real values, then (2.1.12) becomes a gamma distribution (Likeš, 1967). It would seem fair to assert that one would not postulate the Erlang distribution, *ab initio*, as a psychological model but rather start from axioms that incorporated exponentially distributed random variables, for some good reason, and then go on to consider collections of such variables. In that way the Erlang distribution would arise as a natural consequence of the assumptions.

Markov Processes

Probably Markov models of some form have been used more extensively than any other sort by those mathematical psychologists who were concerned to capture the quantitative features of learning, when it is assumed that learning is a stochastic process in real time. To a large extent, therefore, the literature of Markov processes is almost synonymous with that of mathematical learning theory and consequently is both already well covered and outside the precise scope of this review. The texts of Atkinson (1964), Levine and Burke (1972), or Norman (1972) are more suitable for the investigator seeking models of learning or forgetting per se. However, a discrete parameter Markov chain is one form of time series that must be considered despite the comments just made; it is a process in discrete time, where a system can be at one time in one and only one of a finite set of states. The set of states is called the *state space* of the process.

Even in the psychology of nonlearning performance, such as the sustained utterance of a well-known language, there have been numerous examples of the approximate, appropriate, and useful representations that can be achieved with Markov chains. Jaffe and Feldstein (1970) in their study of the rhythms of dialogue found, by defining two states as "silence" and "speech" (together these constitute their state space), that the time series of utterances in both monologue and dialogue are approximately Markovian. Time series in a two-state space are, of course, like series of realizations of a binary variable, such as

000110100111101000111111100111110010100111101101111

It has been suggested that the two states "vowel" and "consonant" lead to a Markov chain representation of some Polynesian languages, because in such languages consonants never follow consonants, but vowels follow vowels with a much higher probability than would be found in European languages.

In a chain, the events observed, spaced at equal intervals, can be taken as the defined states of the system. As a class of events that can only take a finite set of values (such as responses on a rating scale running from "like" to "dislike" through seven statements) may also be readily conceptualized as states of a system, this definition of a chain is extremely wide and will potentially include many time series models in which responses are recorded in a digital data processor.

The additional necessary conditions that make a chain into a Markov chain are by definition as follows:

For any chain longer than two trials, which may be written $j - 1, j, j + 1, \ldots, j + m$, ($m = 2, 3, \ldots$), the distribution of $y(t)$ for $t = j - 1, \ldots, j + m$ depends only on $y(t - 1)$. So, given $\{y^*\}$ as a set of realizations of $y(t)$,

$$p(y(j) = y^* | y(0) = y^*_0, \ldots, y(j - 1) = y^*_{j-1})$$
$$= p(y(j) = y^*_j | y(j - 1) = y^*_{j-1}) \tag{2.1.13}$$

From this definition, it follows that Markov chains are one restricted sort of time series where the sequential dependencies do not run back more than one trial and thus constitute a limiting case of the more general type of time series that may be modeled, as in Chapter 3, as a preliminary to control theory. At the same time, the finite-state Markov chain is one sort of learning model among many Markov models, some involving continuity assumptions or a continuum of states, so the one special case considered here is the common member of two classes of models, time series and learning, that have an overlap but are generally not reducible to one another.

Let us now consider a dynamic process in time that embodies a Markov chain, to illustrate the fact that stochastic models may be used to represent some features of a system that exhibit regularity but are embedded within a more complex, and hence less readily analyzed, structure.

A queue of persons that is both continually served at one end and continually replenishes itself by acquiring new members at the other end, usually called the *tail,* can provide an example of a Markov chain that is said to be embedded within a stochastic process. Queues in a self-service restaurant or at the check-in counter in an airport terminal are an example of a relevant sort; one might wish to set up a model predicting that service personnel will strike for more pay or for more help when the product of queue length × waiting time exceeds some limit and simulate the situation to investigate its possibilities.

In such queues we are interested in the total length of the queue at a given time, and the distribution of service times between customers; some have to wait much longer than others to obtain service.[3] The service times of customers are independent random variables with common expectation and variance, which is another way of saying that the service times are distributed independently of the identity of who is being served but are dependent on the server.

The length of the queue in the time segment when customer C_j has just finished being served is X_j, and it can be shown that the sequence $\{X_j\}$ is a Markov chain.

Further consider a characteristic variable, $\delta(X_j)$, which takes the value 0 if and only if C_j was present when C_{j-1} was being served, and $\delta(X_j) = 1$ if, contrariwise, C_j was not present. Then it is possible to define a recurrence relationship

$$X_{j+1} = X_j - \delta(X_j) + U_{j+1} \tag{2.1.14}$$

and as X_{j+1} can be expressed solely as a function of terms in j and $j + 1$, the embedded process relating queue length to arrivals (U_{j+1}) is a Markov chain.

This result can be generalized a little further. Suppose that instead of using X_j (the queue length) as the dependent variable, which is locked onto the customer

---

[3]Although the time it takes to serve one customer varies in real time, the series of customers could be redefined as one in which one customer is served on each trial (in one unit of notional discrete time), but the number, U_j, of customers arriving and joining the queue at the tail end, during the service time of the current customer, would have a distribution in notional discrete time that is a convolution of the service and arrival distributions in real time.

number j, we redefine our time base so that the times at which the j arrive are special points on a continuum of time. Then take N_n as the new dependent variable, meaning the number of people actually standing in the queue at time n. If the service times have an exponential distribution, then it may be shown that the sequence of $\{N_n\}$ also constitutes a Markov chain.

It is important to note that Markov chains are relatively unrestricted in the content of their state spaces, because the states themselves need not be characterized by numbers, nor need they be in any sense ordered, merely distinguishable. Upon this freedom rests the common use of Markov models in psychology; states such as *ignorance, guessing, overlearned,* and *forgotten* can be used in models of learning. Contrariwise, in time series applications, events typically take values on some metric of magnitude or intensity, discrete or continuous. Hence time series models that are concerned with rates of change are more restricted than Markov chains in the sense of their permissible state spaces, but less restricted in that they allow us to predict outcome to be a function of events on many more trials than the previous trial.

2.2 AUTOCORRELATION STRUCTURE AND POLYNOMIAL REPRESENTATION

Suppose that the record of an experiment is two time series of discrete form:

$$S_1, S_2, S_3, \ldots, S_{j-2}, S_{j-1}, S_j, S_{j+1}, S_{j+2}, \ldots, S_N$$

$$R_1, R_2, R_3, \ldots, R_{j-2}, R_{j-1}, R_j, R_{j+1}, R_{j+2}, \ldots, R_N$$

where the trial numbers $1, 2, \ldots, j, \ldots, N$ are in the (arbitrary) time units chosen for analysis. It is known by an experimental psychologist who has done his or her homework that the results of such an experiment may depend, within limits, on the actual length in absolute time units (seconds, minutes, $\ldots$, years) and the regularity of the time intervals and that the trial length used either must by well chosen for the objectives of the experiment or must itself be a variable that is controllable within limits and is under investigation. In this exposition we take the trial length in real time either as fixed or as having variations in real time of negligible significance; so departures in real experiments from these ideal specifications could constitute one or more discontinuities in the time series. The effects of discontinuities can be spectacular and disastrous for the theoretical analysis and for empirical prediction and control and are considered as a major topic in their own right in Chapter 3.

For further simplification the values of the input series, which are the quantifications of the stimuli chosen, are taken to be *i*ndependent *i*dentically *d*istributed, or as is commonly written to be an i.i.d. (white noise) series. That is, the values

$$X_1, X_2, X_3, \ldots, X_{j-1}, X_j, X_{j+1}, \ldots, X_N$$

which can be taken as abbreviations for

$$X(S_1), X(S_2), X(S_3), \ldots, X(S_{j-1}), X(S_{j+1}), \ldots$$

are independently distributed as a set of normal deviates with zero (or constant) expectation and fixed variance.

This i.i.d. constraint is important; it is necessary for the development of theory and analysis in the more common procedures associated with Box and Jenkins (1970). Indeed, if an input series is not in i.i.d. form, then it may have to be what is called "prewhitened" before analysis can proceed. Fortunately, in psychological and psychophysical experiments a randomized input series is usual practice, partly in order to minimize some sort of anticipatory strategy by the subject that can lead to responses being made without reference to the current stimulus being presented.

The input series that we accept, in multivariate profusion throughout our lives, from the environment in which we live are commonly not random or at least have strong sequential nonrandom properties upon which second-order random perturbations are superimposed. This raises problems for the validity of any result based on experiments in which stimulus properties are generated over trials by a quasi-random process; for if the subject is not going to be able to use the properties of sequentiality that are usually available in the time series that the world provides, will this lack of sequentiality actually enhance or degrade performance on individual trials? Put so generally there is probably no answer to the question, but surprisingly little is known about it considering its fundamental importance in the representation of human behavior.

For comparable reasons the output will be described by

$$Y_1, Y_2, Y_3, \ldots, Y_{j-1}, Y_j, Y_{j+1}, \ldots, Y_N$$

which can be taken as abbreviations for

$$Y(R_1), Y(R_2), Y(R_3), \ldots, Y(R_{j-1}), Y(R_j), Y(R_{j+1}), \ldots$$

The sequential dependency within a series, provided it is stationary, may be represented numerically by the autocorrelation structure of the values taken; that is, it is the sequential structure of the magnitudes of the events and not the *identities* of the events that is to be represented. This point would be irrelevant in applications in the physical sciences, where much of this methodology originated, but in psychology there is always the problem that a subject giving estimates is not responding to magnitudes or sensory intensities but to labels given to identify stimuli from a finite set of alternatives. If a subject does this, then a representation in Markov chain form may be more appropriate than the one being expounded here, at least for some sequences.

We define

$$r(x_j, x_{j-k}) = r(x, x, k) \tag{2.2.1}$$

as the autocorrelation of $\{X\}$ with itself at a lag of k steps, which will be

$$r(x, x, k) = \frac{(N-k)^{-1} \cdot \sum\limits_{j=k+1}^{N} (x_j, x_{j-k}) - (N-k)^{-2} \cdot \sum\limits_{j=1}^{N-k} x_j \cdot \sum\limits_{j=k+1}^{N} x_{j-k}}{\left[(N-k)^{-1} \cdot \sum\limits_{j=1}^{N-k} x_j^2 - (N-k)^{-2} \cdot \left(\sum\limits_{j=1}^{N-k} x_j \right)^2 \right]} \tag{2.2.2}$$

where N is very large compared with k, so that the effect of defining $r(x, x, k)$ over a sample of length N will be little affected by the summations in the denominator being taken over any $N - k$ observations in sequence. If unfortunately N is small and k is large, then the estimate will run into error through end effects and will be generally worse with increasing k. If $r_m(x, x, k)$ is an estimate from a sample time series length m embedded within the longer series N, then the $r_m(x, x, k)$ will exhibit fluctuations that may be misleadingly big according to the starting point of the sample. These fluctuations can be very large and they can exhibit spurious periodicities. One way around this problem is to define the autocorrelations as averages over collections of samples for the time series; these estimates would be said to be based on ensemble averages. The choice of how empirically to proceed is determined in part, at least, by the investigator, prior beliefs about the stationarity of the system parameters in the long run, and the maximum length of time series one can observe at an unbroken session without fatiguing or otherwise altering, locally in time, the characteristics of the behavior being studied. A formal treatment of this problem can be given in Bayesian terms (Eykhoff, 1973, 1974) but presupposes more information that we can consider in this initial presentation.

Defining $r(y, y, k)$ in the same manner as $r(x, x, k)$ gives the output series autocorrelation of lag k. It is more convenient to standardize the $\{X\}$ and $\{Y\}$, if it is legitimate to assume they are distributed normally, with zero mean and unit variance, so that

$$C(x, x, k) = (N-k)^{-1} \sum\limits_{j=k+1}^{N} x_j \cdot x_{j-k} \tag{2.2.3}$$

on a series of length N. Again, if k is very small with respect to N, the summation is over $N - k$ consecutive terms as convenient.

By definition from (2.2.3), it follows that

$$C(x, x, k) = C(x, x, -k) \tag{2.2.4}$$

$$C(y, y, k) = C(y, y, -k) \tag{2.2.5}$$

and if for x_j we put instead y_j in (2.2.1), then the crosscovariance of Y lagged k steps on X is obtained, and

$$C(x, y, k) = C(y, x, -k) \tag{2.2.6}$$

Now importantly the symmetry of (2.2.4) and (2.2.5) is lost, and except by chance selection of values, in general

$$C(x, y, k) \neq C(x, y, -k) \tag{2.2.7}$$

The set of autocovariances of lags 1, 2, 3, ..., k, ..., ∞ is the autocovariance spectrum of a time series. The form of such spectra is an object of investigation because some processes have recognizable spectra; metaphorically one can call the autocovariance spectrum the signature of a dynamic process; working back from a spectrum to the dynamics of a system is an example of identification.

In any stationary process with quantified inputs and outputs there will, therefore, be

an input autocovariance spectrum, symmetrical about $k = 0$, an output autocovariance spectrum, symmetrical about $k = 0$, and a crosscovariance spectrum that is not symmetrical, in general, about $k = 0$.

The characterization of a total bivariate system in discrete time necessarily requires all the three spectra; it can be sufficient for k to be quite small and in psychological processes an upper limit of 8 is generous, provided that this is taken as a rough rule. Note the contrast between a representation outside time, where a single correlation r_{xy} or the two regressions of Y on X and X on Y would be sufficient as a statistical description, and a representation in time that now demands three spectra involving a total of $3k$ covariances. More than that, it is the pattern within those covariances rather than the individual values that may be judged to be informative.

The stationarity of the system has been presupposed as a condition for its representation; in practice the stationarity of the three series, input, output, and input–output, can be regarded as equivalent to the requirement that the $C(*, *, k)$ be independent of the trial number j, for all j and for all k. As shown later, there are more rigorous definitions of stationarity and less rigorous requirements on the stationarity condition for time series analysis than is used in this elementary section.

A system that has no defined $C(x_j, y_{j-k})$ [or as in (2.2.6) $C(x, y, k)$] is one in which future stimuli X_{j+k} do not determine present responses Y_j. Such a system is said to be physically realizable, and we take it that this means psychologically realizable also; to allow $C(x, y, k)$ or $C(y, x, -k)$ to exist would be to model precognition, which is a priori implausible in more usual experiments. The crosscovariances $C(y, x, k)$ and $C(x, y, -k)$ are admissible and are those used. This modeling constraint does not mean that psychological systems (individuals or groups) do not appear to respond to future events with skill and advantage; it means that the formal representation of such behavior within the context of time series analysis is sought by using models that are psychologically realizable in the sense just defined.

It should be emphasized that the whole process of representing time series, and the interrelation between time series, in terms of autocovariances and crosscovariances, is not unique mathematically. For every representation of a time series expressed as a set

$$C(x, x, k), C(y, y, k), C(x, y, k) \qquad k = 0, 1, 2, 3, \ldots$$

there is a completely equivalent (i.e., isomorphic) representation in terms of sines and cosines, or Walsh functions. The trigonometric representation is reviewed in Sections 2.4 and 2.6 to 2.9, and in some cases is computable at much higher speeds than the analysis in terms of correlation spectra. As the two mathematical forms are isomorphic, there is no special status to be given to either, though in many psychological processes the covariance analysis is easier to interpret. It must always be remembered that the interpretability of parameters in a model is as important as its goodness of agreement to data structure.

Though the autocovariances and crosscovariances yield spectra that are intrinsically informative, they are not the end point of analysis nor of process identification. In calculating the covariances the object is to work toward estimates of the coefficients in a general linear equation of the form

$$y_j = v_0 x_j + v_1 x_{j-1} + v_2 x_{j-2} + \cdots + v_k x_{j-k} + 0 \cdot x_{j-k-m} \qquad (2.2.8)$$

where the $\{v_k\}$ are fixed for all j and all m. The status of the $\{v_k\}$ in time series models of dynamic processes is discussed in detail later.

Yule (1926) was one of the first to show that a time series in which successive values are highly dependent (that is to say, autocorrelated) can usefully and mathematically validly be regarded as having been generated from a time series of independent successive shocks $a_j, j = 0, 1, 2, \ldots$.

Precisely how an autocorrelated series can be generated from an i.i.d. series is considered next, in a linear form that is perhaps the simplest available.

This series of independent shocks is, again, an i.i.d. process or can fairly be represented as one. For computational or simulation purposes, it can be given a zero mean and a fixed variance, σ_a^2. Now any series of quantifiable stimuli that are drawn from a sufficiently large (and not trivially constituted) pool of exchangeable acts of sampling is a white noise process in this sense. Here *exchangeable acts of sampling* means alternatives that are drawn in such a way that the experimenter is indifferent as to what is drawn from the pool on a particular trial. In other words, a series of stimuli picked to use in a sequential experiment can be thought of as a series of shocks to the system in Yule's (1926) sense. The reader should be careful here, because shock carries ordinary-language connotations of surprise, and a random sort of series seems to be disruptive because of its very randomness; that is its maximum surprisingness at any point in time. That may be true, but rather less and rather more generality is intended in writing of shocks here; a series of buffets, jolts, perturbations, or displacements conveys the required abstract sense.

The conversion of the i.i.d. series $\{a_j\}$ to an observed autocorrelated series $\{x_j\}$ can be written as a linear equation

$$x_j = \psi_0 a_j + \psi_1 a_{j-1} + \psi_2 a_{j-2} + \psi_3 a_{j-3} + \cdots \qquad (2.2.9)$$

where the $\{\psi_k\}$ are the coefficients of a *linear filter:* The process of transferring from the a_j to the x_j is *filtering;* the algebraic structure of (2.2.9) is *linear*.

As Box and Jenkins (1970) have popularized an alternate notation, using the operator B to mean a backward shift in time by one step, and we wish to cite a general result of time series analysis that is central to identification of dynamic components in a process, this is a convenient point to use B notation.

By definition,

$$B(x_j) = x_{j-1}$$
$$B^2(x_j) = B(B(x_j)) = x_{j-2}$$
$$B^n(x_j) = x_{j-n}$$

so the form of (2.2.9) in B notation is

$$x_j = \psi(B)a_j \qquad (2.2.10)$$

This is in operator form; the ψ tells us the name of the dummy variable used to label the coefficients; the B tells us that a backward difference function of the ψ is used to go from the a_j to the x_j.

It is legitimate to use B in this way because it behaves in a manner consistent with the rules governing operators; they satisfy a calculus. The z transformations of Chapter 3 are completely analogous to B operators, though z transformations have emerged in engineering analysis and B in statistics.

This powerful general result for autocorrelated time series means that regular dynamic features can be represented when modeling the way that the human subject does some tasks, motor or cognitive, as a linear filter. This does not mean that all behavior is suddenly recognizable as the consequences of linear filtering; it means that it can be worth the effort of seeking that sort of representation to give us insights not otherwise available. The concern is with reproducible patterns of behavior, dynamically stationary, and occurring in situations where the subject produces responses to quasi-random series of stimuli. A representation like (2.2.9) or (2.2.10) is tractable if it stops after a few terms or is infinite but strongly convergent, because then it is normally stable and it may be possible to work backward from the x_j to the a_j and identify the ψ_k. To seek for representations like this, as a first preference in modeling when it is suspected the system is dynamic and not open loop, is to take a systems theory approach. Obviously, however, it is only a little part of systems theory.

(The next ruled section may be omitted at a first reading.)

In practice the ψ_k of (2.2.9) are not found exactly but are estimated from finite data samples. The estimates of the v_k in (2.2.8) can be derived by the following argument.

First, restate what it is desired to achieve as a formal representation when x_j are inputs and y_j are outputs:

$$y_j = f(x_j) + e_j$$

where $f(\cdot)$ is going to be some linear transfer function with coefficients $\{v_k\}$ and e_j is noise. The Yule (1926) generalization about autocorrelated series can be written, for this case, as, for some $\{c_k\}$, we may define

$$P_j = c_0 x_j + c_1 x_{j-1} + c_2 x_{j-2} + \cdots$$

for some linear filter of the $\{x\}$, and also we may select $\{d_k\}$ so that

$$P_j = d_0 a_j + d_1 a_{j-1} + d_2 a_{j-2} + \cdots$$

where the a_j are i.i.d.

In the backward difference notation, then,

$$P_j = C(B)x_j$$
$$P_j = D(B)a_j$$

so

$$C(B)x_j = D(B)a_j$$

and rearranging

$$x_j = \frac{D(B)}{C(B)} \cdot a_j$$

This quotient $D(B)/C(B)$, a ratio of two series, we call $Q^{-1}(B)$. This notation is used because later it is inverted. So,

$$x_j = Q^{-1}(B)a_j \tag{2.2.11}$$

or

$$a_j = Q(B)x_j \tag{2.2.12}$$

which means that the transformation is made in the reverse direction. As a_j is i.i.d. by definition, $Q(B)$ is that transformation that will turn the x_j into an i.i.d. series; the operation called *whitening* the input series.

Returning to (2.2.8) written in B notation,

$$y_j = v(B)x_j + e_j \tag{2.2.13}$$

and it is desired to get to this relation, where the x_j are intercorrelated, from a representation in i.i.d. form.

Premultiplying variables from (2.2.13) by $Q(B)$ throughout, using (2.2.12),

$$Q(B)y_j = v(B)Q(B)x_j + Q(B)e_j \tag{2.2.14}$$

This gives new variables created by the operation, which may be renamed thus:

$$\beta_j = Q(B)y_j$$
$$\alpha_j = Q(B)x_j$$
$$\epsilon_j = Q(B)e_j$$

so that

$$\beta_j = v(B)\alpha_j + \epsilon_j \tag{2.2.15}$$

Consider a shift of k steps, in the input series α_j to α_{j-k}. Multiplying through (2.2.15) by α_{j-k}

$$\alpha_{j-k}\beta_j = v(B)\alpha_{j-k}\,\alpha_j + \alpha_{j-k}\epsilon j$$

and considering a long series of j values, the expectation of these terms is by definition a covariance in each case.

$E(\alpha_{j-k}, \beta_j) = \text{cov}\,(\alpha, \beta, k) = $ the covariance of α with β shifted k steps

$E(\alpha_{j-k}, \alpha_j) = \text{cov}\,(\alpha, \alpha, k) = \text{var}\,(\alpha) = \alpha_\alpha^2$

$E(\alpha_{j-k}, \epsilon_j) = 0$ by definition, because ϵ_j is residual noise

Therefore,

$$\text{cov}\,(\alpha, \beta, k) = v_k \cdot \alpha_\alpha^2$$

or

$$v_k = \frac{\text{cov}\,(\alpha, \beta, k)}{\sigma_\alpha^2}$$

Using sample statistics as estimates of the theoretical v_k values gives

$$\hat{v}_k = r(\alpha, \beta, k) \cdot s_\beta \cdot s_\alpha^{-1}, \qquad x = 0, 1, 2, \ldots \tag{2.2.16}$$

It is these $\hat{v}_k$ that are calculated to estimate (2.2.8). Hence the transfer function coefficients can be expressed in terms of sample autocorrelations and standard deviations.

When a set of v_k is obtained from data, it is then necessary to have some means of ascertaining that the observed coefficients lie outside the intervals expected if one or more random processes are the actual generators of what appear to be causal dynamics. There is no general solution to this problem; all statistical tests on the v_k or the associated autocorrelations have to make strong assumptions and are thus limited in their generality. If little is or can be known about the form of the transfer function, or the way that the v_k decrease successively, then the only way to proceed may be to set up, as a simulation, a process that it is required to compare with the observed behavior and then with random inputs to generate large samples of determinations of sample v_k. It is always possible and useful to compare observed time series and their associated parameters against specific competing alternative models; showing that real data are not compatible with some theory is comparatively easy because the computer can be used to predict both deterministically and probabilistically what the theory would generate. However, blanket tests based on some very general null hypothesis are not too useful, and none of the tests cited in the literature should be used in such a manner.

This statement may seem too sweeping, because Box and Pierce (1970) developed what is sometimes called a portmanteau test of the whole set of calculated residual autocorrelations. These constitute what is left of sequential structure after that due to a fitted ARIMA model has been removed. One necessary sort of evidence of goodness of fit of a time series model to real data is that the residual time series approximates to white noise or i.i.d. form. If a model is appropriate, then there should be zero autocorrelation over all lags in the errors, which are the theoretical counterparts of the observed residuals. Such portmanteau tests are now, in some versions, built into computer packages for time series analysis such as the extensive and powerful programs published by the Rothampstead Experimental Station at Harpenden, England. These programs can also calculate approximate standard errors in the estimated v_k, using an algorithm like that of Ljung and Box (1979) and Box and Jenkins (1970, part V, 3.3.).

Portmanteau tests are useful heuristically but can be dangerous if taken as the sole basis upon which to accept or to reject a model. Alternative tests have been developed and in some cases tested, necessarily, by simulation, as the problem is analytically unpleasant.

Ansley and Newbold (1979), Godfrey (1979), Ljung and Box (1979), Newbold (1980), and Poskitt and Tremayne (1980) have reviewed aspects of the problem; we cannot do better than quote Ansley and Newbold when they warn "particularly in small samples, the portmanteau statistic can be difficult to interpret. Moreover, for such sample sizes, the statistic can possess very low power against alternatives involving quite severe misspecification, as shown by Davies and Newbold (1979)."

Even when very simple models are involved, series of over 100 trials are required before one can make safe deductions from significance tests on sets of residual autocorrelations. Tests on single selected autocorrelations are even more dubious, and it is wise to reiterate that pattern and structure, and replicability, mean more in model selection here than do significance levels.

In restricted circumstances, tests are available to assess the significance of individual autocorrelations at different lags and to test for the most likely order of a transfer function. The two questions are in fact interrelated, and modern practice (see Chapter 3) attaches more importance to finding the minimum complexity model of a particular structure, given that the researcher has some idea of what a plausible structure looks like, than in assessing the significance of individual coefficients. Typically one does not test one model against a null hypothesis; one tests a number of competing models, of different order and structure, against the data and thus against one another.

Some approximate results, useful in simpler and well-explored circumstances, are given here; they depend for their accuracy on the way that the successive autocorrelations converge to a minimum. Examples of how series behave are shown in Table 2.2.3. If and only if it is acceptable to assume that a psychological process is of low order (and in fact published cases often are not usefully modeled beyond two lags of input and/or output) and that traces of previous events die out with exponential decay (which is a good approximation in psychophysiological modeling but should be handled with more caution in cognitive theories), then the following procedure is legitimate. It is always valuable, in addition, to compare results with patterns of autocorrelation and partial autocorrelation spectra reported for standard pure processes. (Cases in human operator studies are, for example, given by Shinners, 1974.)

Bartlett (1935, 1946) obtained the approximate results, for the variance of estimated $r(x, x, k)$ in a sample of a process where k is greater than q, and q is the theoretical lag beyond which the autocorrelation function ought to have died out, with the further assumption that the theoretical autocorrelations $\rho(x, x, k) = \phi^{|k|}$ with $\phi < 1$ (an exponential decay form), if N is the sample length,

$$\text{var} \left[r(x, x, k) \right] \underset{\text{approx}}{=} N^{-1} \left(1 + 2 \sum_{v=1}^{q} \rho_v^2 \right) k > q \qquad (2.2.17)$$

which reduces, if a series is random, to

$$\text{var} \left[r(x, x, k) \right] = N^{-1}$$

For a typical psychological experiment, with scaling to make the input and output variances about equal, this gives for 50 trials that the s.e. of $v_k = .14$.

If some information is available about the order of the autocorrelation structure, then more sensitive tests can be devised (Box & Pierce, 1970) but these may presuppose impractically long samples. See also Durbin and Watson (1950, 1951).

The conditions for (2.2.17) in a way anticipate the properties of the simplest autoregressive scheme, named after Markov. The Markov scheme is first-order autoregressive with a noise perturbation superimposed. (It should not be confused with the finite-state Markov chain models used in mathematical learning theory, but it is related to the Markovian linear operator models.)

In this model

$$x_j = px_{j-1} + a_j \tag{2.2.18}$$

where p is a constant, $|p| < 1$. It is easy to show that (2.2.18) is equivalent to

$$x_j = a_j + pa_{j-1} + p^2a_{j-1} + \cdots + p^m a_{j-m} + p^{m+1}x_{j-m-1} \tag{2.2.19}$$

Multiplying (2.2.18) by x_{j-1} gives [after taking expectations as for (2.2.15)]

$$C(x, x, 1) = p \cdot var\ (x)$$

or

$$r(x, x, 1) = p$$

and it follows that

$$r(x, x, k) = p \cdot r(x, x, k - 1) = p^k \tag{2.2.20}$$

The Markov series oscillates in a fairly regular way, so that a subject showing one-stage dependency in his responses might erroneously be taken for exhibiting a simple periodicity contaminated by noise.

It can be shown (Kendall, 1973) that the mean distance between peaks in the Markov oscillations is $(\cos^{-1}(-.5(1 - p)))^{-1}$ and that

$$var(x) = \frac{var(a)}{(1 - p^2)} \tag{2.2.21}$$

If the autoregressive process is extended to two stages, then the simplest model is called a *Yule scheme:*

$$x_j = -w_1 x_{j-1} - w_2 x_{j-2} + a_j \qquad |w_2| < 1 \tag{2.2.22}$$

where it can be shown that

$$r(x, x, 1) = \frac{w_1}{(1 + w_2)} \quad \text{and} \quad r(x, x, 2) = w_2 + w_1^2 \cdot (1 + w_2)$$

It is also possible from recursive equations

$$r(x, x, k) + w_1 \cdot r(x, x, k - 1) + w_2 \cdot r(x, x, k - 2) = 0 \tag{2.2.23}$$

to determine autocorrelations $r(x, x, 3)$ and beyond. The actual form of the correlogram is a damped periodic function. The geometrical properties of this sinusoid are given by Kendall (1973). If the process is stationary, then it follows that the conditions $w_1 + w_2 < 1$ and $w_2 - w_1 < 1$ are met; the process oscillates if w_1 is less than 0, and $-2 < w_1 < +2$, and solutions must lie in the triangle $(w_1, w_2) = (-2, 0), (0, 1), (2, 0)$.

A further statistic that can be useful in diagnostic identification is the partial autocorrelation spectrum; by definition

$$c_1 = r(x, x, 2)$$

$$c_2 = \frac{r(x, x, 2) - r^2(x, x, 1)}{1 - r^2(x, x, 1)}$$

and higher c_m are defined in terms of the quotient of two determinants (Box & Jenkins, 1970). In a situation like (2.2.20) if the partial autocorrelations are observed, they are often negligible and slightly negative after the first term c_1. If a process is autocorrelated and is of order m, then the autocorrelations themselves constitute an infinite series (though perhaps a diminishing one), but the partial autocorrelations cut off abruptly after m lags. Thus inspection of the partial autocorrelations may be sensitive in determining the order prior to fitting a model. In using spectra of autocorrelations and partial autocorrelations, however, there are dangers because some patterns found are a function not only of the process structure but also of the time series sample length. The standard errors of partial autocorrelations are of order $n^{-1/2}$, where n is the sample length, for c_k where $k < m + 1$. Box and Jenkins have discussed the use of partial autocorrelations in identification; they can also be used analytically to see if a time series has been overdifferenced to achieve stationarity, when it would better have been treated as having local transients or perturbations, superimposed upon a stationary and undifferenced series. For interpretation, one may think of the partial autocorrelation at lag k as the autocorrelation at lag k with the effects of all the intermediate observations removed; one might write this as

$$c_k = r((x, x, k):r(x, x, 1), r(x, x, 2), \ldots, r(x, x, k - 1))$$

Worked examples of the use of autocorrelations are given by various authors, including Anderson (1980), Fuller (1976), Montgomery and Johnson (1976), Ostrom (1977), for different contexts, and standard computer programs in various libraries, including the IMSL system (1980) will perform exhaustive descriptive analyses and in some cases identification. The following examples were done using IMSL on a Dec 20 computer.

The Form and Autocorrelation Structure of Two Examples of Autoregressive Processes with Order of Two Lags

The sensitivity of the form of observed time series, and of their associated autocorrelation spectra to quite small changes in their parameters, can usefully be shown by two examples that resemble cases originally used illustratively by Fuller (1976). Here are examined the results of changing the relative weight given to the terms representing one lag and two lags. The examples are useful because they show periodic patterns in both the data samples and, in one case, in the autocorrelations, thus exemplifying comments about apparent periodicities that have already been made in this section. In particular, it is useful to show that periodic changes in output, or in the autocorrelations with increasing lags, are most definitely not of themselves sufficient evidence of some external periodic influence. There is always a natural temptation, when output is periodic or nearly periodic, to look in the environment for some input that has a related periodicity, because one of the simplest ways to produce periodic outputs is to create a system that merely tracks input, and then use a periodic input. That is an open-loop way of approaching the problem. In time series it is important to know what pseudoperiodic effects look like; why autocorrelations over long lags, k, are not necessarily evidence of sequential dependence up to k intervals; and how stable, that is, stationary, process structure arises to random input.[4] In practical time series analysis, it is so often expedient to discount appearances as being direct evidence of process structure or complexity that the surprising capacity of quite simple transfer functions to generate complex and variable sequences should always be in the investigator's mind.

Setting up as generating equations two autoregressive processes of the form $y_j = f(y_{j-1}, y_{j-2})$, the first is

$$y_j = 1.39y_{j-1} - 0.482y_{j-2} + e_j \qquad (2.2.24)$$

where e_j is a random number, in the range 0 through 1. To create some comparison cases, the coefficient of y_{j-1} was decremented by steps of 0.02 leaving the rest of the equation fixed. The values of e_j were produced by a random number function on a Dec 20 computer with a Fortran complier. Table 2.2.1 shows the first 40 terms of some runs of 100 created with $e_1 = 1$ and random inputs thereafter. Four cases corresponding to coefficients of y_{j-1} equal to 1.39, 1.37, 1.35, and 1.33 are tabulated. All the series drift up and down, as the pattern of first differences

$$\Delta^1 y = y_{j-1}$$

given correspondingly in Table 2.2.2, show.

The autocorrelations drop away in a monotone fashion and are given for the first 8 lags in Table 2.2.3. How fast they drop off, and whether or not they go to zero or below, depends on the relative magnitude of the y_{j-1} and y_{j-2} coeffi-

---

[4]This problem arises in evaluating the data of Staddon, King, and Lockhead (1980) who attempt to assess the problem of sequential analysis in category judgments by regression methods, which are not, from a time series approach, valid. See also Kadane, Larkin, and Mayer (1981) for a related problem in reaction-time analyses, with better estimation.

TABLE 2.2.1
Samples of y Series with Different Coefficients of y_{j-1}

Trial Number	y_{j-1} Coefficient			
	1.39	1.37	1.35	1.33
1	1.000	1.000	1.000	1.000
2	1.595	2.301	2.359	2.395
3	2.469	3.368	2.925	3.424
4	3.275	4.286	3.702	3.866
5	3.689	5.033	4.089	3.640
6	3.664	4.865	4.111	3.635
7	3.509	5.227	4.130	4.080
8	3.181	5.275	3.617	3.929
9	3.449	5.412	3.780	3.497
10	3.905	4.990	3.910	3.732
11	3.820	5.026	3.791	3.430
12	4.106	4.918	3.875	3.360
13	4.265	5.180	3.412	2.935
14	4.335	4.894	2.775	2.293
15	4.517	4.986	2.793	2.436
16	5.080	4.747	2.694	2.541
17	5.302	4.786	2.870	2.267
18	5.730	4.404	2.773	2.323
19	5.855	4.586	3.320	2.988
20	5.406	5.025	3.685	3.264
21	4.837	5.486	4.109	3.750
22	4.806	5.278	3.811	3.607
23	4.749	4.616	3.924	3.009
24	4.591	3.805	4.396	2.497
25	4.283	3.078	4.364	2.817
26	4.115	3.188	4.013	3.257
27	3.798	3.520	3.750	3.293
28	3.990	3.867	3.879	3.450
29	4.028	4.246	3.437	3.711
30	4.140	4.105	3.246	3.728
31	4.189	3.895	3.067	3.999
32	4.791	3.616	3.509	3.936
33	4.764	3.820	4.231	4.054
34	4.754	4.408	4.475	4.225
35	4.587	4.886	4.809	4.445
36	4.131	5.062	5.242	3.954
37	4.009	5.541	5.520	3.999
38	3.950	5.281	5.052	4.069
39	4.005	4.750	4.330	4.149
40	4.224	4.899	4.305	3.944

TABLE 2.2.2
First Differences of y Series Shown in Table 2.2.1

Trial Number	1.39	1.37	1.35	1.33
1	—	—	—	—
2	—	—	—	—
3	0.874	1.068	0.566	1.029
4	0.806	0.918	0.776	0.441
5	0.414	0.747	0.387	−0.226
6	−0.025	−0.168	0.022	−0.005
7	−0.154	0.362	0.019	0.445
8	−0.329	0.049	−0.513	−0.151
9	0.268	0.136	0.163	−0.432
10	0.456	−0.422	0.129	0.235
11	−0.085	0.036	−0.119	−0.303
12	0.286	−0.108	0.084	−0.069
13	0.159	0.262	−0.462	−0.425
14	0.071	−0.287	−0.637	−0.642
15	0.181	0.093	0.018	0.144
16	0.564	−0.239	−0.099	0.105
17	0.222	0.039	0.176	−0.274
18	0.428	−0.381	−0.097	0.056
19	0.125	0.182	0.547	0.665
20	−0.449	0.439	0.364	0.276
21	−0.569	0.461	0.424	0.486
22	−0.031	−0.208	−0.298	−0.143
23	−0.057	−0.662	0.114	−0.598
24	−0.158	−0.811	0.471	−0.512
25	−0.308	−0.727	−0.032	0.320
26	−0.169	0.110	−0.351	0.439
27	−0.317	0.333	−0.263	0.036
28	0.192	0.347	0.130	0.157
29	0.038	0.379	−0.443	0.260
30	0.112	−0.141	−0.191	0.017
31	0.049	−0.211	−0.179	0.271
32	0.602	−0.278	0.442	−0.063
33	−0.026	0.204	0.722	0.118
34	−0.010	0.589	0.244	0.171
35	−0.167	0.478	0.334	0.220
36	−0.456	0.175	0.432	−0.491
37	−0.122	0.480	0.278	0.045
38	−0.059	−0.261	−0.468	0.070
39	0.054	−0.531	−0.722	0.081
40	0.220	0.149	−0.025	−0.206

TABLE 2.2.3
y Autocorrelations
$y_j = 1.39y_{j-1} - .48_2y_{j-2} + e_j,$ etc.

Lag	1.39	1.37	1.35	1.33
0	1.000	1.000	1.000	1.000
1	.841	.846	.756	.802
2	.673	.649	.510	.583
3	.541	.464	.265	.421
4	.449	.323	.094	.308
5	.386	.241	.001	.191
6	.332	.193	−.051	.093
7	.276	.177	.026	.012
8	.206	.158	.033	−.070

cients. It can also depend on the series length, but here this is fixed. Note that the autocorrelations are such that conventional significance tests might lead the investigator who did not know the structure to interpret significant lag effects up to $k = 8$, or beyond if the calculations had been done, because $p(r = .164,$ d.f. $= 98) \leq .05$. There is, of course, no functional dependence beyond two lags; the system, whatever its parameter values, has only "memory" two trials back, and all the examples here have the same structure.

The second example is (using z as the variable merely for contrast)

$$z_j = z_{j-1} - 0.88z_{j-2} + e_j \qquad (2.2.25)$$

with the coefficient of z_{j-2} decremented by steps of .02. Table 2.2.4 gives the first 40 terms for cases where the coefficient of z_{j-2} is equal to .88, .86, .84, and .82. The corresponding first differences are shown in Table 2.2.5. The autocorrelations are given, again for up to 8 lags, in Table 2.2.6. The pattern of the autocorrelations now swings between positive and negative values, rather in the manner of a damped pendulum coming slowly through decreasing swings to rest. The oscillating pattern would continue if further lags were examined. It is seen that high correlations at many lags beyond input are possible; again in fact the process does not go back in its generation more than two trials.

Both the y case and the z case here are selected cases of the autoregressive process with both of two lags present; the negative value of the $j − 2$ term stops the process exploding. There is no need to give separate names to each pattern of output or to postulate that they are in some way different processes just because they look different as the parameters change. Given the general structure, the parameter values are a sufficient description both of what is observed and what is expected to happen as the parameters change.

TABLE 2.2.4
Samples of z Series with Different Coefficients of z_{j-2}

Trial Number	.88	.86	.84	.82
1	1.000	1.000	1.000	1.000
2	1.195	1.901	1.959	1.995
3	1.047	1.737	1.340	1.894
4	0.605	0.879	0.580	0.720
5	0.006	0.164	−0.049	−0.691
6	−0.418	−0.565	−0.168	−0.631
7	−0.234	0.273	0.417	0.929
8	0.195	1.210	0.574	1.695
9	1.115	1.669	1.104	1.163
10	1.581	0.738	1.165	0.742
11	0.649	0.090	0.566	−0.067
12	−0.072	−0.115	0.222	−0.084
13	−0.250	0.663	−0.252	0.083
14	0.192	0.920	−0.409	0.155
15	0.951	1.120	0.488	0.884
16	1.666	0.594	1.088	1.158
17	1.238	0.308	1.252	0.490
18	0.573	−0.076	0.531	0.069
19	−0.081	0.510	0.434	0.654
20	−0.565	1.432	0.522	1.003
21	−0.360	1.798	0.887	1.311
22	0.816	0.741	0.481	0.675
23	1.525	−0.786	0.489	−0.387
24	1.104	−1.407	1.013	−0.713
25	−0.056	−0.650	0.916	0.545
26	−0.662	1.358	0.297	1.839
27	−0.477	2.548	−0.044	1.706
28	0.791	1.955	0.450	0.833
29	1.517	0.402	0.488	0.137
30	1.278	−1.134	0.579	−0.097
31	0.311	−1.171	0.505	0.614
32	0.143	0.056	0.946	1.101
33	−0.014	1.799	1.488	1.337
34	0.292	2.662	1.142	1.157
35	0.572	1.796	0.692	0.833
36	0.352	−0.009	0.630	−0.045
37	0.319	−0.601	0.802	0.147
38	0.371	−0.473	0.390	0.832
39	0.529	0.220	−0.124	1.370
40	0.757	1.554	0.434	1.067

TABLE 2.2.5
First Differences of z Series Shown in Table 2.2.4

Trial Number	.88	.86	.84	.82
1	—	—	—	—
2	—	—	—	—
3	−0.148	−0.163	−0.619	−0.101
4	−0.443	−0.858	−0.760	−1.174
5	−0.599	−0.716	−0.629	−1.411
6	−0.424	−0.728	−0.119	0.060
7	0.184	0.838	0.585	1.560
8	0.430	0.937	0.157	0.766
9	0.920	0.459	0.530	−0.531
10	0.466	−0.931	0.061	−0.421
11	−0.932	−0.647	−0.599	−0.809
12	−0.720	−0.206	−0.344	−0.017
13	−0.179	0.778	−0.473	0.168
14	0.442	0.257	−0.157	0.072
15	0.759	0.199	0.897	0.728
16	0.715	−0.526	0.600	0.274
17	−0.427	−0.286	0.165	−0.668
18	−0.666	−0.383	−0.722	−0.421
19	−0.654	0.586	−0.097	0.585
20	−0.484	0.922	0.088	0.349
21	0.205	0.365	0.365	0.308
22	1.177	−1.057	−0.405	−0.636
23	0.708	−1.527	0.008	−1.062
24	−0.420	−0.622	0.524	−0.326
25	−1.160	0.757	−0.097	1.259
26	−0.606	2.008	−0.619	1.294
27	0.185	1.190	−0.342	−0.133
28	1.269	−0.593	0.495	−0.874
29	0.726	−1.553	0.037	−0.696
30	−0.240	−1.536	0.091	−0.233
31	−0.966	−0.037	−0.074	0.710
32	−0.169	1.227	0.441	0.487
33	−0.157	1.743	0.542	0.236
34	0.306	0.863	−0.346	−0.180
35	0.280	−0.866	−0.450	−0.324
36	−0.220	−1.805	−0.062	−0.878
37	−0.033	−0.592	0.172	0.192
38	0.052	0.128	−0.412	0.685
39	0.158	0.693	−0.514	0.538
40	0.229	1.334	0.557	−0.304

TABLE 2.2.6
z Autocorrelations
$z_j = z_{j-1} - .88z_{j-2} + e_j,$ etc.

Lag	.88	.86	.84	.82
0	1.000	1.000	1.000	1.000
1	.549	.565	.523	.535
2	−.270	.293	−.238	−.334
3	−.718	.824	−.624	−.999
4	−.510	.630	−.425	−.518
5	.076	.059	−.029	.164
6	.532	.641	.180	.636
7	.478	.633	.225	.506
8	.124	.093	.146	−.020

2.3 IDENTIFICATION THROUGH BOX–JENKINS METHODS

The methods now to be discussed derive from the work of Box and Jenkins (1970) whose work has been very influential and consequently extensively used in applied statistics (Anderson, 1975). The methods have been almost completely automated by the development of computer programs of considerable sophistication, and the stages in the identificatory cycle of operations, from raw time series data to final model identification and parameter estimation can all be made the subject of algorithms that effectively minimize the role of the investigator. Whether or not this is entirely a good thing is a matter of dispute (Anderson, 1977; Newbold & Granger, 1974) because the process of choosing a model from a set of possible alternatives can and should properly utilize information that is extraneous to the time series data themselves. How this extraneous information can properly be incorporated into the process of model identification is an unsettled question, and there is an element of art as well as science always present. This can be a good thing; it leaves room for the creativity of the theoretician and reduces the probability that blatantly silly theories will receive support from ambiguous data.

The general Box–Jenkins model is called the *representation of an autoregressive integrated moving-average process* (ARIMA for short), which is

$$(1 - \phi_1 B - \phi_2 B^2 - \cdots - \phi_p B^p)(1 - B)^d X_j =$$
$$\theta_0 + (1 - \theta_1 B - \theta_2 B^2 - \cdots - \theta_q B^q)a_j \qquad (2.3.1)$$

where the $\{a_j\}$ are a white noise i.i.d. process, and the $\{X_j\}$ constitute a nonperiodic time series that can be reduced to stationarity by differencing a finite number of times: dth-order differencing can be expressed as $(1 - B)^d$.

The form (2.3.1) is arrived at via two steps in the derivation, first putting

$$W_j = (1 - B)^d X_j \qquad (2.3.2)$$

where B is the backward shift operator, to obtain the stationary nonperiodic time series $\{W_j\}$ from $\{X_j\}$ and then assuming that $\{W_j\}$ is an ARIMA with defining polynomials $\phi(B)_p$, $\phi(B)_q$, so that (2.3.1) in this new briefer notation becomes [as in (2.2.10)]

$$a_j = \left[\frac{\phi(B)_p}{(\theta(B)_q + \theta_0)} \right] W_j \qquad (2.3.3)$$

which is more simply written as

$$a_j = Q(B, p, q) \cdot W_j \qquad (2.3.4)$$

or

$$W_j = Q^{-1}(B, p, q) \cdot a_j \qquad (2.3.5)$$

where $Q(B)$ means a quotient of two polynomials in powers of B. This construction of a quotient of two polynomials will be met repeatedly in time series theory (see Section 3.5) and its form defines the order of the ARIMA as p, q, d. In other words, to identify the process underlying a time series that is the output of an experiment in which the input is an i.i.d. series, it is necessary to know in advance p, q, and d or to fix them for a number of trial solutions in turn and compare the properties and residuals of those solutions, which are themselves competing models in the identification problem. The difficulties and ambiguities center on the appropriate fixing of p, q, and d, on the credit side the Box–Jenkins approach gives us a whole family of possible functions, of great power and generality, and potentially very diverse substantive meaning. So, p is the number of autoregressive terms in the model, q is the number of moving average terms in the input noise, and d is the order of finite differences to which it is necessary to go to obtain stationarity. As seen later, the process of differencing to achieve stationarity in a finite sample can lead to dangerous misidentification unless handled with caution.

The form (2.3.5) can in practice be replaced by a single polynomial to give

$$W_j = v(B) \cdot a_j \qquad (2.3.6)$$

which is the equation of an experiment when the stimulus series is random and the W_j are interpreted as a series of quantitative responses: With a change of notation, (2.3.6) is in fact the (2.2.8) achieved by autocorrelation analysis, to an approximation.

Anderson (1977) has given a meticulous account of the steps that an investigator has to move through in order to perform a valid time series analysis, within the spirit of Box–Jenkins methodology. It is expedient to restate the sense of his comments before looking more closely at actual models and conditions for their correct identification.

It is expedient:

1. To be thoroughly familiar with the relevant psychology and physiology that may have led to the generation of the observed time series.

2. To make an informed specification of the class of models that the experimenter considers realistic and to stay inside that class.

Having defined the psychological and mathematical terms of reference, then the cycle of identification, estimation, and verification is entered and gone round until some convergence upon a satisfactory outcome is achieved. Specifically the investigator has to

3. Make a trial identification of a particular model from the class of models deemed relevant in the light of stages 1 and 2; this means finding p, q, d and some values for $v(B)$ in (2.3.6).

4. Estimate quantitatively the characteristics of the model identified tentatively in stage 3 by using statistically efficient procedures.

5. Compare the predictions of the model in stage 4 with the initial time series data used to fix the parameters of the model and see how well they agree.

6. Further use the model to predict to a new set of data gathered in analogous or related circumstances.

If the model seems to work, then its structure becomes a theory about how time series of the sort being studied are in fact generated. It is from this last step that theory should take off and be extended or restructured.

The stages 3, 4, 5, and 6 can and if necessary should be entered recursively, going back from stage 6 or 5 to stage 3 and remodeling as many times as is feasible, in cost and effort, to show improvement. This is obviously a process of comparative model evaluation within a restricted class, which does lend itself to computerized treatment if the models in the class can be adequately specified in advance, by a seed model and variations thereon by some defined rule, incrementing parameters, for example.

As the use of these methods in psychology will be to analyze and predict sequences of responses, let us write the most common identifiable models that are likely to describe response sequences, always bearing in mind that in fact it is the output of a bivariate series with i.i.d input that is the structure under investigation.

First-Order Autoregression [AR(1)]

$$y_j = v_1 y_{j-1} + e_j, \quad e \sim N(0, \sigma^2) \tag{2.3.7}$$

which in backward shift notation is

$$(1 - v_1 B)y_j = e_j, \quad j = 0, 1, 2, \ldots, N \tag{2.3.8}$$

This AR(1) model has $p = 1$, $q = 0$, $d = 0$ in the general notation of (2.3.1).

Second-Order Moving Average [MA(2)]

$$y_j = a_j + v_1 a_{j-1} + v_2 a_{j-2} + e_j \tag{2.3.9}$$

Here the v_k are usually written as negative, giving in backward shift notation

$$y_j = (1 - v_1 B - v_2 B^2)a_j + e_j \tag{2.3.10}$$

which has $p = 0$, $q = 2$, $d = 0$.

It is usually possible to express an MA model in terms of an AR model or vice versa or to write models that are a mixture of the two processes. This means that solutions are not unique in structure, but if it is known in advance that either MA or AR is appropriate, then it is possible to find the values of the coefficients with some attendant error. But, in order to proceed, conditions on the parameters in (2.3.1) have to be satisfied:

Mathematical Conditions Necessary for Identification

1. The polynomial $\phi(B)$ of order p, which is the autoregressive part of the general equation (2.3.1) describing the behavior of y (the response sequence) has to have roots outside the unit circle. The roots of this polynomial are either real, or complex numbers $\sigma + iw$ and must lie outside the circle radius one in the σ, iw plane. If they lie on the circle, then trouble can ensue; if they are within the circle, then identification becomes impossible.[5]

---

[5]This condition applies in the case where stochastic parameter identification is required in the presence of noise, which is obviously a very general case, and can thus plausibly be advanced as a starting point in psychological experiments (Åström & Eykhoff, 1971). The unit circle condition is related to deeper mathematical conditions that when satisfied assure the nonsingularity of the system parameter covariance matrix, so that it is invertible. The invertibility is the basic requirement here; it means that the weights of the polynomial converge (this is not necessarily a stationarity requirement) and hence recent events are more important in determining the behavior of the system than are temporally remote events. This last property has some direct psychological interpretation in modeling, and so it is reasonable for the investigator to check or explicitly to assume that it is satisfied before analyzing data. The value of expressing the condition in the given form lies partly in that it can be depicted graphically; it also ties in with the algebra of polynomials.

2. The polynomial $\theta(B)$ of order 1, which is the moving average part of the i.i.d. input, is intractable unless its roots also all lie outside the unit circle; if the roots do lie outside the unit circle, then the model is invertible, and the Box–Jenkins system *is* concerned with invertible models.

The procedure for model identification depends in part on examining the structure of the autocorrelation sequence $r(y_j, y_{j-k})$, $k = 0, 1, 2, 3, \ldots$ or, in the case where the input is i.i.d., the sequence $\hat{v}(k)$ of estimates for (2.3.6), and looking at the shape of the $\hat{v}(k)$ distribution with increasing k. The MA(1) model cuts off after lag 1; allowing for estimation error, the v_k for $k = 2, 3, \ldots$ should be near zero. The MA(2) model cuts off after lag 2; the same general comments apply.

The AR(1) model fades gradually away and can show alternating signs, which makes it difficult to separate from an MA(q) model on short and error-loaded data sequences. The AR(2) model can fade away like a damped sinusoid, which may lead to confounding between periodic and aperiodic processes. Models that are mixed MA and AR can resemble an AR model with the terms of low k displaced by the presence of the MA terms.

In this author's experience, psychological time series even within the same experiment (Gregson, 1978) can yield, for different subjects, patterns of coefficients that are plausibly like AR(1) or AR(2) or MA(1) or MA(2); the fuzziness of results makes identification in a positive sense difficult, though it is possible to exclude the MA(p) models in some cases due to lack of a sharp cutoff. The core of the problem is that small coefficients of $v(B)$ will be less than expected noise levels (which are about n^{-1}, where n is the series length, for autocorrelations, and $n \geqslant 200$).

It should be remarked that AR(1) is equivalent to ordinary linear regression, but the remaining models have complications and are solved by hill-climbing techniques or other computer methods for ill-conditioned equations.

Given that a series of estimates $\{\hat{V}_k\}$ has been obtained, the identification of the underlying process model then depends on checking that the residual error is not excessive and is not structured in terms of its own autocorrelation spectrum and then matching coefficients of models that are plausible to the observed $\{\hat{V}_k\}$.

The point about noise minimization is relatively simple and is considered first: The difference between the observed and fitted time series is of the form

$$Y_j - W_j = e_j, \qquad j = 0, 1, 2, 3, \ldots$$

or

$$Y_j - v(B){\cdot}x_j = e_j \qquad (2.3.11)$$

where $\{y_j\}$ is the output series observed, $\{x_j\}$ is the random input series to an experiment, differencing having been carried out if necessary, and $v(B)$ is the series of coefficients convoluted with the input series to make a prediction of the output. The calculated $\{\hat{v}_k\}$ are a truncated estimate of the $v(B)$ and consequently will be an approximation; they have to be used in (2.3.11) and the e_j may be thereby inflated beyond the levels that would obtain if the complete model $v(B)$ were available and were correct. The time series $\{e_j\}, j = 0, 1, 2, 3, \ldots$ has its own autocorrelation structure; it should be that of an i.i.d. process but in practice is taken as acceptably small if it decreases very rapidly monotonically to zero. If, contrariwise, the e_j autocorrelation spectrum shows periodicities or large terms in its tail (lags greater than 3), then all is not well; a different model should be tried and in psychological data the most likely problem is nonstationarity that cannot be sensibly removed by differencing or extracting a linear, or low-frequency periodic, component.

Considering now the estimates $\{\hat{v}_k\}$, whose computational extraction is extremely easy but whose conversion into the polynomial quotient form of (2.3.5) is full of traps and pitfalls for the unwary; there is no substitute for having a considered insight into some aspects of the psychological process being modeled before beginning this stage. The computations used to obtain the approximations yield biased estimates; they are neither sufficient nor efficient statistics in practice; on small samples they can be very unstable and the post hoc identification of bias may require considerable diagnostic skills. The critical problem is that efficient estimation is only possible if the model form [p, q, and d of (2.3.1)] is known but not the individual coefficients; the strategy is therefore to start with the simplest alternatives and the lowest orders of complexity.

The greatest danger lies in creating unnecessarily complicated models; there is a way round this danger by factorizing the polynomials in (2.3.1) and if factors are not extracted when they should be, then unstable estimates can ensue. For example, suppose the correct underlying model is MA(1) so that

$$y_j - \bar{y} = a_j - \theta_1 \cdot a_{j-1} \tag{2.3.12}$$

so that the deviations of output about their mean are a function of an i.i.d. input with a lag of one term, and in error we write a more general ARMA form as

$$(1 - \phi B)(y_j - \bar{y}) = (1 - \theta B)(1 - \theta_1 B) \cdot a_j \tag{2.3.13}$$

then this will have an infinite set of solutions along the line $\phi = \theta$ and it may be impossible to discover that ϕ and θ are actually redundant.

If the transfer function of an experiment is

$$Y_j = v(B)X_j$$

then in terms of (2.3.1), we obtain the identity (Box & Jenkins, 1970, p.346)

$$(1 - \phi_1 B - \cdots - \phi_p B^p)(v_0 + v_1 B + \cdots) = (\theta_0 - \theta_1 B - \cdots$$
$$-\theta_q B^q)B^b \tag{2.3.14}$$

The identification of p, q, b in (2.3.14) may be achieved, for simpler cases, by following tabulated results given by Box and Jenkins for models between $p = 0$, $q = 0$, various b, up to $p = 2$, $q = 2$, various b. It can be shown that the impulse response weights v_k for a given p, q, b model consist of

1. b zero values v_0, v_1, . . ., v_{b-1}.
2. a further $s - r + 1$ values v_b, v_{b+1}, . . ., v_{b+q-p} following no fixed pattern but dependent for the values they take on the system dynamics; these will obviously only exist if q is less than p.
3. values v_k for $k > v + p - q + 1$ that derive from a difference equation

$$v_k = \delta_1 v_{k-1} + \delta_2 v_{k-2} + \cdots + \delta_p v_{k-p},$$

starting with $k = b + q$. *The response to a step input can be derived from the response to an impulse input; if the impulse response coefficients are $\{v_k\}$ and the step coefficients are denoted by $\{V_k\}$, then*

$$v_{(B)} = (1 - B)V(B) \tag{2.3.15}$$

In psychological applications $p = 2$, $q = 2$, $b = 3$ should be about the maximum complexity that it is reasonable to consider. The interplay of the three parameters p, q, and b is subtle; to illustrate in simpler cases within the limits just given, it is again helpful to consider what the response of the system would be to a single nonzero impulse input. The response to such an impulse will be delayed in its onset by b steps; when it does occur, it will be spread over $q + 1$ intervals; the relative magnitudes of the responses within those intervals is given by the coefficients θ_i, $i = 1, 2, . . ., q$ in (2.3.14). The effect of increasing p will be to increase the number of oscillations in the response process, the coefficients ϕ_i, $i = 1, 2, . . ., p$ represent the extent to which the process is underdamped, damped, or overdamped in its oscillations to a limit. Comparison with standard results in published cases, with computer simulations, and with data in which responses to relatively simple impulse inputs can be segregated and identified will obviously facilitate identification.

The simpler sorts of misidentification can arise as follows:

1. If the transfer function (2.3.14) is correctly chosen but the associated noise is not i.i.d., then the noise estimates e_j of (2.3.11) will be autocorrelated but not correlated with the x_j. The form of this spurious autocorrelation is diagnostically relevant.
2. If the transfer function is incorrectly chosen, then the e_j will be cross correlated with the x_j. Within error limits this cross correlation should be zero. If the model has been correctly identified in terms of p, q, b but not in terms of its coefficients, then a χ^2 test on the noise cross correlations is available, but strictly

it is necessary to know the number of non-zero weights in the noise autocorrelation function.

There is a further complication that arises for adequate sample lengths n, but nonrandomized inputs x_j; for a string length n, the variance of the input-noise cross correlations would be of order n^{-1}. But if the inputs are autocorrelated, due to a failure to use randomized inputs, then the cross correlations $r_{xe}(k)$ are themselves autocorrelated across sets of time series. This means that if the x_j are autocorrelated inadvertently or otherwise, then a perfectly adequate transfer function model will give rise to pronounced patterns in the residuals e_j that are spurious and that will disappear if the input is properly randomized.

The major dangers of misidentification can occur on inadequately long time series samples, where extrapolation from fitted models will be hopeless because a model identified as stationary will, in fact, take off or explode when further terms are added. Anderson (1977) has reviewed a number of cases; as the problem of taking too short time series is a perennial one in psychology, particularly in operant or applied behavior modification sequential experiments, Anderson's cases demand detailed study.

A case that is of considerable importance in experimental psychology involves processes where the input is a random series except for rare but quite large jumps, such as occur where there is a change between two successive treatments in an experiment of the sort that goes baseline (with second-order random variations) then first treatment period (with more second-order variations) then a new baseline period for comparison with the first, and so on.

The process

$$y_j = a_j + \Sigma \, h_k, \qquad k = 1, \ldots, j \qquad\qquad (2.3.16)$$

where the h_k are usually zero but sometimes nonzero, with the hiccup being well outside the error range of the a_j terms is a general representation of such sequential experiments. In the Box–Jenkins system, this might be tackled by attempting to create stationarity by using first differences: $d = 1$ in (2.3.1). This in fact complicates the analysis, it is preferable to introduce instead dummy variables at the locations of the jumps and estimate their magnitudes, provided that there are not many of these and that each jump can be given some substantive interpretation. To do this is to perform what Box and Tiao (1975) call intervention analysis. This is examined in greater detail in Section 3.6.

A comment is apposite here on why the experiment of the baseline– intervention–baseline sort (ABA' in some operant notation) cannot be properly analyzed by just fitting three regression lines, one to each phase, by least squares, and then comparing the parameters of those lines; looking at shifts in means and shifts in slopes.

If all successive observations, within all three phases, were independent, then it would be statistically legitimate to fit the three lines of Fig. 2.3.1 and compare means and slopes by tests based on standard regression theory, perhaps improved by the use of Bayes' priors on the parameters (Novick & Jackson, 1974). But as soon as the series are autocorrelated, positively or negatively, in one or more phases, the biases in estimation can be gross. Ostrom (1977) approaches the problem from econometric precedents. Setting up a general model (within each phase) of an autoregressive process where X are inputs, Y outputs (the values regressed in Fig. 2.3.1) and v and u are i.i.d variables,

$$e_j = p{\cdot}e_{j-1} + v_j \tag{2.3.16a}$$

defines autocorrelated residuals with lag 1,

$$X_j = cX_{j-1} + u_j \tag{2.3.16b}$$

defines the autocorrelated inputs (which are apparently taken as all equal within a phase in Fig. 2.3.1 if they are explicitly considered), and

$$Y_j = a + b{\cdot}X_j + e_j \tag{2.3.16c}$$

is the regression observed. It is necessary to constrain $|p| < 1$ *and* $|c| < 1$.

Here a t-test for slope is $b/(\text{s.d.}(b))$, but var (b) is a function of $(1 + pc)/(1 - pc)$ that in practice can mean, which Ostrom shows by simulation, that for very large c and p (i.e., a strongly autocorrelated process that can look like clean data when graphed) that the residual variance is underestimated by nearly 1000% and t overestimated by a factor of 3. Significance is readily found in noise. The situation makes it imperative to test for autocorrelation before attempting to assess the magnitude of intervention effects. This in practice means modeling the time series first. It should be noted that the estimates of the means and slopes of the regression lines can be unbiased when at the same time the residual variance is seriously underestimated in the way just described.

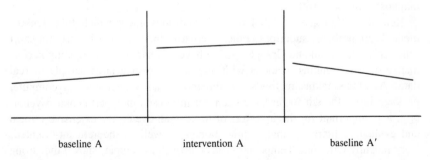

baseline A   intervention A   baseline A′

FIG. 2.3.1   Three regression lines fitted to successive segments of an interrupted time series; raw data not shown.

The second main danger facing the researcher who is making an exploratory analysis with no precedents to guide a choice of plausible models, and with time series of 30 or less observations, is that the autocorrelation structure can be apparently well-behaved even when a process is about to explode. By "explode" is meant that the successive terms suddenly take off and rise to astronomical values or, in an inverse, form die away suddenly to zero. Anderson gives the case of a series of around 30 terms with autocorrelations

$$r(x, x, 1) = +.498, \quad r(x, x, 2) = +.245, \quad r(x, x, 3) = +.118, \quad r(x, x, 4) = +.053$$

and less thereafter. The $r(x, x, k)$ follow an exponential decay; the simplest model would be AR(1), or

$$y_j = 0.5y_{j-1} + e_j \tag{2.3.17}$$

However, unfortunately, the data were generated by the system

$$y_1 = 1$$

$$y_j = 2 \cdot y_{j-1} + e_j, \quad j = 1, 2, \ldots, 30 \tag{2.3.18}$$

which is likely to break loose explosively and follow the strictly deterministic rule $y_j = 2 \cdot y_{j-1}$ by swamping the variance of e_j. If one takes an short run of the same process, it will be even more well-behaved in terms of the rapid monotone decay of its autocorrelations.

If parameter estimation is not efficient, if not all the data are used, then even with checks it is always possible to interpret explosive models as stationary. Particularly this is the case if one uses only the autocorrelation spectra and its derivations in order to make inferences about model structure. The only way to identify explosive processes is to run them long enough for the explosion to begin and to inspect the raw data of the time series as well as any computed statistics. But if it is too dangerous or too costly or unethical to let a process run so far, then a test in terms of the first and second partial autocorrelations may be diagnostically powerful.

Kendall (1973) gives a tabulation of conditions under which Box–Jenkins methods are probably superior to other alternative methods, particularly for short time series. Newbold and Granger (1974) have compared the forecasting performance of Box–Jenkins methods with alternatives over a large sample of real data. As Box–Jenkins methods are the most readily available, in computer package form, though so far have been but little used in experimental psychology, it is important for the investigator to keep an eye on the extensive critical and evaluative literature that is practitioner- as well as theoretician-oriented. Very recently Otter and Tempelaar (1980) have, for example, shown the strong superiority of Kalman filtering (Section 5.4) over Box–Jenkins methods in some contexts. The strength and popularity of Box–Jenkins methods lie in their relative simplicity and small demands in terms of prior knowledge, on the part of the investigator, of process structure. There are many circumstances in which they are not necessarily optimum methods; see McLeod (1977), Nicholls (1977).

2.4 SERIES WITH NATURAL PERIODICITIES

Processes that exhibit regular recurrent patterns of a fixed length in time, and possibly subpatterns repeated many times within a larger cycle, are widespread in nature. Processes that are sufficiently close to exhibiting regular periodicities in real time to be reasonably treated as periodic, over a length of time sufficient to represent a substantial period of interest, can occur in biological psychology and have even been postulated in cognitive performance, where some early theory of Philpott (1932) purported to describe cyclical fluctuations in the output of subjects performing psychological tests. Processes that fluctuate diurnally, perhaps even including sensory acuity (Yensen, 1959, though the evidence is slight) might be relatively common because they are correlated with metabolic processes of the body that in turn depend to some degree on light and darkness or on climate and the seasons. The representation problems that arise in describing cyclical or periodic behavior are treated by fairly standard methods, most commonly by Fourier analysis that involves decomposing a continuous record into a sum of sinusoidal curves of known fixed frequencies (Fourier 1822/1955) or, in the case of a Fourier transform, performing the process in discrete time. These procedures are commonly done, if at all, on a computer using algorithms with an extensive literature of their own.

Two points should be emphasized at once; fitting sums of sine functions to a periodic time series of a priori unknown spectral composition is atheoretic; no model is postulated initially, and consequently analyses based on a finite sample that is relatively short can exhibit components that are bogus. Less well known is the fact that nonsinusoidal representations, actually based on binary functions so that input and output records are at two discrete levels, may be an equally good fit and of greater theoretical defensibility. Such functions, as for example in Fig 2.4.1, are based on Walsh–Hadamard transforms, from work originally by Walsh (1923). Anything that can be done in sinusoidal form could in principle be paralleled in Walsh–Hadamard functions and the latter are in some ways less theoretically restrictive; they relate more naturally to the discrete time representations of Chapter 3. A laboratory example from perception is easily constructed; given a reversible figure such as the familiar Necker cube or the staircase that can be seen as though from above or from below, with two modes of perceived configuration and virtually instantaneous flip between modes, if a subject is instructed to depress a key when he/she sees the figure in one mode and release it so long as it is in the other, then he/she generates a record like Fig. 2.4.1 though not necessarily with regular periodicities. The high segments represent time in one mode, the low segments time in the other. If the process is suspected to be a

FIG. 2.4.1

renewal type, then the analysis of the distribution of interflip times may be of interest, but if it shows some regularities, perhaps after discarding early records, then the regularities themselves are of interest. In this situation most subjects oscillate between perceptual modes and settle down to a pattern, though a detailed time series analysis seems not to have been attempted so it is not clear if the process is stationary periodic, though for some subjects it appears to have an asymptotic mean rate.

Walsh–Hadamard and Fourier transforms have come into increasing importance as the bases of computerized pattern recognition, pattern discrimination, or identification and pattern enhancement for photographic images that are fuzzy but can be sharpened by the removal of some periodic components. If two-dimensional displays can be written as a form of bivariate time series with t_0 set at the origin $(0, 0)$ of the display, some marked economy in the representation of patterns can be achieved based on a very small number of Fourier or Walsh components.

Fourier Analysis Representation

It is well known that periodic functions are stationary once trend components have been removed from them. In practice many real data samples are so noisy that alternative models, periodic with a high number of periodic components, or with a low number of periodic components and superimposed trend and moving average aperiodic components, may be equally good fits, and the choice between them has then to be deferred or based on relative interpretability.

A typical periodic function may be written as

$$f(x) = \sum_{j=1}^{\infty} a_j \sin jx + 0.5b_0 + \sum_{j=1}^{\infty} b_j \cos jx \qquad (2.4.1)$$

or equivalently but more tersely

$$f(x) = \sum_{j=1}^{\infty} C_j \sin (jx + \phi_j) \qquad (2.4.2)$$

where the a_j, b_j, C_j, and ϕ_j are coefficients at the choice of the theorist.

This means that the periodic function may be decomposed into an infinite series of sines and cosines, each appropriately weighted and having a unique frequency. It is the periodicity of the function $f(x)$ that ensures, subject to conditions, its decomposability into the infinite series of simpler periodic functions. The decomposition into sinusoids is not the only one possible but was first discovered and is most used in time series analysis in disciplines that relate to psychophysiology. The decomposition should be thought of as relatively convenient rather than necessary; it obviously makes theoretical assumptions about the nature of underlying processes in time if the sets of coefficients in (2.4.1) or (2.4.2) are given substantive meanings. In practice the summations do not have to be taken to infinity; the first few terms may converge rapidly on an empirically acceptable solution when modeling.

The first term has period 2π [given appropriate choice of the time units; in fact these units may be in time or in space, because (2.4.1) and (2.4.2) are not, at this stage of the argument, necessarily functions in time; it is only the periodicity and not the spatiotemporal domain of the phenomena that is assumed]. This first term has, then, the slowest changing values, and the second and subsequent terms have higher frequencies; that is to say their periods are submultiples of the first term. The second term has period π; the third has $2\pi/3$; and the nth has $2\pi/n$, which means that it completes n cycles for every one cycle that is completed by the first term. The cosine terms, if we use the mixed sine, cosine representation (2.4.1), behave in a like manner.

We can think of the points generating the sinusoidal components as the projections of points on the circumference of a circle, rotating with constant angular velocities, ω as shown in Fig. 2.4.2. The first component does one complete revolution, 2π radians, in unit time; the next rotates twice as fast, so $\omega = 4\pi$; the next three times as fast, so $\omega = 6\pi$; and so on. Both the angular velocity representation and the periodicity representation are commonly used in the relevant literature, and the same concepts may be found written in either form.

Terminology commonly met includes

ω = angular frequency in radians/unit time

$2\pi/\omega$ = wavelength or period = λ

number of cycles per unit time = 1/period = $\omega/2\pi$ = frequency

This means that the periods of terms of a Fourier series are

$$2\pi, \quad \frac{2\pi}{2} = \pi, \quad \frac{2\pi}{3}, \quad \frac{2\pi}{4} = \frac{\pi}{2}, \quad \frac{2\pi}{5}, \quad \cdots$$

and the corresponding frequencies are

$$\frac{1}{2\pi}, \quad \frac{2}{2\pi} = \frac{1}{\pi}, \quad \frac{3}{2\pi}, \quad \frac{4}{2\pi} = \frac{2}{\pi}, \quad \frac{5}{2\pi}, \quad \cdots$$

If the frequencies are, for some reason, defined over an arbitrary time base of $2L$ units (for example, L = six months would be plausible in studying annual

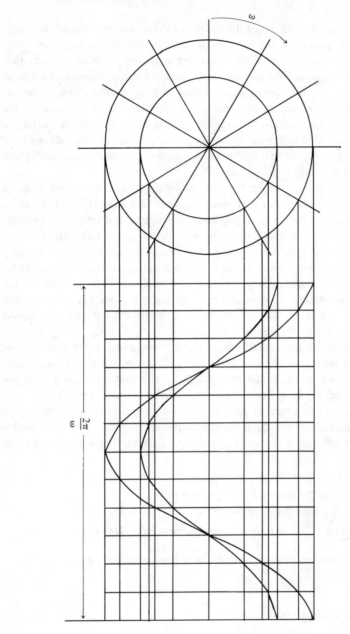

FIG. 2.4.2   Generation of sinusoids from points on a circle rotating with constant angular velocity; two amplitudes in phase are shown.

cycles of behavior that may be linked to the seasons), then the angular frequencies are expressed as $j\pi/L$.

Theoretically the representations in frequency spectrum terms and in autocorrelation terms are deducible from each other, but in practice the relationship may be too complex for the investigator to be able readily to guess what one would be like from an inspection of the other; there is often a case for having both because each contains valuable information but has its own problems in interpretation.

In practice we do not observe periodic processes continuously unless rather clumsy instrumentation exists, and if we observe continuously, then either we obtain many meters of output records that are tedious or intractable, or the very continuity of the observation may interfere with the process being observed. In cost–benefit terms, it may be better not to have complete records but to have records at a series of discrete points in time provided that we are certain by what rules the sampling of the discrete points is achieved. At the finest scale with which the experimental psychologist is typically concerned, the psychophysiology of EEG activity, one observation of a voltage (the cortical potential) is taken in practice about every 3 msec. Computer hardware makes this convenient though real-time sampling can be faster. In psychological experiments with a coarser metric the time unit may be really or virtually fixed as the trial length, T, and we then observe one vector of events per trial, the elements of the vector being taken as simultaneous or as ordered in some special way (see Chapter 4 for examples of this).

Events of higher frequency than π/T or of periods shorter than $2T$ are not detected by such a set of observations in discrete time; it is said they are *aliased*, which means they are completely lost to analysis. This may be good or bad according to what we seek; if the noise in the situation is of higher frequency, then it is expedient to alias it out of the representation. What cannot be detected cannot be included in an analysis or prediction, so the time unit of discrete observations imposes an upper limit on the summations in (2.4.1) and (2.4.2) that become finite and not infinite. This in turn imposes some approximations or limits upon what can be modeled.

Periodic series are of interest when it does not seem to matter, for the investigators' purposes, exactly when the recording of data begins, tomorrow at 10:00 A.M. may be as good as today at 10:00 A.M., though today at 2:00 P.M. might be quite disastrous. Obviously the indifference cannot be carried too far, but most psychophysical experiments are run on the assumption that we start recording when it is convenient, given some broad constraints. In fact, data samples will be collected under conditions such that intracondition stability or equivalence with respect to the series parameters is expected and, given this, intercondition comparisons may be valid. Series incorporating suspected or known learning processes are a very poor bet for periodic analysis, unless the learning process can be expressed as a smooth time trend that can be partialled out from the parameters; in this hypothetical and booby-trapped situation it is not clear a priori whether the smooth component or the periodic components are necessarily of the greatest interest; that is a psychological and not a mathematical question.

Mathematically the idea that the starting point in time is not critical means that the functions describing the time series have to be constant over translations in time; as seen later this is, in fact, a stationarity requirement for a periodic function.

Formally it is required (Brillinger, 1975) that

$$f(t + \theta) = C_\theta f(t) \qquad \text{for } t = 0, 1, 2, 3, \ldots \tag{2.4.3}$$

where C_θ is a scalar function of θ, and $C_1 \neq 0$ to avoid triviality. Now C_θ is an operator, so it can be applied recursively, giving

$$f(t +1) = C_1 f(t) = C_1^2 f(t - 1) = C_1^{t + 1} f(0) \tag{2.4.4}$$

If $C_1 = \exp\{\alpha\}$, then $f(t) = f(0) \exp\{\alpha t\}$. This will yield bounded solutions for $\alpha = i\lambda$, and using the relationship

$$\exp\{i\lambda\} = \cos\lambda + i\cdot\sin\lambda$$

it follows that if $f(t) = \Sigma c_k \exp\{i\lambda_k t\}$, then

$$f(t + \theta) = \Sigma\, C_k \exp\{i\lambda_k t\} \tag{2.4.5}$$

where $C_k = c_k \exp\{i\lambda_k\theta\}$.

In this brief treatment we have taken the function $f(t)$ to be deterministic and shown that sinusiodal definitions can meet the requirement (2.4.3), but if the $f(t)$ is either random or stochastic, then it will be the probability structure [usually the set of moments of the probability density function associated with $f(t)$] that would be invariant under time translation. In this sense the stationarity of the process is the stationarity of its statistical descriptive parameters, that is, its sufficient statistics.

The term *mixing* is found in the literature (Rosenblatt, 1956) to mean a series that has a short span of internal dependence, which we may regard as a loose analogy to a weak memory for its own past record. Sequences of human judgments in a psychophysical experiment might plausibly, a priori, be taken as mixed in this sense. In mixing, if two measures $g(t)$ and $g(t^*)$ are taken at times t and t^*, their correlation should tend rapidly to zero as $|t - t^*| \to \infty$. Not only is this psychologically plausible (Gregson & Paddick, 1975) but it facilitates mathematical analysis.

There are two distinct important concepts to grasp here: The idea that covariance decreases with the lag or separation of points considered, which leads to the idea that the sum of the set of covariances over all lags is a bounded sum, which in turn leads to tractable analysis of the time series in the frequency domain; and the idea that the covariances for any given lag are fixed, which state of affairs is called second-order stationarity or wide-sense stationarity. This more restricted sort of stationarity is generally assumed, even if implicitly, in all the more common forms of time series analysis before those to be considered in Chapter 5. The second-order stationary time series with strong mixing is an obvious starting point for modeling much of human behavior; even if it does not fit, the precise knowledge of how and why it does not fit is informative and would be a necessary stage in the progression to any consideration of nonstationary representations.

Convariance stationarity is defined by fixing two moments of the time series; put

$$C_a(t) = EU_a(t) = C_a$$

for a constant mean, and

$$C_{ab}(t + \theta, t) = \text{cov} \{U_a(t + \theta), U_b(t)\} = C_{ab}(\theta)$$

where $t, \theta = 0, 1, 2, \ldots$ and $a, b = 1, 2, \ldots, r$ where the time series U is r-dimensional, and the covariance matrix C_{ab} will be $r \times r$. This definition obviously covers the univariate time series as well, for $r = 1$.

Continuing with the consideration of this r-dimensional time series, which has r values in a vector at any observable time t, given first- and second-order stationarity,

for $a, b = 1, 2, 3, \ldots, r$ as $|\theta| \to \infty$

we postulate (which is a very weak sort of mixing condition) that

$$\sum_{0=0}^{\infty} C_{ab}(\theta) < \infty \tag{2.4.6}$$

from which we may immediately define the frequency coefficients $f_{ab}(\lambda)$ for $-\infty < \lambda < \infty$, which as a set constitute a spectrum. That is to say, defining

$$f_{ab}(\lambda) = (2\pi)^{-1} \sum_{n=-\infty}^{\infty} C_{ab}(\theta) \exp \{-i\lambda\theta\} \tag{2.4.7}$$

transforms from a representation of the time series in terms of its autocovariances in time to a representation in terms of frequency components. The set of $f_{ab}(\lambda)$ is defined as a second-order spectrum, or the spectral density of the time series when the spectrum is composed of sinusoidal components. If all the coefficients $f_{ab}(\lambda)$ are arranged in an $r \times r$ matrix, then this is called the *spectral density matrix* of the series $U(t)$, where U is an r-vector.

Most of the tractable models used in time series analysis are stationary or made up of sums of stationary series; but before some examples are considered, it is expedient to note some definitions of terms that are widely used in mathematical senses, as formally given here, and as names for processes in engineering and by generalization in biological cybernetics or in physiology, for example, in psychoacoustics.

Suppose we have an operation A, which transforms an r-valued time series into an s-valued time series (the first is a vector of r values and the second a vector of s values at any observable time t). Such an operation is called a *filter* and in this form is so vague that practically any continuing living organism could be thought of as a filter or a set of filters. At this level of vagueness we can do little even though the idea of using a filter as a conceptual building block for describing living systems or subsystems such as color vision does mark an important step away from descriptions that stand outside time. Adding two conditions, linearity and summability, circumscribes the concept of a filter considerably; if $U_1(t)$ and $U_2(t)$ are two series, then:
If

$$A[a_1 U_1 + a_2 U_2](t) = a_1 A[U_1](t) + a_2 A[U_2](t) \qquad (2.4.8)$$

and

$$A[U(t + \theta)](t) = A[U](t + \theta) \qquad \text{for all } t, \theta = 0, 1, 2, 3, \ldots \quad (2.4.9)$$

then A is an $s \times r$ linear filter. This filter may itself be a multivariate series in time; written out in full it would be a series of matrices, or what is called the *coefficients of a matrix polynomial,* of which examples are given in Chapter 6 in experimental applications in cognitive psychology.

In a simple unidimensional case, where both the input and output series are single-valued time series ($s = r = 1$), then

$$y(t) = \Sigma \, a(t - \theta)u(t) \qquad \text{for } -\infty < \theta < \infty \qquad (2.4.10)$$

where the $a(\ )$ are the elements of A.

The form (2.4.10) can be written equivalently instead as

$$y(t) = \Sigma \, a(\theta)u(t - \theta) \qquad (2.4.11)$$

for both the convolution sums of (2.4.10) and (2.4.11) come to the same thing. With the additional condition that the sum

$$\Sigma \, |a(\theta)| < \infty \qquad (2.4.12)$$

the filter A is summable. In practice the terms in negative values of θ are not observable; they mean that effects work backward in time, which is not plausible in psychology, and so the summations in (2.4.10)–(2.4.12) are instead taken over the positive infinite range only, that is, from $\theta = 0$ to $\theta = \infty$. In practice, if the filter A converges very rapidly to zero, then the sum is taken over a very few terms, and the approximation involved is sufficiently close for the following results, defined on linear summable realizable filters, to hold.

The *transfer function* of a filter is given by

$$B(\lambda) = \Sigma \, a(\theta) \exp \{-i\lambda\theta\}, \qquad -\infty < \lambda < \infty \qquad (2.4.13)$$

if the set $\{a(\theta)\}$ is the response of the filter to a single impulse input. If two summable filters, $\{a_1(\theta)\}$ and $\{a_2(\theta)\}$ are applied simultaneously, then they have a transfer function that is the sum of their separate transfer functions; but if they are applied in temporal succession, then the resultant transfer function is the product of the two separate functions; that is, if $a_1(\theta)$ is an $r \times q$ linear summable filter, and $a_2(\theta)$ is an $s \times r$ linear summable filter, then applying first a_1 and then a_2 means that $a_2{*}a_1\,(\theta)$ is an $s \times q$ linear summable filter, with a transfer function that we can call $B_2(\lambda){\cdot}B_1(\lambda)$.

The expression $a_2{*}a_1(t)$ is the *convolution* of two expressions in time; by definition

$$a_2{*}a_1(t) = \Sigma \, a_2(t - \theta)a_1(\theta) \qquad (2.4.14)$$

and the use of (2.4.13) takes what is convolution in the time domain into multiplication in the frequency domain. As we see again in Chapter 3, Fourier transforms and z transforms have the property of taking convolutions in time, which are conceptually difficult to handle (though not difficult to compute or to simulate with adequate facilities) into multiplication in the frequency domain; for many years the latter was the only tractable way of proceeding, and in periodic time series it is the natural way to proceed in the physical sciences and in those aspects of psychophysiology that have periodic physical functions as their usual inputs.

One further formal definition concerning filters is important; that of l-summability. A filter that is l-summable meets, for some $l > 0$, the condition that

$$\Sigma \, [1 + |\theta|^l|] \, a(\theta)| < \infty \qquad (2.4.15)$$

An interesting case of an l-summable filter is the simple operation of taking first differences to replace a series;

$$Y(t) = U(t) - U(t - 1) = \Delta_1 U(t) \qquad (2.4.16)$$

is in fact an l-summable filter for all possible values of l; it has coefficients

$$a(\theta) = \begin{cases} 1 & \text{if } \theta = 0 \\ -1 & \text{if } \theta = 1 \\ 0 & \text{otherwise} \end{cases}$$

By application of (2.4.13) the corresponding transfer function of (2.4.16) is

$$B(\lambda) = 2i \cdot \exp\left[\frac{-i\lambda}{2}\right] \cdot \sin\left(\frac{\lambda}{2}\right) \qquad (2.4.17)$$

which yields a frequency distribution with most of its mass concentrated at $\lambda = \pm n\pi$, where n takes only odd values. The consequence of this rapidly converging function (the summability condition) is to take out slowly varying components but retain rapidly varying components; in time series analysis it is often expedient to difference a series once, or possibly twice, to remove slow periodic components that produce an effective nonstationarity over the sample period being studied.

To summarize these comments on the notion of stationarity within the context of periodic time series, we note three formal definitions that embody some of the definitions given previously and are commonly met.

A sequence of independent identically distributed random variables, called i.i.d., where each variable can be a vector of r terms, is a pure noise stationary time series, it can be defined for time instants $t = 1, 2, \ldots$ and can be added to or superimposed upon any other stationary time series defined at the same set of instants, preserving the overall stationarity. The pure noise process has no dominant or identifiable frequency components; it is equally represented at all frequencies. In practice the noise generated in the internal processes of living organisms would not be expected to be pure noise but might approximate to it for some purposes. The formal definition of (aperiodic) pure noise provides a baseline from which tests of the statistical significance of departures from random expectation can be constructed.

Denote the i.i.d. sequence by $e(t)$, $t = 0, 1, 2, 3, \ldots$ for a scalar series ($r = 1$), and apply to it a summable filter with terms $a(\theta)$, yielding

$$Y(t) = \Sigma \; a(t - \theta) \cdot e(\theta) \qquad (2.4.18)$$

then $Y(t)$ will be a stationary series; and if $e(t)$ is r-valued, and $a(\theta)$ is an $s \times r$ summable filter, $Y(t)$ will become an s-valued stationary series. The filter here is in effect changing the dimensionality of the time series but preserving the stationarity; further, if only a finite number, say m, of the terms of the filter are nonzero, then (2.4.18) is simply a *moving-average process*. A moving-average realization of a stationary process will in general, therefore, be itself stationary.

As a third case, consider again the definition (2.4.2), which, for multivariate generality, we may write slightly differently as

$$Y_k(t) = R_k \cdot \cos (\omega_k t + \phi_k) \qquad \text{for } k = 1, 2, \ldots, r \qquad (2.4.19)$$

where $Y_k(t)$ is r-vector-valued at all t, the R_k are constant scalar coefficients, and the constants ϕ_k, $k = 1, 2, \ldots, 4 - 1$ are uniform over the interval $-\pi$ to $+\pi$, and

$$\Sigma \; \phi_k = 0$$

This multivariate time series (2.4.19) is stationary because if any finite set of points is considered and then shifted by t units of real time, the structure of the series, in terms of its moments, autocovariance, and frequency distribution, will be unchanged. It should be obvious that, given the stationarity properties of each of the distributions, mixtures of these distributions with stationarity would be expected to occur in real psychological processes; the problem of decomposing such mixtures back into their component parts is a problem of identification in the systems theory sense (MacNeill, 1977).

Fluctuations Resembling Periodicities and Produced by Simple Networks

Fluctuations in output of two coupled systems, or perhaps better, alternations between them that bear no immediate obvious relation to the inputs, have been noted by various workers in motivational psychology and in neurology. The periodicities that can be emitted are not smooth, but the switching between competing outputs, with first one and then the other going to zero, may under noisy conditions look deceptively like the consequences of periodic inputs. The simplest case of this family is produced when two organisms (which might be neurones) each are excited by input and each has an inhibiting output onto the other. Figure 2.4.3 shows part of this process in two steps in discrete time; the form given may be used for computer simulations.

Systems like Fig. 2.4.3 have been studied for their properties at least since McDougall (1903); most recently Ludlow (1980) reports various simulations in

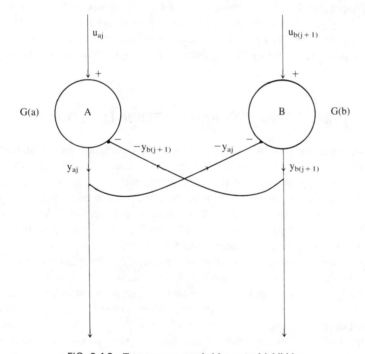

FIG. 2.4.3   Two systems coupled by mutual inhibition.

the context of animal behavior. Some of the behavior of mutually inhibiting subsystems is not readily predictable and depends critically on the relative gains $G(a)$ and $G(b)$, and the sequential structure of the inputs. The main feature of interest is the abrupt discontinuities in the output for slowly varying inputs, or sometimes for constant inputs.

To simulate the sequences, it is convenient to use a unit of discrete time such that each subsystem receives an input every alternate step.

The recurrence relations, with all y positive or zero as a boundary condition, are

$$Y_{b(j+1)} = G(b){\cdot}u_{b(j+1)} - G(b){\cdot}y_{aj} \tag{2.4.20}$$

$$Y_{a(j+2)} = G(a){\cdot}u_{a(j+2)} - G(a){\cdot}y_{b(j+1)} \tag{2.4.21}$$

and it is necessary to fix u_{a1} and u_{b1} and $G(a)$ and $G(b)$ to initiate the process. This assumes that the transmission time in the two inhibiting crosslinks is negligible but that shifts in the input values are slower than the trial intervals.

The critical parameters are $G(a)$ and $G(b)$; if these are both less than unity, then both subsystems will continue to fire. When one exceeds unity, then switching can occur, and this can be quasi-periodic.

As soon as we add some representation of the idea that the gains adapt to steady input, so that if u is constant, then $G(x)$ decreases with time, for completely steady input the outputs will switch repeatedly; the whole system becomes an oscillator. As more subsystems are added to the original two, with all possible pairwise inhibitory links present, very complex sequences of output can result.

2.5 NONLINEAR AND VOLTERRA FUNCTIONS

This section is by way of a digression and can be omitted on a first reading.

In the literature of time series analysis and of control theory, terms such as *functional* and *kernel* are met; these are, historically, borrowings from mathematical developments of the late nineteenth century and in particular derive from the profoundly important work of the Italian mathematician Vito Volterra (1860–1940) who first investigated and solved some of the key problems of analysis, which arise in this area, about 1885 (published by Volterra 1887).

The reader will have noticed that in time series representations of dynamic processes we depart from the idea that an observed response is a function, sufficiently, of those stimulus events who have just occurred in that segment of time we call the *current trial* or in some other notional segment. Instead the current observable behavior is written as a function of a series of events on previous trials and at the start of any analysis of a record of behavior the questions of what previous events, how many previous events, and their functional interrelationships, are very properly open questions. This means that the dependent variable is observed behavior, which is a vector of values at a point in time. The question whether the observed behavior depends on a discontinuous set of previous observations, say on the trials $j - 1$ back to $j - k$, which is k observations in all, or whether instead we choose to conceptualize the previous time segment in which the trials $j - 1$ back to $j - k$ lie as a continuous period in which some independent variable takes values at all instants is treated as of secondary importance, as real experimental analyses of real data have to work in discrete time, on time series records. Obviously the move from discrete to continuous time is mathematically anything but trivial, and historically the description of processes in which a dependent variable was treated as the consequence of a range of values of a function, which itself was continuous, came first. Volterra's contribution was to extend the notion of a function to that of a functional; the latter is in fact a very general case of which the first is a tractable limited form. Again historically functions, and their calculus, preceded functionals by at least 300 years, and the process of education in abstract analysis typically recapitulates history in order; the use of functional analysis in theoretical psychology also appears to exhibit the same historical recapitulation.

A functional is best defined by first restating that a function y of several independent variables $x_1, x_2, x_3, \ldots, x_n$ is written as $y = f(x_1, x_2, \ldots, x_n)$ and the set of n variables is finite. Typically in psychometrics we seek to identify f as a linear regression in the n variables, or in a subset of the n because n is too many, or we seek to replace the $\{x_i\}$ by a new set of mutually independent variables $\{x^*_k\}$ that are also, hopefully, fewer in number than n and are related by a linear function f, or some other not-too-dissimilar function f^* that seems to be easier to read back into some framework of causality from x or x^* onto y. Now, abandon the restriction that n is finite; the set of predictor variables becomes, mathematically, countably infinite and then in the limit continous. To do this the variables x are replaced by a function $x(t)$ that is defined to take values over a range

$$T_0 < t < T_n \tag{2.5.1}$$

and immediately the notion is extendable to make y a functional of several functions $x_a(t), x_b(t), x_c(t), \ldots$ each with its own associated range as in (2.5.1). The functions chosen for a model of functional form

$$y = f(\, x_a(t),\, T_{0a},\, T_{na},\, x_b(t),\, T_{0b},\, T_{nb},\, \ldots) \tag{2.5.2}$$

are themselves independent variables that may be identified through modeling and experiment. Actually the name *functional* for expressions of the sort of (2.5.2) was introduced by Hadamard, though the creation of a general mathematical theory of the functional calculus was initiated by Volterra; the concepts of continuity, differentiation, and integration have to be evolved afresh because they were, in the first instance, defined for functions and not functionals.

Volterra was led, in his search for general theory, to investigate particular equations that are instances of functionals and that he considered (sometimes with ample justification) to be models of processes that arose in the physical and biological sciences; consequently, instances of those special equations bear his name.

We now give some formal results (Volterra, 1959) that underpin some alternative representations of time series models to which attention will be drawn. Note in particular that functionals are not linear in general, and hence representations of time series in Volterra form arise when for some reason it is expedient to abandon the conceptual constraint of linearity in modeling.

A functional can be an ordinary function of its arguments at the same time; this is made clear by the definition:

> y is a functional of the function $x(t)$ in the interval T_a, T_b when it depends on all the values taken by $x(t)$ when t varies in the interval T_a, T_b. If other variables α, β also occur in the function $x(t)$ but are constant, then y is an ordinary function of those variables α, β and not a function of t as is x.

Functionals depending on values taken not by one but by several functions that are connected, as in the form $y = x(t)$, $z = g(y)$, in the intervals, respectively, (T_a, T_b) and (T_c, T_d) can be reduced to functionals depending on a single function.

The regular homogeneous functions of degree n are defined to have the form

$$F_n[y(t)] = \int_a^b \int_a^b \ldots \int_a^b k(\xi_1, \xi_2, \xi_3, \ldots, \xi_n) y(\xi_1) y(\xi_2), \ldots, y(\xi_n) d\xi_1 d\xi_2 d\xi_3 \ldots d\xi_n \qquad (2.5.3)$$

where the function k is called the *kernel* of the function F_n. It may sometimes be assumed that the kernel is symmetric with respect to its n variables, which means in that case the order of the n operations in the multiple integral may be permuted.

Given the form (2.5.3), then in turn we may compose sums of regular homogeneous functions whose highest degree is n, and such sums are called *regular functionals* of degree n, taking the form

$$G_n[y(t)] = k_0 + F_i[y(t)] + F_2[y(t)] + \cdots + F_n[y(t)] \qquad (2.5.4)$$

From the definitions (2.5.3) and (2.5.4) there can be derived a theorem (Fréchet, 1906) that every functional $G[y(t)]$ can in the limit be represented by an expression that is a sum of terms like (2.5.3) for $n = 0, 1, 2, \ldots, n$.

In the context of time series representation, these results imply the following generalization: Given any stationary series that is formed by a linear expression

$$y(t) = \Sigma \, a(t - \theta) u(\theta) \qquad (2.5.5)$$

where, because $u(t)$ is stationary, $y(t)$ is also stationary, then *alternatively* $y(t)$ can be formed through a nonlinear function

$$y(t) = f(U(t), U(t - 1), \ldots) \tag{2.5.6}$$

which may possibly have an infinite number of arguments. If it does have an infinite number of arguments, then it is recognizably a functional, as (2.5.2), over the interval of the time series sample. As the linear stationary forms are not always tractable, Brillinger (1970) and others have attempted to find more tractable forms by the use of nonlinear relations of the functional expansion form derived from (2.5.4), which necessitates a series of kernels as follows:

$$Y(t) = \sum a_1(t - j_1)U(j_1) + \sum \sum a_2(t - j_1, t - j_2)U(j_1)U(j_2) +$$
$$\sum \sum \sum a_3(t - j_1, t - j_2, t - j_2, t - j_3)U(j_1)U(j_2)U(j_3) + \cdots \tag{2.5.7}$$

If $Y(t)$ is given and $U(t)$ is defined as a series satisfying this Volterra expansion (2.5.7), then an analysis in terms of identifying the a_k of (2.5.7) is equivalent to a process of frequency demultiplication, of the extraction in the frequency domain of lower-order harmonics from $U(t)$.

This digression into functionals is made to emphasize that fitting any linear stationary model to a finite sample from a time series is not a unique modeling but a special case that is justified if at all on the grounds of its tractability, simplicity, and interpretability. One could advance plausible psychological reasons, in some contexts, for using at least a low-order version of (2.5.7) as a general approach and this would bear a close resemblance to analyses in the frequency domain, but without stationarity assumptions. The particular attraction of (2.5.7) in behavioral modeling is the possibility of using the higher-order kernels as expressions reflecting interactive products of previous stimulus–response combinations in the recent history of a subject.

The second-order Volterra equation has kernel terms that resemble

$$Cy_j u_{(j - k_1)} u_{(j - k_2)}$$

where each pair k_1, k_2 contributes one element, a covariance, to a matrix of such coefficients. This matrix is in fact triangular because by the symmetry over k_1 and k_2 it is symmetrical about the diagonal of $k_1 = k_2$ terms, and half may be omitted. The use of this second-order kernel [which may be seen as a restricted case of (2.5.7)] is a two-dimensional transfer function that arises instead of one vector of coefficients as soon as the shift is made from the linear to the simplest nonlinear models of this sort (Lee and Schetzen, 1965). The researcher therefore needs to acquire skill in reading and interpreting the patterns in such matrices. In physiological analyses of successive spike and evoked potentials in neurones, Marmarelis and Marmarelis (1978) have made extensive use of this and higher-degree kernels to study the circumstances where successive responses to the same input are not the same (i.e., the system departs from linearity) but may be represented by a second-degree Volterra function because the sequential dependence of two successive response potentials is regular. Marmarelis and Marmarelis give extensive details of computation, without and with digitizing of inputs; they also consider the graphic consequences of computational error, which can be serious.

A series of detailed analyses by Reichardt and Poggio (partly summarized in Reichardt, 1977) of the processes of figure–ground discrimination in the visual system of the common housefly *Musca domestica* provide a powerful illustration of the value and utility of Volterra representations of neural networks. The housefly is studied as one of the simplest prototype organizations using bilateral visual information to control motions in an environment of both absolutely fixed and moving objects; the same processes that enably the fly to make movement and position computations, and hence fly toward targets, also are implicated in its perception of relative motion and its discrimination of a moving figure against a fixed ground. The analysis starts from the hypothesis that relative motion between figure and ground leads to an independent or context-free perception of the figure; figure movement leads to the sharp perception of figure boundaries against a background of the same texture, from which it could not be distinguished when stationary.

The fundamental problem is to build a model, which is adequate as a description and of minimum complexity, to represent functionally (and not necessarily in terms of detailed neural architecture) what the fly has to do, with the sequences of inputs it receives, in order to be able to perform the discrimination implicit in its observable choice behavior. The behavior of interest arises when the fly can reliably move toward or land upon something when its path originates from an arbitrary starting point. This reliable directed behavior has to be demonstrated over a range of different sorts of two-dimensional visual displays presented to the fly.

We do not ask "how does the fly do it?" but rather "what is the simplest way that its functioning, when it shows these invariances of locomotion, can be adequately represented?" Knowing that it takes time, and the input of sequences of very small events to the compound eyes of the fly before it can respond appropriately, leads us to seek a convolution of inputs and detection processes.

The response of the fly at a point in time can thus be conjectured to be the consequence of a sequential string of inputs to the compound eye (which by its structure is a set of discrete elements, the ommatidia) being taken into the relatively simple nervous system of the fly and in some way integrated (summed, multiplied, or convoluted in a network with intrinsic transmission delays) to provide the output signals to the wings, body joints, and legs that then determine the subsequent intended direction of flight of the fly. It is reasonable to suppose that the fly can make corrective movements when in flight on an almost continuous basis. Flies can move onto a moving target, such as another fly of the opposite sex, in midair.

If a signal moves from left to right, say, across the visual field of the fly, then stimuli enter first at one side and then progressively enter other receptors with delays related to the neurophysiological configuration of the fly's eyes. As the animal has two eyes, large discontinuities in the input series may occur when a sharp point stimulation moves out of one visual field into the other.

If one places before the two-eyed fly a sinusoidal grating and moves it at constant speed horizontally first in one direction and then in the reverse direction, the fly responds with a strong direction-sensitive movement, which reverses if the signal direction of movement is reversed. Now it can be shown both by simulation and by theoretical analyses that in order for the fly to be able to do this (and consequently for more complex two-eyed organisms to do it) it must employ a system with at least two inputs and nonlinear signal summations.

If the two receptors are a and b (which in the usual orientation could correspond to left and right eye detection units, or in the fly to two ommatidia laterally adjacent in one eye), the input periodic signals are time series $x_a(t)$ and $x_b(t)$, and the output is a behavioral or turning response (a measured torque in dyne-centimeters exerted by the fly), which we may call $y_{ab}(t)$, then it has been deduced that

$$y_{ab}(t) = \int \int_{-\infty}^{\infty} h_{ab}(k_1, k_2) x_a(t - k_1) x_b(t - k_2)\, dk_1\, dk_2 \qquad (2.5.8)$$

where h_{ab} is a kernel with the antisymmetrical property

$$h_{ab}(k_1, k_2) = -h_{ab}(k_2, k_1)$$

An alternative type of experiment that complements the first involves presenting only a single, narrow, stripe of light, oscillating with small spatial amplitude or alternatively by a stripe that flickers in time so that all eye receptors adjacent to the angular position of the stripe are comparably stimulated with the same frequency and phase. These inputs are to one eye, not to two as in the previous example (2.5.8); the average elicited response is for the fly to turn toward the stimulus, no matter what the initial direction of the stimulation relative to the body axis of the fly. No linear system could be the underlying mechanism that is to perform this computation for the observed response, because it is known that no significant average response, over time, is found to a stabilized retinal image; the average response of a linear system is independent of the input modulation, so the receptor system has to have nonlinearities in it. The simplest adequate input–output relation between one receptor and the output torque response is of the form

$$y(t) = \int \int_{-\infty}^{\infty} h(k_1, k_2) x(t - k_1) x(t - k_2)\, dk_1\, dk_2 \qquad (2.5.9)$$

where the kernel h is now symmetrical.

Further experiments, involving the presentation of two stripes at once and then more complex figures, indicates that lateral inhibitions between adjacent receptors come into operation and complicate the analysis considerably. To support an analysis of figure–ground discrimination, fourth-order Volterra functions appear necessary; these can perform nontrivial computations that will support figure–ground discriminations; they may also support the organism's ability to discriminate between different patterns. Reichardt concluded that in a spatially distributed information processing system the capacity of nonlinear lateral interactions to process information is essentially greater than that of linear systems, because the response of a linear system to complex inputs is the superimposition of the responses to the input components, whereas the response of nonlinear systems can be very different. There is no linear system that could produce the figure–ground discriminative capacities of the fly nor of organisms that can do better than the fly.

The analysis of systems composed of Volterra transfer functions linked together in tandem, one operating upon the output of the other and both within the same black box, is a logical extension and of potential interest for predicting the behavior of complex psychological processes. The treatment is necessarily beyond our present scope but is reviewed by Schetzen (1980).

Bilinear Models

There is, justifiably, a sustained and widespread dissatisfaction with linear time series models, in those areas of economics, biology, and physiology where linear time series have found to be wanting. Some tractable alternatives have recently been studied and their properties are potentially very interesting for theoretical psychologists. An example by Subba Rao (1979) has some most striking properties that can very easily be simulated.

Suppose we have as input a white noise series $\{e_j\}$ and observed output $\{y_j\}$. A model is said to be bilinear if it has cross-product terms in y and e. The coefficients $\{v_{jk}\}$ of the bilinear terms are known as the coefficients of nonlinearity of the process. Small adjustments of the relative values of the nonlinear components can make extreme and spectacular changes in the dynamic output of the system representable by a bilinear model. In particular, under white noise i.i.d. input the system may suddenly flare up, like sunspots, earthquakes, or outbursts of sudden and violent temper, all of which might resemble episodes superimposed upon a quiescent continuous small amplitude process. In other words, the occurrence of sudden very energetic periods that subside as abruptly as they started is no necessary evidence of discontinuity, of a change in the environment, of switching between states, or of temporarily going out of control. An organism with no repertoire of states, but just one bilinear process in which it is presumably trapped, can exhibit episodes of extreme activity at random and fairly rare periods. The potential for the organism to do this is always present, intrinsic to the bilinearity; it is not something that comes and goes and to which a name, such as a *mood,* need be given.

The example given by Subba Rao (1979) is

$$y_j = v_1 y_{j-1} + v_2 y_{j-2} + v_{11} y_{j-1} e_{j-1} + v_{21} y_{j-2} e_{j-1} + e_j \qquad (2.5.10)$$

where $v_1 = .8$, $v_2 = -.4$, $v_{11} = .6$, and $v_{21} = .7$.

This form is related to the Volterra functions reviewed earlier but is much easier to work with (compare Marmarelis & Marmarelis, 1978); the coefficients are identifiable.

The process (2.5.10) can stay quiescent for long periods, and then suddenly explode to tens of thousands of times its usual amplitudes. The starting values y_0, y_1 are not relevant; the relative sizes of v_{11} and v_{21} are critical; the process can be made by careful choice of the coefficients to stay quiet, to explode (or implode) and never return, or most interestingly to have wild periods if given the previous values.

In Fig. 2.5.1 the explosion shown between simulation trials 757 and 779 inclusive is typical; the process may sit for hundreds of trials with $y_j < 3000$ (using starting values of $y_0 = 1$ and $y_1 = 1.1$ and e_j distributed rectangularly over the interval 0,1 and selected by random generation on computer) and then run up briefly to values around 100,000.

A further problem for the interpretation of black box input–output relationships that this sort of process creates arises from the fact that a bilinear time series can have the same covariance structure as an ARMA process of lower

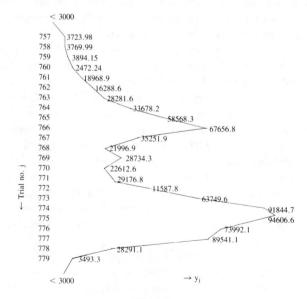

FIG. 2.5.1

order. The covariance structure of a process is thus not sufficient for its identification if the system is capable of remembering, even for a short time span, its own past outputs and inputs. The presence of phenomena like Fig. 2.5.1 are sufficient evidence to justify using, and only using, nonlinear modeling in biological processes. Subba Rao and Gabr (1979) and Gabr and Subba Rao (1979) discuss identification testing in this context.

2.6   PERIODOGRAMS AND POWER SPECTRA

Any analogies or borrowings from the physical sciences into psychology are notoriously uncertain and should be taken with considerable reserve. Using theories of fields of force as metaphors for social processes can be surprisingly empty, for example, and many writers have speculated on mental energies without ever quantifying that energy or seeking laws abouts its conservation. There is, however, some justification for pursuing in detail the idea that the power of a system within a restricted frequency band can be measured; the units in which this power is measured may be arbitrary, but it is valuable to have some way of assessing the way that power is distributed over a system and from this moving to the next step, which is to measure changes in a distribution of power with time and with the action of extraneous variables upon the system.

It is as well to remark that a bivariate time series is a record of a system that does work upon inputs to produce outputs of the same or different form at some other place or time, and this involves the expenditure of energy. Usually, in the sorts of biological subsystems that are of interest to the psychologist, such as the conversion of pressure waves into neural electrical sequences in the ear, the energy expended by the body does not appear anywhere in his or her analysis; we may find mention of the efficiency of one or other of the senses being permanently impaired by an overload in input, through tissues at the transduction point between environment and body being permanently damaged; indeed applied psychologists have worked on problems of protecting man from the dangers of his working environment by devising special clothing or workspaces, but the danger levels identified are expressed in static physical parameters, decibels, light levels, acidities, and so on, not in upper levels of work done per cubic millimeter of receptor tissue. There are obvious practical reasons why this should be so; information should be expressed in a way that leads to practical action in practical situations, but it is easy to lose sight of precisely how a subsystem of the human body does become overloaded or of the problem of measuring exactly what power levels are involved.

If a time series is regarded as the realization of a physical process, then some properties of the series reflect, in an absolute or a relative way, the underlying activity that generates the series. If more energy is expended, then the amplitude of the fluctuations in the series will increase, provided of course that the series is of such a sort, in continuous or discrete time, that it can at any point in time take a number of alternative amplitudes. If the series, either at input or output, is simply a square of Walsh–Hadamard waveform (see Fig. 2.4.1), then the amplitude does not carry information. But the amplitude is not the only measure of expended energy available to us, precisely because of the time-extended nature of the system, which admits of representation in the time or frequency domains. And even if we have no precise analog of a physical system, given some restricted frame of reference so that data samples are always collected in a comparable manner and quantified in the same units, then changes over relatively long time periods, of much much greater magnitude than the units of discrete time used for observation, changes in the expenditure of energy by a system, are fundamentally important in gaining an understanding of what capacity, if any, that system actually has for self-regulation.

One way of noting that a system with time series input and output must be dissipating energy into the environment is to consider the changes in entropy between input and output. At a number of points the elementary linear stationary system with random (i.i.d. or white noise) input and some output that is locally predictable has been mentioned or illustrated. Clearly, if a system converts random or quasi-random perturbations in its input into a steady-state output, then it does this by a reduction of entropy; the information content of the output series is negligible compared with that of the input. The system can only do this by taking energy from somewhere else; if it is conceptualized as closed, and no mention made of its energy consumption, then in effect the system is being credited with an inexhaustible power supply that nowhere features explicitly in its equations or black box representation.

If a series in time, $x(t)$, is considered over the closed interval of time, $-T \leq t \leq T$, then mathematically the energy of $x(t)$ over the closed interval $-T, T$, is given by

$$\text{Energy } [x(t), -T,T] = \int_{-T}^{T} x^2(t) \, dt \qquad (2.6.1)$$

which is, of course, defined over continuous time. The energy is not defined over the integral from $-\infty$ to $+\infty$ because this leads to an impossible infinite energy sum (Koopmans, 1974). The definition (2.6.1) is acceptable with the additional assumption that the process $x(t)$ has about the same energy over all successive observable time intervals of length $2T$,

$$(n - 1)T < t < (n + 1)T \qquad \text{for } n = 0, 1, 2, 3, \ldots$$

which is in fact another sense in which the stationarity of $x(t)$ may be conceptualized.

In engineering, power means the rate, in time, at which energy is expended; consequently the average energy per unit time is called the *power* of a time series. As the integral of (2.6.1) is defined over a range of $2T$ time units, then

$$\text{power } [x(t), -T, T] = (2T)^{-1}(\text{energy } [x(t), -T, T]) \tag{2.6.2}$$

This definition is for a local segment of the time series; in the limit we need a definition of the power of the series over infinite time, and this limit should be finite if it is to be tractable. The power of $x(t)$ is defined as

$$\text{power } [x(t)] = \lim (t \to \infty)(2T)^{-1} \int_{-T}^{T} x^2(t) \, dt \tag{2.6.3}$$

The units in which power is measured by (2.6.3) are squared amplitude. The importance of using the definitions (2.6.1) and (2.6.3) is that transient time series have finite energy and zero power, persistent time series, such as the sinusoidal periodic function, have finite power; and if they are decomposed into a sum of periodic nonzero functions, each of those in turn will have finite power. To put this important result around the other way, the various frequency components of a time series have each power components that when summed make up the total power of the time series; a resolution of a time series into independent frequency components is also a resolution into independent power components. This means that the power contributed by any one component is independent of the amplitudes and frequencies of the remaining components; in applications where a power decomposition is sought, the value of analysis in the frequency domain is therefore obvious. In applications where a power decomposition cannot be given a substantive interpretation, there may be preferred representations in the time domain.

The parallel expression to (2.6.3) in discrete time is, for $2k$ trials,

$$\text{power } [x_j, j - k, j + k] = \lim (k \to \infty)(2k + 1)^{-1} \sum_{-k}^{k} x_j^2 \tag{2.6.4}$$

which is a completely general expression for a stationary series. As a periodic series contains all the information possible about its power in the form it takes in a single cycle, which we can call of length K trials, the power of a periodic time series in discrete time is the power of the vector $\{x_j\}, j = 1, 2, \ldots, K$, *which is*

$$\text{power } [x_j, \text{ period } K] = K^{-1} \sum_{j=1}^{K} x_j^2 \tag{2.6.5}$$

Another way of regarding the power of a time series is to consider it as a variance, given an appropriate definition of the autocovariance of the series. An important result stemming from Wiener (1930) may be cited here:

If the autocovariance of $x(t)$ is defined as based on a finite sample, length $2T$, in terms of the expectation

$$E\left[(2T)^{-1} \int_{-T}^{T} x(t + k) \cdot x(t) \, dt \right] = \hat{C}(k) \tag{2.6.6}$$

where the boundary condition has to be imposed that

$$x(t + k) = 0 \qquad \text{if } |t + k| > T$$

then this $\hat{C}(k)$ is an average that is in fact an instance of the general definition, for a weakly stationary process $x(t)$, that

$$C(k) = E(x(t + k) \cdot x(t)) \tag{2.6.7}$$

The expectation in (2.6.7) is defined over a set of time samples, called an *ensemble*. A single time series is a realization of a statistical process within the time limits used; a set of such time series exemplifies the variation, if any, between realizations due to stochastic (noise) variation, and the set of all possible realizations is called the ensemble of realizations. This ensemble is an unobservable abstraction, in practice some finite collection of records is used as an adequate basis to estimate $C(k)$. The usefulness of ensemble definitions is that they indicate to us what data to collect in order to estimate the $C(k)$. So, an ensemble average is an average over a set of realizations within one time segment, such as might be provided by a group of subjects treated as interchangeable with respect to the parameters of the process being studied, which is a dangerous assumption (Gregson, 1978), or better by a series of samples of comparable length at different sessions under near stationarity.

To assess the usefulness of the approximation $\hat{C}(k)$ in (2.6.6) we define

$$D(T, k) = E\left[(2T)^{-1} \int_{-T}^{T} x(t + k) \cdot x(t) \, dt - C(k) \right]^2$$
$$= E[\hat{C}(k) - C(k)]^2 \tag{2.6.8}$$

and if $D(T, k) \to 0$ as $T \to \infty$, then $\hat{C}(k)$ is a consistent estimator of $C(k)$. Not all time series do meet this condition; Koopmans (1974) discusses in some detail the conditions under which $D(T, k) \to 0$.

In contradistinction to (2.6.6), Wiener (1930) defined the autocovariance as a time average, which is an average in the limit as the sample length, $2T$, increases to infinity. The Wiener definition is

$$C_w(k) = \lim (T \to \infty)(2T)^{-1} \int_{-T}^{T} x(t + k) \cdot x(t) \, dt \tag{2.6.9}$$

$C_w(k)$ is the autocovariance function of the kth order for the time series, provided that $x(t)$ is real-valued with the property that $C_w(k)$ exists and is finite for all k.

If we put $k = 0$, then

$$C_w(k) = \lim (T \to \infty)(2T)^{-1} \int_{-T}^{T} x^2(t)\, dt \qquad (2.6.10)$$

which is the power of $x(t)$ and is finite because of the previous assumption. It can be shown that

$$|C_w(k)| \le C_w(0) \qquad (2.6.11)$$

which means that the autocovariance function is always bounded, in modulus [we need this because $C_w(k)$ can be negative, but $C_w(0)$ is always positive] by the power of the time series. The power is thus an analog of a variance (or better, a covariance of zero lag), and the series cannot have an autocovariance over nonzero lag that is greater than its variance. If the argument is expressed in autocorrelations, it is trivially obvious, but the point of the formal proof is revealed by the next step in Wiener's argument.

Wiener established an equivalence between $C_w(k)$ and the spectral distribution of the time series, $F(A)$, which is the distribution of the amount of power in the harmonic components of the time series (expressed, i.e., in the frequency domain) with component frequencies $f_A \in A$. The equivalence is

$$C_w(k) = \int_{-\infty}^{\infty} \exp\{i\,\lambda\,k\}F(d\lambda) \qquad -\infty < \lambda < +\infty \qquad (2.6.12)$$

In experimental situations, biological systems are often characterized by noise, which is continuous over some frequency range λ', λ'', though not necessarily of even power over that range (which is to say, it is not necessarily white noise), and superimposed upon the noise power distribution will be a discrete spectrum, in which only some fixed frequencies exist with associated finite nonzero power. Call this discrete set $\{\lambda_j\}$. Each of these λ_j is of interest because it potentially corresponds to some psychological or psychophysiological process with stable features.

We would like to be able to take a time series, which is a record of such a system with mixed discrete and continuous components, and separate out the noise continuous spectral distribution from the signal discrete spectral distribution so that analysis may then proceed on the latter only, noting however that the total energies of the two parts of the system together is important because one wants to have an intuitive, or better, measure of the extent to which the system is being swamped by its own noise (Freiberger & Grenander, 1959).

Because of the relation between $C(k)$ and $F(A)$ it is possible to express $F(A)$ as its decomposition into two parts, discrete and continuous, thus:

$$F(A) = F_d(A) + F_c(A) \qquad (2.6.13)$$

where the discrete spectral distribution $F_d(A)$ and the continuous distribution $F_c(A)$ each have an associated term in $C(k)$, because of (2.6.12). So the auto-covariance is expressible as a sum of discrete terms $p(\lambda_j)$ and an integral of a continuous function. As $C(0)$ is a special instance of $C(k)$, the total power in a spectrum can be expressed as the sum of the power in the discrete and continuous components.

Considering only the discrete components

$$F_d(A) = \sum p(\lambda_j), \qquad \lambda_j \in A \qquad (2.6.14)$$

where λ_j is one of the discrete set of frequencies such that $p(\lambda_j) > 0$, and

$$C(k) = \sum_{j=-\infty}^{\infty} \exp\{i\,\lambda_j k\} p\,(\lambda_j) \qquad (2.6.15)$$

$$C(0) = \sum_{j=-\infty}^{\infty} p(\lambda_j) \qquad (2.6.16)$$

In practice it would be easier to start with estimates of the autocovariance from reasonably large samples, and work to the expressions for the power, using the relationship

$$p(\lambda_j) = \lim\,(T \to \infty)(2T)^{-1} \int_{-T}^{T} C(k)\,\exp\{-i\,\lambda_j k\}\,dk \qquad (2.6.17)$$

together with (2.6.16).

Now if the expression

$$\sum p^2(\lambda_j) < \infty \qquad (2.6.18)$$

then (2.6.15) can be shown to be the representation of $C(k)$ as an almost periodic function (i.e., a function that approximates periodicity in a mathematically definable sense). This generalizes the results considerably.

Koopmans (1974) treats this topic in detail and offers salutary reminders that the knowledge of the set $\{C(k)\}$ is not sufficient information to reconstruct the original time series $x(t)$.

The information that is irretrievably lost, when moving from $x(t)$ to $\{C(k)\}$ as a stage in the power analysis, is what engineers call *phase information*. That is, the precise point in real time where the process begins is lost information; power is not dependent on that information; and we cannot reconstruct the harmonic components of the system in its frequency domain representation relative to the point in time where observations began.

Two other points must be made and reiterated later; the process underlying a time series does not have to be strictly periodic, and it does not have to be deterministic (it can be defined stochastically) in order to use a power spectrum representation. The conditions that have to be satisfied center upon the nonrandomness of the autocovariance function, which must tend to a limit. This in fact does occur for a large class of mathematically definable processes that are stochastic, only weakly stationary, and almost but not perfectly periodic. This means that the circumstances in which it is sensible to conduct power analyses on data samples are quite wide, but strictly the legitimacy of performing such analyses in a given situation rests on mathematical criteria that are beyond the scope of an introductory text. It is certainly not proper to offer simplistic generalizations about the validity of analyzing psychological data through time series taken into the frequency domain; the methods are more robust than was apparently at one time thought to be the case. As it is now extremely easy to perform power analyses, through hard-wired computer support, within seconds of collecting data, and one can use the results of such an analysis as feedback to a human subject in visual or analog rather than mathematical form, we should next consider how this is done.

2.7 FOURIER TRANSFORMS AND ANALYSES

The computational processes involved in moving from a representation in the time domain to one in the frequency domain were laborious to the point of intractability until the development of computing facilities and the creation of algorithms that shortened and speeded up the processes. What was intractable has consequently become commonplace and freed the investigator to concentrate his or her efforts more profitably on questions of substantive interest.

The fast Fourier transform, and the fast Walsh transform have extensive literature (Brigham, 1974, Brillinger, 1975) concerning both their theoretical foundations and their empirical behavior when processing real data samples. Univariate or multivariate time series, with real or complex terms, can be analyzed in the frequency domain; it may fairly be stated that the problem is to make sense of the results rather than to perform the computations, for which standard library programs and packages of programs exist.

Notation in this area is not completely standardized, but initial definitions should make it clear, when comparisons are drawn with other sources, to what reference is being made.

Suppose we have some complex-valued function $A(\lambda)$, of period 2π, and impose the usual summability condition that

$$\int_{-\pi}^{\pi} A(\lambda) \, d\lambda < \infty.$$

then the *Fourier series* which is equivalent to $A(\lambda)$ is defined as

$$A(\lambda) = \sum_{\theta = -\infty}^{\infty} \exp\{-i\theta\lambda\}a(\theta) \qquad \theta = 0, 1, 2, \ldots \qquad (2.7.1)$$

where the set $\{a(\theta)\}$ are the *Fourier coefficients* of $A(\lambda)$, and

$$a(\theta) = (2\pi)^{-1} \int_{-\pi}^{\pi} \exp\{i\theta\lambda\}A(\lambda)\, d\lambda \qquad (2.7.2)$$

The definition (2.7.1) is over an infinite summation, which is not practical, and instead what are called partial sums, or sums to the first n terms of the infinite series in (2.7.1), are taken for computational purposes. This raises immediately the question of how accurate are Fourier representations of $A(\lambda)$ that are based on partial sums; empirical examples of what occurs as n increases are given graphically in standard texts.

If the expression (2.7.1) is replaced by a sum over the range $-n$ to $+n$, to read instead

$$A(n, \lambda) = \sum_{\theta = -n}^{n} \exp\{-i\theta\lambda\}a(\theta) \qquad (2.7.3)$$

where n is a real integer, then (2.7.3) is called a *finite Fourier transform* of the sequence $a(\theta)$, $0 = 0, 1, 2, \ldots$, and

$A(n, \lambda)$ is an approximately to $A(\lambda)$ for large n. How good the approximation actually is depends on the shape of $A(\lambda)$; if $A(\lambda)$ is smooth, then the approximation is good for quite small n. An expression for the order of approximation is given by Brillinger (1975).

For two basic examples we consider what the fast Fourier transform (FFT) does to two series, a constant time series $x(t)$, $x(t) = 1$, $T = 0, 1, 2, \ldots, n$ and a periodic function.

$$\text{Given } A(\lambda) = \sum_{-n}^{n} x(t) \exp\{-i\lambda t\} \qquad (2.7.4)$$

as the term $x(t) = 1 = $ constant for all t, then

$$A(\lambda) = \sum_{t = -n}^{n} \exp\{-i\lambda t\}$$

$$= \frac{\sin[(n + 0.5)\lambda]}{\sin[\lambda/2]} \qquad (2.7.5)$$

This sinusoidal expression (2.7.5) has peaks at $\lambda = 0, 2\pi, 4\pi, 6\pi, \ldots$, so the input of fixed amplitude, at discrete points in time, becomes in the frequency domain outputs only at the series of frequencies 0, $m\pi$, and the solutions for values of $m = 2$ and are ignored.

If $x(t) = \exp\{i\omega t\}$, $|t| = 0, 1, 2, \ldots$, then the time series is a periodic function; it, by definition, has frequency ω and no other periodic components.

Now

$$A(\lambda) = \sum_{-n}^{n} \exp\{i\omega t\} \cdot \exp\{-i\lambda t\} \tag{2.7.6}$$

$$= \Sigma \exp\{-i(\lambda - \omega)t\}$$

$$= \frac{\sin[(n + 0.5)(\lambda - \omega)]}{\sin[(\lambda - \omega)/2]} \tag{2.7.7}$$

or (2.7.5) with $(\lambda - \omega)$ written for λ.

Now (2.7.7) has peaks at ω, $\omega \pm 2\pi$, $\omega \pm 4\pi, \ldots$, which is simply the previous case (2.7.5) shifted sideways along the frequency continuum by ω units of frequency. Again, terms above 2π can be ignored if the system is defined as periodic over the interval in time of 2π units.

This example enables us to make a point of importance in considering a black box system that has both as input and as output relatively simple periodic functions in time. If the output is periodic, then it can be so because the black box performs a phase shift and nothing else, discounting changes in amplitude that are changes in scale of measurement, or it can be because the black box is performing an operation like (2.7.6). The situation, viewed from outside the box, is ambiguous as to what process occurs within the box, a brief delay or a change from the time domain into the frequency domain with subsequent output as a time series. The intrinsic ambiguity of black box analyses was remarked on in Chapter 1, this is a formal instance where a process or system cannot be identified on the limited information given by a simple periodic input and corresponding output. It may also be expressed by saying that a physical or physiological mechanism for performing (2.7.6) can be used as a way of performing phase shifts. The combination of the two inputs to (2.7.4) and (2.7.6) will produce a combination of the peaks at output, the peaks of interest being now at 0 and at ω. The zero frequency peak represents an average level of input upon which periodic fluctuating input can be superimposed. So, if the average level is set to zero before applying the FFT, some rather uninformative peaks can be removed; and if the average in fact drifts over time relatively slowly, then it may be removed by taking out a linear trend before representing the sample in the frequency domain.

Time series can be multivariate and of arbitrary length, so the form (2.7.3) needs generalizing to be more useful. Let the input time series be a vector X of finite length at discrete intervals 0, 1, 2, . . ., $T - 1$, call this $X(0)$, $X(1)$, $X(2)$, $X(3)$, . . ., $X(T - 1)$. The FFT can then be defined as

$$A(X; T, \lambda) = \sum_{t=0}^{T-1} \exp\{-i\lambda t\}X(t), \qquad -\infty < \lambda < \infty \qquad (2.7.8)$$

and the conversion from this form to one in summation limits $-n$, n, which is computationally convenient, follows from putting $T = 2n + 1$, n an integer, so that

$$A(X; T, \lambda) = \exp\{-i\lambda n\} \sum_{0=-n}^{n} \exp\{-i\lambda 0\}X(n + 0) \qquad (2.7.9)$$

It was remarked previously that the FFT of two processes, (2.7.4) and (2.7.6), was the sum of the two series, and this additive property is generally true; two time series superimposed in the time domain are additive in the frequency domain, so in symbolic form, where c_1 and c_2 are any two scalars,

$$A(c_1X + c_2X^*; T, \lambda) = c_1 \cdot A(X; T, \lambda) + c_2 \cdot A(X^*; T, \lambda) \qquad (2.7.10)$$

These two series must be defined over the same time interval.

If the two series are convolved and not superimposed, then the Fourier transformation of their convolution is the product of their individual Fourier transformations. It is this particular property that is exploited in the fast Fourier transform (FFT) algorithms (Brillinger, 1975.)

If the two original functions are to be multiplied together, however, then the Fourier transformation of their product is the convolution of their separate Fourier transformations (Kufner & Kadlec, 1971).

The terms of the FFT, $A(x; T, \lambda)$, returning to the univariate case $x(t)$ to simplify consideration of autocovariance terms, have an asymptotically normal distribution under sampling that is expressible in terms of the power spectrum. This result is necessary to enable the investigator to decide if the FFT of some series that is examined differs in some frequencies from what would be expected to arise when transforming a white noise series. The terms of the spectrum also have asymptotic distributions that have been studied; a detailed treatment may be found in Fuller (1976).

To recapitulate and bring results together, if

$$E(x(t)) = T^{-1} \sum_{t=0}^{T} x(t) \qquad (2.7.11)$$

$$C(k) = T^{-1} \sum x(t - k) \cdot x(t)$$

where

$$\sum_{k=-\infty}^{\infty} C(k) < \infty \qquad (2.7.12)$$

then

$$C(k) = \int_{-\infty}^{\infty} \exp\{i\lambda k\} F(d\lambda) \qquad \text{(covariance in terms of power)} \qquad (2.7.13)$$

$$F(\lambda) = (2\pi)^{-1} \sum_{k=-\infty}^{\infty} \exp\{-i\lambda k\} C(k) \qquad \begin{array}{l}\text{(power in terms of} \\ \text{covariance)} \end{array} \qquad (2.7.14)$$

$$A(x; T, \lambda) = \sum_{t=0}^{T-1} \exp\{-i\lambda t\} x(t) \qquad \text{(FFT in terms of the time series)} \qquad (2.7.15)$$

and the asymptotic distribution of the FFT terms expressed as functions of the power terms that correspond are, for three separate conditions, if

$$|\lambda| = 2\pi, 4\pi, 6\pi, \ldots$$

then

$$A(x; T, \lambda) \sim N(T \cdot E(x(t)), 2\pi T \cdot F(\lambda)) \qquad (2.7.16)$$

if

$$|\lambda| = \pi, 3\pi, 5\pi, 7\pi, \ldots$$

then

$$A(x; T, \lambda) \sim N(0, 2\pi T \cdot F(\lambda)) \qquad (2.7.17)$$

and if

$$\lambda = 0, \qquad A(x; T, \lambda) = \sum_{t=0}^{T-1} x(t) = T \cdot E(x(t)) \qquad (2.7.18)$$

The power spectrum $F(\lambda)$ is nonnegative, even, of period 2π with respect to λ. If the power spectrum of an input series $x(t)$ is known when $x(t)$ is expressed in the frequency domain, then an output $y(t)$ will have a distribution that can be expressed in terms of $x(t)$ and an FFT $A(\lambda)$.

If

$$\text{var}\,[x(t)] = \int_{\pi}^{\pi} F(x; \theta)\, d\theta \qquad (2.7.19)$$

and

$$y(t) = A(\lambda) \cdot x(t) \qquad (2.7.20)$$

then

$$F(y; \lambda) = |A(\lambda)|^2 \cdot F(x; \lambda) \qquad \text{for all } \lambda \qquad (2.7.21)$$

From (2.7.20) and (2.7.21)

$$\text{var } [y(t)] = \int_{\pi}^{\pi} |A(\theta)|^2 \cdot F(x; \theta) \, d\theta$$

In the expression (2.7.21) we have just met the squared norm of a Fourier coefficient $A(\lambda)$; the distribution of such terms multiplied by a constant is called the *periodogram;* this is mathematically tractable in various useful ways because its ordinates have a distribution resembling a χ^2 with 2 d.f. when the input is white noise. There are other properties that enable us to draw parallels between a periodogram analysis and an analysis of variance in a manner that is reminiscent of statistical analyses commonly employed in experimental psychology. Fuller (1976) does this by going back to the original definition, as in (2.4.1), of a Fourier representation.

If we have a time series sample length n, then using the first m terms only of the sinusoidal representation, and regrouping (2.4.1) for convenience, with $n = 2m + 1$,

$$x(t) = \frac{a_0}{2} + \sum_{k=1}^{m} \left(a_k \cos \left(\frac{2\pi kt}{n} \right) + b_k \sin \left(\frac{2\pi kt}{n} \right) \right) \qquad (2.7.22)$$

with $b_0 = 0$, and

$$a_k = n^{-1} \cdot 2 \sum_{t=1}^{n} \cos \left(\frac{2\pi kt}{n} \right) \cdot x(t) \qquad (2.7.23)$$

$$b_k = n^{-1} \cdot 2 \sum_{t=1}^{n} \sin \left(\frac{2\pi kt}{n} \right) \cdot x(t) \qquad (2.7.24)$$

then the Fourier coefficients a_k, b_k are in fact regression coefficients, which express the regression of $x(t)$ upon the corresponding periodic functions $\cos \left(\frac{2\pi kt}{n} \right)$ and $\sin \left(\frac{2\pi kt}{n} \right)$. As all these sinusoidal components are mutually independent, for that indeed is the purpose of the representation, the regression of $x(t)$ upon the Fourier series can be decomposed readily into an analysis of variance. It is the variance of $x(t)$ that is to be decomposed, and the sum of squares [component of the total sum of squares $\Sigma\ x^2(t)$] due to the kth coefficients (2.7.23) and (2.7.24) is

$$\left(\frac{n}{2} \right) \cdot (a_k^2 + b_k^2) \qquad \text{with 2 d.f.}$$

So, for each of the Fourier frequencies (see Section 2.4) there will be a 2 d.f., or $2m$ in all. With 1 d.f. for the mean effect, whose sum of squares is $\left(\dfrac{n}{4}\right) a_0^2$, this adds up to n degrees of freedom for the total series $\{x(t)\}$, $t = 1, 2, \ldots, n$.

A minor adjustment is needed if $n = 2m$, that is, if n is even, for then $b_m = 0$, and the sum of squares for the mth frequency is $\left(\dfrac{n}{4}\right) a_m^2$.

If one were performing a proper analysis of variance, one would proceed to the mean squares and then to F ratios, lumping terms of secondary interest to constitute a residual error term. The practice, however, has grown up of working directly with the sums of squares and multiplying the one or two anomalous terms (a_0, and for n even, a_m) by 2.

There are some variations in the way the word *periodogram* is defined; here we have followed Fuller (1976) and, for the discrete frequencies

$$\frac{2\pi k}{n}, \qquad k = 0, 1, 2, \ldots, m$$

defined the periodogram $I_n\left(\dfrac{2\pi k}{n}\right)$ as

$$I_n\left(\frac{2\pi k}{n}\right) = \left(\frac{n}{2}\right)(a_k^2 + b_k^2) \tag{2.7.25}$$

This can be shown to be equivalent to writing

$$I_n(\lambda) = 2n^{-1}(|A(\lambda)|^2) \tag{2.7.26}$$

So the squared norm of the Fourier coefficient at frequency λ is directly proportional to the variance of the time series taken up by regression onto that frequency; the two representations, Fourier analysis and analysis of variance after multivariate regression, are transformable one into the other.

It was stated previously that under restricted conditions the periodogram components were distributed as χ^2 with 2 d.f. This arises as follows:

If the observations in the original time series realization $x(t)$, $T = 0, 1, \ldots, n$ are i.i.d. as $N(0, \sigma^2)$, then the a_k, b_k, being linear combinations of the $x(t)$, will also be normally distributed. The a_k are independent from their corresponding b_k, and vice versa, because they are based on sine and cosine functions that are orthogonal by definition. To express this in correlation form, $r_{a_k b_k} = 0$ for all k, $k = 0, 1, 2, \ldots, m$. From this situation it follows that each $I_n(2\pi k/n)$ will be distributed, after division by σ^2, as χ^2 with 2 d.f. There is nothing to stop us normalizing the original time series by putting

$$x'(t) = \frac{x(t)}{\sigma}, \ x'(t) \sim N(0, 1)$$

and analyzing the periodogram of $x'(t)$ instead, which simplifies the interpretation and facilitates comparison between sets of data. The *amplitude* and the *phase* angle of the kth component are given, respectively, by[6]

$$R_k = [a_k^2 + b_k^2]^{1/2} \qquad \text{(amplitude)} \qquad (2.7.27)$$

$$\phi_k = \tan^{-1}\left[\frac{b_k}{a_k}\right] \qquad \text{(phase angle)} \qquad (2.7.28)$$

and confidence regions for these parameters can be obtained from F distributions; the clearest detailed treatment is perhaps that of Anderson (1971). In graphical presentations, the usual convention seems to be to plot R^2_k as ordinate against the frequency k/n as abscissa and not, despite the name periodogram, against the period n/k.

If the coefficients $(n/2)^{1/2} \cdot a_k$ and $(n/2)^{1/2} \cdot b_k$ are used instead of simply a_k and b_k, then the coefficients are said to be normalized; in this form for any time series, i.i.d., or satisfying (2.7.12), in the limit they are uncorrelated, with zero expectations and having variances that are proportional to the spectral density at the frequency $2\pi k/n$. A proof is given by Fuller (1976, p. 281). These results are very important for testing if any observed time series is more consistent with H_0 or H_1, where these alternatives hypotheses may be written as

$$H_0 : x(t) = \bar{x} + e_t, \qquad e_t \sim N(0, \sigma^2_e) \qquad (2.7.29)$$

$$H_1 : x(t) = \bar{x} + A \cos jt + B \sin jt + e_t \qquad (2.7.30)$$

where in the latter case, (2.7.30), j is known before the test is made. The only term in the two models (2.7.29) and (2.7.30) having nonzero expectation is $\bar{x}$.

Even if a time series is not generated by a normal process, in the limit its periodogram can be treated as a set of chi-squared random variables with different independent expectations. The investigator wishes to search for periodicities or, better, for particular frequencies that he or she believes are psychologically meaningful; at the microevent scale we seek, typically, 10-Hz signals in the electroencephalogram. At a coarser time resolution we may give intermittent reinforcement at an evenly paced schedule every 10 min in some situation where we wish to encourage the continued occurrence of some pattern of behavior. The patterns we expect to find in behavior are instances of (2.7.30), though of course the dependent time series we induce in behavior may be shifted in phase; if it lags input but has the same periodicity or has a nontrivial component with the same

---

[6]The equivalence between the representation in a_k, b_k and in R_k, ϕ_k form has already been anticipated by Equations (2.4.1) and (2.4.2):

$$a_k \cos\left(\frac{2\pi kt}{n}\right) + b_k \sin\left(\frac{2\pi kt}{n}\right) = R_k \cos\left(\frac{2\pi kt}{n - \phi_k}\right)$$

periodicity as the input (or forcing function, to use engineering terminology), then this may be reflected in ϕ_k of (2.7.28) but there will still be a dominance of R_k over other amplitudes. Tests of the largest periodogram ordinate start from the work of Fisher (1929), and the literature of various methods of statistically testing periodigram properties is very extensive, due to a sustained interest in the area by economists.

An ingenious way of investigating the nonrandomness of a periodogram's generating time series is to plot and test the shape of the *cumulative periodogram*. Let us define the normalized cumulative periodogram as

$$\text{Cum}(j;\, m) = \left[\sum_{k=1}^{m} I_n\left(\frac{2\pi k}{n}\right) \right]^{-1} \cdot \sum_{j=1}^{k} I_n\left(\frac{2\pi j}{n}\right), \qquad (2.7.31)$$

$$j,k = 0, 1, 2, \ldots\ldots, m$$

where by definition,

$$0 \le \text{Cum}\ (j;\, m) \le 1$$

As the ordinates of this I_n process are distributed approximately as independent X^2, then Cum $(j;m)$ has the same distribution as an ordered sample of size $m - 1$ drawn from a rectangular probability distribution; for under (2.7.29) the ordinates all have the same expected height. As shown by Durbin (1969), this leads

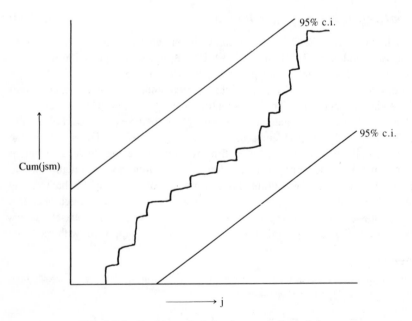

FIG. 2.7.1   Confidence limits on the cumulative periodogram.

immediately to the use of a Kolmogorov–Smirnov one-sample test and the simple graphical methods.

The simplest practical way to find the mean and estimated variance of $I_n(2\pi k/n)$ for a given process is to take repeated samples of fairly large n, sufficient to obtain estimates of all the frequency components in which there is a priori interest, perform a frequency analysis upon each using a fast Fourier analysis (Bloomfield, 1976) with a standard computer library program suitably adapted for local use, and then examine the intersample distributions. This idea is so obvious that it has been a recommended method for some time, originally due to Bartlett (1950). The point of interest is that the sample size, that is, the length of the time series $x(t)$, $t = 0, 1, 2, \ldots, n$, has but little effect upon the accuracy of the estimates of the components of the periodogram, in the following sense. The number of periodogram ordinates we can compute is less than $n/2$; increasing the sample size n increases the number of components that we can compute but does not increase the accuracy of those already computed. The efficiency of the estimate for a particular frequency remains unchanged, once the sample length is great enough to support the computation of that $I_n(2\pi k/n)$. There are immediate practical qualifications to this statement, because of estimation errors in the frequency analysis and complications that follow from the use of filters; but to a first approximation it is sufficiently true to dictate what are efficient data analysis strategies.

2.8   FILTERS AND WINDOWS

The conversion from time domain to an equivalent representation in the frequency domain is defined in terms of a summation over an infinite series, over an infinite range of frequencies. As soon as we move into the real world of the experimental situation, in which it costs money and effort to collect data, we collect samples of finite duration, and we convert as rapidly as we can into a frequency domain representation that only involves some of the lower frequencies, those at the upper end of a possible continuum being usually judged of less meaningfulness to the theoretician. How short a sample is; how fine a recording procedure must be, in terms of its resolution (the interval between successive observations, measured in clock time); how precisely the frequencies must be identified, in hertz; and how stable estimates must be over successive samples or experimental sessions in order to be interpretable are all questions that have to be answered in terms of the precise problem in hand and the characteristics of the laboratory hardware available. Prior knowledge concerning what frequency spectrum to expect is always valuable and naturally leads to Bayesian statistical analyses of frequency spectra and of inference from time series. Some developments in this direction are mentioned in later chapters.

The frequency spectra that are obtained from short samples, say less than 2000 observations long and employing a finite Fourier transform, are all to some degree wrong. Whether or not the errors matter depends on the use to which the terms $I_n(2\pi k/n)$ are to be put, but the possibility of detecting frequencies that are not in fact active bases for power conversion, and missing or biasing the estimated values of others which are, is always present. It was realized by 1900 (by Fejér) that the partial sums of a Fourier series (2.7.3) could be poor approximations to the function under study. Consequently a diversity of methods for correcting and improving estimates have been devised; a detailed but incomplete survey is given by Brillinger (1975). The computational methods for cleaning up frequency distribution estimates are known variously as data windows, tapers, convergence factors, frequency windows, or kernels; they are related to (2.5.3).

Here we consider why data windows are useful and review briefly only two cases. In most practical cases the differences between alternative methods are second-order, and if an available computer program incorporating some particular filter has to be used without modification, it is likely to be a variant of one of the two reviewed here, though the user should always try and check what he has taken off the library shelf, if program listings are available. As fast Fourier transforms are now becoming available as computer hardware, unmodifiable and inaccessible but extremely fast and convenient, the user may have to pay special attention to performance specifications or to calibration trials in any configuration of computer and peripherals that is assembled. The human subject should never be run as a generator of time series data translated into the frequency domain without first running the same situation with known frequencies as benchmark inputs. The results of such checks can be salutary if not demoralizing.

A *digital filter* means a filter that is linear and in discrete time (Koopmans, 1974). Recall that the term *filter* means a time-invariant transformation, any process that satisfies these conditions of linearity, and time invariance, and turns one time series into another time series is a filter. In practice we are only concerned with filters that themselves, if series, have a finite number of terms and operate on finite samples in discrete time. Filters are used to get rid of features of data that are judged to be both present and unwanted before the filter is applied; filters are consequently models of many processes in the physical world, and many of the transduction processes of the human senses, particularly in hearing, are represented in psychophysical theory by filters. Consequently we may use filters of known properties deliberately to modify time series, perhaps by removing trends or periodicities (which is commonly the case in economics) or stopping the transmission of frequencies above or below some nominated value (which is common in electronics and in the instrumentation of psychophysiological experiments), or if we already know that input–output relations of some subsystem resemble those consequent upon filtering, then a filter is a reasonable simulation of the subsystem. Knowing that filtering takes place it is meaningful to seek for mechanisms in the physiological substrate of behavior that could effectively filter signals outside a given frequency range. Deafness, at least of some sorts, is filtering by malfunction. Being able to ride a bicycle, as in our lengthy example in Chapter 1, over a cobbled road surface such as still survives in parts of Europe, is an ability to filter out signals of high frequency from the steering column and handlebars of the cycle, apart from in-phase signals engendering discomfort to the saddle. On a motorcycle the shock absorbers, if good, do the filtering. The words *filter* and *sieve* have comparable meanings both in their physical and functional uses, and a time filter can be metaphorically regarded as a sieve; whether one values what passes through or what is stopped from passing is a matter of choice. Difference operations, averages, and the z transforms reviewed and used in Chapter 3 are all examples of filters. Filters that depend both on a fixed number of previous inputs and a fixed number (not necessarily the same) of previous outputs are said to be *recursive*.

Many of the modeling objectives of the simpler developments in mathematical psychology reduce, consequently, to attempts to write recursive filter specifications. Thus it may be said without being pejorative that much of rigorous theoretical psychology is filter construction; the task is far from being intrinsically trivial or easy. The Kalman filter (Chapter 5) is a recursive filter.

Any random series will, after the sequential application of differencing and integrating filters, resemble a required weakly stationary time series, which will approximate to any continuous spectral density function as closely as desired. The algorithm to implement this very strong generalization is (Koopman, 1974) the recursive filter

$$y(t) = \sum_{j=1}^{q} (-d_j)y(t-j) + \sum_{k=0}^{p} c_k \cdot e(t-k) \tag{2.8.1}$$

where $e(t)$ is i.i.d. input with spectral composition uniform as

$$F_e(\lambda) = \frac{\sigma_e^2}{2\pi}, \qquad -\pi < \lambda \le \pi \tag{2.8.2}$$

$\{d_j\}$ and $\{c_k\}$ are the complex coefficients of two polynomials D and C, so that we may write

$$F_y(\lambda) = \left(\frac{\sigma^2}{2\pi} \right) \left| \frac{C(\exp\{-i\lambda\})}{D(\exp\{-i\lambda\})} \right|^2 \tag{2.8.3}$$

The set of coefficients $\{p, q, c_k \cdot d_j\}$ is at choice. There is a necessary condition placed upon the zeros of the polynomial D that is illustrated in Chapter 6 (in effect to ensure that the quotient in (2.8.3) does not result in an operation like division by zero, the roots should all lie outside the unit circle in the plane of complex numbers in which the roots are representable).

A finite sample of data from preferably an unbroken record in time is the desired output of experiments where conditions are consistent during data collection. Such a sample can be thought of as the result of applying a rectangular filter or, as it is called in this context, a window to a notional time series that started long before the experiment and ran on afterward. By a rectangular window is thus meant an operation that permits the recording, at equal intervals, of those and only those data points that appear in the window. A short rectangular window, length W trials, with averaging of the data in it as its output, at each trial j, is a simple moving average process, picking up one new term at $j + 1$ and losing one term at $j - W$ on each trial. So, by extension, any finite length of data in a time series is the result of convolving an infinite series with a finite data window. This observation is not a pedantic exercise in definition but a preamble to a class of data processing operations that increase the fidelity of analyses in the frequency domain.

Define a finite data window by

$$W(N, t) = 1, \quad 1 \le t \le N; 0, \text{ otherwise} \tag{2.8.4}$$

In an experiment where the starting point of analysis, considered as a system, is the input from the environment $u(t)$, length N, and this input is convolved with a filter whose coefficients as $\{a_k\}$, the observed approximate output $y(t)$ over a length N also, will be given by

$$\hat{y}(N, t) = \sum_{k=-\infty}^{\infty} a_k \cdot W(N, t - k) \cdot u(t - k) \tag{2.8.5}$$

whereas the theoretical ideal output, if we were not restricted to length N, would be

$$y(t) = \sum_{k=-\infty}^{\infty} a_k \cdot u(t - k) \tag{2.8.6}$$

and hence the error consequent on only observing the system for N trials is the difference over those N trials of (2.8.5) and (2.8.6) whose expectation is

$$E(N^{-1}[\, y(t) - \hat{y}(N, t)\,]^2)$$

It can be shown that if $y(t)$ has a frequency spectrum $F(\lambda)$ that is bounded so that its limits are λ^* (lower frequency bound) and Λ^* (upper frequency bound), then

$$2\pi\lambda^* \cdot \Sigma\, a_k^2 \le E(y(t) - \hat{y}(N, t))^2 \le 2\pi\Lambda^* \cdot \Sigma\, a_k^2 \tag{2.8.7}$$

where the summation is over the sample range $t - 1 < k < t - N$. The error in (2.8.7) is sometimes intolerable but can be minimized by replacing the rectangular window, which is not optimal, by windows that are not uniform but taper off toward the ends. The error does not arise if the time series is aperiodic, because then the upper bound in (2.8.7) becomes zero. The replacement of $W(N, t - k)$ by some other tapered filter $\phi(N, t - k)$ in (2.8.5) is discussed in the literature of Fourier transformations under the heading of *convergence factors;* tables of many alternative forms with their properties are given by Brillinger (1975) and also discussed as windows by Anderson (1971) and as kernels by Fuller (1976).

To avoid a discussion of minor differences between filters that are peripheral to our purpose, two models are considered each of which, with parameters suitably chosen, generates commonly used filters as special cases. First, let us observe that the rectangular window with all terms equal, as in (2.8.4), has a Fourier transform that is a sinusoid; this is called the *Dirichlet kernel,* which is

$$D(N, \lambda) = \frac{\sin (N + 1/2)\lambda}{(2\pi \sin (\lambda/2))} \tag{2.8.8}$$

in shape this represents a damped sinusoid and can take negative values. It has its greatest dominant peak around $\lambda = 0$. It is the kernel (2.8.8) that it is desired to modify, to minimize secondary peaks and to get rid of negative values.

The coefficients of the Blackman–Tukey window, $W_{BT}(N, t - k)$, and N and $t - k$ are defined to be

$$\phi_k = 1 - 2a + 2a \cdot \cos \left(\frac{2\pi k}{N} \right) , \tag{2.8.9}$$

with $k = 0, 1, 2, \ldots, N/2$, N even for convenience. The terms $\{\phi_k\}$ are the coefficients of the *lag window* or *data window,* and the Fourier transform of (2.8.9) will be the *kernel* or *frequency window.* The frequency window of the Blackman–Tukey lag window can be expressed as a weighted sum of terms like (2.8.8). Two special cases are important enough to be named; the Hanning window, with $a = 0.25$ in (2.8.9), and the Hamming window, with $a = 0.23$. The very small difference is reflected in the confusable names. To show what these windows do, consider Fig. 2.8.1: In the ideal case the energy of a single frequency is concentrated in a band of negligible width, and there is no energy anywhere else in the adjacent frequency continuum. If, however, a finite sample is taken from the time series whose frequency distribution is characterized by the ideal Fig. 2.8.1, then the finite sample will, if viewed through a rectangular window, exhibit spurious secondary frequencies, called *lobes* of the distribution as in Fig. 2.8.2: The precise size and shape and number of the side lobes depends on the size of the data window. To get rid of the side lobes completely is not possible, but they can be minimized by convolving the data series with the lag window or (the same thing) multiplying the sample frequency spectrum by the frequency window.

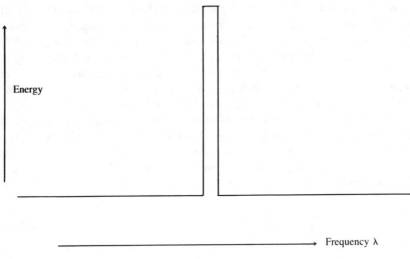

Energy

Frequency λ

FIG. 2.8.1

The Blackman–Tukey window diminishes the largest secondary lobes; with $a = 0.25$ it is computationally simple, with $a = 0.23$ it is slightly more effective: The side lobes are further diminished but the advantage is small. Now that all such calculations are done on computers, preferably on-line, the distinctions become something of historical curiosities. The coefficients of a Blackman–Tukey window are maximal at $k = 0$, the center of the window width N, so that

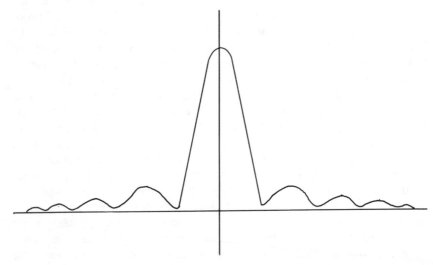

FIG. 2.8.2   Distribution with side lobes.

$$\phi_0 = 1$$

down to

$$\phi_{|N/2|} = 1 - 4a$$

and zero outside the limits of the filter. The applications of such filters in the simulation of communication processes are discussed by Blackman and Tukey (1959).

The Bartlett–Parzen family (Parzen, 1961) of filters has as generating equation

$$\phi_k = 1 - \left(\frac{|k|}{N/2} \right) q \tag{2.8.10}$$

for a data window of width N. If the parameter $q = 1$, the window, called a *Bartlett window*, is triangular; it is quite obviously triangular with height of 1 in the middle and dropping off linearly to 0 at the ends. Parzen has also considered the case where $q = 2$.

The choice of N for a window is a compromise; variance increases with N, but bias decreases. The situation is reminiscent of a general principle of time series analysis, which has been called Grenander's uncertainty principle (with due respect to Heisenberg); namely, that if resolution is increased, then stability of representation decreases; one cannot have both resolution (detailed analysis) and stability (low intersample variance) at the same time, as there is a trade-off between the two desirable qualities.

Assessment of the degree of approximation to a correct frequency spectrum consequent upon filtering may be approached as follows; the frequency window is given from the data window by

$$\Phi(N, \lambda) = (2\pi)^{-1} \sum_{-N/2}^{N/2} \phi \left(\frac{k}{N} \right) \cdot \exp \{-ik\lambda\} \tag{2.8.11}$$

and the estimated power spectrum, c.f. (2.7.14), is

$$f(N, \lambda) = (2\pi)^{-1} \sum_{-N/2}^{N/2} \phi \left(\frac{k}{N} \right) \cdot C(k) \cdot \exp \{-ik\lambda\} \tag{2.8.12}$$

where $C(k)$ is the sample autocovariance, based on the total sample length, which can be greater than the window length.

The estimate of a frequency domain representation, based on a finite sample and computed with a fast Fourier transform, is thus biased and is partly corrected by multiplication by the frequency window:

$$A(\lambda) \doteq \hat{A}(N, \lambda) = \phi(N, \lambda) \cdot F(N, \lambda) \tag{2.8.13}$$

where $F(N, \lambda)$ is a Fourier transform based on a time series length N.

It is desirable to have a measure of how well a window performs its function of diminishing the spurious side lobes and retaining only the narrow energy band around the true frequency. Various alternatives have been suggested, perhaps the simplest and conceptually clearest is that of Parzen (1961) who noted that the area under a filter spectrum can be replaced by a rectangle of the same total area and same maximum height, but whose width would then be equal to 2π (Σ $\phi(k/N)$ $)^{-1}$. This width is narrow if the window effectively concentrates the frequency; a small Parzen bandwidth represents an efficient window, but other conditions such as nonnegativity may need to be met as well. The rectangular data window has a Parzen bandwidth of π/N but, as already observed, has negative values in its Dirichlet kernel. The bandwidths of the Bartlett (triangular) window and the Hanning window are both 2π $/N$, so there is little to choose between them on this basis; they constitute a basis against which other forms may be compared.

The Hanning window is probably the most common in use with computer-based analyses; but once calculation is on-line, the form of kernels is not of great interest unless one is concerned with filter design to achieve a particular end, such as the construction of high-pass or low-pass filters to admit selectively only certain frequency ranges.

There is a conceptual extension of filtering that is important in sensory psychology, because what occurs in the microphysiology of receptor organs, when environmental energy is transduced into neural pulse trains, is filtering of time series with time series as output. Schematically the sequence is thus:

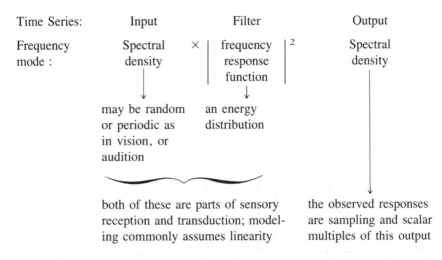

Time Series:	Input		Filter		Output
Frequency mode :	Spectral density	×	frequency response function	2	Spectral density

may be random or periodic as in vision, or audition

an energy distribution

both of these are parts of sensory reception and transduction; modeling commonly assumes linearity

the observed responses are sampling and scalar multiples of this output

If the input process is a mixture of *s*ignal and *n*oise, then the output is contaminated signal, and the filter is the organism's method of removing noise, to some extent that may not be complete but is sufficient for biological functioning in the long run.

Contrast the previous diagram, where inputs and outputs are time series, with the representation in signal detection theory (s.d.t.) where the relatively primitive filtering on an excitation continuum of input signals is simply a cutoff point with the rule

$$\text{if } g(x) > x_c, \text{ then respond } S$$

and

$$\text{if } g(x) < x_c, \text{ then respond } N$$

where $g(x)$ is some monotone function on the input whose time series properties are not explicitly considered. In contradistinction, here the filter can be quite complex and pass only frequencies within a given range, irrespective of the energy level. This sort of filtering in the frequency domain is actually of greater potential interest in some psychophysiological contexts because it comes nearer to being a representation of the functioning of the neural circuits that are implicated in sensation and perception.

2.9 COHERENCE AND RELATED MEASURES BASED ON BIVARIATE FREQUENCY ANALYSES

As this chapter is deliberately an elementary review of more basic conceptual points in a very extensive domain of applied mathematics, focusing on those and only those points that have, in this author's present view, some potential use for the experimental psychologist who wishes to formulate models and experiments that are in time and not outside it in a limbo of abstraction, the multivariate extensions of time series analysis have, in the main, been avoided, although it has been repeatedly indicated that all major results can and, better, should be expressed in matrix form. Doing so, however, in an introductory text can lose a reader who with the courage of successful laboratory applications in univariate analyses, such as a single-channel EEG record, will want to go on to multivariate time series, both on the input and output side.

Some time series methods, however, depend at least on a bivariate situation, or perhaps a situation where input to a system is one time series but output is two or more series that are not independent, not simply described in terms of their common dependence on the input time series. For example, one may examine the interrelation between a flickering lamp of fixed frequency, as the source of visual input, and the EEG records produced on different points of the head; by appropriate representations one can begin to answer questions such as "Is any given output expressible as the product of a linear filter and the input?", which is a question we have anticipated in Section 2.8, or we may also, perhaps more interestingly, ask "Is the variation, in a given frequency band, which two EEG records from different points exhibit, in phase?" If it is, then this suggests that both are being driven in the same way from a common input that itself, at a given frequency band, may or may not be in phase with the two outputs. Such questions have been asked in attempts to locate brain damage by electrical scanning (Gersh & Goddard, 1970) or examine the grosser functional organization of the brain (O'Connor & Shaw, 1978). One may also (see Chapter 4) take a series of univariate judgments, each with its associated response delay, as a bivariate output to a univariate stimulus series. One may then ask if the response times are functionally related (through analyses in the time or frequency domains) to the stimuli, to the responses, or to the responses after a common dependence of both responses and reaction times upon the stimuli has been partialled out.

The last point just made should hint to the reader that correlation theory carries over, virtually intact, into time series analysis, provided that the sets of variables between which correlations are defined are very carefully specified. One might begin by asking why cannot two series in discrete time be treated as one series of bivariate observations and correlated directly? The answer is that one can, but to do so and no more is completely to miss the point of time series analysis, for such a correlation answers one very circumscribed question about the two time series, concerning whether or not they share one linear, possibly periodic, trend component over the interval examined. It may in fact be such a trend component that is of minimal interest to the investigator; the least that it is expedient to do is to compute a series of cross-correlations over a range of leads and lags. As we have shown the generality of decomposition of time series in the frequency domain, it follows that for each frequency bandwidth there will be an analogy of time series cross-correlations over the whole frequency spectrum. This latter series is called the *coherence* of the system. To show the relation among coherence, power analyses, filters, and signal detection through optimal filtering, it is expedient to start again from the definitions of the autocovariances of the time series involved. The treatment is given in terms of univariate series; for the proper formalization with vector time series, the treatment by Brillinger (1975) is lucid. The inversion of frequency matrices corresponding to covariance matrices is involved in any adequate general treatment and computational approach, though filtering methods that avoid the difficulties of matrix inversion have been developed and are touched on in Chapter 5.

The definitions of coherence start from the general assumptions that relate to weakly stationary multivariate stochastic systems, and for a rigorous treatment the reader should refer to such texts as Brillinger (1975), Koopmans (1974), and Rosenblatt (1963) and the source papers of a purely mathematical nature cited therein. The notion of coherence relates to more general, and to the psychologist, more familiar measures in regression or in correlation theory, and formal parallels can consequently be worked out in as great a detail as is desired. The brief treatment here serves simply to make empirical studies comprehensible, where coherence measures are used in a straightforward descriptive manner.

The general case uses $\mathbf{x}(t)_r$ to denote an r-vector input and $\mathbf{y}(t)_s$ to denote an s-vector output of a system (the $\mathbf{x}$ notation here does not refer to state variables but simply follows statistical conventions, not state or control theory notation), and the terms may be defined in general in $r + s$ vector expressions with consequent covariance matrices. Restricting the treatment to the simplest linear case with $r = s = 1$, let

$C(x, x, k)$ be notation for the covariance of $x(t)$, $x(t - k)$
$C(x, x, k) = C(x, x, -k)$ immediately by definition
$C(y, y, k)$ is defined analogously
$C(x, y, k)$ is the cross-covariance of $x(t)$, $y(t - k)$

It should be emphasized that, in general, $C(x, y, k) \neq C(y, x, k)$, because the definition of the cross-covariance of x and y depends both on the lag k and on whether it is x or y that lags. It also follows from the definitions that

$$C(x, y, k) = C(y, x, -k) \tag{2.9.1}$$

and the Schwarz inequality gives us

$$C(x, y, k) \leq (C(x, x, 0) \cdot C(y, y, 0))^{1/2} \tag{2.9.2}$$

for all k, $-\infty \leq k \leq \infty$, provided that the means and cross-covariances are bounded. The terms $C(x, x, 0)$ and $C(y, y, 0)$ are obviously time series variances.

The $C(*, *, k)$ are time domain expressions that can be Fourier transformed, using the general relation

$$f(x, y, \lambda) = \Sigma\, C(x, y, k) \cdot \exp\{-i\,\lambda\,k\} \tag{2.9.3}$$

with $-\infty \leq \lambda \leq \infty$, and the inverse transformation is

$$C(x, y, k) = \Sigma\, f(x, y, \lambda) \cdot \exp\{i\lambda k\} \tag{2.9.4}$$

with $-\pi \leq \lambda \leq \pi$. So, in the single input–output cases, both $\{C(x, y, k)\}$ and $\{f(x, y, \lambda)\}$ are vectors over the set of k or of λ values in which we are interested, and the system is necessarily and sufficiently described in a given domain by the appropriate vector, but both vectors become matrices as soon as the system is multivariate, which affects the form of expressions involving the products or inverses of $C(x, y, k)$ or $f(x, y, \lambda)$. Because the distributions $C(x, x, k)$ and $C(y, y, k)$ are symmetrical, the $f(x, x, \lambda)$ and $f(y, y, \lambda)$ are real-valued; they have no imaginary components. But in contradistinction the cross-spectral distribution $f(x, y, \lambda)$ is generally complex-valued (its terms have imaginary parts that do not vanish upon computation). There is a relation between $f(x, y, \lambda)$ and $f(y, x, \lambda)$ that is called a *partial symmetry*, as it can be shown that

$$f(x, y, \lambda) = \bar{f}(y, x, \lambda) \tag{2.9.5}$$

where the f notation in (2.9.5) indicates a complex conjugate of f.[7]

The fact that $f(x, y, \lambda)$ is a set of complex numbers, the cross-spectral density function, is no bar to its analysis. Because it is a series of complex variates, it is decomposable into two series, which are, respectively, real and imaginary parts:

$$f(x, y, \lambda) = w(x, y, \lambda) - i\sigma(x, y, \lambda) \tag{2.9.6}$$

for all λ.

The real and imaginary parts of the right-hand side (r.h.s.) of (2.9.6) have, respectively, been given the names of *cospectrum* (or cospectral density function) and *quadspectrum* (or quadrature spectral density function). In some sources they are given alternative names or symbols consistent with the cospectrum, quadspectrum terminology.

As the original covariances are based on discrete time data, the computational formulas for (2.9.6) are

$$w(x, y, \lambda) = (2\pi)^{-1} \sum_{k=-\infty}^{\infty} \cos \lambda k \left\{ \frac{C(x, y, k) + C(x, y, -k)}{2} \right\} \tag{2.9.7}$$

and

$$\sigma(x, y, \lambda) = (2\pi)^{-1} \sum_{k=-\infty}^{\infty} \sin \lambda k \left\{ \frac{C(x, y, k) + C(x, y, -k)}{2} \right\} \tag{2.9.8}$$

So, for any λ, we have five expressions of interest, which are

$$f(x, x, \lambda), \quad f(y, y, \lambda), \quad f(x, y, \lambda), \quad w(x, y, \lambda), \quad \sigma(x, y, \lambda) \tag{2.9.9}$$

A distinction must be drawn between two cases: the first case is where the cross-spectral density $f(x, y, \lambda)$ has both real and imaginary parts that are non-zero. Then the *complex coherence* (which is an analog of the familiar Pearson product–moment correlation coefficient) is defined as

$$\gamma(x, y, \lambda) = \frac{f(x, y, \lambda)}{(f(x, x, \lambda) \cdot f(y, y, \lambda))^{1/2}} \tag{2.9.10}$$

As $\gamma(x, y, \lambda)$ is, as has just been remarked, a sort of correlation coefficient, it is employed in time series analysis like a first-order correlation to serve as a building block in constructing other measures such as partial coherences, which

---

[7]If a square matrix B has its j, mth element $(w_{jm}, i\sigma_{jm})$, then the corresponding element of $\bar{B}$, its complex conjugate transpose, will be by definition (σ_{jm}, iw_{jm}). That is, $w_{mj}(B) = \sigma_{jm}(\bar{B})$, $i\sigma_{jm}(B) = iw_{mj}(\bar{B})$. A square complex-valued matrix B is called a *Hermitian matrix* if it is equal to its conjugate transpose, $\bar{B}$. B is positive definite if for any complex vector W, where $\bar{W}W > 0$, $\bar{W}BW > 0$.

serve purposes analogous to partial correlation coefficients. Higher-order or multivariate coherences, where the $f(*, *, \lambda)$ terms are replaced by matrix expressions, parallel multivariate R^2 in correlation theory. The treatment of these topics in more advanced texts on multivariate data analysis, such as Kendall and Stuart (1961), is a useful adjunct at this point.

If in (2.9.10) the term $f(x, y, \lambda)$ is replaced by the real length of the vector in w, $i\sigma$ space that defines $f(x, y, \lambda)$, which is to say the modulus of $f(x, y, \lambda)$ in polar coordinates is taken, then an alternative definition that is in real and not complex numbers evolves as

$$\rho(x, y, \lambda) = \frac{|f(x, y, \lambda)|}{(f(x, x, \lambda) \cdot f(y, y, \lambda)}^{1/2} \tag{2.9.11}$$

which satisfies the inequality $0 \leq \rho(x, y, \lambda) \leq 1$.

It is necessary, as in the definition of a correlation coefficient, to make $\rho(x, y, \lambda) = 0$ when the denominator in the r.h.s. of (2.9.11) is zero.

From (2.9.6) and (2.9.11) it follows that

$$\rho(x, y, \lambda) = \left\{ \frac{w^2(x, y, \lambda) + \sigma^2(x, y, \lambda)}{f(x, x, \lambda) \cdot f(y, y, \lambda)} \right\}^{1/2} \tag{2.9.12}$$

and the phase of the cross-spectral relation, at λ, is given by

$$\theta(x, y, \lambda) = -\tan^{-1}\left(\frac{w(x, y, \lambda)}{\sigma(x, y, \lambda)} \right) \tag{2.9.13}$$

which is a measure of the extent to which the two periodic functions x and y at λ are out of phase so that y leads or lags x in that frequency component. Obviously y can in this representation lead or lag x to varying degrees at different frequency components, a situation that is readily representable in computer simulations but does not lend itself to a clear graphical portrayal if we were to attempt to superimpose all the periodic functions that exist in a broad spectral situation onto one graph. The minus sign in (2.9.13) arises from the $\sigma(\ )$ term being imaginary. The phase in (2.9.13) may be thought of as an average phase lag of y on x or the difference in the input and output phases.

In practice the estimation of (2.9.12) and (2.9.13) is difficult if the series are heavily contaminated with random or white noise fluctuations, and averaging over repeated samples may be necessary before sufficiently stable values can be obtained; but in this case the values of (2.9.12) and (2.9.13) must be thought of as ensemble averages, not some locally invariant property of the system. The lead, in time units, of input x over output y is given, at frequency λ, by

$$t(x, y, \lambda) = \frac{\theta(x, y, \lambda)}{\lambda} \tag{2.9.14}$$

If a periodic time series is passed through filters, then its phase will be shifted, unless the filters are specially designed to have *zero phase shift*. Whether or not some biological process has zero phase shift is an empirical problem. In engineering applications it is possible to design filters that are zero phase shift at all frequencies, but these may not be paralleled in living systems.

A coefficient of coherence should measure the degree of linear association between the input and output time series, by analogy with a correlation coefficient, or a variance partitioning of linear regression. This situation is a representation of what a hypothetical linear filter, transforming the input into the output, would do. To put this another way, given the coherence between two time series that are periodic in each case, then the output can be matched by a linear filter applied to the input that is so constructed that it predicts the same amount of variance in the output as can be predicted from the original series and the coherence. The equivalence between filter and coherence is in terms of the proportion of power at a given frequency that can be predicted from the coherence;

$$\rho^2(x, y, \lambda) = {}_{\text{def}} \text{ proportion of power at } \lambda \text{ in either } x \text{ or } y \text{ that can be predicted from the other treating the coherence as a linear regression}$$

Expressions for the expected mean and variance of sample coherences have been derived in some special cases. See also Jenkins (1961), Jenkins and Watts (1968).

3 Model Structure and Identification in Time

3.1 ORDERS OF COMPLEXITY OF DYNAMIC MODELS IN PSYCHOLOGY

Dynamic modeling, via time series analysis, has decidedly not been the typical paradigm in experimental psychology, and the failure of cybernetics to "take on" in some psychologies has been documented with suggestive reasons, by Powers (1978), writing from a North American standpoint. Critiques of the relevance of cybernetics to psychology have but little international validity precisely because the role of S–R behaviorism has been of very varied impact in different countries; here we eschew the question of why psychologists have not used dynamic quantitative methods as much or as often as they could have, or should have, and instead concentrate on what can or might be done. The intention is forward-looking and not retrospective, without denying that something can be learned from incidents in the history of a discipline; the student first approaching a subject may in a way recapitulate historical trends in the growing understanding he or she achieves of the subject matter being modeled.

Consider Table 3.1.1, which is a simplistic outline of different types and levels of dynamic models that can be used in psychology, the simplest being at the top and the most complex and conceptually adequate for our self-imposed task at the bottom. For comparisons with qualitative and humanistic modes of description, on the far right mention is made of some topics and even of some great writers who might well in their work illustrate, with outstanding skill, the levels and problems involved. Naturally it is not being claimed here that these authors always or only wrote at the level where they are named, and it should also be obvious that we can have quantitative modeling at a very varied range of

127

TABLE 3.1.1
Levels of Dynamic Models

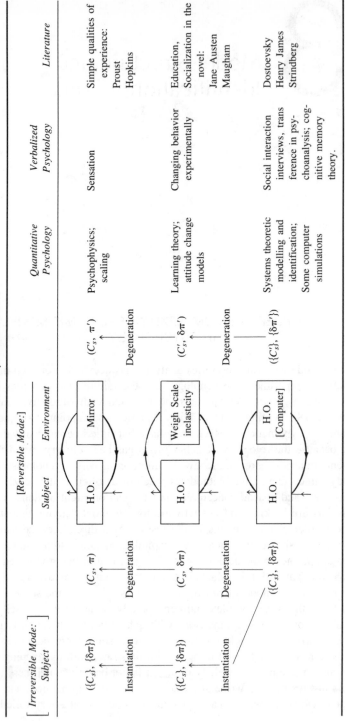

Columns: Literature | Verbalized Psychology | Quantitative Psychology | [Reversible Mode:] Subject — Environment | [Irreversible Mode: Subject]

Row 1:
- Literature: Simple qualities of experience: Proust, Hopkins
- Verbalized Psychology: Sensation
- Quantitative Psychology: Psychophysics; scaling
- Reversible: (C'_s, π') ← Degeneration — Subject: H.O. / Environment: Mirror
- Irreversible: (C_s, π) ← Degeneration ← $(\{C_s\}, \{\delta\pi\})$ Instantiation

Row 2:
- Literature: Education, Socialization in the novel: Jane Austen, Maugham
- Verbalized Psychology: Changing behavior experimentally
- Quantitative Psychology: Learning theory; attitude change models
- Reversible: $(C'_s, \{\delta\pi'\})$ ← Degeneration — Subject: H.O. / Environment: Weigh Scale inelasticity
- Irreversible: $(C_s, \delta\pi)$ ← Degeneration ← $(\{C_s\}, \{\delta\pi\})$ Instantiation

Row 3:
- Literature: Dostoevsky, Henry James, Strindberg
- Verbalized Psychology: Social interaction interviews, transference in psychoanalysis; cognitive memory theory.
- Quantitative Psychology: Systems theoretic modelling and identification; Some computer simulations
- Reversible: $(\{C'_s\}, \{\delta\pi'\})$ — Subject: H.O. / Environment: H.O. [Computer]
- Irreversible: $(\{C_s\}, \{\delta\pi\})$

sophistication for any one of the substantive areas such as education, learning, or social interaction that have been cited as prototypical.

The box-and-line schemes are intended to be read as follows. The top level involves a human observer coming before a mirror, seeing his reflection in the mirror, and then going on his way. The mirror is describable as a physical system, C_s', with fixed parameters π' that are such things as the thickness and opacity of the glass used in its construction. For the purposes of seeing briefly one's reflection and, for example, noticing that one's own eyes are gray in color, the human observer may also be described as a sensory system, C_s, with some parameters π that might describe the myopia of the subject and his color vision. In no way do C_s, π, C_s', and π' change over time. Importantly, the act of interaction between the two subsystems (C_s, π) and (C_s', π') leaves no marks or change on one or the other. The mirror does not wear out (except, perhaps, infinitesimally and below the resolution of experimental measurement, which is an implicit factor in all the three models shown in Table 3.1.1), nor does the observer suffer a change in sensory acuity as a consequence of the simple act of self-regard. The feedback loop is not really feedback but, as shown, is two independent events in sequence, in discrete time. In this paradigm the role of human observer and mirror are interchangeable in a conceptual sense, they both are static C_s^* with fixed parameter set π^*. The mirror is a model of sensation; the observer is a model of the mirror. The simplest sort of psychophysics is just this: Second-order corrections may subsequently be introduced for empirical accuracy (changes in the π^*) or for model validity (changes in the C_s^*) or to correct for the fact that one or both C_s^* are not in fact fixed in time. The latter correction does not occur in classical psychophysics, but corrections for unstable π^* treated as being unstable as a result of time-order errors, or local sequential instability of time-independent π^*, do occur from Fechner (1860) onward.

The middle level is a paradigm of the simplest of learning theories, those that postulate an accumulation-like process in learning or a negative counterpart in forgetting via the irreversible depletion of a memory trace strength. In this metaphor, the observer comes to a weighscale, weighs himself, obtains a reading, leaves the calibration of the weigh scale a very small amount worse as a consequence of using the mechanism, and departs. The weigh scale receives, say, 75 kg; indicates 76.2 kg; and is left in a state whereby next time a weight of 75 kg is put on the platform it will indicate 76.3 kg. The human user came to the scale believing that his weight was 73 kg and left believing it was a compromise between 73 kg and the indicated 76.2 kg. How he states the compromise between 73 kg and the indicated 76.2 depends on his C_s (he may be a good Bayesian or he may be like many human observers typically infra-Bayesian and unable rationally to revise his subjective probabilities about his own weight) but nowhere does the real weight of 75 kg feature in the records of the outputs of the two subsystems. The $\delta\pi$ now represent the changes in the subject's self-regard in terms of weight, and the $\delta\pi'$ represent the changes in the error of the weigh scale as a consequence of interaction with a load. Here we have a simple loop; each action on each side modifies very slightly the parameter characteristics of the other side, in discrete successive steps, but the model structures C_s^* are unchanged. Again, as at the first level, the roles of the two subsystems can be functionally exchanged; C_s^* are fixed and the π^* are modifiable on each side. Any model of learning of the sort that postulates a small change in response magnitude or response probability on each trial as a function of environmental feedback (such as the classical models of mathematical learning theory) put the human operator in the role of the weigh scale and leave the environment in the role of the mirror in the top example. So many learning theories, including some intended to deal with the serial learning of word lists, are a degenerate form of the inelastic weigh scale paradigm; with C_s', π' for the environment (an ordered list C_s' with word elements π') and C_s, $\delta\pi$ for the learner (C_s being his memory structure, $\delta\pi$ the changes in conditioning probability associated with each internal representation within the learner, of the word elements π').

Whether or not such accumulator models are actual feedback models depends on more than the evidence of externally observed learning sequences. The loop structure may be closed intermittently, the top link being open when the bottom is shut and vice versa but not both closed at once. This gives a representation of the $S-R-E$ (stimulus-response-reinforcing event) sequential open-loop behaviorist model but, as Powers (1978) and earlier writers have pointed out, this is an open loop and not a feedback process even if E_k is contingent upon (S_k, R_k) for all k. If the loop is permanently closed (though this can be a closure in discrete time) and also the E_k and R_k depend in an identifiable manner on the *sequence* (S_k), then feedback can be taken to exist.·

The bottom row describes a very general paradigm, two human organisms interacting with one another. Each may mimic the other, learn from the other, teach the other, change his or her mode of functioning on its own initiative or as a consequence of actions by the other. We are now at the level of the smallest social group that the psychologist wishes to study, the dialogue or dyad. This is also the minimum-size interaction in clinical psychology; one therapist and a patient, and the processes of transference and countertransference in psychoanalysis are an attempt, whatever one may think of their scientific status, to cope with the real problem of description and theory construction at this level. When modern cognitive psychologists avowedly set upon the task of constructing dynamic memory models, their formal structures sometimes reach this level of flexibility. We are reminded of an aphorism attributed to Bertrand Russell: "If an account of something is complicated enough, it stands a chance of being true."

Fortunately, even at this level of complication and abstraction, a considerable amount had already been achieved in metatheoretical analysis. This is what systems theory is about; it furnishes guidelines as to what might economically and coherently be said. Formally, now each side of the system has a set of alternative structures $\{C_s\}$, and within each such structure there exists a set of parameter values that is itself in a state of change in time, $\{\delta\pi\}$. Each side of the system is dependent for its present state and parameters at least in part on the other. The two sides are formally isomorphic and can be interchanged; where two human operators are interchanged, each stands both in the role of subject and environment. It is only the experimenter's viewpoint, from outside the total system, that may momentarily distinguish one as agent and the other as recipient. A computer simulation of adequate complexity may stand in the role of either or both subsystems if it meets Turing's test.[1]

Now the description of Table 3.1.1 proceeds back up the page, via the left-hand *irreversible mode* column. So far, in each case, the models as a whole are reversible because in terms of the (C_s^*, π^*) structures of the two subsystems the positions of subject and environment are interchangeable. Further, the weigh scale model is a structurally limited, that is, degenerate case of the general dynamic system model at the bottom; the mirror model is a further degeneration of the weigh scale. It is never possible to work down the page and predict what the general system will do from having a record of its inputs, unless restricted conditions obtain within the general system, mean, in effect, that the weigh scale or mirror constitute local, closed, stationary subsystems within the general system. There are, then, no general rules for inference downward and cannot be, though fortuitous empirical situations can arise that make it possible to describe quasi-closed systems as though they were mirrors or weigh scales.

Suppose now the reversibility of subject and environment, or equivalently the formal isomorphism between the two sides, is lost by making the nominated human operator side, on the left of the diagrams, of maximum dynamic complexity in all cases; that is of structure $(\{C_s\}, \{\delta\pi\})$. The environment, however, will be kept as simple as possible, like weigh scales or mirrors. The defence for this conceptual device lies in that we may use constrained quasi-closed subsystems of the environment as local environments, which are then not dynamic and not generalizable. Such closed subsystems are called *experimental designs;* the problem of their limited ecological validity is the problem that they are made tractable, like mirrors or weigh scales, at the expense of no longer being like other human subjects or like open systems.

The retention at all levels of $(\{C_s\}, \{\delta\pi\})$ in the description of the human operator side of the system is called *instantiation* (meaning: to keep intact the form $(\{C_s\}, \{\delta\pi\})$ as a proper instance of the left-hand subsystem structure at each level). A model with the human subject as $(\{C_s\}, \{\delta\pi\})$ and the environment as degenerated is said to be in an irreversible mode; given this formal asymmetry, it is not legitimate to interchange man and environment in a formal sense.

---

[1]This much cited test, dating from about 1950, is recently discussed again by D. R. Hofstadter, in *Gödel, Escher, Bach: An Eternal Golden Braid,* London: Penguin Books, 1980.

The reader will see, perhaps with exasperation, that much of traditional modeling in psychology has, in the sense of this analysis, been explicitly and deliberately degenerate. It could hardly have been otherwise because the conceptual and computational tools necessary did not exist when psychophysics came into existence (the mirror model, about 1860s) or when learning theory evolved (the learning curve, exponential negatively accelerated, around the 1920s). It is impossible to build or to examine the operation of the models tabulated in the irreversible mode without system theory mathematics and computer simulation. This may in part indicate why the literary mode, leading to the metatheories of psychoanalysis, has run so far ahead in some ways of quantified psychology (Meehl, 1978); it is easier to write discursively about a complex system and its associated phenomenology than it is to analyze its tight structure. It may not even have a tight structure but be at best fuzzy. This is no reason not to try, but it means incidentally that the results of the exercise will not be translatable without significant loss of meaning out of the far bottom left of the table into the levels above or the modes to the right.

In following sections, examples of models and dynamic analyses via time series are reviewed that fall into various places in Table 3.1.1. It should be noted that a particular substantive problem in psychology may be modeled at a diversity of levels; sensation experiments have led to all sorts of systems to represent the actions of transducers such as the eye or ear, and cognitive psychology has produced and is producing models that in the table would be reversible or irreversible, weigh scale or flexible.

3.2 DISCONTINUOUS TIME SERIES IN PSYCHOLOGY

Consider again a sequential experiment; let us look just at a few trials in the middle of the experiment, well after the start and well before the end. The usual psychophysical equations that are used are first-order gain functions that we can write as $R_j = g(S_j) + e_j$.

$$e_j \sim N(0, \sigma_e), \qquad \text{cov } (S, e) = 0, \qquad \text{cov } (R, e) = 0$$

It is a great simplification if each trial can be regarded as an autonomous experiment. Under such ideal circumstances, which apparently were the objective of early 19th century psychophysicists such as Fechner and Wundt, the R_j in Fig. 3.2.1 are solely a function of the current S_j and of nothing else apart from the central processes in the organism that are constant terms, with fixed parameters, on all trials. Making the individual trials into mutually independent experiments was treated as a problem in experimental design; by trial and error the necessary conditions might be found. Unfortunately, if the process is dynamic and has memory, then there may not exist any conditions in which it is both true that the trials of an experiment are mutually independent and also that the pacing

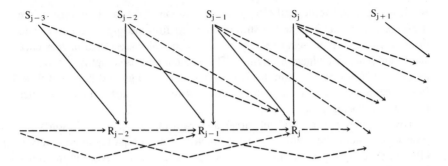

FIG. 3.2.1 Part of an experiment where previous stimuli and responses have lingering effects.

of the experiment in real time remotely resembles the real-world behavior one is trying to understand.

In classical psychophysics it was early discovered, empirically, that trials had a lingering effect upon what came after; these lingering effects were treated as nuisances, masking the invariances of true psychophysical parallelism.

Corrections for the lingering consequences of previous stimulus or response events can take, and have taken, various forms:

1. Ignore them.

2. Average them out by coalescing them with error variance.

3. Model them in an a priori manner and then, if required, subtract their effects to obtain estimates of ''pure'' responses; this can be either a deterministic or a stochastic exercise.

4. Construct a time series model from data with very open, but usually linear, a priori assumptions concerning the structure of the sequential process.

Examples of the first three strategies can be found in the psychophysical literature; the approach 2 is essentially what Fechner and early psychophysicists tried, by conducting experiments with a balance of different local sequences (A before B, then B before A, all possible orders of A, B, C equally often, and so on) and by running essentially the same experiment with different intervals between presentations to see what this does to sequential effects. This is not bad advice; it is indeed still the core of much that is written on experimental design.

Trying explicitly to model sequential effects from a priori models was the approach of Helson (1964a). He devised various specific equations, where effects were either additive or multiplicative. These differed in their algebraic details as his theory evolved, and special cases were created for different sensory or cognitive situations. Helson's models are interesting but ad hoc from the present viewpoint. His core idea was to express a response as a weighted function of the present stimulus, the geometric mean of past stimuli (the adaptation level, or AL), and contextual effects; the separation of the last term reflects the useful psychological insight that stimuli may be partitioned by the observer into discrete classes, some being seen as having a special background or reference status and hence weighted differently. This is a complication that is common in psychological theory. The antithesis between figure and ground in gestalt theories of perception is an example; it is not a distinction that features in simpler time series models at all.

There is thus psychology but rather awkward mathematics in Helson's approach: Consider the status of the geometric mean of past stimuli. Helson (1964b) states quite simply that he arrived at the concept of AL "in the time-honored way found so fruitful in mathematics, physics, and chemistry, i.e., by definition. There are many advantages in defining a concept besides the important one that we then know what we are talking about [p. 26]." He asserted that defining AL as a weighted mean made it possible to determine the weights in his equations, though two difficulties beset his model: the constants need considerable ad hoc adjustment, to fit data in different experimental paradigms; and from a time series approach it may properly be suspected that they are not really constants, because the model is not stationary and should be. In examples of time series models reviewed in Chapter 2, cases are given where the transfer coefficients of past terms die away rapidly, converging to zero, or they are zero after a fixed and known number of terms. But the coefficients are fixed from the start of an experiment; they do not build up as a function of input. This state of affairs ensures stationarity and computability and sometimes identifiability. If every new stimulus comes in to add its own part to a floating AL, then the process is not stationary; the number of implicit terms contributing to the AL is always increasing, though of course the practical consequences of using an unweighted geometrical mean is that later inputs are swamped by the cumulative previous data. Thus the AL should settle down and become relatively impervious to later extreme inputs, unless those extremes have some special status as contextual effects. Hence this essentially nonstationary model becomes, after a settling down period, about the same as a model *not* of short moving-average form but with no lags and an almost fixed mean term. In a sense it ceases to be dynamic because it becomes a set of constants outside time.

Reiterating, the important feature of Helson's (1964a,b) model thus becomes not the sequential structure but the context or anchor term. Special events have a key role in shifting or holding the AL; such special events may be the extreme stimulus values used in an experiment, because they determine the total range of experience available for the subject to scale his or her numerical responses in giving numbers to stimulus events.

Such models provoked interesting empirical studies and suggested alternative forms but did not always fit data well; little invariance of structure or parameter values was tightly demonstrated. There is thus scope for reexamining the psychophysical processes modeled by Helson with modified time series methods, trying to incorporate the particular mechanisms that he noted and that appear to be almost peculiar to psychology. Almost peculiar, because serious problems in econometrics arise when variables are misidentified as exogenous rather than being dependent; to some degree the distinction between contextual and stimulus series inputs in psychophysics may be paralleling the exogenous–endogenous distinctions made by econometricians.

In the simplest form it has been noted that the transfer function for a psychophysical experiment like Fig. 3.2.1 would resemble

$$R_j = v_0 S_j + v_1 S_{j-1} + v_2 S_{j-2} + v_3 S_{j-3} + \cdots + v_k S_{j-k} + \cdots$$

and the set of weights v_k are called the *linear transfer coefficients* or the *linear transfer spectra* (LTF). This equation is both mathematically and in its psychological interpretation the *convolution* of two processes, one in v_k, which is within the observer, and the other in S, which arises from input to the observer. As it has just been written, the process makes the output R_j depend on and only on events S_{j-k} that have already happened. It does not make R_j depend on events in the future that have not yet happened. If we make this reasonable restriction, which only means that we have no terms like $v_{-k} S_{j+k}$ in the right-hand side of the equation, then the system is said to be *physically realizable*.

It is more compact to write the same equation in a briefer notation (one would use this terser notation when writing computer programs to solve for the values v_k or to make estimations), which is

$$R_j = \sum_{k=-\infty}^{k=+\infty} V(j, j-k) \cdot S_{j-k} \tag{3.2.1}$$

in the general case, and with limits for k of 0, $+\infty$ in the physically realizable case. What is physically realizable is presumably the same as what is psychologically realizable, because we do not usually postulate that the subject can respond to future events of which there is no knowledge now, for the experimenter, before those events have occurred. To accept this possibility is to entertain some of the hypotheses of parapsychology.

Under some conditions it is possible to create systems in discrete time that are physically realizable; they do not use future information, and yet they can behave as though they knew what was going to happen on the next trials. They can anticipate events a few trials ahead and respond by reproducing those events before they occur (Krut'ko, 1969). This capacity to anticipate accurately, a sort of very local forecasting with negligible error, depends on the system being able to compute the first- and second-order differences of the input series and use these as a basis for extrapolation. Such systems are a very elementary form of recursive or adaptive filtering, which is introduced in Chapter 5.

The question of realizability is usually treated quite briefly in systems theory derived from the physical sciences, because it refers only to the point of not employing future events when modeling a real transfer function; mathematically it is a constraint on the limits of summation in (3.2.1). In psychology, however, it deserves more consideration because apart from the odd problems of parapsychology that arise if we wish to admit the possibility of precognition, there are limits of a fuzzy sort on what it is sensible to credit a psychological system with being able to remember or to process in the time available between two trials. It is now possible to simulate information-handling processes of much greater speed and accuracy than the human subject could achieve, even if given a long time to execute the task in question. The algorithms that are employed to compute transfer functions are not seriously offered as models of how the subject actually performs, in all details, a tracking or cognitive task, but there has to be some thought given to what has to be stored, in a form resistant to distortion or loss, in order to perform the equivalent of a convolution or even a moving average or geometric mean.

Approaches that review the detailed empirical structure of sequential effects in judgments, without using formal time series modeling but reporting some autocorrelations or autocovariances as contingencies over different lags, have naturally augmented our understanding of what needs to be modeled and have highlighted the persistent nature of sequential effects so that approaches 1 and 2, ignoring or averaging away, are repeatedly seen to be just untenable (Flexser & Bower, 1974; Gregson, 1974; Rabbitt & Vyas, 1974). Empirical studies of recency and frequency effects in temporally extended and repeated tasks are widespread (Mayes & McIvor, 1980). It might be remarked that any models that postulate feedback (Broadbent, 1977) are not treated clearly if represented in the way used by Helson; yet they are representable in many cases by time series. This does not mean that Helson was not aware of feedback; on the contrary he accorded it a fundamental status in his review of basic judgment processes. It means that his algebra was not sufficient to represent his psychological insights, though he anticipated, as an experimental psychologist, later concern with modeling sequential effects such as contrast or assimilation (see Chapter 4).

The constraint on realizability is mathematical but not necessary; if alternative models, both realizable and nonrealizable, were to be set up as competing alternatives, as a way of testing assertions about some observed behavior being consistent with precognition of future events, then there is a direct possibility of using time series modeling and seeking minimum residual or maximum likelihood solutions (Shore, 1980). The question of whether such physically nonrealizable models should be used in psychology is thus a question about the prior credibility of such models.

In the practical methods of computing descriptions of psychological experiments, computationally *as a minimum* the following would be derived and serve as a starting point for testing the appropriateness of any linear models:

1. The autocorrelation spectra of the S_j,

   corr (S_j, S_{j-k}),   for $k = 0, 1, 2, \ldots$

2. The autocorrelation spectra of the R_j,

   corr (R_j, R_{j-k}),   for $k = 0, 1, 2, \ldots$

3. The covariance spectra between input and output for leading
   corr (S_j, R_{j-k}) for $k = 0, 1, 2, \ldots$
   and for lagging
   corr (S_{j-k}, R_j) for $k = 0, 1, 2, \ldots$

(We do not in practice need both these, but they are not the same and must be distinguished.) From the estimates $\hat{v}_k$, which are themselves obtained from spectra 1 to 3, we derive

$$Y_j = \hat{v}_0 S_j + \hat{v}_1 S_{j-1} + \hat{v}_2 S_{j-2} + \cdots + \hat{v}_h S_{j-h}$$

taking h to be typically about 3 and not greater than 8, so that Y is an approximation that is reasonably safe because the series v_k converges rapidly to zero. Then the error of the LTF model is E_j, which is $Y_j - R_j$.

4. The series E_j has itself an autocorrelation spectra, which is

   corr (E_j, E_{j-k}),   for $k = 0, 1, 2, \ldots$

and for the model to be acceptable the series of coefficients of this noise autocorrelation spectra based on E_j must converge to zero rapidly. If this series shows periodicities, then the model is suspect.

This means in practice that one needs all the spectra 1 through 4 as well as the estimates of v_k before one can properly decide if there are any real sequence effects in a psychological process. As many published studies in psychology are cast in a form that does not give this spectral information, they are at best incomplete and cannot be tested. It is important to realize that the LTF is a model of a very general type, for representing a class of possible dynamic processes. The actual number of alternative models that could give the same autocorrelation structure can be quite high, and the number varies as a function of the model structure. In this psychological discussion, a form that is moving average on the stimuli has been taken as a paradigm, but the more general form would involve previous R_{j-k} terms, and the maximum lag of S and R terms plays a part in determining how many alternative models could fit from purely mathematical considerations. The ambiguity is only reduced by bringing psychological considerations to bear, in short by considering the realizability from a viewpoint that draws on what we know about human functioning and performance limits.

Following the general Box–Jenkins approach, the LTF may be written not in terms of the input S and the output R but in terms of the differences of order m of these variables.

If

$$\Delta^1 S_j = S_{j+1} - S_j, \qquad \Delta^2 S_j = \Delta^1 S_{j+1} - \Delta^1 S_j, \qquad \cdots$$

then the first level at which it is possible to write a stationary LTF (i.e., one in which the v_k are constants) may be

$$\Delta^m F_j = \Sigma \; V(j, j - k) \cdot \Delta^m S_{j - k}$$

Fortunately, in psychology it seems unlikely that we ever need to go beyond Δ^2 to obtain a model, if a stationary representation exists.

If a psychological process is dynamically stationary, then it can always be represented by an LTF. This follows because any S–R system with discontinuous input and output can be represented by the convolution of an S series and a V series. The V series, which can be defined very widely and take quite complex forms, are all examples of what are called lattice-σ functions. Thus the *existence* of a model that describes stationary dynamic processes is guaranteed, but this does not stop the estimates of the v_k from being subject to serious error if data samples are small or the estimates of the S and R values are themselves inaccurate.

It is of value to give, without proof, some results that we want to use. Suppose we have two LTFs in parallel, as in Fig. 3.2.2. The system in Fig. 3.2.2 comprises the LTF V1, which we have provided with a feedback loop, and the LTF V2, which has also been given FB, and a rule at the input stage for deciding which of the two LTFs is operative on any one trial [in fact, a weighted mixture of the two could operate, but let us be simpleminded and think of the input rule as something like a switch (English: point) on a railway track, and the successive S as wagons sent down the line from the left of the diagram].

The output needs a combination rule, and this has been connected in such a way that it is dependent on and only on the input it receives from V1 and/or V2, but all the outputs, from V1, from V2, and from the combination rule, go back to the switching rule at the original input. In this way the system is closed and can be stationary. If either the switching rule or the combination rule could be written as functions of environmental variables, independent of and outside the S sequence and the LTFs V1 and V2, then the system would not be stationary, it would not be predictable, and it would not be possible for the experimenter who only has access to the S values to control its behavior.

Now we can state two theorems (Krut'ko, 1969) that enable us to simplify Fig. 3.2.2 back to a single LTF under stationarity:

Theorem 1. For every set of m LTFs in parallel there exists an equivalent LTF for a single system, given stationarity.

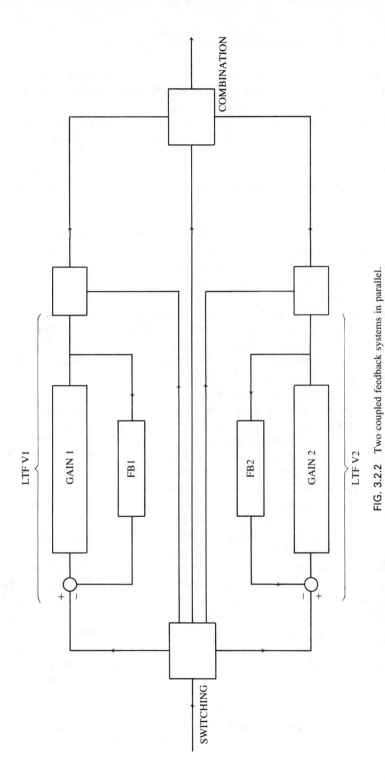

LTF V1

GAIN 1

FB1

+ −

COMBINATION

SWITCHING

FB2

GAIN 2

LTF V2

− +

FIG. 3.2.2   Two coupled feedback systems in parallel.

139

Consequence 1. It is not possible, knowing only the series S_j and R_j, to discover the value of m, the number of independent LTFs within the system, so long as the system remains dynamically stationary.

Theorem 2. For every stationary process that has feedback, there exists an equivalent process, that is, one with the same input–output relationship that has no feedback.

Consequence 2. It is not possible, knowing only the series S_j and R_j, to discover whether or not FB operates, so long as the system remains dynamically stationary.

Combining the consequences of Theorems 1 and 2 we may state that the input–output relations of the system in Fig. 3.2.2 could be exactly copied by an equivalent single nonfeedback system with an identifiable LTF, though the actual form of the LTF, algebraically, would not be the same as the forms of the LTFs it replaces.

But, due to the constraints we placed on the way in which the switching rule and the combination rule in Fig. 3.2.2 were connected, we have to discover the switching rule by experimentally interfering with its operation, if we are to obtain enough information to predict the behavior of the system outside the sequences S that we use in experiments.

Now all time series can be represented as combinations (with suitable weightings) of responses to the basic inputs, the *impulse* and the *step*, provided that the system remains stationary under such inputs of limited magnitude.

In engineering this property immediately suggests that to discover the dynamic characteristics of a system one runs it under various impulses and steps. It is possible to do this with simple physiological systems as well, but a special difficulty can and does arise in psychological experiments.

If a system is representable by an LTF of a few terms, then when input stops, output should continue for a bit longer and not die out abruptly. But, in a psychophysical experiment, often on a trial we have a "ready" signal, followed by a stimulus, followed by some feedback indicating *inter alia* that a trial is over. When these ancillary inputs are used, though they are not themselves part of the stimulus series, the responses are likely to stop abruptly when stimuli stop. We do not usually generate a decaying series of pseudoresponses or judgments to stimuli that might have been presented but were not. At the same time, all the shifts S_j to S_{j+1} in any series of stimuli are steps in sequence, so provided the steps are small and do not involve going to zero for a subsequence of trials, the human observer appears to remain dynamically stationary: After all, if he did not, one could not obtain the approximately static gain functions represented by the well-known psychophysical functions.

It is suggested that a system like Fig. 3.2.2, where one LTF mediates response to stimuli and the other to *absence* of stimulation, is a minimally adequate representation of what occurs in these cases where responding stops abruptly.

3.3 PSYCHOPHYSICAL MODELING AND SEQUENTIAL ERROR

The idea that we might study a time series as an abstract phenomenon, which exhibits some regularities in its mathematical and statistical properties, is naturally neither novel nor unexplored. On the contrary, time series have been the starting point of many economic analyses since the middle of the nineteenth century, and one could defensibly argue that applied sciences of disease and the control of continuous processes in oil refineries are concerned fundamentally with little else but time series and their interpretation. This is, of course, an oversimplification, but it serves to provoke the question:

> Given that psychology aspires to be rigorous and quantified in many areas and given that all behavior and human experience exists in time and creates sequences in time, why have psychologists been relatively ineffective and unoriginal in their contributions to the concepts and methods that are available for the analysis of series of events?

This is a complex and subtle question, admitting of many answers; each of the answers might be true in a circumscribed way. To attempt any answers might take us into a surprising diversity of topics, but two main features of psychology that emerged in the late 1800s can fairly be given some blame for the deficiencies that are discernible. These two features are *time dependencies* in psychophysical data and, hence, by extension in psychometric data and *response metrication.*

Time Dependencies

In setting out the groundwork for his psychophysics, Fechner (1860) gave us not only methods and a primitive scaling theory, he also defined what were for him the nuisance effects that were seen to impede the enterprise of creating his fledgling science. By doing this, he committed himself to a style and level of model building, though obviously he would not have described his work in quite those terms, and he indicated that some features of behavior would be defined as error that was removable by averaging operations on data. There is a distinction to be made here between error that is so defined that it must necessarily be removed by suitable averaging operations and error that is not precisely defined, a priori, in terms of its distributional properties but that seems, after we have done an experiment, to be largely removed by averaging, though the rationale of what is being done may be left opaque or open to dispute. In Fechner's day such distinctions were not drawn with the precision that a modern statistician would require, and so it is not fair to tax Fechner, belatedly, with being unclear on the distinction.

For example, Fechner (in Adler's translation of the 1860 edition of *Elemente der Psychophysik*) wrote:

since our method consists of the comparison of two magnitudes, a successive presentation should be preferred to a simultaneous one, especially since the latter is hardly possible . . . although the observations follow each other closely, each is uninfluenced by the other, and the superposition takes place only in the memory of the observer. The ability to compare magnitudes in this way is . . . very curious. . . . At present we must base ourselves on the fact of its existence [p. 73].

Fechner's distinction between observations supposedly independent and memory involving mutual interference (of traces, presumably) is still a core assumption in some memory models a century or more later. It is not the intention here to accept or sustain Fechner's tradition without criticism; it is not accepted that the ability to compare magnitudes of successive events is a tractable fact until that ability is described and understood in terms of sequential processes that do not suppose that successive observations are mutually uninfluenced by one another.

Fechner goes on to define effects that he called conditions of the temporal and spatial state of the compared magnitudes. "The influence of small differences will be evened out in the long run. . . . The existence of constant errors . . . merely complicates the measurements obtained by our methods, but does not cause them to be inexact [p. 76]."

Fechner then proceeded to make a virtue out of the presence of these persistent errors, in commenting "one must not see a disadvantage in these complications of our methods as caused by the presence of constant errors, but rather an important advantage, inasmuch as the determination of constant error itself becomes a part of the psychophysical measurements that can be made [p. 76]."

The presupposition is that, by averaging some response measure, one averages out the contaminative bias with which that measure is affected. In fact the two operations of averaging and averaging out are not necessarily equivalent unless it is also presupposed that some restricted form of linear model is legitimate; say,

$$\psi = \phi + \epsilon \tag{3.3.1}$$

and additional postulates are necessary concerning the distribution and covariance of the error term ϵ.

In modern inference, particularly in Bayesian statistics, there is a strong obligation to make prior assumptions fully explicit in any model that is set up.

The Fechnerian tradition, which despite S. S. Stevens (1951) repudiation—"to honour Fechner and repeal his law"—persists even more strongly in the latter's work, consists explicitly or implicitly of requiring that the experimenter:

1. Assumes that there is a most appropriate response, R, at some defined point in time, to a stimulus S. Both S and R are represented in the model by real

numbers; R is the value ψ may take with maximum prior probability when ϕ takes S and ϵ takes 0.

2. Assumes that observed ψ, for a given $\phi = S$, are distributed as $G(\psi, \sigma_R^2)$ or, *if this is implausible, as log G(log ψ, $(\sigma_R')^2$)*.

3. Assumes that a component of the observed variance σ_R^2 *is* σ_ϵ^2, the error variance.

4. Assumes ϵ is distributed as $G(0, \sigma_\epsilon^2)$ with covariance cov $(\epsilon, \phi) = 0$.

5. Then from assumption 1 the distribution of

$$R^* = (R - \psi) \tag{3.3.2}$$

is taken to be $G(\zeta, \sigma_R^2)$, where $\zeta = E(R^*)$ and R^* is equated with the observed response contaminated with error or response biases.

These biases are of two sorts, constant and random, and the distribution of R^* is then decomposed into two independent components

$$G(\zeta, \sigma_c^2) \quad \text{and} \quad G_e(0, \sigma_r^2) \tag{3.3.3}$$

6. The first term of (3.3.3) is removable, if the experiment can be so symmetrically constructed that errors of magnitude $+\zeta^*$ and $-\zeta^*$ are all equiprobably for all $\zeta^* \in \{\zeta\}$ or, alternatively, if the distribution of ζ is completely specifiable, a priori. It virtually never is, so the assumption of (3.3.3) is made. If the design of the experiment and the assumption (3.3.3) are compatible with data properties, then $E(\zeta) = 0$ for a sufficiently long experiment.

Further,

$$\text{if } \zeta \to 0, \quad \text{then } \sigma_c^2 + \sigma_r^2 \to \sigma_R^2 \tag{3.3.4}$$

The reader may note that thorough examination and amplification of models of this and alternative related forms constitute part of the classical theory of mental testing. For such an alternative treatment, see Lord and Novick (1968).

In this monograph, assumption 6 is effectively abandoned, and consequently a model that is fundamentally different from (3.3.1) has to be used as a fresh starting point. It is perhaps here expedient to reiterate that although S. S. Stevens (1951) firmly rejected Fechner's basic psychophysical equation in favor of what he called a power function; that is,

$$\psi = a \cdot \phi^b + \epsilon \tag{3.3.5}$$

where under specifiable and restricted circumstances a and b are constants, his treatment of residual error and of departures from (3.3.5) engendered by possible sequential effects is as simplistic and unfounded as Fechner's.

In fact, the issue of whether Fechner's "Massformel" (which is what the equation was called)

$$\psi = \log \phi + \epsilon \tag{3.3.6}$$

or Stevens' (3.3.5) is a better model, when second-order and not-so-second-order sequential processes are treated as removable by averaging, is almost independent of the question of how to treat the representation of sequential processes in human judgments. We say "almost independent" because the possibility exists of writing sequential versions of either (3.3.5) or (3.3.6), but the subsequent problems of experimental design and data analysis need not be equally tractable in the two situations. It is perhaps simpler to use (3.3.5), or forms related to it, provided these are regarded as first-order time-independent approximations to a process properly represented as embedded in time; hence this will be done where feasible.

The basic metatheoretical assumption, which either stems from Fechner or has been independently remade by generations of psychometricians, is that psychological modeling is a search for an invariant mapping of each ϕ value into an associated $E(\psi)$. Any approximate solution to this problem has considerable practical usefulness in problems of engineering design and environmental control.

Coupled with this is the methodological assumption that it is only possible to identify the parameters of the general functional equation

$$g(\psi) = h(\phi) + G_e(\epsilon) \qquad (3.3.7)$$

where g, h are real, positive, single-valued monotone increasing functions of their arguments and G_e is a Gaussian p.d.f., if (3.3.7) is conceptualized in time-independent form.

The point about (3.3.7) that is of concern here is that nowhere in the equation does there appear any mention of when (relative to some zero time) the $\{\phi\}$ were presented and the $\{\psi\}$ were made, and consequently there is no information about the sequential ordering of the $\{\phi\}$ and the $\{\psi\}$. In fact, though data are generated in real time, in real sequences, at real rates of collection, g and h are not functions of time, sequences, or rates as expressed in (3.3.7). Fechner's position, and that of many psychophysicists after him, was that given reasonable and careful experimental precautions there should be invariant and identifiable forms and parameter values for g and h. Obviously, g is postulated independently of h and both are independent of G_e. In the language of systems theory, the functions g, h, and G_e are uncoupled. It is not clear what sort of system they would describe if they were coupled (so that the parameters of one function become functions of the parameters of one or more other functions). If the functions were coupled, then their coupling would be expressed in simultaneous equations involving time and the rates of change of the parameters of g and h in time. The form (3.3.7) will be called time-independent, and all instances of (3.3.7) such as (3.3.1), (3.3.5), or (3.3.6) are thus special cases of time-independent first-order gain functions, by definition.

As the methodology necessary to get round the parameter identification problems inherent in the time-dependent analogs of (3.3.7) did not really become practical before the 1960s, a century after Fechner, the methodological assumptions were pragmatic. But what is pragmatic is not irrevocable, nor necessarily desirable. Released from the necessity of assuming time independence, the question to be asked is whether or not, on balance, it is worth making the assumption.

Response Metrication

Fechner (1860) advanced his psychophysical equation as a step toward the primitive quantification of unidimensional sensory continua. These continua, from the assumptions of psychophysical parallelism, must lie in one–one correspondence with physical continua already definable and measurable by criteria outside a given single observer. The criteria were not, of course, outside the consensus of the class of all informed scientific observers who wish to communicate with one another, for definition of units and measurement procedures in physics is by agreement, and agreement follows from some demonstration of consistency within the mass–length–time system and upon convenience and communicability. Lacking such agreement, or even the demonstration that agreement was feasible, Fechner proceeded by attempting to show that psychological scales existed because physical scales existed at the same time psychophysical correspondences existed, of sufficient invariance to stabilize the psychological continua given their corresponding physical continua. This is not an argument, from the psychologist's standpoint, for equating physical and psychological continua, but it has been used as such by critics anxious to show that the only scales that exist are physical. Such digressions need not detain us, because none of the arguments advanced by such critics of psychological measurement have seriously been put in time-dependent form.

Now, a vicious circle may be discerned. If the proper (unknown) form of (3.3.7) is in fact time-dependent, but contrariwise it is assumed that (3.3.7) and in particular (3.3.5) holds, in order to proceed, then errors will be obtained when the model is fitted to data in a real experiment. Such errors may be confounded with $G_e(\epsilon)$, which itself is hardly likely to be nonexistent. Or, they may be decomposed into

$$B_c(\psi, k) + G_e(\epsilon) \tag{3.3.8}$$

where $B_c(\psi, k)$ is the distribution of constant errors; that is, they are k biases, associated with particular ψ. There may exist yet another better representation of the residual errors in which the decomposition is

$$B_t(\theta, \psi^*, \psi') + G_e(\epsilon) \tag{3.3.9}$$

where B_t is a different bias distribution due to sequential processes θ taking two successive values of ψ, ψ^* and ψ', as arguments. B_t is thus derived from marginal distributions on multivariate distributions, or Volterra functions.

The differences, however, between the goodness of fit of the scaling models following from the two alternative decompositions of residual error, (3.3.8) and (3.3.9), would usually be small in comparison with the magnitude of the residual errors themselves. Thus, within a single experiment, statistical arguments based on classical significance tests to compare alternative models would be unilluminating. However, it might be possible to create an experiment in which var (B_t) can be maximized. As the objective of classical psychophysics was to do precisely the opposite, in other words to find procedures in which var (B_t) was minimized, the sensitivity of experiments to time-dependent processes, whose identification is necessary for an understanding of dynamic features of judgment processes, is in fact minimized or lost.

The circularity just mentioned arises in the next stage of the argument; the assumption that B_c, G_e is an adequate representation is necessary in order to identify correctly the metric of ψ. If, instead of classical psychometric procedures or nonmetric multidimensional psychophysical scaling, we use multidimensional scaling such as Anderson (1974) has developed, the problem is still present.

The metric of ψ has to be identified, with an error tolerance comparable in variance with that of the observational errors on ϕ, before it is possible to state with reasonable a posteriori confidence, in the expression

$$\text{var} (B_c) + \text{var} (B_t) + \text{var} (G_e) = \text{var} (G) = \sigma_R^2 \qquad (3.3.10)$$

that

$$\text{var} (B_t) \ll \text{var} (B_c), \text{var} (G_e) \qquad (3.3.11)$$

But (3.3.11) is a necessary condition for (3.3.7) to be valid, that is, for the mapping $\phi \Leftrightarrow \psi$ to be time-independent. Hence, a condition on (3.3.7) has to be imposed and satisfied before (3.3.7) can be used to test that the condition is satisfied, which is circular. In practice, strong assumptions are made about (3.3.11) that then release the investigator to estimate goodness of fit to (3.3.7) on the assumption that, for some sorts of experiment, (3.3.11) is met.

The question now is, does this circularity matter in practice?

If a time-dependent version of (3.3.7) is used, it is expediently rewritten as

$$g_t(\psi, t) = h_t(\phi, t) + G_e(\epsilon) \qquad (3.3.12)$$

The new functions g_t and h_t have arguments that could be multivariate or even complex, but most important at this stage of the exposition the introduction of t presupposes that instantaneous values of ϕ can be compared with other instantaneous values of ϕ, and analogously ψ at one instant can be compared with ψ at another instant. These are assumptions about the scalability of ϕ and ψ outside time! There is no requirement that comparisons be made between ϕ at t_1 and ψ at t_2 directly, but indirectly there can be such a requirement.

In order to evaluate terms such as

$$g_t(\psi, t_1) = g_t(\psi, t_2) \tag{3.3.13}$$

it is necessary to have a metric on g_t; this metric, which can be called γ_t, has to satisfy properties such as[2]

$$\gamma_t(\psi, t_1) - \gamma_t(\psi, t) = 0 \quad \text{iff} \quad g_t(\psi, t_1) = g_t(\psi, t_2)$$

$$\alpha \cdot \gamma_t(\psi, t_1) - \alpha \cdot \gamma_t(\psi, t_2) = \alpha(\gamma_t(\psi, t_1) - \gamma_t(\psi, t_2)) \tag{3.3.14}$$

$$\alpha \cdot \gamma_t(\psi, t_1) - \beta \cdot \gamma_t(\psi, t_2) = \gamma_t(\alpha\psi, t_1) - \gamma_t(\beta\psi, t_2)$$

where α and β are real positive (scalars), or

$$\frac{\alpha \cdot \gamma_t(\psi, t_1)}{\beta \cdot \gamma_t(\psi, t_2)} = \frac{\gamma_t(\alpha\psi, t_1)}{\gamma_t(\beta\psi, t_2)}$$

This metric γ will be defined as real and single-valued, unless ψ is a vector when it will have dimensionality equal to or less than that of ψ. For this reason, γ_t will only represent some of the potentially quantifiable features of g_t, and some η_t on h_t would be similarly restricted.[2]

The chronic problem of psychology is the absence, in many circumstances, of any pair of metrics γ_t, η_t, though η_t usually exists if ϕ is appropriately chosen.

The analysis of time-dependent processes underlying (3.3.12) leads almost immediately into difference and differential equations, precisely because the focus is on the relative rates of change of ϕ and ψ. It is strange that many elementary texts on experimental psychology have chapters on measurement and scaling, without making it at all clear that the need for ψ to have metric properties is not an end in itself but mainly a prerequisite for setting up time-dependent models (or, for that matter, models in which conjoint dependence of both input and output variables is demonstrably on some third set of variables, not necessarily time).

Models in which there is a restriction to terms of the sort

$$\Delta\psi(t_1, t_2) = \gamma_t(\psi, t_1) - \gamma_t(\psi, t_2) \tag{3.3.15}$$

where t_1 is a point in time that is one elapsed time unit T after t_2 in real time, and

---

[2]The expression *such as* is used here because (3.3.14) are sufficient properties for some scaling purposes, but they have obviously not been derived as a necessary and sufficient axiomatic set. For such formal derivations of nonreducible axioms sets, see, for example, Pfanzagl (1968).

[2]The reader may protest that if one cannot write γ, η as time independent, then no progress is possible; metrics ought to be time-independent functions of the arguments of g and h, or their meaning is distinctly odd. As the existence of strictly time-independent γ_t in psychophysics has not been established yet, we propose here to leave the options open but at the same time assume that the time dependence of γ_t is strictly second-order with respect to the dependence of g_t on the parameter t. If this were not true, then (3.3.14) would not be satisfied within the limits of observation error variance.

$$\Delta^2\psi(t_1, t_2) = \Delta\psi(t_1, t_2) - \Delta\psi(t_2, t_3) \tag{3.3.16}$$

where t_1 precedes t_2 by T, and t_2 precedes t_3 by T, are difference models. The unit T is fixed in real-time units (usually the number of trials in an experiment serves to count T) but the actual value of T, in seconds or minutes, need play no part[4] in expression involving

$$\Delta^m\psi(a, a') \tag{3.3.17}$$

where a and a' are any arguments and m is the order of the difference.

Models in which the gradient of γ_t in real time, or in θ units, is measured and itself serves as a variable are differential equation models. As we have adequate metrics on h_t and can generally write $d\eta_t/d\theta$ and higher derivatives

$$\frac{d^m\eta_t}{d\theta^m} \tag{3.3.18}$$

the problem focuses immediately on the possibility of also writing terms such as $d\gamma_t/d\eta_t$ or $d\gamma_t/d\theta$.

The possibility of writing psychological equations in differential form was explicitly considered in the 1870s, with no progress worth consideration. Generally, however, by extreme contrast with the physical sciences, psychology has been characterized by an almost complete absence both of differential and difference equation models, as has been remarked by Luce (1972). But, more interestingly, the absence of such models indicates an absence of theorizing in terms of rates of change. This is no longer true; Wicklegren's (1968) models of memory storage and decay are explicitly built on coupled differential equations, and other examples have been developed by Grossberg (1976, 1978), but it is still the case that most psychologists are distinctly unhappy and baffled in the face of calculus or finite difference algebra. Skinner (1953) is perhaps the paradigm figure for such a wilfully illiterate response to enumeration. The exception is that minority of workers influenced by control theory or Bellman's (1961, 1967) dynamic programming and cybernetics.

The stylistic differences in conceptualization between (3.3.7) and (3.3.12) can be brought out tersely by reconsidering the question of stability. This question is returned to and looked at in detail later, but a preliminary overview is useful.

There are three related senses in which a psychological system may be considered to be stable. At the level nearest to intuitive understanding, a system is stable if it has the capacity to restore itself to some state after being temporarily displaced, within small specifiable limits, from that original state. The weighted doll that comes back to an upright position after being knocked over is a crude system with limited stability, but it would hardly qualify as dynamic, and so it is

---

[4]For conditions under which T need not be specified, see Section 3.4.

not a good paradigm for the psychologist seeking a model of human behavior. At the same time, the problem of writing the equations that tell us how long it would take such a doll to right itself, how many drunken wobbles it would make on its rounded base before coming to rest, how big each wobble (in degrees deviation from the vertical) would be, and what is the average ratio of two successive wobbles as those wobbles slowly diminish in amplitude as the doll comes to rest, the measure Philpott (1932) calculated (see Section 4.1), are all problems that require dynamic analysis taking into account the real physical parameters of the system. Although the doll is a trivial case as a paradigm of behavior, it is not necessarily trivial as soon as it is required to know the quantification of its capacity to return to rest. Even more interesting is the possibility that the doll might have two different stable positions: upright and lying on its side, and it may only be possible to enter and stay in the latter stable position if it is entered slowly. In other words, stability is a function, in the case of the doll, of inertia. Two abstract higher-order properties, neither of which is directly observable in the sense that size, weight, and movement are observable to the senses, are coupled in a fashion that can only be deduced from experiment and only be expressed in time-dependent equations.

The second sense derives from the first and is closer to the needs of the theory constructor. The behavior of a system, which in psychology is an abstracted part of the individual's total repertoire of skills and acts extending through time (we might monitor the use of speech, without recording associated body postures, for example), is describable if it can be written as a special case of (3.3.12). It is quantifiable and, hence, predictable if g_t and h_t of (3.3.12) are specifiable and if γ_t and η_t exist and satisfy conditions like (3.3.14). A system is said to be stationary if the forms of g_t and h_t are expressible as dependent on some parameters that are all fixed; that is, the parameters of g_t and h_t are time-independent, but the precise relationship between ψ and ϕ that they describe is one that varies, lawfully and systematically, in time and is consequently dependent on where, in time, (3.3.12) is observed.

As equations employed to express the dependence of γ_t and η_t in time are usually linear, this second sense of stability is strictly a special case, linear dynamic stationarity. It is the only sort of stability that is readily available to analysis in psychological experiments. To advance more complex models in psychology would run so far ahead of the experimenter's capacity to approximate to a metrically well-behaved γ_t that it has not, so far as is known, yet been seriously advocated.

If (3.3.12) is expressible as two linear equations in time, which at some level m [m defined as in (3.3.17) and (3.3.18)] are stationary, then the system is said to be *identifiable*, and some identifiable systems are stable. The precise conditions for stability, when the system will be self-correcting for short (in θ units) departures from g_t, are considered later.

The second circularity problem arises here; it is another view of the circularity noted previously. For a finite string of observations, with attendant measurement errors, it is always possible to find a time-independent form (3.3.7) that will approximate to a version of (3.3.12), irrespective of which of the two is appropriate. If (3.3.12) is valid and is also stationary during the finite period of observation, then there must exist an equivalent time-independent form that will exhibit the same input–output relationships. The proofs of this and related theorems are established (see Sections 3.2 or 3.5). The relationships will in practice be expressed as one–many correspondences between ϕ values and their associated $g(\psi)$ distributions. Hence, the identification of a pair of metrics, γ_t, η_t, will enable us to fix two equivalent forms, like (3.3.7) and (3.3.12), but not to choose between them. One form will permit valid extrapolation to other data samples, the other will not, except fortuitously. Stationarity is a necessary condition for identifying a metric, precisely the same condition makes (3.3.7) and (3.3.12) indistinguishable.

An engineer describing the control of systems is faced with this problem, though he or she has the advantage that both his or her input and output usually exist and are known to have time-independent metrics. If stationarity is assumed when it does not hold, then the identification of the parameters in (3.3.12) will in general be wrong. If stationarity exists, then there is ambiguous identification unless transient perturbation of the system can be induced, so that it is locally nonstationary and then returns to stability, and the manner of its return to stability can be quantitatively described as a path through time. Systems describable by (3.3.12) can come back to stability; systems describable by (3.3.7) do not have this property. Hence, the strategy for identifying the form of (3.3.12) without falsely reducing it to an equivalent form under stationarity, as (3.3.7), is to destroy temporarily the stationarity. There is a need to have data on the behavior of a system both under stationarity and nonstationarity before the parameters in (3.3.12) can be estimated.

There exists no general prescription in experimental psychology for studying systems under nonstationarity, though the tradition in some areas of perceptual psychology, of examining how the observer fails to perform in the absence of some types of contextual information upon which he may usually draw, comes close to it. For example, viewing surfaces through a reduction tube and attempting to judge their distance and inclination from small visible patches of surface textural cues is a task set up to examine what information may usually be employed in judging distances of texture surfaces. It would seem, however, that often the precise opposite is advocated; the subject's behavior under steady conditions is considered to be a prerequisite for the quantification of behavior. For another example, the experimental psychologist would set out to quantify the perception of sound levels, if he or she were investigating sound and annoyance in the vicinity of loud sources such as highways or airports, after some subjects had adjusted to recording conditions, had had practice in magnitude estimation, learned by demonstration what, for the experimenter, constituted noise of a given type and what did not, and so on. The end of such an exercise should be a recommendation concerning legal limits on decibel levels of sound generation, but psychophysically as an intermediate step to this a relationship has to be identified, like (3.3.7), with the possible form

$$g^*(\psi) = h(\phi) + C(v_1, v_2, \ldots, v_i, \ldots, v_n) + G_e(\epsilon) \qquad (3.3.19)$$

where the $\{v_i\}$ are context variables (such as attitude, social class, age, personal deafness, and political attitudes toward transport systems) and C is a linear function of the $\{v_i\}$ that effectively shifts ϕ for a given ψ. The effect of C is expressed this way, in this example, because the problem here is to find out what ϕ generates a given ψ, the ψ being a rated level of annoyance. Another way to express the problem is to measure the annoyance enhancement or diminution due to C as the difference, for fixed ϕ:

$$\begin{aligned} g(\psi) - g^*(\psi) &= h(\phi) + G_e(\epsilon) - h(\phi) - C(\{v_i\}) - G_e(\epsilon) \\ &= C(\{v_i\}) \end{aligned} \qquad (3.3.20)$$

The problem here should now be familiar if the reader has pursued the tenor of the argument; if time independence is assumed in (3.3.7) and (3.3.19), then (3.3.20) will be incorrectly identified. In fact, C might also be time-dependent, in the sense of being related to sequence properties of ψ in θ, and if C involves the representation of contrast or adaptation effects, it is a priori more likely to be time-dependent than are g or h. Extending the argument, the identification of a scale of annoyance generated by noise in the environment requires the metrication of g^* in (3.3.19), which is formally better put as the problem of finding γ_t in a time-dependent analog of (3.3.9) where g_t^*, h_t, and C_t are replacements, respectively, for g^*, h, and C.

If the form (3.3.19) is assumed, or even a hybrid with g, h, and C_t, then the metric γ will in general be incorrectly identified under stationary conditions. The approximation inherent in the error may, or may not, be acceptable for applied psychological work; there is no general means of knowing without constructing and testing the approximation in a prediction exercise. But when it is found, post hoc, that scales of psychological measurement appear to lack validity in field situations, this lack of validity can have as its basis the misidentification of a form (3.3.12) as being supposedly of the form of (3.3.19). The circularity of the identification problem associated with (3.3.12) and (3.3.19) imposes an upper limit on the predictive accuracy of metrics as soon as extrapolation is attempted outside the limited range of stationary behavior upon which they were constructed.

The problem of the time dependence of C in (3.3.19) has been empirically examined by Poulton (1979) who points out that there can be unfortunate social consequences if we take C to be stable, when in fact we know that really it can be strongly context-dependent and can show marked "warm-up" effects in the early trials of experiments in which we assess sensory magnitudes.

The third form of stability with which the theoretical psychologist ought reasonably to be concerned is that due to Andronov (1956), a Russian applied mathematician who developed it in the 1930s, as a concept for what he called, appropriately, coarse systems. Let us define what is now called *structural stability* (where the structure here is a dynamic abstraction, not of course a physical construction) in contradistinction from the classical notion of stability that was developed by Liapunov (1947) in the 1890s (see Chapter 1). In the classical sense a system is stable if, when it is displaced, it returns arbitrarily closely to its condition before displacement; temporarily the behavior is not describable by equations with time-independent coefficients, then it reverts to the state where the conditions are again describable. So we may expect that our system input–output equations can be written in time-independent form but that short episodes will occur in which we are temporarily out of control and out of touch with the precise dynamics of the system we aspire to represent and predict; the system for a while escapes our attempts to model its behavior. There are, of course, qualifications to this; the transient perturbations must be slight, and their time derivatives if they exist must be smallish; they must be quantifiable in magnitude and direction multivariably, and the return to stability should occur within a finite and measurable time. Without such provisos the whole modeling exercise becomes vacuous.

It can be shown that systems with classical stability may be qualitatively not the same for small changes of parameters in the model that properly describes them. In terms of (3.3.12), if the variations in g_t and h_t are second-order, their consequences will be detectable in a system (or a cognitive or manual task executed by the human agent) that is classically stable; the stability itself is dependent on the absence of the second-order variability in g_t and h_t that may be all that is necessary to achieve a representation of the first-order transient input–output instabilities.

An elementary example (Tomovič & Vukobratovič, 1972) is given by the system

$$\frac{d^2\phi}{dt} + \frac{2\delta \cdot d\phi}{dt} + \phi = 0 \tag{3.3.21}$$

which is stable if $\delta > 0$ and then exhibits harmonic fluctuations, and is unstable at $\delta \leq 0$. Very small changes of δ in the region of zero can have disastrous long-term effects.

The structural stability concept emerged from the incompleteness of classical work on systems when it was required to model systems that have in a sense robustness, as many biological and social systems appear to possess. The stability of a system, in the face of changes in the parameter values that describe it, is structural stability. A structurally stable system will behave qualitatively in the same manner for a range of small changes in parameter values; geometrically one may visualize a convex region in the parameter hyperspace of the model within which the system is equivalent in input–output relationships—which themselves may, of course, be multivariate. This sort of system need not exhibit classical stability in the face of changes of input in a region of the parameter space exactly coextensive with the region within which it is structurally stable.

We want to suggest here that this structural stability may be of more interest to the psychologist than is classical stability, on the following heuristic argument. The gross features of input–output relationships are all that have been captured by most psychological and psychophysiological scaling exercises. Ekman,[5] for example, noted and made use of the fact that relations between two psychological scaled response measures could be intraindividually more stable, over time, than psychophysical relations involving one or other of the psychological variables in question. For a diversity of reasons, Baird (1975) and Gregson (1976a) have argued that there does not everywhere exist a $d\psi/d\phi$ for (3.3.7), so that (3.3.7) and by analogy (3.3.1) are only definable over closed ranges of either ϕ or ψ. Gregson's argument gave reasons why ϕ might define these closed ranges; Baird's why ψ should, with neither excluding the other. Both arguments, either that input ranges (ϕ) for stability are limited or that output ranges (ψ) are similarly limited, imply that if it is assumed there exists a rate of change of output for input ($d\psi/d\phi$ for continuous ψ and ϕ) when in fact it does not exist, then assuming that it exists will lead to a misidentification of g_t. A system does not have to have everywhere smooth rates of change; it can be unpredictable in its response to some particular inputs or unpredictable after having made some outputs. Misidentification means finding wrong values for the parameters of g_t, which obviously is crucial if the system like (3.3.21) is sensitive to small changes.

If a psychological system, or some sensory system, for a given range of inputs and outputs, however, is structurally stable, then small changes in g_t (its parameters or its structure) will not affect the major qualitative characteristics of that system. Such second-order changes in the parameters of g_t and h_t will be entirely within a range of parameters for which the system is structurally stable, to the degree of accuracy that its inputs and outputs can be measured. The very roughness or fuzziness of the human system in some tasks might coincide with the range of parameter values for which structural stability holds; this makes for biological economy in the sense that precision is not supported where it is not needed.

If a time-dependent system is in fact fuzzy in its output variables, and structurally stable over an appreciable range of its internal parameters, then the conjoint assumptions of continuity and time independence might do no great harm in constructing equations to predict behavior, because within the regions of fuzziness and structural stability it is a matter of indifference to the organism, if

---

[5]Ekman's work spans a series of studies published from the Psychology Department of the University of Stockholm in the 1950s and 1960s. See Gregson (1975, Chapter 3).

not to the investigating psychologist, what actually occurs. The organism and the psychologist are still in trouble if the rate or magnitude of inputs pushes the system into instability.

The interesting, and hopefully disturbing, conclusion at this point is that if a psychophysical system is dynamic (and it is impossible to see how it could *function* as an open-loop system with fixed parameters, though an appropriate *representation* of that form must exist under stationarity), then if it is also stable in Andronov's sense, it will be robust to second-order errors in its representation. Luck is in a way on the psychologist's side, provided he or she has the sense not to attempt parameter estimation to a degree finer than that implied by the minimum univariate diameter of the convex parameter space within which system stability obtains. As much of the literature of psychophysics may try to do just that (as, for example, in estimating Fechnerian thresholds or Steven's power function slope parameters), there is room for consideration that a lot of time has been misspent. The same will surely hold for what some call animal psychophysics.

The argument does not end here, however, because if the coefficients of the equations that define a system are not known exactly, the study of the equation must also include verification of whether or not the system has a stable structure, and this in turn implies that we need a different sort of experiment from that appropriate for parameter estimation under asymptotic stability. We cannot identify the parameters of a stable coarse system until we have established that it is such a system.

As the most popular solution to (3.3.7) has been, in recent years, Stevens'

$$\psi = a \cdot (\phi - \phi_0)^b + G_e(\epsilon) \qquad (3.3.22)$$

with a, b, and ϕ_0 fixed time-independent constants and var G_e second-order, then if the foregoing argument about stability holds, it is required to show that (3.3.22) is a robust misidentification of a class of dynamic systems with functional equivalence consequent in part upon their stability. In short, it is necessary to show that (3.3.22) could arise, as a rough approximation, to a diversity of closed-loop systems so that the validity of (3.3.22) as an approximate input–output relation (which is all the design engineer or social survey organizer might need to know at one point in time) is no guide at all to the classical stability of the system nor even to the existence of its stability. In short, (3.3.22) is not a system identification, which is precisely what a theoretical psychologist should be looking for, and what Fechner's original was, albeit expressed oddly.

The required demonstration has been in part provided some time ago by MacKay (1963) and runs thus:

The variables and processes of MacKay's model can be traced through Fig. 3.3.1; the input is a signal $I(t)$ that varies in time and is observable. This signal I varies in level; in the receptor R it is converted into a frequency f_1, so that magnitude of input maps into frequency of output from R, as the first and independent stage of the model. It is not in fact necessary that f_1 or f_2 should be

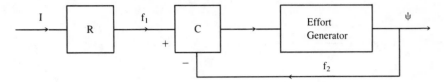

FIG. 3.3.1   Psychophysical feedback model as suggested by MacKay (1963).

regarded as frequencies rather than encodings varying in level, but MacKay chose to make this suggestion in the interests, presumably, of neuropsychological verisimilitude. The transformation within R is assumed to be

$$f_1 = k_1 \cdot \log (I - I_0) + a_1 \qquad (3.3.23)$$

where k_1, I_0, and a_1 are constants characterizing R. The model is written quite abstractly in terms of a single input variable and its subsequent transformations. The output f_1 then becomes one of the inputs to a comparator, C, which is a specific part of the organism isolated as an intermediate stage between the receptor and the ''effort generator''; this latter corresponds to a sort of gain function. The central idea of this model is that the effort generator creates a signal, f_2, which minimizes some loss function in the comparator C; it is a sort of matching of central variables to input variables, and the output is a consequence of this matching. The response made is a reading-out of the level χ within the effort generator, after the system has got as near to a match as it can. So χ is the internal variable under the control of the organisms, and this χ is also converted into a frequency, f_2, for input to the comparator. The transformation involved is postulated, analogously, to (3.3.23), to be

$$f_2 = k_2 \cdot \log (\chi - \chi_0) + a_2 \qquad (3.3.24)$$

As proposed, the transformations (3.3.23) and (3.3.24) are reminiscent of what Fechner assumed in his ''inner psychophysics,'' and not like (3.3.5), which is used as a model of the $I - \chi$ or $I - \psi$ relationships in Fig. 3.3.1. Note that the internal activity level of the gain is $\chi(t)$, which is either read out through some transformation, presumably linear, from I to ψ or converted to f_2 for feedback; both these transformations occur at once. Only I and ψ are directly observable; the f_1, f_2, and χ are not accessible.

The system is postulated to be in equilibrium, which means ready to give a response to the outside observer, when

$$f_1 = b \cdot f_2 + a \qquad (3.3.25)$$

and this equilibrium is reached instantaneously without error in the simple model.

The equilibrium state reduces to

$$\chi - \chi = c(I - I_0)^d \qquad (3.3.26)$$

where

$$\log c = \frac{a_1 - ba_2 - a}{bk_2}$$

and

$$d = \frac{k_1}{bk_2}$$

Equation (3.3.26) is Stevens' form like (3.3.22) even though the transformations (3.3.23) and (3.3.24) are Fechnerian.

The important point MacKay (1963) derived was that if instead of (3.3.23) and (3.3.24) one were to write

$$f_1 = k_1 \cdot (I - I_0)^{a_1} \tag{3.3.27}$$

instead of (3.3.23), and analogously

$$f_2 = k_2 \cdot (\chi - \chi_0)^{a_2} \tag{3.3.28}$$

then the form of (3.3.26) would be unchanged. Thus a black box equation like Stevens' can arise from a diversity of internal transformations, provided that a matching feedback loop is internal to the system. The remaining transformation, to take χ out, or some

$$\psi = q_1 \chi + q_2$$

as a magnitude response, is implicit in the model. As this last transformation is trivial, we equivalently assume that to the human agent his or her own $\chi(t)$ is directly observable and this is what he or she reports when asked to judge $I(t)$. The main objective of Mackay's demonstration was to show the nonuniqueness of Stevens' result, so that necessarily a number of alternative dynamic processes would all be indistinguishable from the outside and commonly appear to support Stevens' model. This denies Stevens' equation the status of a unique psychophysical theory reflecting inner transformations but leaves it viable as an approximation to an overall gain equation, which would be expected to occur commonly in carefully controlled psychophysical tasks, as it does.

Simulation of the MacKay Model with Real-Time Processes

To build a computer simulation of the organism-matching process model that MacKay advanced requires a number of additional assumptions and the fixing of a number of parameter values within intrinsically plausible limits. The exercise is, however, illuminating for the way it brings out the necessary complexity of even a single-loop dynamic model when applied to psychological processes; this gives some idea of the work involved if one were to proceed to models with nested loops as are often advanced heuristically without quantification in modern cognitive and social psychology.

The matching of (3.3.25) was simply stated to occur and to be achieved. For a time-independent model, if the matching can occur between one input, I_n, and the next in order, I_{n+1}, this is sufficient. However, a real organism that functioned analogously would take some time to achieve a matching and might never achieve it within small limits of error in a time short enough to be completed within the period before the next input comes along. Quite a lot is known about the intrinsic response delay and undershooting or overshooting in the response characteristics of many human skills and of some physiological transduction systems within man that facilitate the execution of such skills (McFarland, 1974, Sheridan & Ferrell, 1974), and it seems reasonable, therefore, to incorporate typical features into a simulation that could achieve, in elapsed time with a margin of error, the matching that MacKay postulated. Then it is possible to examine the simulated system as a black box, purely in terms of input–output relations, and see if it is still equivalent irrespective of whether the transformations from signal strengths to encoded frequencies are via log or via exponentiated functions.

The system diagram needs complication and modification as in Fig. 3.3.2.

Before writing plausible functions for the components of the new system, it is pertinent to note that a choice is available between writing the functions in Laplace form or as difference–differential equations in discrete time sequences. As a representation in time is sought and analysis of sequential errors in psychophysics has been almost always in the time domain, time equations are used. This also makes simulation easy.

The input signal from the environment is generated as white noise with a rectangular distribution $0 < I < 10$ and then arbitrarily smoothed via

$$I_s(t) = .4I(t) + .3I(t-1) + .2I(t-2) + .1I(t-3) \tag{3.3.29}$$

which gives an input varying randomly but not very abruptly within a fixed range. This smoothing is done precisely because real organisms spend most of

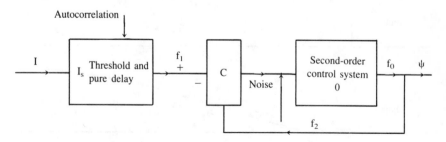

FIG. 3.3.2   Realization of organism matching process in real time.

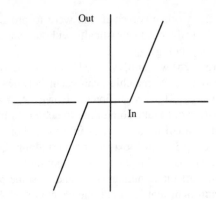

FIG. 3.3.3   For threshold effects (time does not appear in this graph).

their lives in environments that do not change randomly, and they often cannot cope with big random input fluctuations.

The box R is the sensory transducer that produces the frequency f_1: This transduction requires inbuilt delay of the onset of response and a threshold effect in that very small inputs should be treated as zero. Graphically this is shown in Fig. 3.3.3 and 3.3.4. This can be written as a convolution in discrete time; with $x(t)$ as input, $y(t)$ as output, the response to a step in input is

$$y(t + j + d_2) = \sum_{\theta = t}^{\theta = t + j - 1} x(\theta) \cdot \left(1 - \exp\left(\frac{(t - \theta)}{d_1} \right) \right) \tag{3.3.30}$$

where d_1 and d_2 are delay constants.

The observed output is thus a linear summation of overlapping convolutions like (3.3.30); this $y(t)$ is converted to a frequency $f_1(t)$ using

$$f_1(t) = k_1 \cdot \log (y(t) - y_0) + a_1 \tag{3.3.31}$$

or some alternative it is desired to investigate. Here the constants k_1, y_0, and a_1

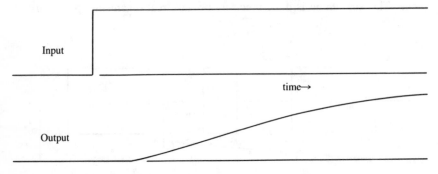

FIG. 3.3.4   A damped response, with initial delay.

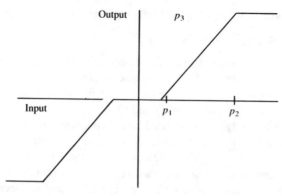

FIG. 3.3.5 Note, again, that time does not appear in Fig. 3.3.5; it is necessary to specify p_1 and p_2; p_3 then follows from the gain function of 0.

have to be fixed and their consequences explored. It is expedient to begin with k_1 = 1, $y_0 \rightarrow 0$ and $a_1 \rightarrow 0$.

The organism box 0 has to be considered in its closed loop and be capable of underdamped or overdamped behavior; when heavily overdamped it will behave like a first-order system such as has been just set up for box R. It is interesting to retain a facility for varying the damping and exploring the consequencies. It is also sensible to allow for threshold and ceiling effects; in many sensory continua the available range of response is distinctly limited (odor is a case in point) and only a subrange of possible physical energy levels of input are represented in output.

Figures 3.3.5 and 3.3.6 show, respectively, the threshold and dynamic features required in the loop. It is required to be able to encompass all the shown dynamic alternative responses to a step function, preferably with one parameter in the model. Response r_2 is probably the most plausible, particularly because the original input is partly smoothed.

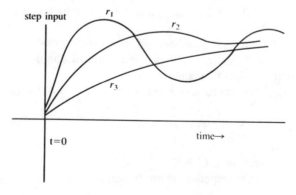

FIG. 3.3.6 Responses in time for a step input at $t = 0$.

0, with some initial level χ^* (to prime the system at $t = 0$) generates f_2; as

$$f_2 = k_2 \cdot \log (\chi - \chi_0) + a_2 = g(\chi) \tag{3.3.32}$$

with k_2, χ_0, a_2 as constants to be fixed arbitrarily. The same comments apply here as for k_1, y_0, and a_1, but it may also be necessary further to restrict the choice of the constants in $g(\chi)$ to make the system converge into stability, given the initial characteristics of (3.3.31) and (3.3.25).

The fact that f_1 and f_2 are postulated to be frequencies and not scalars does not enter into the model; they are treated as scalars, with both treated as inputs to the comparator C, as $+f_1$, $-f_2$. The f_2 values are transformed as $b \cdot f_2 + a$, representing loop gain and bias, and the noise with Gaussian distribution injected on each cycle as an instantaneous value with zero expectation and variance that has also to be fixed as a system parameter. What is of interest here, in terms of dynamics, is the ratio var (comparator signal)/var (noise), but this ratio is not treated as a modeled parameter directly. It can be estimated from simulation records after some trials have elapsed and plotted against overall input–output characteristics.

The signal that the loop tries to minimize, and takes real time to diminish, as in the approach to asymptote in Fig. 3.3.6, is the comparator difference

$$\delta(t) = f_1(t) - b \cdot f_2(t) - a \tag{3.3.33}$$

and 0 adjusts $\chi(t + 1)$ to diminish $\delta(t + 1)$. The dynamic characteristics imply that this modification of δ will persist over some trials.

Let $b \cdot f_2(t) - a = f_3(t)$ for convenience; then $f_3(t)$ for a step input at $t = 0$ will take the paths shown in Fig. 3.3.7, which is just Fig. 3.3.6 drawn upside down, to emphasis that the desired asymptote of $\delta(t)$ is zero. Let the value of $\chi(t + 1)$ be that which could generate $\delta(t + 1)$ (see Hale, 1973; the process is treated as continuous but sampled in discrete time with unit period or in psychological terms once per trial in an experiment) according to

$$\delta(t) = 1 - (1 - \xi^2)^{-.5} \cdot \exp (-\xi t) \cdot \sin (t + \lambda) \tag{3.3.34}$$

where $\lambda = \cos^{-1} (\xi)$ and ξ is the system parameter such that $\xi \geq 1$ implies overdamping.

$.707 \leq \xi \leq 1$ yields one overshoot and no undershoots as in r_2 of Fig. 3.3.6 and 3.3.7, and $\xi = 0$ implies oscillation and marginal stability. It is obviously convenient to keep ξ less than and near to unity.

Equation (3.3.34) is the basis of a convolution of $f_2(t + j)$, for a step input at t,

$$f_2(t + j) = \sum_{\theta = t}^{\theta = t + j - 1} g(\chi) \cdot \delta(t - \theta) \tag{3.3.35}$$

where $g(\chi)$ is defined as in (3.3.32).

The output f_0 to the response system is then at t,

$$f_0(t) = f_2(t) - \delta(t) \tag{3.3.36}$$

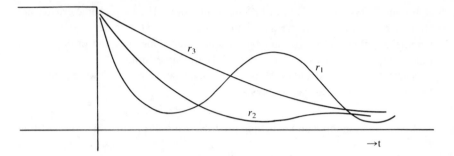

FIG. 3.3.7 Path of $f_3\,(t)$ following a step input, for various degrees of damping.

which has to be converted back to an equivalent χ by

$$g^{-1}(f_0(t)) = \chi(t) = q_1\psi(t) + q_2 \tag{3.3.37}$$

The overall input–output graph is thus $\psi(t)/I_s(t)$, and it is this graph that is asserted to be generally linear irrespective of the substitution for g in $g(\chi)$; log $(\psi(t))/\log(I_s(t))$ is a straight line if MacKay's (1963) demonstration holds for all parameter sets in real time. Otherwise, more reasonably and conservatively, it is postulated that: There exists a parameter set for the model M such that

1. The parameter set is not inconsistent with available psychophysical and psychophysiological data.
2. The alternative substitutions $g^* = \{g_1(t), g_2(t), \ldots, g_m(t)\}$ leave the input–output relation

$$\frac{\log(\psi(t))}{\log(I_s(t))}$$

approximately a straight line, where the set g^* includes MacKay's two instances respresenting Fechner's and Stevens' equations.

This conjecture does not admit of analytic proof, g^* being undefined, but sufficient conditions (i.e., one or more parameter sets in M) may be identified by simulation.

A Small-Scale Simulation

Using $\xi = .2$, $\lambda = .7$, in a simulation of the previous system written for PDP 11 in BASIC, Monte Carlo sequences of 200 trials were run. The input was a nonnegative random rectangularly distributed sequence, smoothed by a convolution over three trials, to remove abrupt discontinuities. The characteristics of Fig.

3.3.3 and 3.3.4 were also built into the simulation. The loop characteristics are slightly oscillatory, with the gain and bias of (3.3.33) both set at 0.1; all the parameter values were arbitrary but chosen after some trial and error to yield input–output sequences within numerically tractable limits.

The autocorrelation and crosscorrelation analyses of $\psi(t)/I_s(t)$ were conducted for all cases, which are as follows:

1. Fechnerian input and matching processes; Input f_1 as in (3.3.23), matching f_1^* as in (3.3.24).
2. Fechnerian input and Stevens output; Input f_1 as in (3.3.23), matching f_2^* as in (3.3.28).
3. Stevens input and Fechnerian output; Input f_2 as in (3.3.27), matching f_1^* as in (3.3.24).
4. Stevens input and matching processes; Input f_2 as in (3.3.27), matching f_2^* as in (3.3.28).

The LTF coefficients $\{v_k\}$ for four simulations are given in Table 3.3.1 as follows:

TABLE 3.3.1
Transfer Coefficients of Four Alternative Models

v_k:	f_1, f_1^*	f_1, f_2^*	f_2, f_1^*	f_2, f_2^*
$k = 0$	.31	.21	.19	.21
1	.57	.39	.39	.48
2	.74	.45	.50	.62
3	.81	.40	.56	.68
4	.79	.35	.58	.64
5	.74	.31	.56	.57
6	.65	.25	.51	.45
7	.50	.19	.43	.31

The point of interest here is that the coefficients $\{v_k\}$ are all positive and peak at about v_3 or v_4; this implies that the input–output dependency is best defined, within this simulation, by a functional equation

$$R_j = f(S_{j-3}), \quad \text{or lag 3}$$

but there are slight differences between models in this respect that could not, of course, show in MacKay's original treatment.

If the $\psi(t-3)$ and $I_s(t)$ are replaced by their respective log $\psi(t-3)$ and log $I_s(t)$ to check (3.3.26), the linear regressions of output on input were typically, on four simulations, given by

Model	Slope	Intercept	$F(1,198)$	Percent Variance
1	.565	.00	92.96	31.95
2	.680	.00	170.67	46.29
3	.693	.12	182.58	47.97
4	.428	.00	44.48	18.34

The equivalence, functionally, of the four models is weak and is critically dependent on the parameters of the loop equations (3.3.33)–(3.3.35). The input–output relations are expressible in all cases as a psychophysical power function, but the actual slope of this function can vary with the form of the internal transformations. It does not, however, follow that it would be possible to identify f_1 or f_2 or f_1^* or f_2^* from the input–output regressions; this lack of identifiability is precisely what MacKay demonstrated analytically, and it is demonstrated that under some simulation conditions the result still holds when real-time delays are entered. The many–one internal–external relations of the matching feedback loop black box thus support Stevens' generalization precisely because there is no identifiability.

3.4   THE z TRANSFORM

The z transform method is fundamentally important in the analysis of sampled data or digital systems and was introduced by Hurewicz (see Jury, 1958) in engineering for that purpose. It has become increasingly useful because of the increased practice of both representing dynamic systems in discrete time as a step toward computer simulation and actually interacting with dynamic systems in a sampled time series in order to control such systems. In principle, man–machine systems or on-line experiments in which a human subject is interrogated by and instructed by a computer once on each trial are appropriately analyzed by the use of z transformations, though there are qualifications to this generalization that center on the problem of the nonlinearity of behavior. All the treatment of z transformations summarized here involves standard results, which may be found in a number of different sources; the selection of topics and algebra given here is directed toward those that have the most a priori chance of being necessary and useful in formalizing simple psychological experiments. In any detailed application it would soon be necessary to go further into the theory or to use standard values of the z transform that are tabulated in more advanced references. In this elementary treatment no effective distinction has been made between digital system theory, in which the system itself is realized in a series of pulses, like a classical $s–r$ model in psychology where one and only one value of each of s and r is deemed to hold on a trial of unspecified finite duration, and events within the trial are not formally represented in the derived $s–r$ relationships (e.g., psychological or psychophysical scaling), and on the other hand a sampled model in which the underlying stimulus and response processes are thought of as continuous variables in time, which are observed only at sampling instants spaced at one per experimental trial. As soon as this distinction is important, and it is potentially a distinction that demarcates psychophysics from psychophysiology, then the interpretation of the system representations achieved through the use of z transformations should be made with explicit caution.

The z transform methods are not necessary, in that they are only mathematical tools for facilitating the handling of convolution summations; the basic idea remains the convolution summation, but considerations of tractability make the z transformations invaluable as soon as systems of higher order have to be studied. As psychologists have readily postulated such systems in models of higher cognitive processes involving feedback, without the attendant numerical analysis being offered in most if not all cases, it behoves us to look ahead and see what is involved if such theorizing is taken seriously. In the case of sampled data systems, as opposed to digital systems, the appropriate mathematics is offered by Russian workers under the name of σ-lattice transforms. The results closely parallel the z-transform properties that are more familiar or accessible to English-speaking readers, but some of the material in the treatment offered here owes indebtedness to both z- and σ-lattice formalizations.

The z transformations make it possible to operate on whole sequences of numbers, real or complex, by converting those sequences into complex numbers that may be multiplied together directly or otherwise more simply manipulated. The time index upon which the transformations are based is denoted by k, k = . . . , $-3, -2, -1, 0, 1, 2, 3, \ldots$, and where an experiment is started at zero time t_0 on the clock, this t_0 corresponds to $k = 0$. For psychological purposes, as actual clock times do not necessarily feature in a model of an experiment, notionally, the values of k may be thought of as trial numbers. In practically all the formulas derived, it is necessary to stipulate as a boundary condition that k never becomes negative. If it is allowed to take negative values, then results are not generally true. This boundary condition is mathematically necessary, and thus remains a condition for translations into computer programming of experimental control and simulation, but negative values of k are meaningless in describing a psychological situation.

Definition: For a sequence $f(k)$ that is 0 for $k < 0$, and for which k takes only integer values (for short, let k be called an *integer function* of time or space in this context), the z transform of f is given by

$$Z(f(k)) = F(z) = f(0) + \frac{f(1)}{z} + \frac{f(2)}{z^2} + \frac{f(3)}{z^3} + \cdots + \frac{f(k)}{z^k}$$

or equivalently

$$F(z) = \sum_{k=0}^{\infty} f(k)z^{-k} \tag{3.4.1}$$

As z may be an arbitrary complex number (of form $\sigma + iw$, where σ is the real part and iw the imaginary, with $i = (-1)^{1/2}$, and note that some engineering texts write instead $z = x + jy$ with the same respective connotations), the $F(z)$ will also be complex. The initial sequence $f(k)$ is called the *generating sequence,* and $F(z)$ is a transformation that acts upon the sequence, converting it into a complex number.

Alternatively $F(z) = Z(f(k))$ expresses the same transformation.[6]

Such a transformation is made because it is much easier to work with $F(z)$ than to work with $\{f(k)\}$. As seen, if it is desired to go back from a z transform to a generating function, then an inverse transformation, $F^{-1}(z)$, will be required; obviously, by definition, $F^{-1}(F(z)) = \{f(k)\}$.

As this process of transforming from sequences in $f(k)$ to complex numbers $F(z)$ and back again is a common mathematical activity in the analysis of systems that are linear and in discrete time, the more frequently encountered results are tabulated and may be looked up as required in the same manner as elementary trigonometric functions or logarithms.

The values that $F(z)$ can take are a picture of a dynamic system; they have to be plotted in two-dimensional space: axis σ (real values) horizontally and iw (imaginaries) vertically. This can only be done when $F(z)$ is finite in both parts, but this is the case for simple and well-behaved systems. The values of z for a given generating sequence as in (3.4.1) can be plotted in the z plane as it is called; for each value $z*$ there will be a corresponding value $F(z*)$ and if $F(z*)$ is finite, then the set $\{z*\}$ in the z plane is the set of all points for which $F(z)$ is finite. This set is called a *region of convergence* of $F(z)$; if however $f(z)$ is infinite, the corresponding z values define a region of divergence. These regions play a part in the mathematical conditions under which z transforms are manipulable; the region of convergence is usually a circle in the z plane with center at the origin, and its radius is denoted by R.

So, if $\{f(k)\}$ is a series of terms in a transfer function, the $F(z)$ is the z transform of that series, and $F(z)$ becomes a shorthand notation for the response of the system under study to some input. The input that is of prime importance, as we are concerned to represent all experiments as series of finite steps, is the unit step input.

The z Transform of the Unit Step Input

This important result can most readily be reached by treating it as a special case of a more general input, so it is sensible to obtain the more powerful result first.

Suppose $f(k)$ is defined as a geometric series for the integers $\{k\}$,

---

[6]This z transformation of a function can be obtained also by finding the Laplace transform of that function expressed in pulse-data form (a series of steps) and replacing the complex variables in the Laplace transform by $T^{-1} \ln (z)$ where T is the sampling interval of the pulse; in other words, the z transform is a special form of a Laplace transform used on digital or sampled-data systems.

$$f(k) = 0 \qquad \text{for } k < 0$$

$$f(k) = a^k \qquad \text{for } k = 0, 1, 2, 3, \ldots \tag{3.4.2}$$

If the values of a and k are positive, this is a physically realizable system; in psychological experiments involving adaptation it would be reasonable to expect a to be between 0 and 1.

If $a = 1$, then $a^k = 1$ for all k, so the step function that moves from 0 to 1 at t_0 is representable as a special case of (3.4.2). Substituting (3.4.2) in (3.4.1),

$$F(z) = \sum_{k=0}^{\infty} a^k z^{-k} \tag{3.4.3}$$

which may be seen to be a geometric series with constant ratio equal to az^{-1}, so the sum to n terms is

$$F_n(z) = \frac{1 - (az^{-1})^n}{1 - az^{-1}} \tag{3.4.4}$$

Now $|az|^{-1}$ is the magnitude of a complex number, and if $|az|^{-1} < 1$, then $(az^{-1})^n$ approaches zero as n increases indefinitely. Hence in the limit as $n \to \infty$,

$$F(z) = (1 - |az|^{-1})^{-1} \qquad \text{for } |az|^{-1} < 1$$

$$= \frac{z}{z - a} \tag{3.4.5}$$

Note that if $|az|^{-1} > 1$, the summation diverges and is unbounded. Processes that diverge in this way are not realizable and are thus not potential representations of reasonably stable psychological processes that persist over a series of trials.

The response to the step function will thus be obtained by putting $a = 1$ in (3.4.5) so that

$$F(z) = \frac{z}{z - 1} \qquad \text{for } |z| > 1 \tag{3.4.6}$$
$$\text{unbounded} \qquad \text{for } |z| < 1$$

if $f(k)$ is a step function at t_0. In geometrical terms, $|a|$ is the radius of a circle centered at the origin of the z plane, so that the *unit circle* (which means the circle radius unity centered at the origin) encloses the *region of divergenze* of response to a step function, and outside the unit circle is the region of *convergence*. To put this in another way, a system that has $F(z)$ outside the unit circle in the z plane has a convergent response to a unit step input.

Poles and Zeros in the z Plane

It can be shown mathematically that most of the z transforms that are of practical importance can be expressed as a ratio of two polynomials. The geometric

TABLE 3.4.1
Some Transforms of Input Series in Discrete Time,
Step Size T secs

$f(k)$ $k \geq 0$	$f(kT)$ $k \geq 0$	$F(z)$ $\Sigma f(kT) \cdot z^{-k}$ $k = 0, \infty$
1 (steady state)	1	$z(z - 1)^{-1}$
k (ramp)	kT	$Tz(z - 1)^{-2}$
k^2 (accelerated)	$(kT)^2$	$T^2 z(z + 1)(z - 1)^{-3}$
exp $(-ak)$ (exponential decay)	exp $(-akT)$	$z(z - \exp(-aT))^{-1}$
$k \cdot \exp(-ak)$ (ramp with decay)	$kT \cdot \exp(-akT)$	$zT \cdot \exp(-aT) \cdot (z - \exp(-aT))^{-2}$
sin ωk (periodic)	sin ωkT	$z \cdot \sin \omega T \cdot (z^2 - 2z \cos \omega T + 1)$

sequence

$$F(z) = \frac{z}{z - 1}$$

under some conditions is such a case, for both z and $z - 1$ are themselves the truncated remnants of polynomials; they can both be regarded as the consequence of the substitution of appropriate values of coefficients $\{b_j\}$ in the general form

$$b_0 z^n + b_1 z^{n-1} + \cdots + b_j z^{m-j} + \cdots + b_m z^0 \qquad (3.4.7)$$

so that if desired we could write

$$F(z) = \frac{b_{m-1} z^1 + b_m z^0}{b_{n-1} z^1 + b_n z^0} \qquad (3.4.8)$$

with $b_{m-1} = b_{n-1} = b_n = 1$, $b_m = 0$. This is hardly profound, but it serves to emphasize that the general expression required, which embodies (3.4.8), is

$$F(z) = \frac{b_0 z^m + b_1 z^{m-1} + \cdots + b_j z^{m-j} + \cdots + b_m z^0}{a_0 a^m + a_1 z^{m-1} + \cdots + a_j z^{n-j} + \cdots + a_n z^n} \qquad (3.4.9)$$

and can be factored.

Any polynomial can be expressed as the product of its factors (and there are standard computer programs in, for example, FORTRAN, or BASIC, available for this using a diversity of numerical methods of differing accuracy and speed of convergence on a solution).

As (3.4.9) can be divided through by a_0 without loss of generality, when factored the equation becomes

$$F(z) = \frac{b_0(z - z_1)(z - z_2)(z - z_3) \cdots (z - z_m)}{(z - p_1)(z - p_2)(z - p_3) \cdots (z - p_n)} \qquad (3.4.10)$$

The roots are the sets $\{z_i\}$ and $\{p_h\}$, $i = 1, 2, 3, \ldots, m$, $h = 1, 2, 3, \ldots, n$. When z takes any of the values of $\{z_i\}$, then $F(z) = 0$, so the values $\{z_i\}$ are the *roots* of $F(z)$. Similarly, the value of $F(z)$ goes to infinity if z equals any of $\{p_h\}$, and the $\{p_h\}$ are called the *poles* of $F(z)$. A plot of the loci of $\{z_i\}$ and $\{p_h\}$ on the z plane is called a *pole–zero diagram* of $F(z)$.[7] In practice, all that can usefully be said about $F(z)$ can be said by specifying $b0$, $\{z_i\}$, and $\{p_h\}$.

In the case of (3.4.5) the geometric series has a zero at $z = 0$ and a pole at $z = a$.

The general result may be put thus: Any z transform that can be expressed as (3.4.10) will have the pole that is farthest from the origin located on the boundary separating the regions of convergence and divergence. In the case of (3.4.5) this boundary is a circle radius $|a|$, and the pole is on the positive σ axis at $(a, i0)$.

The unit step is the case, as already seen, where $a = 1$, so the unit step $F(z)$ is represented by a unit circle. In fact it can be shown that the boundary between convergence and divergence is always a circle centered at the origin, and the parameter of interest is therefore the radius of this circle, R.

The roots that satisfy (3.4.10) will either be real or complex. If they are real, they are represented by points on the σ axis of the z plane; if they are complex, then by conjugate pairs of the form $(\sigma + iw, \sigma - iw)$. A typical data analysis of a psychological experiment can lead to a mixture of real and complex roots (see Section 6.3).

The z transform has a number of different mathematical properties that enable it to be used in the analysis of discrete linear systems, and in particular it is suitable for converting the convolution–summation representation into a form where input–output relations are represented directly by simple multiplication of z transforms, instead of the more cumbersome algebra of convolutions.

To show how convolutions are converted, it is first necessary to describe two other properties that z transformations exhibit. If $f(k)$ is a given sequence, then it is sometimes convenient to decompose it into two or more, say, W, other sequences; that is,

$$f(k) = a_1 f_1(k) + a_2 f_2(k) + \cdots + a_s f_s(k) + \cdots + a_W f_W(k) \qquad (3.4.11)$$

or contrariwise to add two or more sequences together to make a new sequence.

From (3.4.11),

$$F(z) = \sum_{k=0}^{\infty} \{\Sigma\, a_s f_s(k)\} z^{-k}$$

$$= \sum^{W} a_s \cdot f_s(k) z^{-k} \qquad (3.4.12)$$

or

$$F(z) = \sum a_s F_s(z) \qquad (3.4.13)$$

for $z > \max \{R_s\}$, where R_s is the radius of convergence for $F_s(z)$; that is, the

---

[7]The actual observed roots will move between pole and zero loci depending on the open-loop equivalent gain of the system. See examples in Chapter 6.

region of convergence of $F(z)$ is the intersection set of the z for which all $F_s(z)$ simultaneously converge.

If a system consists of delay units and nothing else, then the output is the input unchanged except that it occurs later in time. A left luggage office or a set of lockers that does not mislay or confuse what are deposited in it is such a system; a passenger aircraft, hopefully unhijacked, is another example. When the delay system holding the passengers becomes disconnected from that holding the baggage, then the passengers experience intense frustration and may be moved to litigation, which suggests an interesting formalization of frustration for social psychologists.

The operation of creating a delay in an input signal is called *right-shifting* just because time is conventionally represented as a horizontal line running off to the right of the page, and the delay is shown as a right displacement on this line. So, a system that delays in time by m units (or by m trials in an experiment) is represented by

$$y(k) = f(k - m), \qquad k = 0, 1, 2, 3, \ldots \tag{3.4.14}$$

where both series $y(\ \ )$ and $f(\ \ )$ are identically 0 for $k < 0$.

Writing as before

$$Y(z) = \sum_{k=0}^{\infty} y(k)z^{-k} \tag{3.4.15}$$

$$= \sum_{k=0}^{\infty} f(k - m)z^{-k}$$

$$= z^{-m} \cdot F(z) \qquad \text{for } z > R$$

or

$$Z(f(k - m)) = z^{-m} \cdot F(z) \tag{3.4.16}$$

so that a delay of m units in input gives an output $z^{-m} \cdot F(z)$, which may be checked by substituting back in (3.4.1).

As most psychological systems have one or more delays in them, which are often called *reaction times,* and subjects are conveniently represented as doing two or more things at once (in the sense of trying to respond to two or more inputs in parallel) that may have different attendant delays, it is illuminating to derive the response of a system with a mixed input of a signal and the record of its own previous output with a delay. This is the general case where a subject responds both to current stimuli and a record of his own previous response, combined linearly. The problem of fundamental interest here centers on the legitimacy of assuming that the combination is linear, but this case is considered as a starting point, and the extension to nonlinear systems would be derived later. A failure to fit a linear model may be necessary prior information to the investigator who wishes to embark on trying to derive a suitable nonlinear model.

If

$$y(k) = \alpha u(k) + \beta y(k - 1), \qquad k = 0, 1, 2, \ldots \qquad (3.4.17)$$

where α and β are scalars (they may be thought of as weights reflecting the relative importance of the two functions u and y in determining a response, and in the simplest case $\alpha = 1 - \beta$; $\alpha, \beta > 0$).

From the linearity property

$$Z(y(k)) = \alpha Z(u(k)) + \beta Z(y(k - 1)) \qquad (3.4.18)$$

taking z transformations this becomes

$$U(z) = \alpha Y(z) + \beta z^{-1} Y(z)$$

and it is required to solve for $Y(z)$ as

$$Y(z) = \frac{\alpha z}{(z - \beta)} \cdot U(z)$$

The response of this system to the unit step is

$$Y(z) = \frac{\alpha z}{(z - \beta)} \cdot \frac{z}{(z - 1)} = \frac{\alpha z^2}{(z - \beta)(z - 1)} \qquad (3.4.19)$$

To find what the observed response will be, it is necessary to find some sequence $f(k)$ that generates $Y(z)$, and this is done by using an inverse z transform. Inverses may be solved for using simultaneous or boundary condition equations or, in many cases, read off directly from tables.

Decomposing (3.4.19) yields

$$Y(z) = a + b \cdot \frac{z}{z - \beta} + c \cdot \frac{z}{z - 1} \qquad (3.4.20)$$

where a, b, and c are unknowns.

From tables of the z transform, it can be found that the sequence that generates $Y(z)$ is

$$a \cdot \delta(k) + b(\beta)^k + c(1), \qquad k = 0, 1, 2, \ldots$$

where $\delta(k)$ is the unit pulse input.

The coefficients a, b, and c have to be evaluated by the method of partial fractions from equating (3.4.19) and (3.4.20) (see, e.g., Cadzow, 1973, for a detailed treatment) and the result here is

$$a = 0, \qquad b = \frac{-\alpha \beta}{(1 - \beta)}, \qquad c = \frac{\alpha}{(1 - \beta)}$$

Inserting these values in (3.4.20) yields

$$y(k) = \frac{\alpha}{(1 - \beta)} \cdot (1 - \beta^{k+1}), \qquad k = 0, 1, 2, \ldots \qquad (3.4.21)$$

Transfer Functions

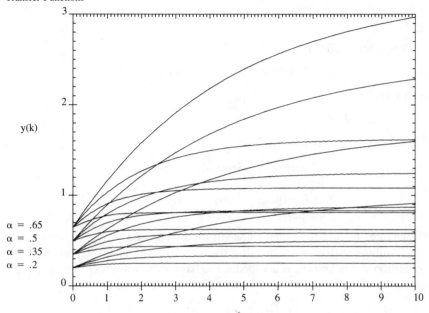

FIG. 3.4.1   Plot of the function (3.4.21) for selected values of α and β. For each value of α, taken as .2, .35, .5, and .65, are shown four curves, which reading upward in each group correspond to β = .2, .4, .6 and .8. Thus the uppermost curve is plotted for α = .65, β = .8.

Other more complex cases are solved by a generalization of this result. These results lead naturally to the representation of input–output relations, given a convolution–summation of a linear discrete system, which in theory can be observed as the response to a unit pulse (Kronecker δ) input. If J is the time span after which the system effectively truncates itself,

$$y(k) = v(0)u(k) + v(1)u(k - 1) + \cdots + v(j)u(k - j) + \cdots + v(J)u(k - J) \tag{3.4.22}$$

where $v(j)$ is the set of l.t.f. (linear transfer function) coefficients, then the z-transforms $Z(u(k))$ and $Z(y(h))$ are simply related provided each sequence is identically zero for $k < 0$.

$$Y(z) = \sum_{k=1} y(k)z^{-k}$$

$$= \sum_{j=0}^{J} v(j) \cdot \sum_{k=0} u(k - j)z^{-k} \tag{3.4.23}$$

Obviously all the terms $v(j)$ can be thought of as acting on a lagged (i.e., right-shifted) system j steps delayed, so

$$Y(z) = \left\{ \sum_{j=0} v(j)z^{-j} \right\} \cdot U(z) \qquad (3.4.24)$$

where $U(z) = Z(u(k))$. But

$$\{\Sigma\ v(j)z^{-j}\} = Z(v(k)) = H(z) \qquad \text{(by definition of } H(\ ))$$

This gives

$$Y(z) = H(z) \cdot U(z) \qquad (3.4.25)$$

A summary tabulation is:

Location	Sequence	z-Transform
Input	$u(k)$	$U(z)$
l.t.f. within	$v(j)$	$H(z)$
Output	$y(k)$	$Y(z) = H(z) \cdot U(z)$

Therefore, to find the output, analytically as opposed to computationally by performing a system simulation directly from the convolution–summation representation if it is known, it is expedient to have a z transform of the input to the system and of the output, and then the filter will be

$$Z^{-1}(H(z)) = Z^{-1}\left(\frac{Y(z)}{U(z)} \right)$$

Using these results in the unit step case again,

$$Y(z) = H(z) \cdot U(z)$$

$$= H(z) \cdot \frac{z}{z-1} = H(z) \cdot (1 - z^{-1})^{-1}$$

where $(1 - z^{-1})$ is a complex number. Multiplying and rearranging gives

$$Y(z) - z^{-1}Y(z) = H(z)$$

which can be satisfied by the difference equation

$$y(k) - y(k - 1) = v(j)$$

or, in words, the first-order difference $\Delta^1(k)$ of the output is the l.t.f., when the input is a step.

It can also be shown that for $u(k) = (\delta)$, $U(z) = 1$, so in this case $Y(z) = H(z) \cdot U(z) = H(z)$, which implies $y(k) = v(j)$, and establishes the result that the response to a unit pulse is the realization of a series of l.t.f. coefficients, in a linear system.

The required sequence may be represented by

$$f(k) = \sum_{i=0}^{k} a^i g(i), \qquad k = 0, 1, 2, \ldots \qquad (3.4.26)$$

Considering the right-hand side of (3.4.26) first,

$$z(a^i g(i)) = G(a^{-1}z) \qquad \text{for } z > aR$$

$\Bigg($ from

$$Z(h(i)) = Z(a^i g(i)) = \sum_{i=0}^{\infty} a^i g(i) z^{-1}$$

$$= \sum_{i=0}^{\infty} g(i)(a^{-1}z)^{-1} \Bigg)$$

where $G(a^{-1}z)$ means evaluate $G(z)$ and replace z by $a^{-1}z$ wherever z occurs. Returning to (3.4.26),

$$f(k) - f(k - 1) = a^i g(i) \qquad \text{for } k = 0, 1, 2, \ldots$$

provided that $g(0) = f(0)$.
   Now

$$G(a^{-1}z) = \sum_{k=0}^{\infty} (f(k) - f(k - 1))z^{-k}$$

or

$$G(a^{-1}z) = F(z) - z^{-1}F(z), \qquad z > R$$

and

$$F(z) = G(a^{-1}z) \cdot (1 - z^{-1})^{-1} \tag{3.4.27}$$

Call the sequence $f(k)$ in (3.4.26) the *cumulation* of $a^i g(i)$; the step function cumulation is again a special case of this sequence for i where

$$g(i) = 0 \qquad \text{for } k = 0$$

$$g(i) = 1 \qquad \text{for } k = 1, 2, 3, \ldots$$

and

$$f(k) = k \qquad \text{for } k = 0, 1, 2, 3, \ldots$$

and

$$F(z) = \frac{z}{(z - 1)^2} \qquad \text{for } z > 1 \tag{3.4.28}$$

   The inverse z transform of this is a staircase (compare a hypothetical case of all-or-none learning of a list of paired associates).
   The z transform is graphically represented by the partition of the z plane (horizontal axis reals, ordinate axis imaginaries) into the stable area inside the

unit circle and the unstable area outside the circle. But for representing responses to a pulse input, it is often more convenient to use the transformation (in complex variables)

$$w = \frac{z - 1}{z + 1} \qquad (3.4.29)$$

and consider instead the w plane, where now the left-hand part (negative reals) represents stable components and the right-hand part represents unstable components. This transformation maps the inside of the unit circle into the left-hand plane, the outside into the right-hand plane, and the unit circle into the imaginary axis of the w plane; Lindorff (1965) gives an extended treatment for sampled-data systems. In Section 6.3 the examples given graphically are in fact in the w-plane representations. The context and the stability conditions usually make it quite clear what representation is being used.

Direct comparisons between representing human tracking behavior (see also Section 4.4) in time series notation (as in Section 2.2) and in z transforms have been made in recent cybernetic studies. These serve well to illustrate some advantages that can accrue from taking a time series approach, provided that boundary conditions on what constitutes a reasonable model are carefully formulated. They also serve to reemphasize the mathematical equivalences between different modes of representation of dynamic processes.

Human dynamics in tracking tasks can be represented using Laplace transforms, z transforms, Fourier analysis, or time series transfer functions. All four methods have by now been used; time series modeling is the most recent but does offer some advantages, not least of which is that a process may be identified with smaller data samples than used in Fourier analysis; however, the calculations required may be longer. Thus time series analysis may be superior for identification but inferior for control in the real-time applications of interest to the engineer.

Shinners (1974) and Osafo-Charles, Agarwal, O'Neill, and Gottlieb (1980) have reopened the question of human operator tracking under different input conditions and with different sampling frequencies. Shinners demonstrated that compensatory tracking to impulse and to step inputs was second-order. In z notation a loop gain, with sampling interval of 0.2 sec, was

$$G(z) = \frac{c_1(1 - c_2 z^{-1})z^{-1}}{(1 - c_3 z^{-1})(1 + c_4 z^{-1})} \qquad (3.4.30)$$

which is a result of the operator trying to eliminate a lag, in which he is not successful. Shinners conjectured that subjects learn both to smooth output and to introduce periodic components.

The details of Shinners' solutions for $G(z)$ were brought into doubt by Osafo-Charles et al. (1980), who used a different sampling interval, 0.1 sec, and perhaps most importantly constrained the parameters when modeling in order to impose steady-state conditions as a limiting case. As these investigators used a mixed low-frequency sinusoidal input that subjects could not anticipate, this condition means that a solution to

$$y_j = \sum_{k}^{n} v_k y_{j-k} + \sum_{h}^{m} w_h x_{j-h} + u_j, \qquad m \leqslant n \tag{3.4.32}$$

where u_j is i.i.d., is what is required. In practice this means identifying n, m, $\{v_k\}$, $\{w_h\}$.

Instead of using Box-Jenkins methods, Osafo-Charles et al. used a derivation of ordinary least-squares regression analysis called *normalized residual criterion* (NRC). In practice this method finds the n, m for which (on a data string of fixed length T)

$$\sum^{T} \frac{\left(y_j - \sum^{n} v_k y_{j-k} - \sum^{m} w_h x_{j-h} \right)^2}{\sum (y_j)^2} = \frac{\|V\|^2}{\|Y\|^2} \quad \text{(by definition)} \tag{3.4.33}$$

is minimized.

It was shown that MA and AR models were inadequate (i.e., that m *and* $n > 0$) and that for both low- and high-frequency tracking it was not necessary to go beyond m, $n = 2$.

An immediate test is provided for the decision, given $m > 1$, to justify increasing n from some value n_1 to a greater value n_2.

$$\Delta = \left| \frac{\|V\|_{n_2}^2 - \|V\|_{n_1}^2}{\|V\|_{n_2}^2} \right| \cdot \left| \frac{T - n_2}{n_2 - n_1} \right| \tag{3.4.34}$$

is distributed as F with d.f. $= (n_2 - n_1, T - n_2)$ for large T (Åström & Eykhoff, 1971).

The additional boundary condition rests on the argument that for sufficiently large j, when complete steady-state behavior is attained after a perturbation,

$$y_j = y_{j-1} = y_{j-2} = y_e$$

$$x_j = x_{j-1} = x_{j-2} = x_e$$

when the perturbation is at $j = 0$.

It can be assumed that the gain of the system is unity, so that $y_e = x_e$, then

$$w_0 = 1 - v_1 - v_2 \tag{3.4.35}$$

in the model $y_e = v_1 y_e + v_2 y_e + w_0 x_e$ where $n = 2$, $m = 1$. Data show this to be appropriate in the low-frequency input range.

In contrast, the high-frequency range requires $n = 2$, $m = 2$ and

$$w_0 = 1 - v_1 - v_2 - w_1 \qquad \text{as a constraint}$$

The constraints are imposed on the regression analysis used to estimate v_1, v_2, and w_1. w_0 is then obtained from the constraints. The actual effect on parameter values is slight, but the constraints make important differences to the dynamics; particularly, the constrained models can settle down after perturbation, whereas the unconstrained ones may never do so.

The comparative forms of the time series transfer functions and the z-transform gains is given in Table 3.4.3. The forms hold for both constrained and unconstrained solutions.

TABLE 3.4.3
Comparisons of Time Series and z-Transform Solutions
in a Human Tracking Task, after Osafo-Charles et al., 1980

	Low Frequency	High Frequency
$G(z)$:	$\dfrac{c_1}{(1 - z^{-1})(1 - c_2 z^{-1})}$	$\dfrac{-c_1(1 - c_2 z^{-1})}{(1 - z^{-1})(1 - c_3 z^{-1})}$
t.s.t.f.:	$y_j = v_1 v_{j-1} + v_2 v_{j-2} + u_j$	$y_j = v_1 y_{j-1} + v_2 y_{j-2} + w_0 x_j + w_1 x_{j-1} + u_j$

The advantage of NRC modeling, in well-understood situations like the previous, is that it is not necessary to calculate the autocorrelations and partial correlations and that estimation occurs in one step. The Box-Jenkins procedures can require a series of trial solutions. Obviously NRC only selects models within the set compared; it would not indicate the existence of better nonlinear solutions, though the form of the residuals to the original $G(z)$ of (3.4.30) hints that this may be possible. In the solutions of Table 3.4.3 the residuals vanished, indicating that a nonlinear model would not fit any better to these data, but it might hold with wider generality over different input conditions.

3.5 ASPECTS OF MODEL IDENTIFICATION

The original impetus within psychology for the study of control and controllable systems mathematically came from Wiener's popularization of cybernetics in the late 1940s. The mathematical and conceptual techniques of this monograph are perhaps in part a belated response to this impetus, but if so must be greatly tempered by the realization that cybernetics did not reach the heart of psychological modeling problems, for a diversity of historical reasons. Neither has general systems theory, which has had the benefit of more extensive and considered formalization (Mesarovich & Takahara, 1975) than cybernetics in its most popular decade ever received, been used as a conceptual framework for the reexamination of psychological problems. Kantowitz (1975) has described this as a "catch 22" situation: where no one can understand either the problem in theory construction nor the solution, without the mathematics, and few if any will learn the mathematics until the need is demonstrated. It is indeed true that practically all the developmental work in time series analysis of dynamic systems, even goal-seeking systems that are characteristically human, came from outside academic psychology. Some of the few counter-examples that might be cited are from outside the United States, which has been the cradle of most mathematical psychology, so the survival of a systems theoretic approach in the behavioral sciences is interestingly international (Buckley, 1968; Powers, 1978).

A closer look at this unprepossessing situation suggests that there are four fundamental difficulties in using a systems theoretic approach in psychology, however rigorous and experimentally well-defined the work may aspire to be.

1. Systems theory models are not constrained to the view that an observed response is the consequence of an observed stimulus that is roughly contiguous in time with the response or precedes it a little.

2. Systems theory models are not constrained to equate the observed response (which may be nothing or nearly nothing) with the output of a system, when behavior is modeled.

3. Purposive behavior is usually conceptualized qualitatively, in terms of drives, motives, and even hierarchical constructions with fuzzy (in the nonmathematical sense) structures and interactions. If psychological deterministic theories have any place within a system theory approach, then it is as special limiting cases, and no more; they have by definition and structure no systematic generality.

4. The mathematical methods of systems theory, and consequently of time series analysis within systems, are means toward system identification and not an end within themselves (Eykhoff, 1974). The identification of the conditions under which the structure of a system can be identified raises problems of great subtlety, the study of which has attracted interest widely exceeding the scope of what we might think of as classical mathematical psychology such as is found in learning theory or test theory. To apply effectively methods of systems identification requires that the investigator knows, at least up to some degree of explicit formal representation, what it is that is being sought. One cannot identify the structure or parameters of a dynamic system unless one knows, a priori, what are the most likely competing explanations of how that system functions. This requires much more than a vague discussion about teleology.

In this section some recurrent aspects of system identification that arise when trying to build bridges between psychology and systems theory, using time series data, are briefly reviewed. There is considerable virtue in avoiding setting oneself impossible tasks in systems identification; some of the formal metamathematics at an advanced level in this area is concerned with trying to spell out precisely what can be done and what cannot. The reader is referred to Casti (1979), Granger and Andersen (1978) or Kalman, Falb, and Arbib (1969) for examples.

Disquiet about the adequacy of open-loop stimulus–response descriptions of behavior goes back at least to Dewey in the 1890s (Slack, 1955) and the very term *stimulus* itself has been open to redefinition in attempts to come to terms with evident self-contradictions that ensue when the stimulus is defined as some event in the environment and no more. In motor-tracking tasks the stimulus is defined as a change in the environment, over time, that is necessary but not sufficient for a response to occur; for a response to occur the subject must also have as stored information where he or she is now, and where he or she wants to be. This latter construct, "where the subject wants to be," is something that can move around in space, obviously must persist in time, but may only be defined at or in some fixed time intervals. The argument thus pursued leads to the idea that the existence of a stimulus presupposes the existence of a common frame of reference between the experimenter (or some part of the environment that plays an experimenter-like role for a while) and the subject and defines the *error* signal as the *difference* between *desired* (intended, target) state and a *present* state. This signal is supposed to be the appropriate stimulus value to use in any model of regular stimulus–response relationships that are to make psychological sense.

To complicate matters, the control decisions that are made recurrently in order to minimize errors depend necessarily on estimates of the error, and the estimates are themselves error-loaded, with threshold and bias terms including serial effects and range effects.

The idea that the input to the human actor is a series of signals each of which signifies fairly precisely the direction of error and rather more fuzzily the extent of error builds readily into control theory models of motivation and purposive behavior and facilitates the formal quantitative identification of feedback parameters. The equivalencing of stimulus with error is not just axiomatic, it takes on a key metatheoretical role in linking the psychology of sensation, perception, and motivation to systems theory. Without this explicit redefinition of the stimulus or input as an error signal, the subsumption of some theoretical psychology into systems theory could not be achieved. The role of time series analysis is to identify what the error reducing subsystems of the human organism are and plot their courses through time, where the records in real time show some invariant features upon being repeatedly elicited. The dynamic regularities of systems in action are the expression of the capacities of such systems to bring error to a tolerable minimum; that is precisely what control means. Systems that survive long enough to exhibit regularities are identifiable and capable of control, in principle.

Given this framework, there remains the fearsome task of explaining how a system capable of self-regulation can also learn and forget. Systems theoretic psychology (Miller, 1978; Powers, 1978; Powers, Clark, & McFarland, 1960) has at some stage to augment even the most complex hierarchical feedback structures with a special adaptive subsystem (one that negates entropy growth locally within the system but not in the system plus its immediate environment) that can perhaps cope with the large-scale nonstationarity of the human organism. Nonstationarity as observed from outside can most easily be thought of as created by hierarchical switching between local subsystems each of which is separately equivalent to one stationary feedback system. It does not follow that this is how nonstationarity is created, but hierarchical systems have an appeal for theoretical psychologists because of their parallels with some neurophysiological structures in the higher nervous system—indeed the lowest-order feedback loops in Powers' models are equated tentatively with spinal reflexes or some cranial nerve sensory functions and the higher-order systems with mediation of complex regulatory and cognitive functions such as the perception of invariant relationships in the environment. It is of interest that similarity judgments, which present many intricate problems in psychometrics (Gregson, 1975), are thought by Powers to need a fifth-order hierarchical system for their mediation.

MacKay (1956) early made the point that if we require the organism to have the capacity to make invariant responses to sequence properties then higher-order control is necessarily implicated. There are difficulties, however; it is imperative to distinguish between control of the probability that if an action occurs, it will take the same form and control of the probability that if an action of a given form is to occur, it shall occur in a given time interval. Quite different system properties are entailed in the two cases, and MacKay noted "since the thresholds governing these probabilities are continually changing the probabilities cannot be interpreted as frequencies in an observable time series [p. 40]," they can only be interpreted as the relative frequencies in an imaginary 'ensemble' or population of similar situations.

The identification of the parameters of a single closed loop with a noisy environment (Goodwin & Payne, 1977) is a paradigm task that serves well to illustrate how we must proceed in order to build a link between theory and quantification at the simplest level. This case will be reviewed in more mathematical detail than it ever receives in typical psychological texts because the subsequent questions about the identifiability of systems that can be serial or parallel, and single loop or multiple loop, that have received attention in cognitive psychology, particularly in the context of models of short-term memory and information processing, rest on this simplest case.

Note that in Fig. 3.5.1 there are three combinational points where different time series are coalesced: the comparator C at the closure of the feedback loop, and two others where noise series e_1 and e_2 are algebraically summed into the loop signals. This is a very general form and special cases can be constructed simply by putting one or more series as null. The part inside the dashed line is internal to the organism at any level, but at the first-order level the gain and information sources G_2, G_3, and G_4 can be in the environment and hence observable independently of the closure of the loop. That is, the lower-order loop in a model of human behavior can be externally perturbed (G_2 and G_4) and closed externally through the environment (G_3).

The series s is set externally, from some source H, which in Powers' treat-

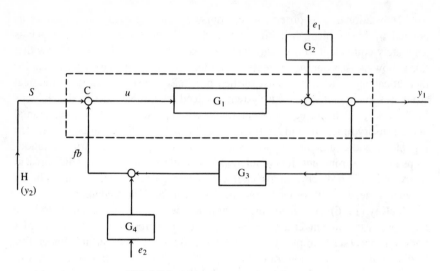

FIG. 3.5.1   Noise perturbed feedback loop.

ment would be the output of a second- or higher-order subsystem. To put this another way, it is not expected that a lower-order feedback system in a living organism sets its own series s, which corresponds to what in engineering terminology is the sequence of set–point values for the loop.

The series s is a time series

$$s = \{s_1, \ldots, s_j, \ldots, s_t\}$$

The actual system input, which is the resultant of the comparator C and is hence an error signal, is the sequence or time series

$$u = \{u_1, \ldots, u_j, \ldots, u_t\}$$

So the input series (which is as close to the simple deterministic notion of a stimulus as one can meaningfully get in considering the functioning of a dynamic system) is a series of algebraic resultants u from the combination of a series fb displacing the system from a desired but noninvariant stability s. The series fb are located in the backward feedback loop path and as shown are themselves generated as a resultant of internal and external signals.

It is important to reiterate that s is not the stimulus series that would be observed from outside; s may be implicit and never seen unless we ask a subject to report something like a series of self-imposed target values or intentions after he or she has received both s_j and fb_j on the jth trial.

The observable input, if the loop is closed through the environment, is e_3 but the sequence fb corresponds to a stimulus series in the sense of a traditional psychophysical experiment, if we distinguish between distal (e_2) and proximal (fb) stimulation. When the output series y has no apparent relation at all to the perturbation series fb, then the experiment is concerned with a system that is functioning adequately under dynamic control, if the output y is within limits equivalent to a fixed gain on the input s. This point is made at length by Powers (1978) using a slightly different algebraic approach. He traces the confusion in psychology about what are the inputs and outputs of a cybernetic loop to Wiener, who conceptualized the picture of Fig. 3.5.1 as a subsystem within an organism, whereas some psychologists have assumed that the cybernetic paradigm is a total organism model, like the psychophysical equations, in which s = stimuli, y = responses, and fb = organismic variables. Although there is little merit in resurrecting dead paradigms, if the feedback loop is to be related to stimulus– organism–response psychology, which is rather a vacuous mapping, then the proper interpretation is stimuli = fb, organismic variables = s, response = y, fb, and noise = e_1, e_2. But there are in fact other more complex ways of mapping the cybernetic loop into behavior.

From the two noise sequences e_1 and e_2 the covariance matrix of error, Σ, is defined for

$$
\begin{vmatrix} \mathbf{e}_1 \\ \mathbf{e}_2 \end{vmatrix} \cdot \begin{vmatrix} \mathbf{e}_1' & \mathbf{e}_2' \end{vmatrix} = \begin{vmatrix} \Sigma_{11} & \Sigma_{12} \\ \Sigma_{21} & \Sigma_{22} \end{vmatrix} = \Sigma \tag{3.5.1}
$$

If it can be said that the process is reasonably, a priori, a single loop closed and perturbed as in Fig. 3.5.1, then the problem can be expressed equivalently as one of asking; Are there meaningful estimates of the transfer functions $\mathbf{G}_1$, $\mathbf{G}_2$, $\mathbf{G}_3$, and $\mathbf{G}_4$ that can be constructed from the observable series, in s, fb, and y?

The analysis of this noisy closed loop has been treated in mathematical detail by Goodwin and Payne (1977); the identification of the quadruple of transfer functions $\{\mathbf{G}_1, \mathbf{G}_2, \mathbf{G}_3, \mathbf{G}_4\}$ may, under restricted conditions, be achieved by computerized solutions of matrix equations in z transforms. There are two main cases to consider: where the two noise sources e_1 and e_2 in Fig. 3.5.1 are correlated, and where they are independent. The latter case is more tractable; the former may have more general a priori relevance to psychological experiments.

For the independence of $\mathbf{e}_1$ and $\mathbf{e}_2$ it is possible to obtain meaningful models, but there are inherent difficulties in establishing if estimates of $\mathbf{G}_2$ and $\mathbf{G}_4$ are of minimum phase, which is a precondition for obtaining correct estimates of $\mathbf{G}_1$–$\mathbf{G}_4$. The problem of identifying the forward path, that is, $\mathbf{G}_1$ and $\mathbf{G}_2$, can be treated separately if the noise sources $\mathbf{e}_1$ and $\mathbf{e}_2$ are uncorrelated. But the models for $\mathbf{G}_1$–$\mathbf{G}_4$ obtained will depend on the factorization (see also examples in Chapter 6) of the input–output z-transform $\Phi_{uy}(z)$, which is a bivariate matrix. Only one of the alternative ways in which $\Phi_{uy}(z)$ can be factored will represent the actual system, as opposed to having an equivalent structure in the sense of fitting observed input–output data reserves.

There is a unique relationship between the quadruple $[\mathbf{G}_1, \mathbf{G}_2, \mathbf{G}_3, \mathbf{G}_4]$ and a matrix $\mathbf{K}$ that, together with the covariance matrix Σ of (3.5.1), defines the transfer function as

$$\phi_{uy}(z) = \mathbf{K}(z) \cdot \Sigma \cdot \mathbf{K}^T(z^{-1}) \tag{3.5.2}$$

This matrix $\mathbf{K}$ can be partitioned into four blocks, corresponding in layout to the terms in (3.5.1), as

$$\mathbf{K} = \left| \begin{array}{c|c} \mathbf{K}_{11} & \mathbf{K}_{12} \\ \hline \mathbf{K}_{21} & \mathbf{K}_{22} \end{array} \right| \tag{3.5.3}$$

and the unique relationship among $\mathbf{G}_1$, $\mathbf{G}_2$, $\mathbf{G}_3$, $\mathbf{G}_4$, and $\mathbf{K}$ is

$$\left. \begin{array}{l} \mathbf{G}_1 = \mathbf{K}_{12}\mathbf{K}_{22}^{-1} \\[4pt] \mathbf{G}_2 = \mathbf{K}_{11} - \mathbf{K}_{12}\mathbf{K}_{22}^{-1}\mathbf{K}_{21} \\[4pt] \mathbf{G}_3 = \mathbf{K}_{21}\mathbf{K}_{11}^{-1} \\[4pt] \mathbf{G}_4 = \mathbf{K}_{22} - \mathbf{K}_{21}\mathbf{K}_{11}^{-1}\mathbf{K}_{12} \end{array} \right\} \tag{3.5.4}$$

(This bordered section may be omitted on a first reading.)

To digress briefly and anticipate some results on state space models (see Chapter 5), it is possible to set up a parallel form of description to Fig. 3.5.1 and to define its relation with the $\Phi_{uy}(z)$ approach outlined previously.

Writing as a general form

$$y_j = \Sigma \, \mathbf{G}(j, k)u_{j-k} - \Sigma \, \mathbf{F}(j, k)y_{j-k} \tag{3.5.5}$$

which is an ARMA with $\{\mathbf{G}\}$ as coefficients of past inputs and $\{\mathbf{F}\}$ as coefficients of past outputs, z transforms can be defined as

$$F^*(z) = \overset{m}{\underset{\Sigma}{}} Fkz^{m-k} \tag{3.5.6}$$

and similarly for $G^*(z)$, $u^*(z)$. The input–output overall system, in z transforms, is

$$Y(z) = H(z) \cdot U(z) \tag{3.5.7}$$

and from (3.5.5) and (3.5.6)

$$H(z) = [F^*(z)]^{-1}[G^*(z)] \tag{3.5.8}$$

The right-hand side of (3.5.8) is called a *matrix factor description* (MFD) of $H(z)$.

As it is the case that

$$\left. \begin{array}{l} F^*(z) = z^m F(z) \\[8pt] G^*(z) = z^m G(z) \end{array} \right\} \tag{3.5.9}$$

we can also write

$$H(z) = [F(z)]^{-1} \cdot [G(z)] \tag{3.5.10}$$

or

$$F(z) \cdot Y(z) = G(z) \cdot U(z) \tag{3.5.11}$$

which parallels the general Box–Jenkins representation as a quotient of two polynomials in backward shift operations.

The alternative state space representation of the process in Fig. 3.5.1 can be written (see Chapters 1 and 5) as

$$\left.\begin{aligned} \mathbf{A}\mathbf{y}_j &= \mathbf{B}\mathbf{u}_j + \mathbf{C}e_{ij} \\ \mathbf{E}\,u_j &= \mathbf{F}\mathbf{y}_j + \mathbf{L}e_{2j} \end{aligned}\right\} \tag{3.5.12}$$

where $\mathbf{A}$, $\mathbf{B}$, $\mathbf{C}$, $\mathbf{E}$, $\mathbf{F}$, and $\mathbf{L}$ are all polynomial matrices in z^{-1}.

There are two MFDs for this system, which are

$$[\mathbf{G}_1 : \mathbf{G}_2] = \mathbf{A}^{*-1}[\mathbf{B}^* : \mathbf{C}^*] \tag{3.5.13}$$

and

$$[\mathbf{G}_3 : \mathbf{G}_4] = \mathbf{E}^{*-1}[\mathbf{F}^* : \mathbf{L}^*] \tag{3.5.14}$$

The (3.5.13) is an MFD for the forward part of the system, and (3.5.14) is for the backward part.

The method, which has been computerized in some cases, is called joint input–output identification. It can be powerful because sometimes it works with a minimum prior knowledge of the structure of the system. Interestingly it is not necessary for $\mathbf{A}^*$ and $\mathbf{E}^*$ to be stable, which means that an open-loop unstable system is potentially identifiable provided that the closed loops within it are stable. The case that is of potential interest to psychological theory arises when we can assume that the noise $\mathbf{G}_4$ is negligible; this means that stimuli are very accurately measurable compared with other measurements of inputs to the system. It is then possible to identify $\mathbf{G}_1$, $\mathbf{G}_2$, and $\mathbf{G}_3$ even if $\{s_j\}$ is never measured or observed.

Goodwin and Payne (1977) extend the analysis to cases of linear systems with time-varying structure and provide a recursive least-squares algorithm. The argument leads into methods resembling a Kalman filter (see Chapter 5), but the previous treatment is valuable for delineating the conditions under which identifiability of the gains within a single loop is formally possible.

Identifiability, in the wider and less rigorous sense, particularly centers on the question of the possibility of deciding if a memory process works in series or in parallel from examination of the inputs and outputs. This question may on the surface seem to resemble the general problem we have just formalized, but in fact it is more complicated, for at least two important reasons. These are, first, that psychologists have generally given sparse and inadequate attention to the problem of what sort of stationarity, if any, they assume when constructing a model of items going into and out of memory (i.e., learning and forgetting) and, second, systems theory models at the level of analysis reviewed here do not involve parametric specification of how long events will take to be transformed through gains and round loops and in and out of comparators, though at all stages it is assumed that things are not instantaneous but take finite time to happen. When these finite times are of the same order of magnitude as the time to go round a loop, or longer, then there are horrendous dangers in the assumption that the system can be analyzed by freezing it in time or treating it as a series of discrete steps in sequence. Powers (1978) gives worked examples; he states

one persistent and incorrect approach to feedback phenomena is to treat an organism as a . . . system, with any feedback effects being treated as if they occurred separately, after one response and before the next . . . qualitatively this seems to work   but . . . (it) . . . fails   quantitatively . . . the   stimulus–response–stimulus–response–stimulus–response . . . analysis seems to succeed only because of the limitations of verbal or qualitative reasoning. [p. 420

He continues: "treating behavior as a succession of instantaneous events propagating around a closed loop will not yeld a correct analysis, no matter how tiny the steps are made [p. 432]."

An extensive contrasting of views on the identifiability questions with respect to cognitive processes is offered by Anderson (1978) and Anderson, Hayes-Roth, and Pylyshyn all separately in 1979, in *Psychological Review*. The dispute there centers on the problem of whether the input–output relations of mental imagery could themselves ever settle the question of how the images of sets of related things are encoded, as sorts of pictures or as propositions taking as arguments the encoded representation of attributes.

There are, of course, at least two other main distinct areas of modeling in which the identifiability question presents special difficulties for theoretical psychologists. As just mentioned, there are: (1) problems of deciding from outputs and the times to produce outputs what the central representation is given that the subject can match, identify from a class of similar alternative events, estimate degrees of similarity consistently, create confusions of identity, exhibit partial recall of attributes from entities, and so on; also there are; (2) problems in deciding if matching operations of output to assorted targets (a recognition or detection paradigm) is serial, parallel, or hybrid serial–parallel in structure; and (3) problems in deciding if central subsystems are open- or closed-loop, serial or parallel given that they process series inputs and produce series outputs.

Cases 1 and 2 involve, as usually raised (Townsend, 1972, 1974), the explicit and indeed central considerations of total processing times, which are virtually synonymous with reaction times, so that a complete failure to identify arises only when two or more models match outputs not only in their content but at least stochastically in their temporal event distributions; this is rather like matching the l.t.f. coefficients but is much more restrictive because of the additional constraints on the plausible form that outputs from a recall and identification process can take. In Case 3, identification is usually in terms of l.t.f.s. for the system as a whole that is quantitatively more precise but conceptually in some ways less complex. So it is possible to invent examples of two systems that would not be identifiable (in the sense of being told apart solely on their input–output l.t.f.s for a given class of stimuli) quantitatively but would be identifiable in terms of the relative probabilities of different classes of outputs (different symbolic representations of inputs, for example), or the converse might hold in which two systems were qualitatively unidentifiable but were quantitatively different, in terms of l.t.f.s or total processing times. Now there are powerful general theorems about identifiability, which are concerned with the identification of the minimum-complexity structure of systems given their quantitative input–output relations and nothing else; unless it can be shown that the argument for identifiability from processing times stands outside these general theorems, the processing times of themselves are not sufficient information to identify a process structure.

Townsend (1972) has clearly offered the most thorough and rigorous analysis of the serial–parallel identifiability problem and demonstrated in a number of reviews that the general question of the identifiability of the two classes of processor is not answerable without very detailed specification of the rules governing the processing of elements and the distribution of processing times. The actual definitions employed change slightly with the development and the mathematical level of analysis; identifiability here is defined over a class of systems rather than over single systems, so that the question of what process is operating is answered and only answered in terms of classes, such as serial models, serial terminating models, parallel models, and parallel intercorrelated models. The process to be identified is defined so that, given any set of elements already processed and their order of completion, the set of processing rates for the remaining elements will be constant. This is readily seen to be a sort of stationarity condition.

Probability mixtures, particularly of parallel systems, may exist, in which case they are defined in such a way that on any one trial one and only one of a set of parallel processes will be in operation. Thus to specify the mixture distribution is also to give the generator for a set of switching rules between processors; this can be like a Markov process specified by a transition probability matrix, where the states of the Markov chain are the different processors. In the more formal treatment of the problem (Townsend, 1972) the distribution of completion times for processing elements is given as an exponential form, but Erlang and gamma distributions are also postulated. By axiomatizing the processes in this way it is feasible to use results from queuing theory and renewal processes (see Section 2.1). The following general results are offered and proved for three parallel channels or for a more general case of n channels.

1. A mixed parallel system cannot be equivalent to a mixed serial system.

2. There exist serial systems for which no unmixed parallel systems are equivalent.

3. The class of unmixed parallel systems can be mimicked by special cases of the class of mixed serial systems.

4. A limited capacity parallel independent model can predict the same as a serial model with respect to the processing times of individual elements or predict the same relation between n, the total number of elements to be processed, and the total processing time.

If we restrict ourselves to the prediction solely of mean processing times, then this would be equivalent to predicting the performance of only deterministic systems, which is predicting at the level of the means but not predicting the distributions or higher moments of processing times.

An input that is a magnitude (tagged by a description) at a point in time reslts in an output that is also a single event; for example, presenting the symbol "4" results in the utterance, after a delay, of the word "four," and how long it takes to utter "four" is of no interest, but how long it takes before the subject begins to utter the word is the critical feature of the information processing system in which we are interested.

As time series, such inputs and outputs are δ functions (1 at some point in time, 0 elsewhere) with, for the output, a response delay of t_r, as in Fig. 3.5.2.

The distribution over replications of the delay t_r is $g(t_r)$, which Townsend initially took as exponential, an empirically realistic and tractable assumption. But it is necessary to establish a more general equivalence in terms of such distributions to prove an existence theorem that equates some parallel to some serial processes and thus contraindicates identifiability in the restricted, class, sense defined previously. It can be proved (Townsend, 1972) by first establishing the equivalence of a mixed serial system to a parallel system by describing $g(t_r)$ as a mixture of gamma distributions. Then it can be shown that some probability mixture of gamma distributions converges to a mixture of δ functions, which in turn converges weakly (i.e., by arbitrary close approximation) to any probability density function whatsoever. This latter step is a general result in the statistics of sampled-data systems (Krut'ko, 1969). This proof of a series of formal equivalences of families of probability distributions upon response delays in processing is necessary in order to demonstrate very generally that we can have, to a desired degree of precision, mimicking and hence loss of identifiability between the mixed serial and parallel classes of processes, where the inputs and outputs are stimuli and responses that can be represented as vectors of qualities occurring instantaneously. The processing here is thus a very restricted, almost limiting case, of the dynamic transfer models considered previously. Townsend provisionally concluded that the evidence of reaction times in disjunctive choice and identification tasks, taken with considerations of information

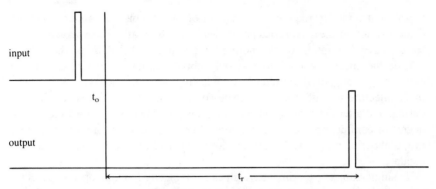

FIG. 3.5.2 Pure response delay.

processing and parsimony of process structure, gives slightly more weight to some forms of parallel processing, but the "parallel serial question should be ruled as unresolved in most of the contexts in which it has been studied."

It should be noted that the previous analyses make no explicit mention of stationarity but do presuppose it. The models set up to describe human memory and performance in cognitive tasks attempt to find parameter values for processes that are invariant across experiments or across classes of experiments. In this sense subjects are taken to be stationary in the parameters of their cognitive processes during fixed experimental conditions, after preasymptotic conditions have been worked through. The general theorems about systems equivalence under stationarity, and only under stationarity, which make identifiability of a system under stationarity from input and output records alone a logical impossibility, are further noted in Section 5.2.

3.6 IDENTIFYING EMBEDDED EPISODES WITHIN TIME SERIES

Within a long time series one may readily expect to find episodes, or short runs, that differ in character from the main series. This can arise either because the experimenter sets out deliberately to make a local change occur, and sustain it for some required period, or because temporarily things get out of control. It is possible to think of such episodes as time periods in which the main process underlying the time series temporarily surrenders control to some other process, only to take back control later. How such episodes, embedded within a longer series, are identified and parameterized depends entirely on what previous knowledge can be brought to bear on their identification and what can be measured or recorded for subsequent analysis. Many psychological experiments are embedded episodes within the life history of the subject, and the quantification of the multivariate properties of response during the specifiable conditions of an experiment typically requires the creation of measurement procedures and the determination of the time series properties before and after the experiment, as a steady-state description of the normal, unperturbed, behavior of the subject outside the specific conditions that only obtain during the experiment. If the experiment is supposed to produce some lasting change in behavior, then to test this conjecture it is necessary to create some measures on time series, before, during, and after the experiment such that it is possible to say, with a specifiable degree of confidence, that the conditions after the experiment are closer to those in the experimental episode than to those that held before the experiment was begun.

In single-subject experiments, such as are typically found in operant psychology or behavior modification studies, the preexperiment time series is called a *baseline condition,* and it is said that control is established over behavior when the mean rate of responding in some previously specified way is raised or lowered during the experiment and returned to baseline levels after the experiment. This process can be repeated during the history of one subject, and very considerable ingenuity has been demonstrated by experimenters in devising what are called schedules of reinforcement, which are in effect quasi-random time series of input variables, to move rates of responding up or down. However, many hundreds of such experiments were successfully done before the possibility of analyzing them as time series with embedded episodes was seriously examined. A very important paper by Box and Tiao (1965), on time series with interventions, created the statistical methodology for embedded episodes of known location but unknown magnitude to be analyzed in the framework of the general linear model. That is, with a suitable choice of transformation of response variables, which presupposes that the ARMA structure of the preexperimental situation is identifiable, and is itself sustained with a single parameter change (i.e., a shift in mean output) during the embedded episode, it is possible to treat the whole time series as a problem akin to an analysis of variance. There are obviously serious problems in this approach, however, before analysis ever begins, because we may very reasonably think that the autocorrelation structure of the time series of responses may be the thing that changes during the embedded episode, and at the same time the mean rate or mean level of responding may be of minor interest. The difficulties are serious precisely because practical experimental designs are typically much too short to facilitate the independent stable estimation of parameters in the episode or intervention within the basic time series, and commonly the preepisode and postepisode samples of the time series are themselves very brief. The common criticism that experiments are not run long enough to establish that the initial state is really dynamically stationary is a justified one. The equally common criticism that follow-up studies, to see if the effects of intervention in an episode are lasting after the intervention has ceased are much too short, is equally pertinent. In a poorly designed study the last observation in the follow-up may be predominantly a response to the onset of the intervention period, when the sequential dependency of the basic process extends over more trials than the intervention. This need not be in any way discernible from visual inspection of the records of behavior over time; only an examination of the structure of the time series, over adequate samples, in either the time or frequency domains, can reveal the minimum length of an interpretable intervention experiment.

The uncertainty about an embedded episode is related to all its features: for example,

1. Uncertainty about the precise onset and end points in time, expressed as prior probability distributions, of the embedded episode. This uncertainty obviously disappears in planned experiments, but it does not disappear in the post hoc examinations of records of quasi-experiments. In fact, records of time series may be collected as a means toward finding out where episodes occurred, if they occurred at all.

2. Uncertainty about the stationarity during an episode; an intervention may be characterized as a local, temporary, loss of stationarity. The mean drifts up or down or breaks loose and meanders erratically; then it returns to stationarity after the episode is over.

3. Uncertainty about covariance stationarity during the intervention, a problem similar to type 2 but more complex.

4. Uncertainty as to whether the embedded episode results in the addition or the superposition of another process in time, or if the basic process is completely replaced by an alternative time series associated uniquely with a single state of the system.

These four sorts of uncertainty are sufficient to make the theorist pause for reflection without adding more; obviously they can occur singly or in combination. The few cases that have been considered in detail (Glass, Willson, & Gottman, 1975) assume that the onset and duration of an intervention episode is known, that covariance stationarity holds, that the intervention results in a shift in a mean level of the forcing or input to the system, and that the embedded episode is additive rather than replacing in its operation. This is, in the previous scheme, one fairly tractable case from a logical possibility of at least 16, some of which have been explored ad hoc in various disciplines, to which we refer briefly.

In what might be called a traditional view of scientific method, any experiment that was beset by two or more of the types of uncertainty given would be called badly designed, or no sort of experiment at all. If there does exist a time series before intervention that does support a detailed dynamic analysis, then the traditional view is excessively conservative. It is as well to recall that the usual advice given about experimental designs presupposes that means and variances will be the sufficient statistics to define behavior within a state or treatment, before some other intervention occurs. In time series analysis this is not true; considerably more information about process structure is and must be available. Consequently there are in principle more ways in which discontinuities in behavior contingent upon intervention, and recorded by an embedded episode, can be detected.

In this section two general problems about embedded episodes are reviewed; first, a problem that arises in searching for features of evoked potentials (which are short time series, about 600 msec long, of fairly stable and reliable form, arising in electroencephalographic records as a response to impulse inputs); second, a comment on some single-subject models, derived from the Box and Tiao (1965) precedent. When searching for evoked potentials, investigators have tried a wide diversity of techniques (some reviewed by John, 1977; John, Ruchkin, & Vidal, 1978) depending on prior information and what particular details of the evoked potential are of interest. Very detailed hypotheses concerning what should happen in a noisy time series, with some energy at fixed frequencies, when the embedded episode is expected to be an evoked potential, can be constructed. Birkemeier, Fontaine, Celesin, and Ma (1978) consider the case of epileptic transients in EEGs. At the opposite extreme a conditioning experiment to modify behavior may not be able to be specified at all precisely in advance, beyond stating the direction in which a mean level of responding would shift. The two paradigms demand, therefore, different approaches.

Consider a data matrix, X, of m time series samples, each N trials long.

$$X = \begin{vmatrix} x_{11} & \cdots & x_{1N} \\ x_{m1} & \cdots & x_{mn} \end{vmatrix}$$

The ensemble averages are then the vectors $(_e x_i)$, where

$$e^x i = m^{-1} \sum_{j=1}^{m} x_{ji} \tag{3.6.1}$$

Let us assume that $x_{ji} \sim N (_e x_i, {}_e \sigma_i^2)$ and that the variance $_e \sigma_i^2$ is a function of the location of a signal in time, measured as elapsed from a defined zero. The data that are given are not time-locked so that they are not phase-locked and unless grossly aliased will necessarily be in most cases mutually out of phase.

Each sample series X_{ji}, $i = 1, 2, \ldots, N$ has embedded in it, with a prior probability not less than $(m - 1)/m$, a sequence, E_i, of length less than N, which is known to be slightly distorted; that is, it is contaminated with noise or drift. This sequence E_i is the realization of an episode, E^*. The precise starting point is not known a priori, so the starting points over the component series of an ensemble may exhibit second-order variation in the starting point denoted by $i = i_0$ and in length of E_i. The variations in amplitude and in the form of E^* will be treated as orthogonal to those in the starting point.

TABLE 3.6.1
Identification of Embedded Episodes
Various Conditions

		Form	
		Known[a]	Unknown
Location	Known	Parameters of scale	Shifts in level or a discriminant problem
	Unknown	Phase-locked identification with unknown parametrization and S/N ratios	Only solvable given stationarity and covariance stationarity of the contextual series and the possibility of phase-locked identification

[a]Known in the affirmative sense; the alternative of being known by elimination up to a restricted set of alternatives is subsumed under "unknown."

The definition of the starting point i_0 has, for practical reasons, to be defined in terms of some x_{ji} that is expected to be outside the mean noise bandwidth. Unless the first element of the set of observations that might be the embedded episode is an outlier from the noise variability in the system, it cannot be picked up by a simple filter using minimal data. It may be necessary to test hypotheses concerning the genesis and observable shape of E. Following the general considerations already outlined about embedded episodes, three cases will be distinguished.

1. The basic process generating x_{ji} can be η, i.i.d.; but when E^* starts, then E_i completely replaces η as though the system can switch instantaneously between two mutually exclusive states, η^* and E^*, of the system. Once the process is in E^*, it runs its course for at least the greater part of its expected length, unbroken, so that it does not transiently relapse back into η^*.

2. The basic process generating x_{ji} is η^* as a continuous i.i.d. series (in discretely sampled time); but when E^* occurs, it is linearly superimposed upon η^* so that what is observed, as y_{ji}, is

$$\alpha \cdot E_i + (1 - \alpha) \cdot \eta_i = y_{ji} \tag{3.6.2}$$

where α is a scalar that is the square root of the expected signal/noise power ratio on the ith trial. For simplicity, $\alpha_i = \alpha$ for all i for which E_i is nonzero within E^*. As η_i is i.i.d., the ensemble average of y_{ji}, $_e y_i$, is given by

$$_e y_i = E_i + _e x_i \tag{3.6.3}$$

if and only if the E_i are phase-locked to start at the same i_0 in all $j \in m$.

3. The observed series (x_{ji}) is a convolution of an input series I_j that is not directly observable but resembles a step function, within a longer autocorrelated process ξ_j, so that

$$\xi(z) = x_{\eta}(z) \tag{3.6.4}$$

across the ranges where I_j does not extend, and

$$x_{\xi}(z) = \eta(z) \cdot I(z) \tag{3.6.5}$$

across the range of the embedded episode E^*. In this case the problem is one of deconvolution, and an observed episode E_i (which may, for example, be an evoked potential within an EEG time series) is interpreted as the output, in time, of the convolution of the series I_j on the process ξ that itself may be thought of as the consequence of applying a filter $\phi(z)$ to white noise such that

$$\xi(z) = \phi(z) \cdot \eta(z) \tag{3.3.6}$$

In practice, for evoked potentials, this would not be the usual way to proceed in the identification problem for E^*; instead the evoked potential is taken to be a replicable phenomenon in the time domain, even if it is generated by some underlying process so that what is observed is $z^{-1}(x_{\xi}(z))$. To identify the process E^* as underlying the realization E_i that is defined by the time-locked average of earlier realizations in a sense avoids, or better perhaps, skates around, the identification and interpretation problems attendant upon (3.6.5) and (3.6.6).

Consider then some problems in identifying embedded episodes in the sense of Case 2, because Case 1 can be derived from Case 2 as $\alpha \rightarrow 1$ and if observed is trivial because visual inspection will suffice for any j. The argument is expressed in terms of an ensemble of records from a single subject, so that variations in parameters between subjects are not considered.

Three identification problems follow:

1. Location of the starting point i_{j0} in the jth realization of E^*.
2. Location of a marker characteristic; a stable first maximum or minimum, which is an empirically reliable extremum value within E^*.
3. Utilization of the total estimated episode E^* by treating $\{E_i\}$ as a set of sufficient statistics. There are two ways of encoding an episode, both of which have their merits. If it is believed that there exists some subset of points $\{B\}$ within $\{E_i\}$, each characterized by a magnitude and a latency (after i_0), which is stable and interpretable under fixed endogenous conditions and that the remaining set $\{E_i - B\}$ is of minor importance, then each $b_i \in \{B\}$ can be characterized by a vector b and the set $\{b\}$ matched to a corresponding set $\{\beta\}$ drawn from $\{x_{ji}\}$ at and after the starting point i_0. This is essentially template matching at critical points only; it throws away information and hence its statistical efficiency is indeterminate. If a series can be filtered before matching, then consideration has to be given to the question of how the filter will enhance the differences between $\{b\}$ and a corresponding set of vectors based on $\{E_i - B\}$.

The Prior Distribution on the Embedded Starting Point

Given that $\eta_i \sim N(0, \sigma_\eta)$ contains the episode and that η^* is i.i.d., if E_i is a realization of E^* of length δ where δ is known; then if

$$E_i \sim N(\theta_i, \sigma_e)$$

the observed

$$x_{ji} \sim N(\theta_i, (\sigma_\eta^2 + \sigma_e^2)^{1/2}) \tag{3.6.7}$$

The starting point $i_0 = 1, 2, \ldots, N - \delta$ is to be found assuming that all embedded episodes are observed completely or not at all.

From a rectangular prior on i_0,

$$p[E^*|i] = \left[\frac{\delta}{(N - \delta)} \right] \qquad \text{for } 1 \leq i \leq N - \delta$$

$$\text{for } \delta + 1 \leq i \leq N$$

$$= 1 \qquad \text{for } N - \delta \leq i \leq \delta + 1 \tag{3.6.8}$$

And

$$p([\eta^*|i]) = \left[\frac{(N - \delta)}{N} \right] \qquad \text{for } 1 \leq i \leq \delta -$$

$$\text{for } \delta + 1 \leq i \leq N$$

$$= 0 \qquad \text{for } N - \delta \leq i \leq \delta + 1 \tag{3.6.9}$$

If $\delta > N/2$, then there exists a set of points that can be asserted to be certainly within E^* in the middle of a sample. This information might be used to phase-lock the episodes between two j, j' in an ensemble without making any a priori assumptions about the shape of the E^* as a template.

The probability that an observed x_{ji} is a member of E_i and hence generated by (3.6.7) is

$$p[E^*|x_i] = \frac{p[x_i|E^*] \cdot p[E^*|i]}{P[x_i|E^*] \cdot p[E^*|i] + p[x_i|\eta^*] \cdot p[\eta^*|i]} \tag{3.6.10}$$

There are two sorts of ancillary knowledge that may be used to simplify the argument (John, 1977); first, that $\sigma_e^2 \ll \sigma_\eta^2$, which is an argument about the relative reliability of E_i as against η_i after phase-locking; second, that there exists a series of peaks (valleys) $\{b\}$ that are well outside $\pm 2\sigma_\eta$. This second point can be combined with (3.6.8) to assist identification.

The posterior likelihood that a peak is in E^* is given by

$$\frac{p[E^*|x_{ji}]}{p[\eta^*|x_{ji}]} = \frac{p[x_{ji}|E^*] \cdot p[E^*|i]}{p[x_{ji}|\eta^*] \cdot p[\eta^*|i]} \tag{3.6.11}$$

which only applies when the peak examined is outside $N - \delta \leq i \leq \delta + 1$, from (3.6.9).

The decision rule entailed by (3.6.11) is, if

$$\frac{p[E^*|x_{ji}]}{p[\eta^*|x_{ji}]} \geq k \tag{3.6.12}$$

then accept E_i, where $k = a$ (expected from first peak of $E^*/1.96\sigma_\eta$) and a is a measure of amplitude.

Instead of $p(x_{ji}|H)$ in (3.6.11), the distribution properties of (3.6.7) may be used, rather than assuming that $\sigma_e^2 \ll \sigma_\eta^2$.

The likelihood ratio of interest is then, a priori,

$$\lambda_i = \frac{P[\theta_i - 1.96\sigma_e \leq x_{ji} \leq \theta_i + 1.96\sigma_e|E^*] \cdot p[E^*|i]}{P[\theta_i - 1.96\sigma_\eta \leq x_{ji} \leq \theta_i + 1.96\sigma_\eta|\eta^*] \cdot p[\eta^*|i]} \tag{3.6.13}$$

But as θ_i is not phase-locked in this expression, it is necessary to replace θ_i with $b_{i - i_0}$, which is the magnitude of the peak expected at $i - i_0$ steps after the start of E_i. Or, more diffusely, we may use the fact that

$$\theta_i \sim E'(\theta, \sigma_\theta)$$

over the episode E^* and replace σ_e in (3.6.13) with σ_θ. Again, (3.6.13) applies outside the range of (3.6.9).

Now, the generalization of λ_i to some subsequence of length δ, which is an estimate of the temporal location of E^*, is

$$\lambda^{(\delta)} = \prod_{k=i_0}^{i_0+\delta-1} \lambda_k \tag{3.6.14}$$

which is more tractable in the log likelihood form of

$$\ln \lambda = \delta^{-1} \Sigma \log \lambda_k \tag{3.6.15}$$

Actually this is not the most efficient use of information, because if (3.6.13) identifies a peak, so that $\lambda_i > k$, then immediately this implies constraints on the values of θ_k at all k in (3.6.14): The set $[b]$ enables the confidence region on $\{\theta_k\}$ to narrow if the form of E^* is a priori stable for at least a subset B.

A strategy that suggests itself is therefore to estimate

$$\lambda_{i_0}^{(\delta)}, \quad i_0 = 1, 2, \ldots, N - \delta$$

or the equivalent log likelihood from (3.6.15), such that for some subset B

$$\lambda_{i_0}^{(\delta)} = \prod_{k \in B|i_0} \lambda_k \tag{3.6.16}$$

and take the maximum of (3.6.16) as an indicator of where i_0 is to be found.

The argument so far has been concerned with finding a single embedded episode in a single realization and then using the location estimates to phase-lock each separate realization before calculating ensemble averages and signal-to-noise ratios. According to John (1977), simple estimates of the form

$$\frac{\sigma_{ei}^2}{(\sigma_{ei}^2 + \sigma_{\eta i}^2)} \qquad i = 1, 2, \ldots, N$$

are suitable (though there are some errors in other formulas given therein).

Yet another device suggests itself for an uncontaminated estimate of $\sigma_{\eta i}^2$, given that the intraensemble or interseries variance in the subset of trials $N - \delta$, $\delta + 1$ is an estimate of the variance where E^* as in (3.6.7) holds.

The analysis given makes negligible use of the autocorrelation structure of η^* and of E^*; in fact, if it is known that E^* is identifiable in its major features by a low-pass filtering leaving those features conspicuous, and if η^* is largely removed by the same filter, then cepstrum analysis (Tukey, 1967; Hassab, 1977) is pertinent. However, remaining in the time domain, the series x_{ji} can be split into three parts, any one of which may be null; these are

$$\eta_1^*, \qquad i = 1, 2, \ldots, i_0 - 1$$

$$E^*, \qquad i = i_0, \ldots, i_0 + \delta - 1$$

$$\eta_2^*, \qquad i = i_0 + \delta, \ldots, N$$

For η^*, the autocorrelation spectrum is $r(x, x, k)$, $k = 0, \ldots, f$ which has $\epsilon(r(x, x, k)) = 0$, $\epsilon(r^2(x, x, k)) = N^{-1}$ (approximately, see McLeod, 1977); whereas for E^*, based on a typical model (E_i), which is fairly smooth and low frequency,

$$r(E_i, E_{i+k}) = \rho^{|k|}, \qquad k = 0, \ldots, f$$

with ρ estimated, as a first approximation. The problem here is the inadequacy of series length for the accurate estimation of the autocorrelations for all but very small f.

However, the series of ratios

$$R_k = \frac{r(E_i, E_{i+k})}{r(x, x, k)}, \quad k = 0, \ldots, f$$

can be calculated for each i_0, $i_0 = 1, \ldots, N - \delta$, as a moving sample base. Transforming the correlations to $z = \tanh^{-1} r$,

$$Rz_k = \frac{\tanh^{-1}(r(E_i, E_{i+k}))}{\tanh^{-1}(r(x, x, k))} \tag{3.6.17}$$

which is a ratio of two normal deviates, each with variance $(n - 3)^{-1}$ for larger samples, having a Cauchy distribution (Kendall & Stuart, 1963). This provides possible confidence limits on Rz_k^2 based on a t-distribution with d.f. $= 2$. If it is assumed that successive estimates of autocorrelations are approximately independent, then for large samples the set $\{Rz_k^2\}$ might be treated as a union–intersection problem in the sense of Rao (1952) or as a multivariate t-distribution, (Dunnett, 1955; Press, 1972). Vectors Rz_k provide a basis for using discriminant analyses to separate samples of embedded episodes into different subclauses; with a Monte Carlo collection of noise records and reference episodes with known origins and properties, discriminant functions can be calculated for the subsequent identification of new episodes.

An Example of the Use of (3.6.17)

Different samples of time series, obtained under conditions about which it is reasonable to predict the occurrence of particular data patterns such as embedded episodes of a specifiable form, can be analyzed in an exploratory fashion using equation (3.6.17). The following example is based on EEG records obtained under two conditions, with and without very brief visual stimulation with pinpoint lights in the periphery of the visual field. These unpublished data were collected by D. A. R. Smith about 1979 at the University of Canterbury, New Zealand, to whom thanks are due. EEG records were fed on-line through an analog–digital converter to a PDP11/10 computer with augmented storage. The program for analysis was written by the author, records of up to 500 msec in length being stored on tape cassettes and accessed as required.

Epochs of EEG recordings, from a single electrode on a normal subject, were made by sampling at 5-msec intervals in time series of 100 observations. This frequency of observation does not alias the frequencies in the low range of interest, and signals above about 45 Hz are filtered by a low-pass filter with some roll-off around that figure. Recordings were made to resting behavior, with no stimulation, and to periods where an evoked potential was expected to be found, starting at a point known a priori, from calibration runs, to within 50 msec. The evoked potential is expected to be an episode, about 300 msec long, of a striking and characteristic form in which the earlier peaks and valleys are linked to physiological processes in the brain and are relatively stable, whereas the later fluctuations, of smaller amplitude, are apparently more labile and can be moved by exogenous psychological processes, such as induced expectations concerning the form of a signal before it occurs.

The recordings were repeated a number of times, so that a pair of series, $\{N_j\}$, $\{E_j\}$, refer first to a series of noise, probably with 10 Hz present, and second to a paired sequence, taken a few seconds later with an evoked potential believed to be present. Separate analyses, displaying the signals on a VDU, and also averaging series and comparing averaged time-locked series with templates, were available as well and were performed in some cases.

The objective here is to assess the comparability of the autocorrelation spectra of the samples; as seen, this is additional information to that provided by the autocorrelation and crosscorrelation spectra themselves.

For four series, $\{N_j\}$, $\{E_j\}$, $\{N_{j'}\}$, and $\{E_{j'}\}$ it is possible to obtain the following:

1. The autocorrelation spectra in each case up to about lag 8.
2. All the six crosscorrelations, $r(N, N)$, $r(N, E)$, $r(E, E)$, and $r(E, N)$.
3. The l.t.f. coefficients $\{v_k\}$ for each pairing in item 2.
4. The terms of the multivariate t-distribution of (3.6.17). Here we just examine, for illustration, four Rz_1^2 series, for $N_1, N_2; N_1, E_2; N_2, E_1$; and N_2, E_2.

We have, then, as hypotheses, that:

1. H:Null: The Rz_k^2 for N_1, N_2 will all be within the 95% confidence limits of the multivariate t-distribution with seven dimensions.
2. H:Potentials: If the samples E_1 and E_2 are sampled within a series at a phase-locked starting point, the subsamples will have Rz_k^2 within the 95% confidence limits of the multivariate t-distribution.

As the differences between the relatively low-frequency spectrum of an evoked potential and the high-frequency spectrum of noise and alpha mixed would be expected to show in the autocorrelations over greater lags, the Rz_k^2 should in the case of mismatches fall outside the 95% confidence limits at the higher k values. As there were no data from previous experiments to assess the distribution of computed Rz_k^2 terms and see if their intersample distribution was in fact multivariate t, these figures should be interpreted with caution; the whole procedure can be hypersensitive to variations within a set of homogenous time series due to nonstationarity over the length of the samples.

The matrix of Rz_k^2 values is shown as (3.6.18):

k	N_1, N_2	N_1, E_2	E_1, N_2	E_1, E_2	
0	1	1	1	1	
1	1.77	.92	1.02	.53	
2	1.57	.96	1.32	.80	
3	.76	1.39	.98	1.78	(3.6.18)
4	3.65	1.34	12.76*	4.67*	
5	1.94	16.78*	.42	3.64	
6	3.55	26.66*	.49	3.69	
7	4.96*	14.02*	.17*	.48	

The corresponding coefficients $\{v_k\}$ are set out in [3.6.19]:

k	N_1, N_2	N_1, E_2	E_1, N_2	E_1, E_2
0	$-.16$	0	.04	$-.37$
1	$-.25$	.19	.10	$-.52$
2	$-.26$	.25	0	$-.47$
3	$-.26$	.36	$-.19$	$-.27$
4	$-.27$	.44	$-.02$	$-.36$
5	$-.21$	.34	$-.11$	$-.27$
6	$-.06$	.33	$-.19$	.09
7	0	.40	$-.07$	.05

$$(3.6.19)$$

Note that in (3.6.18) the row for $k = 0$ must be 1 by definition, as the terms are based on the ratio of two autocorrelations of lag zero, whereas in (3.6.19) the terms for $k = 0$ are based on crosscorrelations of bivariate series. The data in this example were deliberately chosen because they are typically "dirty," being mathematically an ill-defined mixture with nonstationarities and transients. The signs in (3.6.19) are of little import; the two largest coefficients in the last column are where the largest coefficients should be, given the weak phase-locking of the two series. If E_2 is progressively shifted relative to E_1, the last column of (3.6.19) reads, prior to the phase difference of (3.6.19) (i.e., 10 msec earlier), as $-.17$, $-.14$, $-.35$, $-.48$, $-.41$, $-.19$, . . . and after [i.e., E_2 10 msec later than in (3.6.19)], as $-.51$, $-.33$, $-.44$, $-.35$, .04, $-.02$, . . . though each of these have markedly inferior fits in their corresponding $\{Rz_k^2\}$.

As a rule of thumb, it appears possible to tolerate one Rz_k^2 outside the 95% region, (shown as *; the values less than 6.2^{-1} or greater than 6.2 are outside the 98.75% region and less than 8.2^{-1} or greater than 8.2 are outside the 99.5 region and clearly unacceptable), particularly as the v_k for higher k are unstable and have small means. The obvious violations are between N_1 and E_2 or between E_1 and N_2, which is consistent with the hypotheses. The demonstration shows that (3.6.17) is one basis upon which to facilitate the identification of time series with embedded episodes, if a number of realizations of those episodes exist, though their form need not be known precisely beforehand. An alternative frequency domain treatment may be found in Walter (1963).

Intervention Analysis as a Modification of the General Linear Model

A very common experimental paradigm in single-subject behavior modification studies involves, in sequence:

1. A baseline period in which behavior is observed and recorded, in some of its quantifiable aspects, without attempting to change the environmental parameters in any way that would be contingent upon behavior.

2. A period of intervention in which something is done according to a theory that predicts that at least one of the aspects of behavior quantified in item 1 will, as a consequence, change in a consistent and interpretable manner.

3. A return to baseline, in order to see if the patterns of behavior exemplified in item 1 spontaneously reinstate themselves when the intervention procedures of item 2 are discontinued.

There are further obvious complications that ingenuity suggests; a period in which the reverse treatment of item 2 is applied, to produce behavior changes opposite in sense and direction, is often used. If a subject can be manipulated back and forth, then *control* is said to have been established. As seen, this is not control in the same sense as the word is used in control theory but something more restricted. This control of behavior is not the same thing as demonstrating learning; a dynamic system can behave in the manner given without in any way altering the internal parameters of its feedback processes. It is rather a method of discovering what are the experimental factors that constitute the critical inputs of a very nonlinear system.

An extensive technical terminology has been created to describe the procedures of such experiments; here we deliberately avoid commitment to that terminology, because those aspects of the analysis that are relevant to our theme can be fitted into time series and systems theory without augmentation.

The methods of data analysis that have been advocated for single-subject research within the operant tradition (Kratchowill, 1978, et op. cit.) and that explicitly derive from time series analysis originate in an extension of the ARMA model to cope with local shifts in the mean output, which can in turn be reformulated in terms of the general linear model. To show what is involved, the general linear model (Horton, 1978) will be set up, followed by Box and Tiao's (1965) extension, and some comments on special cases that have subsequently been developed and even computerized from automated analysis. This formal approach, rather than a problem-focused one, is adopted to make clearer the origins and vicissitudes of the methods advocated. It should be realized that a number of methods of analyzing single-subject time series experiments have been advocated that are just plain silly. These are critically reviewed by Gottman and Glass (1978) and need not detain us further. If results are replicable, they probably mean something psychologically, but the methods of analysis that have been used do not reveal what it might be.

Suppose that there is a set of N observations of a dependent (output) variable, y, and these are defined to be the consequence of some independent constants, X, and a set of unknown parameters, θ. As real data are being discussed, a set of residual errors, e, with cov $(e, X) = 0$ will also be present. The general linear model states simply that

$$
\begin{vmatrix} y_1 \\ y_N \end{vmatrix} = \begin{vmatrix} x_{11} & x_{1m} \\ x_{N1} & x_{Nm} \end{vmatrix} \cdot \begin{vmatrix} \theta_1 \\ \theta_m \end{vmatrix} + \begin{vmatrix} e_1 \\ e_N \end{vmatrix}
\tag{3.6.20}
$$

Or in matrix notation

$$
\mathbf{y} = \mathbf{X}\boldsymbol{\theta} + \mathbf{e}
\tag{3.6.21}
$$

If a vector $\boldsymbol{\theta}$ is created as an estimate of $\boldsymbol{\theta}$ (because $\boldsymbol{\theta}$ is not directly observable), then the predicted outputs $\mathbf{y}$ are related to the estimates as

$$
\hat{\mathbf{y}} = \mathbf{X}\boldsymbol{\theta}
\tag{3.6.22}
$$

The fitting of $\boldsymbol{\theta}$ by least-squares estimators means, quite simply, that a minimization of $\mathbf{e}$, denoted by $\hat{\mathbf{e}}$, which is also

$$
\hat{\mathbf{e}} = \mathbf{y} - \hat{\mathbf{y}}
$$

is obtained by the minimum of $\hat{\mathbf{e}}'\hat{\mathbf{e}}$.

It can be shown that

$$
\hat{\boldsymbol{\theta}} = (\mathbf{X}'\mathbf{X})^{-1}\mathbf{X}'\mathbf{y}
\tag{3.6.23}
$$

which is a matrix equivalent of the normal equations of regression or analysis of variance. The requirement of (3.6.23) is that $\mathbf{X}'\mathbf{X}$ has an inverse; the output $\mathbf{y}$ has to be measurable in the same sense as in the time series models we are considering throughout the text, namely as a set of continuous or nearly continuous variables.

In analyzing a time series, the interpretation of the terms in (3.6.21) would be, sensibly,

$\mathbf{y}$ = the output series or some tractable transformation of it

$\mathbf{X}$ = the matrix of constants representing the relative mean levels in different episodes of a series; in ANOVA terminology the design matrix of the study

$\boldsymbol{\theta}$ = the regression parameters linking input (marker or design) variables $\mathbf{X}$ to the quantified outputs $\mathbf{y}$

The major conceptual difficulties center on how to interpret the matrix $\mathbf{X}$ that is $N \times m$ and links the m parameters of the system ($\theta' = (\theta_1, \ldots, \theta_m)$) to the N-term realization ($y' = (y_1, \ldots, y_N)$) where the y are equally spaced in time.

An experiment with two successive phases, and where the second phase is expected to have a different mean from the first, would, for example, with four observations in each phase, be when written out in full matrix form

$$
\begin{vmatrix} y_1 \\ y_2 \\ y_3 \\ y_4 \\ y_5 \\ y_6 \\ y_7 \\ y_8 \end{vmatrix} = \begin{vmatrix} 1 & 0 \\ 1 & 0 \\ 1 & 0 \\ 1 & 0 \\ 1 & 1 \\ 1 & 1 \\ 1 & 1 \\ 1 & 1 \end{vmatrix} \cdot \begin{vmatrix} \theta_1 \\ \\ \theta_2 \end{vmatrix} + \begin{vmatrix} e_1 \\ e_2 \\ e_3 \\ e_4 \\ e_5 \\ e_6 \\ e_7 \\ e_8 \end{vmatrix} \qquad (3.6.24)
$$

where the first column of 1's in the X matrix is the average vector for the whole time series experiment; the second column with four 1's in the second phase only represents a superimposed shift in the mean during the second phase. This corresponds to what would be the consequence of an embedded episode in the sense discussed previously. These numbers X are level codings in an analysis of variance, or dummy variables in a regression; their values have no meanings in terms of the units of y. The problem is to estimate θ_1 and θ_2 and then compare them to see if the difference $\theta_1 - \theta_2$ is meaningful. If all the observations $y_1, \ldots, y_8$ were independent, this would not be a time series problem; one would employ a t- or Behrens–Fisher test to obtain posterior confidence regions on the shift $\theta_1 - \theta_2$, which is in effect the shift of mean y values from the first to the second phase. However, for time series this is a completely invalid and potentially seriously misleading thing to do, because of the autocorrelation and sequential dependency of the terms in y. Gastwirth and Rubin (1971) give a detailed analysis of this problem.

As the autocovariance structure of y is precisely what might interest us much more than the shifts in mean levels, it is necessary to proceed with caution.

If the process is nonstationary and is strongly autocorrelated, then it is necessary to choose a model of the time series in the baseline period and then parametrize the change from baseline to embedded episode as a change in mean, that is, in θ. Box and Tiao (1965) considered a very general integrated moving-average process, with a remote origin in time, as the baseline process. Their argument, which has become the model for other analyses in psychological research, proceeds as follows.

Define an i.i.d. input series $\{a\}$, so that the observed output series is $\{w\}$; under stationarity there is a constant v_0 such that

$$
w_j = M + v_0 \sum_{k=1}^{\infty} a_{j-k} + a_j \qquad (0 < v_0 < 2)
$$

and this observed series w_j is interesting because it hasn't any mean (over its total duration there is no first moment) unless $v_0 = 0$ and is nonstationary, but a "local level" at a point in time j is given by

$$L_j = M + v_0 \sum_{k=1}^{\infty} a_{j-k} \qquad (3.6.25)$$

and it is these levels $\{L_j\}$ that shift as a consequence of intervention.

The value of the process at the point where observations begin can be treated as a fixed but unknown parameter L resulting from the unobserved a that were realized before observations commenced, and the observed output will then be

$$w_1 = L + a_1$$

$$w_j = L + v_0 \sum_{k=1}^{j-1} a_{j-k} + a_j \qquad (j = 2, 3, \ldots) \qquad (3.6.26)$$

and it can be shown that

$$L = v_0 \sum_{k=0}^{-\infty} (1 - v_0)^k \cdot w_k$$

This model appears to match closely many real-world applications in a variety of disciplines, given that $0 < v_0 < 1$, without introducing further complications.

Before E^*, (3.6.26) holds, but after E^* begins on trial $n_1 + 1$ and continues until trial n_2

$$w_j = L + \delta L + v_0 \sum_{k=1}^{j-1} a_{j-k} + a_j \qquad (3.6.27)$$

is the appropriate representation, where δL is the effect of intervention upon the local mean.

If v_0 is known, and a transformation of output variables is made (i.e., a synthetic $\{y_j\}$ is written as a function of the original but unobserved $\{w_j\}$), then

$$y_1 = w_1$$

$$y_j = w_j - v_0 \sum_{k=0}^{j-2} (1 - v_0)^k \cdot w_{j-1-k} \qquad (j = 2, \ldots, n_1 + n_2)$$

$$(3.6.28)$$

For simplification, put $(1 - v_0) = x$; then in the format of the general linear model, as in (3.6.20) or (3.6.24), we can write

$$y = \begin{vmatrix} y_1 \\ \cdot \\ \cdot \\ \cdot \\ \cdot \\ y_{n_1} \\ y_{n_1+1} \\ \cdot \end{vmatrix} = \begin{vmatrix} 1 & 0 \\ \cdot & 0 \\ \cdot & \\ \cdot & 0 \\ x^{(n_1-1)} & 0 \\ x^{n_1} & 1 \\ \cdot & x \end{vmatrix} \cdot \begin{vmatrix} L \\ \delta L \end{vmatrix} + e \qquad (3.6.29)$$

$$\begin{vmatrix} \cdot \\ \cdot \\ \cdot \\ y_{n_1+n_2} \end{vmatrix} \quad \begin{vmatrix} \cdot & & \cdot \\ \cdot & & \cdot \\ \cdot & & \cdot \\ x^{(n_1+n_2-1)} & & x^{n_2-1} \end{vmatrix} \qquad\qquad \begin{matrix} (3.6.29 \\ \text{continued}) \end{matrix}$$

The thing of interest is all this is δL, and $\theta' = |L \; \delta L|$, so

$$\theta = \begin{vmatrix} \hat{L} \\ \hat{\delta L} \end{vmatrix} = (\mathbf{X}'\mathbf{X})^{-1}\mathbf{X}'\mathbf{Y}$$

[from (3.6.23)].

It is possible to establish a posteriori credibility intervals on δL, if L, δL, and $\log \sigma_a$ have locally independent uniform prior distributions, because $\hat{\delta L} - \delta L$ follows a t-distribution. The formulas required are complex and are given by Box and Tiao (1965) with several examples under simplifying conditions.

There are two aspects of the model given that are of intuitive importance for the psychologist; the model employed can be shown to be the realization of a process in which the organism is subjected to a series of random buffetings and gives a little, but only a little and proportionately with some resistance, to each stimulus from its environment received in turn. An observer exposed to a series of disparate political messages might sway in his or her attitudes in such a manner, always listening a little to the last advice given. The second point is that the test based on contrasts of the θ in (3.6.23) concentrates on the evidence about the point n_1 in time, when the embedded episode begins, and uses information remote from that point with progressively diminishing weight. It thus concentrates upon behavior at the first impact of environmental changes. This may make very good sense, depending on the psychological assumptions that the investigator brings to bear, concerning L, δL, and the variance–covariance stationarity. Box and Tiao (1965) show that an AR model, as opposed to an MA model, leads to inappropriate conclusions, because testing δL in the AR model weights events remote from n_1 too heavily.

The most critical point, and it is one that anticipates filtering of Chapter 5, is that the model building to locate embedded episodes is and must be iterative, on location in the earlier examples considered, and on mean shift in the later examples. Rarely will the model be parametrized in advance (in θ), but the more prior information on its structure that is available and trustworthy, the sooner should it converge to an acceptable estimation.

The extension of Box and Tiao's models into single-subject research in psychology has been popularised by Glass, Willson, and Gottman (1975) and by Revenstorf, in German (1979). Complications additional to the main model include allowing for drift (the presence of very low-frequency components in psychophysiological studies) in the mean (Glass, 1972) and fitting episodes where the mean is expected to follow some profile $\{\delta L_i\}$, $i = n_1, \ldots, n_2$, which can be specified in advance as a series of weights in the appropriate column of the $\mathbf{X}$ matrix in (3.6.24) or (3.6.29).

It is possible, using the residual error terms after model fitting, to compare alternative hypotheses that state an intervention effect is either gradual in onset and decline or abrupt in onset and abruptly removed or some other combination of these possibilities. This can be done if the nature of the "gradualness" is precisely parametrized in advance in **X**. If, however, the underlying ARMA process has been misidentified, the results of such comparisons would be uninterpretable.

ADDENDUM TO SECTION 3.6

Time-Warping as an Identification Precursor

In the context of word recognition, in constructing algorithms that will "recognize" one spoken word from among an indeterminate finite population of such words, a method of identifying embedded (auditory) episodes has been developed by Itakura (1975) and subsequently employed with some success by Rabiner, Rosenberg, and Levinson (1978). This procedure utilizes a method known as *time-warping* and leads to the development of a distancelike measure for comparing the realizations of an autocorrelated time series that characterize the episode being identified. The methodology here is, as so far developed, unique to auditory recognition but in principle could be used as an alternative to the methods previously discussed in any context where it is possible to set up templates, even if only fuzzy ones, to match against the embedded episodes whose identification is being sought.

The problem, again, is that the shape of a word is a sort of recognizable time series pattern, with some characteristic peaks and troughs, and sequences involving two or more peaks or troughs that have constrained relative magnitudes. The absolute values of the pattern, in terms of length, and the (time, amplitude) coordinates of salient features are only constrained weakly. Under transformation into the frequency domain the power spectrum may only be recognizably unique at some subset of frequencies. However, we do recognize the same word, or sentence, said to us by different speakers, with a prodigious variety of accents, pitches, stresses, speeds of utterances, and so on. At least we do with our own language if we are fairly tolerant to the diversities that occur as soon as we are outside a small regional or socioeconomic group. Even the processes of word recognition that we are trying to model or to reproduce are not perfectably reliable in the human listener with normal hearing. Speech recognition as a general topic is outside our scope, but this particular problem has some interesting conceptual affinities to the problems of locating evoked potentials; in fact once encoded into a discrete time series of continuously varying amplitudes the data in EEGs, speech, or cognitive processes may be indistinguishable apart from their specific parametrizations, so one mathematical method for identification could hold for all areas some of the time but not for all practical cases in any one area.

Itakura (1975) notes that a speech signal is a redundant time series; it is typically strongly autocorrelated to some variable and a priori indeterminate extent. Attempts to use the linear transfer function of a series as a basis of discriminant analysis, to tell feature patterns from one another, were not in fact very successful. Conceptually, it is desired to characterize any speech pattern as a series of linear coefficients and then put these series, one for each pattern of interest, at specific locations in a discriminant space the dimensionality of which would have to be the largest number of coefficients needed uniquely to characterize the most complex of patterns. Unfortunately this appears not to work, because the signals are too complicated and very nonstationary. Consequently, Itakura tackled the much simpler problem: given a short time series, what is the optimal distance measure of the space in which we embed some transformation of that series that is to be used to test a hypothesis that the series was generated by a process having a specified l.t.f.? The idea that some input utterance is a word, with semantic reference, is an additional hypothesis that can be circumvented here.

The discrete time series is assumed to be

$$M = a_1 x_{j-1} + \cdots + a_p x_{j-p} + e_j, \quad e \sim \text{i.i.d.}, \quad N(0, \sigma_e) \quad (3.6.30)$$

In this context, because p is much less than any periodicity in e, the autocovariance of e is asymptotically zero, for adjacent samples. The sequence $\{a_i\}$ is called the set of linear prediction coefficients (abbreviated to LPC) because of the use to which it is to be put. The aspect of the analysis that is of interest, because of its potential generality, is the derivation of the measure of distance (which may be monotone upon but not equivalent to dissimilarity) between a segment $X = \{x_j\}$, $j = 1, 2, \ldots, N$ and the model M^*. The segment is potentially a realization of the model.

The set of parameters $\mathbf{P} = \{\sigma_e, a_j\}$ specify sufficiently the conditional joint probability $p(\mathbf{X}|\mathbf{P})$ and given that $N \gg p$,

$$\log (p(\mathbf{X}|\mathbf{P}) = -\left(\frac{N}{2}\right)(\log 2\pi\sigma^2 + \sigma^{-2} \cdot \mathbf{a}'\mathbf{V}\mathbf{a}) \quad (3.6.31)$$

where $a' = (a_1, \ldots, a_j, \ldots, a_p)$.
$\mathbf{V}$ is the covariance matrix whose elements are

$$V_i = N^{-1} \sum_{n=1}^{N-i} x_i x_{n+i}$$

Two quadratic forms can be constructed: $\mathbf{a}'\mathbf{V}\mathbf{a}$, which is the residual when the signal $\mathbf{X}$ is created from the prediction of the model M^*, and $\hat{\mathbf{a}}'\mathbf{V}\hat{\mathbf{a}}$, when $\mathbf{X}$ is created from a maximum likelihood estimate **a** under the assumptions that both σ_e and $\{a_j\}$ are free to vary. If the model M^* is close to the actual process underlying **X,** then the **â** will be close to the **a** and then

$$d(\mathbf{X}|\mathbf{a}) = \log\left(\frac{\mathbf{a}'\mathbf{V}\mathbf{a}}{\mathbf{\hat{a}}'\mathbf{V}\mathbf{\hat{a}}}\right)$$

will be near to zero because the two quadratic forms will be nearly the same. But if the sample **X** is not generated by a realization of M^*, then $d(\mathbf{X}|\mathbf{a})$ will be large, in fact Itakura notes that $d(\mathbf{X}|\mathbf{a})\cdot N$ is distributed as chi-squared with p d.f. approximately and thus suggests its use as a distance measure between **X** and M^*. There are, however, computational difficulties such that an alternative form is used after the operation of time-warping, to be described shortly. Another problem is that the quotient $d(\mathbf{X}|\mathbf{a})$ depends for its value on what is taken as a data sample and what is taken as defining, by example, the model M^*. In practice, M^* has to be constructed from a large collection of reference data, which leads to further problems in the cluster analysis of reference samples (Levinson, Rabiner, Rosenberg, & Wilpon, 1979).

As the sample **X,** which is possibly a word, may be uttered at any one of a range of speeds, it can be longer or shorter than the reference model M^* and has to be adjusted in length in some definable fashion before the distance between **X** and M^* can be defined and calculated. The rules for this adjustment involve changing the length of the data sample in a constrained but not one-one transformation; alternative forms have been examined by Rabiner, Rosenberg, and Levinson (1978). Consider one of the simplest, though not necessarily the most efficient in practice (as shown in Fig. 3.6.2).

As both the abscissa and ordinate time scales are discretized, the only distances to be computed in assessing the separation between model M^* and data **X** are the set of points inside the rhomboid frame that fixes the limits of the time-warping transformation. A partial axiomatizing of the time-warping is given by Itakura; the boundary conditions can be critical in determining the efficiency of pattern recognition algorithms based on time-warps.

The distance definition $d(\mathbf{X}|\mathbf{a})$ can be rewritten as $d(n, m; k) =$ the distance between the nth segment of input and the mth segment of the reference pattern denoted by $R(k)$; in full,

$$d(n, m; k) = c(m; k) + \log\left(\frac{(b(m; k)r(n))}{(\hat{a}(n)r(n))}\right) \tag{3.6.32}$$

where

$b(m; k) =$ the autocorrelation of the inverse filter of the model in $\{a_j\}$, which means the spectrum of autocorrelations that the process with impulse response $\{a_j\}$ would be assumed to have before

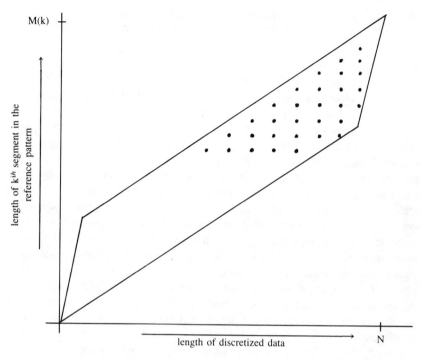

M(k)

length of kth segment in the reference pattern

length of discretized data   N

FIG. 3.6.2   Constrained time-warping transformation.

actual identification, assuming that it takes the simplest form possible as in M^*;

$r(n) =$ the autocorrelation coefficients of the first p lags on input;

$\hat{a}(n) =$ the maximum likelihood estimators of the impulse response coefficients of the process;

$c(m; k) =$ the power of the model, $\Sigma\ a_j^2$.

This expression has to be computed separately for each of the possible coordinates (n, m) within the time-warping function of Fig. 3.6.2, which can take an inordinately long time unless some simplifying strategy is adopted. The sum of all distances $d(n, m; k)$ within the envelope of the time-warping can be denoted by Δ; then the choice of time-warping to optimize identification will be the warp that minimizes Δ for a given class of signals. Then, using the warp that gives minimum distance between a template that is "correct" and a data set of utterances corresponding to that template, one may identify subsequent utterances from among a large set, of which some are correct and some incorrect, by comparing values of $D(k) = \min \Delta$ with a range of observations. The process of creating templates is itself complex and requires sequential interactive algorithms of some subtlety.

3.7 CATASTROPHES, DISCONTINUITIES, AND HYSTERESIS IN TIME SERIES

The limitations of simple stationary models of input–output relationships when living systems are to be described may center on two features; abrupt discontinuities in output at some point in a continuously varying input, and hysteresis.

Figure 3.7.1 illustrates the familiar property of sluggish self-regulating systems, animate or inanimate, which may have at least two input–output relationships, depending on whether input is ascending or descending within some range of input values denoted here by ϕ_0, ϕ_{max}. The notation here is chosen to suggest physical stimulus inputs and psychological response outputs, as the hysteresis problem is a classical one in psychophysics. It probably occurs in many other areas, such as aesthetic evaluation (Gregson, 1968), but has not been sought for, because traditionally in psychology the phenomena of hysteresis and comparable multiple-output-to-single-input relationships have been thought of as a nuisance, to be averaged out or avoided by some ingenious use of stimulus sequences so chosen that the observed ϕ–ψ function lies within the loop in Fig. 3.7.1. As observed, this is an impoverished way of looking at an interesting phenomenon; the existence and magnitude of hysteresis under specifiable conditions constitutes critical information about the internal dynamics of any system that is to be modeled. To be simplistic, it is only linear open-loop systems with very high sensitivity that do not show some hysteresis, and the view taken here is that psychological systems are neither open loop nor very sensitive to small perturbations, unless we can show in some particular instance that the contrary holds.

As shown in Fig. 3.7.1, outside the range ϕ_0, ϕ_{max} the system has no

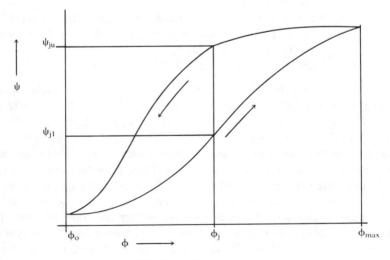

FIG. 3.7.1   Hysteresis Loop.

sensitivity, in psychophysical terminology the inputs are below the (lower) threshold or above the (upper) saturation threshold. Outside the range in which the system both has sensitivity and shows hysteresis, it only has two states of functioning, ψ_{max} and ψ_0, which in degenerate sensory or cognitive tasks correspond to saying "yes" or "no," "present" or "absent," "different" or "same," "signal" or "noise."

It has, of course, been known since Fechner introduced the method of limits around 1860 that sensory systems showed hysteresis; indeed the method of limits is a procedure that is intended to average out the hysteresis loop and replace it with a point estimate, which is a notional threshold located somewhere inside the loop. There are some interesting conceptual problems with this approach if the loop area becomes negative, that is, when the ascending branch is uppermost in Fig. 3.7.1 and the descending branch is below, with respect to the ψ axis. As such behavior in sensory systems would be thought a little atypical, if not paradoxical, the problem has not been properly faced. In fact it is no problem at all if time series modeling is used.

So, the classical psychophysical solution to the problem (and as we read it, the modern solution as well, employing magnitude estimation procedures) is to construct a single-valued

$$\psi = f(\phi)$$

by averaging out corresponding pairs (ψ_{ju}, ψ_{j1}) for each ϕ_j, and using a standard procedure to track up or down the two branches of the loop, which may be, in the limit, to try to destroy the loop by using random stimulus sequences.

There are immediate tiresome complications in psychophysics that are not always paralleled in the physical sciences, though they would be in some biological systems. There are not, in fact, simply two branches or functions, ascending or descending, in sensory psychology, unless the sequences of inputs is strictly increasing or decreasing, but the response will depend on the length of a series $\{\phi\}$ and its starting point; the process of generating ψ_j is expressible as a sort of integrated moving-average process that Helson (1964a,b) attempted in his adaptation-level theory models, which were intended to apply to sensory and social judgments in the first instance. He later attempted to generalize his approach, but in no way did his algebraic structures take on the dynamic shape of the bivariate autocorrelated core that is employed here. To steal a metaphor, Helson's attempt to show that judgments had a reference point that moved and was an average of previous related, weighted, impressions was like trying to make a time series omelette without breaking the time series eggs.

The idea that the hysteresis loop should be averaged out for a proper representation either of some point ψ_t, ϕ_t within the loop, where $\psi_t = 0$, $\phi_t =$ the physical correlate of a 50% threshold, or for some function $\psi = f_m(\phi)$ as in Fig. 3.7.2 is, in the light of dynamic modeling, an impoverished and impoverishing way to treat an interesting problem. The idea possibly persists in balancing

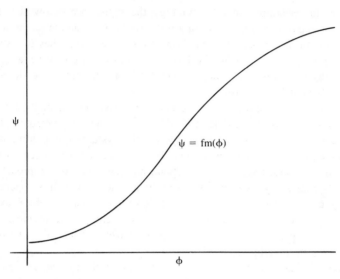

ψ

$\psi = fm(\phi)$

ϕ

FIG. 3.7.2

experimental designs in psychology so that with sufficiently careful experimental control the hysteresis loop should shrink to minimal area, as in Fig. 3.7.3.

To do this, or to hope to do it, again misses the point. The area of the loop represents work done by a system in restoring its own equilibrium. If the area of the loop changes systematically under different external conditions, then this is information about the system and about its capacity to return to states represented in some way by ψ_0 and ψ_{max}. Changes in the area of the loop as a consequence of identifiable extraneous variables imply that the dynamic characteristics of a feedback loop with nonlinearities are modifiable. In short, the system can in a sense learn, if the area A_h is modifiable and then stays modified; whereas it cannot learn but is dynamically complex if A_h is a function (which itself may exhibit hysteresis) of quantifiable conditions (variables) other than $\{\phi\}$, $\{\psi\}$.

Simply hysteresis, as in Fig. 3.7.1, can be produced by an autocorrelated process

$$\psi_j = \psi_0 + \sum_{k=0}^{n} v^k \phi_{j-k} + e, \qquad 0 < v < 1 \qquad (3.7.1)$$

if the input series $\{\phi_j\}$ is locally, over a few trials, strictly ascending and then descending. To illustrate this, some examples have been simulated on a program written in BASIC for PDP11/10, using an input series $\{\phi_j\}$ with a period of 40 trials, $\phi = .6$ for convenience in printout size, $\phi_1 = 0.95$, $\psi_0 = 10$, $v = .75$, $n = 8$, and omitting e completely, gives loops like Fig. 3.7.4, the ψ values are those of the upper branch only; but it can be seen that the loop at its widest is about 6ψ units. Increasing v to .85 as in Fig. 3.7.5 opens up the loop to about 12ψ units at its widest; further increasing v aggravates the hysteresis strikingly.

It can readily be seen, and demonstrated outside the range of the examples, that v is the critical parameter in (3.7.1) in determining the shape (length, area, steepness) of the hysteresis loop.

For greater generality, the mixed model

$$\psi_j = \psi_0 + \sum_{k=0}^{n'} v^k \phi_{j-k} + \sum_{k=0}^{n} w^k \psi_{j-k} + e \qquad (3.7.2)$$

may be considered. With $w = 0$ or $v = 0$ we have the special cases that arise when only input averaging, or only autoregression, can be predicted. For simplification here we put $n = n' = 8$; for large values of k, the ψ terms are negligible beyond $n = 8$, because w has to be small for the process to approximate to stationarity. Series with $v = 0$ and $w = .5$ or more are violently nonstationary; their hysteresis loops never close and are very large.

A typical loop, for the same sawtooth input as previously, but with $\phi = .2$ to squeeze in the diagram, $w = .1$ and $v = .75$ is given in Fig. 3.7.6: The loop is about 7ψ units wide and a different range from that in Fig. 3.7.4. The result of increasing v to .95 is shown in Fig. 3.7.7. By comparison of Fig. 3.7.4, 3.7.5, 3.7.6, and 3.7.7, it can be deduced that without detailed knowledge of the parameters in (3.7.2) the form of the process (AR, MA, or ARMA) is not explicitly identifiable from the loop shape.

An alternative way in which hysteresis can be created in a system, unlike the previous model, is to incorporate deliberately some abrupt discontinuities in the

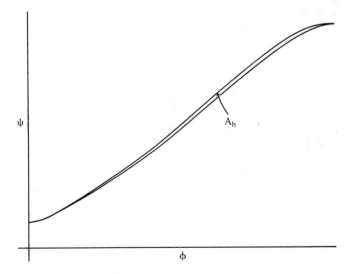

FIG. 3.7.3   Minimal Hysteresis.

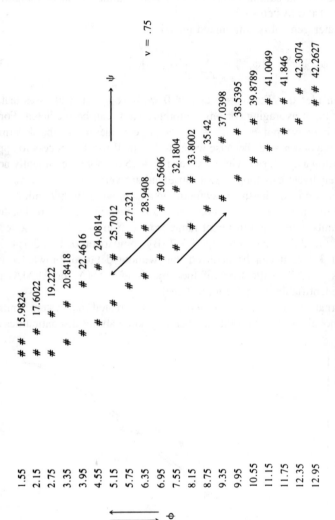

FIG. 3.7.4   Time series generated hysteresis loops.

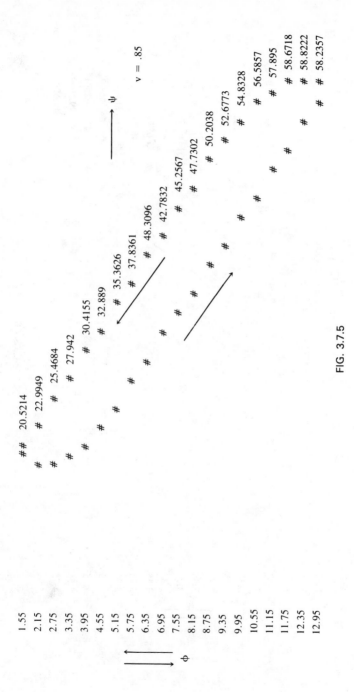

FIG. 3.7.5

213

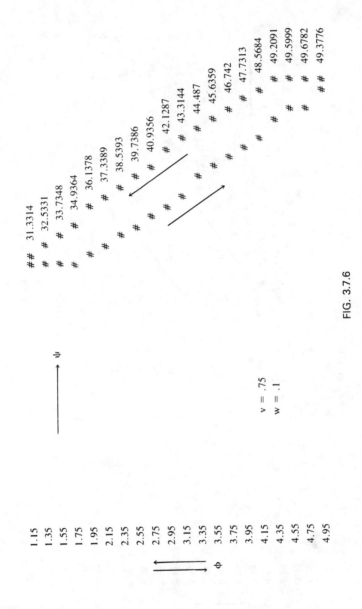

FIG. 3.7.6

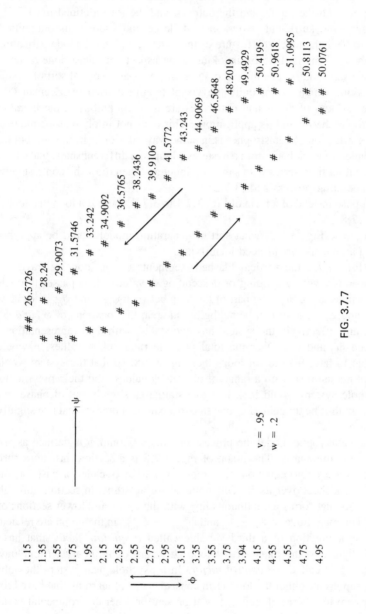

FIG. 3.7.7

output from a continuous input. The previous model obviously assumed continuity in both the inputs and the outputs, and the form defined in (3.7.2) was necessary and sufficient. Now, instead, large and sudden discontinuities are made to be a characteristic feature of the system, which the model structure has to embody. This is done by invoking some aspects of catastrophe theory. We have chosen to introduce the topic of catastrophes as a special sort of hysteresis generation, which is not quite the visual treatment used by Zeeman (1977), whose surfaces of cusps and butterflies are now ubiquitous in the literature of catastrophe theory and its applications. This does not imply that the mathematical classification of catastrophes is in some way inferior or irrelevant, but here it is intended to work back from a hysteresis loop of a different shape that can occur in the output time series with sawtooth input and then draw the contrast between this generating process and (3.7.2).

Suppose instead of a form of Fig. 3.7.1 to 3.7.7, there is a loop that looks like Fig. 3.7.8.

To create Fig. 3.7.8, what sort of generating model would be appropriate? What parameters would need identifying?

In Fig. 3.7.8 the vertical (dashed) segments of the loop are traversed instantaneously with ascending or descending ϕ values, as ϕ passes through the point values ϕ_d or ϕ_u. The part of the loop between ψ_{min} and ψ_{minc}, or between ψ_{maxc} and ψ_{max}, is or can be negligible in area; the locations of ϕ_d *and* ϕ_u are fixed, and effectively the system has two states, with dual representation of ψ between ϕ_d and ϕ_u. Over the total possible range of ϕ values, it would be possible to have a series of loops like Fig. 3.7.8, so that the system would be discontinuous in ψ, with a range of discrete ψ values, and the representation of the whole system would look like two staircases slightly out of phase. Figure 3.7.8 can thus be thought of as one step in a pair of staircases that rise slightly out of phase.

In a catastrophe model the process that maps ψ onto ϕ is defined as always locally minimizing ψ. The graph of Fig. 3.7.8 is a section through a surface, defined by a cubic equation, that represents what is called a cusp, a folding locally of a sheet over itself. This notional surface runs, in section, through the line -.-.-.- that forms a continuous line with the upper and lower sections of the loop. The magnitude of $\phi_u - \phi_d$ and $\psi_{maxc} - \psi_{minc}$ in the graph are related and fixed as a function of a third variable called a *splitting factor* that has axis perpendicular to the plane of the loop. In catastrophe theory terminology the variable ϕ is called the *control factor*. In a psychological system the splitting factor represents either the long-term consequences of learning that have brought the system to where, globally, it is at present or other environmental variables that affect the overall sensitivity of the system.

The segment in Fig. 3.7.8 marked as -.-.-.- inside the loop is part of the notional ψ response surface, but it is virtual rather than a real part of the system. Because the system always minimizes ψ, it cannot come to rest on that line; in

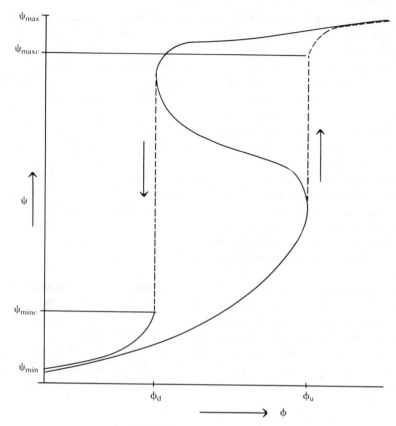

FIG. 3.7.8 A catastrophic hysteresis.

fact, it cannot, unlike the previous example, ever enter the inside of the loop. A contrary system that always maximizes ψ can show the same hysteresis loop but cycled in the reverse sense, which would then be clockwise in Fig. 3.7.8. The point of this extended example is to indicate that abrupt hysteresis loops can be stable phenomena in systems that have $v = w = 0$ in (3.7.2), if the additional constraint of the minimization (or maximization) surface for ψ is imposed. Hysteresis is not, therefore, of itself indicative of a need for a time series or dynamic analysis; but if it does occur as the consequences of sequential effects, then it may show the continuities of Fig. 3.7.1, whereas if it is not, then it can show the discontinuities of Fig. 3.7.8 and cannot be forced within the loop.

The dual representation of Fig. 3.7.8 holds no matter from where a reversal in direction occurs; a ϕ series that starts in $\phi_u - \phi_d$ will, at t_0, be in either the upper or lower loop. It will stay on the loop branch it is in, as shown, until if descending it reaches ϕ_d, and if ascending it reaches ϕ_u. Outside that range the system is effectively single-valued in ψ. But if the hysteresis is a consequence of a sequential structure as in (3.7.2), then it will descend in ψ from any starting point ψ_n on the lower branch as soon as reversal occurs, and correspondingly on the upper branch from ψ_y as shown in Fig. 3.7.9.

Application of catastrophe models, using implicitly the single cusp and hence a hysteresis loop as in Fig. 3.7.8, have been postulated by Zeeman (1977) for a surprising diversity of psychological applications, such as anorexia nervosa (a condition in which the patient switches from gorging to fasting), errors in judgment during driving a car when intoxicated with alcohol, the occurrence of riots in prisons, and other problems arising in psychophysiology and neuropsychology.

As a catastrophe represents, or can sensibly be made to represent, transition between two qualitative states, it would be possible to characterize each state by a function like (3.7.2) with unique parameters. An embedded episode as discussed in Section 3.6 would then be a state shift, temporarily; the behavior exhibited within the state could include a form of hysteresis not shown in the original state. Such complexities are mathematically tractable and have been formalized.

Tong and Lim (1980) have shown that the cusp catastrophe, which gives rise to the discontinuities of Fig. 3.7.8, can be completely represented by a time series with two states; such a process they call self-excitatory threshold autoregressive (SETAR). In such a process each state is characterized by a particular set of autoregression coefficients, of which, in state i, m_i would be nonzero. The rule for switching between states is given in terms of the current input u_j; if u_j is greater than some critical value u_c, then the process goes into state 1, say; if u_j is

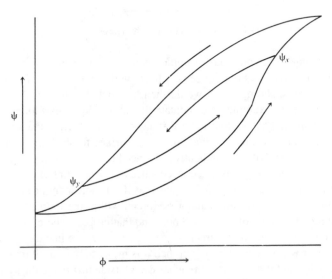

FIG. 3.7.9 ψx, ψy are reversal points.

less than u_c, it goes into state 2. Thus the autoregressive structure fluctuates between two spectra as a function of the input. Tong and Lim have investigated the formal mathematics and the identifiability of such SETAR models; their importance is that they may make it quite unnecessary to postulate catastrophes for some psychological discontinuities but instead use time series whose memories are a function of current stimuli. See also Brillinger (1977).

3.8 APPENDIX TO CHAPTER 3: LAPLACE TRANSFORMS

As emphasized, if time series are discrete, then all the necessary convolution calculations that it is usual to want to carry out can be done in z transforms or directly by computer. However, many texts, particularly in physiological psychology or in areas bearing on motor skill movements that are monitored continuously, will employ Laplace transforms and not z transforms. If the behavior we are interested in is regarded as the output of a sampled-data system, then it can be shown that the z-transform approach is effectively the same as taking the Laplace transformations out of continuous time into a discrete time. For reference, and to enable the reader to check parallel constructions, a few elementary standard definitions and results are given here. The topic has an extensive literature; the notation here seems to be fairly standard.

First the Laplace transform of some function in time, $f(t)$, is defined to be

$$\mathcal{L}\,[f(t)] = \int_0^\infty f(t) \cdot \exp\,(-st) \cdot dt \qquad (3.8.1)$$

where s is a complex number. Note that the r.h.s. in (3.8.1) is an integral over a time period of a function that may be differentiable, and the l.h.s. is an algebraic expression that stands outside time. If $f(t)$ represents a response that extends through time, then it is possible to represent both transient and steady-state components of the response in the Laplace transform. The transforms are tedious to compute but can be used like building blocks to represent complicated situations whose dynamic components can be recorded or conjectured. Extensive tables of the Laplace transforms are used normally by design engineers; for the commonest input series the transforms are as follows:

Defined Input	Algebraic Form		Laplace Transform
The unit impulse (δ)	$f(t) = \infty$	for $t = 0$	1
	$f(t) = 0$	for $t > 0$	
The step function	$f(t) = k$	for $t > 0$	k/s
	$f(t) = 0$	for $t < 0$	

The derivation of this case is as follows: From (3.8.1)

$$\mathcal{L}\,[f(t)] = \int_0^\infty f(t) \cdot \exp\,(-st) \cdot dt$$

$$= \int_0^\infty k \cdot \exp\,(-st) \cdot dt$$

$$= [-ks^{-1} \cdot \exp\,(-st)]_0^\infty \qquad\qquad (3.8.2)$$

At the limits, when

$$t = \infty \qquad \text{then } -ks^{-1} \cdot \exp\,(-st) = 0$$

when

$$t = 0 \qquad \text{then } -ks^{-1} \cdot \exp\,(-st) = -ks^{-1}$$

so

$$\mathcal{L}\,[f(t)] = 0 - (-ks^{-1}) = \frac{k}{s} = F(s)$$

The ramp function

$$\begin{array}{ll} f(t) = kt & \text{for } t > 0 \\ f(t) = 0 & \text{for } t < 0 \end{array} \quad k/s^2$$

The decaying exponential

$$f(t) = \exp\,(-at) \qquad \frac{1}{(s + a)}$$

The Laplace transforms have three properties that make them easier to manipulate than the convolutions of their corresponding functions $f(t)$.

If $\mathcal{L}\,[f(t)] = F(s)$, by definition (see the example for the step function), then

$$\mathcal{L}\,k \cdot f(t) = k \cdot F(s) \qquad\qquad (3.8.3)$$

so

$$\mathcal{L}\,[f_1(t) + f_2(t)] = \mathcal{L}\,[f_1(t)] + \mathcal{L}\,[f_2(t)] \qquad\qquad (3.8.4)$$

$$\mathcal{L}\left[\frac{df(t)}{dt}\right] = s \cdot F(s) - f(0^*) \qquad\qquad (3.8.5)$$

where $f(0^*) = $ the value of $f(t)$ at $t = 0$ approaching from above.

$$\mathcal{L}\left[\int_0^t f(t)\, dt\right] = s^{-1} \cdot F(s) + s^{-1} \cdot [\int f(t)\, dt]_{t=0} \qquad\qquad (3.8.6)$$

The parameter s is nowhere evaluated, because it is simply an intermediate step in calculations that later transform back from the s domain into the time domain. That is to say, we restrict ourselves to cases where if there exists

$$F(s) = \mathcal{L}\,[f(t)] \tag{3.8.7}$$

then also

$$f(t) = \mathcal{L}^{-1}\,[F(s)] \tag{3.8.8}$$

The use jointly of transformations like (3.8.7) and (3.8.8) means that s will appear and disappear again in calculations without at any stage having been given numerical values; the process is analogous to writing a computer program in which we take logs and later take antilogs (exponentiate) to find an output but at no stage see or want to see the intermediate numerical stages. These intermediate stages do not bear any necessary relation to events in the segment of the real process that is being modeled.

Diagrammatically the method of using Laplace transforms is just like using z transformations or time series transfer functions, as in Fig. 3.8.1.

The method of partial fractions, which is employed to help solve inverse z-transform problems, is also used with Laplace transformations. The point is to break up a complicated expression in s into parts each of which will be a weighted term like the examples given for the impulse, step, ramp, and exponential decay forms listed previously.

For example, if an expression in s is $s^{-1} \cdot (s+1)^{-1}$, this can be rewritten as $s^{-1} - (s+1)^{-1}$, so

$$\mathcal{L}^{-1}\,[s^{-1} \cdot (s+1)^{-1}] = \mathcal{L}^{-1}\,[s^{-1}] - \mathcal{L}^{-1}[(s+1)^{-1}] \tag{3.8.9}$$

which from tabled forms $= 1 + -\exp \cdot (-t)$ or

$$y(t) = 1 - \exp(-t)$$

which is the form of a learning curve used often in psychology by Thurstone and later by Hull.

The functions in s can be cascaded; the output of a series of transformations F_1, then F_2, then F_3, and so on will be $F_3(s) \cdot F_2(s) \cdot F_1(s) \cdot x(s)$ where $x(s)$ is the s form of the original input $f(x, t)$.

The use of (3.8.5) is to represent some process that differentiates whatever input it receives, in time, and outputs the result.

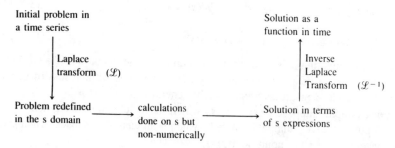

FIG. 3.8.1   Stages in the use of Laplace transforms.

For example, a differentiator acting upon a ramp input produces a step output with step height proportional to the original ramp slope, and if this step is in turn differentiated again, it will turn into a single impulse of size proportional to the step. This can be shown formally by repeated application of (3.8.5) on the original s function ks^{-2}.

The simple feedback loop with continuous input and output can be converted, by Laplace transforms, to the equivalent open-loop form. Suppose that Fig. 3.8.2 represents the input and output series of a stationary process, with each part represented in the s domain.

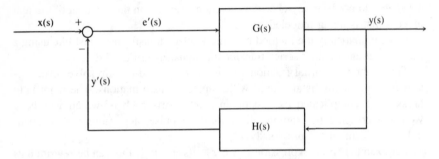

The above loop reduces to the function open loop that will have the same transfer function:

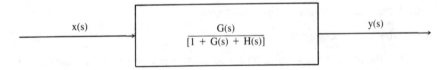

FIG. 3.8.2   Feedback and open-loop configurations in the s domain.

The equivalence in Fig. 3.8.2 can be obtained by writing the equations, which follow by definition, for

The comparator: $e'(s) = x(s) - y'(s)$ (3.8.10)

The gain: $y(s) = G(s) \cdot e'(s)$ (3.8.11)

The loop gain: $y'(s) = H(s) \cdot y(s)$ (3.8.12)

and then eliminating $e'(s)$ and $y'(s)$ to obtain $y(s)$ in terms of $x(s)$. As $G(s)$ and $H(s)$ can be pure delay or even identity transformations without loss of generality, the model constitutes a completely general case.

For example, suppose $G(s) = s^{-1}$, which means G simply integrates whatever input it receives, and let $H(s) = 1$, which is an identity feedback. Then give the system a unit step input, so $x(s) = s^{-1}$. Then

$$y(s) = s^{-1} \cdot (1 + s^{-1})^{-1} \cdot s^{-1} = (s(s + 1))^{-1}$$

from Fig. 3.8.2. The solution to this is given by (3.8.9) so that the input and output will resemble Fig. 3.8.3. If the same system were to be given a unit impulse input instead of a step, the output would be a decaying exponential $y(t) = \exp(-t)$, for the impulse input is $x(s) = 1$, so

$$y(s) = s^{-1} \cdot (1 + s^{-1})^{-1} \cdot 1 = (s + 1)^{-1}$$

and

$$\mathcal{L}^{-1} (s + 1)^{-1} = y(t) = \exp(-t) \tag{3.8.13}$$

As the basic equation of the system, in either open- or closed-loop form, is completely determined by $x(t)$, $y(t)$, $G(s)$, and $H(s)$, given any three one may in principle solve for the fourth expression, which may be an unidentified transfer function.

The Laplace transforms may be used in a simple but useful proof of the manner in which a high-gain loop with low-gain feedback can be used to swamp the effects of noise injected into a system after (i.e., on the output side) the main gain. Consider the closed loop shown in Fig. 3.8.4 where a noise whose s transform is $d(s)$ is injected into the loop as shown. It is assumed that the system is linear and stationary.

To ascertain how this loop will behave, we use the principle of superposition that holds for linear systems and consider first how the loop behaves with no noise and an indeterminate input of form $x(s)$. Call the resultant output $y_x(s)$, and

$$y_x(s) = \left(\frac{G(s)}{[1 + G(s) \cdot H(s)]} \right) \cdot x(s) \tag{3.8.14}$$

whereas the response to pure noise with zero input at $x(t)$ will be $y_d(s)$ where

$$y_d(s) = \left(\frac{1}{[1 + G(s) \cdot H(s)]} \right) \cdot d(s) \tag{3.8.15}$$

and

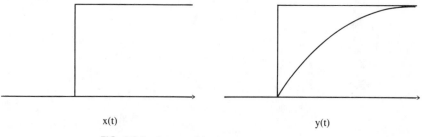

x(t)   y(t)

FIG. 3.8.3   Integrated-loop output to a step input.

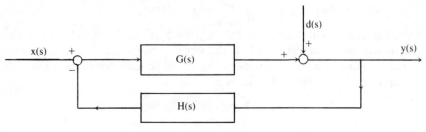

FIG. 3.8.4   A noisy loop.

$$Y(s) = y_x(s) + y_d(s)$$
$$= [1 + G(s) \cdot H(s)]^{-1} \cdot (G(s) \cdot x(s) + d(s)) \qquad (3.8.16)$$

Now, if $G(s)$ is large and $H(s)$ is not large (but is greater than 1), the term in $d(s)$ will be second order relative to the term in $x(s)$, so that $y(s)$ will approximate to $y_x(s)$. As is commonly used in electronics, and can be used in physiological processes where a high gain is not destructive of tissue, a feedback loop with appropriate gain is a selective filter for removing a noise component.

4 The Applicability and Limits of Time Series Representations

4.1   A HISTORICAL COMMENT ON TIME SERIES EXPERIMENTS

It is possible to convert a continuous signal into a discrete series of pulses, evenly spaced in time, and there are a number of different ways in which this can be done, both conceptually and in terms of hardware. If the process of sampling the continuous process satisfies some quite general conditions, then it is said to be a sampled-data system. The whole description and statistical analysis of a sampled-data system is just as rigorous as one in continuous time and, in fact, has a number of advantages; not least for the psychologist is the advantage that a system in discrete time reflects immediately the idea of data being collected by observations spaced in trials in time. There is no constraint to a single stimulus or response observation in each trial; both input and output are generally vectors, and the individual stimuli or responses can be scored so that they only take one of a finite set of values. That is, each variable can be treated as a lattice variable and not necessarily as capable of varying continuously over some range of values defined outside the experiment. There is considerable waste of effort and trivialization, however, if only binary variates are used. The combination of sampling in discrete time, and independently the discretization of the input and output variables, brings us conceptually close to the typical digital computer representation and control of an on-line psychological experiment. Interestingly, it also has parallels with some theorists in multidimensional scaling who have argued for psychological data representation only up to the limit of resolution of a coarse-grained map in multidimensional space; other theorists have gone further and argued that scalings that do no more than locate lattice partitions are *the* proper representations in psychology.

225

The methods reviewed in this and previous chapters, however, often originate from work in continuous-time systems, mostly in engineering where it is sensible to think of inputs as either completely random (white noise) or periodic and to treat outputs as sinusoidal with or without contamination. There are some areas of psychology where this is equally justified; the physics of hearing is obviously such an area and also the extensive work in the representation of electroencephalograms by mathematical models, from the 1940s onward.

As extensively shown, whether or not the record of the output of a system in time is discretized, it can be converted into a frequency distribution that stands outside time and where the energy level of any frequency present in the original series in time can be proportionately characterized. As such a frequency distribution or spectrum in many practical situations drops off rapidly with increasing frequencies and may be consequently truncated without significant loss of information, representation in the frequency domain can be terse and tractable. The other obvious reason for transforming into the frequency domain is the need to be able to calculate transfer functions; for some time the only feasible way of analyzing linear systems was through Laplace transforms (Section 3.8) and analytical procedures derived therefrom. But there are many systems, or sorts of systems, of potential interest to the experimental psychologist that are better analyzed by staying in the time domain and not by transforming into the frequency domain, operating therein, and then finally transforming back to obtain a predicted output. With an increased diversity of methods of analysis available comes an increased responsibility on the part of the investigator to redefine problems even more precisely.

So, although it is not necessary to transform from continuous into discrete time and from discrete time into the frequency domain by treating signals as sinusoidal, it is sometimes very convenient to do so and then exploit the range of methods and computer software facilities that exist; the whole area has been studied in great detail (Bracewell, 1965, Tou, 1959). When the output signals are periodic or are strongly suspected to have periodic components embedded in them, it is most usual to seek a representation as a sum of sine terms each with a fixed frequency. In motor behavior, earlier work on the stability and capacity of the human tracking response was done by transforming into the frequency domain and treating nonstationary behavior as approximately stationary, or what was called quasi-stationary. The incentive to use frequency domain representation has been increased by the development of the fast Fourier transform (Cochran et al., 1967), or FFT, the conversion of time domain into frequency domain information is undertaken for reasons that make obvious good sense in engineering and medical physiology; there design and control are realistic objectives. But, in psychology where the investigator stops with a descriptive analysis and then questions the stability of the description, the justification is less obvious. It is quite proper to use the terms *validity* and *reliability* to refer to necessary and sufficient properties of a time series analysis of sequential behavior, because although one does not immediately think of a time series analysis of behavior samples as a psychological test in the usual sense, any set of parameters from a fitted model can serve as a predictor of subsequent behavior and as a basis for discriminating between individuals. So, the notions of identifiability and stability in time series and systems analysis parallel, respectively, validity and reliability in psychometrics, though it is not fruitful to pursue the analogies at the level of detailed algebraic expressions, and there are problems in considering the representation of unstable and modelable systems that are not usually investigated in test theory but are increasingly the subject of system simulation.

In practice, if it is known that high-frequency components are extraneous, then they may be removed with a low-pass filter before transformation takes place. In engineering practice there is considerable interplay between hardware and software methods of filtering a time series as part of its analysis, and it would be sensible to expect experimental psychology to follow the same strategy; there is much to be said for simplifying the data before methods such as FFT are used, because the interpretation of low-energy frequency components is likely to be speculative.

It would be idle to pretend that the present literature of experimental methods in psychology includes many detailed examples of a problem being conceptualized and then analyzed in time series terms; the intellectual fossilization attendant upon a single-minded devotion to analysis of variance has done much to inhibit the growth of models and methods that are really pertinent to the representation of psychological processes. There are still, in the early 1980s, discussions concerning whether a psychological account of something should aim at being a process model or simply a statistical regression of dependent on independent variables. As there are no grandiose objectives in time series modeling, it could not be asserted that by following any or all of the paradigms in this text an insight must necessarily be gained into how man thinks or functions. At the same time, as soon as one gets away from the simplest of modeling in time, the distinction between statistical regression models and process models becomes rather blurred; the equivalences between the more complex sequential dependencies in multilag and in bivariate time series and models of feedback loops and control show that there is no sharp cutoff between statistically summarizing a set of input–output relations in sufficient complexity to offer a system description (by definition, as outlined in Chapter 1) and modeling some quasi-closed subsystem that has the capacity for process generation and self-regulation. Some metatheoretical disputes in psychology, which go back before the days of artificial intelligence and viable software simulations of problem solving, center on the question of whether or not, as an account of a system increases in its intrinsic complexity and nonlinearity, it will begin to exhibit characteristics that, when man was the only complex source of behavior studied in detail, were thought of as sure evidence of motive, purpose, or intelligence. The view taken here is that many sustained patterns of behavior that are thought of as motivated or directed are properly modeled via some sort of control system, as reviewed in very general abstract terms in Chapter 3. It is possible to be reasonably precise, in systems theory, about what a feedback loop is and does, and when it is identifiable. It is much less easy to avoid ending up in a verbal morass of drives, motives, intentions, goals, and purposes (or their operant analogs) if one adopts what was for a while the mainstream psychological approach to directed behavior and its analysis. Just because verbal analyses of motivation are fuzzy, it is impossible to know if all that is meant is properly subsumable under control theory, though McFarland (1971) made a courageous attempt to do something like that. The proper rejoinder to those who question the value of systems theory generalizations in the area of motivational analyses is to require the verbal theorist to formalize those areas of theory that are potentially outside or not amenable to control analysis with sufficient rigor for it to be clear what is being said. If someone wishes, as is their right, to assert that there are special characteristics of some types of purposive human behavior that are measurable but not capable of being represented within a system theory approach and for which a time series analysis is not a relevant or valid preliminary skirmish with the data, then the obligation, which goes with the right, is to produce formal analyses at a level of rigor and abstraction compatible with the levels employed in systems theory at its best (Mesarovic & Takahara, 1975). To do less is often to indulge in polemic.

No one with a sensible dislike of computational drudgery would have attempted any of the methods described in this and previous chapters before digital computers became ubiquitous. However, there is one early precursor at least who, though methodologically at times horrendous, should be honored with a mention; he was S. J. F. Philpott, working at University College London between the two World Wars. Though very obviously a quantitative psychologist, Philpott was a loner among psychometricians, anticipating the human engineering psychologists of the 1940s but also linking back to the founders of human psychophysics and their preoccupation with time and the experience of time. The earliest work on autocorrelations within time series and between periodic time series owes much to the work of Yule (1926) whom obviously Philpott knew, and though Philpott kept his analyses simplistic in the interests of communicating to his naïve contemporaries, he makes passing references that show that he was aware of better formal methods of transforming his data from the time to the frequency domain and of the hopelessness at that time of trying to use short runs of observations to support strong theories. He earlier saw that one of the key problems (Philpott, 1932, p. 77) was to find a measure of similarity between waveforms in respect of wavelength and phase and attempted by a mixture of log transformations in the time dimension and graphical superposition to show that there were recurrent and invariant periodic components, which he called ''function fluctuations'' in the output of simple cognitive and motor tasks. The sparseness and roughness of his raw data were such as to defeat his purpose and yet leave room for the eye of faith to read into them considerable regularities that today one would question. At times the analyses are numerological speculations of a bizarre kind. His output curves resemble a process in which wavelength increases exponentially with time after the start of a task, and amplitude is progressively damped. Qualitatively this shows in some of the graphs, together with noise, baseline trends, shifts of phase, and behavior, that Philpott sadly labeled "erratic." Though he had no data in the first 5 sec of any task, and the resolution of data was at best about one data point per second, he claimed as a general law that by transforming back he had located the zero point, in time, of the function fluctuations induced by mental work, as lying at 4.076×10^{-23} sec after the origin. How this sort of nonsense could be seriously entertained in a century that had already seen, nearly 2 decades before, the development of general relativity theory, is lost in decent obscurity. Philpott (1932) concluded "we have not been able (to explain the function fluctuations) . . . it is sufficient to have described and systematized them." The problem perhaps is that, like Fechner and his other predecessors, Philpott was looking for the numerical constants of behavior, in the model of 19th century physics, instead of looking for invariance in the process structure that could have generated his data. The alternative to lamenting individual differences is to realize that process can be invariant when the numerical outputs are anything but constant, which is one of the strongest recurrent demonstrations of time series analyses.

The tradition, already extant, to which Philpott (1932) referred in his monograph was concerned with the analysis of experiments on the perception and estimation of elapsed clock time. Perhaps surprisingly it is not our topic to review the very extensive work on the perception of time, though experiments in that area frequently employ paradigms that are, in effect, a time series of signals (usually brief pulses) and a time series of responses to those signals. Each signal may elicit or may fail to elicit a response that will have a delay. Further, the delays will have a time series structure that is autocorrelated. The modeling and analysis of serial time perception studies are reviewed, briefly, in the Section 4.2 to illustrate some ways in which it may be treated within our general framework. It is however proper to make the general point that most experiments on time perception have not been done as time series experiments in the statistical sense and that most time series experiments have nothing necessarily to do with the perception of time. It would be nice if there were two or more quite distinct words to refer to "time" in the two senses just distinguished, but the fact that, at least in English, there are not may in part explain the implicit chain in the spasmodic development of the topic within psychology.

In this chapter some experiments that are paradigms of methods and problems in psychological time series are reviewed. The theory previously covered is drawn on where germane. The lack of time series analyses in experimental psychology has been noted and emphasized, but in the wider areas of the social sciences, and particularly in social and resource planning studies, examples are becoming more plentiful and have obvious implications because often problems of method and conceptualization are solved in advance of finding specific application within psychology. Any excursion into a growing field is a poaching expedition, and the mixup of disciplines and data in large-scale systems modeling has been likened to a quilting bee[1], with the interesting consequences that models have been developed that can be divided into segments so that parameter estimation can proceed in one segment whereas identification is the main task in another; this sort of planning strategy in theory construction reflects the large scale of computing resources and costly data collection that can arise in the social sciences today.

Two very general models that need mention but that do not sit comfortably in any of the specific sections of this chapter that follow must be noted because of the breadth of their implications. There have been attempts at general reviews and classifications of sequential analysis methods in selected areas of the social sciences, at very varied levels of sophistication. Bakeman and Dabbs (1976) offered a catalog of data types of sequential social interaction that they call "behavior streams." These are obviously multivariate time series of behavioral data, and nothing else. They label sequences in which only the states are recorded, but not their times of entry or duration of occupancy, as Type I; if concurrent states are admissible, then the data become Type II. Types III and IV refer, respectively, to data with real-time bases, sequential (single series) or concurrent (multivariate series). Our view, unequivocally, is that it is better to treat all new situations as their Type IV (real time, discrete, multivariate) and only simplify subsequently for particular purposes. The legitimate uses of the simpler structures, inevitably throwing away information about series structure, will facilitate modeling in Markov chain form and make it possible to estimate state transition probabilities as descriptive statistics. However, it is easy to concur with Bakeman and Dabbs that "techniques that can handle the complex interrelations of social behaviour possess a descriptive fidelity that has been lacking in behavioural research [p. 344]." Examples of dialogues, musical phrases, mother–child interactions, and visual gazing between people have all previously been handled by simple transition probability tabulation with or without explicit commitment to some finite state model.

The first of the two general models, which may be seen as helping the researcher bridge the gap between the wide qualitative description of psychological processes on the one hand and the quantitative minutiae of a time series representation on the other, is due to Mitchiner, Crews, Watt, and Brewer (1975) and derives from earlier models by Brewer and co-workers. A general method of constructing and parametrizing simulation models is available, which if a loss in

---

[1]This term is not part of the author's own folklore; it appears to be North American and describes a collective endeavor by housewives to join forces in finishing one bed cover quickly. Cultures less dedicated to private enterprise have collectives that are just as good as metaphors in this context, also implying the patchwork qualities of the output.

statistical inference can be tolerated in the interim, may make rapid headway in constructing models from small samples of multivariate time series. The tentative fixing of a model can clear the way for precise parameter estimation afterward; in this sense the cycle of identification and estimation previously described as associated with the Box–Jenkins approach is generalized.

Suppose an n-dimensional state vector x_j describes the system at time j; with u_j an r-dimensional input, p is an m-dimensional parameter vector to be estimated, and f is a nonlinear n-dimensional vector function. Then the system simulation equation is written as

$$x_{j+1} = f(x_j, j, j+1, u_j, p) \tag{4.1.1}$$

and the object is to apply this recursively to obtain long-term predictions.

Next we assume that q data vectors are available from some partial experiment; these are

$$u_1^*, \ldots, u_q^*$$
$$x_1^*, \ldots, x_q^*$$

and from these input to (4.1.1) the object is to find an estimation set $\hat{p}$.

The "quilting bee" device comes in at this point; first, partition f into the set $\{f_i\}$, $i = 1, 2, \ldots, n$. The partitioning is based on conjectures about how the system might have subsystems that can behave in a closed manner for some parameter values; such conjectures would be psychological and not necessarily mathematical, at least initially in an investigation. This partitioning means that we only seek to solve for the set of parameters p_i that are appropriate to the subset $\{f_i\}$. The minimization criterion chosen is

$$I_i = \sum_{j=1}^{q-1} (x_{i,j+1}^* - f_i(x_j^*, j, j+1, u_j^*, p_i))^2 \tag{4.1.2}$$

which Mitchiner et al. (1975) point out is in contradistinction to the more familiar least squares criterion

$$I_0 = \sum_{j=1}^{q} \{x_j^* - x_j\}' \{x_j^* - x_j\} \tag{4.1.3}$$

The point of using (4.1.2) is that it copes with the intrinsic nonlinearity of f. The key idea is that the $\{p_i\}$ can be chosen so as to be independent sets for different f_i. If two or more $\{p_i\}$ have an intersection, then the associated I_i have to be coalesced and a new minimization sought for the redefined I_i. The strategy here is thus to segregate the minimization problems, so that failure to converge on a solution for a particular $\{p_i\}$ does not inhibit solution in the rest of the parameter space for the total system.

Though the vector x_j has been defined initially as a set of state variables, the distinction between state and input variables has no meaning so far as parameter identification is concerned, within the framework of this approach. The authors point out that once a parameter has been identified as an input variable in one part of the system, it becomes fixed and a state variable for another discrete f_i. To keep a total system model simple, therefore, the number of input variables should be kept to a minimum. A special case of (4.1.1), in terms of rates of change of the x_i, where

$$\Delta_{i,j+1} = \text{def } x_{i,j+1} - x_{i,j} \qquad (4.1.4)$$

is

$$\Delta_{i,j+1} = \alpha_i \left[\beta_i \prod_{k=1}^{s} \phi_{ik} - x_{ij} \right] \qquad (4.1.5)$$

where the product in s is over the set of s partitions f_i, α and β are parameters to be identified, and the ϕ_{ik} are nonlinear functions of x_j, u_j, and p_i.

When the system is in steady state, then the differences of (4.1.5) are zero, so that the regression parameters β_i under fixed system parameters p_i provide a conceptual link between a representation in regression form and a system equation. In the literature of simulation theory, alternative interpretations can be given to the ϕ_{ik}. Their task is to quantify the interactions between hypothetical variables, but as they are themselves rates of change of states, they can be used as state variables to characterize the system. Given (4.1.5), the function (4.1.2) to be minimized has to be rewritten more appropriately as

$$I_i = \sum_{j=1}^{q} \{\Delta_i(j, x_j^*, u_j^*) - \Delta_{i*}(j)\}^2 \qquad (4.1.6)$$

where the Δ_i expression is found by solving the r.h.s. of (4.1.5) repeatedly, and the Δ_{i*} are observed increments. Solution algorithms are based on the joint use of (4.1.5) and (4.1.6). The important features of these simulation strategies are that they will always converge on a prediction solution and that the simulation of what the system will do (i.e., how it will behave) is obtained before the model is identified. After successful simulation has been achieved the identification problems can be approached separately, so the separation of prediction and identification in some applied problems can be formalized and priority given to the more urgent task. Additionally it has been shown that quite complex systems can be simulated in terms of their immediate future behavior with relatively little sample data, using the previous approach. The objectives of experimental psychology are not usually those of prediction without theory construction, though ironically in the area of behavior modification some successes in prediciting behavior from a purely black box approach has encouraged the more empiricist operant psychologists to claim that theory was unnecessary for their purposes. The distinctions raised previously are, of course, replete with difficulties and pitfalls in any real applications, but they serve to emphasize that the prediction of the behavior of very complex systems can be achieved by models that are subject to recursive internal modification and that this success is not evidence, of itself, of process identification but rather a necessary prerequisite to identification. The formal parallels between the algebra used and time series modeling as a step to identification is very close; the intention of the theory constructor and the interpretation given to the terms in a model is often a better guide to the metatheoretical status of the model than the fact that it has inputs, outputs, and states.

An example of modeling that resembles the simulation case but has a precise psychological interpretation has been furnished by Kohonen (1977), in constructing a network representation of associative memory. Cells in a neural assembly that is to be capable of association and the reconstruction of complete images or patterns from partial or fragmented inputs that resemble inputs previously experienced are linked by a network in which the signal transmission properties of a single idealized cell can be written in linear transfer function form. The ideas are those of Chapters 2 and 3 but turned to a different use; events are not just in time but in the space–time of the transmissions within the neural network.

In this case the inputs and outputs of a cell are defined to be frequencies, and the role of a single cell is to summate inputs from those other cells in the network to which it is directly connected and to output the result into the network. The summation within a cell takes place in a time span that is second-order with respect to the unit of discrete time in which input patterns of excitation to the network are defined to occur.

Let

u_i = an input impulse frequency to cell i

y_i = an output frequency from cell i

then, by definition in the network,

$$y_i = u_i + \sum_k c_{ik} \cdot y_k \tag{4.1.7}$$

where the c_{ik} are the elements of an interaction matrix of intercell effects that Kohonen (1977) calls "intercouplings," defined over the set of cells in the network. Call this matrix C.

The summation in j in (4.1.7) has an open upper bound; the size of the network is not taken as a closed system parameter, though the model is intended to capture some of the features of the pyramidal neurons of the neocortex. This physiological correspondence should not be pushed too far, as the model is probably too "crisp" to be a representation of how a stochastic network actually operates. Instead, let us just take it as a process description of a minimum-complexity system that can have associative memory characteristics.

Memory in this model is equated with changes in the elements of C,

$$\frac{dc_{ik}}{dt} = \alpha \cdot y_i(y_k - y_{kb}) \tag{4.1.8}$$

where y_k = a presynaptic impulse frequency from cell k onto i, y_i = the post-synaptic triggering activity of i sending signals onward to the network, and y_{kb} = the value of y_k at which there do not occur any changes in c_{ik}. The idea here is that the intercouplings will be modified by inputs that actually pass through them, and there is a threshold of input intensity above which changes in the elements of C will occur and below which C will remain unchanged. An unchanged C implies that nothing is remembered, in the sense of being put into a memory storage or representation within the network. It is convenient, if only for face validity, to distinguish inhibition where $c_{ik} < 0$, $\alpha < 0$ from excitation where $c_{ik} > 0$, $\alpha > 0$.

The initial conditions require that c_{ik} at t_0 are set at zero, which means that the network is initially open to intercoupling but not interconnected, and all elements of C are equal and null. Memory then consists of progressively changing the elements of C, reducing the entropy of the matrix. The input to the network is an input series, in discrete time, of patterns each of which is stationary in the unit of discrete time but distributed over the space of the network. Call these patterns $\{u_i, j\}$, $j = t_o, 1, 2, \ldots, m, \ldots$. At time m the intercouplings will then have become

$$c_{ik}^* = \alpha \cdot \sum_{j=1}^{m} y_{i,j}(y_{k,j} - y_{kb}) \tag{4.1.9}$$

Then (4.1.7) becomes at time j

$$y_{i,j} = u_{i,j} + \sum_{k} c_{ik} \cdot y_{k,j} \tag{4.1.10}$$

$$= u_{i,j} + \sum_{h=1}^{m} w(j, h) \cdot y_{i,h} \tag{4.1.11}$$

where the kernel $w(j, h)$ represents the similarity between the input pattern at time j and the series of previous input patterns that have already occurred at times h, where h takes some subset of values in the range $1, \ldots, m$. We may write, again with α as a rate constant,

$$w(j, h) = \alpha \cdot \sum_{k} y_{k,j}(y_{k,h} - y_{kb}) \tag{4.1.12}$$

and interpret (4.1.10) as a recollection from memory of what will, in effect, be a weighted linear sum of previous inputs, the weights being proportional to the similarities of what is now recalled to what was input or experience previously. Kohonen (1977) used (4.1.11) as the basis for simulation of the associative recall of two-dimensional patterns and in doing so assumed that the memory cortex was a single two-dimensional layer. The results are quite strikingly successful, requiring about 20,000 elements in C. It should be noted that it does not follow that a two-dimensional system, recalling flat pictures, would imply or require that the matrix C would also be two-dimensional; in fact the representation of C in a spatial net, with the strength of intercouplings proportional to their proximity, may need a higher dimensionality than any of the patterns recalled.

The review of these models at this point in the chapter is intended to remind the reader, by noting analogies and differences, that the typical time series models and convolution integrals or sums bear a very strong relationship to models that have psychological importance but a slightly different, though related, structure. The mathematical parallels are not fortuitous, but the interpretation of the parts within the models in the simulations involves more implicit assumptions about the process in psychological terms; it is as though the identification had already been achieved in all but a few details, by translating the qualitative ideas about processes into algebraic structures that turn out to resemble special cases of time series models. But at the same time the examples quoted have a complexity and inherent generality, which are necessarily lacking in the more specific and more prosaic cases associated with narrow, circumscribed (but important) problems that are reviewed next. The simulation models can often be constructed on very small data bases because of the prior commitment to model structure; there is a trade-off between how much it is possible to assume about systems and how much data it is necessary to collect to confirm what is suspected but still unconfirmed. To end by returning to the ill-fated example of Philpott's function fluctuations, if one wished again to take seriously his ideas, then it would be possible to make some headway by using a mixture of on-line experiments, simulation, and possibly time series identification, but in developing the methods, hardware, and concepts to do all that one has necessarily, along the way, acquired quite a different view of what a plausible model of human performance should look like. It is not that the runs of data were never long enough to test the sorts of stationary theory that were borrowed from physics to represent nonstationarity in performance, it is that now the models are intrinsically nonstationary from the moment of construction, and their algebraic style is different.

4.2 THE PERCEPTION OF TIME ITSELF, REACTION TIMES, AND SOME RELATED TIME SERIES

Of time you would make a stream upon whose bank you would sit and watch its flowing.

Kahlil Gibran, The Prophet, 1923.

The experimental psychology of time perception and time estimation is extensive and has been an active area for many years; for present purposes only a few examples of one type of time estimation experiment will be considered, and that will, perhaps surprisingly, be grouped with experiments on choice behavior and identification choice. The rationale for taking these together is as follows. In a choice experiment in which the subject is asked to say, as soon as possible, whether or not an event that has just occurred fell into a specific class, the latency or reaction time after stimulus presentation is measured, and the correctness of the judgment when it occurs. In some sorts of time estimation experiment, one asks a subject to say as accurately as possible when some interval of time has elapsed; it may be an interval designated by a label, like "ten seconds," or it may be matched to another unlabeled interval that has previously been experienced. The subject is required to mark out the end of a time period that is just as long as a previous time interval whose start and finish had been signaled by the experimenter. There are many methodological complications to delight the curious, such as presenting time intervals that are filled with sounds or are silent, such as encouraging subjects to count to themselves or trying by all ethical means to stop them counting. What matters in this context is that the time that the subject is supposed to mark out, by responding to signal its end or completion, can be thought of as an internal event to be identified and responded to by an appropriately chosen response (Creelman, 1962). The distinction between the time estimation experiment and the identification choice experiment is, in this classification, a distinction between internally and externally presented stimuli from which an identification choice is to be made.

It transpires, as might be expected, that the analysis and representation of what happens in a sequence of identification choices made in real time is complex and as yet no general solution exists. A multivariate time series representation of the paradigmatic experiment could be set up, and to some extent this has been done in recent years. In this section are examined some of the more complex attempts to model sequences of responses where the time to make a response is of greater interest than the response itself. This is typical of choice identification experiments where there are only a few possible alternative events.

In the two-choice identification paradigm, the stimulus series is a random sequence of instances of S_1 and S_2, where S_1 and S_2 may or may not be readily discernible, but the intrinsic physical properties of the stimuli are not represented in the model and play no part in the analysis. Of greater interest may be the actual time in milliseconds between successive stimuli or between stimuli and some time limit upon responding. The experimenter chooses to present the random sequence with fixed probabilities, π_i for S_i, $i = 1, 2$. It may also be necessary to introduce nonrandom subsequences at quasi-random locations; for example, runs of $S_1 S_1 S_1$ may be interspersed in an otherwise random sequence. The sequential dependencies up to any order are at the choice of the experimenter, and there is particular interest, in reported studies, in either runs of one stimulus or in regular alternating sequences. The subject may or may not be told in advance that $p(S_1) = \pi_1$; obviously in the two-choice situation $\pi_1 = 1 - \pi_2$. The permitted responses may be partitioned into two disjoint sets, designated R_1 and R_2, where R_1 is "appropriate" for S_1 and R_2 for S_2. More formally, we may say that there exists an identification function R such that $R(S_i) = R_i$, $i = 1, 2$. In fixed choice experiments, no provision is made for other responses such as $R_3, \ldots, R_n$.

After each trial we have a quadruple that characterizes what happened:

$$S_j, \quad R_j, \quad T_j, \quad E_j \qquad j=1, \ldots, t$$

where $S_j \in \{S_i\}$, $R_j \in \{R_i\}$, $0 < T_j \leq \infty$, because $T_j \leq 0$ is inadmissible by instruction, as it is the case of false anticipatory responding. E_j is a feedback from the experimenter, so that if

$$R_j = R(S_j) \qquad E_j = \text{``right''}$$
$$R_j \neq R(S_j) \qquad E_j = \text{``wrong''}$$

Some writers use a characteristic variable, taking values $(0, 1)$ to redefine E_j.

The problem is to see if the distribution of T_j, $h(T_j)$ can be sufficiently characterized by a stationary function f, where

$$h(T_j) = f(\{ S_k \}, \{ R_k \}, \{ E_k \}, \{ T_k \}, k = 1, \ldots, j) \qquad (4.2.1)$$

Obviously this is a formulation that is a catchall and therefore vapid as a model; strong simplification of the form of f and the constraint of its arguments is sought. There are various simplifications that have intuitive appeal, both mathematical for tractability and psychological for process simplicity and plausibility. Treating the problem as a multivariate time series, with single (stimulus) input and multiple (vector) output, is one possibility.

Falmagne (1965) reduced the problem, by a series of postulates, to what was essentially a Markov chain representation by introducing a variable $K_{i,n} = $ the level of preparedness of the subject with respect to the ith stimulus on the nth trial. Setting up the transition probability matrix for $\{K_{1,n}, K_{2,n}$ to $K_{1,n+1}, K_{2,n+1}\}$ because K is defined as two-valued (i.e., preparedness is all-or-nothing), in terms of two model parameters c and c', Falmagne obtained predictions of the reaction-time distributions under all S, R conditions on the nth trial. According to Falmagne (1965), the justifications for proceeding this way were "a model of r.t. which does not include an inherent mechanism for selective preparation or anticipation of the choice of response would have difficulty in explaining experimental results to date [p. 78]" and that "interdependence of r.t.'s has an appealing simplicity; it suggests that a model might be constructed based solely on sequential effects [p. 79]." Unfortunately this one-stage sequential dependency model does not fit all data properties well, and an alternative approach, allowing higher-order dependencies, is needed. This was shown in a monograph by Laming (1968) that is about as complex and penetrating an analysis as is likely to be supportable by real data. Laming made more progress with the problem by using multiple regression models, not quite time series analyses in the standard forms given in Chapters 2 and 3, as exploratory tools for locating the functional structure of time series of reaction times for choices. As Laming's notation is very complex and specific to his formulation of the two-choice task, his original equations will be expressed in a looser functional form from which it is easier to relate to time series and state models.

The interest in Laming's (1968) approach is that he used alternative formulas, all of a mulitiple linear regression type, but used error as a first-order explanatory independent variable. There are in fact two main theoretical problems: (1) predicting the sequence of response choices (which is the same as predicting the error sequence given that the stimulus sequence is known); and (2) predicting the sequence of reaction times. One may plausibly be interested in the first problem, without wishing to solve for the second, but it is difficult to make sense or progress with the second if the actual response sequence does not feature in the model, because r.t.'s are contingent, apparently, on the response sequence structure ($\{R_j\}$, cov $\{R_j, R_{j+k}\}$).

The prediction equation for T_j, given the system record up to that trial and including S_j, R_j, was postulated by Laming to be of the form

$T_j = f_1$(autocorrelation of T_j, T_{j-k}) + f_2(state variable determining the autocorrelation process) + f_3(signal, response, and error covariances with r.t. up to $j - 1$) + f_4(local sequential repetition/nonrepetition of the signals, which is a degenerate local signal autocorrelation) + f_5(increment in r.t. consequent upon error in the identification response)

$$(4.2.2)$$

From the given $f_1, \ldots, f_5$, the last one f_5, is the only process that is not plausibly postulated in advance from very general considerations of cognitive psychology but rests on specific psychological knowledge.

The model (4.2.2) is advanced by Laming (1968) as purely descriptive; it is a regression analysis of the microstructure of the decision process. Its value lies in the fact that its solution enables us to specify the minimum complexity account that will predict sequential reaction time behavior, though in the form of a multivariate time series model there may well exist a process or system description that is simpler and more elegant than the aggregate of parts that makes up (4.2.2).

There is an important distinction, as already noted, between the sequential structure of r.t.'s, as in (4.2.2), and the sequential structure of error responses. A family of regression models are necessary to cover the range of prediction problems involved; the coefficients in these models are classified by Laming into the following:

1. Preceding sequences of $S_{j-1}, S_{j-2}, \ldots, S_{j-k}$ where a_k are coefficients relating error E_j to the $\{S_{j-k}\}$ and u_k are coefficients relating r.t. T_j to the $\{S_{j-k}\}$.
2. Pairings $\{S_j, R_j\}$.
3. Aftereffects of an error, which are $\delta R_{j+1}, \delta R_{j+2}, \ldots, \delta R_{j+k}$ following E_j.
4. Covariances on $\{T_j, T_{j+k}\}$, h_k.
5. Coefficients on the interaction of cov (T_j, T_{j+k}) with (S_j, R_j).   (4.2.3)

The empirical results have three main features that invalidate a simple Markov chain representation and make a complex time series analysis plausible:

1. The coefficients a_k rise from a_1 = approx .010 to a_2 = approx. .020 and then fall monotonically to a minimum around a_7 = approx .002 (Laming, 1968, p. 104, Fig. 8.2).

2. The coefficients u_k similarly peak at u_2 = approx .020 and then drop back rapidly to around noise level at .005.

3. The r.t. covariances h_k are maximal at h_1 and fall off to noise at about h_4.

This indicates that the reaction times are generated by a process that is in some ways more dependent on lag 2 than on lag 1 inputs but also could have components extending over about four trials. This not only invalidates a Markov representation in any tidy form, it also implies psychologically that local alternation induces the expectation in the subject of more alternation in the input series. The effect of this expectation is confounded with the effects of stimulus frequency.

The intertrial interval critically affects the sequential interactions of reaction times; as the intertrial interval decreased in Laming's (1968) data from 4096 msec down to 1 msec, the interaction terms (5) in (4.2.3) increased greatly and came to dominate the process. At very short exposures the mean rate of extraction of information from the signals presented is less after an alternating sequence of signals than it is after a run of one signal. This decrement in performance with alternating signals and very short intertrial times is sometimes accompanied by a "mental image" in the subject, which it is claimed "gets in the way" of doing the task. But one has to be cautious here, as the decrement in performance can occur without this phenomenological counterpart being reported.

Laming's results are the most complex to date, using a representation in the time domain. It has been suggested by Green (1971) that r.t. data can be represented by a Fourier analysis in the frequency domain, starting from the idea that the reaction-time distribution $h(T)$ can be written as the convolution of two stages,

$$h(T) = \Sigma\ d(T) \cdot e(T - k) \tag{4.2.4}$$

where $d(T)$ is a distribution of sensory decision latencies, and $e(T)$ is a distribution of residual latencies. The idea is that the sensory latencies are generated by a process that occurs first, in series with the other residual delays in the system that follow within more central processing. The deconvolution of (4.2.4) is intended as a step toward the identification of $d(T)$. The distribution $h(T)$ is the histogram of reaction times from a given experiment under specified conditions; it was postulated that $e(T)$ is bounded, which means that its density function only exists inside a range whose bounds can be the subject of prior specification. In a given task we can set limits on the reasonable upper and lower values of a mean observable reaction time. The distribution of $d(T)$ was postulated to have a Poisson-like form with an exponential tail and to exist in two variants, one corresponding to events before a signal onset (in time) and one for events after that onset. Green and Luce (1974) used this model for $d(T)$ in order to solve for the form of $e(T)$ in the frequency domain, employing a FFT. The result was incompatible with the reaction time for intense signals, a task in which detection is not involved but response latency is measured more or less uncontaminated, so the model for $d(T)$ was rejected. There are complications, not least because the form of $h(T)$ is in part a function of the waiting time between signaling the onset of a trial and the signal itself. The analysis could have been performed in the time domain, but this point is not critical to supporting or rejecting the model for $d(T)$.

The peculiar local phenomena in sequences of identification judgments and their associated reaction times, particularly with respect to the effects of alternation in the stimulus series, had of course been known for some time, and various attempts to model or quantify the major effects and to disentangle them from one another are to be found (Howarth & Bulmer, 1956; Senders & Sowards, 1952; Skinner, 1942; Verplanck, Collier, & Cotton, 1952) in which the time series analyses are either wrong or incomplete. Attempts to explain what was happening was somewhat circular; for example, Skinner (1942) conjectured "the more natural response tendency is for repetition, but . . . subjects' concepts of chance alter their behaviour in such a way that responses are alternated rather than repeated [p. 501]." In this sort of explanation the cognition drives the behavior, but the cognition of sequential probabilities has to be built up from experience of previous time series, which implies some nonstationarity in the process. At the same time most published analyses have been of local stationary higher-order dependencies. Some of these earlier studies were made in the context of sequential judgments of stimulus magnitudes and will be commented on in the section on psychophysical time series with particular reference to the classical problem of time order errors.

The most thorough analysis of sequential effects in time estimation has been given by Michon (1965, 1967), and his major findings are readily describable with the methods of autocorrelation analysis and feedback modeling.

Figure 4.2.1 is our revision of one scheme offered by Michon (1967) as paradigmatic of most theories of sequential time estimation, when expressed in flow process steps. This representation is particularly useful because it leads directly into computer simulations of the response of the system under impulse or step inputs and enables us to trace out the consequences of changing the coarseness, in milliseconds, of the internal pulse counter. The counter in Fig. 4.2.1 is activated by a psychophysiological mechanism to provide a time base in discrete steps. This is supposed to be a process of fairly stable characteristics; it has to behave as though it has a very short discrete step counter in order to accommodate a diversity of data, and about 0.1 msec appears to be a plausible bound on the necessary fineness of this counter. Experiments that are about time percep-

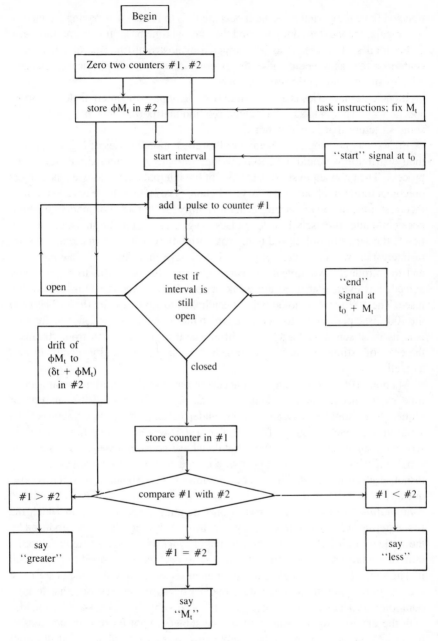

FIG. 4.2.1 Flow process of a time estimation decision structure; parallel presentation paired comparison paradigm (modified from Michon, 1967, with additions).

tion and have n external periodic inputs are thus to be taken as having a total of $n + 1$ inputs, the n external inputs, and the internal time base. It is the performance of the total system that is to be compared against real time; particular interest centers on the cases where one of the external inputs is a real physical clock (i.e., a series of constant period time signals).

If one external series is a clock, it may pulse or pace the internal clock in some special way. That is to say, the autocorrelation matrix ($n + 1 \times n + 1$) can have some structure that is not stationary.

Errors may be generated in any or all of the notional boxes of Fig. 4.2.1, and their distributions would have to be written into any computer simulation of the process. The precise physiological basis of the internal clock has been the subject of conjecture for about a century. Michon (1967) lists at least 23 alternate theories; none have very strong generalizability. At the level of modeling here it does not matter precisely how the pulses are generated, but the statistical properties of the series of pulses and their crosscorrelations with external processes are of interest. It would be perfectly possible to have more than one internal clock and to introduce switching rules between them. It does seem to be generally agreed, however, that there are weak periodicities of about 100 msec and 700 msec. The 100-msec periodicity has been linked to alpha rhythm (9 to 12 Hz) and the 700-msec periodicity to a point at which the subjective experience of duration is at its most sensitive, in terms of difference thresholds. Away from 700 msec the error of estimation increases, though there may be modality-specific effects as well.

Michon (1967) commented that accelerations and decelerations in subjective time experience occur and their occurrence gives surprise, ''the analysis of sequential relations is essential to our understanding of the functioning of the serial timing mechanism [p. 14].'' Baker (1962) was one of the first to perform sequential analyses in this context, but they have not been extensively used. The serial experiment where a subject is required to tap, or to make some crisp response at an even rate, has to be provided with a standard or reference sequence. This task as it is usually structured by experimenters is either one of *continuation* (a method of reproduction extending through time) in which the first m terms are produced externally and the $m + 1$ to nth terms are produced by the subject or alternatively the task is one of *synchronization* where the external train of signals continues unbroken and the subject has to respond in phase with it. The subject may be asked to try to tap in exact synchrony, in which case he or she has to respond in an anticipatory manner because each response has a finite duration and needs to be begun before its observable part occurs and coincides with the external signal. Alternatively the subject might try to respond so as to bisect as accurately as possible the intervals in the external series. It does not necessarily follow that the internal standard or sequence in the extrapolation task functions in the same way as the external standard sequence in the synchronization task.

It is because synchronization requires constant monitoring of input that the flow diagram (not given here; the exercise in constructing it will help the reader to obtain a real feel for the depth of the conceptual problem involved) becomes more complicated; we have now to consider ways in which information from the $j - k, j - k - 1, \ldots, j - 2, j - 1$ cycles become integrated into the matching process that would resemble Fig. 4.2.1 on the jth cycle.

The continuation task shows nonstationarity; according to Michon a trend with polynomial terms up to degree 7 exists (this is probably a gross overestimate due to autocorrelations of residuals that should have been removed by differencing to an appropriate degree), but we may accept that a marked change with practice occurs in this context. Surprisingly the synchronization task appears to be quite stationary. The results shown in Fig. 4.2.2 for the continuation task suggest that a Markov representation such as

$$y_j = v_0 + v_1 y_{j-1} + u_j, \qquad v_1 > 0 \tag{4.2.5}$$

is appropriate, whereas in the synchronisation process, the $R(1)$ autocorrelation is negative, and possibly also $R(2)$ and $R(4)$. See Fig. 4.2.3; the oscillation suggests that the Yule process

$$y_j = v_0 + v_1 y_{j-1} + v_2 y_{j-2} + u_j \tag{4.2.6}$$

with appropriate choice of coefficients is an economical model. Actually it may in some circumstances be an oversimplification.

There is some internal sequential dependence in the synchronization sequences; the difference Michon (1967) considered "probably reflects the generic difference between an external and an internal standard [p. 36]." The externalization of the standard brings with it the possibility of successive compensations or second-order corrections that themselves will have an autocorrelation structure. The ability of a subject to correct for an error in estimating depends in part on the size of the time interval being judged; Weber's law does not hold exactly, but the error does increase in an average way expressible by

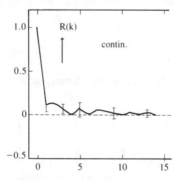

FIG. 4.2.2   Autocorrelations in the continuation paradigm, after Michon (1967).

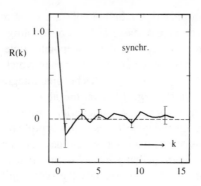

FIG. 4.2.3   The synchronization autocorrelation spectrum corresponding to Fig. 4.2.2.

$$\delta t = k \cdot t_{av}^{1.5} + a, \qquad k = .04 \tag{4.2.7}$$

and this relation holds for both continuation and synchronization. Hence whatever the mechanism of correction is, the loop is closed differently in the two procedures but the loop sensitivity is not enhanced.

Of great potential interest is a phenomenon first noted in detail by Ehrlich (1958) that involves transient shifts into a second state during the series of estimations. The subject becomes as it were "unhooked" from the input pacing series in the synchronization task and thus for an indeterminate period is monitored only by the internal clock. The response process in the long run gets hooked up again. Switching between systems under conditions of overload, as a theoretical possibility, is discussed in Sections 3.2 and 5.3. Michon considers the possibility that the internal standard follows the fluctuations in output to some extent (which means that there is a nontrivial crosscorrelation spectrum between the residual errors of the responses and the internal counter, a possible link not shown in Fig. 4.2.1). Obviously the external standard will not be coupled in that way. This point is interesting because it suggests an adaptive filter, anticipating Chapter 5, with state variable x_j, response y_j, input u_j, and

$$x_{j+1} = Ay_j + Bx_j \tag{4.2.8}$$

$$y_j = f(x_j, y_{j-1}, u_j) \tag{4.2.9}$$

but this coupling may only occur within limits, so it is necessary to clarify the functional relation (4.2.8)

$$\left.\begin{array}{l} y_b \le y_j \le y_a \leftrightarrow x_{j+1} = Ix_j \\[2mm] y_j < y_b, \quad \text{or} \quad y_a < y_j \leftrightarrow x_{j+1} = Ay_j + Bx_j \end{array}\right\} \tag{4.2.10}$$

which resembles some of the details in our simulation extension of MacKay's model in Section 3.3.

The process just described is self-regulatory but has sensitivity that decreases with the input magnitude. Michon (1967) suggests, in offering an explanation of how this could be so, that (4.2.9) arises from the time-order error. Implicit is the notion that there is a fixed probability of an error of increment or decrement at one step of the counter (see Fig. 4.2.1) and this will therefore generate a random walk in time, the variance of the total cumulative error is a function of the distance of the random walk from the origin. It is also necessary to postulate that the step size in this random walk is a function of the average response size, which is something like Weber's law extended through time. The derivation of the transfer function of the system follows from axioms as follows:

Axiom 1: If the input series $\{u_j\}$ is isochronous, with interval $= C$ sec,

so that

$$t_j - t_{j-1} = t_{j+1} - t_j \tag{4.2.11}$$

then if

$$t_j - t_{j-1} = C_j$$

$$\psi C_j = C_j \qquad \text{for all } j > 2$$

where ψC_j is the response (i.e., the reproduced interval on trial j).

Axiom 2: The system has error-free recall for C_{j-1} and no recall at all for $\{C_{j-2}, \ldots, C_{j-n}\}$

Axiom 3: If C_j is now made $\neq C_{j-1}$, to generalize Axiom 1, then an error will occur in ψC_j; call

$$\psi C_j - C_j = E_j$$

It is assumed that E_j is compensated for immediately and completely at the next interval. So if

$$C_{j+1} = \delta C + C_j$$

then
$$\psi C_{j+1} = \psi C + E_j = \psi C + \delta C$$

which gives

$$\psi C_j = C_{j-1} + (C_{j-1} - \psi C_{j-1})$$
and as

$$\psi C_j = C_{j-1} \qquad \text{for isochronic series}$$

$$\psi C_j = 2C_{j-1} - C_{j-2} \qquad \text{with varying } C_j \tag{4.2.12}$$

The z transform of (4.2.12) leads to

$$H(z) = (2z - 1)/z^2 \quad \text{for a closed loop} \tag{4.2.13}$$

and

$$G(z) = H(z)/(1 - H(z)) = (2z - 1)/(z^2 - 1) \quad \text{for an open loop} \tag{4.2.14}$$

The actual response of the system to step function inputs is consistently slightly different from the model, as shown in Fig. 4.2.4.

The departures from the predictions of (4.2.12)–(4.2.14) are caused by longer sequential dependencies than one lag. Michon rewrites $G(z)$ of (4.2.14) to become

$$G'(z) = \alpha G(z) \tag{4.2.15}$$

and splitting $G(z)$ into a delay

$$P(z) = (1 - \beta)^{-1}(z - 1)^{-1} \tag{4.2.16}$$

and a damping of oscillations

$$Q(z) = (1 - 2\beta)\cdot(1 - \beta)^{-1}(z - \beta)^{-1} \tag{4.2.17}$$

we have from (4.2.15) that

$$G'(z) = \alpha(2z - 1)\cdot(z - 1)^{-1}(z - \beta)^{-1} \tag{4.2.18}$$

This leads to a messy but useful expansion in

$$\{ C_{j-1}, \ldots, C_{j-6} \} \text{ of } \psi C_j$$

which fits data closely.

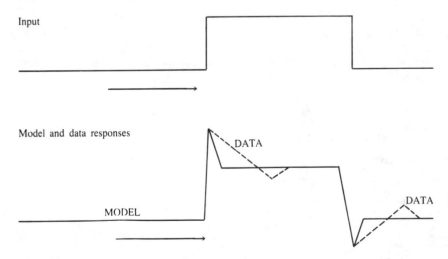

FIG. 4.2.4 Inputs and outputs to step function showing data departure from the model of (4.2.13), (4.2.14).

The difference between synchronization and continuation in terms of the autocorrelation structure of error sequences has been modeled by Voillaume (1972); the postulated sequential dependencies only lag by one interval, so they would be inadequate for the reasons given previously.

Extensive experiments, from 1936 to 1974, involving sequences of both visually and auditorily presented stimuli, are reproted by Chmelař and Osecký (1974, 1975); these involve paradigms where isochronic series of stimuli of different types are used. The interest is not in the reaction times nor in the stimulus magnitudes but in whether or not a detection response is given to stimuli designated as being of a control type and other stimuli deliberately ignored. The task thus resembles vigilance or signal detection studies, but the theoretical framework is one of "active attention or distraction." However, the substantive details are error sequences, and the models set up are two-state Markov processes. The states are attentive, X, and distracted, Y, so that a sequence of state occupancy, of time segments of varying length, represents the state variables. The stimulus series, of control and other types is a second discrete series, and the response process is mediated by a third sequence of response states. This is shown in Fig. 4.2.5 with some augmentation. In Fig. 4.2.5 the series X, Y always alternates and is unobservable. The discrete isochronic series C, $\bar{C}$ is a random i.i.d. two-state series generated by the experimenter; the actual stimulus durations involved in each presentation are not important as they are equal or less than the period, t, of the system. The two states U and V are products, logically, of the series above; given that the task is to detect a C-type stimulus when it occurs, the state U covers correct detection and the state V failure to detect a C-type stimulus. The resultant series of correct responses, R_c, and implicit correct responses that would be available if elicited, shown as (x), are the observed outcome. Failures to detect are shown as F, which is the type of error series to be described statistically in the models developed by Chmelař and Osecký. In other words, some properties of a subset of a time series are to be represented in a model with parallel two-state sequences, each of which is postulated to be a sort of Markov process realization. If the jth occupancy of X in the top series of Fig. 4.2.5 is X_j (without specification of duration) and similarly for Y_j, X_j always being followed immediately by Y_j, then the length of the periods are distributed exponentially

$$E(X_j) = \chi$$

$$p(X_j = x) = \chi^{-1} \cdot \exp(-x/\chi)$$

$$E(Y_j) = \phi$$

$$p(Y_j = y) = \phi^{-1} \cdot \exp(-y/\phi)$$

$$(4.2.19)$$

where χ and ϕ are parameters of a given observer. From these two parameters

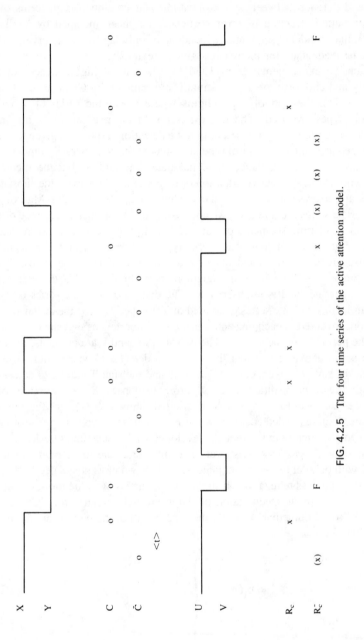

FIG. 4.2.5 The four time series of the active attention model.

248

the model enables us to derive two other parameters of greater psychological interest, which are $d = \phi/(\chi + \phi)$, meaning the probability of being distracted at any moment, and θ, which is a coefficient of attention inertia, implying relative ease of distraction.

$$\theta^{w/t} = \exp\left(-w/\chi - w/\phi\right) \tag{4.2.20}$$

where w is the mean length of an interval between two C-type stimuli (or the mean number of stimuli in a run of irrelevant stimuli) and t is the trial interval as shown in Fig. 4.2.5. It should be noted from (4.2.20) that θ is independent of the trial interval. This situation therefore does not resemble that of Laming (1968) where the interstimulus interval became critical for some process parameters.

All the models reviewed briefly here suggest, or explicitly involve, jumping between states and nonstationarity. Interactions between time intervals in different sensory modalities in the context of relative psychophysical scaling of time elapsed has also been suggested to occur by Eisler (1977).

Time-Order Errors

In the context of sequential estimates of the relative duration of periods of elapsed time, the time-order error (or time error, or TOE or TE) has been studied and modeled as a special case by Eisler (1975) and by Hellström (1977a) who considered the relative fit of alternative models to data from a diversity of experimental paradigms. The Eisler theory states that the sequential comparison of two intervals is done within the organism by using two registers (compare Fig. 4.2.1); in register #2 the second duration is stored, in #1 the total duration of the first and the second stored without a break. Then the two are compared. Psychophysical transformations and trace decay effects will operate, if at all, on the contents of the two registers during or after their being filled. Actually there have been many theories about how and why TOEs are generated. To summarize their general sense, though few have been submitted to adequate detailed quantitative analysis with the exception of Hellström's, which will be reviewed shortly, it is expedient to have a fuller notation. Let the stimulus at time j be S_j, the input series being $\{S_j\}, j = 1, \ldots, m$. Let the internal representation of S_j at time k, k can take any value $1 \le k \le m$, be $I_{j,k}$. Let the relative judgment of S_{j-1}, S_j at time k be $R(S_{j-1,j})_k$, and so on.

Representing this as a process in discrete time we have Fig. 4.2.6. The models of Hellström, and simpler predecessors, are to be considered as micromodels of the general multivariate series and its generated products $R(X, Y)_{j+k}$ as shown in Fig. 4.2.6.

What can validly be said for time errors of duration judgments, as a generalization, was said many years ago and has been known since as *Vierordt's law*. The TOE is positive for shorter durations (approximately less than 1 sec) and

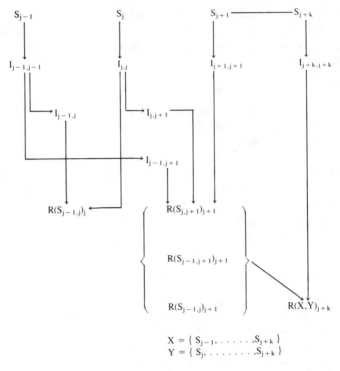

$$X = \{ S_{-1}, \ldots \ldots, S_{j+k} \}$$
$$Y = \{ S_{j}, \ldots \ldots, S_{j+k} \}$$

FIG. 4.2.6 Sequential comparisons of stimulus magnitudes that generate time-order errors.

negative for longer durations; that is, the first stimulus of a physically *equal* pair of durations is *overestimated* for short durations, relative to the second, and thus *perceived* to be longer. The reverse, underestimation, occurs for longer durations. There are also secondary complications; the gap in time between two stimuli, and the actual sensory modality in which the durations are presented, can modify results quantitatively to a smaller degree. Some findings reported are less readily replicable and subject to considerable intersubject variation.

To obtain a model of wide generality, Hellström (1977a) considered a three-category response system, so that in our notation of Fig. 4.2.6

Relation		*Condition*		*Response*		*Frequency*
$R(S_{j-1,j})_{j}$	$\Leftrightarrow$	$I_{j-1} > I_{j}$	$\Leftrightarrow$	"First greatest"	$\Leftrightarrow$	n_1
	$\Leftrightarrow$	$I_{j-1} < I_{j}$	$\Leftrightarrow$	"Second greatest"	$\Leftrightarrow$	n_2
	$\Leftrightarrow$	$I_{j-1} = I_{j}$	$\Leftrightarrow$	"Equal"	$\Leftrightarrow$	$n_{=}$

The judgments are mapped onto a single continuum, for condition k, as in Fig. 4.2.7:

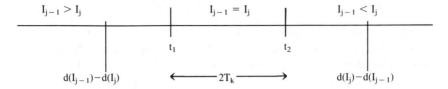

FIG. 4.2.7   Stimulus continuum for time period comparisons.

The stimuli as internally represented each have discriminal dispersions $d(I)$ onto the continuum so that when the $d(I_j)$ are rectangular distributions,

$$D = E(d(I_{j-1} - I_j))$$
(4.2.21)

and alternative formulations with $D(I_j)$ distributed normally with the same expectations are also available. It would be preferable to regard each as a special case of a beta distribution of unknown parameters and solve for them, for this makes some Bayesian methods readily available, and the parameters may then be interpretable.

It is only possible to solve for D/T for a given stimulus pair (and not to identify D or T alone); let the pair be i under condition, or subject, k. Hellström considered two models (his 1a and 2a of 1977a) that were particularly encoded to deal with temporal data (as opposed to stimulus magnitude experiments; see Section 4.3).

$$\frac{D_{ik}}{T_k} = B_{1k} \cdot \phi_{1i}^\beta - B_{2k}\phi_{2i}^\beta + c_k$$
(4.2.22)

where the B are fixed biases, the Φ_{ji} are the physical durations of the first and second stimuli in the ith pair, the form

$$B_{jk}\phi = \left(\frac{B'}{T}\right) \cdot \phi_i^\beta, \qquad \text{where } \phi_i^\beta = I_i$$
(4.2.23)

if the B are split into biases and scaling constant parts.

The alternative is to write

$$\frac{D_{ik}}{T_k} = B_{1k}(\phi_{1i}^\beta + \phi_a^\beta) - B_{2k}(\phi_{2i}^\beta - \phi_a^\beta)$$
(4.2.24)

which fits data marginally less well but may be preferred because of the status that can be given to ϕ_a, which is less ad hoc than the c_k in (4.2.22).

It can be shown, assuming the rectangular distribution of $d(I)$ on ϕ, that $D/T = (n_1 - n_2)/n_=$ (cf. the figure on p. 254). However this model takes no account of the covariance between $d(I_{j-1})$ and $d(I_j)$ and assumes that T is fixed when it may be a variable. The comparatal dispersion (Gulliksen, 1958), which is the s.d. of $d(I_{j-1} - I_j)$, denoted by σ_c, also may be written as

$$\sigma_c = f(S_{j-1}, S_j) = f(\, d(I_j),\, d(I_{j-1}),\, \text{cov}\,(I_j, I_{j-1})) \qquad (4.2.25)$$

The psychophysical question is whether the TOE arises due to variation at the level of the $d(I_j)$ or at the level where the $R(X, Y)j_{+k}$ are generated in Fig. 4.2.6. The models that Hellström developed assume that the two comparisons are not carried further back than S_{j-1} for the construction of $R(S_{j-1,j})_j$, but as seen later a more elaborate representation is necessary. Results of experiments rule out response bias, criterion bias, and mediating absolute responses as main factors constituting the TOE effect and strongly support a perceptual interpretation, which in our Fig. 4.2.6 means implicating processes at the bottom of the picture. This disposes of a number of earlier alternative theories, so Hellström (1977a) concludes "the use of a single number to describe the time error leaves out most of the important features of the phenomenon. A comprehensive account of the process of comparing successive stimuli is obviously needed [p. 21]."

If it is accepted that

$$\psi t = \alpha(\text{time})^\beta \qquad (4.2.26)$$

is a model of perceived duration, ψt, then β is usually a little above 1, (Björkman & Holmqvist, 1960; Eisler, 1976) but itself will have a distribution over subjects. Clearly (4.2.26) is built into (4.2.23) and (4.2.24). In the case of (4.2.24) the term ϕ_a is an adaptation level, which is a function of prior stimulus exposure (a weighted moving average of the prior inputs $\{S_{j-1}, \ldots, S_{j-k}\}$; strictly $\phi_{aj} \neq \phi_{aj-1}$ depending on the local relative values of the series $\{\phi_{am}\}$, $m = j, j - 1, j - 2, \ldots, j - k$. The ratio B_{1k}/B_{2k} is reliably about 0.72 in time duration estimation experiments, but the model (4.2.24) can fit cases in which $B_{1k} > B_{2k}$.

If it were desired to rewrite (4.2.23) and (4.2.24) in a linear transfer function form on any input, so that $R(S_{j-m,j-n})_{j-k}$ is a general comparison at a point in time of two l.t.f.s sampled after delay, then the general equation for the shape of the trace decay of a stimulus I_j with time has to be found. There is some evidence that shows this is a complex problem in that a trace first rises and then decays gradually; yet the actual amounts of rise and fall and the rate of fall are functions of the initial input magnitude. In short, the process is nonlinear and requires kernels of second-order for its representation (see section 2.5).

4.3   SEQUENTIAL EFFECTS IN PSYCHOPHYSICAL JUDGMENTS

This section reviews common themes and some diverse results in modern models of sequential psychophysical judgments. The common theme is that the judgments are of the magnitude or perceived intensity of sensations. The subject does not just make a binary response, yes or no, as in the time estimation paradigms reviewed in the previous section; he or she also says how big each detected event is at the time of detection. So the sequential properties of the task can be reflected in an added dimension to the sort of model previously considered; the new dimension is a set of stimulus magnitudes, and if both the input and output sides of the model are to incorporate this new information, then two dimensions are added, but generally one input series, the stimulus physical magnitudes or intensities, is sufficient. It will be seen that intermediate phases in models are introduced; these intermediate phases are themselves time series of constructs that represent some stage in information processing between input and output. It may in some cases be appropriate to treat these intermediate constructs as state variables of the system, in the sense used in Chapter 5, q.v.

The sequential relationships that empirically are found to hold between errors or biases in the estimation of stimulus magnitudes may be complex (Possamai, Granjon, Reynard, & Requin, 1975), or at the other extreme nonexistent; attempts to generalize on what happens have been rather incomplete and untidy. An adequate model of sequential psychophysics would aim to entrap all the time series properties within one algebraic framework, covering all measurable aspects of each stimulus and response event. This objective has so far not been attained. Luce and Green (1974a) attempted a "state of the art" summary at the restricted level of single variable (i.e., single physical input dimensions of variation) processes because little is known of multivariate systems. They reviewed some predominantly American work and essayed the conclusions that sequential effects are: (1) small in simple auditory detection tasks; (2) large in probability prediction of visual events; (3) relatively large in tasks of recognition of intensity; and (4) smaller when feedback is provided. Probably all of these conclusions are too sweeping, being dependent on limited data from a restricted range of stimulus values and response constraints. Some counter instances are certainly given in other studies cited subsequently. It is clear that the various psychophysical tasks of detection, discrimination, recognition, identification, magnitude estimation, and similarity estimation, for which no general theory exists, have each their own peculiarities when their sequential structure is considered.

A salient parameter in determining the sort of sequential relationships in psychophysical tasks is information feedback; the experimenter designates some subclass of responses, which may be expressed via some fuzzy functions of stimulus properties, as "correct," and the information as to whether one or more responses lie within the fuzzy set will, if fed back to the subject, sometimes modify some aspect of behavior upon subsequent trials. Most earlier models of human judgment did not use the inherent sequentiality of responding as a theoretical starting point for assessing the intrinsic sensitivity of the human observer, but eventually interest shifted toward sequential phenomena as regular and informative data (Atkinson, Carterette, & Kinchla, 1962; Howarth & Bulmer, 1956; Kirby, 1975).

Sequential shifts in thresholds, as a function of runs of one out of two of the alternative stimuli used in a simple choice experiment (one of which might be a null-valued stimulus, a dummy, blank, or noise trial) were analyzed by Wertheimer (1953) and by Howarth and Bulmer (1956) by counting the relative frequencies of ''no'' (nondetection) responses after runs of three identical stimuli. The weak conclusion was that nonrandom stimulus sequences have the effect of varying the frequency of detection responses, raising the frequency to a more probable stimulus and lowering it to a less probable one. This has a sort of beneficial ecological payoff in that it reduces errors in detection by the organism; as most real-world stimulus sequences are anything but random, our chances of long-term survival in a partially hostile world can be enhanced by having such features inbuilt or learned. Stimuli were flashes of light viewed in the dark; the interest in these early studies lay in demonstrating that the sequentiality was more due to response choice autocorrelation than to fluctuation in the detection threshold. The statistical analyses were not such as to demonstrate this conclusively.

As a process model the situation requires three time series, as in Fig. 4.3.1, which is not fully analyzable by the simpler methods used in reported work. The linkages in Fig. 4.3.1 between $E_j = f(S, T)$ and $R_j, R_{j+1}, \ldots, R_{j+k}$ are the special interest of adaptation level theory (Helson, 1964). The trial-by-trial fluctuations of E_j and of R_j, whether or not the mapping

$$R_j = g(E_j) \tag{4.3.1}$$

is taken as sufficient instead of writing

$$R_j = g(E_j, E_{j-1}, \ldots, E_{j-n})$$

were reviewed by Parducci (1963, 1964) who focused attention on conditions supposedly necessary for the phenomena of ''assimilation'' (a tendency to repeat judgments because a later R_{j+k} is dependent on E_j) and ''contrast'' (a tendency to shift E_j as a consequence of T_j being positively correlated with S_{j-1}). Parducci (1963) wrote that the first experimental problem is to find a situation for which

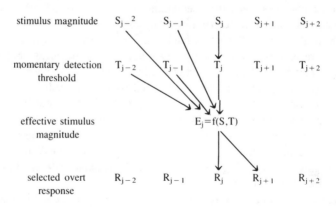

FIG. 4.3.1

the remembered values of the stimulus extremes would be relatively unstable. This should attenuate any anchor effects provided by the ends of the stimulus ranges, which have been long known to play a salient role in quantitative judgmene phenomena.

In Parducci's (1963) (and also Helson's) notation, AL = adaptation level:

$$AL_j = [j - 1)/j] \cdot AL_{j-1} + j^{-1} \cdot S_j \qquad (4.3.2)$$

and

$$p(R = R_j) = K(S_j - AL_j) + C \qquad (4.3.3)$$

where R_j is the response predefined as most appropriate to S_j, and C, K are constants. The response is strictly defined in terms of its probability of falling in one category, say, "very heavy," of an ordered set of categories.

Note that (4.3.2) takes the AL to an asymptote; for more trials and more stimuli, the more stable the AL. But in fact Parducci found that sequential effects were of comparable size in the second 150 and the first 150 trials of sequential two-choice experiments. This is sufficient to invalidate (4.3.2) but could leave (4.3.3) valid within some other model. The alternative

$$AL_j = a \cdot AL_{j-1} + (1 - a) \cdot S_j \qquad (4.3.4)$$

which is obviously the same as

$$x_j = ax_{j-1} + (1 - a)u_j \qquad (4.3.5)$$

if one takes the AL as a state variable of the system, and

$$y_j^* = k \cdot (u_j - x_j), \qquad y_j^* = y_j - c \qquad (4.3.6)$$

so that (4.3.5) and (4.3.6) constitute a state model, two properties of which are

$$x_j = E(u)$$

with long response series, and if the input series is homogeneous and then has a large step, the sensitivity of the system to the step (y_j^* greater than some critical threshold value) increases with the run length. These properties are in fact not appropriate; the probability of a correct [in the sense of (4.3.3)] response was found to be independent of the prior homogeneous run length. Further attempts to patch up this class of model by involving two ALs at once were not much better but naturally had marginally smaller residuals. Parducci and Sandusky (1965), in two-choice experiments using an analysis in terms of the four pairs $L_jL_{j+1}, L_jR_{j+1}, R_jL_{j+1}, R_jR_{j+1}$ (here L = left; R = right) that are the primitives of the system, found that all sequential effects in judgment for two-response alternatives disappeared. Hence, short-term alternation and repetition effects are obviously preserved, as the primitives fall into alternations and repetitions. Clearly, as soon as we define the primitives over longer runs, the situation is more complex.

Some slight further improvement was achieved by redefining the effective stimulus (E_j of Fig. 4.3.1) as

$$E_j = S_j - [a \cdot B + (1 - a) \cdot S_{j-1}] \qquad (4.3.7)$$

where B is a fixed parameter dependent on context cues. There are quite different sequential structures for detection and for recognition if these results are generalizable.

The previous studies were run without feedback; feedback in magnitude estimation tasks aggravates (or facilitates, according to one's view of the problem) both assimilation and contrast (Holland & Lockhead, 1968). The sequential structure of "absolute" category judgments, for example, k physically defined stimulus values and a response choice of k alternatives, one for each of k psychological magnitudes, is according to some writers expected to run back up to eight trials. Figure 4.3.2 is adapted from Holland and Lockhead (1968) is a typical pattern of results; the error on the vertical axis is defined in terms of a category shift, taking the categories as having the interval scale structure of the stimulus set, up to some scalar multiplier. The error is written as a conjoint function of S_{j-k} and k for R_j, and the error is minimal if S_{j-k} is about the average of the stimulus range, the whole process being symmetrical about the middle of the stimulus range.

Much of this sequential effect has a very dubious status, as shown by computer simulation by Gregson (1976a). The very regularity of the phenomenon hints that it may be, at least in part, an artefact of misidentification. Very long sequential dependencies have been shown (Chapter 3) to be a result of misinterpreting an autocorrelation spectrum as a direct representation of the order of a process, so that, for example, an autocorrelated process of order 1 or 2 may show

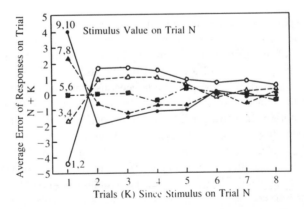

FIG. 4.3.2   The effect of the stimulus on a given trial on the responses on the next eight trials (from Holland & Lockhead, 1968).

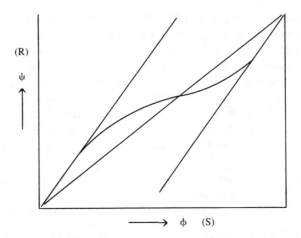

FIG. 4.3.3   Gregson's (1976a) four-parameter model.

monotonically decreasing autocorrelation over a longer run than two trials. But there is another difficulty here, which is psychologically more interesting and important. If the psychophysical function, which is an averaged first-order gain function of output on input, is not in fact monotone increasing but has one or more breaks in it, then falsely assuming that it is single-valued and continuous will lead to the identification of sequential relationships that do not exist. Gregson (1976a) constructed as an alternative a four-parameter model, in which the psychophysical function takes as its form two linear segments, with an ogival transition between them, as in Fig. 4.3.3. The observed patterns of pseudosequence effects and average first-order gain functions can be efficiently recovered by permitting the two line segments notionally to continue, each with decreasing probability as serving as a psychophysical gain function, in indefinite extension. The two ends of the psychophysical continuum can be thought of as upper and lower thresholds or as upper and lower anchor points. The pervasive effects of anchor values at the extremes of psychophysical tasks has been remarked on previously. Gregson's conclusions, after reviewing a number of studies and simulating the sequential properties of experiments with various parameter values in the model of Fig. 4.3.3., were as follows:

1. There is consistent evidence of second-order departures from the simple psychophysical model

$$\log R = a + b \cdot \log S$$

in a wide range of studies; the exceptions are sufficient to constitute the basis of a new model if the second-order departures have intrinsic substantive interest,

2. The reported form of data is often inadequate to determine what sort of

discontinuous model is appropriate because only the average responses to each stimulus value are plotted, and it is strictly necessary to know the sequential structure of the stimulus and response sequences and their crosscorrelations, but the four-parameter model can be fitted to a wide range of cases.

3. If the four-parameter model is true and we falsely assume that a single psychophysical function is appropriate, then we can generate pseudosequence effects in the dependency of error upon lagged input. Other real sequential effects may also exist, but they have to be disentangled from the pseudoeffects before it can be stated what is happening in the psychophysical process.

The process assumptions of Holland and Lockhead (1968), corrected by the given qualifications, are psychologically reasonable and anticipate some features of the process that later workers have tried to model. To summarize so far:

1. For an absolute judgment with feedback, the stimulus one trial back serves as a standard for comparative judgment.

2. The memory of the standard is contaminated by and, hence, is displaced toward traces of past stimuli (this is continuous assimilation).

3. The sequential contamination is monotone decreasing on temporal remoteness, so stimuli experienced some time back have relatively little bearing on current behavior (a trace decay assumption).

4. The memory of a numerical feedback one trial back is generally veridical.

The sequential structure of a psychophysical experiment with feedback can perhaps more clearly be conceptualized by thinking of the input series to the system as a series

$$\ldots S_{j-2}F_{j-2}S_{j-1}F_{j-1}S_jF_jS_{j+1}F_{j+1}S_{j+2}F_{j+2} \ldots$$

which reflects the fact that the input is locally structured as an alteration of stimuli, and of feedback concerning what a response should have been. The question of whether "what a response should have been" is the same or not the same as "what the stimulus was" depends on the prior defined correspondence between the stimulus set and the response set employed in the experiment, in standard terminology, upon the identification function of the experiment mapping stimuli into the partitioned set of correct and incorrect responses. This of course raises the nice point of whether the S, F, S, F, . . . series should be treated as univariate or bivariate; if it is bivariate, then the suffices should be modified to emphasize the fact that the S and F terms are staggered in time and do not coincide. Using the notation adopted in Fig. 4.2.6, that $X_{j-1,j}$ implies X inputted as time $j - 1$ and stored until an operation at time j is performed upon the representation of X, and $R(S_{j,j+k})_{j+m}$ means a comparative judgment response to the pair of stimuli inputted at j and at $j + k$, made later at $j + m$ (obviously $m \geq k$ unless we are studying forecasting behavior), consider Fig. 4.3.4:

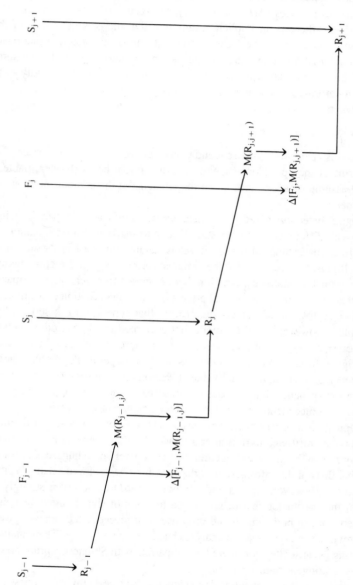

FIG. 4.3.4 Sequential psychophysical judgments with feedback provided.

In the process of which Fig. 4.3.4 is a partial representation (we have not shown the functional dependence of F_j on S_j, nor that of R_j on earlier terms in the series of first-order differences $\{\Delta[F_j, M(R_{j,j+1})]\}$ between feedback and memory of past responses), there is an implicit assumption that the operation M is of the form of an inverse, F^{-1}, because the subject has to use the information to answer the internal question "did I make the appropriate response to that stimulus?" if the F information is taken to be information about the identity of S_j rather than information about what R_j should have been. Error arises in the process, when

$$M(R_{j,j+1}) \neq F_j \quad \text{for all } j \tag{4.3.8}$$

and unless this error arises, the sequential structure of Fig. 4.3.4 is not identifiable in terms of the operations shown, though it might be partly identifiable if additional assumptions are made about the latencies of the component comparison judgments.

The signal detection paradigm, where weak stimuli are compared against noise or weak differences between stimuli lead to inefficient discrimination, is different from magnitude estimation in many details, not least in its sequential structure. It must be observed that the simplest forms of signal detection theory, which is a branch of statistical decision theory applied to psychophysics, makes absolutely no provision for sequential effects because by definition each stimulus or noise is a realization of a stochastic process that generates i.i.d. series when time sampled. However, the s.d.t. model has been modified by various writers to try to incorporate sequential effects even though these are obviously a nuisance for the original formation of the model. As an s.d.t. experiment involving noise and a number of alternative signal values takes on the character of a magnitude estimation experiment with absolute response categories, the sequential problems of s.d.t. experiments are treated for convenience in this section.

The typical s.d.t. experiment involves a vast number of trials, and the data analysis is often restricted to runs after a steady state has been attained; warm up and preasymptotic behavior can apparently extend over some hundreds of trails. Studies that discard the information in the unstable phases are of relatively little interest to us. However, Speeth and Mathews (1961) came down strongly in support of the conclusion that behavior is a function of signal, signal + noise, and the sequence of both stimuli and responses that preceded the behavior, even though previously autocorrelation analyses had been inconclusive. Their analysis is interesting because they considered it compatible with Skinnerian principles of control by contingent reinforcement.

There is a risk that sequential dependencies may be completely missed in psychophysical experiments with feedback if an inappropriate time series analysis is used; the previous example of finding long lag dependencies that are not really present can be matched by cases where the sequential structure is completely missed. An autocorrelation analysis of the response sequence is not informative if the subject is highly responsive to feedback, shadowing the previous trials instead of responding to present trials, and at the same time the feedback, admittedly veridical, is simply an echo of a random series of stimuli. For analytical and empirical reasons it is desirable to have the stimulus series in effect prewhitened at the stage of designing an experiment, but the considerations that lead both time series analysts and experimental psychologists to use random input series do not presuppose that feedback is an integral part of the task; the use of i.i.d. stimulus series is not advanced in the context of Fig. 4.3.4. As Speeth and Mathews (1961) noted, "indicating the correct answer to the subject, though essential for good performance, may influence his subsequent response in a manner not correlated with either the preceding response or the signal on the next trial [p. 1047]."

The effect of feedback diminishes, as might be expected, as $(S + N)/N$ increases (a ratio of energy levels, commonly expressed in audition as decibels (dB) (signal + noise)/noise and so a dimensionless number) and should be maximal with feedback that is useless to the subject, except as a basis for response biases, on $(S + N)/N$ pairs that are in fact so nearly equal in energy level as to be indiscriminable. However, the dependency of subjects on a feedback as a basis of response choice is not constrained; the subject can ignore it in theory. Marked individual differences on the degree of reliance upon feedback are found; the guessing strategies of subjects are themselves representable as autocorrelated sequences with idiosyncratic spectra. It should be noted that the perseveration, or nonperseveration, of responses can be quite independent of any sequential dependency in correctness per se.

To test the longer lag dependencies, the response records in the Speeth and Mathews (1961) study (blocks of 500 trials, 10,000 responses per subject) were recoded in binary form, with a characteristic variable defined by

$$X_j = 1 \leftrightarrow R_j = R_{j-1} \quad \Big\} \tag{4.3.9}$$
$$X_j = 0 \leftrightarrow R_j \neq R_{j-1} \quad \Big\}$$

From a theorem on the collapsibility of Markov chains, it was found that it was sufficient to check subsequences not longer than six trials for sequential dependence. A state of the system is then definable as an n-tuple of X's from (4.3.9).

Specimen response state transition matrix (X-defined) for a single subject, from data of Speeth and Mathews (1961).

	1	10	100	000	
1	.4	.6	0	0	
10	.2	0	.8	0	$= M_x$
100	.3	0	0	.7	
000	.2	0	0	.8	

(4.3.10)

Matrix M_x is defined in terms of response chains; analogous matrices can be defined by creating another characteristic variable X_j', which is defined on the basis of the responses that the feedback has given as correct on a previous trial. The psychologically important point that these analyzes emphasize is that the number of states in the system, and consequently the matrices like (4.3.10), change their structure and eventually collapse to a simple two-state system as the $(S + N)/N$ ratio increases. In other words, the sequential structure of behavior becomes more complex the more difficult the psychophysical detection or discrimination task being performed or attempted.

Under null feedback conditions, results on sequentiality are apparently contradictory (Tanner, Rauk, & Atkinson, 1970). Using a model that is a stochastic extension of the structure in Fig. 4.3.4, see Fig. 4.3.5:

The trace M has a distribution

$$M(S_{j-1,j}) \sim T_j \leftrightarrow N(t_j, \sigma_T^2) \tag{4.3.11}$$

The signal can only take in the s.d.t. paradigm two realizations, t_0, t_1 with common variance σ_T^2. The original signal is also similarly restricted;

$$S_j \sim I_j \leftrightarrow N(s_j, \sigma_I^2)$$

Again, the two values of s_j are s_0 and s_1, with common variance σ_I^2. The fixed prior probability of $s_1 = p(s_1) = \gamma$, and so $p(s_0) = (1 - \gamma)$. For simplicity, it is then assumed that, for some $0 \leq \alpha \leq 1$,

$$\left. \begin{array}{l} t_1 = \alpha + (1 - \alpha)\gamma \\ t_0 = (1 - \alpha)\gamma \end{array} \right\} \tag{4.3.12}$$

As $R_j = _{def} \Delta(S_j, T_j)$, and S_j and T_j are defined to be independent,

$$R_j \sim E(t_j - s_j), \qquad var\ (R_j) = \sigma_T^2 + \sigma_I^2$$

In this model the structure of sequential dependencies can be shown to be dependent *both* on feedback and on the provision of prior information concerning

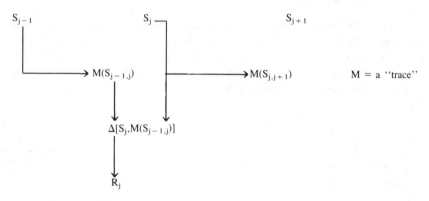

FIG. 4.3.5   Trace-mediated judgments without feedback.

the relative frequencies of the alternative stimuli. The model (4.3.11), (4.3.12), which the authors called the memory–recognition model (not a very useful name, because it describes virtually any time series model of sequential judgment!) fits well under some conditions. The decision rule for the subject to choose his or her response is set, quite simply, as

$$\Delta(S_j, T_j) > d_0 \leftrightarrow R_j = R_1 \tag{4.3.13}$$

$$\Delta(S_j, T_j) < d_1 \leftrightarrow R_j = R_0$$

and if

$$d_0 > \Delta(S_j, T_j) > d_1 \leftrightarrow R_j = R_{j-1}$$

Here the d_0, d_1 are the criterion values of the s.d.t. process.

If s_a is the current stimulus value, t_b is the trace of the previous trial, d_c is the decision criterion previously used, then it can be shown that

$$p(R_1 | S_a A_b S_c) = \Phi\left[\frac{(s_a - t_b - d_c)}{\sigma(R_j)} \right] \tag{4.3.14}$$

where Φ is the cumulative normal distribution. Special cases of (4.3.14) arise when $a = c$. The extension of the model is to assume that two perseverative processes, repeating a response, and reporting a repetition of a signal (as defined by feedback) are linearly additive effects combining to generate the current response probabilities. Why two strategies that cannot both occur at once should be pooled in this manner, rather than treated as states of a system between which the transition rules are formalizable, is not clear; but as the model does not fit uniformly well, the convention is probably inappropriate. In the sense of more recent approaches (reviewed in Chapter 6), it is of greater interest to predict trial-by-trial behavior than to calculate probabilities over an ensemble of trials equivalent in some sense.

The relation between the instability of successive response ratios, r, where $r = R_j/R_{j-1}$ and the difference of successive stimuli $S_j - S_{j-1}$ is, in magnitude estimation tasks, often given by a shape like Fig. 4.3.6:

The curvilinear relationship of Fig. 4.3.6 was first reliably found (though not in all subjects studied) by Green and Luce (1974) and Green, Luce, and Duncan (1977), who actually plotted the coefficient of variation $[\sigma_r/E(r)]$ of R_j/R_{j-1} and found the phenomenon in both magnitude estimation and in magnitude production. To summarize results, Green, Luce, and Duncan used a single linear regression

$$Y_j = \gamma X_j + \alpha X_{j-1} + \beta Y_{j-1} + \delta \tag{4.3.15}$$

where, for estimation, $Y_j = R_j$, $X_j = S_j$ and, for production, $Y_j = S_j$, $X_j = R_j$.

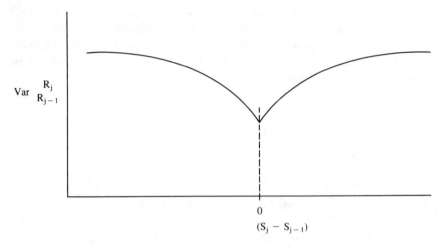

FIG. 4.3.6 Relation between response ratio variation and stimulus difference in some magnitude estimation tasks.

[The coefficients in (4.3.15) are nothing to do with (4.3.12); the notation here follows the original text.]

Mean values found for the coefficients in (4.3.15) are, with associated multiple R,

	γ	α	β	δ	R^2
For production	.205	−.083	.339	.254	.908
For estimation	.219	−.087	.531	−.120	.732

The familiar dominance of the current trial input, the negative small coefficient of one trial back input, and the strong previous output coefficients are not surprising. As no bilinear models (with $X_j Y_{j-k}$ terms) were used, the structure is not properly identified by comparison of alternatives; but it is psychophysically parsimonious. Further checks on contributions to the R^2 by component terms of the regression showed that the variance taken up by the Y_{j-1} and X_{j-1} was second-order compared with X_j in both regressions, Y_{j-1} slightly dominating X_{j-1}. As X_{j-1} precedes in time Y_{j-1}, the time series of inputs to the subject, using $M(Y_j)$ for the recall of Y_j and considering the input on one trial as the sequence $M(Y_{j-1})$, X_j, to produce Y_j and then putting the terms in serial order,

$$
\begin{array}{ccccc}
M(Y_{j-2}) & X_{j-1} & M(Y_{j-1}) & X_j & Y_j \\
? & -.087 & .531 & .219 &
\end{array}
$$

increment in

$$
\begin{array}{cccc}
R^2 & .013 & .019 & .603
\end{array}
$$

The pattern of responding was given an interesting interpretation by Green, Luce, and Duncan (1977); they postulated what is in effect a two-state filter, including a limited bandwidth of intense attention within which sensitivity was maximal. Signals falling outside this band are only weakly perceived. Signals falling inside the band are represented in output by a gain of an order of magnitude greater. If two signals fall within the band, their ratio is computable by the observer; but if one or both falls outside the band, then their ratio is not computable and the observer will be forced to guess. This result very properly leads these workers to reject (4.3.15) as an adequate model, because cov (Y_j, Y_{j-1}) can be written as a function of $\Delta^1 X_j$, but what that function is varies with X_j. If we were to attempt to construct a state model from (4.3.15) by reforming it, then at least two states would be needed; in each state β would be a function of X_j and X_{j-1}, which is neither linear nor stationary but could be simulated (compare Section 2.5).

The following bordered section may be omitted at a first reading.

Some differences have arisen between those workers using the form just described, two states with the structure

$$Y_j = f(X_j, X_{j-1}, Y_{j-1}, e_j)$$

in each state (Jesteadt, Luce, & Green, 1977), and an alternative single-state model (Staddon et al., 1980), where

$$Y_j = f(X_j, \ldots, X_{j-k}, Y_{j-1}, e_j), \qquad k \Rightarrow 8$$

The dispute cannot be reconciled because the methods of parameter estimation used in some studies were regression and not time series, which can produce a difference in the order (maximum lag) of the fitted models, and because Staddon et al. (1980) did not transform their raw variables before model fitting, as did Jesteadt et al. (1977) by taking logs. Cleaning up data by examining first-order regressions before using time series estimation is standard practice, if only to facilitate the identification of suspect outlying records that are evidence either of error or of local nonstationarities; in unpublished work in olfactory psychophysics, the present author found that taking logs of raw variables before proceeding to a linear time series analysis with the Genstat computer package, in the Box–Jenkins tradition, can in some cases improve fit and simplify structure. Unless and until investigators concerned with the psychological presence and meaning of long stimulus–response lags routinely perform time series analyses with alternative initial transforms and report standard errors on all parameter estimates (Ansley & Newbold, 1979), the questions necessarily remain unsolved. In general, if no strong prior theory exists, then a model low-order in both input and output ARMA structure is to be preferred, but the investigator in any psychological study should allow as a possibility that the lags may be variables and not constants. The autocorrelation structure would then not be stationary. This leads to a consideration of SETAR models (see Section 1.3), which if multistate and not two-state may not, in the limit, be identifiable but would fit badly some of the higher lags of the nearest linear one-state model. An attempt to rewrite and improve the single-state multilag model has been made by Wagner and Baird (1981) for data using numerical stimuli and responses. They suggest that subjects use different strategies according to local sequence properties. Full consideration of this possibility leads naturally into models discussed in Chapter 5, as their revision is multistate and nonlinear.

The role of the ratio of successive responses used in the first part of the previous analysis had featured (Luce & Green, 1972, 1974a) in a model of the psychophysical process of intensity estimation that incorporates precisely formulated time series concepts at two levels of description, psychophysiological and psychological or, perhaps less preemptively, microstructure and macrostructure.

The first level assumes that the output of a sensory transducer is a series of neural pulses (which is true) and that the critical parameter is the mean interarrival time (IAT), μ (compare Section 2.1), in a Poisson process (which is a reasonable approximation). If the mean IAT is monotone increasing on signal intensity (which is an assumption about the transducer characteristics at the very first stage of psychophysiological input), then possibly this monotone relationship is approximated by a power function in the sense of

$$\log (\text{IAT}) = a + b \cdot \log (\text{physical input})$$

There are two simple rules that a system that monitors its own IATs could use to support decisions about the existence or magnitude of inputs; *either* set a number, k, and then observe until this number of impulses have gone past the monitoring point and note the time taken for k to happen (some inbuilt clock is obviously required; compare Section 4.2), which is timing for a fixed count, *or* the process is observed for a fixed time and a count of impulses taken (which requires a counting mechanism with a fixed periodicity). Even more simple than counting for a fixed time is, equivalently, setting a criterion IAT and recording a response when the first IAT less than the criterion occurs (this requires an internal clock of greater precision than the timing for a fixed count). For the comparison of two signals (which means two trains, or two sets of trains, of neural activity) more complex versions of counting in fixed time or timing for a fixed count are needed.

Sensation input processes are not single channel but at least based upon a multiplicity of channels functioning in parallel with some indeterminate cross-correlations between channels. The pattern of excitation over a set of channels can carry information about the qualitative nature of stimulation; Luce and Green (1974a) restrict their formalization to a set of channels that are in effect re-duplicative or mutually redundant and are concerned with the transmission of quantitative information about stimuli. Defining

J = number of parallel channels
k = number of IATs collected before responding
β = a criterion against which a mean IAT is compared,

these three parameters are required to be independent.
The process is also limited in accuracy by the upper bound on the amount of information about IATs that can be stored and compared against the criterion; this is represented by a buffer store capacity K. There are conceptual problems in theorizing this way because the operation of all the parameters is really stochastic. The response latencies exist because a system conceptualized in this way must take time to make any decision.

The observed reaction times y have a distribution in time, $y(t)$, which is given by the convolution integral

$$y(t) = \int_0^t l(\theta)r(t - \theta) \, d\theta \qquad (4.3.16)$$

where $l(\theta)$ is a distribution of latencies consequent upon using the rule for monitoring pulse trains to criterion β, and $r(\theta)$ is a residual distribution for processes within the organism that follow the pulse train monitoring. There has to be made some provision for the time to make the overt response (e.g., to say "I hear it!"), which cannot occur until after the operation of the criterion β. By using Laplace and inverse Laplace transforms (see Section 3.8), the shape of $r(t - \theta)$ is identifiable, given data $y(t)$ *and* a model for $l(\theta)$.

From these axioms, Luce and Green (1974a) derived results identical to or compatible with signal detection, magnitude estimation, mean reaction times for judgements with random foreperiods, and a prediction for Weber's law. The inverse relation between reaction time and stimulus intensity was also confirmed, and parametric consistency to the model fitted to various experimental paradigms was achieved.

However, the powerful conclusions of the neural trace model at the microanalysis level do not extend to the more gross sequential effects in, say, series of magnitude estimations. The timing or counting processes as given do not lead without modification to models that will exhibit the required sequential effects in judgment that are well known to exist. So, Green and Luce (1977) suggested a structure like Fig. 4.3.7; the stimuli are transformed into two internal representations, ψ_1 and ψ_2, as though two carbon copies were made of the input S, as a prerequisite to making sequential comparison judgments.

In the theory of Fig. 4.3.7 the internal representations $\psi_{1,j}$, $\psi_{2,j}$ are destroyed when they are used by the subject to generate a response (a ratio judgment) into which they enter as numerator and denominator. If the experimenter asked for a whole series of m judgments involving ψ_j, then it would presumably be necessary to store $\{\psi_{1,j}, \psi_{2,j}, \ldots, \psi_{m,j}\}$ to support the responses. There is a quaint

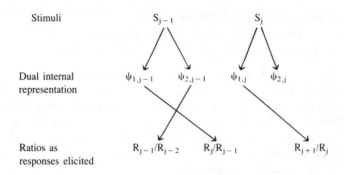

FIG. 4.3.7   Dual internal representation and series of ratios of magnitudes.

problem here; if we are running an experiment in which the subject is told in advance, perhaps truthfully, how many judgments he is going to be asked to make involving S_j, how should this in Fig. 4.3.7 affect his behavior? There is some conceptual imprecision or implausibility in the notion of a finite store of destroyable or destroyed representations, unless instead the ψ process is redefined as continuous in time but sampled at discrete points during which time it alerts and decays but in a manner unaffected by the sampling. There is an aphorism that one cannot step into the same river twice, and this is a better metaphor, in time series modeling, than the carbon copy idea. Quantitatively the important point is that ψ_1 and ψ_2 are defined to be independent, which in the discrete sampling process means that the errors on some mean ψ_j are i.i.d. It can, however, be shown that even with cov $(\psi_{1,j}, \psi_{2,j}) = 0$ there may be some sequential effects of considerable interest. If this covariance were not zero, then the effects would be different and probably more marked.

Sequential effects will occur in the multiple trace process if it is allowed that the $\psi_{1,h}$, $\psi_{2,h}$ have definable expectations, when S_h is the physical magnitude of a stimulus (trial number not specified), each ψ being a stochastic variable. Define

$$F_{1,h} = E(\psi_{1,h}) \tag{4.3.17}$$

$$F_{2,h} = E\left(\frac{1}{\psi_{2,h}}\right) \tag{4.3.18}$$

and the ratio of expectations has itself an expectation on the jth trial, for the total set of distinct stimulus values that exist in an experimental trial j, $\{S_h\}_j$, $h = 1, 2, \ldots, m$, as

$$B = E[F_{1,(h)} \cdot F_{2(h)}] \tag{4.3.19}$$

Over the total situation, once stability has been attained, it can be shown that

$$\frac{E(R_j|S_j = h, S_{j-1} = h')}{E(R_j|S_j = h)} = \frac{F_{1,h'} \cdot F_{2,h'}}{B} \tag{4.3.20}$$

which is unity if there is no sequential dependency but otherwise less than or greater than unity. The presence or absence of bias in R_j/R_{j-1} depends on the value of B; for if $\psi_{1,h}$ and $\psi_{2,h}$ are identically distributed, it is demonstrable that

$$F_{1,h} \cdot F_{2,h} \geq 1$$

(see Green & Luce, 1977, corollary 2, p. 4).

In real experiments, B will take time to settle down even if the subject operated in a manner perfectly consistent with (4.3.17)–(4.3.19). Estimates of (4.3.20) over a wide range of studies show that the function is monotone increasing with the value of S_{j-1}.

It should be emphasized that R_j/R_{j-1} is the ratio judgment $R_j/R_{j-1,j}$, which is a function of ψ_j, ψ_{j-1}, and $j - j - 1$ is a real time interval and not the ratio of two separate overt responses. R_j/R_{j-1} is a number calculated by a subject after the subject has separately estimated internally R_j and R_{j-1}, a single response to a pair of stimuli experienced separately, in sequence. The extent to which sequential effects are present, and their direction (assimilation or contrast) varies with the sensory modality of the $\{S_j\}$ (Jestead et al., for an example in audition, 1977) and may be embedded in many other types of bias. Poulton (1979) lists a range of processes that render the judgment of sensory magnitudes anything but constant and includes under the heading of "transfer" sequential effects predicating stimuli, judgments, and responses. Quite complicated solutions are offered by Poulton for running experiments in such a way as to minimize biases, which may yield more clear data for applied purposes but will inevitably destroy much of the interesting evidence of how the subject functions dynamically.

The facility with which sequential or time-order error may be demonstrated particularly in loudness judgment experiments was used by Hellström (1977a, 1977b) in later studies consonant with those reviewed in Section 4.2 for time estimation. The notion that TOE in magnitude estimations is solely due to response biases, by which is meant response preferences or shifted response criteria, as in mapping the partitions of a response category scale onto a sensory continuum of intensities, is firmly discounted. Helström concluded that "TOE is a differential weighting, in the formation of the judgment, of the sensory effects of the first and second stimulus," and consequently not representable by a single number, as early psychophysicists had thought. This is, of course, compatible with a linear transfer function model of sequential judgments but rather different from the approaches of Luce and Green. Hellström extended consideration of the finer details of TOE to include the actual interstimulus interval, in seconds, and in the case of tones the duration of each stimulus. If the second stimulus is made longer than the first, this will increase the efficiency with which relative judgment task is performed. Even more complex paradigms, with stimuli (anchor values) presented before, between, or after the comparison pair, have been used. The presence of extra stimuli in the series can reverse the direction of assimilation (or contrast) effects between the members of the comparison pair (compare

Fig. 4.3.2). The theories in this area generally treat the input and output events as point values combined with scalar weights, sequence parameters (more weights), and context stimuli (more weights), rather than as the convolution of filters and processes extending through time, sampled at discrete intervals. It is probable that in most of these models the level of description of the sensory–cognitive process is set too coarsely; a time series analysis at a more detailed level is needed to bring some coherence and invariance to the findings. Models that effectively have the subject compare the present stimulus (a point value) with the memory of the previous stimuli (a vector of point values) are inadequate, as noted by Hellström (1977b) in rejecting earlier models.

Very little evidence using time series analysis in psychophysics bears on modalities other than hearing, although the long slow adaptation and recovery characteristic, supposedly, of olfaction should make that modality potentially interesting. The difficulty of quantifying the stimulus concentration in olfaction until the development of modern olfactometry is obviously a contributory reason for the neglect of the problem experimentally. An autocorrelation and l.t.f. analysis of sequential effects in odor intensity ratings, which is not the same as adaptation in detection thresholds, was performed by Gregson and Paddick (1975). The stimuli were acetophenone and eugenol; 11 subjects were used and the coefficients v_0, v_1, and v_2 calculated for each. Very big individual differences in the goodness of fit of a power law were found, but for nearly all subjects v_0 dominated strongly, and the coefficients dropped off thereafter. An interesting difference emerged in the v_2 coefficients: These were negligible in size, but in 10 out of 11 cases were negative for acetophenone and in only 2 cases out of 11 negative for eugenol. This means that small coefficients can carry important information that is only revealed by its consistency across subjects. The results indicated that the self-adaptation characteristics of the two substances differed markedly under the time intervals used, which were the same for all conditions. Correlations across subjects suggested that there was a marked linkage between v_0 for eugenol and v_1 for acetophenone, stronger in fact than that between the v_0 coefficients themselves. This suggests a marked and regular difference in the form of the transfer function for the two substances. If within-modality differences are so marked, generalizations across modalities should be treated with reserve.

This analysis obviously differs from the auditory models of Luce and Green reviewed above, where successive differences of stimuli were shown to be more informative than stimulus values. So little is known about olfaction by comparison with audition, and the rate of stimulus presentation and the amount of information transmittable in the sensory channel are so different in the two cases, that caution is needed before results are seen as either compatible or incompatible. It is in principle possible to reanalyze any bivariate transfer function such as that used by Gregson and Paddick (1975) to see if a specific nonlinear model, with the provisions introduced by Luce and Green, is more illuminating; indeed some recent work by time series analysts centers strongly on such questions. Luce, Baird, Green, and Smith (1980) extend and explore their sequential models in an attempt to synthesize some previous results; they meet with some serious problems in model identification but are able to reject a range of models.

4.4 MOTOR SKILLS AND REGULATION

The field of human motor skills, where a human agent controls or regulates a mechanical system by closing continuously or intermittently one or more loops, was the first to be extensively analyzed using control theory. Consequently it has its own extensive literature with little or no reference back to mainstream psychology. This historical evolution has been remarked upon in previous sections; here a few sources and concepts are brought together for the convenience of the reader and to contrast developments with other sections of this chapter.

Under the heading of engineering psychology, studies of very varied sophistication in skill analysis have been surveyed in the *Annual Review of Psychology* by Fitts in 1958, Melton and Briggs in 1960, Chapanis in 1963, Poulton in 1966, Noble in 1968, and Alluisi and Morgan in 1976. Specialist journals such as *Ergonomics* should also be consulted and Poulton (1974). Successive writers attest to the changes in, and theoretical proliferation of, the area and the impossibility of reviewing the whole area as though it were homogeneous. The most coherent treatment of general methodology is offered by Sheridan and Ferrell (1974) who cover a wider range of systems analysis methods than is implied by time series analyses alone, linking into information theory and decision modeling.

Ellson (1949) under the rubric of operational analysis considered linear superposition of inputs and outputs as ''a direct parallel in engineering of the behavioural approach in psychology [p. 9].'' He went on that ''the relationships between input and output are the basic functions and they may be investigated without reference to intervening mechanisms [p. 10].'' Such a very empty black box approach has been abandoned both in theory and in practice by the disciplines that Ellson sought to set in parallel: What is interesting is the strict adherence to linear systems being used to sustain the correspondence with a simplistic behaviorism. There is, however, a special justification for adhering to this correspondence within the deliberately restricted scope of man–machine systems that would be neither necessary nor plausible nor fruitful in the wider area of cognition. In man–machine systems it was only the input–output characteristics that were reliable, regular, and fairly linear, which could be exploited by the designer by being written as component subsystem specifications into the larger aggregate of subsystems that the engineer wished to control. As Ellson argued, it is possible that in certain practical situations tracking behaviour may be sufficiently well isolated by means of instructions and training. Whether or not it can be isolated, and on being so isolated become stationary and linear, is an empirical question. We now know that it does not matter whether or not it is precisely stationary and linear; what matters is its controllability. It so transpires that in some constrained tasks human motor skills are very close to a linear representation; it is always an economical strategy to see if some linear representation is useful, if we are working in complete ignorance. The possibility that a human operator has a set of different linear models and will switch from one to another as the situation demands was anticipated in theory and is reported by various writers such as Welford (1976) and Stassen (1979) who covers important work in human engineering.

A key problem is that of deciding how to incorporate, functionally, the operator into the loops of the system. Modern representations tend to be simple but nonlinear; earlier ones were linear but complex. For example, Stankovic and Kouwenberg (1973) treat a single closed-loop compensatory task with abrupt perturbations as Fig. 4.4.1.

To proceed as in Fig. 4.4.1 requires a dichotomization of the loop characteristics into a linear system and what is called the *remnant,* defined as the component in the operator's response resulting from stochastic time variations of parameters P and the disturbance function $\eta(j)$.

There is a general, almost metatheoretical question as to whether compensatory tracking, where the operator physically shifts controls or switches to bring the system output back with a range of target values, is equivalent to intermittent monitoring behavior where the operator samples and integrates information from

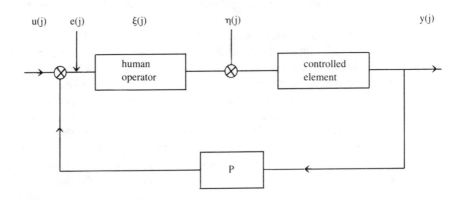

$\eta(j)$ is a noise perturbation between the operator and the element to be controlled

P represents discontinuities and state changes in the environment

FIG. 4.4.1   Compensation with perturbations.

displays of the state of a system and then makes servo control adjustments that do not themselves involve physical effort to any significant extent.

The comparison is, approximately, that of Fig. 4.4.2 and 4.4.3.

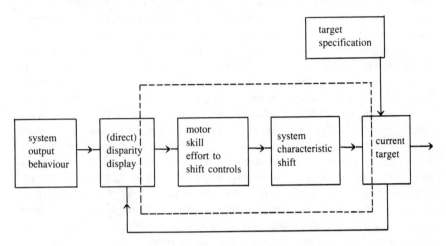

FIG. 4.4.2   System representation of a tracking task.

The part inside the box of dashed lines is the subsystem that is functionally inside the operator.

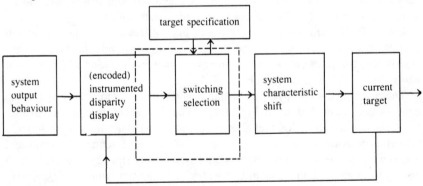

FIG. 4.4.3   System representation of instrument reading and appropriate corrective action: compensation.

Again, the box of dashed lines encloses the human operator's functional contribution. He or she can now handle more information about the system state because of the preencoding; the switching (which is a lightweight motor skill) also permits target respecification semicontinuously. If this progression is developed, we end up with an operator and a graphic display at the periphery of a computer controlled system, occasionally changing the state specifications for a system that is largely self-regulatory. The logical progression, where the human operator's role is less and less motor and more and more cognitive, at the high level implied by intermittent intervention to sustain a policy rather than the details of program execution, is a recapitulation of an historical trend where the increasing capacity of mechanical systems to control themselves and to set their own long- and short-term objectives reduces the required human labor force even in decision-making roles. The interface between operator and a physical subsystem, where the operator interfaces with the machine environment as a whole, has shifted; the physical environment encompasses more and more stages in the largest control loop that may intermittently exist to set the total system policy. For this reason much of the methods and theory of man–machine systems must be ephemeral; it represents a succession of compromises at some intermediate states of the art that in any one case may or may not obtain a transient embodiment in real man–machine system, like an airplane with some degree of automatic pilot control that is less than 100%. Pseudocontrol may be retained; high-speed trains are run by computer control either on board or through signals fed in on carrier frequencies through the track or motive power supply, and the driver's role becomes almost symbolic and hence hardly representable in a formal systems model that gives the operator something real to do. However, the results of models of past stages in man–machine automation have lessons for us in theoretical psychology, at least they may be valued representations of how the human operator would behave if the environment left him that much, and no more and no less, of critical functioning in his hands (and brain).

Baron and Kleinman (1969) incorporated intermittent monitoring with system control (in actuality control of the movements of some vehicle) to allow explicitly for vision as a data sampling process, which puts tracking as the response into a discrete time model; see Fig. 4.4.4.

The perceptual–cognitive part of this hypothetical system is enclosed in the inner box of dashed lines in Fig. 4.4.4. The data reconstructor was mathematically made to be a Kalman filter (see Chapter 5) and a least-mean-squared predictor in tandem. In order to proceed with the representation, Baron and Kleinman postulated a set of displays, and an observer strategy to decide *which* display to monitor at any instant, by employing a sampling rule. This obviously presupposes a limited channel capacity on the part of the observer, a dwell time for any choice to observe a given display, and rules about when to change between displays. Even with a Bayesian strategy to decide and to revise continuously the probabilities that important information will be lurking at any moment on a given display (either the one one is watching or some other), the representation problem is complex for the model builder and one would not think that the human observer would become very near to optimality without extensive practice in interacting with such a system. The situation implies that a cost function on attending to displays (i.e., the cost of missing critical information by looking in

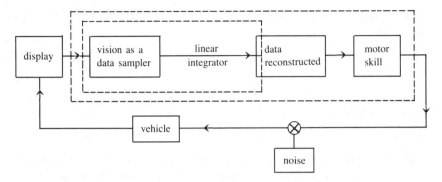

FIG. 4.4.4   Tracking in discrete time.

the wrong place at any time) can be written over the total set of alternative displays, in the long run. This in effect writes a control policy, which is a stochastic ordering of outcomes or target values for given inputs and degrees of perturbation, into the model. Having done this it is then possible to use some variant of optimal decision theory to define efficient behavior.

A critical feature of instrument monitoring behavior treated in this way is making the time sampling rates efficient and economical in effort. The variance of the noise levels across the set of alternative displays plays a crucial role in determining the expediency of switching attention between displays. The dwell time, which is the time the observer spends in attending for an unbroken period to a particular display (from amongst alternatives), has a distribution that is a function of the noise variance and of the demand characteristics of the system. Consequently it is not possible to define a global optimum strategy without knowing the parametrization of the system (Beggs, Saksteini & Howarth, 1974).

Motor tasks that are repetitive and simple, such as tapping a Morse key, from the pacing of internal control (the message in dots and dashes that the subject is trying to transmit) and not external signals (as in Section 4.2) are a hybrid of time estimation and motor skills modeling. Wing and Kristofferson (1973) advanced a model in which the distribution of time keeping and the distribution of motor delays in subsequent response execution could be separated.

Defining

$$I_j = t_j - t_{j-1} \quad \text{where } t_j \text{ is a point in time}$$
$$= \Delta t_j$$

The responses are assumed to be evenly spaced by an internal timekeeper, as

$$C_j = \text{constantly distributed} \sim N(C, \sigma_C)$$

and an independent superimposed delay

$$D_j \sim N(D, \sigma_D)$$

As D_j operates on C_j's output; because the two processes are independent and in cascade,

$$E(\Delta^1 t_j) = E(C_j) - E(D_{j-1}) + E(D_j) \tag{4.4.1}$$

$$= C - D + D = C$$

and for a single interval

$$I_j = C_j - D_{j-1} + D_j \tag{4.4.2}$$

If $C \sim N(C, 0)$, that is, a very consistent timekeeping process (in practice if $\sigma_C^2 \ll \sigma_D^2$, s will suffice), and D is exponentially distributed (see Section 2.1 on renewal processes), then I_j will have a Laplace distribution that McGill (1962) found in some data from neurophysiology of possible relevance. For a specification of the Laplace distribution, see McGill's treatment.

The lag zero covariance of the interresponse interval series

$$\text{var} (I_j) = \text{cov} (I_{j,j}) = \sigma_C^2 + 2\sigma_D^2 \tag{4.4.3}$$

because of the independence in (4.4.1).

The lag 1 covariance is $-\sigma_D^2$ and the process shows the strong negative sequential dependence in that a long delay in one trial produces a long interresponse interval and then on average a short interresponse interval on the next trial: The autocorrelation of lag 1 is

$$r(j, j - 1) = -\left(2 + \frac{\sigma_C^2}{\sigma_D^2} \right)^{-1} \tag{4.4.4}$$

and this result is considered important because it furnishes a mechanism where $r(j, j - 1)$ is negative without any feedback being present, in other words the negative value of $R(j, j - 1)$ is not of itself sufficient basis for identifying the sequential consequence of feedback in a serial task. It can be shown that (4.4.1) imposes bounds on $r(j, j - 1)$ in the form

$$0 \leqslant r(j, j - 1) \leqslant - 1/2$$

Data show that $\bar{s}_C^2 = a(\bar{I} - b)$, where a and b are regression constants, is an approximate relationship. The distinction between pursuit and compensatory tracking anticipated earlier was reformulated by Briggs (1966) in the following manner:

At one extreme we have the 100% pursuit display in which there is no compensating component; the subject merely attempts to follow a display pointer or cursor with a control, seeking always to minimize local (in time) error. The two points to be matched are in the instantaneous display to the subject, who is thus being fed the error signal symbolized in diagrams as located at the comparator element in the join of the feedback and input. In 100% compensation the target is fixed, and the cursor that is the following element is under control and under perturbation at the same time, so that after displacement it can be brought back on target by corrective movements that are opposite in sense and equal in magnitude to the error of the cursor, unless multipliers and nonlinearities in the feedback are also introduced. So the operator compensates by correcting the cursor for its visible disparity from the target.

Between the two extremes any mixture is mechanically possible; the action of the operator can be partly to track the target display with the cursor and partly to compensate for the wandering of the cursor from where it is intended to be. Consequently, varying the pursuit–compensation proportions constitutes a variable for experimental investigations of the characteristics of closed-loop tracking.

The relative accuracy of tracking performance depends on the frequency components of the target input; only under very low frequencies and without mechanical drag on the motor controls can compensation be better than pursuit. At very low frequencies there are periods (in the rise and fall of a sinusoid where the second derivative d^2x/dt^2 is approximately zero) where the input is effectively a ramp with fixed slope. There the operator can use the dynamics of steady ramp change to operate an open loop instead of a closed loop; this is behaving like an amplifier and not like tracking. If the loop is closed, then error and acceleration information is utilizable. Hence with slow periodicities as input, the system in time series terms alters its sequential structure periodically, fluctuating between first difference and second or third difference summations of input. This is a strictly predictable form of nonstationarity, which is examined more formally in Chapter 5.

If a machine inputs an abrupt violent jerk, then the dynamics involve higher-order terms, d^nx/dt^n, $n \geq 2$. The operator needs to be able to control, on the response side, derivatives of the same order or else risk the loop going into oscillations with positive amplification, which is the path to violent instability.

In engineering terms, there have to be integral transforms in the control system that match the derivatives of the error sequence in the input subsystem.

In practice the human operator does not get beyond the second derivative matching double integration with acceleration, but there are special strategies available to cut out the higher-order dynamics that cannot be tracked continuously or even discretely at high frequency. In other words, by going into discrete time of a sufficiently low sampling fraction, control may be sustained. One way this can be done is by introducing a wobbling component into the corrective motor responses. If the operator adds to the control movement a medium-frequency low-amplitude oscillation, then this increases the amount of tractable information in the feedback; by time sampling this augmented feedback, a higher-order system behaves so far as the operator is concerned like a simple first-order system. This is a type of filtering that aliases the higher-order components but appears not to have been studied in detail; it is not known exactly how it is done.

The existence of the strategy just described emphasizes that the information feedback, to close the control loop, critically affects the precision of execution; this is hardly surprising. Bilodeau (1966) considered this a crucial issue in motor skill analysis. Information feedback is definable as the discrepancy between target and actual responses; it is thus that and only that information that matches the input from a comparator to a gain element in a control loop.

Let us concentrate here on one restricted aspect of the problem of optimization of information feedback (IF) to facilitate human learning, simply to link in explicitly with a time series paradigm. The motor skill experiment with discrete IF is, putting IF and R in the same units of measurement,

$$R_{j-1}IF_{j-1}R_jIF_jR_{j+1}IF_{j+1} \cdots \tag{4.4.5}$$

In motor skill execution the actual time elapsed between events in the series (4.4.5) may be critical, because of the mechanics of causing limbs with inertia to stop and start, as well as because of neural transmission lags. Defining

$$D_{j-1} = t(IF_{j-1} - R_{j-1}) = \text{delay}$$

$$P_{j-1} = t(R_j - IF_{j-1}) = \text{post-IF delay}$$

$$D_{j-1} + P_{j-1} = T_{j-1} = \text{trial duration in seconds,}$$
or intertrial interval $ITI_{j,j-1}$

The locus of IF is defined to be

$$L_{j-1} = \frac{t(IF_{j-1} - R_{j-1})}{t(R_j - IF_{j-1})} \tag{4.4.6}$$

As the locus, delay, and ITI are confounded variables, little data exist to disentangle their effects; P_{j-1} and $ITI_{j,j-1}$ are commonly correlated.

A decline in accuracy with increasing ITI can occur even if P_{j-1} is brief; to demonstrate this, a paradigm with reduplication of IF is used, as in Fig. 4.4.5:

The results of experiments reported by Bilodeau (1966) seemed generally to support the position that L_{j-1} does not matter so far as performance accuracy or rate of acquisition are concerned, within the paradigm of Fig. 4.4.5. However, there is, as might sensibly be expected, a limit to how much IF may be delayed without degrading its effective utilization. Temporally displacing IF_j until it occurs between R_{j+k} and R_{j+k+1}, $k = 1, 2, 3, \ldots, n$ will eventually, for $k \geq 4$, impede learning; though, for $k < 4$, some learning will take place. If IF is discretized, then error increases slightly with the coarseness of resolution of the IF scale.

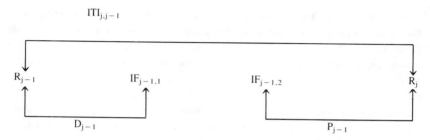

FIG. 4.4.5   Reduplicative *IF* paradigm.

Deliberately degrading *IF,* so that within a band around zero error no *IF* is available, and then outside this band underdisplaying or overdisplaying the extent of error, has been tried. Changes in the width of the dead zone around a target value affect the rate of learning but unless this zone is very wide, they have little effect upon asymptotic performance. It is probable that this result is also found in cognitive tasks with a similar bandwidth definition (Gregson, 1980).

The sequential and bandwidth properties of motor feedback dynamics must be taken to hold only if the subject is not fatigued. The consequences of fatigue on sequential task performance have been summarized by Welford (1976). Of special interest in this context is the effect of fatigue upon the disorganization of sequences of action. Preprogrammed response sequences that are by definition locally independent, over a run of trials, on input, are disrupted. The timing of actions in a sequence are made irregular compared with their unfatigued execution, and in the limit order inversions within a sequence can therefore occur.

Avoidance of disruption by the sequential consequences of fatigue is in some cases possible by predicting events, that is, using local sequence properties to prepare anticipatory responses, and by pacing of performance. All these strategies should result in the local reduction of the rate of choice or decision (which is quantifiable in bits/second) and in the use of *IF.*

There is, however, some disagreement concerning how much sequences of motor acts are preprogrammed into runs or blocks rather than being under the quasi-continuous control of *IF.* Representation of either view in multivariate time series models is radically different from the other; the identification of open-loop preprogrammed blocks rather than closed-loop sequences with rapid feedback is feasible, in principle, because the limiting factor is the rate of corrective action; if the steps of a sequence with repeatable structure can be shown to occur faster than the minimum time for feedback to close and effect correction, then the preprogrammed interpretation is valid for at least some sequences. The situation is not, however, that simple. Glencross (1977) and Klapp and Greim (1979) summarize a diversity of interpretations; Adams (1977) reviews evidence specifically pertinent to the timed movement of the limbs, and Beggs, Saksteini & Howarth (1974) consider intermittent control.

At least three distinct theories have been advanced to account for the performance of skilled motor sequences: the peripheralist view, where sequences are dependent solely and almost immediately upon input, the centralist view where sequences are a consequence of output from higher-order control processes independent for long periods (relatively) of input, and a hybrid view that is more plausible, advanced by Glencross (1977) that both a closed-loop executive system and an open-loop motor program can be implemented, the second being initiated, to run its own course, under the control of the former. The shift from open to closed loop and vice versa must depend on input monitored at the same time, or on central processes that are input independent but can be overridden. A switch back from open loop to closed loop can occur during the execution of a sequence if errors become too large to be tolerable. One can postulate a strictly hierarchical system in which the higher-order levels decide, on their own feedback, the transitions between subsystems. This sort of theory that Powers (1973) postulated is easy to invent and almost impossible to identify. Glencross does not consider the role of this necessary higher-level monitor but emphasizes the strong centralist position; once control is central, the identity and sequence of a set of muscle commands is completed before it is executed and then becomes autonomous of central control until its completion.

The central control processes are hypothetical; they are proposed because of the following:

1. Some learned motor sequences are executed with precise regularity and reliability.
2. Sequences are executed so fast that interruptions between steps to make corrections is only thought to be possible at some points, not at any point.
3. The alternative hypothesis is that feedback is (a) available and (b) utilizable to modify subsequent phases; yet these two conditions have not been generally demonstrated to hold.

The visual-motor corrective feedback loop is digitized with a loop delay of about 200 msec overall, but as will be seen this figure may be misleading. Alternative feedback loops may function in parallel, involving different sensory systems, and consequently a more defensible representation is one in which IF is a vector, with different attendant delays for each component therein.

The variability in kinesthetic-loop delays leads to the suggestion that there are two sorts of delay in series, a long delay for response sequence initiation and a short one for the amendment of a sequence once initiated. To put this another way, the observed initiation loop delay is the two phases in series; if the required rate of change is above a critical level, as it will be if a step input is requested (as in abrupt initiation of a sequence), then a slower response will be observed. Only within a limited bandwidth of rates of change (i.e., a bandwidth about zero change) can a revision of output be achieved through one loop.

Two types of motor sequences are of interest for their theoretical implications: arpeggio sequences and ballistic movements. The arpeggio is, of course, a rapidly executed run of notes on an instrument such as a piano or violin; subsequences are executed and only intermittently sampled. One observed corrective strategy is for subjects to drift back onto target after a slow drift away, in either direction or timing, has occurred. These drifts are very low-frequency components superimposed on the cycles of higher-frequency execution. It is of interest that in periodic tasks, such as turning a handle, the response-produced feedback will always be out of phase but with the same period as the task and can be utilized. It is not clear if it is continuously utilized or only when it can be treated as rate open-loop information as in the case described previously. Ballistic movements (very fast, like a projectile) are out of control during execution but have a limited range; otherwise our limbs would somewhat messily snap off and fly away if we moved them very quickly. Involuntary whiplash movements imposed on the human body during severe accidents can of course produce such dramatic consequences.

Clearly, the motor program has to be modifiable by feedback during slow execution, or the program could never be learned. In speeding up a program there will be changes in the relations of the moves within it as the periods of acceleration and deceleration reach a limit relative to fixed rate or stationary moments. If the feedback loop is of fixed delay, then its utilization will be more and more delayed in relative terms as a sequence is speeded up during learning; as feedback is optimum only if delay is minimized; acceleration of a sequence degrades the value of feedback until in the limit one is better without it.

Welford (1976) postulated three stages in motor skill execution:

1. Analysis and brief storage.
2. Matching response to signal.
3. Response execution.

Glencross (1977) preferred to treat stages 1 and 2 as a single feedback loop and stage 3 as the subsequent open-loop consequence of selecting a program that then runs autonomously.

The execution of a sequence may involve some or all of the three stages; if only amplitude gain is to be corrected and not sequence and target specification, then correction can be rapid enough to change an arpeggio-like run in "mid flight." changes in gain will imply changes in timing one element relative to its precursors and successors, with cumulative effects in later stages given that movements are fixed velocity and variable amplitude. The control of sequences can be preplanned and made faster and more sensitive to error by feedforward loops in which current action presets sensory receptors to be optimal for future predicted input scanning (as in linear extrapolation). This can be done by responding to first-order differences and making a brief lead anticipatory response.

Klapp and Greim (1979) attempt to identify some of the more precise questions about the central storage of preprogrammed motor sequences, in tasks where muscles are controllable both by visual and kinesthetic feedback. It would appear that short movements are preprogrammed but that long movements are under feedback control. The interaction between precision of target specification (the psychological correlate of physical target size) and movement amplitude is such that short movements decrease in rate as precision is increased, but large amplitude movements do not.

The more uncertainty is introduced into the future course of a movement, by making the movement one of a set within which a decision has to be made at onset, the more information is needed, but there is a limit to how many different sequences can be anticipatorily programmed at the same time. Only if two sequences have the same time base (i.e., overall duration from onset to target) can they be jointly preprogrammed. The general picture, when feedback is multivariate but there is also a central limit on what can be preprogrammed, suggests that the covariance structure of brief extrapolatory time series of responses depending on different programs is a limiting factor in the system's capacity to function and store those programs for alternative execution. Little is known on this question.

Even the simplest tasks have varying temporal structure and varying autocovariance of response times, according to whether the input is selectively controlled by previous responses or by current stimuli. Rabbitt and Vyas (1979) again take up the multivariate character of the input information on which sequences are based, pointing out that information about (1) signals, (2) mapping rules from stimuli to responses, (3) decisions to be made, and (4) particular motor responses can all be independently stated and stored in memory. Importantly, in addition they offer evidence that a hierarchical structure is imposed on these sorts of information and higher-order characteristics of skills that can determine choice responses over a sequence of trials are preserved independently of psychophysically represented stimulus properties. This is an explicitly centralist position from which it is deduced that the degree of sequential dependency in a response sequence can increase with the centrality of the level of control.

The contrary view, seeking for a neurophysiological mechanism at the periphery, to mediate the timing and positioning of motor movements, has been advanced in detail by Adams (1977). He comments "in the absence of an organ of time it must be assumed that timing is governed by an undiscovered brain mechanism or is a derived function of one or more of the senses [p. 505]." He attempts to invoke the temporal distribution of discharge rates from receptors in the limb joints as a sort of internal clock that is in turn monitored by some controlling mechanism, spinal or cortical. It is possible to argue that if some process with monotone decreasing activity levels extending over a long time after step input will serve as a time base (which is what the limb joints provide), then any such mechanism would serve. So a central mechanism has as much right as has a peripheral one, though a peripheral one close to the muscles being controlled would minimize the length of some neural circuitry.

Sequences observed by Adams (1977) have a form like Fig. 4.4.6, where θ denotes the current error in the sense

$$\theta = R_{j-1} - \text{current target specification}$$

and e_j is a noise distribution. $R_{j,j+1}$ implies the trace of the response made at j that is still active at trial $j + 1$.

The input signal is the error θ, referred to a target that we can take to be locally constant, which produces a noise biased input (θ confounded with e) which is conjointly input to the response selection process together with a trace $R_{j-1,j}$ of the previous limb position and the rate of execution. To be precise, all θ e, R should be thought of as multivariate. As the internal clock is supposed to be paced independently of the trial spacing and input–output identities, we may put

$$\frac{\Delta R_j}{\Delta t} = |R_{j,j+1} - R_j| \qquad (4.4.7)$$

The neurophysiology that might mediate (4.4.7) by comparing the firing rates against elapsed time involves two types of receptor: SA = slowly adapting (Ruffini, Golgi endings) and RA = rapidly adapting (Paccinian capsules). SA receptors can monitor position and velocity; RA can map velocity and acceleration. Between them, therefore, they could exert three-term control (see Chapter 5) that involves the simultaneous utilization of location, x, and dx/dt and d^2x/dt^2. Periodic inputs up to 250 Hz can in fact be tracked. There is an approximate linear relationship between the SA, RA outputs and psychophysical judgments of limb movement, but this (though conveniently simple) is not necessary for the system to function.

The process of static timing, where a subject moves a limb, then holds it

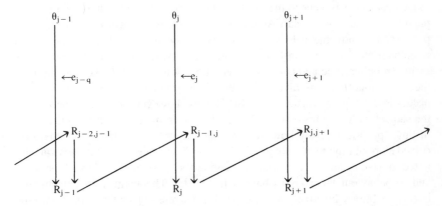

FIG. 4.4.6 Movement monitoring with response-actuated neurological feedback.

immobile for a limited period, and then moves it again, raises a problem for theory; how is it done, and done accurately? How does the subject receive cues concerning how long the limb has stopped, before he moves it again? When it is in motion, the joint receptors SA, RA will fire at a higher rate proportionally to the dynamic moments of movement, but the only firing that takes place when a limb is stationary is in the decay phase. This phase persists for a long time, at almost the same rate, after movement has produced a transient peak in the firing rates.

Adams (1977) postulates that the next move of a limb occurs when "a certain portion of the decay phase is passed." The rate of firing is supposed to be recognizable as a timing cue. As this rate drops off at first rapidly and then more slowly, it would be expected that a rough analog of Weber's law in the timing of intermovement intervals would ensue. How this process is distinguishable from another in which the peak firing rate is taken as a t_0 marker, after which the timing mechanism located centrally (see Section 4.1) takes over, is not clear.

The two theories (joint receptors firing rates versus central neural clock firing rates) are distinguishable in principle; the second would function if only the peak rate signals reached the central nervous system, so it could be disrupted by inputting centrally but not at the same time peripherally a bogus peak signal unrelated to limb movement. The peripheral process would be disrupted presumably only by bogus peripheral signals.

Experiments on interlimb timing, where one limb times another, such as foot tapping to play a clarinet in strict tempo, do provide some support for the notion that the joint receptors firing provide a clock basis. If they do not, then a complex system of feedback with respect to the central clock is required. It is found that the gap between one limb stopping and the other starting can be controlled accurately and that the accuracy is a function of the magnitude of the initial movement of the first limb before the interlimb pause. As distance, velocity, and time of a movement are necessarily interrelated, given that any one is fixed, the second can serve as a cue to the third, so it is empirically difficult to sort out what parameter, if any, is critical. Adams and co-workers conjecture that a record of past executed movements leaves a *perceptual trace* that is temporally extended in a multivariate sense; it constitutes a paradigm against which subsequent movement can be matched and corrected. See Fig. 4.4.6 and 4.4.7. As they put it "a theory without time can travel a theoretical distance but, after all, no movement occurs in a temporal vacuum [p. 514]." This, however, confuses time outside the subject with time inside the subject. Viewed from outside all movements are in time, proprioceptively however one may move so fast or so slow that perceived elapsed time seems not to be related to the change when it is subsequently noted to have occurred. The argument continues "all behaviour has a time base, and so behaviour theory must have it [p. 514]." This confuses a sequentiality basis of arbitrary but fixed (approximately) discrete steps with a clock marking out the elapsing of even time in seconds. The first is necessary; the second is not

Input p-vectors

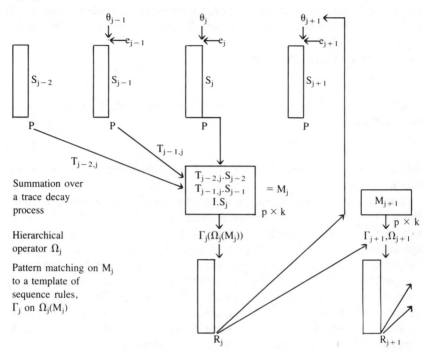

FIG. 4.4.7 Time series with operators replacing convolution sums.

though it is a special case of the former and one to which one or more biological systems, in parallel and interconnected, may approximate. The argument that because we may perceive a sequence, either of inputs or self-generated, as moving faster or slower, or even fast or slow, there must be an internal representation of a physical steady paced clock has little cogency; we do need two or more time series that can get out of or into phase, locally, but this does not require that any one should have the fidelity of a good digital watch. It is partly for this reason that the representation of time series used throughout this review are set in discrete time but not in specific or fixed intertrial units.

A general picture that emerges from the very complex data relationships on sequential motor tasks is not one of a linear stationary time series, univariate or multivariate. From what explanations will not work, we can tentatively identify the minimum complexity account that might serve and comment on one feature that is importantly different from the majority of models described in earlier chapters and sections. Previous models used at some stage a convolution sum in discrete time or a convolution integral in continuous time to generate a transfer function. Now we use a different concept, operators on a matrix whose terms are not summed. This is diagrammed in Fig. 4.4.7.

The diagram of Fig. 4.4.7 is obviously incomplete, not all the links are shown except for the jth trial, to avoid cluttering up the picture; the whole flow from θ, e, S, M, $\Gamma(\Omega(M))$ to R and back to update the operators and input is intended to occur on each trial.

The key to the process is the term

$$\Gamma_j(\Omega_j(M_j))_{p \times k}$$

which replaces a multivariate linear convolution sum which if it occurred would be of the form

$$\mathbf{R}_j = \mathbf{V}_k \cdot \mathbf{S}_{j-k} \tag{4.4.8}$$

where $\mathbf{R}_j$, $\mathbf{S}_{j-k}$ are p-vectors and $\mathbf{V}_k$ is a $p \times p$ matrix summing over k terms, that is, a matrix polynomial.

Instead of a convolution, each k-vector of terms $T_{j-k,j} \cdot S_j$ is not summed but instead held as an ordered set and scanned in priority defined by the set of operators Ω_j of which there are p or less. This defines the relational hierarchical operation of each of the p dimensions in generating output on trial j, Ω_j is itself subject to revision from trial to trial. The scanning process need not be exhaustive, and Ω_j may be degenerately a vector of binary $(0, 1)$ coefficients that leaves a small subset p^* as the basis of action, in short, a filter. The Γ_j take each k-vector of p^* and compares it in its turn with a template of length k; actions adopted are a function of the similarity or disparity between the k-vector and the template in its current form, for each of the p^* vectors. The theory of Adams (1977) monitors the trace of limb joint receptors as a Γ_j in our sense. The results of this sequential application of operators to the matrix M_j, which is necessarily limited in size by memory storage capacity, is

$$\Gamma_j(\Omega_j(M_j)) \rightarrow R_j \tag{4.4.9}$$

The operations of (4.4.9) are obviously not commutative; the output is a vector that in part determines an overt motor response and in part presets the error detectors, which are essentially terms of Γ_j, for the next trial input S_{j+1}.

It may be objected that this model destroys entirely the whole point of reviewing in detail mathematical models that are linear, stationary, and generate tractable transfer functions. This is quite wrong. In fact the process (4.4.9) could be simulated with a lot of additional housekeeping assumptions (when it is seen to be a blueprint for a class of models, not a single model), but it is not totally identifiable for reasons some of which are mathematical and some of which are psychological and have been referred to in previous discussions of identifiability and incompleteness, or uniqueness. In particular, realistic models would require a probabilistic loss of information at each stage; the computation and storage of M_j, $\Omega_j(M_j)$, $\Gamma_j(\Omega_j(M_j))$, and R_j.

To a first approximation the core $\Gamma_j(\Omega_j(M_j))$ can be treated as the operation of nonlinear state variables on the input, in one of the ways to be referred to in

Chapter 5. In practice, either the hierarchical operator model here or a more abstract state space model would be so complex that its behavior would have to be explored by simulation rather than analytically. The system of Fig. 4.4.7 is readily programmable for low-order matrices; its plausibility, interestingly, rests in part on whether or not it is inherently unstable and so goes out of control or fails to track input in the same manner as human subjects. As the model is essentially a formalization of some major ideas and conjectures from the studies cited previously it is sufficiently complex to be realistic.

4.5 SOME TIME SERIES IN SOCIAL PSYCHOLOGY

In social psychology a long succession of publications—it seems wiser not to write of a *series* of publications here—has centered on what has become known as the "sleeper effect." There been alleged demonstrations of the existence and of the nonexistence of this effect, and disputes over its existence, definability, and measurability. Arguments of this sort shade inevitably into philosophy of science issues concerning the possibility of proving the null hypothesis. There is no need to follow the argument into the arid wastes of dialectic; here the argument about the sleeper effect will be used, with deliberate oversimplification, to illustrate the construction of a time series model about a filter. At the end of the exercise it will be possible to make a rich diversity of predictions, on the interplay of attitudes and memory, according to what boundary conditions and initial conditions the investigator likes to add. Our objective here is to build a skeleton theory to show a style of theorizing that is compatible with time series as interpreted in the rest of the monograph, and in particular to provide a precursor to some of the more rigorous methods reviewed in Chapter 5. This example is to answer the question "what happens if the problem is recast in this fashion?" and not to give a final answer to what sleeper effects exist. It is hoped that the reader may begin to think that the whole dispute is a storm in a fuzzy teacup, which is what usually happens if concepts and measurement procedures are not unambiguously defined in the first instance.

The area has been thoroughly reviewed by Gruder, Cook, Hennigan, Flay, Alessis, and Halamaj (1978), and their treatment is the starting point for this modeling exercise. No attempt has been made to capture every nuance of theory or data that they review.

The idea of the sleeper effect is quite unstartling after seeing some of the shapes that linear transfer functions can take. A message is presented to a group of subjects and the message has a putative source. The message has content and inherent credibility, and the source has a credibility of its own. Both the recall of the content of the message after elapsed time and the credibility of the message after elapsed time can be measured. The amount and accuracy of the message recalled at various times after one initial presentation can be quantified [the best ways of doing this would use information theory measures, (Klix, 1973) but most published studies have been much cruder in their metrication], and the credibility of the source as recalled can also be scaled.

Early studies found in some cases that a message from a source with low credibility was not believed, but after some time it was favorably recalled. The argument to explain this outcome runs that after the putative source of the message is gradually forgotten, the message alone is recalled and comes to be accepted on the basis of its intrinsic credibility. So, the hearer of the message has recall that decays over time (simply because anything gets forgotten with the passing of time, eventually), and he or she has recall for the identity of the source. The credibility of a message at a point in time is a function of the initial credibilities and the rates of change of credibilities of the message and source, and the probabilities of either the message or the source identity being recalled at all.

As soon as we have this complexity of modeling, with undefined rates of change of different parts of a system, prediction becomes more than a little vague. If theories are purely verbal, and theorists want to give a separate name to any outcome that could happen, and postulate a different competing psychological process to explain any different outcome, then nothing is unexplainable. Combine this with no defined ground rules for scaling the memorability and credibility and accuracy of recall of messages and comparison of different published studies is hardly worth the effort. However, Gruder et al. (1978) have made the effort and have tried a semiquantitative reconciliation of the conflicting results. One of their main conclusions is that variables have been inadequately operationalized; in simpler language, it is not clear what is a measure of what.

In writing of a sleeper effect, psychologists have apparently meant either (1) a delayed increase in the credibility of a message (which can be a swing from disbelief to belief) or (2) the "discounting cue" hypothesis, which is a more positive assertion than item 1; that the source of the message lacks credibility and this is the reason for the initial disbelief in the message, though the message content is not forgotten.

Experiments bave been designed to manipulate independently the two processes, though in a real-world situation the two may be inextricably confounded. Within the framework of an associationist psychology a process has been postulated whereby the strength of association between the credibility of a message and the recall of the content of a message goes from positive to negative. It is clear that the simplest systems model capable of representing this process in time requires a large number of parameters, rate equations, and boundary conditions. The intrinsic complexity tells us that a diversity of outcomes are to be expected and will have to be predictable for the model to have validity.

The sleeper effect situation can be modeled by a process in time that is recursively modified by a filter. This filter is a set of simultaneous equations that update the values of all the key parameters in the process from time to time. The example to be sketched out here is a very elementary case that probably presupposes too much and explains too little. The objective is to show what a filtering model of a cognitive process looks like; rigorous examples of greater generality are reviewed in Chapter 5. Filter models are in fact often surprisingly easy to run on a small computer, and the exercise speedily makes plain any incompletenesses or contradictions in a theory. Translating a verbal theory into filter form, as is being done here (even at some violence to the original), lays out to view what variables will need defined quantification and what variables will have to be measured with sufficiently good scaling to support statements about rates of change and relative rates of change over time.

Start the process at time t_0. The subject has some initial strength of belief b_0 (this is a degree of assent). The message content is some strength and direction of a proposition, which can be weakened and then lost to recall with time.

The message is presented at time t_1, which is a little after t_0. Call the content at time of presentation m_1; this could strictly be called the "signed content" as it could take negative values if m is so encoded. The rate of forgetting of the message content with time is dm/dt. In practice the model would run in discrete time so the rates are the theoretical parameters of a sampled data system. Forgetting is commonly assumed to be initially rapid and progressively slower (Wickelgren, 1974) so that dm/dt is not constant.

The message source is to be given fixed credibility c_s. This is a scalar and can be taken as positive; the units are immaterial. The message also has a theoretical intrinsic credibility that it has in the absence of any attributed source; call this c_m. Again, c_m is a positive constant. The experimental condition of presenting a message to a control group without any contextual information about its putative source has been tried by some investigators (Gruder et al., 1978). One might argue that all messages or propositions have an implicit attributed source, which the subject infers from the style and content of the proposition and the experimenter's behavior, but this will vary from subject to subject whereas c_s and c_m are fixed parameters from a homogeneous group of subjects. The cognitive simplicity of these theories about attitude shift may give rise to disquiet, but the next step in constructing the filter is not paralleled in verbal theories so far as can be deduced.

At any point in time, t, the message has a credibility c_t, and this changes in time as a function of changes in a mixing equation with one parameter, α, $0 \leq \alpha \leq 1$. Define

$$c_t = \alpha \cdot c_m + (1 - \alpha) \cdot c_s \qquad (4.5.1)$$

so that

$$\frac{dc}{dt} = \frac{d\alpha}{dt} + c_m + \left(\frac{1 - d\alpha}{dt} \right) \cdot c_s \qquad (4.5.2)$$

The idea of the sleeper effect is represented here quite simply by stating that the credibility bias parameter, α, changes over time. If $d\alpha/dt$ is positive, then the importance of the source credibility diminishes over time.

The remaining equations are housekeeping to keep the model running; they are tabled without comment, merely defined.

Initial Constants.   These reflect different experimental conditions or treatments that may be applied to subjects or groups, if suitable scaling exists.

b_0:   initial belief about message content
m_0:   recall threshold intensity
m_1:   initial message content
c_m: message credibility
c_s: source credibility
k_1, k_2:   rate constants
α_0:   initial credibility bias
$d\alpha/dt, t = t_0$:   initial gradient in credibility drift $= -1$
$d_m/dt, t = t_0$:   initial memory decay gradient $= 0$

Parameters of Model in Time.   These are process outputs.

c_t: credibility of the message at time t
b_t: acceptance–recall of the message at time t
m_t: degree of recall at time t
α_t: credibility bias at time t

Filter Equations.   These are solved recursively, starting from the boundary conditions.

$$\frac{dm}{dt} = \exp(-k_1 \cdot t) \tag{4.5.3}$$

$$\frac{d\alpha}{dt} = k_3 \exp(-k_2 \cdot t) \tag{4.5.4}$$

$$\frac{dc}{dt} = \frac{d\alpha}{dt} \cdot c_m + \left(1 - \frac{d\alpha}{dt}\right) \cdot c_s \qquad \text{[see (4.5.2)]}$$

$$b_t = c_t \qquad \text{iff } m_t > m_0 \tag{4.5.5}$$

$$b_t = 0 \qquad \text{iff } m_t \leq m_0 \tag{4.5.6}$$

Ancillary Equations.   These are required to compute current values of m and α, to use in the filter equations.

$$m_t = m_0 - \int_0^t \exp(k_1 \cdot t) \cdot dt \tag{4.5.7}$$

$$\alpha_t = \alpha_0 + \int_0^t k_3 \exp(-k_2 \cdot t) \cdot dt \tag{4.5.8}$$

As the process is now expressed, the empirical questions about observed behavior will center on the value of c_t according to the choice of b_0, m_1, c_m, and c_s. The parameters α_0, k_1, k_2, and k_3 are necessary and critical to the numerical values of outputs; they do not, however, figure in the literature but have to be added to make the psychology into a system theoretic model.

From a few simulations performed in the parameter range $k_1 = .1, \ldots, .4$, $k_2 = .02, \ldots, .27$ and $k_3 = .1, \ldots, .4$, the behavior of the process can be readily discerned; it is a race between the message gaining credibility before it is forgotten by a decay process that can be faster or slower than the shift in credibility. For example, setting $b_0 = 6$, $m_0 = 4$, $m_1 = 10$, $c_1 = 30$, $c_2 = 5$, $\alpha_0 = .25$, if $k_1 = k_2 = k_3 = .1$, then the credibility c_t rises from $c_1 = 13.6$ to $c_{15} = 30$, but the recall strength drops from $m_1 = 9.05$ to $m_9 = 4.09$ and then at $m_{10} = 3.74$ drops below the recall threshold when $c_{10} = 26.9$. In this case the message is forgotten before it ever gains full credibility.

Setting $k_1 = .2$ and the rest of the parameters exactly as before, m_t asymptotes at about 5, above recall threshold, and $c_t = 30$ so that complete message credibility is regained and held.

For $k_1 = .3$, $k_2 = .27$, $k_3 = .1$, the recall asymptotes at about $m_t = 6.7$ reached by trial 14; the credibility asymptotes at about 20.3 reached by trial 17. A diversity of steady states, above or below recall threshold, for both memorability and credibility are attainable by the same process just by suitable choice of parameters. Note that this model makes no use of the autocorrelation properties in the process to generate the filter equations; clearly the process is highly autocorrelated in the outputs but that is of little psychological interest.

An an elementary aid to modeling a sample program is given in Table 4.5.1.

Our next case of special time series in social psychology is the birth-order model of Zajonc and Markus (1975), which is a form of lagged parallel interaction in parametrized growth curves. It is a particularly important example not only because of its elegance and close match to data but because of the very large data base against which it was developed.

The problem of assessing and predicting the average effects of birth order, within a family of siblings, upon relative intellectual level as indicated by intelligence tests, has generated some confusion and apparently conflicting findings. The reconciliation of these findings has been achieved with clarity and deceptive simplicity by Zajonc and Markus starting from the intellectual growth curve of a single child, from birth onward. Measured in a consistent fashion the absolute intellectual level of a child is a monotone function of its age, to a first approximation represented by a curve

$$y_j = 1 - \exp\left(- k^2 j^2\right) \tag{4.5.9}$$

where y_j is the mental performance level at age j years, and k is a constant. To cope with individual differences it is simple to add a parameter to represent the final ceiling level of attainment and put

TABLE 4.5.1
Listing of Simulation Program

```
5    REM B0=INITIAL BELIEF ABOUT MESSAGE, M0 IS RECALL THRESHOLD INTENSITY
6    REM M1=INITIAL MESSAGE IMPACT, K1=RATE CONSTANT, K2=RATE CONSTANT
7    REM C1=MESSAGE CREDIBILITY, C2=SOURCE CREDIBILITY, N=NO. OF TIME STEPS
9    C$="#" \ B$="$" \ M$="*"
10   READ B0,M0,C1,C2,N
11   PRINT "INPUTK1,K2,K3"; \ INPUT K1,K2,K3
20   D1=-1 \ D2=0 \ T=0
30   T=1
31   X=.1
40   D3=C1*D1+(1-D1)*C2
42   PRINT "T";T;"DC/DT";D3
55   A=.25 \ M2=0
60   FOR T1=.1 TO T STEP X
70   A1=K3*(EXP(-K2*T1))*X
80   M=-EXP(-K1*T1)*X
90   A=A+A1
100  M2=M2+M
120  NEXT T1
121  IF A>=1 THEN A=1
122  IF A<=0 THEN A=0
123  M2=M1+M2
124  PRINT "A";A;"M";M2;"B";B1
130  C3=C1*A+C2*(1-A)
140  IF M2>=M0 THEN B1=C3
150  IF M2<M0 THEN B1=0
155  REMC3=CREDIBILITY AT TIME T, B1=ACCEPTANCE-RECALL OF MESSAGE AT T
156  REMM2=DEGREE OF RECALL AT T
157  REM A=ALPHA (=F(TIME))
159  IF C3<=0 THEN 164
160  PRINT TAB(ABS(C3));C$;C3
161  PRINT TAB(ABS(M2*5));M$
162  PRINT TAB(ABS(B1));B$
163  GO TO 170
164  PRINT (ABS(C3)); "-";C$;C3
165  PRINT TAB(ABS(M2*5));M$
166  PRINT TAB(ABS(B1));B$
170  T=T+1
180  IF T>N THEN STOP
190  D2=EXP(-K1*T)
200  D1=K3*EXP(-K2*T)
205  GO TO 40
210  DATA 6,4,10,30,5,30
250  END
```

$$y_{ij} = a_i \left(1 - \exp\left(-k^2 j^2\right)\right) \tag{4.5.10}$$

where a_i is a scalar constant characterizing the ith individual, over some period of years governed by the same intellectual developmental process. These curves all start from zero at birth, and the units are scalable for convenience so that the average within a family can have an asymptote of 100 units. The curves climb first with positive and then with negative acceleration and flatten out completely at around 18 years, the rate of climb and ceiling being completely fixed by the parameters.

Now generalize the model so that it can be stated for the first, second, third, (and so on) children of any family of reasonable size, say, up to about nine. The interest is in the final asymptote of the process (4.5.10) as a function of the birth order and the total family size. The whole analysis can be complicated by distinguishing the two sexes as well, but this will be left out here. The main data base used to develop the model was a study of over 386,000 males, the entire population of the Netherlands men who attained 19 years of age between 1963 and 1966 inclusive. This cohort is interesting in part because some of the older men were little children during the period of German occupation and may have suffered a loss of adequate nutrition either before or after birth.

If the average IQ of solo children (i.e., children with no siblings) is rescaled at 100 units, using the Raven's Progressive Matrices Test as our measure, then the brightest child on average will be the firstborn of two (about 100.6 units), the next brightest the firstborn of three (100.4), and then the firstborn of four (100.1). The second born of two or three are about 100.1–100.2; the rest are less bright and fall off to the ninth of nine with an average of about 96.3. The effects are small but consistent in the total pattern created across birth order and family size. Both these variables are deleterious modifiers of intelligence expectation. Being born later and being born in a large family are disadvantages. What is most interesting is the relationship, a drop off, between the intelligence of the penultimate and the last child in families from two to nine in size; this drop off is consistent and marked.

Disentangling this time series problem[2] starts by fitting the intellectual level curve (4.5.10) for a single child. Values of about $k = .1$ characterize the growth of perceptual skills for boys, $k = .07$ fits verbal abilities, but clearly k is distributed across individuals. The value of a_i is associated with the ith position in a family, where i denotes the number of younger children around. This assumption characterizes what Zajonc and Markus (1975) call a confluence model.

That is, a firstborn has a parameter a_0 when he or she is born at time b_1, so his or her intellectual growth curve is given by

---

[2]With increasing family size, other variables that might be related to intellectual development change are per capital income, per capital housing space, vulnerability to contagious illness, etc. The effect of these variables is lumped together in the parameters $\{a_i\}$, which themselves might show long-term drift.

$$f_1(j) = a_0(1 - \exp(-k^2 j^2)) \tag{4.5.11}$$

but as soon as a second child appears at time b_2, then the first child shifts in his or her intellectual progression to a new growth curve parametrized as

$$f_1(j) = a_1(1 - \exp(-k^2 j^2))$$

and the new child starts at b_2 with

$$f_2(j) = a_0(1 - \exp(-k^2 j^2))$$

When the next child comes along at b_3, then again there is a shift for the previous siblings, so that

$$f_1(j) = a_2(1 - \exp(-k^2 j^2))$$

$$f_2(j) = a_1(1 - \exp(-k^2 j^2)) \tag{4.5.12}$$

$$f_3(j) = a_0(1 - \exp(-k^2 j^2)).$$

To map the intellectual growth of a single child in this parallel interactive process, we need to integrate the $f_i(j)$ over the limits b_i, b_{i+1}, b_{i+2}, ... For example, at b_4, writing for convenience $c(j) = c\exp(-k^2 j^2)$, the firstborn attains

$$f_1(b_4) = \int_{b_1}^{b_2} a_0 c(j) \, dj + \int_{b_2}^{b_3} a_1 c(j) \, dj + \int_{b_3}^{b_4} a_2 c(j) \, dj \tag{4.5.13}$$

The secondborn attains

$$f_2(b_4) = \int_{b_2}^{b_3} a_0 c(j) \, dj + \int_{b_3}^{b_4} a_1 c(j) \, dj \tag{4.5.14}$$

The thirdborn attains

$$f_3(b_4) = \int_{b_3}^{b_4} a_0 c(j) \, dj \tag{4.5.15}$$

and if a fourth child arrives at b_4, then $f_4(b_4) = 0$.

The intellectual facilitatory and inhibitory effects (which are relative, not necessarily absolute) between children are thus functions of the interarrival intervals

$$b_2 - b_1, \qquad b_3 - b_2, \qquad b_4 - b_3, \dots$$

and the constants $a_0, a_1, a_2, a_3, \dots$, though there is an additional correction necessary as seen in the following.

The family of curves (4.5.12) exhibits features that are consistent with average data patterns; the presence of a second child is generally facilitatory for the firstborn, but the empirical distribution and average gaps in months between births, for each ordinal position in a family of a given size, have to be known. Having children close together is not helpful to the intellectual development of the family as a whole; if gaps were sufficiently large, then intellectual level might show an increase with birth order, but usually it does not.

The relatively lower intelligence of only children as compared with the first-born of two is argued by Zajonc and Markus (1975) to be a consequence of another effect, the lastborn defect. Only children are obviously firstborn, last-born, and sibling-free, which means that their performance could be inferred from an interesting diversity of confounded arguments. As the average drop in performance between the penultimate $(m - 1)$th, and last mth, child is about three times that between any other successive i, $i + 1$ pair in birth order, a correction is necessary for this last position that can be written in the regression of intellectual level on birth order as

$$y_{im} = 101.31 - .31i + .01i^2 - .37m + .48d \qquad (4.5.16)$$

where d is a characteristic variable; if $i = m$, then $d = 0$, and if $i \neq m$, then $d = 1$. The y_{im} in (4.5.16) is the terminal level reached as a consequence of integrating expressions analogous to (4.5.13). The correction in (4.5.16) could be more neatly expressed as a condition upon the last integral of (4.5.13); the numerical effect would be the same.

Our last example from social psychology is taken from an unpublished study by Zimmer (University of Oldenburg, 1977) concerning the analysis of sequencies in a prisoner's dilemma game situation.

On any one play of a prisoners' dilemma game, each of the two participants makes one choice from the two choices open to him or her. The 2×2 payoff matrix of the game is so structured that the two choices made by the two players together constitute a cooperative pair or a defecting pair. The notional game is against a third player, the experimenter taking this role. When the two participants cooperate, they can maximize their takings from the experimenter; when one defects from his or her partner and joins forces with the experimenter, then in sum both players lose to the experimenter, though one alone may do marginally better than if he or she had cooperated. Hence the dilemma, whether to cooperate, and to continue to cooperate, in the face of potential defection by the other player. Over a series of plays by the same two players, the whole task takes on a sequential and stochastic strategic quality. As a time series such a game is a two-state process for each player, and the records of the two players constitute a bivariate time series. Zimmer had two groups of subjects; each subject had an opponent who was never seen (in fact, a fictional colleague–adversary); in one group the opponent was stated to be a student, like the player, and in the other group a blue-collar worker. The imaginaries were made to be the same sex as the real players, so sex was not a variable in this sense.

Twenty plays in succession were made by all subjects; the fictional opponents played the same sequence in all the games, so that the proportions of cooperative and defective strategies was much the same for all players. The distinction between the group playing imaginary opponents who were also students of the same sex and the group playing imaginary workers of the same sex showed in the sequential dependencies of the strategies used. Zimmer used an autocorrelation analysis of the pooled and individual data, separating out those subjects whose showed stationarity, and established strong differences between the two conditions; those subjects playing against imaginary students showed a range of forward planning over up to 10 trials. This appeared to be lacking when playing against imaginary workers. There is no penetration to this analysis that shows how the result comes about; its heuristic interest lies in the direct application of the autocorrelation and crosscorrelation methods and the fact that such analyses appear to reveal differences that are not shown, nor could be shown, by Markov or Bayes' models.

4.6   SPECIAL PROBLEMS IN PSYCHOPHYSIOLOGY

Detailed analysis of transduction processes in the more extensively studied sensory modalities, and in corresponding processes in the central nervous system, has produced many mathematical models that convert energy sequences from time to frequency domain or vice versa. These rarely exploit analytical or conceptual procedures that have not been covered at least in outline, so to review them broadly would be reduplicative. The reader should consult advanced texts on sensory physiology for examples that are of substantive interest to the specialist in some area of psychophysiology. Here are briefly reviewed some cases that illustrate points of wider potential interest; there is absolutely no pretension to an exhaustive or representative coverage in a potentially vast area. General reviews have appeared on the use of systems theory and control theory modeling in the biological sciences, and special applications are found in such sources as the *IEEE Transactions on Systems Science and Cybernetics*. Some areas such as cardiovascular functioning have been modeled repeatedly with increasing refinement and complications; they obviously have some relevance to behavior in a wide sense but are not usually included in psychological texts.

The interrelations among time series analysis, control theory, information theory, and the spatiotemporal extensions of time series analysis that have special pertinence in vision, are demonstrable through a few case studies, and some points made therein are obviously generalizable.

It is convenient to choose examples of time series analysis from work done on the EEG and evoked potentials generated at the human scalp, but bare description of the frequency spectrum, however precise and however faithfully it captures the nonlinearities and nonstationarities, leaves important questions unanswered; what sort of system would be expected to have EEGs as its characteristic output? How complicated would it have to be to produce the mixtures of patterns, and the shifts between patterns under different input and central conditions, which are known well enough to be identifiable? Given that the central nervous system (CNS) has some self-regulation, how is this fact reflected in the particular energy spectrum it dissipates? Farças (1977) advanced one possible feedback system that will replicate some EEG phenomena. The central idea used is that the excitation level of a brain has to be held within limits for effective functioning; the average of such excitation levels is called the *cortical tonus*. It is argued that learning by the CNS requires the existence of structures that can regulate tonus; hence Farças postulates a feedback system between inhibitory and excitatory centers and the cortex, whose activities in turn give rise to EEG amplitude and spectra. Adapting slightly Farças's notation, the inputs and outputs of this self-stabilizing network are (where each may be regarded as a multivariate vector)

$x_1(j)$ sensory input to the cortex

$x_2(j)$ input from a motivation center that reflects drive states

   This center in turn receives input from other CNS centers or the endocrine systems.

$x_3(j)$ sensory input to activating centers

$y_1(j)$ is the central tonus; it is the output that through the
         filtering of the scalp is monitored by the EEG recorder

$y_2(j)$ is the output of a generalized or nonspecific inhibition

$y_3(j)$ is the output of nonspecific excitation

It is postulated that $y_2(j)$ and $y_3(j)$ are generalized output to all central neurones, which is probably a quite unnecessary assumption; a subset of such neurones with appropriate network connections would be sufficient.

The diagram of the system is shown in Fig. 4.6.1.

Note that in Fig. 4.6.1 the pathways y_2 and z_3 carry negative (i.e., inhibitory) signals; the rest are positive. The term δ is a loop delay associated with some pathways to and from the cortex.

The generating equations of the model are three simultaneous differential equations in temporal variables. That the system is written in this form implies there is appreciable delay in the loops and that the components are sluggish in their adjustments; the rates of change of outputs are written as functions of the current inputs and outputs. Also there are threshold effects in the operation of the two $z(j)$ variables. It can be shown by simulation that more second-order corrections to the outputs are needed if the system is to approach output asymptotes without overshooting; we omit consideration of this for simplification.

Given that excitation and inhibitions in the model are real nonzero positive numbers, then

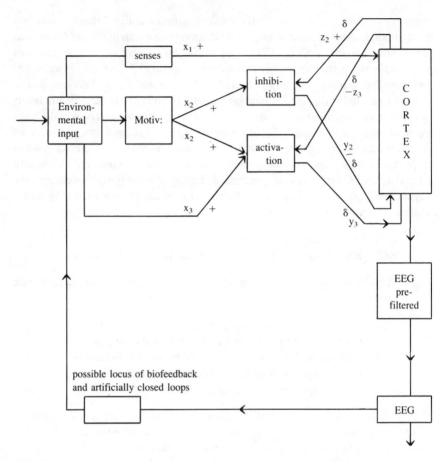

FIG. 4.6.1 Generation of EEG-type output from cortical tonus regulation, after Farças (1977) with amendments.

$$\frac{dy_1(j)}{dt} = -c_1 \cdot y_1(j) + x_1(j) + c_2 \cdot (y_3(j - \delta) - y_2(j - \delta)) \qquad (4.6.1)$$

$$\frac{dy_2(j)}{dt} = -c_2 \cdot y_2(j) + c_4 \cdot (x_2(j) + z_2(t)) \qquad (4.6.2)$$

$$\frac{dy_3(j)}{dt} = -c_3 \cdot y_3(j) + c_4 \cdot (x_2(j) - z_3(j) + x_3(j)) \qquad (4.6.3)$$

where

$$z_2(j) = \begin{cases} y_1(j - \delta) - c_5 & \text{if } y_1 \text{ is positive} \\ 0 & \text{otherwise} \end{cases} \qquad (4.6.4)$$

$$z_3(j) = \begin{cases} y_1(j - \delta) - c_6 & \text{if } y_1 \text{ is positive} \\ 0 & \text{otherwise} \end{cases} \qquad (4.6.5)$$

and c_1, c_2, c_3, c_4 are scalars or vectors.

For simulation the inputs and limits are arbitrary but must be compatible; some typical values that will work are $c_1 = .01$, $c_2 = 70$, $c_3 = .01$, $c_5 = 400$, $c_6 = 100$, $\delta = 4$. The input $x_1(j)$ is generated as a binomial with mean of 8 units. The critical variable for simulation is $x_2(j)$. Its values seriously affect the system characteristics: $x_2(j) = 0$ gives delta waves; $x_2(j) = 125$ gives alpha (around 10 Hz); $x_2(j) = 350$ produces desynchronization and high-frequency outputs.

Hence the system will mimic alpha and delta waves of the EEG and will desynchronize under heavy input. It is of course a minimum complexity representation, in which the inhibitory subsystem x_2, y_2, z_2 corresponds heuristically to the thalamic relays and the excitatory subsystem x_2, x_3, y_3, z_3 to the reticular ascending tracts.

If $x_2(j) = x_3(j) = 0$, then, interestingly, the whole system will eventually collapse despite the network being intact. This is a simple analog of the idea that the CNS needs input to function; studies on sensory deprivation cast equivocal light on this point.

The collapse of the output with zero input as a long-term consequence is acceptable, but the EEG does have a steady-state spectral form with eyes closed and the subject in a state of conscious quiescence. As the EEG is an output, its waveform and autocorrelations within loci and crosscorrelations between loci are the consequences of filtering some other prior signals that are very different. That is, the identification problem is:

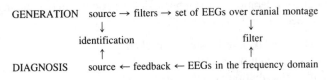

FIG. 4.6.2 EEG analysis as partial identification.

In Fig. 4.6.2 the identification is a matching process; the filter on the right between the two lines is a fast Fourier transform or equivalent.

Let us concentrate on the smaller problem of the relation between the (unobserved) cortical output and the (observed) EEG in the bottom right corner of Fig. 4.6.1. If there is an ensemble of Poisson time series signals (see Sections 2.0 to 2.2) generated in parallel and then pooled *through a network* by superposition, it can be shown that this linear addition gives as aggregate a stationary random process that has a rectangular spectral distribution (white noise within a limited bandwidth) plus a distinct fixed frequency component. So, if it is assumed

(Drösler, 1963) that the generic source of a collection of EEGs is a random generation of signals with fixed ensemble probabilities and that these signals are then pooled through a network with different output delays in each component path, the output for the network as a whole will be the linear sum of the various Poissons, where the pathway delays are themselves representable as a Gaussian distribution of delays in time. The autocorrelation spectrum of this network output can represent an exponentially damped oscillation that will approximate to cortical output over the limited range 0–16 Hz (alpha + theta + slow delta waves) but not properly represent the higher-frequency beta wave energy spectrum. The conclusion is that the filter and the source are not linear, but another possibility, which has been analyzed at some length mathematically (Ten Hoopen & Reuver, 1967) is that the original signals are not random but are perturbed by delay processes. The argument in this case leads back to renewal process models. To make this approach tractable, it is necessary to constrain the delays to sufficiently small magnitudes, such that the sequence of delays does not suffer inversion in order. Let us call such delays "noninverting." The model developed within this context is one of considerable generality, being potentially applicable to cardiac activity, neuronal transmission across synapses, the queuing of oil tankers at bunkering ports, and so on.

There are several identification problems in this area, because a series with regular input and exponentially distributed noninverting delays will produce an output that might equally well have been generated by an exponential waiting distribution with superimposed constant delay. In fact, of course, an infinite set of waiting distribution–delay distribution pairs can yield the same output. The statistics of the output or response distribution can still be summarized. The autocorrelation structure of the output does however eliminate many models from potential consideration. If the input series is periodic, maximum interval T, and it is assumed to be distributed as

$\phi(j)$, which is taken to be sharply peaked,
the delay distribution is $\psi(j)$,
the output distribution is $p(j)$,

and if

$$\phi(j) = \delta(j - T) \tag{4.6.6}$$

where δ is a delta function such that $\psi(j)$ has no distribution for $\phi(j)$, $j > T$, then

$r\Delta^1(j, j - 1) = -0.5$ (a serial autocorrelation of first differences)

a result established by McGill (1962). But if the delay is constant, which means that $\psi(j) = \delta(j)$, then the autocorrelation of $p(j)$ is the same as that of $\phi(j)$, which can be anything that we choose to create. Ten Hoopen and Reuver (1967) give derivations and references for the autocorrelation structure of various delay distributions.

One way of expressing the perturbed periodicity of a series with delays is by finding the probability distribution $e(\theta)\,d\theta$, which is the probability of an event occurring in the interval θ, $\theta + \delta\theta$ given that it has occurred at $\theta = 0$ (compare the renewal processes of Section 2.1).

If the input and delay distributions are

$$\left.\begin{array}{l} \theta(j) \sim N(\xi, \sigma_\phi) \\[16pt] \psi(j) \sim N(\eta, \sigma_\psi) \\[16pt] \text{then} \\[8pt] p(j) \sim N(p, (\sigma_\phi^2 + 2\sigma_\psi^2)^{0.5}) \end{array}\right\} \tag{4.6.7}$$

provided that $\psi(j)$ is recurrent. So a Gaussian distribution of output intervals $p(j)$ can be created by all manner of recurrent ϕ and ψ processes in a variety of values of σ_ϕ and σ_ψ; thus inspection of the intervals of the output tells us little about the input intervals. But using the distribution of $e(\theta)$ may provide information that narrows down the possible range of σ_ϕ/σ_ψ. The periodicity of $e(\theta)$ is lost and smoothed out as the variances σ_ϕ and σ_ψ increase.

It is a safe generalization that the irregularity of CNS cell discharge is caused partly by irregular input and partly by irregular synaptic delays. If both are recurrent series, then, for $p(j)$,

$$0 \geqslant r\Delta^1(j,j-1) \geqslant -0.5$$

In other words, if the $\psi(j)$ are in a distribution of random form [which means that the $\Delta^1(x_j)$ of the series x_j that gives rise to $\psi(j)$] are independent, or i.i.d., that is, $r\Delta^1(j \cdot j - 1) = 0$ for input, and also $r(\phi(j), \psi(j)) = 0$; yet the output intervals $p(j)$ [or $\Delta^1(y_j)$ of the output series] can have a nonzero autocorrelation spectrum.

The distribution $e(\theta)$ of a thalamic neurone can be approximated with a Gaussian series superimposed upon a Poisson series with dead times (there is a refractory period after firing before a new spike potential can be generated). Cells in the retina of the cat's eye are reported to have

$$-0.10 \geqslant r\Delta^1(j, j - 1) \geqslant -0.24$$

but also

$$r\Delta^1(j, j - k), \qquad k > 1 \simeq 0$$

This finding appears to be general for some other types of nerve fibers including human motor neurones. Irregularities in these autocorrelation spectra appear to have diagnostic value in monitoring cardiac malfunctioning. If there exists a large aggregate of neurones firing in rough synchrony, and there are recurrent excitatory and inhibitory events for the aggregate as a whole, then a linear distributed feedback system constitutes a useful model. The generation of evoked potentials superimposed upon EEGs can be modeled in this manner (Freeman, 1964). The transfer functions permit very close modeling to data but are too complex to review in detail; the methods of analysis follow from Sections 3.4 and 3.8. If it is assumed that the neurones constitute a network in which the density of interconnections falls off exponentially as the distance from a source element is increased, and that transmission delay also increases exponentially with distance, then the network has a standing waveform which is sinusoidal and which can be amplitude modulated by the input. Such a network has the capacity of being stable in the face of violent inputs and will show nonlinear saturation of the feedback gain with increasing input signal.

Again, the broad strategy in modelling these systems is to create nearly periodic time series inputs, randomly perturb them, pass them through a network which in a very large scale behaves virtually continuously in its characteristic input-output transformations, and into that network link an adequate substrate for feedback, a whole network apparently functioning on the gross level as a single loop in its performance characteristics. The analysis of the standing waveform, or evoked potentials, of such a loop expressed in signal-to-noise ratio terms has been achieved through z transforms by Coppola, Tabor, and Buchsbaum (1978). Related approaches using partial autocorrelation coefficients have been used by Jindra (1977).

The use of the EEG in studying olfaction creates new complications because an adequate characterization of the system requires spatially as well as temporally extended results. That is, the experience of a particular odor sensation is postulated, to be dependent on the sequence of excitation through space and time over the set of receptors that constitutes the olfactory epithelium and its immediate neural connections. Characteristic bursts of neural activity are found in the olfactory bulb of the brain following stimulation; the problem is to describe tersely such complex spatiotemporal series in a few parameters and then relate these parameters to sensation characteristics. Freeman (1978) found that over successive bursts of electrical activity the induced wave frequency, duration, and mean amplitude varied unpredictably, as well as the shape of the envelope of the power-frequency spectrum (see Section 2.6) but that relative amplitudes and latencies (with reference to the mean parameters of the total spatial array of receptors under excitation) were fairly stable. Results, after passing signals through windows and computing autocorrelations, were that different odors elicit activity in the same areas of the olfactory bulb, thus disposing of a theory of Adrian's that specifically localized responses to different odors in different volumes of tissue. However, "the EEG amplitude patterns do have the range and complexity of variation that are required to reflect responses to odours or perceptual states, but they have not as yet been found to correspond to odours" (Freeman, 1978, p. 601). Barabasz and Gregson (1980) studied human EEG responses to real and imaginary odors in subjects living in Antarctica at a research station 1300 km from the South Pole and found that responses were related as much to suggestion and contextual psychological variables as to the specific odors used.

The analysis by the visual system of inputs that are time series, such as flickering lights (this refers to flicker in intensity of white light, lights varying sinusoidally about a mean wavelength over a narrow range seem not to have been studied extensively, if at all), provides insight into the information resolution of the optical system:

retina → optical tracts → visual cortex

Visibility of gratings, as opposed to their fusion into an apparent homogeneous field, depends on the rate at which they are scanned laterally, at right angles to the lines of the grating, or for a fixed direction of viewing upon the rate at which they pass sideways before the eyes. The two situations are not exactly equivalent. Fourier analysis has been applied to the problem (Campbell & Robson, 1968), though interest in contrast and visibility of fine detail in a visually presented display obviously goes back centuries.

Under restricted conditions it is possible to calculate, knowing the contrast sensitivity (the difference threshold for luminance) of the visual system at a given wavelength or for white light, what the contrast threshold for a grating would be. There are complications in this problem because the neural networks involved do not have linear properties. The typical relation between contrast sensitivity (a difference threshold measure) and spatial frequency (cycles of grating luminance fluctuation per degree of angle subtended at the eye = cpd or c/deg) is as shown in Fig. 4.6.3:

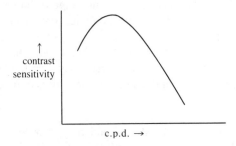

FIG. 4.6.3 Typical relation of contrast sensitivity to spatial frequency.

The actual location of the curve in Fig. 4.6.3 depends on the waveform of the grating (sine, square, wedge, or ramp, and so on) and the ratio of the width of bright light to the total waveform cycle of light and dark; in other words, the waveform is made to have other than a symmetrical form about its mean luminance; in Fourier series terms, it has odd as well as even harmonics (see Section 2.6).

Campbell and Robson (1968) found, *inter alia*, that a square wave grating is perceived to be different from a sine wave when the third harmonic of the square form reaches its own luminance threshold, which in turn increases as the spatial frequency increases. Contrast between sine and sawtooth forms is possible when a second harmonic of the sawtooth reaches its own threshold. There is doubt that any harmonic higher than the third can have much part to play in vision; see Ganz (1975), Nachmias, Sansbury, Vassilev, and Weber (1973), and Maffei and Fiorentini (1973). If the source flickers in time but is stationary in space, for the flicker fusion frequency, when the fluctuations blur into a continuous level of apparent brightness, above 10 Hz the threshold is entirely predictable from the threshold to the base frequency of the waveform; the higher harmonics play no part in detection. In fact, this simplifies the representation problems for the theory constructor because what the visual system can do is behave linearly and only linearly in this respect. The reason why the visual system is incapable of tracking high-frequency inputs lies in the diffusion process within the neural network; diffusion takes place in real time and so the system is inherently sluggish. Looked at the other way round, diffusion involves local signal integration in space and time and it takes time to compute a convolution integral. Probably the most considered theory in this area, involving two or more feedback loops and selective filtering, is that of Kelly (1971).

So, the higher harmonic components have less effect in discrimination tasks than their relative contrast sensitivities, when they are the fundamental frequencies, would suggest. The only simple way that these phenomena can be accommodated is for there to be a set of functionally separate mechanisms in the visual system, each responding maximally at some spatial frequency, λ, and not responding outside the range $\lambda/2$, $2/\lambda$. The identification question is, how many such receptor systems are needed to cover the range of human texture perception? Harvey and Gervais (1978) present and review data indicating that four are necessary and sufficient.

The functional path is thus represented by Fig. 4.6.4; what eventuates in the brain is mathematically a two-dimensional frequency–amplitude spectrum representing an image, encoded into a three-dimensional mass of tissue and extending in time.

The eye composes frequency transforms and may also compose phase transforms; the process is referred to as the modulation transfer function (MTF) of the eye. The channels dm_i, $i = 1, 2, \ldots$ correspond to the processes with critical peak sensitivities.

The channel sensitivities in Fig. 4.6.5, which is essentially four curves of the type of Fig. 4.6.3 superimposed, mediate a broad sensitivity spectrum, V, of undifferentiated brightness (1) and low-, medium-, and high-frequency bands, (2), (3), and (4), respectively.

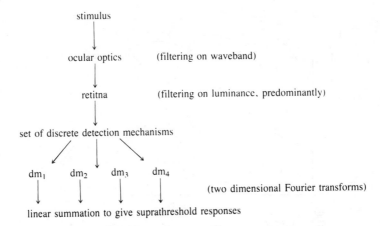

FIG. 4.6.4   Simplified frequency analysis of visual inputs.

Alternative simpler mathematical models with four filters resembling Fig. 4.6.5 were found by Harvey and Gervais (1978) to be inferior to the synthetic model shown; the total system operates by linear summation of the four filters at any cpd, and the output is a single sensitivity. A test of the psychophysics of the model in part rests on its compatibility with the data available concerning the confusability or perceived pairwise similarity of samples of two-dimensional textures. This was attempted by these authors by taking 30 different samples and performing a multidimensional scaling in Euclidean space and then relating the m.d.s. dimensions to the underlying filters, as though the filters are the defining coordinates of each texture when appropriately weighted; the linear summation hypothesis entails that they should be so representable. In fact,

m.d.s. dimension $\# 1 \leftrightarrow H$ to L
$\# 2 \leftrightarrow V$ concatenated with M
$\# 3$ does not map simply into the
filter system

This interpretation is not Harvey and Germain's; it is this author's. The results may reflect in part the use of an inappropriate similarity scaling algorithm (Gregson, 1975, 1976b).

It is obvious that the auditory sense is concerned with multivariate time series inputs converted to multivariate time series neural representations, so the impetus for a considerable range of transfer function identification procedures ought in the first instance to have arisen in the psychophysics of hearing. Indeed, hearing might be characterized as the short-term spectral analysis of input, with the aim of retaining information-bearing features of the acoustic signal (Flanagan, 1967). The quantitative objectives of psychophysics rest on the identification of a transfer function from input to neural encoding. The auditory

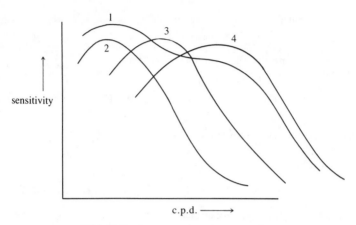

FIG. 4.6.5   Four-channel texture perception.

signal has a number of dimensions, such as average energy levels, frequency spectra, and bandwidth limits, which are determinants in a complex manner of what is perceived. A diversity of mathematical models, apart from the very simple linear relations of psychophysics, exist to account for such phenomena as the relation between detection threshold (decibels) and frequency (hertz) (Biondi, Giani, & Grandori, 1977). Yet much of psychophysical research on observer sensitivity does not use the sequential properties of the stimulus but takes, as input variables, frequency of amplitude expressed as scalars outside time. Perhaps oddly, therefore, the sense that is most concerned with periodic variations in time at high frequencies does not add as much to the repertoire of modeling problems and methods in time series as might at first be expected.[3] Theories of auditory transduction through the resonance of bone or neural circuits are examples of narrow-pass filtering and are handled by standard circuit and control theory; many cases can be found in the *Journal of the Acoustical Society of America,* in *IEEE Transactions on Audio and Electroacoustics,* and in Plomp and Smoorenberg (1970).

One form of periodic psychophysical time series that deserves mention is the family of circadian rhythms in hormone secretion levels. Vagnucci, Liu, and Wong (1977) have identified the serious statistical problems involved in data collection in this area, which in terms of its practical limitations resembles much of applied experimental psychology. Time series are typically discrete, as in taking samples of serum every 2 hours from a patient, and associated psychophysiological results are taken at or near the same points in time. The total duration of sampling may be limited to 24 hours, and so concatenation of a series

---

[3]In fairness, the expansion of time series identification methodology postdates much fundamental work in auditon by at least a decade (Lewis, 1970).

of 1-day samples, phase-locked to a point in time, is required in order to generate a single long time series that is sufficient for analysis. There have been some studies attempting to track diurnal fluctuations in gustatory acuity (Pangborn, 1959; Yensen, 1959) that could have a hormonal basis, though in those cases frequency analysis was not attempted.

The circadian data typically have a low-frequency high-power component with a period of 24 hours (though longer cycles in sexual function are the more familiar) and a number of higher-frequency components are superimposed. One may in fact regard the diurnal variation as a carrier upon which the other variations are superimposed, in which case it becomes a nuisance to be partialled out by periodic trend analysis so that only the residuals may be examined.

Concatenation is forced upon the researcher in this context because for practical or ethical reasons there is at the most only a single cycle of the dominant periodic component over which any single subject may be observed. The concatenation is legitimate if there does in fact exist a narrow bandwidth of phase-locked variation that is sufficiently well defined to be interpretable a priori. The individual differences will then come out as noise. Hence the concatenated time series are a series of realizations of the same stochastic process independent in their generation but assumed to be dynamically homogeneous, phase-locked, and strung end to end and whose regular component of periodic variance bears an obvious relation to an ensemble average.

The analysis of a concatenated time series resembles or can be made conveniently to resemble an analysis of variance; the methods of component variation here have been set out by Bliss (1970). A Bayesian extension of these methods is obviously called for if each subsample is taken to define some constraints on the spectral decomposition of later samples, within a concatenation that is extended through a long time. If the Fourier coefficients of the ith harmonic component are a_i, b_i (see Section 2.7), then the linear model is, for the first two components of the stochastic process underlying the considered time series,

$$\hat{x}_{i,j} = \mu + \alpha_{1j} + \beta_{1j} + \alpha_{2j} + \beta_{2j} + w_j + e_{ij} \tag{4.6.8}$$

where μ is the mean level of response

$$\alpha_1 j = a_1 \cos (2\pi\omega j) \qquad \beta_{1j} = b_1 \cos (2\pi\omega j) \left.\begin{array}{c}\\\\\end{array}\right\}$$

$$\alpha_2 j = a_2 \cos (2\pi\omega j) \qquad \beta_{2j} = b_2 \cos (2\pi\omega j) \tag{4.6.9}$$

and the Fourier variance components are

$$a_1^2 + b_1^2 \quad \text{and} \quad a_2^2 + b_2^2$$

in this case where only two harmonics are sufficient to describe the observed periodicities. If there are n samples, each of length T, of intervals j, $j = 1$, $2, \ldots, T$, the variance components are

Source	d.f.
1 Between intervals (j) over the set T	$T - 1$
decomposed orthogonally into	
1.1 $a_1{}^2 + b_1{}^2$ First periodic component	2
1.2 $a_2{}^2 + b_2{}^2$ Second periodic component	2
. . .	.
. . .	.
. . .	.
1.k $a_k{}^2 + b_k{}^2$ k^{th} periodic component	2
1.k+1 residual scatter w_j	$T - 2k - 1$
2 With intervals e_{ij} (variations across the n samples each of length T intervals)	$T(n - 1)$
3 Total variance	$nT - 1$

The null hypothesis is an aperiodic structure that is

$$H_0: \hat{x}_{i,j} = \mu + e_{ij} \tag{4.6.10}$$

and the expected variance components under (4.6.9) and (4.6.10) are given by Vagnucci et al. (1977). The ratio

$$\text{var(between intervals)/(total var)} = h \tag{4.6.11}$$

is conveniently defined as the *homogeneity* of the concatenation. This makes possible an F test of the legitimacy of concatenation, for

$$F, \text{ d.f.} = (T - 1, nT - T), \text{ is } T(n - 1)(T - 1)^{-1}(h^{-1} - 1)^{-1} \tag{4.6.12}$$

It should be noted that the previous ANOVA is applied, if necessary, after data have been filtered through a Hanning window; autocorrelation analyses of these concatenated series is rather risky. Consequently making a test of h as a precondition to autocorrelation analysis offers some protection against the false positive identification of low-frequency components. Using prior background psychological knowledge to decide on the plausible order and power spectrum is also expedient. As an additional check the variance ratio based on w_j/e_{ij} gives a test of goodness of fit after the set of identified Fourier components have been fitted.

The restricted conditions under which it is legitimate to concatenate need to be reemphasised, because the use of this method, if defensible, enables the investigator to circumvent many of the restrictions that properly have to be placed on time series methods in psychological experiments. The samples of time series forming an ensemble must have the following:

1. Identical length, measured in j units.
2. Identical periodicity with regard to major periodic components, preferably the ones that so dominate the variance structure that they are virtually all that need be considered.

3. The expectation of the within sample mean should be fixed.
4. The standard error of the mean should be second-order.
5. The samples should be in phase with regard to any major component.
6. Bounded amplitude, though the amplitudes need not be initially comparable.

Obviously extensive preliminary experiment is desirable to establish that these conditions are in fact met. The conditions 1 through 5 are necessary and sufficient for concatenation. A low homogeneity measure can result from either large noise or an absence of periodic components and no noise. Concatenating samples that are not properly phase-locked will result in low h; in the limit, white noise (i.i.d. series) gives $h = n^{-1}$.

To adjust real data as a prerequisite for concatenation means that each time series sample must be adjusted with regard to the mean, but it is not necessary to standardize the variance. Indeed, this point reiterates condition 6; one may also wish to consider that the variance is the zero-order covariance of the process, and obviously none of the covariances can be standardized without destroying some of the information that the concatenation seeks to extract and make plain. The method is very sensitive to phase shift between samples; in this respect it resembles the problem of identifying embedded episodes (Section 3.6). An extension of this approach to nonstationary data is given by Goodrich and Caines (1979).

The coherence measure (Section 2.9) has been advanced as a ''new'' statistic for psychophysiological research (Porges, Bohrer, Cheung, Drasgow, McCabe, & Keren, 1980); the interest is in how patterns of activity within one frequency band at input may excite in a regular fashion output at another frequency band. Simpler statistics may completely fail to detect such cross-links that can have clear psychophysiological meanings at the substrate level. Porges et al. take as an example the relations between heart-rate and respiration patterns. In effect they are using the coherence as an analog of a correlation, but in the frequency domain; consequently, it is a descriptive statistic and not necessarily evidence of causality.

4.7   TIME SERIES APPLICATIONS IN CLINICAL PSYCHOLOGY

There is not, in principle, any reason why much of the data of clinical psychology should be more or less amenable to a time series representation than data from any other area of psychology. Indeed, provided that some inputs and outputs to the clinical situation, which typically extends through time for weeks if not months or years, are quantifiable, then there is little new to be said. However, there is resistance to quantification in many areas of therapeutic endeavor for reasons that have nothing to do with the scalability of data but may have much to do with the practical possibilities of collecting extensive, reliable, accurate, and uncensored samples of observations that exemplify the multivariate time series quality of a therapeutic transaction between a therapist, or a drug regime, as input, and the behavior of one or more patients as output.

In those areas of clinical psychology where the therapeutic program is conceived and designed in some detail to be applied behavior modification, with a sequence of baseline, treatment, baseline, and follow-up segments along the lines already discussed in Chapter 3 when considering the identification of embedded episodes in quasi-experiments, there is nothing fresh in quantitative principles that it would be sensible to enunciate. However, many clinical interventions are not so tightly structured in advance but are still amenable to ongoing monitoring of the detailed changes that do take place, and their outcome has to be assessed (at least by any responsible clinician).

The fact that a series of clinical interviews or treatment sessions does not have a fixed objective or expected date of termination at the time it is initiated does not exclude it from ongoing quantitative analysis, though obviously it is going to be difficult to assess the psychological (as opposed to the statistical) magnitude of any changes in behavior outside those guidelines furnished by very general criteria of what is well and what is ill or maladaptive behavior. It is, as Bellman and Smith indicated in their (1973) simulations of clinical interviews, quite possible to define what is convergent, or divergent, or recursive and reentrant in a sequence of verbal interactions even if we have no prior knowledge of what the patient is suffering from, what his or her behavior would be like if he or she were "cured" and whether the therapist is initially correct or incorrect in the putative diagnosis employed to justify exploratory analysis or treatment. This is a dangerous area in which to generalize, precisely because the payoff from a wrong initial strategy that leads to inappropriate surgery, exploratory or irreversible, is large and negative. There is thus, in efficient therapy, a premium on rapid and efficient changes in therapeutic strategies consequent upon rapid accurate feedback. This means, in our terminology and conceptual framework, that if one embarks on time series modeling of clinical processes to aid in our understanding of the microstructure of the clinical process itself, then the models must have inbuilt representation of some sort of adaptive filtering. Only nonlinear models of the interaction between therapy and patient could hope to represent the adjustment of the content and direction of therapy as a consequence of changes in the responsiveness of the patient during therapy. This situation in effect parallels, at a global level, the modeling problems in psychophysiology that have led to the development of nonlinear filters for EEG representation, as described in Chapter 5.

The extensive use of time series analysis in clinical psychology has been pioneered and ably advocated by Revenstorf (1979), and some of his applications need special mention.

In therapeutic programs for drug addiction, such as smoking or alcohol, it is possible sometimes to collect with the patients' cooperation a day-to-day record of the motivational state of the subject and the amount of drug consumed. There are obvious problems in that asking a subject frequently to record such self-descriptive information does not necessarily produce the truth about either consumption or about the will to abstain and its erratic swings and changes, and it is also possible that the relation between self-reported motivational levels and consumption will be changed as a consequence of asking for one or both to be recorded in the manner of a diary. Granted this, the data still constitute a bivariate time series whether in an accurate or in a biased form. In the absence of any better data, self-report deserves analysis; self-report and its interrelations with other behavior is something about which an accurate theory should make specific predictions.

In the case of smoking cessation programs (Revenstorf, Henrich, & Schwarze-Bindhart, 1978) the data are amount smoked in cigarettes per day and self-rating on a scale of determination to give up smoking. These are both in a sense output variables; the input is some indeterminate set of variables that come from the environment including the therapist's activity. However, if a simple cognitive theory is adopted, then the motivational state is a necessary precursor to the level of consumption; whereas if a simple behavioral theory is instead preferred, the level of consumption determines the motivation, which is a variable of secondary importance. Both these theories are clearly too simple as they stand and would not be accepted as a fair summary of the more complex modern learning theories. As it is possible to change cognitive states with or at the same time as changes in behavior are induced, then from learning theory it is possible to change the motivation before the smoking, if some other implicit variables are also involved. This is not readily testable but it is logically possible, which attenuates the possibility of excluding any learning theory analysis from time series results. It can be said, however, as pointed out by Revenstorf et al., that the temporal precedence of behavior before motivation is clearly less compatible with cognitive theory, unless the cognitive theory also allows implicit variables with delayed consequences.

The time series analysis used in the smoking cessation study is not quite standard but derives from a form of factor analysis developed over some years by Jöreskog at Uppsala, Sweden, and called Lisrel. The variables are records of 42 days sequential behavior, for one patient. On each day there are two data points, smoking and motivation that in all generate a 42 + 42 × 42 + 42 triangular matrix, as shown in Fig. 4.7.1.

Comparisons were made between the autocorrelational structure of the series of smoking levels and motivational levels during the early and late parts of therapy. At the start, an autoregressive model of second-order fits motivation changes, but by the sixth week the order has to be increased to third to obtain a reasonable representation with low residuals. The smoking behavior itself appears to be even more intractable, a second-order process, in terms of days lag, fits initially, but something higher than fourth-order was appropriate toward the

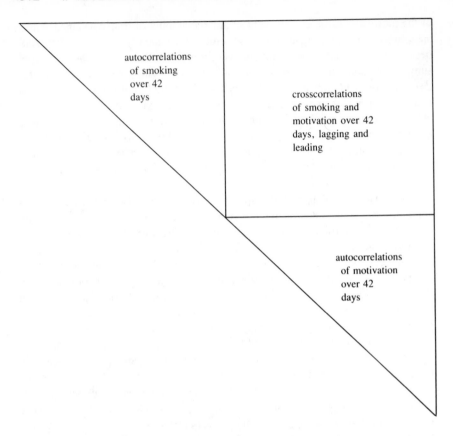

FIG. 4.7.1   Schematic triangular autocorrelation matrix.

end of the therapy. The problem with real data of this sort is that they are collected in a world where the weekend has a special significance; this imposes a cyclical pattern upon the consumption and upon the motivation as the individual typically moves from a work into a leisure situation and back again. So smoking goes up at the weekend and motivation to stop smoking goes down and vice versa during the week. Statistically this cyclical pattern would have to be partialled out and the crosscorrelational structure of the two output variables examined on the residuals. Unfortunately there is a suggestion of an interaction between the cyclical pattern and the crosscorrelational spectrum that changes over time, so that stationary analyses are invalidated. The analysis of residuals in the matrix requires us to be able to partial out the cyclical effects with a model of fixed periodicities, but the nonstationarity makes this impractical. Some of the difficulties in this sort of problem may arise from correlated errors of measurement between the observed variables.

The data are sufficient to reject some sequential structures. Among the possibilities that are of potential clinical interest, Revenstorf et al. (1978) distinguish these; the terms are causal links in the sense of Section 1.1:

$$X_j \rightarrow Y_{j+1} \quad \begin{matrix} X_j - Y_{j+1} \\ Y_j \rightarrow Y_{j+1} \end{matrix} \left. \right\} \quad \text{dependence} \quad\quad (4.7.1)$$

$$\left. \begin{matrix} X_j \rightarrow Y_{j+1} \\ Y_j \rightarrow X_{j+1} \end{matrix} \right\} \quad \begin{matrix} X_j \rightarrow X_{j+1} \\ Y_j \rightarrow Y_{j+1} \end{matrix} \quad \text{interdependence} \quad\quad (4.7.2)$$

$$\left. \begin{matrix} X_j \rightarrow Y_j \\ Y_j \rightarrow X_j \\ X_j \rightarrow Y_{j+1} \end{matrix} \right\} \quad \begin{matrix} X_j \rightarrow X_{j+1} \\ Y_j \rightarrow Y_{j+1} \end{matrix} \quad \text{dependence and reciprocity} \quad (4.7.3)$$

Of the alternatives shown, in each structure it is possible to map one variable, X, into smoking or motivation and the other, Y, into the remaining variable. This gives five models in all; two sorts of dependence and two of dependence and reciprocity, interdependence being symmetrical.

Only a model combining interdependence and reciprocity had a fit to data that could not be rejected at the .10 level, based on a χ^2 with 22 d.f., for the first week. The conclusion is interesting because it overturns so many theories at once: "motivation is neither a mere side effect of behavior change nor is behavior change a direct result of motivation." The interdependence relations are of a similar magnitude in both directions.

The detailed autocorrelational structures of smoking records are univariate time series, with periods of embedded episodes of therapeutic intervention. In this problem again Revenstorf (1975) started from a matrix form, by observing that if

$$x_j = a \cdot x_{j-1} + e_j \quad\quad (4.7.4)$$

is a sufficient representation of the sequentiality in a smoking record, then this is obviously a Markov process and the correlation matrix of a run of k unbroken days records is a simplex matrix. The structure of the simplex was first examined by Guttman; for its major properties, see Morrison (1967).

The inverse is important because its elements are closely related to the partial correlations of the time series; with the observed structure, which is as the reader will see virtually the definition of the Markov process, the partial correlations between nonadjacent events vanish. So if the process is truly Markovian, then the form of its inverse autocorrelation matrix will have the characteristic form shown in Fig. 4.7.2, with some noise. If therapy is consistent and gradual in its effects, beneficial or harmful, then the output matrix will show the diagonalized form.

The Markov model also can be used as a test of the failure of therapy in a way that is unfortunately ubiquitous with smoking cessation programs; in short the

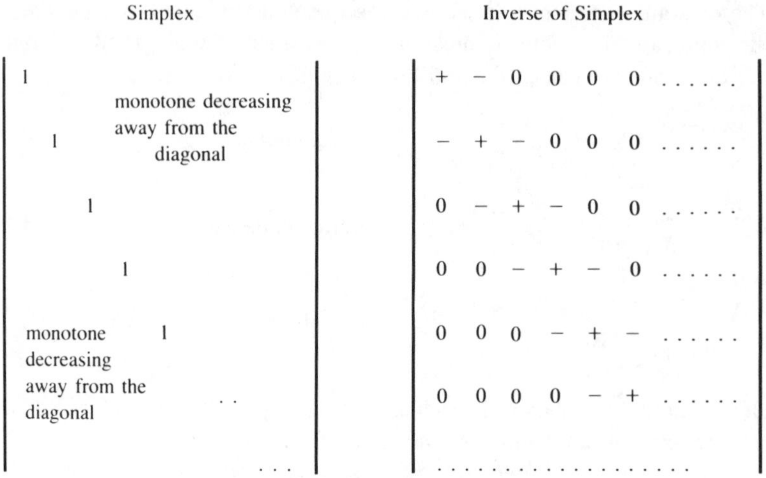

Simplex	Inverse of Simplex

FIG. 4.7.2   Theoretical simplex and its inverse arising from a run of a Markov series.

program fails because after a while the smoking, which was apparently extinguished, reemerges. This reemergence can happen after a long quiescent period. In the first flush of success, smokers stop, and programs receive a good reputation for their effectiveness. Follow-up studies over a sufficiently long period tell a much less encouraging story. Because the smokers who smoked most before stopping temporarily are also observed to be the ones who smoke most when they start again, the consequences of relapse are to produce nonzero entries far off the diagonal in the inverse simplex matrix.

A group therapeutic experiment is a set of time series in parallel. The outcome of such an experiment is definable in terms of the mean shift induced, and the extent of interindividual variation; it is often considered undesirable to achieve an average improvement at the expense of a great spread in outcomes, so that some are worse at the expense of others who are better. This argument is also used in the evaluation of programmed learning (Atkinson & Crothers, 1964; Atkinson & Paulson, 1972) and the psychology of instruction. Various outcomes of group therapy can be represented in terms of their statistical and time series properties. In the context of the Markovian model just considered, Revenstorf (1975) identified four outcomes; slightly modified they are as follows:

1. No change in the mean of individual series compared with the starting levels and with high autocorrelations in each series. This is what is expected if therapy is useless.

2. No change in the mean, but increased variance between subjects; the intrasubject autocorrelations tend to be lower than the intersubject reliability. It should be noted that by James–Stein effects the variance

of subject means should decrease through time even if no therapeutic effect exists, so an increase in the scatter across subjects is evidence of some therapeutic intervention even if there is no shift in the overall mean.

3. All series have a mean shift of comparable size and direction; the autocorrelations show marked interseries variation; this implies that the effect of therapy is homogeneous with respect to reduction in unwanted behavior, eventually, but that the rate at which asymptote is achieved varies between individuals. This is what we might sensibly expect a priori.

4. All series have a mean shift of comparable size and direction; the autocorrelations are homogeneously high. This means that therapy has a consistent effect, though not necessarily a desired effect. Statistically only case 1 is sufficiently well-behaved to be representable as a Markov process; the rest exhibit marked nonstationarities as the result of any effective therapeutic interventions. So the Markov model is a control model for the stable null case.

The value of treating therapy data as fitting/not-fitting a lag 1 model is the exposure, as residuals, of long-term covariances showing that some habits (usually bad) are superficially extinguished but come back in proportion to their original severity. Obviously an ideal therapy does not show this. The case of addiction modification is clinically important but not intrinsically very tractable nor very rich from a time series analyst's point of view. A bridge between time series analysis and test theory is created when a set of time series in parallel, all subject to some intervention, is treated as a case of longitudinal factor analysis (Mulaik, 1972).

A potentially richer situation is offered in the study of interpersonal interactions in married couples extending through time; in system theory terms this is a dyad each of which is the input to the other and receives the output of the other. If only one sort of quantifiable behavior is emitted by each, then the whole system can be treated as one feedback loop, and the conditions for stability of the system as a whole is expressed in terms of the loop gain of the dyad. The loop gain for the dyad has to have a gain factor less than unity if the system as a whole is not to explode, but this can be achieved if only one part is stable, that is, has a gain less than unity. If the parts are h and w (for $h$usband and $w$ife, say) then

$$\left.\begin{aligned} x_{h,j} &= h \cdot y_{w,j-1} \\[2mm] x_{w,j+1} &= w \cdot y_{h,j} \end{aligned}\right\} \qquad (4.7.5)$$

are the equations of the system if the two parts alternate and have outputs y_h, y_w and inputs x_h, x_w. The equations (4.7.5) have been written on the assumption that gain only occurs in converting an output into an input between the two parts of the system. In fact it does not matter if the system is conceptualized that way or the gains written within each subsystem if and only if an input x is converted to an output y. The loop gain, which necessarily and sufficiently determines stability, is wh; the condition for stability is simply $wh < 1$.

The single-loop model is too simplistic because each may be the generator of an output at the same time, and the lagged consequences may be distributed differently for one from the other, over a different number of trials. In diagrammatic form we have Fig. 4.7.3 as a possibility.

The nonzero gain factors in Fig. 4.7.3 are $x_g, \ldots, x_{g,-2}$ and $y_g, \ldots,$ $y_g, \ldots, y_g, \ldots, y_{g,-3}$. The diagram gives the structure of one part of the system, which would be linked to the other part by equations like (4.7.5).

Anecdotally it may be remarked that in couples cohabiting the behavior of one partner elicits a delayed reaction in the other and vice versa. The wife in a marriage may be depressed; the husband attempts to cheer her up and then becomes depressed in turn (perhaps as a result of the unrewarding effort); the woman after a delay does become cheerful and tries in turn to help the partner out of his induced depression. Neither may have any insight into the interactive nature of the process and simply sees the other as having mood swings and being difficult to live with as each is emotionally out of phase with the other. Taking this lifelike scenario more seriously, Hahlweg, Revenstorf and Schindler (1977) and Revenstorf, Hahlweg, and Schindler (1979) compared the relative efficiency of various forms of marital therapy. Records were available on a day-to-day basis for a period of 8 to 12 weeks, which were measures of the time spent together as perceived by each partner, in joint activity, conversation, tender relations, quarreling, and a rating by each partner independently of the feeling of togetherness experienced. An ARIMA model was fitted by Box–Jenkins methods (see Section 2.3). In marital couples there is observed a 1-day lag dependence across a pair (one for each spouse) of series of one sort, though obviously the two records kept by husband and wife show a close agreement much of the time. There is some cyclic fluctuation; the weekends have time-locking effect forcing the patterns into phase. Time series analysis brings out the weekly cycle that is often not clearly discernible in raw data records: "the regression coefficient predicting

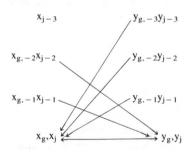

FIG. 4.7.3   Part of a dyad with differently distributed lags.

today's behaviour from what has happened before is in general above 0.40.'' Short-term negative autocorrelations are shown in "feelings of togetherness" in some respondents, which does not augur well for their mutual contentment. Some relations between variables are clearly dependent, but an activity variable can serve as a lead for a later feeling:

$$(\text{time spent together})_{j-1} \rightarrow (\text{feeling together})_j$$

The complete crosscovariance matrix polynomial of the set of variables is thus well worth examination. The interesting point emerges from the analysis given by Revenstorf and co-workers that the more subtle affective lag relationships may not be perceived by a therapist who relies upon a series of interview impressions of what is happening; these relationships are also unperceived by the couple themselves. The disparities in the interpersonal lagged crosscorrelations for wife to husband and husband to wife are themselves the apparent cause of mutual hostility. Naturally there are serious practical difficulties in conducting these studies because the effort of keeping records and the seeming arbitrariness of the task cannot be justified in advance unless there already exists some positive relationship between the therapist and the couple; this may create more implicit variables in the time structure of the process and thus limit the generality of the findings.

5 Systems Theory and Time Series

5.1 SYSTEM REPRESENTATIONS

Although it is tautological that human behavior consists of series of events in time, there are no grounds for jumping to the assertion that the only, or the best, way to go about building psychological models is to construct time series analyses.

A time series representation is not a desirable end in itself; it is too near, in structure and content, to the phenomena it seeks to represent. If there was nothing to be done with a time series model but record it, the often considerable computational labor involved would be futile. It has often been complained that psychological investigations end with the reporting of statistical significance levels, giving us no insight into the effective magnitude or persistence of the effects detected. Not only are the statistical methods of inference inconsistent and overdue for Bayesian revision, but the objectives of the experiment are lost; the reader is entitled to be reminded of what model is being implicitly fitted and why it was thought to be a priori plausible; he or she frequently enjoys neither experience. There is little point in adding another layer of abstract algebra, even further removed from direct observation than the means and correlations with which a typical time-independent analysis stops, unless there is some underpinning by a clear commitment to a theoretical position. A time series analysis that is not purely exploratory is undertaken because it leads, with some high probability, back into a view of a psychological process or phenomenon as a system.

What is being asserted strongly here is that those regularities in psychological data that are sufficiently well-behaved to be the subject of scientific description are, at a formal level, the sorts of regularities that are exhibited by closed subsystems. It should therefore be possible to use the methods of systems theory to investigate psychological data if a bridge can be built between data and system modeling by using a time series representation.

So it is basically necessary to state parts of systems theory that are potentially applicable to psychological data. The statement of systems theory can be done fairly tersely, following Zadeh and Desoer (1963).

In an abstract, uninterpreted sense, a *system* is a collection of objects or events united by some form of interaction or interdependence. This is not a very useful definition because almost anything is a system or can be thought of as part of a system. The eye, the hypothalamus, beliefs about democracy, and ways of holding cutlery within the bounds of politeness are all systems of potential interest to a psychologist. Some systems are obviously thought to be scientifically important objects of study; others are not.

However, the next definition is less familiar and circumscribes our interests considerably; a *state of a system* at any given time is the information needed to determine the behavior of the system from that time on. A fundamental problem in seeking a system representation of some behavior is thus to find out what the states are; there is not a unique answer to this question, but discovering a formal mathematical representation of the system and its states is called *solving the problem of identification*. It is not always possible to do this, so at the metatheoretical level considerable work has been done on the problem of what systems have identifiable states; this is clearly the problem of *identifiability*. Even if a system is identifiable in principle, the task may be so complicated and laborious as to be impractical; questions of the *computability* of solutions can arise. These abstract questions of obvious and serious importance for the general systems theorist are beyond the scope of this study, but they are always lurking in the background, and with the increasing use of computer simulation in psychology they may be expected to intrude in the evaluation of research programs and projects.

As soon as measurement and quantification, even at the degenerate (binary) level is available, a system is redefined as a set of input–output pairs. Such a set is ordered in time when collected as data but may not be ordered when presented as a sufficient description of the system. In this sense a system is an abstract structure, of which the familiar psychological stimulus–response accounts of behavior are special interpreted cases; the interpretation comes when psychological meaning is given to input as stimulation and output as responses. The interpretation makes the psychologist feel "at home" among some abstractions; it may convince the reader that psychology thought of at least something first before systems theory came along (which is of course true) but of itself it is not very helpful in deciding what are legitimate manipulations to get from a stimulus–response record to a model of the internal relationships holding, invariantly over some time period, between stimuli and responses. In one sense, however, knowing that input models stimuli and output models responses is extremely important; when both stimuli and responses are quantified, then the system is about their quantified aspects per se, though it may only be possible to make stochastic statements about these aspects. When stimuli or responses, or both, have marked limits on the range of values they may take in the real world, or limits on the rate at which their values or their derivatives with respect to time may change in real time, then a representation outside these limits is empty of meaning. If the real-world system moves outside some range, it ceases to function and perhaps destroys itself; what these ranges are can only be discovered empirically and then written as boundary conditions onto the inputs and outputs of the abstract system. As all human behavior, like all living systems, is sensibly thought of as working within limits even when these limits have never been discovered, boundary conditions are an intrinsic part of any system model of behavior, not something grafted on afterward to create plausibility.

It is reasonable, therefore, to consider in the beginning only abstract systems with boundary conditions written onto the inputs and outputs. The quantitative estimation of a boundary condition always requires experimental investigation.

The uninterpreted system in this context is defined to be a family of ordered pairs of observables in real time, where that time will generally be taken to be discrete, and most usually the elements of that discrete time will be interpreted as the notional trials of an experimental record, unless otherwise stated. The observables are taken to be inputs and outputs, but in a system these are replaced with functions of the inputs and outputs; it is only *some* measurable aspects of the real-world events that even concern the model builder. Even multivariate inputs and outputs are not in some abstract sense complete representations. For inputs (stimulus values) it is common to use u as a variable name, and for outputs (response values) to use y. The variable x is reserved, often, to name states within the system; the scheme is as follows:

Locus of action psychologically	System component	Variable name or notation
Stimulus values s	Inputs at time j	u, u_j, u, $u(j)$
Organism variables o	States	x, x_j, x, $x(j)$
Response values r	Outputs at time j	y, y_j, y, $y(j)$

where the equivalences imply that in a psychological application it is sensible to interpret the algebraic variables in the sense of the familiar s, o, r labels when a model appears to make a contribution to understanding the relationships between the three classes of variables involved. There is relatively little difficulty in making interpretations of u or y but often considerable difficulty in selecting and understanding state variables; they offer conceptual problems that are more subtle than are direct records of behavior.

The input and output functions of a state are at initial time t_0, $U(t_0, j)$ and $Y(t_0, j)$, and they may be regarded as composed of segments; that is, the set of values taken by U, $\{u\}$, and by Y, $\{y\}$, may be regarded as closed under segmentation (Zadeh & Desoer, 1963), which means the record of the behavior of a system can be regarded as made up of a collection of segments that abut but do not overlap in real time. In psychological applications a simple segment, which is a u, y pair at one point in time j, is called the record of a single trial. The parallelism between the language and concepts of systems theory on the one hand and a semi-abstract representation of a psychological experiment on the other can thus be traced intuitively at this level of description. There is one fundamental difference that must be made clear; in some writers in behaviorist psychology it is usual to regard a response as made to a stimulus. So, the response value r_j^* is to be associated stochastically to the stimulus value s_j^*. If I am presented with a sound of 20 dB above the background sound level, as measured physically, and I respond with a rating "46 units of (my) perceived loudness," then the experimenter recording these events seeks to pair the 20 with the 46; the 46 is taken as belonging in a very special, almost exclusive, way to the 20; not only are the two in the same time segment, j, they are thought to be causally related. It may strike the reader as both pedantic and trivial to remake this elementary point; it is being made precisely because it has been abandoned, as a necessary prior assumption, or as a starting point in theory construction, throughout this monograph. It is abandoned for two reasons; it is theoretically unnecessarily restrictive and plays no part in systems theory, and it is empirically as a strong generalization in psychology almost certainly quite false. What is sought, in systems theory, is an economical representation of the relation, in mathematical terms, between an ordered set of inputs and an ordered set of outputs, in the same series of segments of discrete time.

The term *memory* is found in both systems theory and psychology with a diversity of connotations, and when in systems theory one writes of models with finite memory, the expression has a precise meaning that may not be what it would have had if used in the context of a psychological description. In psychology the notion of finite memory might mean that an individual could only retain learned items for a given time (not considering termination by death) or that the total number of items of a given sort that could be learned and held accurately in memory for a specified time was bounded. The latter meaning is probably not defensible, partly because of a case history documented by Luria,[1] and the former meaning is of limited usefulness because the parameters that determine the storage and retrieval of sets of items in memory include specification of the interitem similarities, which are obviously a function of the particular items put into memory and so subject to change as items are added to or subtracted from the total set presently held in memory.

By contrast, the definition of a finite-state system with a finite memory is both more formal and makes fewer assumptions about anything that happens in some

---

[1]Luria, A. *The Mind of a Mnemonist* (1968).

internal information store that may be called the memory. For example, Gill (1962) proceeds as follows:

A finite-state system is said to have finite memory if two conditions are satisfied for all values of j;

$$Y_j = G(u_j, u_{j-1}, u_{j-2}, \ldots, u_{j-m}, y_{j-1}, y_{j-2}, \ldots, y_{j-m})$$

for some finite m, and G is a real function of its arguments, and

$$Y_j \neq G(u_j, u_{j-1}, \ldots, u_{j-m-1}, y_{j-1}\,y_{j-2}, \ldots, y_{j-m-1})$$

That is to say, the system has the memory at level m if the inputs and past outputs are sufficient to determine the present output and also at the same time if such a determination is impossible when m is reduced by 1.

The given formalization does not mean that the behavior represented by U and Y would be exhibited by a subject whose memory could only hold m items at once, or $2m - 1$ items; it has the more restricted meaning that the observed regularities in behavior represented by the triple $\{G, U, Y\}$ require no greater record to predict behavior with assumptions of linearity than that involved in going back m trials. A finite-memory system is thus a representation of some behavioral regularities in the repertoire of a subject who has a memory of unknown capacity, not necessarily fixed, and can use reliably records of events on m previous trials together with the current stimulus values to generate his present behavior but cannot do this consistently with a smaller record.

Systems in Discrete Time

Systems in discrete time are not always conveniently represented in the forms that have been used in previous chapters; the assumptions that are necessarily built into the linear stationary models that have found application in physiology and psychology are limited and inherently implausible because human behavior, at practically any level of analysis we may care to adopt, is replete with irregularities and discontinuities. Such irregularities can be ironed out some of the time in the laboratory in tasks that are rendered somewhat trivial in part because of their very regularity. In recent years there has been a call for more realistic experimental psychology that gets nearer to working or social situations in which most behavior of interest actually takes place; one way to achieve more realism is to relax constraints upon what behavior may be recorded and, at the same time, seek to model that unconstrained behavior with models that are complicated enough to capture some of the recurrent forms of transient or nonstationary phenomena that psychological systems can exhibit.

It is often plausible to think of the human subject as having a repertoire of states, be they personality types, moods, cognitive strategies for problem solving, or altered states of consciousness. Given such states, then behavior is an endless peregrination between them, and the two fundamental problems are to define what state an individual is in at some point in time and to define the rules for moving between states. The states are not required to be observable; occupancy of a state may only be expressed as a probability statement at a point in time for at least some states of a system, and the rules for moving between states can be stochastic and not deterministic. These generalizations have become commonplace because of the extensive use of finite-state models in mathematical learning theory, and Markov models where states are, for example, each associated with a degree of sleep, or a form of conditioning or learning are familiar and successful as descriptive or exploratory models.

The simple time series models have one and only one set of coefficients, but if a process with two or more states is thought to be plausible, then it may be set up in such a way that each state has one and only one unique LFT associated with it, and over and above these LFTs is some rule that determines the switching between states as a function of input characteristics. It is quite easy to synthesize such systems by computer simulation, and by trial and error it is possible to match the dynamic characteristics of some behavior sequences. But it is another matter, and one fraught with difficulty, to work backward from the given input–output relationships of a complex system that is only known as a black box and attempt to discover laws of behavior that must depend on being able to identify each of the subsystems and the hierarchical relationships holding between them. There is no guarantee that this can be done, there is no general method for doing it. If, in fact, a system is dynamically stationary and the only data available are the input and output records, then some results can be established that sharply point up the indeterminacy of any theorizing based only on stimulus and response relationships. It is possible to generalize about what cannot be identified (from a set of alternative possibilities), but it is not possible to find unique dynamic representations if a wide choice of internal states may be postulated more or less at will.

In the face of these general considerations, concerning nonstationarity, multistate models, and dynamic predictability and identifiability, some results and methods of great value can however be given. The problems put at such an abstract level are not the problems of psychology but the problems of systems representation that are the common inheritance of various experimental sciences.

State Space Representation

As an alternative to transforming into the frequency domain as a method of analyzing systems in time, the state space method that remains in the time domain throughout has come into increasing use. For its fullest exploitation it requires a judicious selection of parameters to characterize the internal relationships of the process being modeled. However, the choice of what are meaningful parameters is extremely wide, and coefficients of difference or differential equations may be used.

In the notation of state space representations there is some consistency of usage:

1. The set of inputs is $\{u_i\}$, and as a variable in time the ith input will be denoted by $u_i(j)$ at discrete time j.
2. The responses are $\{y_k\}$, and analogously $y_k(j)$ is a value at time j.

The internal state variables characterizing the systems are $\{x_q\}$ and again these can be made functions of time $x_q(j)$. The facility to let the internal state parameters vary is intrinsically rich and leads to a wide diversity of models, only very few of which might have potential application in a given problem area. If models are not to be trivial, they must be economical and so the crucial issues center on developing rules for the selection of the state variables, given that their number must be minimal. The state variables have to be selected to satisfy the condition that if, at discrete time j, their values $x_q(j)$ are known, and also the values of u_i (j, $j + 1, j + 2, \ldots, j + m$) are known (in other words, the future inputs are known or predictable), then for discrete times $j, j + 1, j + 2, \ldots, j + m$, the output variables y_x ($j, j + 1, j + 2, \ldots, j + m$) and the future values of the state variables $x_q(j + 1, j + 2, \ldots, j + m)$ are completely determined.

If the conditions of complete determination and minimality are met, then it is said that a state space representation is not unique for a given input–output process, but all valid state space representations will have the same minimum rank, which is called the *order* of the system.

A state model of a system in its simplest form consists of two recursive equations in discrete time:

Let the order of the system be n, and the dimensionality of the input be m; then the first equation relates state recursive revision to inputs in the form

$$\mathbf{x}(j + 1) = \mathbf{A}\mathbf{x}(j) + \mathbf{B}\mathbf{u}(j) \tag{5.1.1}$$

where $\mathbf{A}$ is an $n \times n$ system matrix, $\mathbf{B}$ is an $n \times m$ input matrix, and the output is related to the states and the inputs by

$$\mathbf{y}(j) = \mathbf{C}\mathbf{x}(j) + \mathbf{D}\mathbf{u}(j) \tag{5.1.2}$$

where there are p outputs, and $\mathbf{C}$ is an output matrix $p \times n$ and $\mathbf{D}$ is a transmission matrix $p \times m$. It would be most likely in psychological systems that $m = p$, the outputs and inputs matching one to one, and most experiments in such areas as psychophysics traditionally have $m = p = 1$. Equations (5.1.1) and (5.1.2) necessarily and sufficiently characterize a simple state space system.

This bordered section may be omitted, if desired by the reader.

Suppose that a system is of the very general sort where

$$y(j) + a_1 y(j - 1) + \cdots + a_n y(j - n)$$
$$= b_0 u(j) + b_1 u(- 1) + \cdots + b_n u(k - n)$$

then this will have a LTF in z transforms of

$$H(z) = \frac{b_0 + b_1 z^{-1} + b_2 z^{-2} + \cdots + b_n z^{-n}}{a_0 + a_1 z^{-1} + a_2 z^{-2} + \cdots + a_n z^{-n}} \tag{5.1.3}$$

where $a_0 = 1$.

It is possible to analyze the system by factoring the two polynomials as done in Chapter 3, but errors can cumulate in higher-order systems and circumvention of factoring is therefore sometimes desirable. This can be done by what is called direct programming; the estimation of the state variables is then obtainable from a matrix equation in the coefficients $\{a\}$, $\{b\}$.

In z transforms,

$$Y(z) = H(z) \cdot U(z)$$

so from (5.1.3)

$$\frac{Y(z)}{\sum_{j=0}^{n} b_j z^{-j}} = \frac{U(z)}{\sum_{j=0}^{n} a_j z^{-j}} = Q(z) \tag{5.1.4}$$

From (5.1.4)

$$Q(z) = U(z) - Q(z) \sum_{j=1}^{n} a_j z^{-j} \tag{5.15}$$

and

$$Y(z) = Q(z) \sum_{j=0}^{n} b_j z^{-j} \tag{5.1.6}$$

The state variables are selected to satisfy the relations

$$X_q(z) = z^{-q} Q(z) \qquad q = 1, 2, \ldots, n \tag{5.1.7}$$

and from the recurrence relationship (5.1.5) it follows that

$$z X_q(z) = X_{q-1}(z) \qquad q = 2, 3, \ldots, n \tag{5.1.8}$$

or, in scalar form, from inverse z transforms,

$$x_q(j + 1) = x_{q-1}(j) \tag{5.1.9}$$

By rearrangement of (5.1.5) and (5.1.7) is obtained

$$z K_1(z) = U(z) - \sum_{q=1}^{n} a_q X_q(z) \tag{5.1.10}$$

which in discrete time for scalar quantities may be written as

$$x_1(j + 1) = u(j) - \sum_{q=1}^{n} a_q X_x(j)$$

and

$$y(j) = b_0 u(j) + \sum_{q=1}^{n} (b_q - a_q b_0) x_q(j) \tag{5.1.11}$$

For the solution of practical problems it can be useful to write the last two equations in matrix form:

$$x_q(j+1) = \begin{vmatrix} -a_1 & -a_2 & \cdots & -a_{n-1} & -a_n \\ 1 & 0 & \cdots & 0 & 0 \\ 0 & 1 & \cdots & 0 & 0 \\ \cdot & \cdot & & \cdot & \cdot \\ \cdot & \cdot & & \cdot & \cdot \\ \cdot & \cdot & & \cdot & \cdot \\ 0 & 0 & \cdots & 1 & 0 \end{vmatrix}_{n \times n} \cdot \begin{vmatrix} x_q(j) \\ \cdot \\ \cdot \\ \cdot \\ \cdot \end{vmatrix}_n + \begin{vmatrix} 1 \\ 0 \\ \cdot \\ \cdot \\ \cdot \end{vmatrix}_n \cdot u(j)$$

$$y(j+1) = \begin{vmatrix} (b_1 - a_1 b_0) & \cdots & (b_n - a_n b_0) \end{vmatrix}_n \cdot \begin{vmatrix} x_q(j) \\ \cdot \\ \cdot \\ \cdot \end{vmatrix}_n + b_0 \cdot u(j) \tag{5.1.12}$$

For example, consider an imaginary system that has order 3, and an LTF in z form of

$$H(z) = \frac{1 + 2z^{-1}}{1 - 2_z{}^{-1} + 3z^{-2} + z^{-3}} \tag{5.1.13}$$

The coefficients can immediately be read off directly as

$$b_0 = 1, \; b_1 = 2, \; b_2 = \cdots = b_j = 0, \; a_0 = 1, \; a_1 = -2, \; a_2 = 3,$$

$$a_3 = 1, \; a_4 = \cdots = a_j = 0.$$

so

$$\begin{vmatrix} x_1(j+1) \\ x_2(j+1) \\ x_2(j+1) \end{vmatrix} = \begin{vmatrix} 2 & -3 & -1 \\ 1 & 0 & 0 \\ 0 & 1 & 0 \end{vmatrix} \cdot \begin{vmatrix} x_1(j) \\ x_2(j) \\ x_3(j) \end{vmatrix} + \begin{vmatrix} 1 \\ 0 \\ 0 \end{vmatrix} \cdot u(j)$$

and

$$y(j) \quad = | \; 4 \quad 3 \quad -3 \; | \cdot \begin{vmatrix} x_1(j) \\ x_2(j) \\ x_3(j) \end{vmatrix} + u(k)$$

Alternative methods exist of solving the state equations, and different sets of results may derive from these methods, though the input–output dynamics described will be the same. Hence although a general state space analytical method is available, the interpretability of the state variables still requires knowledge of the substantive properties of the system being modeled. It is possible, given a state space representation, to derive the LTF and other properties such as the response to an impulse or to a step input. The $n \times n$ system matrix **A** plays a key role in such manipulations, and given a model of the form of (5.1.1) and (5.1.2) it can be shown that

$$\mathbf{H}(z) = \mathbf{C}[z\mathbf{I} - \mathbf{A}]^{-1}\mathbf{B} + \mathbf{D} \qquad (5.1.14)$$

and the sequence of LTF coefficients $\{v_k\}$ can then be written as

$$v_0 = \mathbf{D}$$
$$v_k = \mathbf{CA}^{k-1}\mathbf{B} \qquad \text{for } k = 1, 2, \ldots \qquad (5.1.15)$$

A much fuller coverage is given by Cadzow (1973) whose treatment has in part been followed in this section. It is obvious that Equation (5.1.15) should be solved by computer routines and that the coefficients $\{v_k\}$ are as given in matrix form; each is p outputs $\times$ m inputs. Compare the use of multivariate time series analysis in Gregson (1978) for an example of LTF coefficients that are matrices, so that $\mathbf{H}(z)$ is a matrix polynomial. So far there are few explicit treatments of psychological processes in state space form outside human engineering applications, but the theory of this section sets up the problem and discussion of the extensions into nonstationary modeling that is covered at an introductory level in this chapter.

5.2 EQUIVALENCE OF SYSTEMS UNDER STATIONARITY

Control theory has a beguiling fascination for some theoreticians who seek to represent the self-stabilizing and hierarchical characteristics of human behavior by elaborate diagrams of boxes and lines. Sooner or later everything is joined directly or indirectly to everything else, and the reader may be told of the rich potential of boxes and lines for explaining the problem on hand. Unfortunately there is not a number in sight, and often no clues as to how the reader might invent some plausible numbers for himself or herself and put them into a model to see what happens. By painstaking experiment and analyses of reaction times for complex decision tasks there have been built up enough data to show that it is very sensible to regard the way in which we perform many tasks as being under some sort of hierarchical control; we have processes, other processes that override the lower levels and switch between alternative ways of doing the same task, and it has seemed necessary to some theoreticians to pile up these hierarchies in depth to describe the more complex human abilities. There is, as yet, no psychological model to explain how people come to write the sort of applied mathematics used in this book rather than doing something else slightly different to try and achieve the same ends, but it is not fanciful to guess that when such a theory appears, it will have hierarchies of decision and information processing in it. The objection to much of this activity was spelled out in Chapter 1 but needs restating here slightly differently as a lead-in to the general question of modeling nonlinear systems.

The problems of identifiability and of the order of a system model are naturally interrelated; there are limits to identifiability, which means that some alternative models can never be differentiated between in terms of their input–output relations. In one sense this does not matter, for there is always an infinite number of alternative representations of a real process to some given degree of accuracy of measurement, however precise, and any empirical result always excludes an infinite number of other models. In another sense it matters very much, because the alternative models that can fit the data may include two or more that are fundamentally different in structure and that can make widely different predictions as soon as small changes are made in the experimental conditions. When such disparate alternatives are considered to be serious contenders for the position of favored theory, then it is said that a problem of identifiability exists. This situation can be given some coherent treatment in Bayesian terms, by noting that in an identification problem, where an adequate model of minimum complexity is sought, we only put into a relative likelihood expression (of data given model parameters and structure) the alternative models for which we have nonnegligible prior probabilities.

The question of identifiability is very important; we seek to identify the internal structure of a dynamic process; we need to know this before we can predict the circumstances in which behavior will be smooth and regular and the circumstances in which it will break down, or at least become unstable and erratic. This sort of question is, of course, of great interest to clinical psychologists, because when behavior becomes uncontrolled in some way, a person may be judged to be mentally ill or antisocial.

Despite the importance of the questions associated with the identification of a dynamic process, and the potential losses contingent upon its misidentification, however, most experiments in the tradition of experimental psychology have sought to create periods, locally in time, when the human subject was dynamically stationary within the context of the experimental task. Both conceptually and in terms of subsequent data analysis, accounts of behavior have been almost exclusively stationary, and the idea of letting the behavior run wild or even more recently the idea of monitoring the quantifying nonstationarity as a descriptive parameter of behavior in its own right do not fit into traditional experiment or data analysis at all comfortably.

The dilemma that arises is that to do some sorts of experimental psychology at all, say in the area of sensory psychophysics, stationarity must be induced or assumed, and to predict behavior outside the sequence of trials within the experiment there must be a way of predicting what happens as soon as the input series of stimuli is replete with discontinuities. In the mathematical sense in which identifiability is used we are required to be able to specify the following:

1. The form of the general equation, usually an LTF, that will represent a dynamic process.

2. The actual values of the parameters in that equation or, more generally, the meaning of the states of the state space representation.

3. The limits on input and output characteristics within which the equation is expected to be a satisfactory representation.

The basic difficulty arises because many different equations will reduce to the same LTF under stable conditions; stable input–output relations are never the unique consequence of some one model but only of the class of models having the same LTF. As stated after (5.1.13), even the method of solution of the state space equations has inherent ambiguity, which does not stop the approach from being used extensively to solve many problems of control that are important and not amenable to stationary representation.

As psychologists such as Powers (1973) have already attempted to build models that are hierarchies of feedback systems, the questions of importance are as follows:

1. How complicated do models of hierarchical control have to be put in order to describe or predict what is observed?

2. Are any of the models advanced actually testable in the form in which they are expressed?

We have already seen that unquantified models are inherently untestable, so the first question is only worth asking in terms of quantified models. The focus of interest is on the depth of hierarchical ordering, or sequential ordering, of loops, which are necessary in a model.

Note, in particular, that we cannot, just from records of simple experiments, decide how many feedback loops are responsible for controlling the stability of human behavior; it is necessary to bring together results from a diversity of situations.

There are two theorems, which can be proved mathematically but which we can put into words as well, that bear on the problem of identifiability.

3. Any process with k feedback loops that is in a steady state (there are no sudden irregularities in input or output) can be represented by a single feedback loop with a mathematically equivalent gain function.

This means that a person whose behavior is describable by very simple equations is not necessarily doing what he does in a very simple way, and from the record of his stimuli and responses we have no way of telling how complicated his real functional description is.

4. Any process with closed feedback loops that is in a steady state can be represented by an open loop with an equivalent gain function.

This means that a record of steady behavior need give no clues at all to the external observer that it is in fact self-regulatory behavior. Looked at from the outside, behavior that is perfectly under internal control shows no external signs, which can be measured, of that internal control and how it is exercised.

The key words in these two theorems are *in a steady state*. If these words are not true, the theorems do not apply. The first theorem says nothing about how the k loops are combined; they may be in series, in parallel, or hierarchically linked. The fact that loops in series or in parallel can be reduced is important precisely because it provides a way of analyzing the behavior of complex systems by reducing them to simpler equivalent systems, under stationarity.

5.3 DISCONTINUITY IN HUMAN RESPONSES

It has repeatedly been asserted in the limited literature of psychological control theory applications that the human operator exhibits discontinuities in his or her stimulus–response relations; discontinuity, nonlinearity, and locally erratic behavior are not of themselves reasons for not trying to model behavior, as most real-world systems are at best stochastic and certainly not linear or mathematically very well-behaved. There does not exist some grand review of science to which we can turn and look up the relative intractability of the typical data of different sciences; there is a tradition that the softer sciences have data that cannot be readily represented in numerical form, and one of the possible attractions of catastrophe theory (Zeeman, 1977) was that it furnished a way to talk coherently about the limited sorts of discontinuities observed in some systems that locally minimize a loss function of some sort. But it is not possible to make dogmatic assertions that the data of psychology are necessarily more intractable than those of engineering; a comparative review of the form and nature of intractability in the two disciplines would be pretentious and probably vacuous. It remains true that many systems that depart greatly from the mathematically ideal simple cases have been usefully modeled, and many systems in living behavior have never been modeled at all when in fact they could be less complex than systems that have been modeled. The reasons why some systems have been modeled and others not should be sought in the economics of analysis and outcome utilization; it may be very necessary to know how a power station will function under fluctuating load, for many people will be inconvenienced, even run the risk of lethal accident, if it fails. By contrast, the modeling of social interaction processes in married couples can be done (Revenstorf, 1979), but the payoff involves fewer people and may be more difficult to demonstrate convincingly, even though it involves fewer variables and less data in a typical case.

To illustrate what is involved in even the smallest psychological experiment where the potential for discontinuity is great, an example first popularized by McFarland (1974) will be used. An experiment in control with long response lags, performed by Cooke[2] at Oxford, involved setting up a feedback loop as follows. A mercury-in-glass thermometer was hung visibly in a beaker of water standing upon an electrical heating coil. The current in the coil was controlled by a rheostat under the continuous adjustment of an operator, whose behavior was under study. The operator could see the thermometer and read off the instantaneous temperature and could adjust the rheostat to heat up the water or to let it cool down if the water rose above room temperature. The control loop in the causal direction is hand–rheostat–heater–beaker–water–thermometer temperature as indicated-temperature as perceived-cognitive decision-hand.

The control task exists in real times because there is a preset target temperature that the subject is told to get to as quickly as possible. Let us examine the sources of imprecision and discontinuity in this very simple system. For simplicity the time constants between rheostat and heater current can be ignored and the problem put mainly in terms of heat transfer. Heat goes from the heater to the water in the beaker, and most of it is lost to the atmosphere; but if more heat goes in than is lost by convection and radiation, then the temperature rises, until stability is reached. It is possible to obtain stability at any one of a range of temperatures because the heat losses are proportional to the difference in temperatures of water and atmosphere (raised to a power) and so a higher voltage will support a higher steady-state temperature, provided that people do not keep opening and closing doors in the vicinity of the experiment. The subject either knows all this or soon finds out. There are thus time lags in moving heat from the heater to the water and from the water to the thermometer. When the human operator watches the mercury level in the thermometer and adjusts the voltages, he sees the level rise or not rise as fast as he wishes; then a closed loop is created.

The heat transfer part of the system in z form may be written as

$$\text{voltage} \rightarrow \frac{M}{z + A} \rightarrow \text{beaker temperature} \rightarrow \frac{N}{z + B} \rightarrow \text{thermometer temperature}$$

---

[2]See also Crossman and Cooke (1974), in Chapter 6.

where M, N, A, and B are fixed physical parameters concerned with heat transfer.

If the response of the subject is proportional to the error ratio T/D, where T is the current observed temperature and D is the desired target temperature, the feedback loop involving the operator and the physical system can be shown to have a z transform

$$H(z) = \frac{KMN}{(z + A)(z + B) + KMN} \qquad (5.3.1)$$

where K is a constant. Now (5.3.1) when multiplied out has terms in z^2; that is, it is of order 2, and it can oscillate when approaching the desired target temperature D as asymptote. In fact it may asymptote to some other undesired target temperature in the short run.

This system can overshoot, undershoot, or oscillate, and what actually happens depends on the constants of the system. The constant K is the subject's gain on the error, in other words how much he or she underreacts or overreacts to T/D in adjusting the rheostat. If the operator only uses proportional control, as in (5.3.1), then he or she can only respond to the amount of error, and the evidence he or she finds in the thermometer occurs some time after the cause in the heater element. The time of this lag is a crucial variable, because a long lag increases the time it takes to bring the system under control. Parenthetically, note that this argument about the undesirability of delay in feedback is used in some policy arguments as a justification for getting quick approximate information to aid governments.

Now the information that is given to the subject, or which he computes for himself in the part of the control loop that was facilely labeled "cognitive decision," can be expressed in various ways:

$$E(j) = T(j) - D, \qquad j = 1, 2, \ldots, j^*, \ldots \qquad (5.3.2)$$

or

$$E^*(j) = T(j)/D \qquad (5.3.3)$$

which we had before, or the error can be integrated over time

$$I(E) = \sum_{j}^{j+j} E(j) \qquad (5.3.4)$$

and even perhaps the rate of change of error over time, which as the process is being expressed in discrete time might be written as

$$\frac{[E(j + j^*) - E(j)]}{j^*} = \delta E(j, j^*) \qquad (5.3.5)$$

Human operators can in fact do these things at least some of the time; if they could not, then complex skills such as landing a glider might be impossible. Now it is possible to add together three sorts of feedback based on, respectively, (5.3.2), (5.3.4), and (5.3.5) and obtain a sort of dynamic system called by engineers "three-term control," which is often very efficient. One could set up an ideal model of dynamic control by postulating such a system and then comparing actual behavior against it, measuring its efficiency by its shortfall against three-term control. Efficiency would be measured at least three ways, by the integral of error over time (which is what the score in some tracking tasks represents), time to reach asymptote (more appropriate in the temperature regulation example under discussion), or the amount of the asymptotic error. A combination of (5.3.5) and (5.3.2) is better than (5.3.2) alone, so if nothing else is known about the situation, it is better to combine (5.3.4) and (5.3.5) with (5.3.2) if it is feasible.

Cooke showed that, in this task, initially subjects used only proportionate control (5.3.3), which results in overshooting; but later as the task is learned, derivative (5.3.5) and even integral (5.3.4) control are brought into use. The subject thus alters his basic dynamic characteristics; he learns to become a different system requiring quite different representation at the level of (5.3.1).

What is more interesting, and even more intractable, is that as subjects become more skilled, they dispense with continuous feedback altogether and use a sort of discontinuous open-loop control, which is sometimes called bang-bang control. This sort of control can only be used effectively when the characteristics of the system are well known to the operator. One may meet this sort of bang-bang control in use by captains of small ferryboats. On some harbors where there are ferry services run by boats with propellers at both ends and loading and docking facilities that enable the ship to tie up end-on to a jetty, a captain gives short bursts of power to the propellers, forward and reverse, and between times lets the boat drift up to the jetty, which it finally touches with very little impact. The boat has large inertia and drag in the water, so the captain has to learn to give bursts of power whose outcome, in terms of the motion of the boat, is experienced after some delay. The more confident the captain, the larger and more infrequent may be the bursts of power used, to achieve the same end of negligible terminal velocity on meeting the jetty. It is tempting to speculate that a boat in water might be an analogy of some attitude change processes, under the influence of bursts of propaganda, but until one can quantify in some plausible way the intensity of propaganda at a point in time, and the magnitude of delayed response to it, the analogy is not very fruitful.

In the water heating example, bang-bang control consists simply of turning the heat up full for a short burst, then turning it off completely and watching what happens, and then giving one or more secondary bursts as the system nears asymptote, but stopping heating at all but a low level before asymptote is reached. If the heater setting to maintain equilibrium at a target temperature is known, then the final heater setting in a series of bursts would be at this level, but the task requirement that target be reached as quickly as possible demands that other higher settings are used on the way to asymptote. This example has been discussed at length because it exemplifies the interaction between form of control and system parameters that we must expect to happen if the human operator learns a task as part of a control system in which his own response parameters are part of the system. It is a potentially dangerous state of affairs if the system can be destroyed by error in its operation, as happens with a moving vehicle. If, however, the system is innocuous like most psychological experiments, and the interest is in human behavior per se, then interest centers on discovering what makes the subject change his or her modes of control. To put this another way, it is required to learn what are the rules, if any, governing the major dynamic discontinuities of the system. About this question very little is known that can be expressed in control theory or systems theory terms.

In engineering design, the policy is often to take the derivate components (5.3.5) out of human control, leaving man with only the (5.3.2) response to make, and perform the corrections dependent on integration elsewhere in the system. Power-assisted steering systems would in some cases do just this.

As Licklider (1960) commented, even within a homogeneous situation, human response characteristics drift, and the subject may be insensitive to very weak signals and have overload limits that cut out very strong signals. He also observed that personal time scales appeared, in motor tasks, to be quantized, though this is now no problem. Even then, linear models were found useful provided that the system in which the human operator is embedded does not have so many abrupt changes that it never has a chance to settle down and exemplify what its dynamic characteristics are in one or more of its component modes of functioning. Slow drift can be taken out, parameters can be handled if they are allowed to make jumps at rare intervals (here *rare* means with respect to the units of discrete time in which representation is sought), and operation is within the underload and overload limits.

A problem that has interested some psychologists, particularly in developmental research, is that of novelty. If a novel stimulus is introduced into the world of an animal or a child, then suddenly the total range of available stimulation is increased, and the new stimuli are explored by the child and the older things around are neglected. Adults do this with new clothes and new cars and invent elaborate rationalizations for what they are doing. It is possible that much of the analyses attempted by psychologists of behavior immediately after a novel stimulus is introduced into the environment of a laboratory animal, or a child in a playpen, are unsound for the following reasons. If a subject is not responding to stimuli but also to derivative and integral functions of stimulation as reported previously, then an abrupt change in behavior at the time of exposure to new stimuli is not evidence of response to novelty as such, because confounded with the introduction of novel stimulation is a step increase in the value of (5.3.5), and a subsequent change can be taken to be a lagged response to that step increase. It would be necessary to separate changes in stimulation levels and the derivatives of stimulation in time from changes produced to the same degree by the use of novel stimuli, by which must be meant stimuli not met before in the controlled environment of the subject. The problem is that there is no ready metric of degree of novelty, nor of the level and derivatives of total stimulation level, to enable us quantitatively to disentangle the question.

The simpler LTF models in the time domain, or transformed into the frequency domain, are not adequate to achieve a representation of the interesting features of discontinuous behavior, as has been intimated already. Models that derive from the state space approach show more promise, though necessarily are more complex and their parameters are likely to be even further removed from immediately observable input and output sequences.

5.4 KALMAN FILTERS

The problem of predicting where a noisy dynamic system will go in the next instant of time is the problem of constructing a filter.

Ideally we have a system that generates a series of nonrandom outputs, by responding to nonrandom components within a series of inputs that are contaminated to some a priori unknown degree by random noise. The problem may thus be thought of as one of partitioning the input into two components, and the identification of the regularities in the system can never be better than a statistical minimum-loss estimate; the residual indeterminacy arises from the stochastic nature of the noise and from our prior uncertainty of the appropriate representation of the deterministic components in the series.

This is obviously a fundamental problem of great difficulty; it is hardly pretentious to assert that it is *the* problem of experimental science if the objective of science is to construct regular and coherent accounts of phenomena that exist sequentially in real time. So, a number of attempted general and particular solutions have been offered, progressively increasing in power and generality. Most modern accounts of this area date effectively from Wiener (1949) who produced solutions for the extrapolation of time series and separated signals from random noise under restricted conditions of stationarity (in particular for cases of continuous input with forms that are pertinent to engineering applications and mathematically tractable). Obviously Wiener himself was drawing on mathematics that went back to Gauss and Fourier, and the feasibility of what he derived in practical applications owed much to considerations of computability. None of the examples in this earlier work looked very hopeful for analyzing the ill-behaved data of experimental psychology, but Wiener was a prophet as well as a polymath, and the implications of his work was traced out in many disciplines and has had some lasting mark on styles of theorizing in cognitive psychology and neuropsychophysiology; interest here centers, however, on the harder question of data analysis rather than the diffuse question of what are preferred metaphors and styles in theoreticians of a somewhat literary persuasion.

The almost immediate result of Wiener's (1949) breakthrough was the solution of special cases and the simplification and extension of his original results, particularly to systems with limited memory and some types of nonstationarity. It should be noted that each such extension of Wiener's original scope brings the modeling in principle closer to the types of nonstationarity that are thought to characterize the behavior of living systems. That is, with each extension of theory and methodology in this area of filtering, the objections to trying the exercise in psychology have less and less justification and take on a more and more irrational quality. This is not to say that useful results will inevitably follow but that the exercise has now a defensible rationale where formerly it had not.

Two major problems arose in the use of Wiener's (1949) methods; the mathematics were opaque to the potential user group who could not therefore readily trace out the underlying assumptions and know if they were satisfied; secondly, as soon as the methods were applied to digital computation, problems of noncomputability arose.

Kalman (1960) and Kalman and Bucy (1961) revised the available algorithms with the now much-cited Kalman filter, which has had some limited use in areas touching on psychology, particularly EEG analysis. But the Kalman filter itself is in the process of being augmented by other methods that are computationally better behaved, and one must expect the process of revision to continue and to evolve increasingly specialized filters for specific applications. Most of the impetus for this work has apparently come from the space flight sciences, but there are a few examples in the biological sciences that may lead to a rapid expansion if the usual ogival curve of publication cumulative total shows in this area as it has shown in many other areas of scientific endeavor. As writing in the early 1980s gives the benefit of hindsight, it is sensible to look for filters with robust properties and potential applicability to psychological data analysis and be more cursory in considering earlier versions that can be found cited in substantive applications made when they were the best available.

The Kalman procedures are recursively applied; that is to say, as each new trial in a series gives new information, this is fed into the algorithm and the prediction equations are updated. The Kalman method is also known as recursive minimum variance estimation for reasons that will hopefully become apparent later.

The filter is therefore a set of recursive equations that have to be solved in immediate succession within one trial to give a minimum-loss estimate of the parameters in the filter and hence the extrapolation in time to the next trial (but possibly further by successive application) that is desired (Leondes, 1970).

To derive a simpler version of Kalman's filter, it is expedient to follow, for example, Bierman (1977) or Bennett (1979), as Kalman's original expositions are much deeper and more formal in their presentation. Kalman goes into details on the conditions for the existence of solutions to the linear filtering problem; by restricting the presentation to its essentials, some of the analogies (surprisingly) with the assumptions of psychological test theory may be exposed. It is remarked, *en passant*, that the prediction of test or achievement scores with progressive aging, or with both aging and education, could be treated as a filtering problem. If on one trial are observed m variables, $\{y_1, \ldots, y_h, \ldots, y_m\} = \mathbf{y}$ and the parameters of the model that are to be recursively adjusted as new data are compared with predictions are $\{x_1, \ldots, x_i, \ldots, x_n\} = \mathbf{x}$, where $n < m$, and further the $\mathbf{y}$ have associated noise so that each $\mathbf{y}_h$ is observed as $\mathbf{y}'_h = \mathbf{y}_h + \mathbf{v}_h$, where $\mathbf{v}_i \sim \mathbf{N}(0, 1)$ (a standardized error distribution), then the $\mathbf{v}_i$ are an m vector of errors. A fixed matrix of coefficients that relates the parameters to the observables is called $\mathbf{A}$ (or order $m \times n$), and the linear system is represented by the equation

$$\mathbf{y} = \mathbf{Ax} + \mathbf{v} \tag{5.4.1}$$

and it is required to choose a set of values $\mathbf{x}^*$ that will minimize the error variance Err $(\mathbf{v})$, which is defined to be

$$\text{Err } (\mathbf{v}) = \Sigma \, v_i^2 \tag{5.4.2}$$

The bordered section may be omitted by the reader if desired.

For a given set of $\mathbf{x}$ values,

$$\text{Err } (\mathbf{x}) = (\mathbf{y} - \mathbf{Ax})'(\mathbf{y} - \mathbf{Ax}) \tag{5.4.3}$$

It can be the case that more than one $\{\mathbf{x}^*\}$ will minimize Err $(\mathbf{x})$ and then one chooses the set for which $\Sigma \, (x_i^*)^2$ is minimal. This condition is obviously computable, and it can be shown that it is mathematically well-behaved.

The expression (5.4.3) is nonnegative and it is necessary and sufficient for a minimum error solution that δ Err $(\mathbf{x})/\delta\mathbf{x}$ must vanish for all $\delta\mathbf{x}$. This condition is met when the $\mathbf{x}^*$ chosen satisfy the so-called normal equations

$$\mathbf{A'Ax} = \mathbf{A'y} \tag{5.4.4}$$

where, by rearranging,

$$\mathbf{x}^* = (\mathbf{A'A})^{-1}\mathbf{A'y}$$

given that $\mathbf{A'A}$ is nonsingular and that $\mathbf{A}$ has rank n. Then

$$\mathbf{A'Ax}^* = \mathbf{A'y} = \mathbf{A'Ax} + \mathbf{A'v} \tag{5.4.5}$$

follows from (5.4.4). Here $\mathbf{A'A}$ is the information matrix, where information is used in the statistical sense of an inverse variance, and the error covariance matrix is $(\mathbf{A'A})^{-1}$.

By definition,

$$(A'A)^{-1} = E((x - x^*)(x - x^*)') \tag{5.4.6}$$

If prior information is available about both the x, which can be called x_p (as in the sense of a Bayesian prior distribution), and also about the covariance structure of the system that can be expressed in a matrix L_p (which corresponds in dimensions and interpretation with $A'A$), then the normal equations that must be satisfied can be modified to incorporate L_p.

With such prior information, the x^* must now satisfy

$$(L_p + A'A)x = L_p x_p + A'y \tag{5.4.7}$$

There is an important aspect to this result that strengthens its applicability, namely, that x_p and L_p do not have to be known completely; it is permissible and computationally tractable initially to enter zeros for unknown elements of either prior, or in some cases we may use unit values or indifference distributions where all values are initially equal. As the conditions are to be satisfied recursively, as soon as observations are added, the x and A begin to fill up. Obviously, if $L_p = 0$, then all its elements are zero, and (5.4.7) reduces back to (5.4.4). The term $(L_p + A'A)$ on the left-hand side of (5.4.7) may be considered as the revised information matrix when there is prior information.

It is desirable, and a practice in some Bayesian analyses (Novick & Jackson, 1974), to find some way of replacing prior estimates by equivalent additional observations. If we have a system with data, and prior information, the two should be combined into one system of augmented size. The augmentation will necessarily increase the total information in $A'A$.

To achieve this simply, a number of researchers have developed a square root filter in which

$$L_p = R'R \tag{5.4.8}$$

is a factorization of L_p into the product of a square root matrix R' and its transpose. Such square root matrices are not unique, but if R_1 and R_2 are any two such matrices, then by definition $R_1 R_2' = L_p$ and $R_1 = R_2 T$, and $T'T = I$ is satisfied, given T is an orthogonal transformation. It is a requirement that L_p is symmetric with nonnegative eigenvalues (a condition familiar in principal components analysis and other areas of multivariate statistics used in linear modeling for psychometrics).[3]

Now defining

$$y_p = R x_p$$

---

[3] A derivation of the Kalman filter algorithm from results in factor analysis was developed by Priestley and Subba Rao (*International Journal of Control*, 1975, *21*, 471–475). The analogy unfortunately does not carry through to obtaining the dimensionality of the system in state space.

it can be shown that the minimization requirement Err (**x**) is met when

$$
\left| \begin{array}{c} \mathbf{y}_p \\ \mathbf{y} \end{array} \right| = \left| \begin{array}{c} \mathbf{R} \\ \mathbf{A} \end{array} \right| \mathbf{x} + \left| \begin{array}{c} \mathbf{v}_p \\ \mathbf{v} \end{array} \right| \tag{5.4.9}
$$

where the $\mathbf{v}_p$ can be treated as initial Gaussian noise.

The Kalman filter is thus an algebraic way of using both the current behavior of a system, based only on input and output records, together with a model of the system's internal structure, to make predictions about what the system will do in the next step in time. As soon as data from a new trial become available, they are fed into the filter, which has the capacity immediately to revise its internal structure and its parameters in order to minimize the expected prediction errors on the next trial.

Important features of the practical use of the Kalman filter, and related methods, center on its prior information needs, which are necessary to set the recursive algorithm working and to keep it working on successive trials and on the specification of the circumstances in which it will work and in which it will fail. The reader should always bear in mind that the Kalman filter is one of a family of related methods; none are universally applicable, but it has been shown that the Kalman filter can be potentially useful in some psychological cases, given that the system to be modeled is fairly simple (not necessarily univariate) and is autoregressive. The Kalman filter is available as a standard computer routine, for example, in the International Mathematical Subroutines Library package (IMSL 1979) but may need augmentation to stop the filter dying in the middle of a data series.

The most coherent way to give a general perspective of what this filtering does is to regard it as a Bayesian process. The filter uses on any one trial an updated record of previous outputs, because its function is to model closely the time series properties of the outputs using at all times the maximum available data. Let us call the response series up to trial j

$$
\mathbf{y}_j = \{y_0, y_1, y_2, \ldots , y_j\}
$$

and the parameters to be revised A. The observation equation will be

$$
y = \mathbf{A}x - v
$$

as defined already; v has zero expectation and a definable autocorrelation structure.

The Kalman filter derives a conditional probability distribution, given the model structure, which can be written (Bennett, 1979) as

$$
p(A_{j+1}|\mathbf{Y}_{j+1}) = p(A_{j+1}|y_{j+1}, \mathbf{Y}_j). \tag{5.4.10}
$$

This can be expressed in Bayes' form as

$$p(A_{j+1}|y_{j+1}, \mathbf{y}_j) = \frac{p(y_{j+1}|A_{j+1}) \cdot p(A_{j+1})}{p(y_{j+1})} \qquad (5.4.11)$$

As the paremeters A at each trial are optimally revised, using (5.4.11), the use of Bayes' theorem in this form is an optimal means of combining old information about the A_j with new information based on the disparities between y_{j+1} and the prediction of y from A_j and the states x. Figure 5.4.1 shows this concept as a flow chart.

The Kalman filter is particularly relevant to psychological experiments that are series of evenly spaced trials, because it is in discrete time and also because the system model used in it has neither to be linear nor to be stationary in its

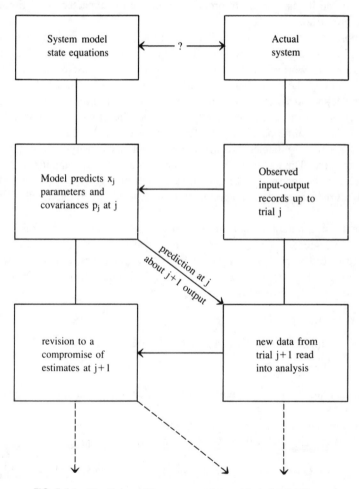

FIG. 5.4.1   The Kalman filter as successive revision of estimations.

parameters. It is very sensitive, in some configurations, to what is used as starting information about the state variables. It may also be necessary to impose boundary conditions in order to stop the estimate of the parameter covariance matrix **P** degenerating to a zero matrix. If this should happen, it blocks new information from entering the algorithm, and predictions start to diverge from the output sequence y_j that is being predicted. One may say that the capacity of the Kalman filter to cope with nonlinear and nonstationary systems rests on the one-trial-ahead recursive properties. To predict further ahead requires better behaved systems, more information about the system's structure, different filtering algorithms, or all three combined.

An aspect of filtering that is potentially informative in data analysis concerns points in time where the experimenter (or the environment) intervenes to create some local episode with special features (as already described in Section 3.6). The intervention can create two fairly abrupt dynamic discontinuities in the system's behavior, one at the start and the other at the end of the intervention period. It is not necessarily the case that both discontinuities will occur (see Chapter 6; if there is a real induced change in system structure, the second change may be absent) but in the immediate vicinity of a discontinuity a recursive filter will temporarily fail closely to track and predict the output. That is, the expected sequence of residuals, $\{v_j\}$, will be a random walk with the mean and autocovariance properties of an i.i.d. process. The process may, of course, be a multivariate random walk. The i.i.d. properties will hold except at the discontinuities, when the residuals will include outlier or extreme values, and the autocovariance structure will be locally disrupted. Heath (1981) has exploited these properties in a diversity of psychological applications.

The relation between the coupling of the Kalman filter to a system that it does closely resemble and the parameters of the state equations in a simple form (omitting some gain and stochastic noise terms at input, for which the full model can make provision) is schematically laid out in Fig. 5.4.2.

In Fig. 5.4.2,

K_j is the Kalman gain
zI is a unit pure delay operation
L is a feedback
x_j are the state variables

and the observed input common to both system and filter is u_j. The outputs are shown.

Given that the observation equation is

$$y = Ax + v$$

then the filter generates corresponding least-squared-error estimates, y^*, such that

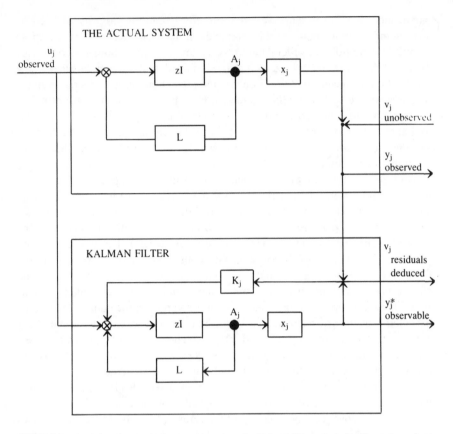

FIG. 5.4.2 A minimum-complexity representation of a Kalman filter coupled to the system whose behavior is to be predicted.

$$\mathbf{y}^* = \mathbf{L}\mathbf{y}_p + \mathbf{K}\mathbf{y} \qquad\qquad (5.4.12)$$

In (5.4.12) the $\mathbf{y}_p$ are the prior estimates of the output, derived from (5.4.11); the $\mathbf{y}$ are new data; and the $\mathbf{y}^*$ are the weighted compromise predictions (as in the lower left box of Fig. 5.4.2). As $\mathbf{L}$ is fixed, $\mathbf{K}$ is adjusted to achieve the desired result.

The $\mathbf{y}^*$ are required to be unbiased estimators of the $\mathbf{y}$ in the model, which are not directly observed. Rewriting (5.4.12) as

$$\mathbf{y}^* = \mathbf{y}_p + \mathbf{K}(\mathbf{y} - \mathbf{A}\mathbf{y}_p) \qquad\qquad (5.4.13)$$

illustrates the fact that minimizing the error in $\mathbf{K}$ will minimize the error in $\mathbf{y}^*$. The error in $\mathbf{K}$ is mathematically the posterior error covariance trace in a multivariate system, which is the sum of the leading diagonal cells of the covariance matrix generated by products like $(\mathbf{y}^* - \mathbf{y}) (\mathbf{y}^* - \mathbf{y})'$.

The algorithm has to be primed with initial values to start its recursive operation. It needs the following:

1. A vector of parameters, x_0.
2. A covariance matrix, P_0, of the parameter values.
3. A nominal estimate of the predicted residual variance, σ_0.

The predicted residual is

$$\mathbf{v}^* = \mathbf{y} - \mathbf{A}\mathbf{y}^* \tag{5.4.14}$$

and the observed residual is

$$\mathbf{v}_j = \mathbf{P}_j\mathbf{A}_j \tag{5.4.15}$$

with associated variance

$$\sigma_j = \mathbf{A}_j\mathbf{v}_j = 1 \tag{5.4.16}$$

The Kalman gain is made to take the form

$$\mathbf{K}_j = \sigma_j^{-1}\mathbf{v}_j \tag{5.4.17}$$

by definition, which as Bennett (1979) notes thus minimizes the least-squares deviation of the estimated filter $\mathbf{A}_j$ from the actual system $\mathbf{A}_j$ (see Fig. 5.4.2). Other filters use alternative criteria at this point, which may for null prior information converge upon the same parameter estimates.

From

$$\mathbf{v}_j^* = \mathbf{y}_j - \mathbf{A}\mathbf{y}_j^*$$

the state vector $\mathbf{x}$ is revised as

$$\mathbf{x}_{j+1} = \mathbf{x}_j + \mathbf{K}_j\mathbf{v}_j^* \tag{5.4.18}$$

The covariance matrix $\mathbf{P}$ has to be revised as

$$
\begin{aligned}
\mathbf{P}_{j+1} &= \mathbf{P}_j - \mathbf{K}_j\mathbf{v}_j' - \mathbf{P}_j\mathbf{A}_j\mathbf{K}_j' + \mathbf{K}_j\mathbf{v}^*\mathbf{K}_j' + \mathbf{K}_k\mathbf{K}_j' \\
&= \mathbf{P}_j(1 - \mathbf{A}_j\mathbf{K}_j') - \mathbf{K}_j(\mathbf{v}_j' + \mathbf{v}^*\mathbf{K}_j' + \mathbf{K}_j')
\end{aligned} \tag{5.4.19}
$$

Equations (5.4.18) and (5.4.19) are the output of the filter; they represent the consequences of applying a process in which the gain is finely adjusted to make a prediction of the state $\mathbf{x}$. This prediction is a compromise between linear extrapolation of the past values and the currently observed values. It can thus be taken as a model of a biological process in its own right,[4] though it has not usually been advanced in this sense.

Although the Kalman filter method has been extensively used, because it

---

[4]A biological system that has the capacity to behave like a predictive filter obviously has more survival potential than one that does not.

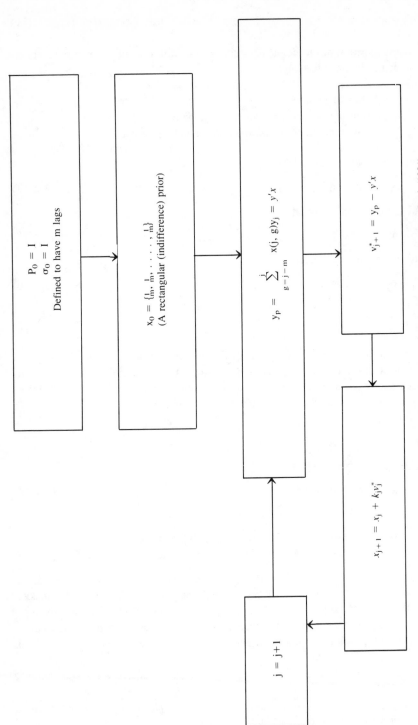

FIG. 5.4.3 Univariate Kalman filter on a purely autoregressive time series as used by Heath (1981).

The boxes in the figure contain:

$$P_0 = I$$
$$\sigma_0 = I$$
Defined to have m lags

$$x_0 = \{\tfrac{1}{m}, \tfrac{1}{m}, \ldots, \tfrac{1}{m}\}$$
(A rectangular (indifference) prior)

$$y_p = \sum_{g=j-m}^{j} x(j, g) y_j = y'x$$

$$v_{j+1}^* = y_p - y'x$$

$$x_{j+1} = x_j + k_j v_j^*$$

$$j = j + 1$$

extended time series extrapolation in the discrete case, and the idea is found incorporated into other methods, it appears to have intrinsic computational difficulties. The Kalman filter replaced the earlier Wiener filter for the two reasons, that it is in discontinuous time and that it avoids difficult computation and matrix inversion. It has been the subject of extensive research and modification, and in advanced applications such have occurred in the space flight technologies; these modifications have been discussed in detail by Bierman (1977) who gives a bibliography.

Once the Kalman filter had achieved a significant breakthrough in filtering methodology, by avoiding problems of matrix inversion and being fast enough for on-line implementation, other filters that derive from the Kalman approach were created in some profusion. Such filters underpin the connections between systems theory and time series. As yet few examples exist in experimental psychology, though the flexibility of discrete time filters and related methods make them quite appropriate for modeling otherwise intractable psychological processes, provided that those processes are purely or dominantly autoregressive.

Heath (1981) has used a simpler linear univariate model with a Kalman filter to examine, illuminatingly, the dynamics and discontinuities in heart-rate

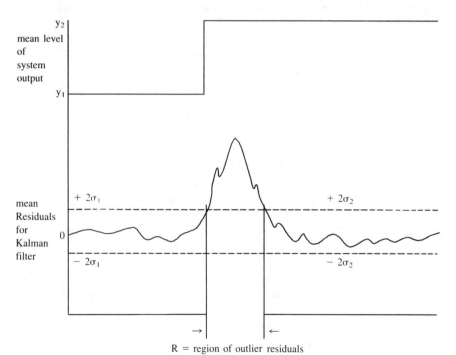

FIG. 5.4.4   Enhanced residuals near a system discontinuity.

changes, signal detection, and cognitive judgments and pattern recognition in young children. A flow diagram of this simpler case is given in Fig. 5.4.3, where the terms are defined as in the previous discussion.

The use of the random walk properties of the residual series $\{v^*\}$ to detect discontinuities is shown pictorially in Fig. 5.4.4. Its effective employment requires some stability (i.e., absence of discontinuities but not necessarily stationarity) in the initial period in order to establish a credibility interval on the step size of the random walk process.

The $\pm 2\sigma$ limits on the residuals need not be the same in the two phases shown but should be almost constant within a phase. The region R depends for its length in time on the rate of convergence of the filter back into stability after the local perturbation induced at the step input.

5.5 COMPUTABILITY AND REPLACEMENT FOR THE KALMAN FILTER

When the solution obtained from a Kalman filter is stable, then the system can be predicted and controlled; the usual objective of doing the calculation is, obviously, to achieve control within acceptable limits. If, instead of taking control as the objective, it is required to use the filtering to see if a model that presupposes a stable $\mathbf{A}$ is a valid representation of the system, then the same calculations may be run but the interest is in a post hoc comparison of predictive accuracy with model assumptions; control may not be an end in itself but only evidence that modeling is accurate. In a valid representation, given the linear assumptions of the Kalman filter, the matrix $\mathbf{A}$ is fixed, and the $\mathbf{x}$, $\mathbf{P}$ are a record of what happened under fixed $\mathbf{A}$. The contribution to theory is $\mathbf{A}$, because $\mathbf{A}$ is the major part of what is usually understood by a model of behavior in psychology, and the measure of acceptability is Err $(\mathbf{x})$. Alternative theories are alternative substitutions for $\mathbf{A}$ and the actual set of states. If $\mathbf{A}$ cannot be confirmed as stationary, then no model has been fitted.

When the filtering fails, either in a control application or, more relevantly here, in a model identification exercise, various courses are open: (1) If it is believed that the system is in fact linear and stationary, then another $\mathbf{A}$ and another filter may have to be tried, either or both can be inappropriate; (2) the nonlinearity is accepted, the system is then chopped into parts each of which is linear and resynthesized from the parts (Young, 1974); or (3) a completely nonlinear but nevertheless identifiable type of system has to be postulated, formalized, and tested.

The first two approaches are used in the technologies, of which EEG is an example perhaps most familiar to psychologists. In these two approaches, analyses are complicated and typically treated as special cases; essentially $\mathbf{A}$ has to be written as a function of time that has empirically identifiable discontinuities. It is necessary to be able to locate with some precision when strong changes in **A** happen. As Walter and Brazier (1968) wrote, we would like a model of our experiment to include a partially regular function of time. The third approach is fundamentally different and raises questions concerning the very objective of science if the shift to it is accepted. The feedback approach is tenable for systems with first-order negative feedback, in short what has been called the "cybernetic paradigm" (Sutherland, 1975); but this paradigm has become progressively less convincing as an appropriate model of biological systems. The failure of the cybernetic paradigm as a general systems model (as opposed to a model of some controllable systems where it works very well) is a question of particular importance to psychology because the cybernetic model is translatable into s–r behaviorist language and vice versa; there is an isomorphism between the two types of theory (Arbib, 1964) so that invalidation of one becomes invalidation of the other. There are systems whose properties are not deducible from negative, positive, or nth-order feedback; homeostasis is not enough. It is pertinent to remind ourselves that time series models with fixed a priori states are closed systems, whereas psychological systems outside the more circumscribed and trivially contrived laboratory situation are open; in other terminology, the psychological experiment is not a zero–sum game, and the experimenter often fails to specify the net gain or loss with respect to such aspects as entropy, information capacity, or the set of states themselves.

A problem of analysis arises when the system to be studied can be conceptualized as closed but is intrinsically so complex that only a few of its states, and the covariance of its states, can be monitored. This is the case of an open system embedded in a closed system; it epitomized quite well many problems in cognitive or physiological psychology. In such a situation the investigator who wishes to build a model of behavior may resort to a form of sampling control, where at any point in time a few states are monitored and corrected and the critical parameter then becomes the periodicity of sampling of states in the filtering. It is not fanciful to use this idea of sampled states and intermittent discrete control as a model of some processes of human learning or education, but the argument becomes diffuse without quantification of inputs and outputs. Certainly, a system that controls itself by sampling subsets of states and filtering these is at a level of complexity above the simple servocircuit; the complexity of such systems imposes limits on the speed, in real time, at which they can operate.

Questions about the realizability of systems that are more complex than a feedback loop are raised repeatedly in contemporary psychological theory, under various guises. The locus of vagueness in the feedback model is, of course, the comparator itself. The sorts of errors or disparities between input and output that cannot be anticipated or detected and corrected for at an adequate speed are the errors that invalidate the feedback model. If data show that a subject, in a task, is correcting up to a point for all the errors created in the experiment by the imperfect control or prediction that he himself exercises, then the cybernetic model is potentially viable. If the subject cannot correct for some of his or her own errors, then the model fails, at least in part, but we are free to look for regularities that will predict, at some other level, the nature and extent of failures in control. This ideal is not often attained; it is true that many of the difficulties in psychology begin with the fundamental problem that the input and output variables are not well quantified, but this of itself is insufficient to explain the poor impact that cybernetic thinking has had in psychology since the efforts of Miller, Galanter, and Pribram (1965) with TOTE theory. This generalization does not, of course, extend to Soviet psychologists (Lefebvre & Batchelder, 1981; Leontiev, Luriya, & Smirnov, 1966). Cybernetic models in which variables are fuzzy are feasible but as yet little explored, whereas speculative models in which variables are not even quantified fuzzily but loops are piled hierarchically upon loops proliferate with seeming abandon. Such heuristic models are utterly unanalyzable, so there is no point in reviewing them.

The problem of where, in practice, it is legitimate to reject a linear feedback model and go for the more variable representation discussed in Section 5.6 is not so simple; it is not just a case of finding that a linear model cannot cope and replacing it, there may be technical defects in the attempted data analysis. Akaike (1976) has reviewed some of the simple problems of autocorrelation analysis that might pertinently arise in a time series experiment, in which alternative models have to be compared.

Models for special sorts of nonstationarity, deriving from the Kalman filter approach, have been derived in a number of cases where special applications and relevant empirical knowledge concerning the likely form of nonstationarities make this feasible. One approach that has been used in EEG analysis and that can be compared in its efficiency with FFT analysis has been developed in detail by Bohlin (1976). It has a number of interesting features that show well the necessary interplay between model structure and interpretation on the one hand and prior knowledge of the general sequential features of typical data on the other.

The parameters of the model are allowed to vary linearly with time, in a form that may be put as

$$\boldsymbol{\theta}_{j+1} = \boldsymbol{\phi}_j \boldsymbol{\theta}_j + \mathbf{w}_{1j} \tag{5.5.1}$$

$$\mathbf{Y}_j = \mathbf{H}_j \boldsymbol{\theta}_j + \mathbf{w}_{2j} \tag{5.5.2}$$

where the output is the vector $\mathbf{y}$ at time j, the parameter vector is $\boldsymbol{\theta}$, and it is the parameter vector varying in time (in defined and permitted ways) that constitutes the fundamental departure from the simplest case of Section 5.4. The vectors $\mathbf{w}_1$ and $\mathbf{w}_2$ are random normal; Bohlin (1976) comments that the fact that the coefficient matrices can be functions, not necessarily linear, of past inputs and outputs is not generally known, but it is valid to use (5.5.2) as a description of the process dynamics and to use (5.5.1) to describe the parameter variation in time. To begin estimation of the process, it is necessary to use approximate estates of ϕ and the covariance matrix R on the outputs and covariance of rates of change of the parameters. This may only mean, in practice, knowing that the parameters vary very slowly as compared with the output variations.

The autocovariance structure of the $\mathbf{w}_1$ and $\mathbf{w}_2$ is denoted by $\mathbf{R}_1$ and $\mathbf{R}_2$, respectively. The rate of change of the parameters θ is to be estimated in an average sense over some extended period, and the parameter that represents the assumed average rate of change of θ_i is μ_i. This μ_i and the vector μ play a central role in the modeling of nonstationarity. The investigator is faced with deciding what ϕ, $\mathbf{H}$, $\mathbf{R}_1$, and $\mathbf{R}_2$ should be like and what physical variables should be represented in the system. As Bohlin (1976) succinctly puts it, the physical problem, the purpose, and a priori information are given in an unstructured way; the mathematical framework is set by the problems we can conveniently solve; and our task is to squeeze as much as possible out of the former with the latter.

Once having set up a model, the nonstationarity has to be captured as accurately as possible by minimizing an expression in the residuals, where the coefficients of the expression themselves vary stochastically. This is

$$e_j + a_{1j}e_{j-1} + \cdots + a_{nj}e_{j-n} = b_{1j}u_{j-1} + \cdots + b_{mj}u_{j-m} + k_j + w_{2j}$$
(5.5.3)

to express this relation in the form of (5.5.1) and (5.5.2), put e for y; for simplification, consider the case where e is a scalar and then the matrix product $\mathbf{H}\theta$ becomes a vector product in which

$$H_j = (-e_j, \ldots, -e_{j-n}u_{j-1}, \ldots, u_{j-m}1)$$
(5.5.4)

and

$$\theta'_j = (a_{1j}, \ldots, a_{nj}b_{1j}, \ldots, b_{mj}k_j)$$
(5.5.5)

In this representation, if the a priori assumptions hold, the parameters in θ will be zero; if the assumptions do not hold, then the residuals will be intercorrelated, and the model has accordingly to be modified in real time to adjust continually the estimations until the required result is achieved. Setting up a nonstationary model implied two related problems, predicting a few trials ahead, which turns out to be relatively easy, and estimating the model parameters, which is considerably more difficult and involves recursive estimation through a system of equations more complex than the Kalman filter but embodying the latter. In practice this recursive estimation is to be done on-line, while data are coming in, and so there has to be a trade-off between speed and fidelity. This trade-off is achieved by imposing an upper limit on the fraction of data that can be used, either by taking short blocks of data spaced in time or by adjusting the sampling interval (the trial length, effectively, in seconds), denoted by h.

In using nonstationary modeling of the form (5.5.1), (5.5.2), the matrices $\mathbf{R}_1$ and $\mathbf{R}_2$ play key roles, and $\mathbf{R}_1$ in fact is involved in an intricate fashion because it does three things at once: specifies the average rate of change of the parameters

θ, affects tracking ability of the algorithm by controlling the rate at which past data are forgotten in estimating future data, and affects the current accuracy of estimation. R_2 can be interpreted as the variance of the one-trial-ahead prediction error of the behavior of the system when its parameters are known; when noise is of high frequency and can be prefiltered out before the algorithm operates, then R_2 is unimportant.

The case of EEG analysis is relatively tractable because we know in advance that the frequency spectrum is mostly in the range 2 Hz to 25 Hz, and the gradual changes of the parameters of the system are of much lower frequency. Signals with greater than 30-Hz frequency can be readily prefiltered, and the characteristics of the commoner transients, such as so-called spikes, can be described approximately. In other words, the sort of description achieved qualitatively by visual inspection of long EEG records under a diversity of conditions provide us with grosser hypotheses to put bounds on the probable spectral forms of signals, transients, and nonstationarities. If the approach discussed here is to be extended to other sorts of psychological data, then a comparable familiarity with such features is obviously desirable. Zetterburg (1969) proposed then the EEG might be sensibly modeled as

$$y_j + \cdots + a_n y_{j-n} = \lambda \ [w_j + \cdots + c_m w_{j-m}] + k \qquad (5.5.6)$$

under stationarity with constant sampling interval of h. The constant λ is a scaling factor; the sets of coefficients $\{a\}$ and $\{c\}$ are also the coefficients of the z transforms $A(z)$ and $C(z)$, respectively.

The interest is in the power spectrum

$$S(f) = \lambda^2 h \left| \frac{C(z) \ (\exp 2\pi i f h)}{A(z) \ (\exp 2\pi i f h)} \right|^2 \qquad (5.5.7)$$

which approximates a continuous spectrum in the range $0 < f < \frac{1}{2}h$. The conceptual device introduced here is the key to the analysis; (5.5.7) approximates what is required with the quotient of two polynomials, but it could be approximated equally well (provided that we tolerate a few more terms) by a single polynomial. So, it is permissible to let the EEG spectrum itself be characterized by the $A(z)$ polynomial only, and let the $C(z)$ polynomial be common to all the signals in the system, with the EEG thought of as embedded in the totality of signals. Then the $\{a\}$ and k in (5.5.6) are allowed to vary randomly with time, and this generates a model in which four recursive relations hold:

$$e_j + a_{1j} e_{j-1} + \cdots + a_{nj} e_{j-n} = \lambda w_{0j} + k_j \qquad (5.5.8)$$

$$a_{ij} = a_i(j-1) + \mu w_{ij} \qquad (5.5.9)$$

$$k_j = k_{j-1} + \mu_1 w_{n+1(j)} \qquad (5.5.10)$$

$$y_j = e_j + c_1 e_{j-1} + \ldots + c_m e_{j-m} \qquad (5.5.11)$$

where the w_{ij} are independent sequences of uncorrelated variates $\sim N(0, 1)$, that is, white noise input.

In effect, here one particular nonstationary EEG is being specified from among the set of all nonstationary EEGs with the same class of model as (5.5.6), and this specification is achieved by the coefficients $\{a\}$. The variability in time of the parameter set $\{a\}$, k has to be chosen to be much less than the signal variability; that is, the spectrum of $\{a\}$ and k is in a frequency range much below that of the EEG being modeled. The parameter μ in (5.5.9) expresses how the power spectrum changes slowly with time, such as occurs when the eyes are opened for a while and then closed again, and the amount of activity in the range around 10 Hz changes. The parameter μ_1 in (5.5.10) is a model constant and not a part of the EEG. As the model (5.5.6) stands, the parameters $\{a\}$ are not interpretable at all simply in physical terms, and as the whole object of the nonstationary analysis is to obtain parameters that more obviously relate to putative physical events in the brain, it is more reasonable to redefine the power spectrum so that it is based on a local sample (called an ensemble in some texts) rather than an average over an extended time span, as is more usual. This entails the revision of (5.5.7) as, locally at j,

$$S(f:j) = \lambda^2 h \left| \frac{\mathbf{C}(z)\ (\exp\ 2\pi i f h)}{\mathbf{A}(z)\ (\exp\ 2\pi i f h:j)} \right|^2 \tag{5.5.12}$$

which, defined in this way, makes the estimates depend only on the very recent properties of the output series.

There are various estimation tasks to be done in order to obtain a description of the process: estimation of $\{a\}$ and k, which requires that a rule for the rejection of local transients from the data record is available; interpretation of the physical bases of the process, which implies computing (5.5.12) given n, m, $\{c\}$, $\{a_j\}$, and λ, and estimating the extent of nonstationarity itself for which λ, μ, and μ_1 are required. As μ_1 is the rate of change of k, the low-frequency disturbances, it is set greater than zero only when prefiltering is considered to be expedient.

Bohlin (1976) points out that it is preferable to have a measure of nonstationarity that is independent of scale, and this is given by

$$d = r \cdot m \cdot s \cdot (y) \cdot \mu/\lambda \tag{5.5.13}$$

for which a maximum-likelihood estimation procedure is available, in terms of recursive functions of $\mathbf{R}_{yy}$ and $\hat{\mathbf{Y}}$, the covariance and estimations of the output, respectively.

As much of the previous work in this area had advocated the use of fast Fourier transforms to obtain the spectral decomposition of the EEG, the differences between the nonstationary (5.5.12) and the FFT should be noted. With an FFT it is possible to sample at a much higher rate, but the accuracy is inferior because it assumes stationarity, and the sample length has to be long, say 128 or 256 trials in discrete time. In contradistinction the method of (5.5.13) can use samples as short as 20 trials, which appears to be near the limit on what is possible.

Summarizing this section, the use of nonstationary autoregressive series is expedient when it is difficult to realize stationarity, which for most psychological experiments would be the case, when the characteristics of a record change suddenly and spontaneously in time or when a change in the process is introduced by the stimuli and the transient course of the change is the object of interest.

5.6 BAYES FILTERS AND THE ABANDONMENT OF STATIONARITY RESTRICTIONS

One of the most powerful, and conceptually different but related, ways of treating the prediction problem, the Bayesian forecasting of Harrison and Stevens (1976) is selected for discussion because its flexibility matches the irregularities that can beset psychological data and thus defy more conventional representations. Harrison and Stevens begin with the observation that real-time series in large-scale noisy situations, such as businesses, have large inbuilt discontinuities and that practitioners in the technologies or in marketing realistically expect and exploit such discontinuities; it is a mark of professional competence to use such information in the policy sciences. The difference in scale from the typical psychological laboratory is obvious, but if a completely general model, to map such discontinuities, is to be constructed, then its objectives encompass at least some of the modeling problems that are, in principle, found in the laboratory. The algebra of discontinuous time series is a priori uninterpreted, and there is no fundamental objection to giving it a psychological interpretation, though the subsequent identification problems may be unusual. To set up a general model is, by the correspondence principle, to set up a model from which the well-behaved linear time series already discussed can be derived as special cases. If it had been desired to have been completely abstract, one could have started this monograph with the general abstract case and imposed constraint after constraint until the simplest case was finally reached, thus passing psychological data coming up as the theory went down, so to speak. The whole objective of modeling is to restrict abstract general cases to a level of simplicity commensurate with data properties of interest, and those same data properties increase in complexity with successively more refined instrumentation in each generation.

Models underlying discontinuous time series are state space models; for example, Harrison and Stevens (1976) remark that the sequential relation

$$2y_j = 3y_{j-1} - y_{j-2} \quad \text{for } j = 1, 2, \ldots \qquad (5.6.1)$$

can arise from the simultaneous equations

$$y_j = m_j$$

$$m_j = 0.5m_{j-1} + b_j \qquad (5.6.2)$$

$$b_j = b_{j-1}$$

where m and b are the parameters of mean level and trend in recent time, respectively. But (5.6.1) can be generated as the realization of other models besides (5.6.2); that is, (5.6.2) is not identifiable from (5.6.1). Typically we should be faced with the problem of choosing between alternatives (5.6.2) even if (5.6.1) is a valid functional relation within the series $\{y_j\}$.

The parameters of the model could be redefined stochastically, as in (5.6.3), and thus come closer to reality. But this can have as a consequence that the state parameters are never identifiable. It might be thought that this is a fundamental objection, but Harrison and Stevens (1976) show that in some cases the predictability of a system can be achieved (at least in the near future) even if it states are never identified. The control of behavior, in the empirical sense that has interested some behaviorists, can be achieved locally in time without having identified sufficient of the structure of a process to achieve a description in the dynamic sense. This is a reconfirmation, in formal terms, of a conclusion reached earlier.

The stochastic equivalent of the example of (5.6.2) is

$$y_j = j_m + e_j$$

$$j_m = 0.5m_{j-1} + b_j + \delta m_j \qquad (5.6.3)$$

$$b_j = b_{j-1} + \delta b_j$$

where var (e), $E(\delta m)$, var (δm), $E(\delta b)$, and var (δb) are known at time j but are not necessarily fixed for all j.

In forecasting y_j values (which is the empirical problem of interest to applied statisticians), prediction involves moving from $\{y_1, \ldots, y_j\}$ to $\{m_j, b_j\}$ and thence from $\{m_j, b_j\}$ to $\{y_{j+1}, \ldots, y_{j+k}\}$. Various ancillary assumptions have to be made about the costs of error in prediction and what has to be minimized in making predictions.

The important relaxations of the traditional approach achieved here, which completely upsets the standpoint usually adopted in psychological applications of control theory, are as follows:

1. The observed series is no longer stationary (the δm and the δb can change with time, and may do so erratically).

2. The predictions involve the stochastic parameters and the latter are not constrainted to be linear functions of the $\{y_1, \ldots, y_j\}$.

3. Importantly, the influence of single wild observations or transients may be diminished, in which case the criterion of optimal prediction is not that of least-square errors.

A dynamic linear model (DLM) is set up, incorporating the Kalman filter but at the same time relaxing some of the assumptions that were originally embodied in its use. This DLM is not directly translatable from the form used to introduce the Kalman filter at (5.4.10); to be nearly comparable it has to be written in three steps:

$$\mathbf{z}_j = \mathbf{A}\mathbf{x}_j + \mathbf{e}_j \tag{5.6.4}$$

$$\boldsymbol{\theta}_j = \mathbf{G}\boldsymbol{\theta}_{j-1} + \mathbf{w}_j \tag{5.6.5}$$

and

$$\mathbf{x}_j = \boldsymbol{\theta}_j\mathbf{x}_{j-1} + \mathbf{v}_j \tag{5.6.6.}$$

where Equation (5.6.6) may be noted to be a Markovian property on $\{x\}$ if $\boldsymbol{\theta}_j = \boldsymbol{\theta}$ = a constant. The $\mathbf{w}_j$ and $\mathbf{v}_j$ are random normal vectors. Harrison and Stevens (1976) telescope Equations (5.6.4) and (5.6.6) into, effectively,

$$\mathbf{z}_j = \mathbf{F}_j\mathbf{v}_j + \mathbf{v}_j \tag{5.6.7}$$

but now, except in the restricted case where the $\mathbf{F}_j$ is fixed this $\mathbf{F}_j$ no longer can have the same interpretation as the matrix $\mathbf{A}$ ($m \times n$) in the previous Kalman model, though it is, of course, still ($m \times n$). The change arises because in the usual Kalman algorithm the matrix $\mathbf{A}$ may, if desired, be written as $\mathbf{A} = f(t)$ to account for gradual time trends that are potentially identifiable and interpretable, but not as $\mathbf{A} = f(z_1, z_2, \ldots, z_{j-1}, t)$. Here however $\mathbf{F}_j$ can be written as $\mathbf{F}_j = f(z_1, z_2, \ldots, z_{j-1}, t)$ and in the case of an autoregressive time series would be so expressed. The evolution of $\mathbf{z}$ is thus concealed within the changes in $\mathbf{F}_j$ and to make things more complex the evolution of $\boldsymbol{\theta}_j$, which is specified by $\mathbf{G}$ in (5.6.5), also must be considered.

Thus, the extension of the original filter ideas to the model in (5.6.4)–(5.6.6) is an extension in depth; the model is in a sense hierarchical because stochastic changes depend in their turn on other stochastic changes, and one has to go one step further from the observable data relationships before a linear model with some fixed parameter, $\mathbf{G}$, is found. This has metatheoretical implications that have not, as yet, been fully worked out; if invariance is sought in a representation of a psychological process, then the success of the DLM models suggests that such invariance should be sought at a level further removed from data and observables than many psychologists, raised in the tradition of so-called operational definitions, have been accustomed to look.

Standard forms of time series models, dealing with a steady state, autoregression, linear growth, or moving averaging, can be shown to be subsumable under the DLM paradigm. However, such standard models are often of greater interest to economists than to experimental psychologists and it is a different aspect of the DLM that is pertinent. Clearly the DLM is a general case that might model the transient discontinuities so readily observed in the microstructure of a psychological experiment. The momentary distraction from a series of judgments when a slide jams in the experimenter's projector or a door slams in an adjacent room could be modeled in their effects instead of being hopefully ignored, though in honesty one often lacks the theoretical insight to know what to do with such analyses if one had them. Here forecasting has run ahead of the conceptual demands implicitly placed on an experiment, because experimental design as the psychologist understands it has so long been predicated on assumptions of a well-controlled steady-state environment, at least during the duration of an experiment. Anything else has been labeled, apologetically, a quasi-experiment. The irony is that the emergence of models such as the DLM might be interpreted as justification for suggesting that the quasi-experiments, coupled with the DLM and extended in time, are the real experiments of psychology.

More precisely, in principle there are, at any point in an experiment, conflicting predictions as to what will happen next, and some of these conflicts are not trivial. A potentially informative experiment is one in which there is uncertainty on at least a subset of trials, concerning which model obtains from a finite set of models we can postulate, none of which may be adequate. Harrison and Stevens (1976) write:

> One of the advantages of using a DLM is that at any time, $t - 1$, the only information required to forecast an observation at the next period, t, is a DLM which describes the evolution of the process in the time interval $(t - 1, t)$ together with the probability distribution of the relevant parameters $(\theta_{t-1} \{y_1, \ldots, y_{t-1}\})$. It is thus clear that the DLM used to describe the evolution of the process at one time can be different from that used by the modeller at other times; this is a very important feature of the Bayesian approach [p. 224].

In this situation a multistate model, where any one state is a model $M^{(k)}$, 1, 2, ..., k, ..., N, and the transition between states is governed by a matrix of one-state transition probabilities, covers the general case. It is interesting that in adopting this definition of the multistate model we have come to a theoretical position that resembles in some ways that adopted by mathematical learning theorists such as Restle who used Markov chains with subjective hypotheses as states in seeking representations of concept learning; the big difference here is that the states are models of some complexity, and each state is definable by

$$M_j^{(k)} = \{F_j, G, V_j^{(k)}, W_j^{(k)}\} \tag{5.6.8}$$

where the V and W terms are known at time j. The transition matrix between states, given that π_{kk*} is the posterior probability of being in $k*$ given that the system is initially in k, is

p_{kk*} with an associated state vector p

Only situations in which these probabilities and transition probabilities are time-independent are presently anything like tractable.[5] Some success in the identification of alternative autoregressive models has been achieved by Akaike (1974) and Shibata (1976) using information theory measures. A review of such methods applied to discrete series is given by Akaike (1976); it is of interest here to summarize Akaike's procedure for choosing a best representation of a time series, though the full analysis in terms of canonical forms with minimum possible order is beyond our introductory treatment.

5.7   IDENTIFICATION IN THE AUTOREGRESSIVE CASE

In fitting an autoregressive model to a single time series of outputs y_j, where the input series x_j is a realization of a normal random variable, for lag k,

$$\text{cov }(k) = N^{-1} \sum_{j=1}^{N-k} y_{j-k} \cdot y_j \qquad (5.7.1)$$

and the autoregressive estimation of the coefficients $\hat{v}_k$ in the relation

$$y_j + y_{j-1} \cdot v_1 + y_{j-2} \cdot v_2 + \cdots + y_{j-M} \cdot v_m = x_j$$

is essentially the same process as estimating the sample convariances cov (k) for $k = 1, 2, 3, \ldots, M$. The estimates $\hat{v}_k$ are completely specified by the values of the first $M + 1$ cov (k), so the accuracy of the estimators is critically dependent on the chosen M that the investigator selects in order to perform an analysis. So, unless the value of M is specified a priori, the process of model fitting is not well defined, but as seen already (Chapter 3) we must properly use ancillary information, that M is not in a psychological context likely to be large and that the sequence $\{\text{cov }(k)\}$ should degenerate rapidly with increasing k; both these conditions impose bounds on the plausibility of solutions. This however leaves unsolved the formal problems of finding a best point estimate of M, given that some real constant M exists. The choice of M is not trivial because M is related to the form of the implicit dynamic model.

Akaike (1976) proceeds as follows: First, assume a model that specifies $f(x|\theta)$ with parameter θ and then find a maximum likelihood estimate of θ, say $\hat{\theta}$, by maximizing L with respect to θ where, by definition,

$$L(x_1, x_2, \ldots, x_N | \theta) = \prod_{j=1}^{N} f(x_j | \theta) \qquad (5.7.2)$$

---

[5]However, extensions of theory to other classes of models, with state-dependent parameters, is an active area. See Priestley (1980) and Young (1978).

In practice it is expedient to work with $\log_e L$, so   [compare (5.7.1)]

$$\ln L = N^{-1} \sum_{j=1}^{N} \ln f(x_j|\theta) \tag{5.7.3}$$

There is a parallel between information measures and likelihood measures that can be exploited to facilitate the argument; the value of θ, which maximizes $\ln L$, say θ_L, also minimizes an expression, called Kullback's information quantity, which is, where $g^*(x)$ is a model,

$$I_L = \int \ln \left(\frac{g^*(x)}{f(x|\theta)} \right) \cdot g^*(x)dx \tag{5.7.4}$$

This I_L is a measure of the likelihood of obtaining $g^*(x)$ as the identified model of the system when the true situation is $f(x|\theta)$. Now it can be shown that if there are several competing models, then a quantity called the AIC (average information content) is to be minimized in order to select the most appropriate model. The

$$AIC = -2(\text{max } \ln L) + 2(\text{number of independently adjusted parameters in the model used}) \tag{5.7.5}$$

and an ancillary rule is immediately necessary, namely, that if two or more models have the same AIC, then the model with fewest free parameters should be chosen.

Because of the relation between (5.7.3) and (5.7.4), and the difficulty of deriving (5.7.3) in time series due to the complexity of the analytic treatment required, Akaike (1976) proceeds via (5.7.4) to develop estimates of the Kullback measure and thence works toward an AIC. For example, consider the case (Akaike, 1976) of fitting an autoregressive model to a single time series, as previously mentioned. We begin by assuming that the order of the process is M; so

$$y_j + a_1 \cdot y_{j-1} + \cdots + a_k \cdot y_{j-k} + \cdots + a_M \cdot y_{j-M} = x_j \tag{5.7.6}$$

where $\{x_j\}$ is a sequence of independent normal random variables, with $E(x) = 0$, var $(x) = C$, cov $(x_j, y_{j-k}) = 0$ for all k. Also note that $a_0 = 1$ by definition. Let j denote the vector $(\{a_k\}, C)$; then if N is the length of the data sample, the estimate of I_L may be defined as

$$\hat{I}_L = -\frac{1}{2} \cdot \ln (2\pi C) - (2C)^{-1} \sum_{k=0}^{M} \sum_{k'=0}^{M} a_k a_{k'} \text{ cov } (k - k') \tag{5.7.7}$$

where

$$\text{cov } (k) = N^{-1} \sum_{j-1}^{N-k} y_{j+k} y_j \qquad \text{for } k = 0, 1, 2, \ldots, M \tag{5.7.8}$$

and

$$\text{cov } (k) = \text{cov } (-k) \qquad \text{for all } k \tag{5.7.9}$$

It is required to select the coefficients $\hat{a}_k$ that maximize $\hat{l}_L$. [These $\hat{a}_k$ clearly parallel the $\hat{v}_k$ used in previous LTF forms; but as here the input–output relations are defined as in (5.7.6), it is clearer to preserve the distinction.] The required coefficients are obtained by solving

$$\text{cov } (k'_v) = -\sum_{k=1}^{M} \hat{a}_k \cdot \text{cov } (k'_v - k) \qquad k' = 1, 2, \ldots, M \tag{5.7.10}$$

and

$$\hat{C} = \text{cov } (0) + \sum_{k+1}^{M} a_k \cdot \text{cov } (-k) \tag{5.7.11}$$

Two simple cases are tractable and interesting.

A unidimensional case in which two or more autoregressive models of different orders, say, M, M^*, are compared can be shown to reduce to a very simple form of *AIC* that for each model is

$$AIC = N \cdot \ln (\hat{C}) + 2M \tag{5.7.12}$$

In the multivariate case, where y_j has t dimensions, the autoregressive model of order M requires to be defined by the set of matrices $\{A_m\}$ and C each of order $t \times t$, where C is the covariance matrix of the t-dimensional multivariate normal x_j.

It is now necessary to redefine

$$C(k) = N^{-1} \sum_{j=1}^{N-k} y_{j+k} y'_j \qquad k = 0, 1, 2, \ldots, M \qquad \begin{matrix} (5.7.13) \\ (\text{c.f. } 5.7.6) \end{matrix}$$

$$C(-k) = C(k) \qquad\qquad\qquad\qquad\qquad\qquad \begin{matrix} (5.7.14) \\ (\text{c.f. } 5.7.9) \end{matrix}$$

and the *AIC* associated is

$$AIC = N \cdot \ln (\det (\hat{C})) + 2Mt^2 \tag{5.7.15}$$

The *AIC* measure has been shown by subsequent workers to rest on an incomplete analysis and thus possibly to lead to misidentification of the order or structure of a process. Wyman (1976) offers a criterion to be minimized that has four terms, thus being an extension of Akaike's (1976) criterion and incorporating it. The development is too complex to review here but rests on dividing the criterion expression into terms that are parameter dependent and terms that are structure dependent. By a stepwise algorithm it could be possible to minimize both parts in turn, convergent upon an overall solution. The formal nonexistence of a single global solution to this identification problem having been established, it seems that iterative numerical methods are imperative.

Kashyap (1979, 1980) shows that the *AIC* rule is inconsistent for estimating the unknown order of a time series that is compatible with an autoregressive form. He showed that the lower bound on the probability of error of identification when the sample size, n, is large, is 0.156, and the situation does not improve with n tending to infinity. Thus the *AIC* rule is not consistent in this case.

An alternative that appears to be related to the *AIC* but is conceptually and computationally better behaved has been advanced by Rissanen (1978, 1979); it is safer to use in autoregressive identification. It is the shortest data description approach, in which by finding a model with minimum length one finds simultaneously estimates of both integer-valued structure parameters and real-valued system parameters. The results resemble another criterion devised by Schwartz (1978) from a Bayesian analysis of posterior model probabilities. The Rissanen approach penalizes strongly the overparametrization of a model and so by comparison with the *AIC* should yield simpler representations.

Maklad and Nichols (1980) offer further criticism of the *AIC* and develop an alternative criterion, *COMP,* which is more versatile and powerful but more laborious to compute. This alternative satisfies by a compromise two criteria at once, that the residual time series after fitting a model should be white noise and that the parameters should be accurately estimated. *COMP* involves calculating the parameter covariance matrix, the autocorrelation of residuals, and a comparison of the variance of these autocorrelations with the observed values. It has two strong advantages; it can compare linear and nonlinear models, and it can predict in absolute terms the residual of a satisfactory model of a given order for a data series of fixed length. This the *AIC* does not do.

Identifying Volterra models (Section 2.5) can in simple cases be achieved by a related method due to Kaya and Ishikawa (1971). Woodside (1971) also gives some results for linear system order estimation.

5.8 A NOTE ON THE SHANNON–GELFAND–YAGLOM INFORMATION MEASURE

The idea of using information as in (5.7.4) to decide if a process has been correctly identified derives from some fundamental results in information theory due to Shannon, and their subsequent extension by two Russian workers, Gelfand and Yaglom (1959). Intuitively, the idea is to represent the nearness of two spectral densities by a measure of the amount of information about one that is predicted from the other. Shannon originally considered the cases of Gaussian and white noise signals in information channels; the ideas are extendable to provide a way of evaluating the value of transfer functions in continuous time, which has some application in neurophysiological studies of the psychophysics of acoustics, for example. The results briefly noted here are thus given in the frequency domain but could be paralleled with z transforms.

Consider the system represented in the frequency domain by

$$Y(f) = H(f) \cdot X(f) + E(f) \qquad (5.8.1)$$

where $y(j)$ would be the output vector, dimension s; $x(j)$ the input vector, dimension r; and $e(j)$ is uncorrelated noise.

At frequency f we may write spectral density matrices, which are effectively covariance matrices in the frequency domain, as

$$\mathbf{S}_{yx}(f), \qquad \mathbf{S}_{yy}(f), \qquad \mathbf{S}_{xx}(f) \quad \text{and} \quad \mathbf{S}_{ee}(f)$$

It can be shown that the residual $\mathbf{S}_{e^*e^*}(f)$ has a spectral density given by

$$\mathbf{S}_{e^*e^*}(f) = \mathbf{S}_{yy}(f) - \mathbf{S}_{yx}(f) \cdot \mathbf{S}\bar{x}\,\hat{x}(f) \cdot \mathbf{S}_{yx}(f)^{cct} \qquad (5.8.2)$$

where cct denotes the complex conjugate transpose of the matrix $\mathbf{S}_{yx}(f)$.[6]

The S–G–Y information measure of the information in $x(j)$ about $y(j)$ is

$$I(y(j)|x(j)) = \int_{-1/2}^{+1/2} \ln \frac{|\mathbf{S}_{yy}(f)|}{|\mathbf{S}_{e^*e^*}(f)|}\, df \qquad (5.8.3)$$

where the terms within the parallel rules in the integral are determinants of the spectral density matrix of the contaminated output and the residual. The formula (5.8.3) is a generalization of one given by Shannon. If $r = s = 1$, then the system has one input and one output, and (5.8.3) reduces to the simpler form

$$I(y(j)|x(j)) = - \int_{-1/2}^{+1/2} \ln (1 - \omega^2(f))\, df \qquad (5.8.4)$$

where $\omega^2(f)$ is the square of the spectral coherence at frequency f (see Section 4.4 for definitions) and is

$$\omega^2(f) = \frac{|\mathbf{S}_{yx}(f)|^2}{\mathbf{S}_{yy}(f) \cdot \mathbf{S}_{xx}(f)} \qquad (5.8.5)$$

which resembles a correlation coefficient. See also Baram and Sandell (1978). A multivariate extension applied to EEG identification is given by Gersch, Yonemoto and Naitoh (1977).

---

[6]For a definition of the complex conjugate transpose of a matrix whose elements are themselves complex numbers, see, for example, Robinson (1967). See also Section 2.9.

6
Extensions into Complex or Nonstationary Processes

6.1 PREDICTION OF BEHAVIOR AND LEARNING

Time series analysis as an area of applied statistics arose in part because of a need for accurate prediction at varying distances into the future; indeed much work in time series in higher dimensions, such as mappings onto the surface of a sphere, arise in weather forecasting. The mathematics are specialized, difficult for a beginner, and have no immediately obvious psychological application (Mendel & Gieseking, 1971). But describing the autocorrelated structure in detail from a series of data points, univariate or multivariate, is not an end in itself even though it provides insights about how a system functions that are not available from direct inspection nor from static analysis. Reducing a messy record to a partitioning of stationary components, linearly or nonlinearly added, and a residual independent noise, is a means of "getting a handle" on process structure in order to increase our confidence in statements about what will happen next, or some time ahead.

The sciences where the payoffs for accurate forecasting are huge include engineering, economics, and medicine; consequently many developments in the forecasting applications of time series (Montgomery & Johnson, 1976) were developed in the first two and applied in the third subsequently. So reasons why psychology lags in the use of time series analysis must be sought not in the quality of psychological data, which are often as well-behaved and scaled or better as much of the information that engineers, economists, or medical researchers use—indeed it is sometimes the same data put to different use—but in the relative sparsity of prediction in psychology. Many psychological studies stop with description or predict in terms of a criterion level but not in terms of the detailed time course of future behavior. For example, we may use an intelligence test to predict future scholastic performance at a series of points in time where examinations are to be taken; one may predict the proportion, from an original cohort, of students who will pass and go on or fail and stop at each successive examination. The information is used to plan educational funding and resources in a centrally planned economy. But to some extent the predictions are unfalsifiable because the pass or admission rate at each successive step can be adjusted to match resources in competition with other demands upon those resources, these exogenous criteria dominate the need to verify predictions made at the start of the exercise.

It is thus rare for a record of intellectual development in a single individual to be kept, say, longitudinally at 6-month intervals for a child from age 7 to 17, and then predicted performance on these data compared with achievement data on the same individual at 6-month intervals from ages 17 to 27. This can in principle be done, at a cost; one of the reasons it is not done is that the intelligence growth curves flatten out in late adolescence and do not move very interestingly thereafter. Also, an individual moves from an educational to a working environment and the environmental variables later are supposed to matter more; their variance will swamp that due to an extrapolation of earlier processes within the individual.

The breakdown of the antithesis between description and prediction, loosely paralleled by interpolation and extrapolation, was established mathematically by the filtering methods of Kalman and Bucy and/or Harrison and Stevens, described in Chapter 5; it may be remarked that the distinction would not have persisted so long in psychology if Bayesian methods in statistics had been sooner and more extensively used where appropriate. It is no longer meaningful, once time series methods are adopted, to regard the building of models of behavior as directed exclusively to either description or prediction. Prediction by interpolation and by extrapolation are both methods of model testing, as also is filtering into the immediate future. Forecasting into the remote future is both a basis of decision making now and of delayed confirmatory analysis, of both the prediction and of the appropriateness of the decision. The data to test interpolation and filtering predictions are in principle available when the prediction is made; they are held in abeyance to test the prediction as a stage in recursive parameter estimation. The established technique of fitting a model to half the data and checking it on the other half (by first splitting the data randomly into halves) is a precursor to the full method of recursive estimation, where each new datum or data vector on the next trial is incorporated by a filter to update the parameters in a provisionally identified model. When this degree of recursive revision is attained, estimation and prediction have been quasi-continuously treated as parts of one process, but the long-range forecasting is still available as another exercise by the investigator. Using data recursively at the moment of generation to revise and update a model does not exclude that same data from also being the basis of forecasting. Rather the contrary, it optimizes forecasting but the forecasts are under continuous revision even if they are not seen much to change. With recursive estimation goes recursive forecasting; the recursion of filter prediction is based on data as they are immediately to hand, but the forecasting is not confirmed until the predicted event arrives and intermediary recursive forecasting may in fact never be used as a decision basis though it is in principle available.

The accuracy of prediction decreases with future extension in a process that is stochastic and stationary; it can decrease even more for one that is determinate and nonstationary; it will decrease even more for one that is stochastic and nonstationary, unless fortuitously the process meanders back to where the nearest deterministic process would have reached. Random walks meander back to their origin under some conditions, but the prediction of such an arrival is not considered the result of statistical insight; on the contrary, knowing the expected distribution of such arrivals in time, and the attendant uncertainty of an arrival in any one time segment is a sufficient description of the process.

If a model is fitted to a part series, then the credibility intervals on future predictions generally widen monotonically as we extrapolate further and further into the future. We can, using the methods of dynamic root identification (Sections 3.4 and 6.3), break up a time series into predictable components, periodic or divergent–convergent (usually exponential functions of time) that will assist in extending the more precise prediction into the future; but the residual error variance is still the basis for a random walk with its consequent divergent credibility intervals.

The best that can be done is to reduce the variance (or step sizes) of the random walk relative to the predictable variance (process amplitude or range). There are, however, exceptions to this; if a process has a nominated target at all times between now and the future point in time to which prediction is to be made *and* it is internally self-correcting, error minimizing in the sense of Section 4.4, or even a Kalman filter (Section 5.4), then it obviously can be predicted at all stages. A complete future forecast is available from now until the error minimization process has local conditions that cause it to fail. So, forecasting is quite a different statistical exercise for a system that has both a prenominated sequence of objectives and a capacity for self-regulation, as long as the objectives and the self-regulation parameters are fixed, or are formally predictable continuously over the time span over which it is desired to forecast.

In practice various models, which resemble time series analysis to some degree, can be ranged all the way between fitting a linear or polynomial regression trend to a fixed sample of noisy data, with little confidence in extended forecasting, to continuously recursive filtering that will track all the vagaries of input as they occur and constantly incorporate new data. But the most bare, if not barren, of forecasting models are those that make a point prediction from a point estimate, with no regard to the intervening elapsed time between the two points.

Drösler (1978) has indicated that classical psychometric test theory is in fact bare in this way "neither classical testing theory . . . nor latent trait theory . . . contain axioms . . . concerning the growing uncertainty of prognosis with forecasting range . . . . This is contrary to experience in psychology [p. 533]." Consequently he advocates the extension of test theory, using convolution integrals. As he notes "introduction of a time dependent form of analysis leads to a dynamic perspective of the psychodiagnostic process [p. 534]."

The forecasting problem, from j to $j + k$, is equivalently one of minimizing

$$E = \Sigma \ [f(j + k) - f^*(j)]^2 \tag{6.1.1}$$

where $f(j)$ is the measure of performance at j, and $f^*(j)$ is an estimate at a previous time, of $f(j)$.

If a linear regression analysis is used, then

$$f^*(j) = \sum_{i=0}^{h} v_i^* \cdot f(j - 1) \tag{6.1.2}$$

where h is the time span of observations already available as a basis for forecasting to a point $j + k$, when at j; but the v_i^* are now not l.t.f. coefficients but regression weights for the purpose of predicting $f(j + k)$.

In diagram form, this is Fig. 6.1.1.

The autocovariance of the set $\{f(j - h), \ldots, f(j)\}$ will be denoted by a matrix;

$$(\text{cov} \ (f(j, j - g))_h) \cdot (v_j^*)_h = \text{cov} \ (f^*(j), f(j + k))_h \tag{6.1.3}$$

The r.h.s. of (6.1.3) is the covariance vector of the chain of observed scores (the data base) being used for the prognosis at time $j + k$. It can be shown that (6.1.3) is the parallel of a continuous analytical equation, the Wiener–Hopf equation that arises in communication theory (Wiener, 1949). This equation is sometimes soluble by Laplace transforms (see Section 3.8).

Using data from Bayley (1940), on cognitive measures of children between 8 and 48 months of age, the autocovariance decreases exponentially with span of forecasting. The drop is so rapid that prediction 40 months ahead from 8 months of age is worthless:

$$\text{cov} \ (f(j, j+ k)) = .94 \ \exp \ (-k/6) \tag{6.1.4}$$

where the units are in months; if the .94 is the concurrent validity of the test (its autocorrelation at negligible time intervals between retesting), then within 6

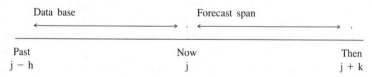

Data base	Forecast span
Past	Now	Then
j − h	j	j + k

FIG. 6.1.1 From data to long-term forecasting.

months the predictive validity drops to $.94/e = .346$ and in 12 months to $.346/e = .127$.

The alternative is to predict from a time series; it can be shown, however, that if the autocovariance function is exponentially declining with lag, then it is of no additional value if measures at one point in time are error-free to make additional observations; prediction from a point value, now, is optimal. This situation can be looked at another way; a process that has only local significant autocorrelation resembles a Markov chain and so has no predictive value before the penultimate trial. However, fortunately it can be shown for age ranges above those just considered that validities of achievement tests do not always drop off exponentially; they may remain high for a period and then drop off sharply, in a concave (negatively accelerated) form, which is an opposite sort of curvature to the exponential decay. This appears to hold if the start point for forecasting is 4 years of age or more. The concave functions are rather intractable mathematically; they cannot be handled by Laplace methods but will yield to numerical analysis. Drösler (1978) found that the optimal weight of past results for prediction in this common case resembled Fig. 6.1.2:

It is pertinent to note that this form is commonly found (see Sections 4.2 and 6.3) in analyzing cognitive judgment sequences, which suggests that the judgment of slowly changing processes can be filtered in a manner approaching optimality, though the time scale is obviously grossly different in the case of predicting test scores outside a laboratory experiment and predicting years ahead in intelligence or personality development.

The case just considered is viewed as an extension of classical test theory; a test is administered repeatedly and the scores kept for forecasting at a point outside the temporal range, $j - h$ to $j,$ of data collection. If prediction can be recursively revised, then the test used at each stage would be changed in its parameters to reoptimize it; this strategy has been used in the psychology of instruction by Atkinson and co-workers (Atkinson & Paulson, 1972). The necessary conditions for making optimum revision of a learning process are that a mathematical model of the learning is available and that a target performance is definable. The optimality may be achieved by a repeated application of Bellman's methods, which are a type of recursive filtering to a nominated target, in which the process approaching the target is redirected at each stage to take a minimum energy path to the target. Clearly this is not stationary; the optimality principle is itself invariable; but the process changes its parameters as a step function of the disparity between the optimal path and the present location, given an algorithm for the calculation of that optimal path to the target, no matter what the instantaneous location of the process in its parameter space. No matter where a process has got to in approaching a target and no matter whether its path up to that point was optimal or not, the optimal path parameters for the remaining part of the process' trajectory can be defined, given some minimization criterion to be satisfied over all the remaining path. This method, which Bellman (1961) called

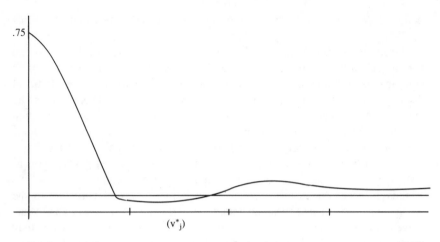

FIG. 6.1.2   Optimal weights for prediction, given monotone negatively accelerated decreasing autocorrelation spectrum.

dynamic programming, is neither descriptive nor predictive but rather prescriptive; it thus stands, very appropriately, in contrast to the methods of time series analysis. It is thus more use as a tool for planning feedback to approximate to optimal learning sequences.

The existence of dynamic programming as a recursive means of directing a process, given that it can be influenced, and filtering as a recursive means of predicting where a process will go, even if it cannot be influenced, suggests a duality between the two and indeed leads in engineering to the problems and methods of design for optimum feedback and optimal stability in control systems, the results of which provide an upper limit against which actual behavior, as a path through discrete time, can be compared. In this sense, therefore, the psychology of spontaneous unlearning is perhaps more easy to describe as a time series with linear structure than is learning and may resemble random walks to absorbing barriers (this simple model fits well the relapse of cohorts of alcoholics, heroin addicts, and others released from full-time therapy and abstinence) or may be parameterized in a way that is highly autocorrelated as, for example, in trace strength models of memory (Wicklegren, 1974). There is thus a metatheoretical difference between modeling learning or modeling forgetting on the one hand and on the other modeling dynamic processes that are psychologically a fairly steady state, with none of the acquisition or loss of input–output relationships that characterize learning or forgetting. The central problem that causes confusion is simply put and practically difficult; a dynamic system displaced from equilibrium and later returning to a steady state does not in fact learn or forget anything, but the curves of performance against time that it traces out will look like learning curves, remarkably like the sorts of curves that are commonplace in behavior modification studies.

If the input to an experiment is defined as the reinforcement rate, measured in units/unit time, and the output is defined as a response rate, acts/unit time; the reinforcement is not then on an individual response but on a local integrated average of responses. Then further suppose that reinforcement rate is regarded as an inverse error signal; reinforcement increases as proximity to a defined target response rate is achieved and is maximal at zero error, that is, when the desired rate of response emission is exactly achieved (with a tolerable bandwidth) and neither underachieved nor overachieved. Compare this paradigm with a tracking task; call the new task *rate emission*. See Table 6.1.1.

It should be noted that if the feedback is in terms of a rate of change [Δ^1 (error), Δ^1(reinforcement)], then it is not logically necessary to specify a target performance level at any stage before that target is, in fact, reached. Hence, as Powers (1978) and others have emphasized, the target does not have to be fixed nor does it have to be decided in advance by the experimenter; but it does have to be definable at any point in time. What is in principle definable and what is fixed in advance are not the same thing. This holds for both paradigms in Table 6.1.1; to use rate and directional feedback does in fact require the experimenter or the subject to have a nominated target direction (from where the system currently is) but not a specific target value; so nothing is available to be learned about target values until the subject is in the immediate vicinity of the desired output, such that deviations in any direction are unreinforced or fed back as error. Examples of differential reinforcement schedules, designed to produce either low or high response rates, are reviewed by Kramer and Rilling (1970); a specific example with somewhat ambiguous outcome is given for the task of reading aloud by deaf children, by Wilson and McReynolds (1973).

Here, then, we have paradigms in which what looks like a learning process or a change in the input–output set of relations that defines and characterizes a system in fact can involve absolutely no learning or system change though it involves changes in overt behavior that can be quite dramatic, even if short-

TABLE 6.1.1
Formal Comparison of Tracking with Rate Emission Modification

Paramter	Tracking	Rate Emission
{ Adjustment to change response:	Control setting Current position (or rate)	Response acts General response rate
Target	Nominated location or magnitude of output	Nominated rate of output
{ Error signal for comparator	Algebraic disparity between locus or magnitude of current behavior and the target; or local gradient of error	Difference between current reinforcement and some unknown maximum, hence replaced by local (gradient) difference of reinforcement

lived. Even more adverse to a superficial equation of learning or control with the manipulation of overt behavior, if the responses of the system are defined to be staying on target and not going to the target through time, then there need not be any overt change in behavior through an interpolated episode that involves changes in the feedback parameters. Powers (1973) makes effective use of this point in considering perceptual processes.

If the two systems of Table 6.1.1 are isomorphic and also completely defined dynamically a priori by their ability to track target values, then they will apparently learn, sluggishly, and unlearn again about the same sluggish rate when the target returns to its predisplacement levels if the reinforcement feedback is removed. With no differential feedback in error signals or reinforcement terms, the system drifts about a spontaneous level of activity. It is therefore appropriate to review possible conditions for differentiating between a dynamic system, linearly responsive, without any capacity for system parameter change, and a system that can learn and forget but that may not be linear and need not be dynamic in the sense of being capable of self-regulation under a wide range of inputs.

Suppose we have an experimental record that resembles Fig. 6.1.3:

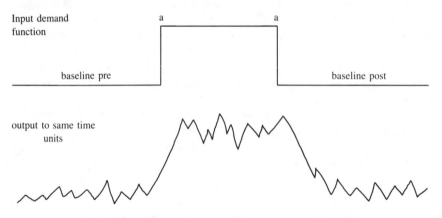

FIG. 6.1.3   Dynamically ambiguous data records.

Instead of presupposing an l.t.f. and seeking its identification, the question of what is happening in Fig. 6.1.3 may, if learning is a serious alternative contending model a priori, be reviewed by listing some alternatives, of which instances may not be amenable to any of the standard forms of analysis that have been studied for their tractability.

6.1.A A system that can be thought of as tracking, by following in sluggish pursuit, *or* responding to moving averages *or* minimizing errors locally and characterized by an l.t.f. of order >1, will behave like the figure. At no stage do the internal parameters of the system change. The only change is in the input levels. Before the record begins, one might, anthropomorphically, assert that the system has already learned or "knows" that it has to follow the input. But there is absolutely no way in which the input–output relationships of the system have to change during the record, and as learning is by definition a change in S–R pairings, there is no necessary evidence of learning.

6.1.B A system that learns quickly and forgets comparably quickly, so that it changes as much as it can change within a small part of the duration of the interpolated episode $a-a$ has at last one different system parameter after it has responded to the change in input and reverts approximately to the original parameters after "forgetting." Grossly this is the same behavior as in case 6.1.A, there is no way to differentiate the two cases from the given data. Experiments that report only the type of record shown in Fig. 6.1.3, which are quite common, are in fact uninterpretable and cannot of themselves constitute evidence of change in the system parameters. It is not necessary, *inter alia*, that the form of the forgetting curve should be the mirror image of the learning curve if 6.1.A holds, merely that they should be opposite in trend.

In order to demonstrate a difference it is necessary to make an extension of theory and to perform ancillary experiments. Distinguish between external or augmented information on the error, internal or system intrinsic feedback on error, and the current nominated target level, which can be regarded as a sort of demand function. The term *demand characteristics* for describing some features of an experimental situation has come into use; it can be interpreted in the same sense as a demand function here, though it is not required that demand be invariant. The simplest learning experiment will require that the external reinforcement (both external information and internal feedback) and the target are coupled in the episode $a-a$ of Fig. 6.1.3 and uncoupled afterward: the process after $a-a$ leaving the target or demand level of performance unchanged at what it was set in $a-a,$ and the process staying on target by internal feedback alone. In such a representation the system has no capacity to change its target spontaneously but will, after it is brought into alignment with a new target by the application of a simultaneous change of target and the auxiliary feedback provided, sustain and monitor its performance at the new level by using internal feedback.

The characteristics of the internal feedback loops do not have to change; as a result of the parallel provision of external information, during $a-a,$ the internal feedback is slowly induced to level out on a new target about which error can be minimized. In other words, it is proper to distinguish between changes in the system that are solely in terms of nominated target values and changes in the parameters of the loops that monitor error about the target values. Either or both can be changed by a learning process, but they are not necessarily coupled so that changing one changes the other. In cognitive psychology one may distinguish between learning strategies and learning solutions in problem-solving behavior; in some ways the distinction might be said to parallel that drawn here.

There will be at least four possible reasons why behavior drifts back to the original output levels that obtained before $a-a$:

1. The target actually drifts and the internal feedback tracks it.

2. The system becomes unlocked from the target and reverts to an equilibrium level of output; the notion of an equilibrium level is perhaps easier to defend if the target level is not a *locus* but a *rate* of responding, as in operant psychology.

3. The augmented feedback was to a pseudotarget, in which the bandwidth of error tolerance in the augmented feedback (which corresponds to sensitivity in a discrete system) was held narrow, but the bandwidth of the internal feedback was temporarily widened, to a considerable degree, by the overriding action of the augmented feedback. In this case the external information temporarily both changes the target and substitutes one set of feedback parameters for another. When the augmented feedback is removed, the bandwidth of the internal feedback decreases (sensitivity increases) and the original target being continuously present in internal representation, the system reverts to its original stability.

4. The system can be switched from one configuration of target coupled with internal feedback to another configuration of a different target with different feedback; only in the presence of a paired target and feedback will the system function at an enhanced level as in $a-a$. This idea may, in a loose qualitative form, be found in the theory of state-dependent learning; it is claimed that learning some tasks when intoxicated results in their superior recall under subsequent intoxication. It is true that alcohol modifies the feedback parameters of motor skills (Gregson, Smith, Strelow, & Brabyn, 1978), but this analogy should be treated with caution; the methodology of state-dependent learning research may still need considerable refinement.

In all the four cases just described, when the system is in any one of the three parts of Fig. 6.1.3, initial, $a-a$, and postintervention, very small deviations will be self-correcting, but if the system shows large deviations, then its intrinsic stability and, hence, its capacity to return to the nominated target locally must be questioned. It is the property of compensating for small displacements, after there has been an initial phase of stability within a part of the experiment, that constitutes evidence of a genuine change between the three parts, and of dynamic stability both in target and in feedback parameters within a time period. Close examination of the results, presented graphically, of many experiments using the paradigm of Fig. 6.1.3 suggests that they do not offer sufficient evidence for us to distinguish what is happening in terms of the four alternatives given. Indeed, the intrinsic logic of the situation is that the input–output record of the type of experiment depicted in Fig. 6.1.3 is not sufficient data to decide, though the

differences between the four cases are psychologically meaningful and important. Unless we know which obtains in a given situation, forecasting is impossible and the ecological long-term validity of the results is nil. Time series analysis, if there exist sufficient data with the three parts, can assist in the identification problem that the existence of the four alternatives poses. It is suggested
that it is the solution of this sort of identification problem that provides a link
between learning theory and the dynamic analysis of steady-state processes that
are our main concern throughout this review.

6.2 SPATIOTEMPORAL AND CHRONOTEMPORAL PROCESSES

There are some environmental structures or processes, mostly mediated through
vision or hearing, that give rise to time series as their only natural form of
stimulus input and that are appropriately represented in most cases by the same or
closely related mathematical expressions. Those that involve patterns extended in
space that need elapsed time to span and perceive we shall call *spatiotemporal*
and, by analogy, those that are samples of time series recurrently presented in a
patterned fashion in time we shall call *chronotemporal*. Their properties are best
defined by example, as formal abstract analysis tends to run ahead of data.

The obviousness of time series has already been remarked (Chapter 4) in the
cases of sound pressure or light intensity variations that, when they have some
regular periodicities, give rise to sensations of pitch or color, but there are other
instances that are less familiar and at the same time share common problems of
representation or analysis. To demonstrate the pervasiveness of series that are
doubly extended in the sense of this section, three areas are chosen each of which
has a more detailed experimental and theoretical literature to which reference
should be made before attempting data analysis.

A spatially extended structure, in one or more dimensions, that is scanned by
an observer located at one point in space, and where the scanning is achieved
either by moving the structure or moving the observer, it being sufficient that one
moves relative to the other, and where the direction of motion is orthogonal to at
least one periodically varying spatial component of the display, will generate one
or more time series of stimulus inputs. In this situation, the total structure shows
periodic or aperiodic patterns, when represented statically simultaneously in the
visual field. If this were not so, we could not draw any graphs to represent time
series. The constraint considered here is one that ensures that the observation of a
small part of the structure that generates stimuli, at one point in time, shows no
dynamic characteristics and gives no information about what would be experienced next if the observer and structure were to move relative to one another.

As soon as there is movement or there is an opportunity to scan simultaneously an extended part of the structure, then this structure can be encoded in

time, or a temporal structure can be encoded in space. Mathematically this is a key idea in time series analysis; it is the basis for seeking representations in different domains, as in Chapters 2 and 3. Now we are noting that in some sensory tasks the observer performs, in a fuzzy manner, a filtering operation in order to identify the structure. It is this filtering that is the psychological analog of time series analysis, though the output is obviously not a psychological equivalent of a linear transfer function in quite the same way that a magnitude estimation judgment may be thought of as the psychophysical counterpart of a physical energy level.

In tall buildings that are flexible (and such flexibility is a deliberate design feature to withstand typhoons and earthquakes), either earth movements or wind will induce periodic movements of varying amplitude and acceleration. The movement is often harmonic, perhaps complex with higher-frequency components, but will have maximum acceleration near the ends of the metronomelike motion and maximum velocity where acceleration is least, in moving through the static resting configuration of the building (corrected for the mean-wind vector). The motion is often unpleasant and frightening to the occupants, particularly when accompanied by creaking and cracking noises from the fabric and fixtures. What a building can be designed to do quite safely as a dynamic structure may be intolerable to the occupants; they can be sick or frightened at levels of movement well inside the safe performance range of the building.

Yamada and Goto (1977), through motion simulation experiments in a room built as a tall building simulator, examined the psychophysics of human responses under periodic input conditions. As the input increases, the system can induce impairments in motor and in visual skills, make subjects feel nauseated, shift furniture around, and make it difficult to walk about without falling or hurting oneself on objects. The results are thus complex but the system input is adequately described by the two parameters, period of movement and acceleration. This is an alternative to using as system parameters the period and full amplitude; there are only two free parameters if the form of the periodic motion is specified completely as harmonic.

What human observers can actually tolerate as earthquakelike motion varies widely depending on sex, age, posture, and orientation of the body axis relative to the major amplitude components of motion. Age is confounded with prior experience in countries like Japan and New Zealand that have earthquakes often, though mostly slight. Experience modifies the fear induced by suprathreshold motion, for better or for worse. The body is an articulated (i.e., loosely coupled) system with inertia and with natural resonance frequencies associated with the component masses of the limbs, but the induced acceleration of the head relative to the body plays a critical role in inducing unpleasant sensations. In the graphs of Fig. 6.2.1 and 6.2.2 the unit *gal* is defined as 1 gal $= g \times 10^{-3} = 981 \times 10^{-3}$ cm/sec^2.

The zones in Fig. 6.2.1 are approximate but serve as a guide to design

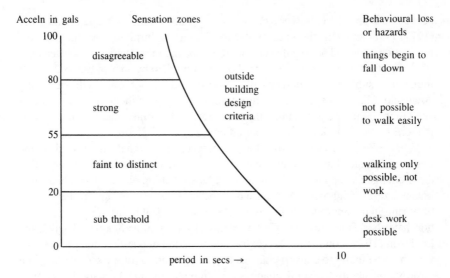

FIG. 6.2.1   Relation between induced head acceleration and response.

engineers; more detailed experiment shows that the threshold for motion has a curvilinear locus in the acceleration-period graph, as in Fig. 6.2.2.

As most engineering research on this problem is based on periods of less than 1 sec, that is, frequencies higher than 1 Hz, the relationships of Fig. 6.2.2 have not been extensively studied. The critical parameter for design is the acceleration; it would be hoped that buildings that swayed stayed within 10 gals. Motion sickness can be induced by prolonged exposure between 10 and 25 gals; whereas

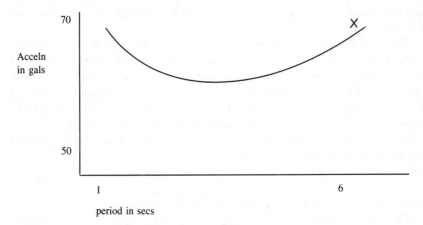

FIG. 6.2.2   Locus of movement-detection threshold zone.

between 25 and 40 gals work becomes impossible, and as Yamada and Goto (1977) comment "in the case of the movement of furniture and fixtures, the production of sound at 40 gal is considered to be the factor which strikes terror in (the) inhabitants' hearts [p. 68]." In the region marked by an X in Fig. 6.2.2, it is found that subjects can perceive the motion and cannot walk without falling down and injuring themselves on furniture. Perception of the movement is facilitated more by the period than by the acceleration, but impairment of motor skills is more by acceleration than by periodicity.

When objects move relative to an observer, the signals they send to the observer change, but the visual system is still left with the task of interpreting these changes as apparent motion and not as something else such as changes in image size or brightness. Motion has to be seen as motion, and to be seen as occurring in the appropriate direction. The physiological bases of motion perception have been the impetus of a lot of model building; as Sekular, Pantle, and Levinson (1978) comment: "To extract information about direction of motion a way must be found to convert changes in spatial position (of the seen object) into information about temporal changes. All models of direction-specificity ultimately solve this problem in the same way; crosscorrelation . . . all reduce to the same basic computational strategy [p. 88]."

The core structure of the autocorrelation model is obtained by postulating one input, an intensity function of time, and two (or more) receptors. In the case of two receptors, the rate of movement of the input is such that the second receptor is excited k time units after the first.

If the input is x_j, the output autocorrelation is

$$r(j, j - k) = \Sigma \, x_j \cdot x_{j-k} \tag{6.2.1}$$

in discrete notation. Here the delay k is in effect a tuning constant for a delay circuit that will maximize output, $r(j, j - k)$, when the input achieves some specific combination of direction and rate; that is, the autocorrelation circuit has a resonant velocity input.

This is a slightly different interpretation of the crosscorrelation of two elements in a network from that used previously. But the extension to a matrix of $r(j, j - k)$ over all the pairwise relations of a set of detectors is consistent with (6.2.1) and Chapter 4. Sekular et al. (1978), deriving from Foster (1971) and Poggio and Reichardt (1973), extend and qualify (6.2.1) as follows; it can be shown that many motion detection models with n inputs and one output can be reduced to a sum of expressions like (6.2.1). The output that serves as the basis of motion detection may thus be written

$$\Omega = w_h \cdot \Sigma \, w_{jk} \cdot x_{hj} \cdot x_{h(j-k)} \tag{6.2.2}$$

where the w_h, w_{jk} are real, and the $w_h > 0$.

Physiological data suggest that receptors separated physically in the retina by a range of distances are involved in the input to Ω; it is also expedient to allow the receptors to decay rapidly after excitation in the mode, so that for fixed object velocity the w_h in (6.2.2), if the x_h are on an array parallel to the direction of motion, and for convenience if $w_1 = 1$,

$$w_{jk} = \alpha \cdot \exp(-\beta k) \tag{6.2.3}$$

where α, β are scalars, ≥ 1 for $k > 0$ and $\alpha = 0$ for $k \leq 0$.

Any network operating as (6.2.2) will be sensitive to both spatial and temporal stimulus properties; the extent of the field covered by the stimulus and its velocity are both reflected in Ω. Hence phenomena of pseudomovement or changes in perceived size with movement have to be explained by suitable choice of parameters in models compatible with (6.2.2).

Sekular et al. (1978) again comment ''the problem that the nervous system solves in order to extract motion information from a visual stimulus is the same problem (that) it solves in other modalities [p. 90].'' This statement underlies the ubiquitousness of convolution integrals in psychophysiology.

There are still difficulties with a model as simple as (6.2.2), (6.2.3); its strength is that it makes motion perception a function involving the structure of the neural network rather than the stimulus properties alone; its weakness is that it is still not complicated enough quantitatively to account for some phenomena of pseudomotion. Sekular (1975) notes evidence that indicates apparent rate of motion is a function of length of observation, which means the w_{jk} in (6.2.2) are not fixed; apparent motion induced by successive point simulation in the two separate loci is extended to the perceiver over a spatial distance many times the real distance, which implies that adjacent elements in a network are mutually exciting even if not direct input to one or other occurs. The network underlying (6.2.2) should have additional diffusion processes added that will also take place in real time, spreading from one element to another and dying away thereafter.

Filtering series into patterns is also performed in two auditory models of pitch perception. Wightman (1973) has suggested that pitch is mediated by transformation through approximate Fourier transforms of the input signals, which is then scanned in its frequency domain form and turned into a pattern resembling an autocorrelation spectrum. This is a coarse structure theory; it is deliberately coarse because pitch perception is insensitive to phase shifts, and hence fine structure theories would postulate the capture of stimulus properties that are, in fact, either not used or filtered out.

The problem is, tersely, as follows: The frequency X Hz from various sources such as different musical instruments is still identified by the human observer as, say, ''B flat.'' The inputs that are equivalent in this special sense have then to be transformed, initially, into similar internal representations; ''the transformed peripheral activity patterns of all stimuli with the same pitch will look alike.'' This means that information that is not about the pitch must be lost, for the specific purpose of pitch recognition. Wightman assumed that what was lost was phase information about stimulus pattern components. The pitch is then defined as mapping into the autocorrelation of an input sample, autocorrelation being chosen precisely because of its phase insensitivity.

Although it is true that mathematically there is an equivalence between frequency and time domain encodings, the neural auditory system has poor spectral analysis, and temporal limits in that positive and negative parts of waveforms are encoded asymmetrically. For these reasons, neural analog computation of signals in the frequency domain will not be necessarily the same as in the time domain. As it can be shown that a time domain autocorrelation process would be phase sensitive on short samples as inputs (see Section 2.2), Wightman therefore chose a Fourier analog instead.

The input pattern to the process is a two-dimensional distribution of activity; location x level. This passes through a limited resolution power-spectrum analysis; location maps into frequency and level into power. The power spectrum is then Fourier analyzed by a network, the output of which is an approximate autocorrelation series. This output is again postulated to be two-dimensional; location corresponds to autocorrelation lag and level maps into autocorrelation magnitude. The comparison of two patterns, to decide if the same "pitch" is represented in each, thus requires the comparison of two autocorrelation spectra to match for peak values. This model is spatiotemporal in the sense that neurological networks are postulated to filter by spatial encoding the parameters of a frequency domain analysis of a time series input; there is a switching between domains in the successive stages of filtering.

The capacity of the auditory system to create periodicities out of inputs that should not be perceived as having such regularities in time is intriguingly illustrated by a chronotemporal type of series devised originally by Pierce, Lipes, and Cheetham (1977) and studied by Pollack (1978, 1979). The PLC series, as they have become known, are constructed out of short bits of time series. Each bit is a brief sample of white noise, obviously having a zero autocorrelation spectrum. These bits are then treated as pulses and can be positive or negative in form; any one can be mirror imaged. Such pulses are said to have opposite polarities; they can be symbolized by a binary series, $+ + + - - + - - - + - \ldots$ If the area under the amplitude waveform of a pulse, in time, is A, the rate of pulses per second is N, the duration of a pulse is $N^{-1} = T$ (about 2 msec), and the binary sequence of pulses is randomly generated, then the pulses can be filtered to have a constrained waveband and still be white; the power spectrum is given by

$$p(f) = 2NA^2 \tag{6.2.4}$$

At low N these series sound like a series of clicks; as N increases, the sequences become like the hiss of white noise. Suppose that the following conditions are imposed:

1. The areas e of opposite polarity are exactly balanced.
2. The shapes (in the frequency spectrum) of pulses should balance.

3. Intervals in time between pulses of opposite sign should have the same duration–frequency distribution as intervals between pulses of the same sign.

Then there are no specific frequency components to give any clues to the listener about N. The theoretical power spectrum is flat, but the short-term power spectra from samples have a periodic structure proportional to N, with harmonics.

Pollack (1979) showed, however, that if we take a string of such PLC pulses, say, $+ + - - + -$, and call this string a pattern and then replicate the pattern and present the successive replicates, the periodicity of the sequence will be detected by the human observer. This periodicity was judged in Pollack's studies by a method of matching, a variable periodic signal under the subject's control being adjusted to match the presented PLC series in apparent dominant frequency. It can be shown that such matching is equivalent to maximizing a crosscorrelation of frequencies between two time series, which is a coherence analysis (see Section 2.9). As it can be shown that PLC's are discriminable even if their pulse lengths T are shorter than a limiting auditory sampling period for detection in simple psychophysics, it appears to be the case that phase information, or integration of samples, is used to establish the coherences. The reliance of this psychophysical model upon coherences based on short samples must be taken with caution; it could be both its strength and its weakness, because coherence is an extremely sensitive measure and susceptible to bias (Bogert, Healy, & Tukey, 1963). It has also been conjectured that at lower frequencies (less than 500 Hz) signals are identified by matching in the time domain, whereas at higher frequencies they are handled in the frequency domain; such a conjecture is clearly at odds with an unqualified version of Wightman's (1973) theory.

The PLC patterns, from which information is extracted somewhat paradoxically by the listener, bear a resemblance at an abstract level to spatial patterns such as random bar figures or checkerboards of unequal bar width. Such spatial patterns have a general representation in Walsh functions, which can be thought of as binary analogs of Fourier series. A complete set of the Walsh functions, called *masks,* of maximum period 8, in two dimensions, are shown in Fig. 6.2.3; they are shown in Cartesian coordinate form but can equally well be mapped into circular form by using polar coordinates instead of into squares; when plotted onto circles, their family structure is a little less obvious to inspection.

The mathematics of these two-valued functions was first explored by Walsh in 1923, as the discrete counterparts of sinusoidal functions. Harmuth (1977) discusses them extensively with respect to applications in engineering; see also Haralick, Shanmugan, and Dinstein (1973). The arrangement of the 64 masks in Fig. 6.2.3 is by the property called *sequency,* which corresponds to frequency in continuous sinusoidal functions. The sequency of one-dimensional Walsh masks is defined as half the number of zero crossings; the variables x and y that generate

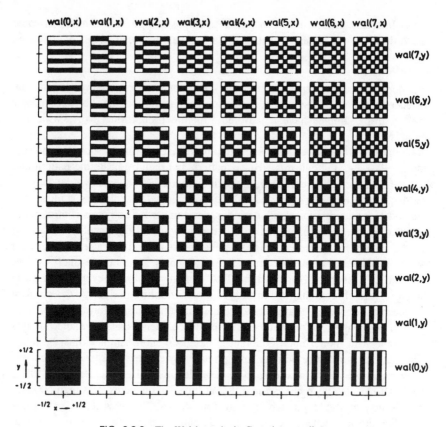

FIG. 6.2.3   The Walsh masks in Cartesian coordinates.

the masks are defined as ranging between -0.5 (say, black) and $+0.5$ (say, white) with no values in between, so the number of patches of black and white that make up a mask (ranging, in Fig. 6.2.3 from 1 for wal $(0, x)$, $(0, y)$) to 64 for wal $((7, x), (7, y))$ and the rest from 2 to 56 inclusive) are its two-dimensional sequency; these values are the products of corresponding one-dimensional sequencies.

Walsh masks are a form of bivariate time series representation; their use raises serious problems for perception theory because, according to a diversity of quantitative models of similarity that have been constructed and used with other types of stimuli (Gregson, 1976b, reviews some prototypical instances), all the $^{64}C_2$ ($= 64 \times 63/2 = 2016$) possible pairwise similarities between masks in the sequency 8, 8 set of Fig. 6.2.3 ought to be the same. Chignell (1979) showed that this was definitely not so; subjects perceive the similarities to vary so that it is possible to represent the 64 stimuli as falling into clusters rather than lying at the vertices of a regular simplex, which is what they would do in multidimensional perceptual space if the models were appropriate.

At the same time the stimuli can be compared and can be shown to vary in the extent to which they are perceived to possess properties such as jaggedness, or symmetry; on the basis of such judgments, either singly or in comparison, they can be cluster analyzed and represented in multidimensional space. It is not necessarily the case that the results of a scaling obtained this way will be tidily isomorphic with one obtained from pairwise similarity estimates. Chignell (1980) tentatively identified such cognitive–perceptual dimensions as two-dimensional sequency (dominant), complexity, and graininess. It is easy to define mathematically a host of properties of geometrical patterns, but over a finite set many will inevitably intercorrelate very highly so that it becomes meaningless to ask which physically definable property is serving as *the* basis for discriminability or perceived degree of similarity. Chignell suggests that the way in which these spatial series are represented as collections of attributes may be a function of the task situation and the demands imposed therein by the experimenter; the representation thus cannot be invariant. Hence there is little evidence of a cognitive filtering of spatial sequential properties that can be represented by some fixed operation like a linear transfer function. Contrariwise, some sort of adaptive filtering could be postulated, which would partition the set of Walsh masks into subsets, as feedback during the task enabling the filter to change the weighting of its parameters. This sort of adaptive network has been postulated in neurological models of pattern perception but leads outside our subject area.

The increased interest in the environmental sciences has been impetus for an expansion of work in spatial and spatiotemporal time series. Initially this was largely to aid our understanding of physical systems that extend over the Earth's surface, such as weather, but there have been extensions into social and economic processes that can be traced through space and time as they diffuse or interact, grow, and diminish, in the areas and the populations they involve. Bennett (1979) gives a thorough review of such models.

6.3 MULTIDIMENSIONAL TIME SERIES EXPERIMENTS

There are as yet few examples of time series experiments in psychology in which there are measured a number of inputs and a number of outputs simultaneously on each trial; in reality most psychological experiments are necessarily beset with collateral inputs and potential outputs that are not elicited as responses but they are not recorded. Methodologically multivariate experiments are an extension in many ways of the simpler bivariate experiment in discrete time (Quenouille,

1957), but there are additional complications that affect the analysis and interpretation (Wilson, 1973, Box & Tiao, 1977). Consequently some examples are reviewed here in detail, taken from Gregson (1974, 1978).

In a cognitive experiment the subject makes a series of judgments; hopefully each such judgment refers to some identifiable quantifiable event in the stimulus environment or to a construct that the subject creates from the input and about which the experimenter has a theory that is modelable. For example, we might have such outputs as the following:

1. The perceived magnitude of a stimulus attribute or some other psychophysical judgment.

2. The similarity of two stimuli presented together, with respect to some specified basis of comparison.

3. The subjective probability that some parameter, such as is defined in items 1 or 2, is larger or smaller than on the current trial.

4. The subjective probability that some event in the total stimulus set in use, explicitly or implicitly, will appear on the next trial.

5. The confidence of a judgment on the current trial.

6. The confidence of a prediction for an event on the next or more future trials.

One could also have detection or discrimination responses, but as these are by definition binary and so yield degenerate time series, they will not be considered here.

From the physical specification of the stimulus attributed available, and in the case of derived properties such as similarities or probabilities, a precise or bounded prediction of a model (see Gregson, 1976a,b, for alternative examples) the inputs can be created that maximally correspond to the outputs. It may be objected that the inputs come first, but their identification can in fact follow from the observation of the outputs; the problem in a multivariate psychometric experiment is to use the time series structure, the known outputs, and a set of inputs of potentially redundant composition, to identify from alternative autocorrelation and crosscorrelation structures what is a necessary and sufficient set of inputs to the total judgment process. Thus the identification is of both structure and inputs together by trying alternative models of the total system. This is not inevitably an horrendous task, but the posterior confidence that the structure and the input variables have been economically identified is a subject for caution. This is analogous to the problem of finding the minimum order ARIMA model that has been discussed in Sections 5.7, 5.8; unless the structure is known a priori the order can be overestimated.

In setting up a multivariate psychometric time series it is therefore expedient to build on what is known previously about the *constituent* experiments. By constituent experiments is meant the set of possible bivariate experiments which, if done one at a time, would yield an approximate estimate of the psychophysical or psychometric functional dependencies of response dimensions upon stimulus dimensions. What is being added when the experiment becomes multidimensional is the set of crosscorrelational spectra that, in the $n \times n$ experiment are the off-diagonal terms of a matrix in which each cell is a polynomial.

If the basic bivariate experiment has the form

$$R_j = f(\{v_k\}, \{S_j, \ldots, S_{j-k}\}) \tag{6.3.1}$$

where for generality we can allow f to be nonlinear, then the corresponding multivariate experiment of order $n \times n$ is

$$\left| \begin{matrix} R_{j1} \\ R_{jn} \end{matrix} \right| = \phi \left(\left| \{v_k\} \right|_{n \times n}, \left\{ \left| \begin{matrix} S_{j1} \\ S_{jn} \end{matrix} \right|, \ldots, \left| \begin{matrix} S_{j-k,1} \\ S_{j-k,n} \end{matrix} \right| \right\} \right) \tag{6.3.2}$$

where ϕ is now a function of up to, possibly, n dimensions.

If the n input dimensions are to be matched one to one with the outputs on psychophysical grounds, then one might expect that the diagonal cells of the matrix $|\{v_0\}|_{n \times n}$ in (6.3.2), with if necessary rearrangement, will strongly dominate the off-diagonal terms; for the later v_k, only weak predictions can be made.

The use of similarity judgments as one or more components in a multivariate cognitive experiment needs some comment, by way of explanation rather than justification, as it is a requirement of the current approach that a theoretical numerical similarity exist on each trial and that the response be scaled in an analogous manner. The quantification of similarity should be effectively continuous over some range of values exemplified in the trials of the experiment. Much weaker assumptions are often made about the nature of similarity judgments by workers employing such data simply as input to multidimensional scaling algorithms. The theoretical and empirical stance here is quite different and has been set out in detail (Gregson, 1974) for the case of a single bivariate time series using three-component stimulus figures. Thus the stimuli have three dimensions of variation but yield a single input variable, the theoretical similarity, on each trial. It is possible to construct, given measurable physical stimulus properties, the predicted scaled pairwise similarities (from 0 to 1 = identity) with sufficient accuracy to be able to reflect, in the v_k estimates, what a subject is using as a strategy of selective attention. Consider the following alternatives that are cognitive sets that the subject can adopt:

C0: Attending only to the current trial stimuli, with no conscious and deliberate regard to intertrial consistency.

C1: Attending not only to the current trial but selectively taking into account what has just been done on the previous trial, with correction to increase consistency where necessary.

C2: Taking account not only of the present and previous trials but also the trial before those; attempting to be consistent over three trials in the short term.

The agreement between v_k spectra and the strategy that subjects are told to employ is not perfect, partly for the obvious reason that what subjects do, what they think they are doing, and what they are told to do are not mutually consistent over all trials (or perhaps in the worst cases on any trials). Results suggested that $\{v_0, \ldots, v_3\}$ are a sufficient set of parameters to modify static models of similarity judgments and obtain an asymptotically good fit. This bivariate demonstration means that one can, in the simplest case, have confidence simultaneously in the similarity values generated by theory and the structure of the l.t.f., and these together will model some of the differential consequences of C0, C1, and C2.

Gregson (1978) considered the case where two stimuli on each of 90 trials were presented each with three variable components (actually color-coded geometrical elements; circles, triangles, squares) and the input variables were as follows:

S1 Similarity, $0 \leq \text{sim} \leq 1$.
S2 Probability that the left-hand stimulus on the next trial would be bigger, overall, than the current left-hand stimulus.
S3 Probability that the right-hand stimulus on the next trial would be smaller than the current right-hand stimulus.

The conditions left-hand, right-hand, bigger, smaller in S2 and S3 were permuted over the subjects but the order of elicitation of judgments was fixed on all trials so that S1 came first. This complication is of minor interest but imposes an extra test on the validity of the modeling.

The S1 values were calculated from the model used by Gregson (1975, Eq. [5.44.1]) in previous related work, the S2 and S3 were recalculated iteratively on each trial by a recursive algorithm and hence were the exact values, given the stimulus series employed.

The responses nominated were as follows:

R1 Perceived similarity, $0 \leq \text{sim} \leq 1$.
R2 Perceived probability, $0 \leq p \leq 1$.
R3 Perceived probability, $0 \leq p \leq 1$.

It should be noted that the S2 and S3 are independent, and so unless the subject adopts an irrational strategy R2 and R3 should also be independent. The experiment as a whole is thus a 3×3 multivariate time series in discrete time with all variables defined or constrained into the closed range 0, 1. The stimulus values were so chosen as to make the S1 theoretical similarities a random series, after some deliberate presentation of very high and very low similarities in the first few trials. No feedback was given, though it can be shown that feedback would marginally modify similarity responses and change their autocorrelation structure (Gregson, 1974). As will be seen, this is probably true for most cognitive judgment processes, similarities are not peculiarly labile nor peculiarly robust.

Methods of modeling multivariate time series were exemplified by Robinson (1967) and originally applied to the geology of submarine searches for oil-bearing strata; mathematically this simply shows the generality of the problem and its potential analysis.

Using z-transform notation,

$$Y = f(A(z))$$

is a system of n variables, where

$$A(z) = a_0 + a_1 z + a_2 z^2 + \cdots + a_k z^k + \cdots \tag{6.3.2}$$

where Y is an n-vector, a_i is an $n \times n$ matrix of constants, $i = 0, 1, 2, \ldots, k$, and z is the dummy variable.

The r.h.s. of (6.3.2) thus has as its set of coefficients a matrix polynomial, which has a determinant; call this det (A), which is in turn itself a polynomial (see Robinson, 1967; Takahashi, Rubins, & Auslander, 1970) so it may be written as

$$\det (A) = a_0^* + a_1^* z + a_2^* z^2 + \cdots + a_k^* z^k \tag{6.3.3}$$

where the a^* are new coefficients, but now they are scalars and not matrices. The stability of the multivariate process as a whole is assessed by examining these $\{a_k^*\}$ and not by attempting to make inferences, which would not be valid, from the $\{a_k\}$.

Under stationarity the factorization of the polynomial determinant when set equal to zero is a product of roots and is of the form

$$Y = a'(I - b_1 z)(I - b_2 z)(I - b_3 z) \tag{6.3.4}$$

and the stability characteristics of the system are identifiable directly from examination of the roots. It is the system as a whole that has, or fails to have, stability. In the multivariate case, stability is not a meaningful concept for each of the constituent experiments; one cannot in terms of stability decompose a multivariate time series. Instead an equivalent system is defined in terms of (6.3.4) and studied per se. The theorem defining a minimal delay system in discrete time, which is a desired condition for stability, may be stated thus:

A time series a_j^* of numerical coefficients defined for integer time indices j represents a minimum delay operator provided that:

1. Coefficients for negative time vanish.

2. $\sum_{j=1}^{\infty} a_j^* < \infty$

3. all the zeroes of the z-transform (see Section 3.4) lie on or outside the unit circle in the z-plane.

By extension, if all the zeroes are inside the unit circle, it is maximal delay. A mixture of zeroes inside and outside the unit circle is mixed delay, which is what one would expect in practice for a psychological system. The longer the delay, the less the efficiency of the system. If it is desired to specify the characteristics of an inverse system that would, under stationarity, if coupled in series after the human operator, recreate the original inputs from the human responses (outputs), then it would have transform $A^{-1}(z)$.

For one subject the polynomial $A(z)$ is given, as an example, in (6.3.5).

$$A(z) = \begin{vmatrix} 0.801 & -0.399 & -0.185 \\ -0.280 & 1.146 & -0.150 \\ -0.771 & -0.096 & 1.144 \end{vmatrix} + \begin{vmatrix} 0.231 & -0.022 & -0.068 \\ -0.184 & -0.233 & 0.093 \\ -0.280 & -0.078 & -0.036 \end{vmatrix} z$$

$$+ \begin{vmatrix} 0.152 & 0.015 & -0.009 \\ -0.183 & 0.068 & -0.174 \\ -0.197 & -0.281 & 0.293 \end{vmatrix} z + \begin{vmatrix} 0.297 & -0.148 & -0.134 \\ -0.132 & 0.057 & 0.046 \\ -0.391 & 0.068 & -0.032 \end{vmatrix} z^3$$

$$+ \begin{vmatrix} 0.232 & -0.053 & 0.013 \\ -0.182 & 0.091 & -0.104 \\ -0.216 & -0.045 & 0.047 \end{vmatrix} z + \begin{vmatrix} 0.141 & -0.141 & 0.130 \\ -0.216 & 0.025 & 0.066 \\ -0.138 & -0.154 & -0.357 \end{vmatrix} z^5$$

(6.3.5)

The polynomial (6.3.5) has as determinant

$$\det A(z) = 0.696 - 0.095z + 0.178z^2 + 0.030z^3$$
$$+ 0.066z^4 - 0.220z^5 - 0.052z^6 - 0.083z^7$$
$$- 0.089z^8 - 0.066z^9$$

(6.3.6)

which is obtained by using Newton–Raphson methods or some equivalent method of numerical analysis. Standard library programs are widely available, working to double precision may be expedient.

If, in (6.3.5), the three output variables were the consequence of and only of the corresponding input variable, so that $R_i = f(S_i)$, $i = 1, 2, 3$, then the matrices a_k would become diagonal. If the sequential effects were negligible for derivatives of the input higher than the nth-order, then the matrices a_{n+1}, a_{n+2} would tend to zero and would solely be due to noise or to error in the identification of the structure of the process rather than of its order. The pattern of numerical coefficients shown in (6.3.5) is typical for most subjects, though anomalous subjects, who from subsequent interview are found to misunderstand or to have misperformed the task exist and, indeed, may also readily be identified independently by examination of the a_k.

It is the dominance of the diagonal terms in a_0 that make it possible for psychophysical or cognitive processes erroneously to be represented, to a good first numerical approximation in the short run, as time independent. It must also be emphasized that it is the neglect both of the off-diagonal elements in a_0 and of the total set of elements in $\{a_1, a_2, \ldots, a_k\}$ that at the same time destroys what evidence exists of dynamic structure and induces error when prediction is attempted. Of particular psychological interest are cases where subjects are essentially identical in their a_0 coefficients but differ in some higher order matrix.

The roots of (6.3.6) on a root locus diagram, where the axes are σ (real components) and $i\omega$ (imaginary components) look like Fig. 6.3.1.

There are in fact only three roots here: one complex pair $-\sigma_1 \pm i\omega_1$ in the left-hand plane, one complex pair $+\sigma_2 \pm i\omega_2$ in the right-hand plane, and one real root $+\sigma_3$ on the σ axis on the right. These three roots represent the dynamic components of the system, into which it is linearly decomposable. A system represented solely by roots in the left-hand plane is under dynamic control; in any psychological experiments in which the "correct" responses are not in some way nominated, or provided by feedback, the control must be something imposed by the subject upon himself or herself. Consistency in response style will be expected to be a sufficient but not a necessary condition for stability, but it

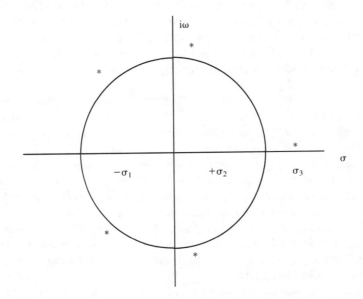

FIG. 6.3.1   Roots of Equation (6.3.6).

must also be the case that the response strategy adopted should be a formalizable relationship to the quantified input variables. Each of the possible loci of roots in Fig. 6.3.1 corresponds to a dynamic pattern, stable or unstable, an l.t.f. of one component of the system. The roots at $-\sigma_1$ represent an l.t.f. that oscillates but whose envelopes decay exponentially; it is damped and converges toward zero. As such oscillations are only observable in discrete time, they represent a series of pulses alternating in sign.

The roots at $+\sigma_2$ represent an oscillating response that increases in amplitude with time, so that if it were the only component present and were to continue indefinitely, it would go wild and fluctuate to extremes. The real component at σ_3 also represents a nonoscillating response that increases with time. However, the interpretation has to be taken further (Gregson, 1978) because the roots on the left-hand plane dominate those on the right-hand plane, and roots outside the unit circle will dominate those inside. It is expected that stable (left-hand) roots should dominate in cognitive tasks because it is known that sequential effects typically only carry over for a few trials and then die away, and if input becomes zero, in some cases response immediately becomes zero as well. This is evidence in itself of nonlinearity; linear systems should have some output after input has finished, as though the subject went on making responses to the residual effects of previous stimuli in the absence of current stimulation, for a brief period measured by the span of the lags of the l.t.f. This is not the same phenomenon as afterimages caused by physiological processes in the receptor organs.

Computationally there are a variety of checks, that the set of roots extracted and plotted is all the roots and not more than the roots and is not reduplicative. If the factorization algorithm is applied too often, then roots will be extracted that, when plotted, superimpose almost exactly on some previous pair or single value. This is called *cancellation* (van den Boom & van den Enden, 1973), and such reduplicative roots are ignored as probably bogus and above the real order of the system if counted.

As Gregson (1978) summarized "if the representation of the . . . situation examined here could have been adequately achieved with a time-independent first-order function then each subject would have had one and only one root on the real axis, in the left hand plane [p. 288].'' In no case did this occur; the evidence is thus completely incompatible with a static representation but at the same time shows some between-subject consistency and leads as a necessary next step to a search for the parameters that determine between-subject parallels and differences in the root loci. Inspection of plots in the experiment described shows that differences relate to what subjects misunderstood the task to be; as the computer had no information fed into it concerning what cognitive states the subjects were in, but only the input–output relations, the method is potentially viable for state identification.

It is obvious that in some limiting cases, where the dominance of the diagonal coefficients in a_0 is extreme, that a static (first-order) model will suffice, as in classical psychophysics. But we cannot know whether or not this limiting condition holds without first performing the dynamic analysis, which has the required generality completely lacking in the static world. One cannot post hoc reconstruct from a static model what the dynamic representation would have been.

A multivariate time series experiment by Kennedy (1977) in which the inputs and outputs were temporal durations and perceived elapsed time has a slightly different structure illustrates different representation problems. The experiment is not symmetric in inputs and outputs but is multivariate and has a cascaded internal structure. It is multivariate because on each trial subjects were asked to give confidences of their current judgments, predictions for the next trial, and confidences for those predictions. The structure is thus

$$\text{input} = x_j = \text{physical time elapsed between two events displayed on a screen}$$

$$\left.\begin{array}{c} y_{1j} \\ y_{2j} \\ y_{3j} \\ y_{4j} \end{array}\right\} = \text{output judgments} \left\{\begin{array}{l} \text{time perceived on trial j} \\ \text{confidence in } y_{1j} \\ \text{time predicted; estimate of } y_1, \\ \text{confidence in } y_{3j} \end{array}\right. \qquad (6.3.7)$$

In this task the sequence of judgments within a trial is precisely

$$x_j \rightarrow y_{1j} \rightarrow y_{2j} \rightarrow y_{3j} \rightarrow y_{4j}$$

and such a sequence can itself be analyzed as a set of multivariate transfer functions;

$$\begin{array}{ll} x_j \rightarrow \{y_{1j}, y_{2j}, y_{3j}, y_{4j}\} & \text{as given in (6.3.7)} \\ y_{1j} \rightarrow \{y_{2j}, y_{3j}, y_{4j}\} \\ y_{2j} \rightarrow \{y_{3j}, y_{4j}\} \\ y_{3j} \rightarrow \{y_{4j}\} \end{array}$$

To do this is to represent each output as input to another linear system in cascade, immediately downstream from its predecessor. All the models discussed previously can be applied to each subsystem; it does not follow that all the possible relations will be nonnull.

In setting up an analytic framework this way, where the judgments are dependent on previous judgments, we depart strongly from traditional psychophysics; it may of course be argued that asking for all these judgments induces a sequential dependence that is circumvented in a simpler experiment, but the precise objective here is to obtain a dynamic representation when the task is explicit rather than implicit. Meredith (1972) has commented that "nothing could be said or written, let alone constructed or acted, without processes in which the temporal order is psycho to physical, the science of psychophysics cannot continue indefinitely to hop along on one foot."

Rouse (1973) treated the prediction of the future states of a discrete time system as having the recursive form

$$x_{j+1} = c_0 \cdot y_{j+1} + C' X_j \qquad (6.3.8)$$

where

$$X_j' = [x_j, \Delta^1 x_j, \Delta^2 x_j, \ldots, \Delta^n x_j] \qquad (6.3.9)$$

and

$$C' =]c_1, c_2, c_3, \ldots, c_k] \qquad (6.3.10)$$

which is a vector of scalar constants. In practice, $n = 2$ is a sensible assumption in (6.3.9). In Rouse's study, subjects were given both feedback on the current trial j that meant the response for trial $j - 1$ and also a record of the previous 10 trials. In such an experiment the feedback is available before the next trial, as in some paradigms summarized in Section 4.4. Here however there was no feedback, but the prediction $y_{3j} \rightarrow y_{1,j+1}$ and the perceived $y_{1,j+1}$ are immediately comparable, and the subject can alter the confidence $y_{4,j+1}$ given the y_{2j}, y_{4j} and the disparity $\delta(y_{1,j+1}, y_{3j})$. Precisely how confidence judgments are revised, in time series terms, is not known. It is known that subjective confidence and subjective probability are not the same psychologically (Rothbart & Snyder, 1970); mathematically well-behaved subjective probabilities will approximate to those defined by probability axioms, though they may not sum exactly to one over a closed event space, and their revision with new evidence is not optimal as defined by Bayes theorem. Confidence judgments, even if scaled individually to lie in the range 0, 1 are not so well-behaved; in this respect they may resemble more readily the quantifiers of fuzzy set theory (A. Kaufmann, 1975).

In the experiment of Gregson (1978) making similarity and probability predictions, the dynamic structure differed between subjects, though there was an identifiable majority consensus. But the same consistent pattern was found by Kennedy (1977) over all nine subjects, as shown in Fig. 6.3.2.

Two roots, a stable oscillating pair in the left-hand plane and a dominated real root in the right-hand plane, are also found in the previously described experiment involving similarities. There is thus some common dynamic component in the way the two judgment tasks are executed, but the similarity and probability judgments generated a more complicated structure. It is of interest that it is apparently possible to model similarity judgments in this manner to a closer approximation than the associated subjective probabilities; that is, the agreement between theoretical and observed similarities can be closer than that between real (mathematical) and subjective probabilities. As mathematical probability theory is much more extensively and rigorously formalized than is similarity theory, the finding has wider implications.

An additional interpretation of the root loci was possible in Kennedy's experiment; in the case of the positive component of the complex root, its absolute value $|\omega_1|$ determines the shape of the envelope of a convergent oscillating

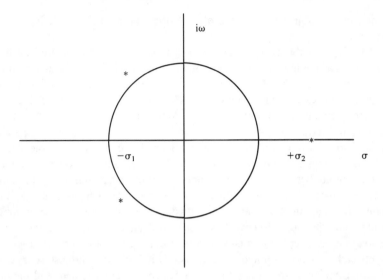

FIG. 6.3.2   Root loci for a complex time estimation and prediction task, from Kennedy (1977).

response. The larger the value of ω in $\sigma \pm i\omega$, the faster the process converges to zero. The rate of convergence, c_r, in seconds, is defined to be $1/\omega$. In each period c_r, the response amplitude reduces by 36.8% of the initial value in that period, so the smaller the c_r, the faster the decay (Chen, 1975). In this analysis, it was found that for the seven out of nine subjects who made the most accurate time estimations there was a clear monotone increasing relation between the value of $|\omega_1|$ (in the range 0–0.5) and the percentage of variance predicted for the time intervals, from the subjective estimates (in the range 80–96). Short time intervals are not very difficult to estimate, but the relationship is in the expected direction; a subject with a rapidly decaying stable transfer function component should indeed do better, given that the model fits to a good first approximation.

None of the studies described here varied the actual time intervals between trials in a systematic way within experiments. Within limits, this should, if done, alter at least the numerical values of the roots if not their configuration. For a thorough system identification, such exploration is necessary; the generation of response errors may have quite a different dynamic interpretation as the pacing of a series is changed, even if the errors themselves, in terms of stimulus misidentification or misestimations, are distributed over the stimulus $\times$ response product set employed in substantially the same manner.

6.4   ON-LINE NONSTATIONARY CONVERGENT
EXPERIMENTS

In this section are briefly reviewed the features of experiments that can arise if the requirements of stationarity and linearity in modeling are abandoned, but the notion that a subject in an experimental situation is a self-regulating system is preserved.

The simplest dynamic paradigm used throughout this book treats the input time series as having structure and statistical properties but is silent as to how the input series itself is regulated; it is given as an independent series of environmental parameters extending through time, and sampled. The behavior of the system, and the eventual output, are dependent. When this paradigm is changed so that the system becomes self-regulating, it does this by breaking down the parallel of the divisions between independence and dependence and between the state variables of the system and the output. The loops are closed between output and system but not between output and input. The concern is to model processes that achieve self-regulation in the face of environmental changes that they cannot control but may anticipate and not to model processes where the environment is brought into the loop. However, as soon as two subsystems, each capable of self-regulation, are coupled in a closed dyad (not in series, nor in parallel with open inputs and outputs), as noted in Sections 4.7 and 3.1, one of these subsystems is the environment to the other. In such a system the environment and the human operator as it were "chase each other's tail," and they may thus converge upon a sort of mutual dynamic partial stability.

One can express this distinction between uncoupled and coupled systems another way: normally a time series analysis is of an open system, in which the input is from outside, and the consequences of the output go back to the external world, and what happens afterward is of no concern to the theory builder. If the input source is completely specified, and its parameters that determine change (its state variables) are written sufficiently as functions of the subject's output, then we have a closed system. Some of the bivariate time series already examined can be conceptualized in this way; for example, the dyadic interaction of married couples monitored on depression scales, where each is defined as the total input to the other for the specific and restricted function of depression generation, is closed. No consideration is given to, or is needed for, exogenous variables outside the marital couple.

To turn an open system experiment into a closed system experiment is to make the input on trial $j + 1$ necessarily and sufficiently contingent upon, and hence a function of, the previous inputs and outputs on trials $\{j, j - 1, \ldots, 2, 1\}$ and the zero (initial) conditions of the system, if the system is not Markovian.

Closed systems with very slow response rates, whose expected approach to stability may take of the order of 2 hours, have been studied in process control (Edwards & Lees, 1974). The classic water-bath study of Cooke, cited in Chapter 5 as evidence of instability and switching between closed-loop and open loop control, is in essence an attempt to set up the major dynamic characteristics of industrial process control in a laboratory task. It can be shown that two dynamic systems with the same or closely related transfer functions that differ only in their time scale may be very different in the ease with which they can be controlled;

the slower system can be appreciably harder to bring onto a target output level. Attwood (1974) noted that a submarine and a powered aircraft are dynamically analogous but for their time scale, but it is more difficult to place a submarine upon the seabed than to land an aircraft. A prediction giving a graphic display of where the submarine will be in the next 7 minutes is found to be a very useful aid to navigation. The capacity of human subjects to integrate trajectories is distinctly limited, and their incompetence probably becomes even more striking as the order of the autoregression of the time series involved goes up (van Heusden, 1980). Obviously as systems become more complex, the human operator may fail to use information not just, or not even, because they involve higher-order integration but because the information overload is reached at the input stage. However evidence suggests that we need external aids to simplify information and to integrate it in time. Much of modern cognitive psychology is concerned with how information is encoded, "chunked," put into storage networks, and so on within the nervous system. What is being noted here is that complex self-regulating systems of which the human operator is a subsystem will only work if much of the encoding and integrating is done outside the operator, which is what increasing computer control of processes is doing anyway. The investigators in this area repeatedly comment that the human operator is more flexible and more economical to deal with very rare contingencies, but if contingencies are not rare and are formalizable, then they can be controlled automatically.

Attwood showed, by altering the water-bath experiment to include what is called a "distance velocity lag," that the process may then be uncontrollable for a novice. The crucial new factor is a device whereby the material being controlled is not a single mass of material (as in the water-bath experiment) but a stream, instrumented at one point as it passes by, and the stream characteristics are modified by action upstream in space and time from the point at which monitoring is performed. Such systems are very easily forced into oscillation by a human operator. It is of interest that if the control is discretized in time (made into a sampled-data system) but not in its control parameters, then oscillations tend to be diminished and control sensitivity improved. This sampling will alias out the error-inducing higher frequencies.

Replacement of a human operator by automatic control has, of course, been achieved in many well-behaved processes, and prediction of human operator performance is mathematically the same sort of problem; for example, Kalman filtering has been employed to predict and describe human control operators (Sriyananda & Towill, 1973). The emergent consensus since the early 1960s (Crossman, 1960) is that human behavior is nonstationary and nonlinear and thus cannot adequately be characterized by any model that strongly presupposes linearity and stationarity. There are, however, qualifications to be noted here:

1. As the nature of control tasks becomes more cognitive and less motor, the processes implicated become more dynamically irregular.

2. The performance of subjects of low intelligence on simple control tasks is dynamically characterizable by linear models precisely because subnormal subjects cannot integrate or compute trends or rates of change, or their cognitive equivalents.

3. The slower the system, the more difficult it is to control even if it is dynamically linear.

From these points we may deduce that no single order of dynamic model is going to hold over a wide range of subjects and situations but that the progression from one dynamic system to another should make psychological sense. The variability with which we rely on memory in control and decision tasks is loosely paralleled by shifts from closed- to open-loop behavior.

In these control paradigms, the parameters but not the dynamic structure of plant can be changed by the operator; the operator changes his own dynamic structure (and possibly his parameters with learning) as a consequence of the feedback that he receives from the plant. The operator and the plant intermittently are a closed loop, but the plant does not attempt to build an internal representation of the operator whereas the operator attempts to build an internal representation of the plant, successfully or otherwise. In fact, some researchers note that the operator constructs quite erroneous notions about how the plant works, which may in the short run give him a viable control strategy. Obviously when the human operator attempts to construct a representation in his head of a dynamic environment, he does not perform formal tests of goodness of fit in the sense of model identification, so if a complex system with the capacity to identify the transfer function of an operator is coupled in a closed loop with that same operator, there will always be asymmetries between the two.

At the same time, the idea that systems with the capacity to identify the structure of other systems could be coupled and would then approach identification recursively is a very attractive one (Bellman, 1961). No longer do we construct control processes that attempt to achieve identification in one bang but rather converge upon solutions slowly. Precisely how to do this optimally is not a solved problem (Söderström, Ljung, & Gustavsson, 1974), but it is certain that human performance will always be suboptimal. One would like to postulate that the relation between subject and environment is in the most general sense one of recursive system identification, but this is vacuous at such a level of abstraction. The existence of the problem is widely acknowledged, and the dynamic multivariate nature of recursive decisions has been attacked as a sort of regression problem (McCann, Miller, & Moskowitz, 1975). The legitimacy of tracing such processes by regression-type models is restricted (Einhorn, Kleinmuntz, & Kleinmuntz, 1979).

Some current models in use in adaptive system estimation attempt to allow for sudden and unpredictable perturbations (Tugnait & Haddad, 1980), and this runs well ahead of regression techniques; as noted earlier, the models with most

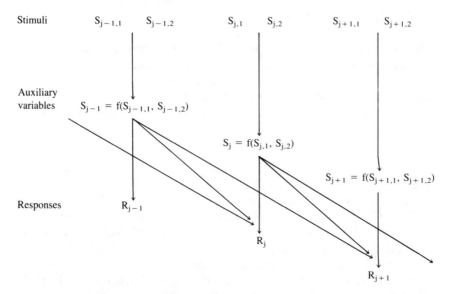

FIG. 6.4.1   Schematic outline of process with auxiliary variables acting as basis for moving-average output; all variables may be scalars or vectors.

psychological face validity seem to be those whose application in psychology is the most belated. It was realized by engineers some time ago (Chandrasekaran & Shen, 1968) that the way for a subsystem to identify another might be to have variable structure and converge (variable structure means, virtually, an ability to learn) upon identification.

This approach, where the human subject under study is coupled with a dynamic system so that each can converge upon a partial representation of the other is thus recent and unusual, if we exclude the interview situation where both subsystems are human and thus incompletely specifiable. Both conceptually and experimentally it could not have been done before the 1970s. Gregson (1980) provides an example with detailed analysis that will be briefly reviewed here for its conceptual features. For details of experimental controls and complete parameters, the reader is referred to the original source.

The study was concerned with comparing two (or more) alternative models that apparently predict closely the values of numerical similarity judgments. An experiment is thus a time series with auxiliary mediating variables that are unobserved constructs, as in Fig. 6.4.1.

We have already met this construction in Section 6.3; here the judgments are univariate (each R_j is a scalar in the discrete set $\{0, (0.1), 1.0\}$), the auxiliary variable is here a theoretical similarity, $\mathscr{S}$, and the parameters of the various f are adjustable, given the stimulus specifications (two vectors for the pair), to minimize a residual error on a linear function

$$R_j = \Sigma \ v_k \ \mathcal{S}j_{-k} \tag{6.4.1}$$

The additional complication introduced in the 1980 experiment, treating model evaluation as on-line system identification, is to have calculated on each trial the prediction of two or more alternative auxiliary variables (different models, f, or the same model and different parameters operating upon the same stimuli). The responses, either R_j or $\Sigma \ v_k R_{j-k}$ are the basis for calculating a residual error, say for the model h,

$$E_{j,h} = |R_j - \mathcal{S}_{j,h}| \tag{6.4.2}[1]$$

and then selecting from the set $\{E_{j,h}\}$ that $\mathcal{S}_j$ that minimized $E_{j,h}$. This becomes the basis for estimating the parameters in $\mathcal{S}j_{+1,h}$ for all h, and for selecting from the set $\{\mathcal{S}j_{+1,h}\}$ which model will serve as the basis for feedback after R_{j+1}, which indicates to the subject if R_{j+1} is within a tolerable bandwidth of permitted "correct" responses. Schematically we now have Fig. 6.4.2.

The key problem in this approach is the modification, by Λ, of the parameters of the set of models $\{f_h\} \rightarrow \{f_h'\}$, or in a more general notation to indicate the sequentiality of the revisions, within each model,

$$\{f_{h,j}\} \rightarrow \{f_{h,j+1}\}$$

Each f_h has a set of parameters that are multipliers or additions on the input components of the vectors that define S_1, S_2. The actual core models compared by Gregson (1980) were similarity equations that take as input the physical specification of the stimuli on each trial and yield for each stimulus pair a real positive scalar, $0 \leqslant \mathcal{S} \leqslant 1$. The modifications are achieved to these models by exploring the parameter space for each model in the vicinity of the current values and moving in a direction that locally reduces the corresponding E_h. This is a sort of hill climbing in numerical methods terminology. It is possible therefore to become trapped in a false local solution. The actual set of models used, in terms of their parameters, need never be exactly the same from one trial to the next. If they were, it would be possible to make this a stopping rule of the algorithm, under the assumption of stationarity. But if the processes converge, then at least one of the models will tend to stability or to second-order oscillations in its parameters. One might regard the transformation rules Λ as a set of rules for changing the state variables of the system or, more properly here, the state variables of a set of hypothetical systems in parallel. Each of the systems can by the operation of Λ and the minimization rule implicit in (6.4.2) be brought back on target, the target being the response behavior of the subject, provided that the parameter space of the given hypothetical system does intersect with the set of

---

[1]It makes little difference in practice if the absolute or the squared residual error is used here.

possible representations if that system is used as a model of the process $\psi\mathscr{S}$ (the psychological judgment process that yields similarity responses given the stimuli on trial j).

The additional closed-loop complication here is that the subject makes R_j with a knowledge of the previous stimuli and responses and also, in the 1980 method, with feedback informing the subject of any incompatibility between R_j and the predictions of the $f_{h,j}(S_{j,1}, S_{j,2})$ associated with min E_h. In this way are revised, to an extent and in a direction determined by Λ, and hence inbuilt by the experimenter, the values of $\psi\mathscr{S}_{j+1}$ to converge on one of the $\{f_h(S_{j+1,1}, S_{j+1,2})\}$. The implicit state variables of $\psi\mathscr{S}$ as a system are thus coupled, in discrete time, to the process Λ and the set $\{f_h\}$, and the objective is to bring the two subsystems, $\psi\mathscr{S}$ and $\Lambda,\{f_h\}$, into compatibility. Another aspect needs comment. The transfer function that determines (6.4.1) can be approximated linearly, with considerable improvement in fit over that obtained with the simple assumption that $R_j = a + b\mathscr{S}_j$. Using $k = 0, 1, \ldots, 5$ in (6.4.1), it was found that up to 97% of response variance may be fitted for one subject under some selective attention conditions. Here "selective attention" refers to component dimensions of the original $S_{j,1}, S_{j,2}$ that are each input in vector form and that may be premultiplied by weight vectors representing selective attention strategies employed under instruction by the subject.

The transfer functions of the various f_h in terms of Λ is not determined in the algorithm used by Gregson (1980); but it will be the case, because the parameters of each $f_h(S_{j,1}, S_{j,2})$ are only changed slowly by Λ and may in some cases abruptly jump back to a zero bias condition if the model drifts progressively away from good fit to responses, that the process is definitely nonlinear and subject to discontinuities. It was deliberately constructed in that form after early versions, referred to in the original paper, did not exhibit convergence or could even badly diverge. It is interesting that discontinuities in this model bear a resemblance, of heuristic importance, to those met in the efficient behavior of process control operators. This does not mean that this form of comparative model evaluation (within the set $\{f_h\}$) is necessarily a model of how human operators learn process control. It is certainly not demonstrated that it can converge optimally or by optimal selection from $\{f_h\}$ in a Bayes sense. Modern theory of systems identification has advanced a number of schemes that are Bayes optimum and it is consequently suggested that a proper long-term objective for theoretical psychology using paradigms like Fig. 6.4.2 as a starting point is to identify optimum paths to solution and to assess quantitatively how suboptimal the human operator actually is when he is coupled dynamically to systems that are themselves capable of learning and capable of modeling what it is that the operator is currently doing, and even of adjusting their own behavior in the light of his suboptimality. For the representation and analysis of such paradigms, time series analysis is an indispensible tool; a systems theoretic approach is a sufficient justification for the use of that tool.

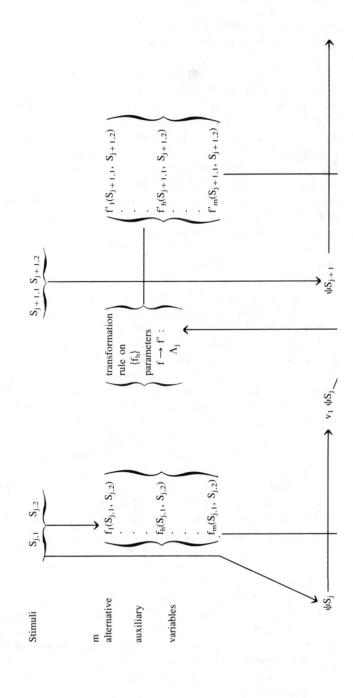

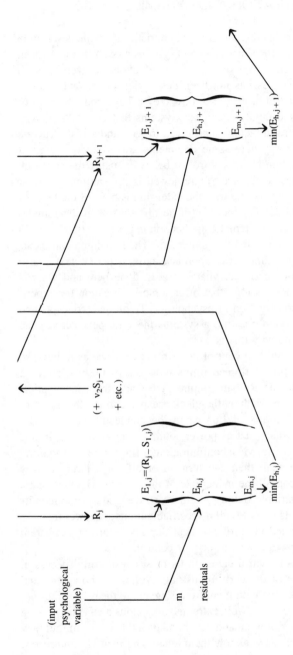

FIG. 6.4.2 Model evaluation via on-line system identification, as used by Gregson (1980).

6.5   SELF-REGULATION AND DYNAMIC CONTROL

As presented in formal mathematics, and as used heuristically in the description of psychological experiments, the time series and systems models that have been reviewed are essentially descriptive. However, the motivation for inventing such methods in the physical sciences has not been description per se but control. Complex systems are studied in order to see how they behave under a range of predictable and unpredictable input sequences. Systems that are well-behaved are preferred to those that are intractable and given to wild and self-destructive variability. In this remaining review some comments are offered on what it means to extend the description to the control of behavior, using the approach developed. The mathematics so far used or reviewed is the starting point for some theories of controllability; necessarily the extension is beyond the level of an introduction and of considerably more intrinsic difficulty than the foundations. As it has not so far found systematic application in psychology, though in principle it could, it is not covered in this monograph. The remaining comments are merely intended to put the time series approach into a wider context and to make some contradistinctions between what has been done here and what is implicit in many texts on methodology that offer some justification for experimental design and theory construction in psychology. Traditional concepts and approaches do not sit comfortably within a systems theoretic perspective, and some comments may indicate why this is so.

A system or device that could so control its own performance as to have an output that remains within predetermined limits is as old as the water clock, which goes back at least to the Roman Empire. We could trace its practical realization through mechanisms such as the clock escapement and the mechanical toys that delighted the courts of Europe in the eighteenth century. But clocks, as devices, do not usually act as power sources; they have a negligible output and one devoted to display, via a configuration of fingers, or to triggering some light switching mechanism than can turn on or off some larger energy source but not in any way control the magnitude of that source. The idea that a large power source, with variable output, could be so designed to monitor its own performance and keep its output within specifiable limits, is newer than the clock and emerged in a related class of practical devices before any coherent theory was developed to describe such a form of control.

The physical realization of control dates, in its most consistently successful forms, from the millwrights of the early industrial revolution who spread and took their ideas and constructions with them from England to the rest of Europe, between about 1780 and 1830. They were extremely ingenious men at harnessing and controlling first the power of wind and water and then that of steam, but they were not theoretical engineers as we know them today, and many left no record of their names. The social divisions between the philosopher and the artisan, which shrunk as one became the natural scientist and the other the design engineer, for some time kept theory and practice apart. As psychology left the apron strings of philosophy much later than other sciences that properly had a concern with the conceptualization and representation of control, and the areas of applied mathematics that were involved with control theory were not those usually taught to psychologists, two areas of human inquiry that in retrospect might have had a common theme had virtually no point of contact. When the idea of the control of behavior by schedules of reinforcement grew in popularity in psychology, it emerged with no avowed indebtedness to the control theory that had been in existence over a century, rather the contrary; some few terms were shared but the resemblance was superficial.

There is, of course, considerable emotional resistance to any idea that behavior can be controlled in the same way that a machine can be controlled; some sorts of control are politically and morally repugnant to us, though precisely what they are varies from one society to another, and political and moral objections to psychologists who have written about control, of whom B. F. Skinner is best known and who has attracted the most criticism, are not usually phrased with enough precision to be analyzable at the level with which we must necessarily be concerned here. Skinner's theories about building society on behavioral control procedures derived from the experimental analysis of behavior may infuriate or offend, and they may be wrong as human individual or social psychology, but at least they have the merit of being defined heuristically in terms of laboratory procedures and measurements that can be reexamined in some cases from the point of view of control theory. This can hardly be said for criticisms of an ethical or sociological sort that use words like *control* or *equilibrium* or *stability* but cannot be translated into the notions of control theory that bear similar or the same names.

The process of observing and recording the output of a system is quite distinct from the operation of exerting control. But the process of predicting the output of a system is related to the control of that system, and in mathematical terms the relation between modeling prediction and modeling control is called a *duality*. The proof that under some conditions the prediction of how a system will behave in the next few periods of observation is related to the specification of an efficient means of controlling that same system is relatively recent and necessarily a difficult problem. It will do no harm to remind the reader yet again that we are analyzing systems, and systems are part of behavior, not the totality of man. As Bellman (1967) puts it: "we will adhere to the classical convention that observation of the output is exact, instantaneous and free. Obviously this is never the situation in the study of real systems. But the practising scientist is reconciled to the fact that reality can only be approached through unreality."[2]

The idea that it is appropriate to analyze the behavior of human beings by treating them as dynamic systems was first seriously exploited in military ap-

---

[2]R. E. Bellman. *Introduction to the mathematical theory of control processes* (Vol. I). New York: Academic Press, 1967.

plications during and after World War II; for the first time in history some experimental psychologists had access to relatively sophisticated apparatus for recording continuously in time the detailed performance of quite complex systems in which the human operator was but one link, albeit an indispensible link, in a network that showed some overall capacity for self-regulation and self-correction. The applications were mainly military; the performance of tank turret guns and bomb sights in aircraft requiring human operation under constantly changing conditions was to be evaluated. The common feature of the tasks imposed on the human operator in such circumstances, and hopefully in more peaceful ones, was tracking. A target moved, some pointer or sighting mechanism was to be kept within a small error of alignment, and the ability of the subject to do this was rapidly found to depend on, apparently, a host of variables such as the shape and size of control levers and the legibility of information displays.

The methods of analyzing systems with self-regulatory capacity usually derived from control theory, which mathematically can be traced back to Maxwell in the mid-nineteenth century but more importantly to Liapunov, as noted in Chapter 1. By the time that experimental psychologists became involved in the interdisciplinary systems design exercises that military needs generated, the engineers involved had built up a tradition of constructing and analyzing, mathematically and experimentally, the type of devices that are often called servomechanisms. This is a shorthand word for mechanisms, incorporated into a machine, that regulate the rate or amount of performance within or around a specified range. However, the capacity for self-regulation played an indispensable part in the spread of mechanical rather than animal power and, again in this century has played a similar central role in displacing man from man–machine systems in which he was originally the controller and regulator. A popular example would be the high-speed trains in Japan, which at speeds of 200 km/hr are controlled by a computer on the train; the driver who sits at the front of the train may only control the movement when entering or leaving stations. Many aircraft in short flights within Europe are virtually under the control of on-board computers; the highly paid human pilot may function as a reserve emergency control system, though many passengers would feel uncomfortable if he were absent, or if he were replaced by an equally competent woman. Human feelings about the control of complex machines and systems are rarely either informed or rational.

Despite these developments, the psychology of self-regulation is in its theoretical infancy and at the time of writing is probably behind theory and experiment in psychophysiology in this respect. There is no general reticence on the part of physiologists to use servo models as paradigms for the processes they simulate or aim to control, but there is a marked reticence in psychology to involve the investigator in the same demanding and toughminded level of abstract modeling.

If a servo system is to be built, then there are various ways in which the designer has the option of incorporating human responses as a subsystem. The objective is to optimize the performance of the whole system, within given cost limits, if possible. These alternatives were being faced by designers when psychologists investigated motor skills in the 1940s and 1950s, and the diminution of the part played by human operators in some control systems was in part a consequence of the relative evaluation of the alternatives; the human operator is very flexible but not always the most reliable under stress or complex loading, or under conditions of protracted vigilance where nothing may happen for hours and then rapid and complex corrective actions be suddenly demanded of him.

The alternatives facing the designer are as follows:

1. Totally human system in which input, output, and corrective actions are all processed within the human agent.

2. The human aided by a servomechanism, with the proviso that the servo can be overruled or bypassed by the human operator at the latter's discretion.

3. The servo aided by a human operator, the servo can cut the human out of the system, with or without warning, if the human exhibits (to the servo) dynamic response characteristics that are outside permitted bounds,

4. A totally mechanical (or hydraulic or electronic) servo system; human intervention limited to the original design and switching the power supply on or off.

In all the alternatives listed here, an analysis of their characteristics under dynamically changing load is needed in order to understand and predict what they will do. This is much easier in most cases for the mechanical part of the system; there are two reasons for this state of affairs that commonly but not necessarily hold. First, in the mechanical (or hydraulic or electronic) parts of the system, the input and output variables are quantifiable and can be monitored continuously or almost continuously (here "almost continuously" means that the minimum interval between two observations of a variable is much less than the time delay factor of the shortest feedback loop in which the variable is involved in the system as a whole). Second, a priori it is much more probable that the dynamics of the mechanical servo are stationary than is the human operator.

The early reports of work in this area are characterized by features that need no longer give concern but that were thought to be crucial at the time. The experimental psychologist working on tracking tasks was not so much concerned with models of man, as models of man–machine systems; the preferred models for studying man, if his interaction with a machine was not the focus of attention, continued to be those of learning theory or factor analysis. The tasks studied were ones that are much more reliably performed by machines as soon as the total system becomes very costly and the associated cost of failure to perform the tracking task is literally astronomical; the problem of landing a manned space capsule on the surface of the moon is a case in point.

Work in the 1940s and 1950s antedated accessible computers. Ellson (1949, 1959) comments that a 2-minute tracking experiment could take 100 hours of desk calculation to analyze; if we were now interested in replicating such a study, the analysis would be done on-line and completed within a few minutes, if not at the most seconds, of the data gathering itself. These early experiments were concerned with the effects of the detailed physical design of systems upon the mean error rates of performance. Analyzed at such a level, results were often contradictory; mean error rates are not appropriate indices of performance in dynamic systems.

There were a number of theoretical difficulties that hindered advancement in this area, which it is expedient to spell out:

1. The psychologists working in this area were few, and apparently entirely dependent on engineering mathematics for their models; no specifically psychological theory seems to have been coherently developed.

2. The available models derived from classical control theory, usually Fourier analyses of continuous input and output relations, were already developed to cope with the dynamic properties of the engineering systems with which the human operators were going to interact; the object was to see if the human operator could be described in a form equivalent to some mechanical system with which, in functional equation terms, he might be thought of as exactly interchangeable. Though the human operator has interesting and exasperating qualities for the system designer, this was about the limit that analysis could then offer.

3. The choice of response measures was restricted in that only one could be considered at a time; multivariate methods were not available either theoretically or computationally.

4. The results that psychologists produce, when expressed in terms of mean error scores under different performance conditions, are critically incomplete for the systems analyst attempting a dynamic optimization of a man–machine servo system. Consequently in later work the engineers appear to have taken the problems into their own hands. When a man–machine problem emerged, then if possible it was completely circumvented by adopting a completely robotic solution. Many of the applied problems upon which psychologists worked in the 1940s and 1950s seem to be ones that were later to be solved by installing an on-line microcomputer or minicomputer with preprogrammed hardware for a specific control function.

5. Theorizing in published reviews (Ellson, 1959; Licklider, 1960) repeatedly emphasized the linearity problems, and devoted perhaps more space to considering why linearity is or is not a strict requirement for modeling human behavior then in presenting the results of modeling that same behavior by making tentative linearity assumptions. As the whole problem of how justified it is to assume linearity, or nonlinearity, in order to identify the dynamic parameters of

human performance, is strictly a quantitative one, this stumbling block is not what at first it seems to be. The evidence of the early studies was concerned with response to high rates of input variation, and for slowly changing inputs it was never doubted that good approximations to dynamic behavior could be obtained with linear models. The better results suggested that between 84% and 96% of the response variance could be represented in linear or quasi-linear models for some tracking tasks. Insufficient evidence existed to make it possible to decide, in many cases, between the appropriateness of nonlinear models with fixed parameters and linear models with variable parameters. In this sense, therefore, the advancement of any particular mathematical model of the human servo as definitive is an instance of the mathematics running ahead of the data. It could be that the complete dependence of psychology on linear S–R models and the computational intractability of nonlinear systems in engineering at that time, taken with repeated evidence of the instability of human behavior within many but not all of the tracking tasks that were attempted, induced a feeling of exasperation in investigators that the justification for linear modeling itself being attempted was more important in a presentation to the mathematically naive reader than the communication of data analyses that were intrinsically both very complex and at the same time tentative.

The problem is, of course, that the proper analysis of feedback systems is impossible without mathematics and the skilled matching of mathematical concepts to the system's behavior, which put such analysis out of the reach of many psychologists. In due course, tracking studies largely obsoleted themselves from an engineering standpoint by being concerned with the details of mechanisms and systems that were soon to be supplanted and cut themselves off from mainstream psychology by being, if written coherently, couched in a form of mathematics that was outside the comprehension of psychologists. This state of affairs, called a "catch-22 situation" by one reviewer (*Contemporary Psychology,* 1975) where none will learn the mathematics unless its usefulness is demonstrated, and no one can follow a demonstration of its usefulness unless they first learn both it and the concepts that are expressible in it and only in it, and where learning those concepts entails adopting a fundamentally different view about the form and purpose of explanations of behavior extending in time, presumably arises in the social history of all sciences. The shift from alchemy to early chemistry and revisions in biology under the impact of evolutionary concepts furnish examples of periods that have to be worked through, leaving some behind and carrying others with them. Bellman (1961) comments analogously on the resistance to changes in the style of writing models of dynamic systems.

The comments just offered on linearity as a core problem also hold in part for the problem of discontinuity. One sort of nonlinearity in dynamic systems arises when the system is subject to abrupt changes in its mode of functioning, and those changes come at somewhat unpredictable times. Within any one state the system may be stochastically stable and representable by a linear model with some level of tolerable noise attached, but the system as a whole, over all the states it can occupy, is nonlinear. This offers problems in some engineering systems; yet most airplanes fall into the description just offered, but they can be flown. The idea that a nonlinear system can be cut up into subsystems, each linear, is used and accepted in modern systems theory; the intrinsic discontinuities are themselves capable of being simulated or may only exist because the investigator's representation cuts up the total system that way.

The continuity assumptions, at the micro level, of classical theory were both necessary and reasonable to anyone trained initially in the physical sciences. They reflect both the form of available mathematics and the intuitive feel of the engineer for the behavior of mechanical systems. But there has always been doubt, in psychology, as to the legitimacy of continuity assumptions, either at the micro level or in more gross terms. Fechner's j.n.d. and sensory quantiles or multiple detection threshold theories all reflect the feeling that the human sensory and perceptual systems are prone to local jumps and discontinuities. The existence of a refractory period, immediately following a motor response, led some investigators of tracking to postulate a discontinuous system with a time unit of about one-fifth of a second; they did not, however, employ the mathematics of discontinuous time series to analyze their experiments in most cases. It is possible to build a psychophysics explicitly incorporating a finite set of major discontinuities in the response quasi-continuum to a stimulus or input continuum that is taken to be truly continuous (Gregson, 1976a).

But there evolved, not from psychology but from the statistical dynamics of time series, a complete discontinuous analog of the mathematics used by the applied psychologists investigating tracking. Conceptually, therefore, the continuity problem has been circumnavigated, and the appropriate methods of analysis compatible both with a psychology that does not wish to assume continuities and with the intrinsic logic of digital, as opposed to analog computation, are readily available. The effective demonstration of a parallelism between time series analysis by Fourier transforms and spectral decomposition and by autocorrelation analysis as a step toward the construction of linear transfer functions appears to be later than the first attempts to use servo models of human behavior. The one major investigator who did start from an autocorrelation analysis is treated with reservations, on this account, by Licklider (1960), in his comprehensive review of work up to the mid 1950s. The parallelism between continuous and discrete models is not one that was of much interest until both approaches were rapidly accessible on a computer. However, to the extent that some earlier models were dictated by a then unavoidable commitment to continuity, they may now be obsolescent.

Consequently we have now reached a point where many of the difficulties and objections have been overcome. It is now feasible to set up experiments to analyze the behavior of systems, which are only locally linear, are discontinuous at some level of measurement, and are multivariate, knowing that the analysis of any experiment coupled to a computer of reasonable capacity will follow rapidly. The problem is now not when *can* we abandon the formulations and presuppositions of experimental design and analysis that have been built outside the context of dynamic systems modeling, but when *should* we? In the area of motor performance studies there are probably no objections, but the current interest of this monograph is in cognition and sequential judgments. Restricting consideration to psychological processes where input and output can both be quantified in some way, a time series representation can be sought in the first instance and time-independent models can be treated, where plausible, as special limiting cases. This creates the position where any model that appears to represent some relationships in behavior should be derivable as a special case from the new wider representation; if it can not, then the wider representation is probably wrong. This situation can be summarized by adhering to what is known as the *correspondence principle:*

> That every new theory should contain, in as formal a way as its methods allow, a limiting transition to the old theory it replaces. If the old theory has fitted the data of some sound experimentation, then the new theory should concur in predicting those results with a comparable degree of accuracy.

6.6 DYNAMIC EXPLANATIONS IN PSYCHOLOGY

The term *dynamic* has been preempted in psychology by some schools of psychoanalytic thought and therapeutic practice that are far removed from the sense of this text. If the analogy with systems theory and dynamic modeling, which in the physical sciences and technologies has given rise to much of the mathematics we have found relevant, had been ruthlessly pursued, then it would have been justified to call this monograph "dynamic modeling in psychology" but to do so could have been to attract an audience who by their training and presuppositions would be, to say the least, baffled. We are not original in noting this state of affairs; indeed Blauberg, Sandovsky, and Yudin (1977), three Soviet writers examining the impact of systems theory on various sciences, point out that "psychology seems to be about the most favorable field for the application of systems ideas" but are hard put to find any examples apart from the qualitative theorizing of Vygotsky and Piaget.

Indeed many psychologists who are profoundly interested in problems of control and self-regulation have not shown any general awareness that those same topics, in the abstract systems theory context (Bellman and Kalaba, 1964), have a far more extensive and rigorous treatment than has been offered by psychologists who stop at analogies of water pumps, and simple mechanistic metaphors or "laws" about the relative frequencies of different classes of stimuli and responses.[3]

Zadeh in a programmatic stance suggested that systems theory has, as its problems: signal representation and classification, and systems characterization; classification and identification; analysis and synthesis; control and programming; optimization, learning, and adaptation; reliability, stability, and controllability. Though this intimidating catalog was inspired by an engineering viewpoint, it does not, after allowance is made for the terminology, read very differently from the programs of some psychologists. In fact the chapter headings of abstract systems texts (Kalman, Falb, & Arbib, 1969) could be taken from a sort of theoretical psychology; whether this is necessary or fortuitous was a motivating question for this monograph.

The proper study of mankind as systems was, of course, assiduously promoted by Ludwig von Bertalanffy (1953), and his aphorism that "the organism should be likened not to a crystal nor to an atom but to a flame" is intended to emphasize the ever-changing form of a system under the influence of external forces and internal processes, which he considered a better starting point for the biological sciences than the static, frozen-outside-time, models of physics or of stimulus–response psychology. Von Bertalanffy's preoccupation with questions on a grand scale, such as that of the isomorphism of laws of dynamic systems in diverse areas of science, left him little time to work out the detailed implications of his ideas in theoretical psychology. The only subsystem that has repeatedly arisen in different forms in neobehaviorist psychology is the cybernetic paradigm of the feedback loop; yet from von Bertalanffy onward there have legitimately been doubts expressed that this is the appropriate way of representing psychological systems. The problem of the intrinsic inadequacy of the feedback loop as a sole representation of the processes of control and self-regulation in human behavior arose repeatedly. The cybernetic model of a black box, with postulated closed loops within, is a form of stimulus–response theory but has not been the grounds for some attempted rapprochement between behaviorism and systems theory. On the contrary it appears instead to have provoked critical reviews of the cybernetic paradigm and its intrinsic limitations in describing open systems, among systems theorists themselves. Yet, at the same time, cybernetic psychology has an important role that is perhaps more distinctive outside the North American tradition. Writers such as Klix (1973) in Germany have used information theory as a binding framework for the interpretation of research, and a number of Soviet theoretical psychologists are, or have been, located in Institutes of Cybernetics. A systems approach to modeling has a distinctly international

---

[3]Dockens (1975) has essayed a link between operant conditioning and a general systems approach at a strictly verbal level, but he is atypical and has been in constructive dispute with this author for some years.

character, with borrowing from other disciplines such as electrical engineering, so that some sociologists (Cortes, Przeworsky, & Sprague, 1974) have even advanced the view that a systems theory approach has a neo-Marxist flavor and that the use of systems modeling is indicative of the sort of functionalism that Marxists describing social institutions have used as a tool. However, it is quite false to deduce any necessary as opposed to fortuitous connection between a political philosophy and a preferred mode of scientific theorizing. Blauberg, Sandovsky, and Yudin (1977) state ''it is quite obvious that no ideological significance can be attached to a system of network planning or to the principles of stratified description of hierarchical multilevel systems [p. 114].'' This does not exclude the possibility that the retention of a particular metatheoretical stance during a period of what has been called paradigm change could have ephemeral political connotations, but our interest here has involved looking at the methods and applications of concepts that are, for many psychologists, a new paradigm. This is task enough without digressing further into the sociology of science.

The connection between abstract general systems theory and the practical techniques of systems and control theory modeling is in fact a loose one, and the descriptive boxes-and-lines-of-influence models that are used in cognitive psychology derive more from the prescriptions of general systems theory, to see the world as systems of systems, some open and some closed, than from the relatively tough-minded approach of control theory that starts from mathematical axioms. Any organism or function of an organism in some restricted sense can be studied as a system, in the elementary sense that it is ongoing and temporarily self-contained, by using traditional stimulus–response notions, or the same collection of events can be the object of a systems theory analysis. The two are not the same, and the latter implies the use of some methods and concepts that include modeling compatible with time series analysis; the former practically never has. So, in different tasks chosen by the investigator, one and the same object may be studied as a system or as a nonsystem. To quote Blauberg, Sandovsky, and Yudin (1977) again ''A description of a succession of events in a . . . process differs importantly from a determination of the structure of that process . . . only in the second case does the researcher treat it as a system. Consequently the object as such, irrespective of the goals of the study and the conceptual instruments used, cannot be given an absolute characterization of a systematic or non-systematic one, as the case may be [p. 118].'' To put this another way, the system properties of the representation of a series of events, some sequence of behavior, lie in the model chosen to capture the regularities in the behavior and not in the behavior itself.

The point being led up to here is that models of neobehaviorist psychology are not generally systems in the sense that systems theory would require; this does not mean that stimulus–response models are necessarily inadequate or inaccurate, but it should mean that in the cases where stimulus–response psychology has been successful in achieving close quantitative descriptions of behavior, such as in psychophysics, mathematical learning theory, and some aspects of cognitive psychology, the models used should be realizable as special limiting cases of a dynamic systems model that is more general in its implications. To say this is to lay oneself open to the charge of setting up a grand scheme for scientific psychology in all the vague pretentiousness of the 1930s, or of von Bertalanffy (1968) himself at his most diffuse. This comment about the desired dynamic form of generalizable models in psychology is not therefore to be read as programmatic but is simply a prediction that in the long run the static or time-independent models that are easily treated as limiting cases of the simpler and more tractable sorts of dynamic models will, *ceteris paribus,* survive longest.

Differences between a systems approach and what psychologists have called a black box analysis are not clear, precisely because the term *black box analysis* seems to have meant one thing to psychologists and another confusingly similar thing to control theorists.

The general criticism of black box analysis from the psychology of the 1960s (Kleinmuntz, 1968) was essentially one of saying, justifiably, that the modeling of data regularities, by the linear presuppositions of analysis of variance or regression, is not the same thing as the modeling of the associated process structure. Nonlinear processes can readily generate linear input–output relationships; systems can produce periodic outputs with aperiodic (random, or white noise) inputs; and so on.

The problem, put succinctly, is that two or more processes with different input–output relationships cannot be the same, but two or more different processes can have the same input–output relationships, up to an arbitrary level of description, within the same set of conditions over a finite time sample. It is interestingly aggravated in psychology because the verbal or written protocols produced by subjects doing sequential tasks are used, very properly, as a sustained probe of central processes. These additional data have been used to support conjectures about the central processes themselves, on the argument that they have a quasi-logical structure that is, in some manner, closer to that of the central process logic than is the output of responses that are themselves the intended end product of the central process.

For example, suppose we present, visually, two isosceles triangles of physically different base angle but the same base length, in the same orientation with bases horizontal, and ask the subject to say "right" or "left" according to which triangle is perceived to be the more "squat." Thus far, the experiment might be a way of teaching native speakers of some other language to use the word *squat* correctly, if some contingent reinforcement is added by the experimenter. The input to the task is a series of triangle pairs, side by side on each trial. We can play experimenter's games by having trials on which there are two identical triangles, or a triangle of base angle 89.9°, and so on, to disturb the complacent subject if a subset of responses shows "perseveration," which means that responses show strong serial autocorrelation and bear no clear relationship to the stimulus properties, but let us leave the complications aside. The simplest in-put–output relation is a plot of difference in triangle base angle against frequency of saying "right" or "left." Taking arbitrary transformations of base angle differences and of response measures including latencies is not fundamentally different; such transformations hopefully put the input–output relationships into straight-line form but leave them completely outside dynamic process analysis.

The next step toward process analysis in this imaginary example is to collect protocols on judgment processes; for example, one might go "let me see, the left-hand triangle doesn't seem to be so high as the right-hand one, and the lower a triangle is the more squat it is, at least I think that is what squat means, so I will say *left*." Subject then utters "left." The protocol could be interpreted as a description of a process in which the image of the left-hand triangle is superim-posed on the right-hand one, and the magnitude and the sign of the resultant difference leads to response selection through a series of stores of vocabularies. Such an interpretation is then to be tentatively reconciled with ancillary data, such as error patterns and response latencies, and if compatibility is achieved, then the form of the cognitive process could be said to be identified.

The sort of process *identification* implied in the data reconciliation just illus-trated is interestingly different from the more general and more formal sense of *identification* as the term is used in systems analysis. Sometimes the two pro-cedures will reduce to the same thing, and this occurs when the models that the cognitive psychologist sets up have a form that is recognizably isomorphic with some abstract models already extant in systems or control theory. The process identification of cognitive psychology might be considered as yet another attempt to find the body–mind interface somewhere in the central nervous system, but it is more than that, if only because it necessarily involves setting up a three-way correspondence. It presupposes some continuing correspondence among an un-observable process, and the quasi-logical sequential structure of the protocol, and the final judgments made and designated responses. We can allow some stochastic sloppiness between the three pairings here, though in some cases the matchings can be very close indeed. It is the closeness of the matchings among the structure of a central process model (such as a memory store with predictable access times) and protocol structure, and response sequences that, when it oc-curs, is the strength of cognitive psychology and the justification of the en-deavor.

As has been hinted, in the language of systems theory the terms *identified, identification, identifiability* have some parallels with the sense of identifying a cognitive process in the psychological experiment. To sharpen the distinction, the role of protocol data in demarcating possible central mechanisms should be emphasized. If the protocol data can themselves be coded into some quantitative form, perhaps by adding marker (0, 1) variables to the occurrence or nonoccur-rence of some elements within typical protocols, then they can be interpreted in two ways.

1. They can be treated as an additional output series and together with the responses that are the nominated output of the sequential task they then constitute part of the total output of a multivariate system. In the example given previously, there can be defined one input series: the angular differences or the height differences in the isosceles triangles, with some process operation upon the series after input, and then two outputs, each of which may be multivariate; the protocol marker variables and the nominated responses with their associated latencies. In this representation there are no central or state variables; the black box is empty. This is not the way cognitive psychologists prefer to think of the representation, after going to the trouble of reintroducing the protocol data in the face of the extreme behaviorists' injunctions not to look inside the box, but at the same time from a systems theory viewpoint there is nothing necessarily between the inputs and the outputs, only more outputs; and in the model there is no assumption about the relative nearness of different outputs to a notional central process.

2. The protocols are not outputs, but a noisy representation of state variables, which both functionally and in a literal physical sense mediate the input–output relationships. This is a strong psychological metatheoretical stance, in which some behavior is defined as responses to inputs (stimuli) and task instructions (which have an equivocal status as inputs or as constraints on potential input), and the observable behavior is then the result of the process monitoring itself while it is generating the nominated output. In this position the response latencies have always been taken as indicators of central processes and not as responses, since late nineteenth-century psychophysicists first studied them systematically.

The second position is psychologically quite different from the first, the distinction being reminiscent of that drawn between stimulus–response and stimulus–organism–response psychologies, but it is equally compatible with an alternative systems theory description of the total situation, one in which the state variables are partly constrained in advance by the protocol data instead of being left to be identified by modeling on records of input–output relations with auxiliary hypotheses about the system structure. As a fundamental and recurrent problem in systems theory is that of the appropriate choice of tractable state variables to support a discrete time model of a process, the second position might be thought, *prima facie,* to be closer to a cybernetic psychology. This has not apparently been the case.

The impact of cybernetics on psychology dates from the 1950s, and was unfortunately neither as quantified nor as conceptually rigorous as it should have been. Theorists have played with the ideas of feedback and self-regulation and built analog models invoking electromechanical systems; yet no great breakthrough, no paradigm shift, emerged (Anliker, 1976; Sayre, 1976). In retrospect it is not clear what was hoped for; without the hard labor of the necessary mathematics, little could have been expected. However, there is an important point to be made in noting the limitations of both general systems theory and of the cybernetic paradigm in particular. Neither of those two approaches are quite the same as the view of systems theory taken in this monograph, and the force of the criticism of them both should be kept distinct.

Systems theorists such as Mesarovic (1964) have appropriately defined a system as ''the mapping of one subset of terms (inputs) into another (outputs)'' and the key term here is *mapping;* the definition shifts the problem of saying anything tangible from global statements about systems into local problems of mathematizing models.

One might wish to argue that a strict behaviorism, predicating stimulus–response relationships, was the proper starting point for a systems representation, because the laws of psychophysics, human or animal, are a sort of mapping in the sense defined previously. However, a strong objection to this comes quite explicitly from systems theorists; Angyal (1969) rejected fundamentally the notion that a system could ever be properly characterized by a set of binary relationships. He asserted that a system as an integral organization could not be reduced to binary relations and therefore had a fundamentally different structure. Rannap (1971) carried this argument into a formalization of a system, S, as a class of sets,

$$S = \{M_s\} \tag{6.6.1}$$

and $\{M_s\}$ has subsets, $M_s^a, M_s^b, M_s^c, \ldots$ such that for any pair, a, b, there exists a many-to-many correspondence. This is written

$$\psi_{ab} = M_s^a \to M_s^b \qquad \text{for all } a, b \tag{6.6.2}$$

and this very abstract notion provides a necessary and sufficient basis for hierarchical structures to emerge within the system.

Using many-to-many correspondences as the building blocks of models in psychology has not been a popular starting point, with the possible exception of multivariate theorists such as Cattell (1966), and certainly has not featured widely in loosely cybernetic modeling like TOTE theory (Miller et al., 1965). But the definition (6.6.2) is still not sufficient; it has to be supplemented by a characterization of the hierarchical structure that any real system exhibits and consequently needs describing at, at least, three levels: (1) from an external, integral viewpoint; (2) from the point of view of internal structure; and (3) from the point of view of considering the current system as a subsystem of a larger system. In fact most psychological theories that are testable are circumscribed in such a way that the third viewpoint is the only tenable one; if a model of feedback in auditory perception is advanced, it presupposes the auditory subsystem to be pseudo-closed but receiving energy and steady-state inputs from the organism of which it is a part. The organism and its immediate environment constitute the first level of system closure that is met when the frame of reference is extended from the subsystem.

Von Bertalanffy (1968) was at pains, in his only text on theoretical psychology, to distinguish between cybernetics and general systems theory, and then to equate the cybernetic paradigm with the familiar stimulus–response scheme, with the feedback loop added to make the system self-regulating. "In contrast general systems are non-mechanistic . . . regulative behaviour is not determined by structural or machine conditions but by the free interplay of forces." This equation between cybernetics and stimulus–response theory is not accepted readily by some psychologists who have recently reviewed changes in the theoretical presuppositions of learning theory. For example, Estes (1975) writes that "the first-order laws of learning are systems concepts expressing the way in which the organism modifies its behaviour . . . over some period of time or sequence of trials." In the sense either of modern control theory or of general systems theory it is however very doubtful, to say the least, if any of the simpler laws of learning are couched in a form that is systems theory rather than theorizing about a system in a way that antedates modern system theory.

It might be thought, on the basis of a false antithesis, that science is concerned either with description or with prediction, but not with both at once.

Suppose for a moment longer that the dichotomy between description and prediction is taken as a canon of scientific method; it frequently is implicitly in textbooks of experimental design. Then it is proper to do a self-contained finite-length experiment in which behavior is described as accurately as possible in terms of the properties and relations between properties, which we can observe and record. From this experiment a descriptive model is subsequently obtained that cannot be unique but that is one of a set that could all predict the results of subsequent experiments equally well on any measure of goodness of fit of data to theory that might be devised after the first experiment was done. By extension from this tradition, the constant search for new models and methods in time series analysis is not a search for a unique model but a search for greater accuracy of prediction, with a marginal increase or preferably a decrease in model complexity, over a wider diversity of prediction and measurement situations and without sacrificing computability. This means in practice there has to be a trade-off among accuracy, complexity, and computability, and there are no general rules for deciding when an optimum trade-off has been achieved. This is all a way of saying that the sorts of analyses that have been reviewed are, in the hands of the practitioner, an art as well as a science. It is the author's view that this situation offers a challenge that cannot be met if one starts from the traditional premises of some standard methods in experimental psychology. To be ponderous, there is such a thing as an irrelevant metatheoretical stance, and it has been taken up by psychologists anxious to have one clear set of rules on how to do an experiment.

If one is not to do either descriptive or predictive science, what is one to do? The answer is, both at once. The same procedure has to do both tasks at the same time; it has to yield a model that is constantly sensitive to its own mismatch with data and that is capable consequently of continuous self-correction. In this sense it is possible to have dynamic models and dynamic strategies for discovering models, and the distinction between the two ceases to be important because both are systems extending through time. To set up such a method of experimenting, in which modeling is combined with controlling behavior to some degree, is to create a form of hybrid experiment that has features of both traditional scaling and learning experiments. However, when the two are combined, the new form takes place in the discrete time of the experiment and not outside time as is the case for more static psychological or psychophysical scaling. The time series nature of data records has to be preserved because the statistical structure within and between time series provides the only effective information about the dynamic characteristics of the process that is being observed, or induced, or superimposed.

The statistical theory of linear stationary time series has a very extensive and rigorous literature; it is becoming apparent that little new of radical import will be added to what is already understood and available for use (Chatfield, 1975, 1977). But the theory and practical analysis of nonlinear and nonstationary time series is still, comparatively, in its early stages of development. It is in this area that discoveries could have serious and powerful implications for the psychologist whose data are known to be ill-behaved and unstable. Precisely because changes and developments are occurring so rapidly, featuring in new publications such as the recently founded *Journal of Time Series Analysis* (started in 1980) and the numerous conferences on time series organized by O. D. Anderson and co-workers, it is hazardous to conjecture what will emerge. It is certain that, to make effective use of the new methods, the investigator has to conceptualize his or her beliefs about the nature of psychological processes in a different way from the static tradition that derived from Fisher's (1929) prescriptions for agricultural experiments and field trials. If psychology is a science about dynamic processes, then it is empirically about systems and about time series. That much is inescapable.

REFERENCES AND RELATED SOURCES

Adams, J. A. Feedback theory of how joint receptors regulate the timing and positioning of a limb. *Psychological Review,* 1977, *84,* 504–523.

Aigner, D. J. A compendium on estimation of the autoregressive-moving average model from time series data. *International Economic Review,* 1971, *12,* 348–371.

Akaike, H. Markovian representation of stochastic processes and its application to the analysis of autoregressive moving average processes. *Annals of the Institute of Statistical Mathematics,* 1974, *26,* 363–387.

Akaike, H. Canonical correlation analysis of time series and the use of an information criterion. In R. K. Mehra & D. G. Lainotis (Eds.), *System identification: Advances and case studies.* New York: Academic Press, 1976.

Anderson, J. R. Arguments concerning representations for mental imagery. *Psychological Review,* 1978, *85,* 249–277.

Anderson, N. H. Algebraic models in perception. In E. O. Carterette & M. P. Friedman (Eds.), *Handbook of perception* (Vol. 2), *Psychophysical judgment and measurement.* New York: Academic Press, 1974.

Anderson, O. D. *Time series analysis and forecasting: The Box–Jenkins approach.* London: Butterworths, 1975.

Anderson, O. D. Time series analysis and forecasting: Another look at the Box–Jenkins approach. *The Statistician,* 1977, *26,* 285–303.

Anderson, O. D. *Analysing time series.* Amsterdam: North Holland Pub., 1980.

Anderson, T. W. *The statistical analysis of time series.* New York: Wiley, 1971.

Andronov, A. *Collected works* (in Russian). Moscow: Soviet Pub. House, 1956.

Angyal, A. A logic of systems. In F. E. Emery (Ed.), *Systems thinking: Selected readings.* Harmondsworth: Penguin, 1969.

Anliker, J. Biofeedback from the perspectives of cybernetics and systems science. In J. Beatty & H. Legewie (Eds.), *Biofeedback and behavior.* New York: Plenum Press, 1976.

Ansley, C. F., & Newbold, P. On the finite sample distribution of residual autocorrelations in autoregressive-moving average models. *Biometrika,* 1979, *66,* 547–553.

Arbib, M. A. *Brains, machines, and mathematics.* New York: McGraw-Hill, 1964.

Arbib, M. A. Memory limitations of stimulus–response models. *Psychological Review*, 1969, *76*, 507–510.

Äström, K. J., & Eykhoff, P. System identification—A survey. *Automatica*, 1971, *7*, 123–162.

Atkinson, R. C. *Studies in mathematical psychology* Stanford, Calif.: Stanford University Press, 1964.

Atkinson, R. C., Carterette, E. C., & Kinchla, R. A. Sequential phenomena in psychophysical judgments: A theoretical analysis. *I.R.E. Transactions in Information Theory*, 1962, *8*, 155–162.

Atkinson, R. C., & Crothers, E. J. A comparison of paried-associate learning models having different acquisition and retention axioms. *Journal of Mathematical Psychology*, 1964, *2*, 285–315.

Atkinson, R. C., & Paulson, J. A. An approach to the psychology of instruction. *Psychological Bulletin*, 1972, *78*, 49–61.

Attwood, D. The interaction between human and automatic control. In E. Edwards & F. P. Lees (Eds.), *The human operator in process control*. London: Taylor and Francis, 1974.

Baird, J. C. Psychophysical study of numbers, IV: Generalized preferred state theory. *Psychological Research* (Springer-Verlag), 1975, *38*, 175–187.

Bakeman, R., & Dabbs, J. M. Social interaction observed: Some approaches to the analysis of behaviour streams. *Personality and Social Psychology Bulletin*, 1976, *3*, 335–345.

Baker, C. H. On temporal extrapolation. *Canadian Journal of Psychology*, 1962, *16*, 37–41.

Barabasz, A. F., & Gregson, R. A. M. Antarctic wintering-over, suggestion and transient olfactory stimulation: EEG evoked potential and electrodermal responses. *Biological Psychology*, 1980, *9*, 285–295.

Baram, Y., & Sandell, N. R. An information theoretic approach to dynamical systems modelling and identification. *IEEE Transactions on Automatic Control*, 1978, *AC-23*, 61–66.

Baron, S., & Kleinman, D. L. The human as an optimal controller and information processor. *IEEE Transactions on Man-Machine Systems*, 1969, *MMS-10*, 9–17.

Bartlett, M. S. Some aspects of the time-correlation problem in regard to tests of significance. *Journal of the Royal Statistical Society*, 1935, *98*, 536–556.

Bartlett, M. S. On the theoretical specification and sampling properties of autocorrelated time series. *Journal of the Royal Statistical Society, Series B*, 1946, *8*, 27–41.

Bartlett, M. S. Periodogram analysis and continuous spectra. *Biometrika*, 1950, *37*, 1–16.

Bartlett, M. S. *An introduction to stochastic processes with special reference to methods and applications*. Cambridge, Mass.: Cambridge University Press, 1966.

Bartlett, M. S., & Kendall, D. G. The statistical analysis of variance heterogeneity and the logarithmic transformation. *Journal of the Royal Statistical Society (Supplement)*, 1946, *8*, 128–138.

Bayley, N. Mental growth in young children. *Yearbook of the National Society for the Study of Education*, 1940, *39*, 11–47.

Bayliss, L. E. *Living control systems*. London: English Universities Press, 1966.

Beggs, W. D. A., Saksteini, R., & Howarth, C. I. The generality of a theory of the intermittent control of accurate movements. *Ergonomics*, 1974, *17*, 757–768.

Bellman, R. E. *Adaptive control processes: A guided tour*. Princeton, N.J.: Princeton University Press, 1961.

Bellman, R. E. *Introduction to the mathematical theory of control processes* (Vol. 1). *Linear equations and quadratic criteria*. New York: Academic Press, 1967.

Bellman, R. E., & Kalaba, R. *Selected papers on mathematical trends in control theory*. New York: Dover, 1964.

Bellman, R. E., & Smith, C. P. *Simulation in human systems: Decision-making in psychotherapy*. New York: Wiley, 1973.

Bennett, R. J. *Spatial time series*. London: Pion Ltd., 1979.

Berglund, U. Dynamic property of the olfactory system. *Annals of the New York Academy of Sciences*, 1974, *237*, 17–27.

Bierman, G. J. *Factorization methods for discrete sequential estimation.* New York: Academic Press, 1977.

Bilodeau, I. McD. Information feedback. In E. A. Bilodeau (Ed.), *Acquisition of skill.* New York: Academic Press, 1966.

Biondi, E., Giani, L., & Grandori, F. Some psychophysical performances of the auditory system analyzed by means of mathematical modelling techniques. In J. Rose & C. Bileui (Eds.), *Modern trends in cybernetics and systems* (Vol. III). Berlin: Springer-Verlag, 1977.

Birch, G. G., Latymer, Z., & Hollaway, M. Intensity/time relationships in sweetness: Evidence for a queue hypothesis in taste chemoreception. *Chemical Senses*, 1980, *5*, 63–78.

Birkemeier, W. P., Fontaine, A. B., Celesin, G. G., & Ma, K. M. Pattern recognition techniques for the detection of epileptic transients in EEG. *IEEE Transactions in Biomedical Engineering*, 1978, *BME-25*, 213–217.

Bjorkman, M., & Holmqvist, Q. On the time order error in the construction of a subjective time scale. *Scandinavian Journal of Psychology*, 1960, *1*, 7–13.

Blackman, R. B., & Tukey, J. W. *The measurement of power spectra.* New York: Dover, 1959.

Blauberg, I. V., Sandovsky, V. N., & Yudin, E. G. *Systems theory: Philosophical and methodological problems.* Moscow: Progress Pub., 1977.

Bliss, C. I. *Statistics in biology.* New York: McGraw-Hill, 1970.

Bloomfield, P. Fourier analysis of time series, an introduction. London: Wiley, 1976.

Bogert, B. P., Healy, M. J. R., & Tukey, J. W. The quefrency analysis of Time Series for Echoes: Cepstrum, psuedo-autocovariance, cross-cepstrum, and saphe cracking. In M. Rosenblatt (Ed.), *Time series analysis.* New York: Wiley, 1963.

Bohlin, T. Four cases of identification of changing systems. In R. K. Mehra & D. G. Lainiotis (Eds.), *System identification: Advances and case studies.* New York: Academic Press, 1976.

Box, G. E. P., & Jenkins, G. M. *Time series analysis, forecasting and control.* San Francisco, Ca.: Holden-Day, 1970.

Box, G. E. P., & Pierce, D. A. Distribution of residual autocorrelations in autoregressive integrated moving average models. *Journal of the American Statistical Association*, 1970, *65*, 1509–1526.

Box, G. E. P., & Taio, G. C. A change in level of a nonstationary time series. *Biometrika*, 1965, *52*, 181–192.

Box, G. E. P., & Tiao, G. C. Intervention analysis with applications to economic and environmental problems. *Journal of the American Statistical Association*, 1975, *70*, 70–79.

Box, G. E. P., & Tiao, G. C. A canonical analysis of multiple time series. *Biometrika*, 1977, *64*, 355–365.

Bracewell, R. *The Fourier transform and its applications.* New York: McGraw-Hill, 1965.

Briggs, G. E. Tracking behavior. In E. A. Bilodeau (Ed.), *Acquisition of skill.* New York: Academic Press, 1966.

Brigham, E. O. *The fast Fourier transform.* Englewood Cliffs, N.J.: Prentice-Hall, 1974.

Brillinger, D. R. The identification of polynomial systems by means of higher order spectra. *Journal of Sound and Vibration*, 1970, *32*, 301–313.

Brillinger, D. R. *Time series data analysis and theory.* New York: Holt, Rinehart & Winston, 1975.

Brillinger, D. R. The identification of a particular nonlinear time series system. *Biometrika*, 1977, *64*, 509–515.

Broadbent, D. E. Levels, hierarchies, and the locus of control. *The Quarterly Journal of Experimental Psychology*, 1977, *29*, 181–202.

Buckley, W. *Modern systems research for the behavioral scientist.* Chicago: Aldine, 1968.

Cadzow, J. A. *Discrete-time systems: An introduction with interdisciplinary applications.* Englewood Cliffs, N.J.: Prentice-Hall, 1973.

Campbell, F. W., & Robson, J. G. Application of Fourier analysis to the visibility of gratings. *Journal of Physiology*, 1968, *197*, 551–566.

Carmone, R. AEP, a new approach to time series analysis and forecasting. In O. D. Anderson (Ed.), *Analysing time series*. Amsterdam: North Holland Pub., 1980.

Casti, J. *Connectivity, complexity, and catastrophe in large-scale systems*. New York: Wiley, 1979.

Cattell, R. B. (Ed.). *Handbook of multivariate experimental psychology*. Chicago: Rand McNally, 1966.

Chandrasekaran, B., & Shen, D. W. G. On expediency and convergence in variable-structure automata. *IEEE Transactions on Systems Science and Cybernetics*, 1968, *SSC-4*, 52–60.

Chatfield, C. *The analysis of time series, theory and practice*. London: Chapman and Hall, 1975.

Chatfield, C. Some recent developments in time series analysis. *Journal of the Royal Statistical Society Series A*, 1977, *140*, 492–510.

Chen, C-T. *Analysis and synthesis of linear control systems*. New York: Holt, Rinehart & Winston, 1975.

Chignell, M. *A new stimulus for psychology: The properties and uses of Walsh functions and their derivations*. Paper presented at the 49th Congress of the Australian and New Zealand Association for the Advancement of Science, Auckland, N.Z., 1979.

Chignell, M. *Cognitive mechanisms of categorization*. Unpublished Ph.D. thesis, University of Canterbury, New Zealand, 1980.

Chmelař, V., & Osecký, P. Matematické Modely Průběhu Aktivní Pozornosti. *Sborník Prací Filosofické Fakulty Brněnské University*, 1974, *19*, 17–51.

Chmelař, V., & Osecký, P. The Markov model of active attention. *Studia Psychologica* (Bratislava), 1975, *17*, 94–104.

Cinlar, E. *Introduction to stochastic processes*. Englewood Cliffs, N.J.: Prentice-Hall, 1975.

Cochran, W. T., Cooley, J. W., Favin, D. L., Helms, H. D., Kaenel, R. A., Lang, W. W., Maling, G. C., Nelson, D. E., Rader, C. M., & Welch, P. D. What is the fast Fourier transform? *IEEE Transactions on Audio and Electroacoustics*, 1967, *AU-15*, 45–56.

Coombs, C. H. *A theory of data*. New York: Wiley, 1964.

Coppola, R., Tabor, R., & Buchsbaum, M. S. Signal to noise ratios and response variability measurements in single trial avoked potentials. *Electroencephalography and Clinical Neurophysiology*, 1978, *44*, 214–222.

Cortes, F., Przeworsky, A., & Sprague, J. *Systems analysis for social scientists*. New York: Wiley, 1974.

Cox, D. R., & Lewis, P. A. W. *The statistical analysis of series of events*. London: Methuen, 1966.

Creelman, C. D. Human discrimination of auditory duration. *Journal of the Acoustical Scoiety of America*, 1962, *34*, 582–593.

Crossman, E. R. F. W. The information capacity of the human motor system in pursuit tracking. *Quarterly Journal of Experimental Psychology*, 1960, *12*, 1–15.

Crossman, E. R. F. W., & Cooke, J. E. Manual control of slow-response systems. In E. Edwards & F. P. Lees (Eds.), *The human operator in process control*. London: Taylor and Francis, 1974.

Davies, N., & Newbold, P. Some power studies of a portmanteau test of time series model specification. *Biometrika*, 1979, *66*, 153–155.

Dockens, W. S., III. Operant conditioning: A general systems approach. In W. S. Dockens (Ed.), *Applications of behavior modification*. New York: Academic Press, 1975.

Drösler, J. Untersuchung des Ruhe-Elektroencephalogramms und seiner Bezichung zum weissen Rauschen. *Zeitschrift für Experimentelle und Angewandte Psychologie*, 1963, *10*, 471–485.

Drösler, J. Extending the temporal range of psychometric prediction by optimal linear filtering of mental test scores. *Psychometrika*, 1978, *43*, 533–550.

Dunnett, C. W. Approximations to the probablity integral and certain percentage points of a multivariate analogue of student's *t*-distribution. *Biometrika*, 1955, *42*, 258–260.

Durbin, J. Tests for serial correlation in regression analysis based on the periodogram of least-squares residuals. *Biometrika*, 1969, *56*, 1–15.

Durbin, J., & Watson, G. S. Testing for serial correlation in least squares regression. I. *Biometrika*, 1950, *37*, 409–427.

Durbin, J., & Watson, G. S. Testing for serial correlation in least squares regression, II. *Biometrika*, 1951, *38*, 159–178.

Edwards, E., & Lees, F. P. *The human operator in process control.* London: Taylor and Francis, 1974.

Ehrlich, S. Le méchanisme de la synchronisation sensori-motrice; étude expérimentale. *L'Année Psychologique*, 1958, *58*, 7–23.

Einhorn, H. J., Kleinmuntz, D. N., & Kleinmuntz, B. Linear regression and process-tracing models of judgment. *Psychological Review*, 1979, *86*, 465–485.

Eisler, H. Subjective duration and psychophysics. *Psychological Review*, 1975, *82*, 429–450.

Eisler, H. Experiments on subjective duration 1868–1975. A collection of power function exponents. *Psychological Bulletin*, 1976, *83*, 1154–1171.

Eisler, H. Attention to visually and auditorily presented durations. In S. Dornic (Ed.), *Attention and performance VI*. Hillsdale, N.J.: Lawrence Erlbaum Associates, 1977.

Ellson, D. G. The application of operational analysis to human motor behavior. *Psychological Review*, 1949, *56*, 9–17.

Ellson, D. G. Linear frequency theory as behavior theory. In S. Koch (Ed.), *Psychology: A study of a science* (Vol. 2). *General systematic formulations, learning and special processes*. New York: McGraw-Hill, 1959.

Estes, W. K. (Ed.). *Handbook of learning and cognitive processes* (Vol. I). *Introduction to concepts and issues*. Hillsdale, N.J.: Lawrence Erlbaum Associates, 1975.

Eykhoff, P. (Ed.). *Identification and system parameter estimation* (Vols. I and II). Amsterdam: North Holland Pub., 1973.

Eykhoff, P. *System Identification Parameter and State Estimation*. New York: Wiley, 1974.

Falmagne, J. C. Stochastic models for choice reaction time with applications to experimental results. *Journal of Mathematical Psychology*, 1965, *2*, 77–124.

Farças, D. D. Simulation of electroencephalographic waves by means of a feedback system. In J. Rose & C. Bilciu (Eds.), *Modern trends in cybernetics and systems* (Vol. III). Berlin: Springer-Verlag, 1977.

Fechner, G. *Elemente der Psychophysik.* Leipzig: Breitkopf und Härtel, 1860.

Findley, D. F. (Ed.) *Applied time series analysis*. New York: Academic Press, 1978.

Fisher, R. A. Tests of significance in harmonic analysis. *Proceedings of the Royal Society, Series A*, 1929, *125*, 54–59.

Flanagan, J. L. Spectrum analysis in speech coding. *IEEE Transactions on Audio and Electroacoustics*, 1967, *AU-15*, 66–69.

Flexser, A. J., & Bower, G. H. How frequency affects recency judgments. *Journal of Experimental Psychology*, 1974, *103*, 706–716.

Foster, D. H. A model of the human visual system in its response to certain classes of moving stimuli. *Kybernetik*, 1971, *8*, 69–84.

Fourier, J. B. *Théorie analytique de la chaleur*. Paris, 1822. (Reprinted in English, New York: Dover, 1955.)

Fréchet, M. Sur quelque points du calcul fonctionnel. *Rendiconti del Circolo Matematico di Palermo*, 1906, 22, 1–74.

Freeman, W. J. A linear distributed feedback model for prepyriform cortex. *Experimental Neurology*, 1964, *10*, 525–547.

Freiberger, W., & Grenander, U. Approximate distribution of noise power measurement. *Quarterly Journal of Applied Mathematics*, 1959, *17*, 271–283.

Fuller, W. A. *Introduction to statistical time series*. New York: Wiley, 1976.

Gabr, M. M., & Subba Rao, T. A note on the estimation of the bispectral density function of a stationary time series. *Department of Mathematics U.M.I.S.T., Technical Report No. 123*, 1979.

Ganz, L. Temporal factors in visual perception. In E. C. Carterette & M. P. Friedman (Eds.), *Handbook of perception* (Vol. V). *Seeing*. New York: Academic Press, 1975.

Gastwirth, J. L., & Rubin, H. Effect of dependence on the level of some one-sample tests. *Journal of the American Statistical Association*, 1971, *66*, 816–820.

Gel'fand, I. M., & Yaglom, A. M. Calculation of the amount of information about a random function contained in another such function. *American Mathematical Society Translations*, 1959, *12*, 199–264.

Gersh, W., & Goddard, G. V. Epileptic focus location: Spectral analysis method. *Science*, 1970, *169*, 701–702.

Gersh, W., Yonemoto, J., & Naitoh, P. Automatic classification of multivariate EEGs using an amount of information measure on the eigenvalues of parametric time series model features. *Computers and Biomedical Research*, 1977, *10*, 207–318.

Gibbon, J. Timing and discrimination of shock density in avoidance. *Psychological Review*, 1972, *79*, 68–92.

Gill, A. *Introduction to the theory of finite-state machines*. New York: McGraw-Hill, 1962.

Glass, G. V. Estimating the effects of intervention into a nonstationary time series. *American Educational Research Journal*, 1972, *9*, 463–477.

Glass, G. V., Willson, V. L., & Gottman, J. M. *Design and analysis of time series experiments*. Boulder, Colo.: Colorado Associated University Press, 1975.

Glencross, D. J. Control of skilled movements. *Psychological Bulletin*, 1977, *84*, 14–29.

Godfrey, L. G. Testing the adequacy of a time series model. *Biometrika*, 1979, *66*, 67–72.

Goodrich, R. L., & Caines, P. E. Linear system identification from nonstationary cross-sectional data. *IEEE Transactions Automatic Control*, 1979, *AC-24*, 403–411.

Goodwin, G. C., & Payne, R. L. *Dynamic system identification*. New York: Academic Press, 1977.

Gottman, J. M., & Glass, G. V. Analysis of interrupted time-series experiments. In T. R. Kratochwill (Ed.), *Single subject research: Strategies for evaluating change*. New York: Academic Press, 1978.

Granger, C. W. J., & Andersen, A. P. *An introduction to bilinear time series models*. Göttingen: Vandenhoeck and Ruprecht, 1978.

Green, D. M. Fourier analysis of reaction time data. *Behavior Research Methods and Instrumentation*, 1971, *3*, 121–125.

Green, D. M., & Luce, R. D. Counting and timing mechanisms in auditory discrimination and reaction time. In D. H. Krantz, R. C. Atkinson, R. D. Luce, & P. Suppes, (Eds.), *Contemporary developments in mathematical psychology*. San Francisco, Ca.: Freeman, 1974.

Green, D. M., Luce, R. D., & Duncan, J. E. Variability and sequential effects in magnitude production and estimation of auditory intensity. *Perception & Psychophysics*, 1977, *22*, 450–456.

Gregson, R. A. M. An aesthetic hedonic contrast paradox. *Australian Journal of Psychology*, 1968, *20*, 225–231.

Gregson, R. A. M. Sequences of similarity judgments as time series. *Acta Psychologica*, 1974, *38*, 429–445.

Gregson, R. A. M. *Psychometrics of similarity*. New York: Academic Press, 1975.

Gregson, R. A. M. Psychophysical discontinuity and pseudosequence effects. *Acta Psychologica*, 1976, *40*, 431–451. (a)

Gregson, R. A. M. A comparison evaluation of seven similarity models. *British Journal of Mathematical and Statistical Psychology*, 1976, *29*, 139–156. (b)

Gregson, R. A. M. A cognitive multivariate time series and its analysis. *Acta Psychologica*, 1978, *42*, 277–291.

Gregson, R. A. M. Model evaluation via stochastic parameter convergence as on-line system identification. *British Journal of Mathematical and Statistical Psychology,* 1980, *33,* 17–35.

Gregson, R. A. M. Time series in psychology: A case study in olfactory psychophysics. *Proceedings 4th International Time Series Meeting, Valencia, 1981.* Amsterdam: North Holland Pub., 1982.

Gregson, R. A. M., & Paddick, R. G. Linear transfer spectra for olfactory magnitude estimation sequences. *Chemical Senses and Flavor,* 1975, *1,* 403–410.

Gregson, R. A. M., Smith, D. A. R., Strelow, R., & Brabyn, J. Acute effects of alcohol on measures of walking performance. *Applied Psychological Measurement,* 1978, *2,* 203–220.

Grossberg, S. Adaptive pattern classficiation and universal recoding, II. Feedback, expectation, olfaction, illusions. *Biological Cybernetics,* 1976, *23,* 187–202.

Grossberg, S. Behavioral contrast in short term memory: Serial binary memory models or parallel continuous memory models? *Journal of Mathematical Psychology,* 1978, *17,* 199–215.

Gruder, C. L., Cook, T. D., Hennigan, K. M., Flay, B. R., Alessis, C., & Halamaj, J. Empirical tests of the absolute sleeper effect predicted from the discontinuing cue hypothesis. *Journal of Personality and Social Psychology,* 1978, *36,* 1061–1074.

Gruder, W. A., & Grisell, R. D. *Simulation and identification in biological science.* Claremont, Calif.: International Multidisciplinary Research Association, 1977.

Gulliksen, H. Comparatal dispersion, a measure of accuracy of judgment. *Psychometrika,* 1958, *23,* 137–150.

Hahlweg, K., Revenstorf, D., & Schindler, L. *Comparison of two behavioral intervention techniques in the area of marital therapy.* (Contingency management and communication training.) Paper presented at the 7th Conference of the European Association of Behavior Therapy (EABT), Uppsala, 1977.

Hale, F. J. *Introduction to control system analysis and design.* Englewood Cliffs, N.J.: Prentice-Hall, 1973.

Hannan, E. J. *Multiple time series.* New York: Wiley, 1970.

Haralick, R. M., Shanmugan, K., & Dinstein, I. Textural features for image classification. *IEEE Transactions on Systems, Man and Cybernetics,* 1973, *SMC-3,* 610–621.

Harmuth, H. H. *Sequency theory: Foundations and applications.* New York: Academic Press, 1977.

Harrison, P. J., & Stevens, C. F. Bayesian forecasting. *Journal of the Royal Statistical Society, Series B.* 1976, *38,* 205–247.

Harvey, L. O., & Gervais, M. J. Visual texture perception and Fourier analysis. *Perception & Psychophysics,* 1978, *24,* 534–542.

Hassab, J. C. Derivatives of statistical measures on the cepstrum. *IEEE Transactions on Information Theory,* 1977, *IT-23,* 540–543.

Hayes–Roth, F. Distinguishing theories of representation: A critique of Anderson's "Arguments concerning mental imagery." *Psychological Review,* 1979, *86,* 376–382.

Heath, R. A. *Adaptive filtering and detection of change: A general methodology for information processing research.* Paper presented at the Eighth Australian Experimental Psychology Conference, Adelaide, 1981.

Hellström, Å. Time-errors for duration: Nondependency on judgment mode. *Reports from the Department of Psychology,* University of Stockholm, 1977, No. 496. (a)

Hellström, Å. Factors producing and not producing time-errors: An experiment with loudness comparisons. *Reports from the Department of Psychology, University of Stockholm,* 1977, No. 497. (b)

Hellström, Å. Differential sensation weighting as the basic cause of time-errors. *Reports from the Department of Psychology, University of Stockholm,* 1977, No. 498. (c)

Helson, H. *Adaptation level theory.* New York: Harper & Row, 1964. (a)

Helson, H. Current trends and issues in adaptation-level theory. *American Psychologist,* 1964, *19,* 26–38. (b)

Holland, M. K., & Lockhead, G. R. Sequential effects in absolute judgments of loudness. *Perception & Psychophysics*, 1968, *3*, 409–414.

Horton, R. L. *The general linear model*. New York: McGraw-Hill, 1978.

Howarth, C. I., & Bulmer, H. G. Non-random sequences in visual threshold experiments. *Quarterly Journal of Experimental Psychology*, 1956, *8*, 163–171.

Itakura, F. Minimum prediction residual principle applied to speech recognition. *IEEE Transaction on Acoustics, Speech and Signal Processing*, 1975, *ASSP-23*, 67–72.

Jaffe, J., & Feldstein, S. *Rhythms of dialogue*. New York: Academic Press, 1970.

Jenkins, G. M. Cross-spectral analysis and the estimation of linear open loop transfer functions. In M. Rosenblatt (Ed.), *Time series analysis*. New York: Wiley, 1961.

Jenkins, G. M., & Watts, D. G. *Spectral analysis and its application*. San Francisco, Ca.: Holden-Day, 1968.

Jesteadt, W., Luce, R. D., & Green, D, M. Sequential effects in judgments of loudness. *Journal of Experimental Psychology: Human Perception and Performance*, 1977, *3*, 92–104.

Jindra, R. H. EEG analysis by means of the Parcas coefficients. *Biological Cybernetics*, 1977, *28*, 51–54.

John, E. R. *Neurometrics: Clinical applications of quantitative electrophysiology*. Hillsdale, N.J.: Lawrence Erlbaum Associates, 1977.

John, E. R., Ruchkin, D. S., & Vidal, J. J. Measurement of event-related potentials. In E. Callaway, P. Theting, & S. H. Koslow (Eds.), *Event-related brain potentials in man*. New York: Academic Press, 1978.

Jones, R. R., Vaught, R. S., & Weinrot, K. Time-series analysis in operant research. *Journal of Applied Behaviour Analysis*, 1977, *10*, 151–166.

Jury, E. I. *Theory and application of the Z-transform method*. New York: Wiley, 1958.

Kadane, J. B., Larkin, J. H., & Mayer, R. H. A moving average model for sequential reaction-time data. *Journal of Mathematical Psychology*, 1981, *23*, 115–133.

Kalman, R. E. A new approach to linear filtering and prediction problems. *Transactions of the ASME: Journal of Basic Engineering*, 1960, *3*, 35–47.

Kalman, R. E., & Bucy, R. S. New results in linear filtering and prediction theory. *Transactions of the ASME: Journal of Basic Engineering*, 1961, *4*, 95–104.

Kalman, R. E., Falb, P. L., & Arbib, M. A. *Topics in mathematical system theory*. New York: McGraw-Hill, 1969.

Kantowitz, B. H. On the beaten track. *Contemporary Psychology*, 1975, *20*, 731–733.

Kashyap, R. L. Optimal choice of AR and MA parts in autoregressive moving average models. *Technical Report, School of Electrical Engineering, Purdue University*, January 1979.

Kashyap, R. L. Inconsistency of the AIC rule for estimating the order of autoregressive models. *Technical Report, School of Electrical Engineering, Purdue University*, February 1980 (also in *IEEE Transactions on Automatic Control*, 1980).

Kaufman, L. *Sight and mind: An introduction to visual perception*. London: Oxford University Press, 1975.

Kaufman, A. *Introduction to the theory of fuzzy subsets* (Vol. I). New York: Academic Press, 1975.

Kaya, Y., & Ishikawa, M. Test of goodness of fit of impulse response model. *IEEE Transactions on Automation and Control*, 1971, *AC-16*, 247–254.

Kelly, D. H. Theory of flicker and transient responses, I. Uniform fields. *Journal of the Optical Society of America*, 1971, *61*, 537–546.

Kendall, M. G. *Time-series*. London: Griffin, 1973.

Kendall, M. G., & Stuart, A. *The advanced theory of statistics* (Vol. I). London: Griffin, 1961.

Kendall, M. G., & Stuart, A. *The advanced theory of statistics* (Vol. II). London: Griffin, 1963.

Kendall, M. G., & Stuart, A. *The advanced theory of statistics* (Vol. III). London: Griffin, 1968.

Kennedy, J. C. *A dynamic analysis of a time estimation task*. Unpublished dissertation, Department of Psychology, University of Canterbury, New Zealand, 1977.

Kirby, N. H. Serial effects in an eight-choice serial reaction time task. *Acta Psychologica*, 1975, *39*, 205–216.

Klapp, S. T., & Greim, D. M. Programmed control of aimed movements revisited: The role of target visibility and symmetry. *Journal of Experimental Psychology: Human Perception and Performance*, 1979, *5*, 509–521.

Kleinmuntz, B. *Formal representation of human judgment*. New York: Wiley, 1968.

Klix, F. *Organismische Informationsverarbeitung*. Berlin: Akademic-Verlag, 1973.

Kohonen, T. *Associative memory: A system theoretic approach*. Berlin: Springer-Verlag, 1977.

Koopmans, L. H. *The spectral analysis of time series*. New York: Academic Press, 1974.

Kramer, T. J., & Rilling, M. Differential reinforcement of low rates: A selective critique. *Psychological Bulletin*, 1970, *74*, 225–254.

Kratochwill, T. R. *Single subject research: Strategies for evaluating change*. New York: Academic Press, 1978.

Krut'ko, P. D. *Statistical dynamics of sampled data systems*. London: Iliffe, 1969.

Kufner, A., & Kadlec, J. *Fourier series*. London: Iliffe, 1971 (Translated from Czech original by G. A. Toombs).

Laming, D. R. J. *Information theory of choice reaction times*. London: Academic Press, 1968.

Lee, Y. W., & Schetzen, M. Measurement of the Wiener kernels of a non-linear system by cross-correlation. *International Journal of Control*, 1965, *2*, 237–254.

Lefebvre, V. A., & Batchelder, W. H. The nature of Soviet mathematical psychology. *Journal of Mathematical Psychology*, 1981, *23*, 153–183.

Leondes, C. T. (Ed.). *Theory and applications of Kalman filtering*. Los Angeles: UCLA, 1970.

Leontiev, A., Luriya, A., & Smirnov, A. *Psychological research in the USSR* (Vol. I). Moscow: Progress Pub., 1966.

Levine, G., & Burke, C. J. *Mathematical model techniques for learning theories*. New York: Academic Press, 1972.

Levinson, S. E., Rabiner, L. R., Rosenberg, A. E., & Wilpon, J. G. Interactive clustering techniques for selecting speaker-independent reference templates for isolated word recognition. *IEEE Transactions in Acoustics, Speech and Signal Processing*, 1979, *27*, 134–141.

Lewis, P. A. W. Remarks on the theory, computation and application of the spectral analysis of series of events. *Journal of Sound and Vibration*, 1970, *12*, 353–375.

Liapunov, A. The general problem of the stability of movement (in Russian, 1892). Reprinted in *Annals of Mathematical Studies* 1947, No. 17. Princeton, N.J.: Princeton University Press.

Licklider, J. C. R. Quasilinear operator models in the study of manual tracking. In R. D. Luce (Ed.), *Developments in mathematical psychology*. Glencoe, Ill.: Free Press, 1960.

Likeš, J. Distributions of some statistics in samples from experimental and power-function populations. *Journal of the American Statistical Association*, 1967, *62*, 259–271.

Lindorff, D. P. *Theory of sampled-data control systems*. New York: Wiley, 1965.

Ljung, G. M., & Box, G. E. P. The likelihood function of stationary autoregressive-moving average models. *Biometrika*, 1979, *66*, 265–270.

Lord, F. M., & Novick, M. R. *Statistical theories of mental test scores*. Reading, Mass.: Addison-Wesley, 1968.

Luce, R. D. What sort of measurement is psychophysical measurement? *American Psychologist*, 1972, *27*, 96–106.

Luce, R. D., Baird, J. C., Green, D. M., & Smith, A. F. Two classes of models for magnitude estimation. *Journal of Mathematical Psychology*, 1980, *22*, 121–148.

Luce, R. D., Bush, R. R., & Galanter, E. (Eds.). *Handbook of mathematical psychology* (Vol. I). New York: Wiley, 1963.

Luce, R. D., & Green, D. M. A neural timing theory for response times and the psychophysics of intensity. *Psychological Review*, 1972, *79*, 14–57.

Luce, R. D., & Green, D. M. Detection, discrimination and recognition. In E. C. Carterette & M.

P. Friedman (Eds.), *Handbook of perception* (Vol. 2), *Psychophysical judgment and measurement*. New York: Academic Press, 1974. (a)

Luce, R. D., & Green, D. M. The response ratio hypothesis for magnitude estimation. *Journal of Mathematical Psychology*, 1974, *11*, 1–14. (b)

Ludlow, A. R. The evolution and simulation of a decision maker. In F. M. Toates & T. R. Halliday (Eds.), *Analysis of motivational processes*, London: Academic Press, 1980.

Luria, A. R. *The mind of a mnemonist: A little book about a vast memory*. London: Cape, 1968.

MacKay, D. M. Towards an information-flow model of human behaviour. *British Journal of Psychology*, 1956, *47*, 30–43.

MacKay, D. M. Psychophysics of perceived intensity: A theoretical basis for Fechner's and Stevens' laws. *Science*, 1963, *139*, 1213–1216.

MacNeill, I. B. A test of whether several time series share common periodicities. *Biometrika*, 1977, *64*, 495–508.

Maffei, L., & Fiorentini, A. The visual cortex as a spatial frequency analyser. *Vision Research*, 1973, *13*, 1255–1267.

Maklad, M. S., & Nichols, S. T. A new approach to model structure discrimination. *IEEE Transactions on Systems, Man and Cybernetics*, 1980, *SMC-10*, 78–84.

Marmarelis, P. Z., & Marmarelis, V. Z. *Analysis of physiological systems: The white noise approach*. New York: Plenum Press, 1978.

Mayes, J. T., & McIvor, G. Levels of processing and retrieval: Recency effects after incidental learning in a reaction time task. *The Quarterly Journal of Experimental Psychology*, 1980, *32*, 635–648.

McCann, J. M., Miller, J. G., & Moskowitz, H. Modeling and testing dynamic multivariate decision processes. *Organizational Behavior and Human Performance*, 1975, *14*, 281–303.

McDougall, W. The nature of inhibitory processes within the nervous system. *Brain*, 1903, *26*, 153–191.

McFarland, D. J. *Feedback mechanisms in animal behaviour*. New York: Academic Press, 1971.

McFarland, D. J. *Motivational control systems analysis*. New York: Academic Press, 1974.

McGill, W. J. Random fluctuations of response rate. *Psychometrika*, 1962, *27*, 3–17.

McGill, W. J., & Gibbon, J. The general-gamma distribution and reaction time. *Journal of Mathematical Psychology*, 1965, *2*, 1–18.

McLeod, A. I. Improved Box-Jenkins estimators. *Biometrika*, 1977, *64*, 531–534.

Meehl, P. E. Theoretical risks and tabular asterisks: Sir Karl, Sir Ronald, and the slow progress of soft psychology. *Journal of Consulting and Clinical Psychology*, 1978, *46*, 806–835.

Mendel, J. M., & Gieseking, D. L. Bibliography on the linear-quadratic-Gaussian problem. *IEEE Transactions on Automatic Control*, 1971, *AC-16*, 847–869.

Meredith, P. The psychophysical structure of temporal information. In J. T. Fraser, F. C. Haber, & G. H. Müller (Eds.), *The study of time*. Berlin: Springer-Verlag, 1972.

Mesarovic, M. D. *Views on general systems theory*. New York: Wiley, 1964.

Mesarovic, M. D., & Takahara, Y. *General systems theory: Mathematical foundations*. New York: Academic Press, 1975.

Michon, J. A. De Perceptie van Duur. *Nederlands Tijdschrift voor Psychologie*, 1965, *20*, 391–418.

Michon, J. A. *Timing in temporal tracking*. Soesterberg, Netherlands Institute for Perception RVO-TNO, 1967.

Miller, G. A., Galanter, E., & Pribram, K. H. *Plans and the structure of behavior*. New York: Holt, Rinehart & Winston, 1965.

Miller, J. G. *Living systems*. New York: McGraw-Hill, 1978.

Milsum, J. H. (Ed.). *Positive feedback*. London: Pergamon, 1968.

Mitchiner, J. L., Crews, W. B., Watt, K. E. F., & Brewer, J. W. Delta approximation: Parameter identification for simulation models of human behavior. *IEEE Transactions in Systems, Man and Cybernetics*, 1975, *SMC-5*, 189–201.

Mohler, R. R., & Ruberti, A. *Theory and applications of variable structure systems*. New York: Academic Press, 1972.

Montgomery, D. C., & Johnson, L. A. *Forecasting and time series analysis*. New York: McGraw-Hill, 1976.

Morrison, D. F. *Multivariate statistical methods*. New York: McGraw-Hill, 1967.

Mulaik, S. A. *The foundations of factor analysis*. New York: McGraw-Hill, 1972.

Nachmias, J., Sansbury, R., Vassilev, A., & Weber, A. Adaptation to square-wave gratings: In search of the elusive third harmonic. *Vision Research*, 1973, *13*, 1335–1341.

Newbold, P. The equivalence of two tests of time series model adequacy. *Biometrika*, 1980, *67*, 463–465.

Newbold, P., & Granger, C. W. J. Experience with forecasting univariate time series and the combination of forecasts. *Journal of the Royal Statistical Society, Series A*. 1974, *137*, 131–164.

Nicholls, D. F. A comparison of estimation methods for vector linear time series models. *Biometrika*, 1977, *64*, 85–90.

Norman, N. F. *Markov processes and learning models*. New York: Academic Press, 1972.

Novick, M. R., & Jackson, P. H. *Statistical methods for educational and psychological research*. New York: McGraw-Hill, 1974.

O'Connor, K. P., & Shaw, J. C. Field dependence, laterality and the EEG. *Biological Psychology*, 1978, *6*, 93–109.

Osafo-Charles, F., Agarwal, G. C., O'Neill, W. D., & Gottlieb, G. L. Application of time-series modeling to human operator dynamics. *IEEE Transactions on Systems, Man and Cybernetics*, 1980, *SMC-10*, 849–860.

Ostrom, C. W. *Time series analysis: Regression techniques*. Sage University Series on Quantitative Applications in the Social Sciences, 07-009. Beverly Hills and London: Sage Pub., 1977.

Otter, P. W., & Tempelaar, D. T. Kalman and Box-Jenkins estimators in a simulation study. In O. D. Anderson (Ed.), *Analysing time series*. Amsterdam: North Holland Pub., 1980.

Pangborn, R. M. Influence of hunger on sweetness preferences and taste thresholds. *American Journal of Clinical Nutrition*, 1959, *7*, 280–287.

Parducci, A. Range-frequency compromise in judgment. *Psychological Monographs*, 1963, *77*, 2(565).

Parducci, A. Sequential effects in judgment. *Psychological Bulletin*, 1964, *61*, 163–167.

Parducci, A., & Sandusky, A. Distribution and sequence effects in judgment. *Journal of Experimental Psychology*, 1965, *69*, 450–459.

Parzen, E. An approach to time series analysis. *Annals of Mathematical Statistics*, 1961, *32*, 951–989.

Parzen, E. *Stochastic processes*. San Francisco, Ca.: Holden-Day, 1962.

Pfanzagl, J. *Theory of measurement*. Würzburg: Physica-Verlag, 1968.

Philpott, S. J. F. *Fluctuations in human output. British Journal of Psychology Monograph Supplement XVII*. Cambridge, Mass.: University Press, 1932.

Piaget, J. *Main trends in psychology*. London: George Allen, 1973.

Pierce, J. R., Lipes, R., & Cheetham, C. Uncertainty concerning the direct use of time information in hearing: Place cues in white-spectra stimuli. *Journal of the Acoustical Society of America*, 1977, *61*, 1609–1621.

Plomp, R., & Smoorenburg, G. F. (Eds.). *Frequency analysis and periodicity detection in hearing*. Leiden: Sythoff, 1970.

Poggio, T., & Reichardt, W. Considerations on models of movement detection. *Kybernetik*, 1973, *13*, 223–227.

Pollack, I. Periodicity measures for repeated random auditory patterns. *Journal of the Acoustical Society of America*, 1978, *63*, 1132–1144.

Pollack, I. Discrimination of uniform spectrum pulse sequences. *Journal of the Acoustical Society of America*, 1979, *66*, 115–122.

Porges, S. W., Bohrer, R. E., Cheung, M. N., Drasgow, F., McCabe, P. M., & Keren, G. New time-series statistics for detecting rhythmic co-occurrence in the frequency domain: The weighted coherence and its application to psychophysiological research. *Psychological Bulletin*, 1980, *88*, 580–587.

Poskitt, D. S., & Tremayne, A. R. Testing the specification of a fitted autoregressive-moving average model. *Biometrika*, 1980, *67*, 359–363.

Possamai, C. A., Granjon, M., Reynard, G., & Requin, J. High order sequential effects and the negative gradient of the relationship between simple reaction-time and foreperiod duration. *Acta Psychologica*, 1975, *39*, 263–270.

Poulton, E. C. *Tracking skill and manual control*. New York: Academic Press, 1974.

Poulton, E. C. Models for biases in judging sensory magnitudes. *Psychological Bulletin*, 1979, *86*, 777–803.

Powers, W. T. *Behavior: The control of perception*. Chicago: Aldine, 1973.

Powers, W. T. Quantitative analysis of responsive systems: Some spadework at the foundations of scientific psychology. *Psychological Review*, 1978, *85*, 417–435.

Powers, W. T., Clark, R., & McFarland, R. A general feedback theory of human behavior. Parts 1 and 2. *Perceptual and Motor Skills Monograph*, 1960, *11*, (*1* and *3*, Serial No. 7).

Press, S. J. *Applied multivariate analysis*. New York: Holt, Rinehart & Winston, 1972.

Priestley, M. B. State-dependent models: A general approach to non-linear time series analysis. *Journal of Time Series Analysis*, 1980, *1*, 47–71.

Pylyshyn, Z. W. Validating computational models: A critique of Anderson's indeterminacy of representation claim. *Psychological Review*, 1979, *86*, 383–394.

Quenouille, M. H. *The analysis of multiple time series*. London: Griffin, 1957.

Rabbitt, P. M. A., & Vyas, S. M. Interference between binary classification judgments. *Journal of Experimental Psychology*, 1974, *103*, 1181–1190.

Rabbitt, P. M. A., & Vyas, S. M. Memory and data-driven control of selective attention in continuous tasks. *Canadian Journal of Psychology*, 1979, *33*, 71–87.

Rabiner, L. R., Rosenberg, A. E., & Levinson, S. E. Considerations in dynamic time warping algorithms for discrete word recognition. *IEEE Transactions on Acoustics, Speech and Signal Processing*, 1978, *ASSP-26*, 575–586.

Rannap, E. R. (In Russian) The systems analysis for description of inventions, scientific and technological information, Series 2: *Information Processes and Systems*, 1971, *6*, 5–10.

Rao, C. R. *Advanced statistical methods in biometric research*. New York: Wiley, 1952.

Reichardt, W. Figure-ground discrimination by the visual system of the fly. In R. Heim & G. Palm (Eds.), *Theoretical approaches to complex systems lecture notes in biomathematics*, 1977, *21*, 117–146. Berlin: Springer-Verlag.

Revenstorf, D. A mathematical model for the analysis of therapies. In J. C. Brengelmann (Ed.), *Progress in behaviour therapy*. Berlin: Springer-Verlag, 1975.

Revenstorf, D. *Zeitreihenanalyse für klinische Daten*. Weinheim und Basel: Beltz Forschungsberichte, 1979.

Revenstorf, D., Hahlweg, K., & Schindler, L. Lead and lag in aspects of marital interaction. *European Journal of Behavior Analysis and Modification*, 1979, *2*, 1–12.

Revenstorf, D., Henrich, G., & Schwarze-Bindhart, U. Linear models for the analysis of the relation between motivation and therapy outcome. *European Journal of Behavior Analysis and Modification*, 1978, *1*, 115–125.

Rissanen, J. Modeling by shortest data description. *Automatica*, 1978, *14*, 465–471.

Rissanen, J. Consistent order estimates of autoregressive processes by shortest description of data. *International Symposium on Analysis and Optimization of Stochastic Systems*. Oxford: University of Oxford, 1979.

Robinson, E. A. *Multichannel time series analysis with digital computer programs.* San Francisco, Ca.: Holden-Day, 1967.

Rosenblatt, M. Some regression problems in time series analysis. In *Proceedings of the Third Berkeley Symposium on Mathematical Statistics and Probability, 1954, 1,* 165–186. Los Angeles, Ca.: University of California Press, 1956.

Rosenblatt, M. (Ed.). *Proceedings of the Symposium of Time-Series Analysis held at Brown University, 1962.* New York: Wiley, 1963.

Rothbart, M., & Snyder, M. Confidence in the prediction and postdiction of an uncertain outcome. *Canadian Journal of Behavioral Science,* 1970, *2,* 38–43.

Rouse, W. B. A model of the human in a cognitive prediction task. *IEEE Transactions on Systems, Man and Cybernetics,* 1973, *SMC-3,* 473–477.

Sayre, K. *Cybernetics and the philosophy of mind.* London: Routledge & Kegan Paul, 1976.

Schetzen, M. *The Volterra and Wiener theories of nonlinear systems.* New York: Wiley, 1980.

Schwartz, G. Estimating the dimension of a model. *Annals of Statistics,* 1978, *6,* 21–26.

Sekuler, R. Visual motion perception. In E. C. Carterrette & M. P. Friedman (Eds.) *Handbook of perception* (Vol. V). *Seeing.* New York: Academic Press, 1975.

Sekuler, R., Pantle, A., & Levinson, E. Physiological basis of motion perception. In R. Held, M. Leibowitz, & H. L. Teuber (Eds.), *Handbook of sensory physiology* (Vol. VIII). Heidelberg: Springer-Verlag, 1978.

Senders, V. L., & Sowards, A. Analysis of response sequences in the setting of a psychophysical experiment. *American Journal of Psychology,* 1952, *65,* 358–374.

Sheridan, T. B., & Ferrell, W. *Man-machine systems: Information control and decision models of human performance.* Cambridge, Mass.: MIT Press, 1974.

Shibata, R. Selection of the order of an autoregressive model by Akaike's information criterion. *Biometrika,* 1976, *63,* 117–126.

Shinners, S. M. Modeling of human operator performance using time series analysis. *IEEE Transactions on Systems, Man and Cybernetics,* 1974, *SMC-4,* 446–458.

Shore, R. W. A Bayesian approach to the spectral analysis of stationary time series. In A. Zellner & J. B. Kadanc (Eds.), *Studies in Bayesian econometrics* (Vol. 2). Amsterdam: North Holland Pub., 1980.

Skinner, B. F. The processes involved in the repeated guessing of alternatives. *Journal of Experimental Psychology,* 1942, *30,* 495–503.

Skinner, B. F. *Science and human behavior.* New York: MacMillan, 1953.

Slack, C. W. Feedback theory and the reflex arc concept. *Psychological Review,* 1955, *62,* 263–267.

Söderström, T., Ljung, L., & Gustavsson, I. *A comparative study of recursive identification methods.* Report No. 7427, (1974) of the Department of Automatic Control, Lund Tekniska Hogskolan, Sweden.

Speeth, S. D., & Mathews, M. V. Sequential effects in the signal-detection situation. *Journal of the Acoustical Society of America,* 1961, *33,* 1046–1054.

Speyer, J. L., Samn, S., & Albanese, R. A stochastic differential game theory approach to human operators in adversary tracking encounters. *IEEE Transactions on Systems, Man and Cybernetics,* 1980, *SMC-10,* 755–762.

Sriyananda, H., & Towill, D. R. Prediction of human operator performance. *IEEE Transactions on Reliability,* 1973, *R-22,* 148.

Staddon, J. E. R., King, M., & Lockhead, G. R. On sequential effects in absolute judgment experiments. *Journal of Experimental Psychology: Human Perception and Performance,* 1980, *6,* 290–301.

Stankovic, S. S., & Kouwenberg, N. G. M. Some aspects of human operator identification in real time. In P. Eykhoff (Ed.), *Identification and system parameter estimation* (Vol. I), Amsterdam: North Holland Pub., 1973.

Stassen, H. G. Man-machine systems: Manual and supervisory control tasks. In J. A. Michon, E. G. J. Eijkman, & L. F. W. de Klerk (Eds.), *Handbook of psychonomics* (Vol. II). Amsterdam: North Holland Pub., 1979.

Stevens, S. S. (Ed.). *Handbook of experimental psychology*. New York: Wiley, 1951.

Subba Rao, T. On the theory of bilinear time series models, II. *Department of Mathematics U.M.I.S.T. Technical Report, No. 121,* 1979.

Subba Rao, T., & Gabr, M. M. A test for linearity of stationary time series. *Department of Mathematics U.M.I.S.T. Technical Report No. 105,* 1979.

Sutherland, J. W. System theoretic limits on the cybernetic paradigm. *Behavioral Science,* 1975, *20,* 191–200.

Takahashi, Y., Rabins, M. J., & Auslander, D. M. *Control and dynamic systems.* Reading, Mass.: Addison-Wesley, 1970.

Tanner, T. A., Jr., Rauk, J. A., & Atkinson, R. C. Signal recognition as influenced by information feedback. *Journal of Mathematical Psychology,* 1970, *7,* 259–274.

Ten Hoopen, M., & Reuver, H. A. Analysis of sequences of events with random displacements applied to biological systems. *Mathematical Biosciences,* 1967, *1,* 599–617.

Toates, F. *Control theory in biology and experimental psychology.* London: Hutchinson Educational, 1975.

Tomović, R., & Vukobratović, M. *General sensitivity theory.* New York: American Elsevier, 1972.

Tong, H., & Lim, K. S. Threshold autoregression, limit cycles and cyclical data. *Journal of the Royal Statistical Society, Series B.* 1980, *42,* 245–292.

Tou, J. T. *Digital and sampled-data control systems.* New York: McGraw-Hill, 1959.

Townsend, J. T. Some results concerning the identifiability of parallel and series processes. *British Journal of Mathematical and Statistical Psychology,* 1972, *25,* 169–199.

Townsend, J. T. Issues and models concerning the processing of a finite number of inputs: In B. M. Kantowitz (Ed.), *Human information processing: Tutorials in performance and cognition.* Potomac, Md.: Lawrence Erlbaum Associates, 1974.

Tugnait, J. K., & Haddad, A. H. Adaptive estimation in linear systems with unknown Markovian noise statistics. *IEEE Transactions on Information Theory,* 1980, *IT-26,* 66–78.

Tukey, J. W. An introduction to the calculations of numerical spectrum analysis. In B. Harris (Ed.), *Advanced seminar on spectral analysis of time series.* New York: Wiley, 1967.

Vagnucci, A. H., Liu, T-S., & Wong, A. K. C. Concatenation and homogeneity of biological time series. *IEEE Transactions on Systems, Man and Cybernetics,* 1977, *SMC-7,* 483–491.

van den Boom, A. J. W., & van den Enden, A. W. M. The determination of the order of process and noise dynamics. In P. Eykhoff (Ed.), *Identification and system parameter estimation* (Vol. 2). Amsterdam: North Holland Pub., 1973.

van Heusden, A. R. Human prediction of third-order autoregressive time series. *IEEE Transactions on Systems, Man and Cybernetics,* 1980, *SMC-10,* 38–42.

Verplanck, W. J., Collier, G. H., & Cotton, J. W. Nonindependence of successive responses in measurements of the visual threshold. *Journal of Experimental Psychology,* 1952, *44,* 273–282.

Voillaume, C. Modèles pour l'étude de la régulation des mouvements cadencés. *L'Année Psychologique,* 1972, *72,* 347–358.

Volterra, V. Sopra le funzioni che dipendono da altre funzioni. *Rendiconti Lincei,* 1887, *IV,* (III), 97–105.

Volterra, V. *Theory of functionals and of integral and integro-differential equations.* (reprint of 1927 edition.) New York: Dover, 1959.

von Bertalanffy, L. *Biophysik des Fliessgleichgewichts.* Vieweg: Braunschweig, 1953.

von Bertalanffy, L. *Organismic psychology and systems theory.* Worcester, Mass.: Clark University Press, 1968.

Wagner, M., & Baird, J. C. A quantitative analysis of sequential effects with numeric stimuli. *Perception & Psychophysics,* 1981, *29,* 359–364.

Walsh, J. L. A closed set of normal orthogonal functions. *American Journal of Mathematics*, 1923, *55*, 5–24.

Walter, D. O. Spectral analysis for electroencephalograms: Mathematical determination of neurophysiological relationships from records of limited duration. *Experimental Neurology*, 1963, *8*, 155–181.

Walter, D. O., & Brazier, M. A. B. Advances in EEG analysis. *Electroencephalography and Clinical Neurophysiology*, 1968. Supplement 27.

Welford, A. T. *Skilled performance: Perceptual and motor skills.* Glenview, Ill.: Scott Foresman, 1976.

Wertheimer, M. An investigation of the "randomness" of threshold measurements. *Journal of Experimental Psychology*. 1953, *45*, 294–303.

Wickelgren, W. A. Unidimensional strength theory and component analysis of noise in absolute and comparative judgment. *Journal of Mathematical Psychology*, 1968, *15*, 102–122.

Wickelgren, W. A. Single-trace fragility theory of memory dynamics. *Memory & Cognition*, 1974, *2*, 775–780.

Wiener, N. Generalized harmonic analysis. *Acta Mathematics*, 1930, *55*, 117–258.

Wiener, N. *Extrapolation, interpolation and smoothing of stationary time series.* New York: Wiley, 1949.

Wightman, F. L. The pattern-transformation model of pitch. *Journal of the Acoustical Society of America*, 1973, *54*, 407–416.

Wilson, G. T. The estimation of parameters in multivariate time series models. *Journal of the Royal Statistical Society, Series B.*, 1973, *35*, 76–85.

Wilson, M. D., & McReynolds, L. V. A procedure for increasing oral reading rate in hard-of-hearing children. *Journal of Applied Behavior Analysis*, 1973, *6*, 231–239.

Wing, A. M., & Kristofferson, A. B. The timing of interresponse intervals. *Perception & Psychophysics*, 1973, *13*, 455–460.

Wold, H. *Bibliography on time series and stochastic processes.* Edinburgh: Oliver and Boyd, 1965.

Woodside, C. M. Estimation of the order of linear systems. *Automatica*, 1971, *7*, 727–733.

Wyman, B. F. Linear difference systems on partially ordered sets. In G. Marchesini & S. K. Mitter (Eds.), *Mathematical systems theory: Proceedings of the International Symposium, Udine, Italy, 1975. Lecture Notes in Economics and Mathematical Systems* (Vol. 131). Berlin: Springer-Verlag, 1976.

Yamada, M., & Goto, T. Human response to tall building motion. In D. J. Conway (Ed.), *Human response to tall buildings (CDS/34).* Stroudsburg, Pa.: Dowden, Hutchinson and Ross, 1977.

Yensen, R. Some factors affecting taste sensitivity in man. I. Food intake and time of day. *Quarterly Journal of Experimental Psychology*, 1959, *11*, 221–229.

Young, P. C. Recursive approaches to time series analysis. *Bulletin of Institute of Mathematics and its Applications*, 1974, *10*, 209–223.

Young, P. C. General theory of modelling for badly defined systems. In G. C. Vansteenkiste (Ed.), *Modeling, identification and control of environmental systems.* Amsterdam: North-Holland Publ., 1978.

Yule, G. U. Why do we sometimes get nonsense-correlations between time-series? A study in sampling and the nature of time-series. *Journal of the Royal Statistical Society*, 1926, *89*, 1–64.

Zadeh, L. A., & Desoer, C. A. *Linear system theory: The state space approach.* New York: McGraw-Hill, 1963.

Zajonc, R. B., & Markus, G. B. Birth order and intellectual development. *Psychological Review*, 1975, *82*, 74–88.

Zeeman, E. C. *Catastrophe theory, selected papers 1972–1977.* Reading, Mass.: Addison-Wesley, 1977.

Zetterburg, L. H. Estimation of parameters for a linear difference equation with application to EEG analysis. *Mathematical Biosciences*, 1969, *5*, 227–275.

Zetterburg, L. H. Recent advances in EEG data processing. In W. A. Cobb & H. Van Duijn (Eds.), *Contemporary clinical neurophysiology* (*EEG Suppl. No. 34*). Amsterdam: Elsevier, 1978.

Zimmer, A. *A harmonic analysis of sequencies in a prisoner's dilemma game*. Paper read at the meeting of Psychometric Society, June 1977.

Author Index

431

Subject Index